Cases on Instructional Technology in Gifted and Talented Education

Lesia Lennex
Morehead State University, USA

Kimberely Fletcher Nettleton
Morehead State University, USA

A volume in the Advances in
Early Childhood and K–12
Education (AECKE) Book
Series

Information Science
REFERENCE
An Imprint of IGI Global

KH

Managing Director: Lindsay Johnston
Production Editor: Christina Henning
Development Editor: Erin O'Dea
Acquisitions Editor: Kayla Wolfe
Typesetter: John Crodian
Cover Design: Jason Mull

Published in the United States of America by
        Information Science Reference (an imprint of IGI Global)
        701 E. Chocolate Avenue
        Hershey PA 17033
        Tel: 717-533-8845
        Fax: 717-533-8661
        E-mail: cust@igi-global.com
        Web site: http://www.igi-global.com

Library of Congress Cataloging-in-Publication Data

Cases on instructional technology in gifted and talented education / Lesia Lennex and Kimberely Fletcher Nettleton, editors.
    pages cm
 Includes bibliographical references and index.
 ISBN 978-1-4666-6489-0 (hardcover) -- ISBN 978-1-4666-6490-6 (ebook) -- ISBN 978-1-4666-6492-0 (print & perpetual access) 1. Gifted children--Education--Computer-assisted instruction. 2. Instructional systems--Design. 3. Information technology. 4. Educational technology. 5. Digital media. I. Lennex, Lesia C., 1964- II. Nettleton, Kimberely Fletcher, 1960-
  LC3993.2.C38 2015
  371.95--dc23
                        2014026477

This book is published in the IGI Global book series Advances in Early Childhood and K-12 Education (AECKE) (ISSN: 2329-5929; eISSN: 2329-5937)

British Cataloguing in Publication Data
A Cataloguing in Publication record for this book is available from the British Library.

5/9/16

Advances in Early Childhood and K–12 Education (AECKE) Book Series

Jared Keengwe
University of North Dakota, USA

ISSN: 2329-5929
EISSN: 2329-5937

MISSION

Early childhood and K-12 education is always evolving as new methods and tools are developed through which to shape the minds of today's youth. Globally, educational approaches vary allowing for new discussions on the best methods to not only educate, but also measure and analyze the learning process as well as an individual's intellectual development. New research in these fields is necessary to improve the current state of education and ensure that future generations are presented with quality learning opportunities.

The **Advances in Early Childhood and K-12 Education (AECKE)** series aims to present the latest research on trends, pedagogies, tools, and methodologies regarding all facets of early childhood and K-12 education.

COVERAGE

- K-12 Education
- STEM Education
- Standardized Testing
- Special Education
- Individualized Education
- Performance Assessment
- Poverty and Education
- Urban K-12 Education
- Head Start and Pre-K Programs
- Common Core State Standards

IGI Global is currently accepting manuscripts for publication within this series. To submit a proposal for a volume in this series, please contact our Acquisition Editors at Acquisitions@igi-global.com or visit: http://www.igi-global.com/publish/.

Titles in this Series

For a list of additional titles in this series, please visit: www.igi-global.com

Cases on Instructional Technology in Gifted and Talented Education
Lesia Lennex (Morehead State University, USA) and Kimberely Fletcher Nettleton (More-head State University, USA)
Information Science Reference • copyright 2015 • 585pp • H/C (ISBN: 9781466664890)
• US $185.00 (our price)

Exploring the Effectiveness of Online Education in K-12 Environments
Tina L. Heafner (University of North Carolina at Charlotte, USA) Richard Hartshorne (University of Central Florida, USA) and Teresa Petty (University of North Carolina at Charlotte, USA)
Information Science Reference • copyright 2015 • 481pp • H/C (ISBN: 9781466663831)
• US $185.00 (our price)

Critical Practice in P-12 Education Transformative Teaching and Learning
Salika A. Lawrence (William Paterson University, USA)
Information Science Reference • copyright 2014 • 317pp • H/C (ISBN: 9781466650596)
• US $175.00 (our price)

Transforming K-12 Classrooms with Digital Technology
Zongkai Yang (Central China Normal University, P. R. China) Harrison Hao Yang (State University of New York at Oswego, USA & Central China Normal University, P. R. China) Di Wu (Central China Normal University, P. R. China) and Sanya Liu (Central China Normal University, P. R. China)
Information Science Reference • copyright 2014 • 409pp • H/C (ISBN: 9781466645387)
• US $175.00 (our price)

Cases on 3D Technology Application and Integration in Education
Kimberely Fletcher Nettleton (Morehead State University, USA) and Lesia Lennex (More-head State University, USA)
Information Science Reference • copyright 2013 • 359pp • H/C (ISBN: 9781466628151)
• US $175.00 (our price)

DISSEMINATOR OF KNOWLEDGE

www.igi-global.com

701 E. Chocolate Ave., Hershey, PA 17033
Order online at www.igi-global.com or call 717-533-8845 x100
To place a standing order for titles released in this series,
contact: cust@igi-global.com
Mon-Fri 8:00 am - 5:00 pm (est) or fax 24 hours a day 717-533-8661

Editorial Advisory Board

Table of Contents

Section 3
Arts and Humanities and the Gifted/Talented Student

Section 4
Voices from the Schools

Detailed Table of Contents

Section 1
What is Giftedness?

Gifted students come from every socio-economic level and from every background. Identification of gifted students varies widely from school to school, state to state, nation to nation. Defining characteristics, culled from the several researchers, are integrated into a cohesive picture of a gifted student.

Giftedness is not present only in childhood. It persists for a lifetime. However, even though most colleges/universities provide special needs services for appropriate students, most if not all college faculty might not believe it necessary to provide any accommodations for gifted/talented students either at undergraduate or at the graduate level. In order to accommodate one or more gifted/talented students in a class, faculty need to rethink their pedagogy and assessment strategies. At the college/university level accommodations are usually absent because faculty do not perceive a need to do so in their courses. In courses for pre-service teachers, some instructors provide practices in courses including how to teach gifted and talented students in basic education settings for K-12 grades. This chapter presents a brief overview of gifted and talented education in the United States focusing more specifically on gifted and talented at the University (or adult) level.

Section 2
Science and the Gifted/Talented Student

Chapter 3

Edward L. Shaw Jr., University of South Alabama, USA
Rebecca M. Giles, University of South Alabama, USA

The answer to educating gifted and talented students in heterogeneous classrooms may lie, at least partially, in using instructional technology to motivate learning and enrich lessons. This case study explores one aspect of effective instruction for gifted second graders during lessons conducted in their general education classrooms. This chapter summarizes the development and delivery, students' performance and perceptions, and professional implications of an elementary science lesson utilizing interactive whiteboard technology to convey science content and elicit participation. It also emphasizes the importance of teacher educators' modeling the use of interactive whiteboards for the purpose of differentiating instruction in teacher training programs to better prepare future teachers for the diverse learners who will fill their classrooms.

Chapter 4

Amy Eguchi, Bloomfield College, USA

Using educational robotics as a learning tool fosters gifted and talented students' learning, helping to instill the qualities necessary for them to be successful 21st century citizens and innovators who can profoundly affect the future US economy. Educational robotics provides a stimulating hands-on learning environment in which students constantly encounter problems that trigger inquiries, inspiring them to develop new solutions, test them out using the physical robots, and reiterate the process until they successfully solve the problems. The chapter presents the theories behind ideal Robotics in Education (RiE) approaches, introducing tips to ensure effective student learning and to maximize the potential of able students to display giftedness.

Chapter 5

Emily Bodenlos, Morehead State University, USA
Lesia Lennex, Morehead State University, USA

It is a controversial topic for some teachers: biological change. By definition, biological change teaches about biological systems and their related geology and ecology. In practice, the concept of Biological Change has become oppositional to some religious beliefs. For those that oppose the concept, it becomes a matter of actual teaching of the concept. It is sometimes glossed over in favor of other, more acceptable, concepts. Kentucky science achievement data for Biological Change indicated that middle grades students had little achievement compared to other concepts. The prior grade level for teaching this concept was fourth grade. A case study was designed to address the needs of three Fourth Grade classrooms. As part of No Child Left Behind (NCLB), language arts scores were supplemented with science and social studies. Objectives for the study were production of science and social studies curriculum using 3D instructional technologies for fourth grade in the following Kentucky Core Academic Standards (KCAS) Language Arts: Reading Standards for Informational Text K-5, Writing Standards K-5, Language Standards K-5, Range-Quality-and-Complexity of Student Reading; Core Content 4.1 Science Standard Biological Change; Core Content 4.1 Social Studies Standard Geography. Important findings for heterogeneous populations were made regarding the use of instructional technologies apps VoiceThread and Pangea Safari.

Chapter 6

In an effort to help special needs students in the classroom, many teachers work very hard to differentiate curriculum for their struggling students. The one group of students in American schools who make little or no yearly progress are the gifted students in the classroom. Enriching the curriculum for gifted students does not appear to be a high priority for teachers. Increasingly, teachers turn to the computer to provide independent work for students, relegating education to a solitary endeavor. Social skills and collaboration are traits encouraged in many classrooms. Instead of isolating gifted students, technology can be integrated into instructional strategies in order to enrich the curriculum for all students. Enrichment can become an integral part of instruction. Technology can create learning environments that challenge gifted students.

Chapter 7

Fostering creativity amongst our students has become increasingly important to prepare them for the complex work environments of the 21st century. It has been mentioned that gifted students may not necessarily just be the ones who have high IQ and perform consistently well in their examinations but also those who are able to showcase their creative talents through content and skills gained in their academic subjects. In Singapore, students who do not perform well in the national

Primary School Leaving Examination (PSLE) to qualify for the traditional academic streams are placed in the Normal Technical (NT) stream in secondary schools. This chapter highlights how a class of 37 secondary two students in the NT stream, averaging 14 years of age, has been able to showcase their creative talents in science through a toy storytelling project. This project was carried out over eight weeks during regular curricula school hours. In this project, students worked in groups to present short fairy tale stories to younger children (3 to six 6 of age) who are less fortunate than them, as part of their Community Involvement Program (CIP). Part of the requirements of this design task was for them to design and fabricate toys that function on scientific principles, and prepare colourful slides with animations in support of their presentation. Each group was given 5-10 minutes to present their stories through their toys and slides. It became apparent to the students that in order to complete the project, they had to make use of knowledge of graphic and animation skills.

Section 3
Arts and Humanities and the Gifted/Talented Student

Chapter 8

A partnership between the Morehead State University Art Education Program and the Lake County Alternative School was established in Fall 2011. This ongoing collaboration provides opportunities for Art Education students to teach art and work with at- risk middle and high school students. It also allows LCAS students, who otherwise have no coursework in art, the opportunity to work creatively with visual art media.

Chapter 9

From November 1 to November 30, students around the world participate in an annual challenge called the National Novel Writing Month Young Writers Program (NaNoWriMo YWP) in which they develop and compose a long narrative story. In the fall of 2011, 16 fourth and fifth grade gifted students at McKeel Elementary Academy took on this challenge through their twice-weekly pull-out gifted programming. Through use of a three-phase program implementation, NaNoWriMo YWP resources and online community, dynamic technology tools, and extended blocks of uninterrupted writing time, these students engaged in advanced writing instruction and practices in order to meet or surpass a personal narrative writing goal. As a result of the program, each of the participating gifted students met the school's learning objectives by identifying and applying advanced writing skills and improving knowledge and application of a personal goal-setting process. This chapter outlines the program's alignment with best practices in gifted education, the program implementation's educational goals/objectives, the specific strategies and practices used in implementing the program, the outcomes to student learning, and recommendations for educators who plan to participate in the program with their gifted and talented students.

The purpose of this chapter is to discuss, explain, and share how the author has used culturally relevant instructional methods (i.e., hip-hop pedagogy) and Digital Audio Workstations (DAWs) in K-12 classroom environments to impact learning motivation and learner achievement from 2005 to 2012. Emphasis is placed on the elements of hip-hop culture (i.e., rapping, graffiti art, beat making, and break dancing) combined with DAWs to impact learning motivation and learner achievement in the heterogeneous Gifted and Talented (GT) classroom. Recommended hardware and software is discussed. Examples include audio interfaces, cables and microphones required, recommended audio recording software, and classroom environment preparations. Photographs and illustrations are included to make the chapter applicable to practitioners in classroom environments and educational researchers.

Section 4
Voices from the Schools

This vignette presents a special case production in World Geography from a group of sixth graders in a rural setting. The group had 23 students, averaging 12 years of age, with a composition of 15 males and 8 females. Among these students were 6 gifted students and 2 special needs students. Presentation using iMovie with captions and voiceovers of Central and South American countries was the culminating event. By encouraging creativity, all students had the opportunity to demonstrate agility with instructional technology.

Chapter 12

Kristen Renee Waller, Morehead State University, USA

This vignette presents a case production by gifted fourth through sixth grade students of motivational videos. Thirty-eight students in a small, independent school district in a semi-rural part of eastern Kentucky were part of the project. The 38 students consisted of 8 fourth graders, 22 fifth graders, and 8 sixth graders: 11 boys and 27 girls. The students are identified as gifted in language arts, math, science, social studies, general intelligence, leadership, and creativity.

Section 5
Teacher Training

Chapter 13

Debra R. Sprague, George Mason University, USA
Beverly Shaklee, George Mason University, USA

There is no doubt that many gifted students have access either at home or through school to instructional technologies. A review of state and local guidelines on technology competencies for students (not just gifted students) primarily focuses on collaboration and communication, creativity and innovation, and critical thinking skills. It is no longer enough for students to master technology skills. They now need to be able to use technology to analyze, explore, and learn.

Chapter 14

Jennifer G. Beasley, University of Arkansas, USA
Marcia B. Imbeau, University of Arkansas, USA

This case study highlights the essential components of differentiating instruction to meet the needs of all students, including those most advanced, as well as English Language Learners by using a variety of technologies. In the district where the case study takes place, many teachers have access to technology, but have received limited professional development to know how to apply the technology effectively. Several roadblocks that many teachers encounter as they move forward in their knowledge about the tools of technology are identified with possible solutions for addressing those concerns offered. The recommendations provided for addressing concerns that classroom teachers face are (1) how to differentiate instruction for all learners, (2) how to learn and sustain growth in using the tools of technology in lesson planning and implementation, and (3) how to manage all of the various components so that chaos does not ensue and every students' learning is maximized. A review of all of these issues can be beneficial to other teachers in heterogeneous classrooms who want to use technology as tool for differentiating instruction.

Chapter 15
   Shigeru Ikuta, Otsuma Women's University, Japan
   Diane Morton, University of Saint Joseph, USA
   Mikiko Kasai, Hirosaki University, Japan
   Fumio Nemoto, University of Tsukuba, Japan
   Masaki Ohtaka, Takashima Special Needs Education School, Japan
   Mieko Horiguchi, Otsuma Women's University, Japan

The authors use a new communication aid in conducting many activities at preschools, special needs schools, and general schools. They use dot codes printed on paper and linked with multimedia such as voices, sounds, movies, web pages, html files, and PowerPoint files. More than one audio file can be linked with a single dot code, and other multimedia files can be further linked to the same dot code in addition to the audios. Just touching the dot code with sound pens (Speaking Pen and G-Talk) can produce the original voices and sounds clearly. If a G1-Scanner pen is connected to a tablet or a personal computer, the multimedia can be replayed on its screen. This chapter reports recent advancements in software used to create handmade teaching materials as well as several case studies from preschools, special needs schools, and general schools.

Chapter 16
   Judith Bazler, Monmouth University, USA
   Letitia Graybill, Monmouth University, USA
   Meta Van Sickle, College of Charleston, USA

There are a number of factors that potentially influence the motivational trajectories of both conventional and gifted students. The most significant role that the gifted adult student plays with his/her peer group both inside and outside of the classroom relies on their innate leadership abilities, depth of content knowledge, and ability to work with young children and adolescents. While university honors programs provide a readily available peer group for many of the brightestincoming students, these honors programs are designed to provide talented students the opportunity to excel with a group of peers having a similar level of ability, motivation, and prior academic achievement. The challenge lies in the identification of the gifted among a selection of students who have met university entrance requirements on the undergraduate level and have degrees granted by accredited colleges and universities, especially if the education program is not informed about the honors designation of the teacher candidate. Consequently, science methods and other education faculty must learn to identify and then differentiate instruction for this population. Some key questions are, How do we challenge the gifted among an already select group of teacher education candidates? What differentiation of teaching methods needs to occur? and What products should the instructor expect from the gifted and talented teacher education candidate? These questions must be answered because the general characteristics that all future teachers hold is a desire for autonomy, a desire to study a topic in depth, and the ability to be creative with lesson planning and classroom implementation and projects that motivate future teachers and include integrated curricula and activities in either solo or group work that also meet the social needs of the gifted student.

Section 6
Teacher Education

Chapter 17
JeongWon Choi, Korea National University of Education, Korea
SangJin An, Korea National University of Education, Korea
YoungJun Lee, Korea National University of Education, Korea

This chapter aims to analyze cases in which programming was educated via e-learning in informatics gifted classes in Korea and provide developmental direction. The gifted class, which aimed to improve computational thinking and problem-solving ability, received the algorithm and programming education and experienced the design and implementation process of a programming project entitled "Interactive Movie Production through Scratch Programming" through the creation of a learning group. The learners received gifted education via e-learning systems, such as video lecturing, video conferencing and smart phones. However, there was much difficulty in providing appropriate feedback and scaffolding to resolve the trial-and-error issues experienced during the programming learning process, which involved learning flow interruptions of the learners which in some cases caused them to give up on the learning process. To overcome this difficulty, the selection of educational content appropriate for distance learning was regarded as important, and algorithm learning utilizing puzzles was proposed as an alternative. Puzzles can encompass learning content using texts and images while also providing feedback and scaffolding appropriate for learners via suitable learning document compositions and descriptions of the problem solving process while also evaluating the learner's ability in detail.

Chapter 18

Masahiro Nagai, Tokyo Metropolitan University, Japan
Noriyuki Matsunami, Nishi-Tokyo Shi Sakae Elementary School, Japan

Japanese parents are genuinely concerned about their children's education, especially if the latter display exceptional abilities. Such parents also believe that the public education system insufficiently nurtures their gifted child's potential. Consequently, parents frequently enroll their children in private schools and afterschool programs at cram schools(juku), which feature accelerated, condensed curriculums. The authors discuss the state of Japanese gifted education before highlighting e-learning's effectiveness in this context based on practical educational research at a Tokyo elementary school.

Chapter 19

Geri Collins, Mercer University, USA
Jeffrey Hall, Mercer University, USA
Bridget Taylor, Mercer University, USA

The purpose of this chapter is to examine the rationale of clustered classrooms and to explore methods of using technology to enhance the educational outcomes of gifted students in clustered classrooms. The chapter includes research-based strategies for facilitating clustered classrooms, provides ideas for incorporating technology across multiple content areas, identifies what exemplary student products should look like, and offers a sample lesson plan that can be adapted to cultivate problem solving skills, critical thinking, and collaboration in a clustered classroom. By highlighting and examining these issues, the authors hope that more teachers will utilize the clustered classroom model, providing outstanding educational opportunities that can benefit all students.

Chapter 20

Jana Willis, University of Houston – Clear Lake, USA
Douglas J. Steel, University of Houston – Clear Lake, USA
Vanessa Dodo Seriki, Loyola University Maryland, USA

This collective case study explores the use and impact of instructional technology, by three university faculty members, on fourth grade Gifted and Talented (GT) students' engagement and motivation to learn. Through this exploration, the authors were able to modify their use of instructional technology to suit the needs of the heterogeneous group of GT learners. Although the level of use, purpose for use, and how students used the instructional technology varied between the courses, this case reveals that all three authors recognized or learned that the heterogeneous nature of the GT students necessitated a flexible approach to instruction and use of IT in order to maintain high levels of engagement and motivation. While these findings are not novel, they do add to the discourse regarding teachers' perceptions of gifted students and how those perceptions inform instructional practices. This chapter intends to stimulate critical self-reflection, among GT teachers and teacher educators, regarding their perceptions of GT students and the impact those perceptions have on instructional practices.

Foreword

Advocates for children all want the same thing. We want to see children thrive in environments that value and respect their abilities, provide challenges for growth, and enhance talent potential. We want them to grow into successful happy adults who contribute to society in myriad ways.

Sometimes certain groups of children in their academic journeys through our schools encounter barriers to their learning. Gifted children are one such group. These barriers are often the unintended consequences of best intentions or the results of mistaken beliefs based on a mythology of incorrect information.

One myth that gets a lot of traction is the myth that gifted children do not need any special help. Therefore, GT classes are pulled away or services are "pushed in" to the general classroom where differentiation is to occur even though the general classroom teacher has had little to no training in gifted education pedagogy. As advocates for gifted children, we know that doing nothing to the general classroom curriculum to help it match the needs of these unique learners is actually doing something. That something is to not allow a child the challenge and fun of learning new materials or to make continuous progress. As a result, we have gifted children who may be proficient and yet underachieving.

What do we do to help educators present curriculum and instruction to meet the academic needs of gifted children? We advocate for change. Sometimes our advocacy takes the form of research, as this book has done. The research explores strategies that work not only for the classroom teacher but also enhance the classroom experience for gifted learners. Instructional technology, cluster grouping, creativity, culturally relevant instructional methods, narrative writing, and differentiating instruction have all been found to have a place in the classroom. How the general education teacher translates using them to offer curriculum to gifted children becomes the key to maximizing their potential. Research makes the translation easier.

I applaud the authors for recognizing that the academic needs of gifted children go beyond their primary and secondary education and extend to the gifted adult student at the university level. It is an area to which we give little thought. We "assume" and believe the myth that it is not necessary to provide accommodations for the adult gifted student at the undergraduate or graduate level. We assume that because they have met the university's entrance requirements, all is well. By identifying and providing differentiated instruction to gifted adult students who become educators, universities produce classroom teachers who have experienced and practiced the skills necessary to differentiate instruction for their students. These teachers are better able to recognize and integrate activities that meet the needs of gifted students.

This book reflects a commitment to providing tools for the proper matching of curriculum and instruction for all children but especially gifted students. As an advocate for gifted children who seeks changes to mindsets about appropriate educational opportunities for gifted children, I look forward to this book becoming a part of classroom teachers' libraries. I look forward to knowing that knowledgeable teachers have the means to remove barriers to learning for gifted children.

Lynette Baldwin
Kentucky Association for Gifted Children, USA

Lynette Baldwin *is the Executive Director of the Kentucky Association for Gifted Education (KAGE), a non-profit volunteer group of parents, teachers, administrators, educators, and citizens interested in being advocates for appropriate educational opportunities for gifted and talented youth in Kentucky. In her role as executive director, she plans workshops and conferences to inform educators and parents of the needs of gifted children, makes numerous presentations to groups on the topic, lobbies for change with the KY General Assembly, and works with various organizations to affect appropriate educational changes for gifted children. She currently represents KAGE on the Advisory Council for Gifted and Talented Education. Ms. Baldwin is retired from the Paducah Public Schools, Paducah, KY, where she was first an elementary teacher and then teacher/coordinator of the district's Gifted Talented Creative Program.*

Preface

Teaching gifted and talented students of any age can be an enormous challenge. Teachers are often unaware of the needs of their brightest students. The capabilities of gifted students often hide their needs. While instructional technology may be used as a tool to offer opportunities for enrichment, teachers need help in discovering ways in which the planned, purposeful use of technology can support implementation of differentiation. This casebook has examples of real classroom practice designed to augment the heterogeneous classroom. All students deserve to have extensions to their learning with appropriately current technologies and opportunities to explore those technologies. The activities and supporting research in this book will allow teachers to bring needed differentiation to their classes to address the needs of all students.

Teacher education courses on instructional technology have usually focused on either teacher usage or teacher constructed applications. Problem-based learning, inquiry learning, can be supported with technology-based instruction. In the past, P-12 teachers were encouraged to use technology with gifted students by using research skills or by providing students with online courses. This casebook not only addresses appropriate methods of using technology in the gifted and talented populations; it also gives a concrete means by which the technology could be implemented in P-20 classrooms and be used to provide differentiated instruction for all students.

This casebook best serves the needs of P-20 teachers. The target audiences for this casebook are P-12 classroom teachers, undergraduate and graduate curriculum/methods courses, and teachers of P-20 gifted and talented students. The book provides wonderful support for Science, Technology, Engineering, and Mathematics (STEM), instructional technology curriculum, and teacher training courses. A companion book provides essential questions about each case study/vignette, lessons learned, and additional resources. Several chapters also offer unique insight to gifted and talented instruction with arts and humanities. Classroom teachers need research-based instructional methods to enrich classroom curriculum. The collected cases provide research-supported ideas for implementation. Teacher education faculty can use the cases to support pre-service teachers as they learn to differentiate instruction for all learners.

The case studies in all six sections were written to provide practical examples of research-based instruction for gifted students. Using instructional technology in a variety of forms, the researchers examined everything from under-identification of gifted students to the diverse needs of the gifted. The case studies provide a framework for improving instruction for all gifted and talented students from elementary to college age. While most of the instructional strategies can easily be implemented into heterogeneous classrooms, the strategies provide ideal opportunities for gifted students to learn in unique and challenging ways. The emphasis of each of the case studies is on gifted and talented students. However, the instructional strategies are easily differentiated to provide challenging curriculum for all students.

The casebook is divided into six sections. Each section scrutinizes a different aspect of gifted education. The first section, "What is Giftedness?" explores the definition of giftedness and gifted education in the United States (USA). After developing an understanding of gifted and talented students, the second section of the book, "Science and the Gifted/Talented Student," explores STEM concepts. STEM is an area that is receiving a great deal of attention, and it is an area where gifted students can grow through practical application of research. The third section of the book, "Arts and Humanities and the Gifted/Talented Student," takes creative thought and instructional technology in a different direction. Creativity is one identification area that is hard to identify, and the case studies provide a research-based platform to promote opportunities to fuse innovative thinking and technology. After examining practices in STEM and the humanities, Section 4, "Voices from the School," provides an insight into how gifted students interact with movie making technology. In Section 5, "Teacher Training," the case studies focus on providing quality classroom instruction. Instructional strategies, creative lesson design, and the needs of gifted college students are researched. The final section, "Teacher Education," examines the ways in which teachers should be supported through research-based training.

In the first section, "What is Giftedness?" Kimberely Fletcher Nettleton lays the foundation for all of the cases in "Defining the Undefinable: What Does it Mean to be Gifted?" by exploring the definitions of gifted and talented students and building an understanding of the diverse characteristics of gifted students. Gifted students learn at a faster rate and in more depth than most students, but enrichment does not always occur in the classroom. This chapter also discusses the twice-exceptional gifted child, the child who has a learning disability or other special need in addition to being gifted. The author discusses both intellectual and emotional traits of the gifted child.

In their chapter, "Historical Overview of Adult Gifted Education in the United States," Judith Bazler, Letitia Graybill, and Meta Van Sickle share the historical underpinnings of gifted education in the United States. Gifted and talented students do not cease to be gifted when they enter higher education. The authors make a case for continued education of gifted students at the university level, suggesting that professors should be more responsive to students' educational needs. This chapter opens a new dimension in gifted instruction as the question of the ongoing need for enrichment for gifted adult learners has rarely been explored.

The first chapter in Section 2, "Science and the Gifted/Talented Student," is Edward Shaw, Jr., and Rebecca Giles's case study, "Using Technology to Teach Gifted Students Science in a Heterogeneous Classroom." The researchers examined the connections between motivation, instructional technology, and gifted students. This chapter summarizes development and delivery of instruction, students' performance and perceptions, and professional implications of an elementary science lesson utilizing interactive whiteboard technology to convey science content and elicit participation. The importance of teacher educators' modeling procedures with interactive whiteboards is emphasized. The authors suggest that using interactive whiteboards in teacher training programs for the purpose of demonstrating differentiated instruction will better prepare future teachers for the diverse learners who will fill their classrooms.

In "Integrating Educational Robotics to Enhance Learning for Gifted and Talented Students," Amy Eguchi presents the theoretical background behind ideal Robotics in Education (RiE) approaches. The study of robotics is an effective blend of STEM skills. Eguchi argues that through robotic programs the potential of able students to display giftedness is maximized. Eguchi introduces valuable tips to ensure effective student learning when teaching with robotics and researches the effectiveness inherent in robotic programs.

Emily Bodenlos and Lesia Lennex discuss using the iPad applications (apps), *VoiceThread* and *Pangea Safari*, to improve concept attainment in a fourth grade science classroom. Detailed lesson plans and alternative app summaries are provided in "VoiceThread and iPad Apps Supporting Biological Change Concept." As students studied biological change using the apps, Bodenlos and Lennex analyzed how students and teachers use technology to create a learning environment that was both challenging and appealing for gifted and talented students.

Integrating technology into Environmental Education is the case study topic in Kimberely Fletcher Nettleton's chapter, "To Boldly Go: Instructional Technology and Environmental Science." Nettleton examines how using technology in an outdoor classroom experience created a learning environment that enhanced collaboration skills. The fifth and sixth grade students explored science through an integrated survival/environmental theme that spanned the school year. In addition to learning critical thinking skills, the gifted students were supported in the development of skills in leadership and creativity.

Mohammed Nazir Amir explores STEM and creativity in the case study "Showcasing the Creative Talents in Science of the Academically Less-Inclined Students through a Values-Driven Toy Storytelling Project" and demonstrates how a class of 14-year-old students was able to represent their knowledge of science through the use of toys. Students in the project worked in groups to present short fairytale stories to younger children (3-6 years of age) as part of their Community Involvement Program (CIP). Students designed, fabricated, and animated toys in addition to preparing electronic media to support their creation. The juxtaposition of creativity and STEM provides a segue into the third section of the book.

Jeanne Petsch examines how art education and technology can be used effectively in "Creating Our World: An Art Program for Alternative School Students." This is the first case study in Section 3, "Arts and Humanities and the Gifted/Talented Student." Pre-service art teachers worked with middle and high school students in an alternative school. The case study explores how building relationships with troubled students and art experiences led to the discovery of unidentified gifted students.

In "From Student to Author: Engaging Gifted Learners in the National Novel Writing Month Young Writers Program," Nancye Blair Black writes about the National Novel Writing Month Young Writers Program (NaNoWriMo YWP). In this program, fourth and fifth grade students developed and composed a long narrative story. Through use of a three-phase program implementation, NaNoWriMo YWP resources and online community, dynamic technology tools, and extended blocks of uninterrupted writing time, these students engaged in advanced writing instruction and practices in order to meet or surpass a personal narrative writing goals. This chapter outlines the program's alignment with best practices in gifted education, educational goals/objectives, the specific strategies and practices used in implementing the program, the outcomes to student learning, and recommendations for educators who plan to participate in the program with their gifted and talented students.

Students who are gifted in the visual and performing art not only create through art and writing, but with music, too. Chris Deason, in "Culturally Relevant Applications of Digital Audio Workstations in the Heterogeneous GT Classroom," brings music into the gifted and talented classroom. The chapter discusses his work from 2005-2012 with Digital Audio Workstations (DAWs). Special emphasis is placed on the elements of hip-hop culture (i.e., rapping, graffiti art, beat making, and break dancing) combined with DAWs to impact learning motivation and learner achievement in the heterogeneous gifted and talented classroom.

Section 4, "Voices from the School," examines how two classroom teachers encouraged students to make movies. The teachers wrote short vignettes to explain how they used movies for different purposes and discovered the creative energy of their students. Cletus Turner, a middle school teacher, discusses how filmmaking was integrated into his sixth grade social studies classroom. His vignette, "iMovies and Gifted Grouping," shares what he learned about cluster grouping and student synergy. Using small-group collaboration to create movies, Turner experimented with group composition and analyzed the results.

Kristen Waller, an elementary school gifted and talented teacher, shares her first-person account of what happened when her principal challenged the gifted students to make a motivational video for high-stakes testing. In "Motivational Video for State Testing," Waller provides an inexpensive road map for using smart phones and computers to create a learning experience that supports students gifted in creative thought, visual and performing arts, and/or leadership. The final project was used to energize the school as it prepared for end-of-year testing.

Debra Sprague and Beverly Shaklee's case study, "Differentiating through Technology for Gifted Students," is the first case study in Section 5, "Teacher Training." Sprague and Shaklee investigate how pre-service teachers use technology when working with gifted students in the classroom. Pre-service teachers worked with classroom teachers to differentiate instruction for gifted students. Sprague and Shaklee emphasize the versatility of technology and the many ways in which it can support enrichment.

Jennifer G. Beasley and Marcia B. Imbeau also investigate differentiation and instructional technology in their case study, "Differentiation 2.0: Using the Tools of Technology to Meet the Needs of all Learners." As they studied the ways in which teachers supported students' interactions with technology, they identified areas in which teachers needed more training. Additional development of skills in differentiation, technology use and integration, and classroom management were recommended.

Shigeru Ikuta, Diane Morton, Mikiko Kasai, Fumio Nemoto, Masaki Ohtaka, and Mieko Horiguchi present a unique method of communication for gifted and talented special needs students in "School Activities with New Dot Code Handling Multimedia." Dot codes printed on paper and linked with multimedia such as voices, sounds, movies, Web pages, html files, and PowerPoint files are used as an effective teaching modification. More than one audio file may be linked with a single dot code, and other multimedia files can be further linked to the same dot code in addition to the audios. Their research illuminates the many ways the dot codes may be adapted in educational settings.

Judith Bazler, Letitia Graybill, and Meta Van Sickle investigated underserved gifted college students in "Designing Instruction for Gifted Future Science Teachers." Bazler, Graybill, and Van Sickle explored the ways in which teacher education preparation programs address the needs of gifted student in science education courses. Identifying and serving the gifted teacher education candidate is challenging. This chapter studies the challenges of differentiated teaching and planning for gifted college students.

The final section of the book, "Teacher Education," begins with Jeong Won Choi, SangJin An, and YoungJun Lee's, "A Case Study of Distance Education for Informatics Gifted Students." Choi, An, and Lee analyzed cases in which curriculum programming was informed via e-learning. With the goal of improving computational thinking and problem-solving ability, the class received algorithm and programming education. The class experienced the design and implementation process of a programming project titled "Interactive Movie Production through Scratch Programming" through the creation of a learning group. The learners received gifted education via e-learning systems, such as video lecturing, video conferencing, and smart phones. The study provides new considerations for applications of technology and gifted education.

In "Gifted Education and One Case Solution through E-Learning in Japan," Masahiro Nagai and Noriyuki Matsunami examine the effectiveness of e-learning as it relates to equal access education. Nagai and Matsunami provide an understanding of gifted education in Japan, reform movements in education, and the lack of acceleration opportunities for gifted students. Many Japanese students are enrolled in private, after school programs called *juku*. This is a privately funded extracurricular activity. This chapter describes the use of e-learning as an alternative to traditional *juku*.

"The Role of Technology in Providing Effective Gifted Education Services in Clustered Classrooms," by Geri Collins, Jeffrey Hall, and Bridget Taylor, provides needed research-based strategies for gifted students. Collins, Hall, and Taylor studied the need for facilitating clustered classrooms and the incorporation of instructional technology across several content areas. From games to science to mathematics, Collins, Hall, and Taylor suggested the use of technology as a foundational element in providing appropriate instruction to gifted students. The researchers provide sample lesson plans as a guide for practicing educators.

In the last chapter, Jana Willis, Douglas J. Steel, and Vanessa Dodo Seriki describe using instructional technology to motivate fourth grade gifted and talented students in a heterogeneous classroom. Their chapter, "Instructional Technology and the Nature of the Gifted and Talented," describes the flexible approach necessary to maintain an appropriately challenging classroom. Their research examines how gifted students interact with each other. A rich technological environment stimulates student learning. Willis, Steel, and Seriki suggest the need for educators to be more aware of the diversity that exists between gifted students.

This casebook clearly serves the needs of P-20 gifted and talented teachers. P-12 classroom cases present research-based strategies for implementation of differentiation for gifted and talented students. Cases with teacher education courses present needed information for building robust differentiation curriculum. Much has been written about gifted and talented populations, but few have given voice to the actual students and their needs. This casebook is a resource rich with experienced teachers presenting classroom cases, both in P-12 and teacher education, which supports teachers in truly teaching to our nation's gifted and talented students.

Lesia Lennex
Morehead State University, USA

Kimberely Fletcher Nettleton
Morehead State University, USA

Section 1
What is Giftedness?

Chapter 1
Defining the Undefinable:
What Does It Mean to be Gifted?

Kimberely Fletcher Nettleton
Morehead State University, USA

EXECUTIVE SUMMARY

Gifted students come from every socio-economic level and from every background. Identification of gifted students varies widely from school to school, state to state, nation to nation. In the USA, gifted students are identified in the following areas: visual and performing arts, leadership, talent in a specific academic discipline, creativity, and overall high intellect (U.S. Department of Education, 1993). Twice-exceptional students are gifted students with a learning disability or other special need. Defining characteristics, both intellectual and emotional, are integrated into a cohesive picture of a gifted student. Identification of gifted students is the first step towards providing educational services.

SETTING THE STAGE

Who Are the Gifted?

There are many definitions of gifted students. The most often used definition of gifted and talented students is that of the federal definition of giftedness as that of students who have

DOI: 10.4018/978-1-4666-6489-0.ch001

. . . outstanding talent, perform or show the potential for performing at remarkably high levels of accomplishment when compared with others of their age, experience, or environment. These children and youth exhibit high performance capability in intellectual, creative, and/or artistic areas, possess an unusual leadership capacity, or excel in specific academic fields. They require services not ordinarily provided by the schools. (U.S. Department of Education, 1993, p. 26)

The National Association for Gifted Children (NAGC) estimates that there are over three million children in the US who are gifted. This translates into approximately 6% of a school's population (2014). This is probably a low estimate, as many students are never recognized. Each state has created its own criteria to determine how gifted students will be identified. The lack of uniform identification means that the types of services and identification depends largely on where a student lives (NAGC & Council of State Directors of Programs for the Gifted, 2011).

Identification is made difficult because gifted children are unique. In addition to the gifted population having a wide range of IQ scores, an IQ score cannot measure all areas of giftedness. Renzulli (1982) separates giftedness into two areas: schoolhouse giftedness and creative/productive giftedness. Schoolhouse giftedness is the type most easily adapted to the educational system because students are able to demonstrate their giftedness in the classroom and on tests. These students are fairly easy to identify, as high, standardized test scores are usually used for identification (Van Tassel-Baska, 2008).

Creative/productive giftedness requires a different means of identification. A student with creative giftedness develops new and original ideas (Renzulli, 1982). These ideas do not have to be original in the sense that they are totally unique. Ideas only need to be original to the child. For example, in a conversation, a sixth grader explained his theory of black holes, the cosmos, and how the universe worked. Although he did not have the background, mathematical skills, and vocabulary to articulate his theory in an elegant manner, his explanation paralleled Hawking's explanation of the universe. For this child, this was original, creative thought. It does not matter that someone else already thought of it. The creative/productive gifted child is rarely identified through a cognitive ability test or worksheets in the classroom. Thus, it is difficult for many teachers to identify gifted students in this area, but it is crucial that these children are identified (Davis, 2003).

Visual and Performing Arts

Early identification of students gifted in performing or visual arts rarely happens in the classroom. Students gifted in visual and performing arts may be identified by their teachers after their talent has matured, but classroom teachers rarely have the expertise to determine if students are gifted in this area. An expert in the field may provide the necessary identification of the talented student. While teachers understand that these gifted students need special instruction, supportive instruction usually takes place outside of school in special programs. Some state may require identification of students in the visual and performing arts, but most school systems are not prepared to meet these students' needs A few large cities have created special schools for visual and performing arts, but students must live within traveling distance. These schools are typically available to middle and high school students, leaving gifted elementary students without the support needed to develop their gifts.

In the United States, it is understood by most people that athletes who have special abilities should have their skills and talents nurtured. These students may need special coaching to reach their full potential. Parents may move to be near coaches or training centers. Students gifted in visual and performing arts may have to move or find instructors for their children. Parents of students who are intellectually gifted are rarely supported in their decisions to provide better instruction for their children.

Leadership

Another area of gifted identification often overlooked in schools is leadership. Children who are leaders may often be leaders outside of the classroom. Due to their very sensitive natures, these gifted students may be involved in service projects outside of the school day. Girls are often overlooked in this area, as their skills are often characterized as bossiness, not leadership (Silverman, 2000). Girls may also be a behind the scenes leader, urging members of a group, putting forth ideas, but never taking direct charge. This may be due to several reasons, from lack of confidence to cultural expectations for being self-effacing or modest (Crothers, Field, & Kolbert, 2005).

Another reason why students gifted in leadership may be overlooked is because, in the words of one teacher, "They choose to use their gifts for evil, not good." Many students, identified as ringleaders with their distracting behaviors, are not usually recognized as needing help in developing their gifts. Silverman (2000) found that many children identified as behavior problems often have high IQ scores. Their behavior is a barrier to identification. Gifted children may be among the brightest in the classroom, but they are not always the best behaved. Many teachers need to look beyond behavior problems and analyze student behaviors. Leadership is an area of giftedness that is not usually developed in schools.

PROBLEMS OF IDENTIFICATION

As in most areas of education, the problem of identification is often made more difficult based on where students live and their racial backgrounds. Just as identification depends on each state's specific criteria, the variations among schools and communities are largely dependent on the ability of teachers to identify children (Moon & Brighton, 2008). Children of diverse backgrounds are underrepresented in the identified gifted population (Baldwin, 1994; VanTassel-Baska & Stambaugh, 2007). There are many factors involved in perpetuating the problem. The first is that teachers are much more adept at identifying students as gifted if they are good students. (Neumeister, Adams, Pierce, Cassady, & Dixon, 2007; Renzulli, 2000). This makes sense, as this is the area where teachers are most knowledgeable. Children who come from families whose language or culture are different than the mainstream will enter school already behind. If a child has not had access to intellectual stimulation, he/she will enter school with deficits in knowledge that will have to be overcome.

Evans (2000) suggested that teacher bias is only one factor in identification. Many children dealing with prejudice may work very hard to fit in and mask their giftedness. Underachievement is very widespread. This is especially likely if the culture does not encourage educational achievement (Ogbu, 1992; Steele. 2010). When undervaluing education is a pervasive belief in a community, friend and family encouragement are crucial components to supporting a gifted student's education (Robinson, 2008). Cultural gender expectations may strongly affect the ways in which males and females are encouraged at home and in their community (Steele, 2010; 1997). Two important factors in the development of *all* gifted students are a stable, supportive family and teacher expectations. Teachers can work with families to give value to the accomplishments of gifted children (Ford, 2003).

TWICE EXCEPTIONAL GIFTED STUDENTS

The difficulty in identifying gifted and talented students is exacerbated by the problem of twice exceptional students: students who have a learning disability and are gifted. Students who are twice exceptional are often unidentified because they are able to create their own methods of circumventing their exceptionality (Silverman, 1989). A child who has a problem with reading may memorize a great deal of information, develop listening skills, and generate strategies that allow him/her to fit in with the rest of the class. These children may initiate a personal modification program for themselves, never realizing that as long as their intelligence allows them to function in the classroom at grade level; they will never receive the help they need to reach their full potential (Johnson, 2011). In fact, if learning disabilities of any kind are identified, gifted students are often released from or denied special education services once their skills reach grade level (Brody & Mills, 1997). Student potential is not considered a factor when determining services for gifted students under current special education guidelines. Students who are at grade level are not eligible to receive special education services.

Misidentification is often a problem with gifted students. Many creative students, with high levels of curiosity have been misidentified as AD/HD. Children who are bored find it difficult to concentrate on classroom activities and lessons. It is hard to tell if a child does not finish an assignment through lack of interest or through lack of focus. Misdiagnosed children are often medicated. Some of the very indicators that identify gifted children are listed as warning signs of AD/HD (See Table 1 Comparison of AD/HD and gifted indicators). Gifted children are not immune to being AD/HD. When this occurs, the children are considered to be twice exceptional. Overlapping characteristics may provide a doubtful diagnosis. A clear understanding of the characteristics of giftedness is an important consideration when evaluating children.

Over-Excitability

Another reason misidentification of AD/HD often occurs is because the social and emotional characteristics of the gifted child are often much stronger than that of other students. Piechowski (1991) examined over-excitability in gifted children and found that while gifted children generally had greater sensitivity to others, their intensity caused many of their psychomotor traits which masqueraded as AD/HD (Shetky, 1981). Gifted children, who feel intense emotions and have a hard time sitting still, resemble AD/HD children. Excited about sharing fascinating information, they may talk compulsively. As their minds quickly make connections, they appear to act on impulse, although their minds are just more engaged and following a different path than the rest of the class. Their behaviors may be overwhelming to both themselves and the other students in the classroom (Dabrowski & Piechowski, 1977).

Gifted children may also be extremely sensitive to input from their senses. On the positive side, sensual sensitivity may manifest itself as receiving pleasure from art, music, or language. A piece of music or art may resonate with the gifted child. A gifted child may write poetry, or love the way words flow together to make a story. The search for just the right metaphor or simile may increase the time it takes to create a story or answer a question. Many gifted children may also be perfectionists, who will refuse to be hurried when it comes to completing their own creations. In fact, gifted children may have an end product so firmly planted in their minds that if their skills do not match their vision, they may have emotional meltdowns as a consequence.

Table 1. Comparison of AD/HD and gifted indicators

AD/HD Indicators	Indicators of Giftedness
Quickly moves between activities Doesn't finish tasks Makes careless mistakes	Learns rapidly Wide range of interests Impatient with routine or drill and practice
Daydreams Easily distracted Forgetful	Long attention span (if interested. If not interested, may stop paying attention) Imaginative Creative Keen observer Lose track of time (intense concentration)
Fidgets Loses belongings Handles a variety of objects	Curious
Moves often	High degree of energy
Emotions not always under control Risk taker	Over-excitability Sensitive (feelings hurt easily) Morally sensitive Shows compassion Concerned with justice, fairness Question authority
Blurts our comments Impatient Talks excessively	Intense Tends to dominate conversations, situations
Trouble getting along with peers Often Interrupts others May not take turns	Prefers older companions or adults Often finds and corrects other's mistakes Judgment often mature for age Perfectionistic
Additional characteristics of giftedness	
Early or avid reader Sense of humor Extensive vocabulary Reasons well Makes connections Sees patterns Excellent memory Retain information with less repetition	

Sources. The National Institute of Mental Health, 2014; Center for Disease Control, 2014; *Project Bright Horizon*, 2014; Silverman, 2014.

However, in a typical school day, many gifted children have problems with oversensitivity to sounds, smells, or textures. For example, the textures of many foods may create a picky eater. Clothing sensitivities may mean only wear certain fabrics or styles can be tolerated. Noise in the school cafeteria or classroom may be too much for a student to handle. Overstimulation from any sensitivity may lead to withdrawal as the student tries to cope with the barrage on his/her senses (Freed, 1990; Meckstroth, 1991; Piechowski, 1991).

Emotional Overload

In the rollercoaster world of adolescent emotions, it may be difficult to ascertain if the emotion observed in the classroom originates from normal mood swings or the overstimulation of the senses that is typical of many gifted children. Just as intellect or talent in the gifted adolescent may be much more than what is expected of peers, the emotional fervor shown by a gifted adolescent may also be outside of the norm. In class, gifted students may become so excited that they interrupt at inappropriate times. For many teachers, it may seem as if their gifted students overreact to everything.

Empathy can be especially debilitating for some adolescents, because in a very real way, they are able to feel what their friends feel. If a friend is depressed, the friend's problems become the problems of the gifted child. The gifted child may spend an inordinate amount of time and emotional energy worrying and trying to solve the problems of others. One college student, Joey, said,

I couldn't understand why I always felt depressed in high school. I had a loving family and no real worries of my own, but I had a hard time remaining cheerful. Then I looked at my friends. One was worried that his family would have to leave the country when their visas expired, another had parents who were divorcing, and one was flunking. I worried that my best friend would not make it into college because he didn't have much money. Their problems became my problems and after a while, I realized I needed to find some cheerful people to be around just so I could refresh my batteries.

Gifted adolescents may become strongly attached to friends or pets. One mother of a gifted child, bewildered when her sixth grade son started crying one night about his dog that had run away, commented:

I mean, it's not as if he hadn't cried before. And I know it was natural that he should miss Yogi occasionally, but tears were streaming down his face and it took him a long time to calm down. I wanted to be sympathetic, but after all, it happened four years ago.

As adolescents leave elementary school, old friendships may disappear as they enter the wider social network of middle school. For some, this is devastating and hard to understand. Because of their ability to form deep friendships, they are often blindsided when friends vanish. Due to their increased sensitivity, their emotional responses maybe more passionate and powerful than that of typical adolescents.

While strong emotions may lead gifted adolescents to organize an event to raise awareness of social injustice or spearhead a campaign for a charitable purpose, there is a dark side to intense passion. There may be a strong concern with death or depression. Gifted students often commit suicide over issues that many people would take in stride. Many gifted students are perfectionists and are unable to reconcile their personal self-worth and any sense of failure, real or perceived. (Schultz & Delisle, 2003). Cross (2013), suggests that depression in adolescents identified as gifted in visual and performing arts appears to be higher than students identified in other areas of giftedness. According to the Center for Disease Control and Prevention (CDC), the number of suicides for adolescents is around 4,600 while the reported number of attempts is around 157,000. A higher number of girls admit to trying to attempting suicide. Sadly, boys are much more successful than girls at taking their lives, as 81% of all suicides in the 10-24 year old range are male (2013). The number of gifted adolescents committing suicide is not measured in the United States due to nonstandard identification practices and because the data collected on suicide does not include information concerning gifted identification (Cross, 2013; Neihart, Reis, Robinson, & Moon, 2002). Cross (2013) suggested that while gifted adolescents may not attempt suicide in greater numbers than other adolescents, they may be more successful due to their abilities for planning.

Introvert or Extrovert

The Myers Briggs' Type Indicator test examines the psychological preferences of through a series of questions. When completed, responses are categorized into dichotomies indicating personal preferences. These paired dichotomies are: Extroversion and Introversion, Sensing and Intuition, Thinking and Feeling, and Judging and Perception (Myers & McCaulley, 1985). While there are no values attached to any one of these areas, a marked inclination towards one or the other within a pair provides insight into how someone interacts with the world. While the normal population's preference for Introversion is around 35%, the preference for introversion by the gifted population is at 50%. Silverman (1986) found that the higher the IQ, the greater the incidence of introversion over extroversion. Students with IQs over 160 have an introversion rate of 75%. Introverts, as opposed to extroverts, require time to work by themselves in order to learn. While there are fluctuations among the scores, many in the introverted gifted subset of the general population need to spend more time thinking through ideas. This means that instead of discussion, students need time to reflect and explore ideas internally (Sak, 2004). Teachers may encourage time to think and allow students time to work independently if desired. Providing students with the option to complete projects on their own will provide gifted students with the chance to problem solve and make connections. Understanding this need may furnish an enriched learning environment to gifted students.

Unfortunately, this need for reflection may have a deleterious effect on timed tests. In this era of high stakes assessment tests, many schools devote a great deal of time to review of core content and discipline related facts. The gifted student needs very little review time. Instead, these students need to know test-taking strategies. Due to the assumption by teachers that these students need little in the way of help, gifted children are not usually provided with much pre-test support. However, many gifted students tackle every problem and will work until they find the correct response. The idea of returning to a troublesome problem after answering easier ones is not considered as an option. For those who are perfectionists, finding a problem they cannot zip through results in an inordinate amount of time puzzling out the answer. If test results for gifted students show a string of correct responses and then a sudden stop before test completion, teachers need to investigate. Even with a teacher's assurance, some students may never believe it is ok to skip a question and return to it.

Teachers are often surprised when their top students fail to finish tests, but another stumbling block for gifted students and their interaction with timed tests exists. A great many gifted students overanalyze questions (Lovecky, 1994). A teacher whose student asks, 'If they mean this, then the answer is B, but if they meant that, then the answer is E,' will need to spend time helping these students trust with their instincts or first choice responses. By overanalyzing, many gifted students never complete timed tests.

GROWING UP GIFTED

By the time gifted children reach third grade, a great number have learned to hide their knowledge and skills. In many classrooms, gifted children are made painfully aware that they do not fit in. Socially, their discussions and interests are well beyond their peers (Robinson, 2003). In an effort to have balanced classrooms, many schools further exacerbate the problem by carefully doling out gifted children, like prizes, to teachers. A common way of keeping balanced classrooms consists of placing one gifted girl, one gifted boy, nine average female students, nine average male students, and two special education students in each class. Gifted children have very few intellectual peers in the classroom. To find a friend whose mind works in the same way as theirs, gifted children often have to cross the gender divide to make a friend in their classroom. And as they age, very few children are comfortable crossing the divide. Social skills may suffer or not develop. And this separation can continue until the gifted child reaches middle school and beyond.

For many gifted students, middle school offers their first chance to develop a broader circle of friends who are at the same intellectual level. In many middle schools, the gifted children may still be parceled out between teachers, but a larger school provides a wider pool from which to make friends. In addition to the usual hormonal challenges that this age brings, many gifted students are suddenly lost in the larger arena. No longer the brightest in the class, they have to learn how to negotiate with others, create friendships, and share the limelight. If this is the first time gifted students have a chance to make friends, their social skills may make it hard for them to navigate the social strata of middle school.

For some gifted children, middle school may be the first time they do not receive high grades for minimal effort. Used to being able to tune out the teacher, for some students, middle school is the first time they have to pay attention in class. Students can flounder because they have never learned study skills. One high school student, Sarah, discovered,

Until the end of eighth grade, I just read while the teacher talked. When I had to do any work, I just read the directions and did the work. I usually had my homework finished before I went home. If I didn't get it done, I just handed in my paper. I don't think the teachers ever really looked at it, because I always got good grades even when it was incomplete. Until I was in an AP class, I didn't even know I had to take notes.

For children who have never been identified as gifted, middle school is often the turning point. Several years of boredom have taken their toll and if middle school is not challenging, it will become harder to keep these children interested in education (Reis & McCoach, 2002). Children with an IQ of 140 waste as much as 50% of the school year because they are not learning new or challenging material, while children with an IQ of 170 or higher waste 99% of their school year (Renzulli & Reis, 1991). Their exasperation or confusion with the educational system may solidify and they are no longer interested in trying to learn. While the exact number of gifted students who drop out of high school each year is unknown, Renzulli and Parks (2000) conducted a study of over 1200 dropout students and found that approximately 27% were gifted students. The number of non-identified children who drop out has not been measured.

INSTRUCTIONAL TECHNOLOGY AND APPROPRIATE EDUCATION

Just as special education students need to receive an appropriate education, gifted students also need an appropriate education (Colangelo, Assouline, Gross, 2004). Gifted students need course work that challenges their minds and imaginations. Traditionally, this has often meant that if enrichment or acceleration happens, it has happened through solitary, independent learning. The computer has provided online courses as well as opportunities for independent research for students. Instructional technology (IT) should be more than just a means for independent work however. It is versatile enough to bring together all the students in the classroom, so that both gifted and non-gifted students can learn together. Increasingly, online courses and study groups are available for gifted students.

Unfortunately, the versatility of IT is often not realized. Just as a violin is played with artistry, skill, and precision in the hands of a musician, it can also be used to adorn a fireplace mantle in the hands of someone with no comprehension of how to play. More often, the vast majority uses IT for utilitarian purposes, although it can be a multi-faceted tool in the hands of a reflective teacher. Inclusive classrooms should engage all students at all levels, and skillful use of IT can be the means of achieving full participation and learning. By understanding that gifted students have many unmet needs in the classroom, an insightful teacher can purposely use IT to provide a rich learning environment for everyone.

CONCLUSION

Identifying gifted students is not an easy task. It requires understanding the unique individuality of people. While there are many theories of identification, to some extent, they all rely on at least two attributes when identifying gifted people: an ability to think and process information much more quickly than the norm and the ability to put ideas or information together in new and different ways. While teachers generally identify gifted students who characterize Renzulli's (1982) schoolhouse giftedness, they are less likely to identify students gifted in leadership, visual and performing arts, or even creative thought. Many gifted students are misidentified due to being twice exceptional. Problems with reading, math, processing, or other learning problems can mask student abilities. Gifted students can be misdiagnosed for AD/HD because of overlapping characteristics. Knowing the identifying traits of giftedness will help parents and teachers understand gifted children.

The emotional side to giftedness is often characterized by greater sensitivity or excitability than the mainstream. Gifted students may feel more passionately or more intensely than their peers may. A strong sense of right and wrong, social justice, and empathy is often associated with gifted students.

Gifted student education can be supported by instructional technology. The ways in which technology is used to provide education in the classroom determines the type of education available to gifted students. Classrooms can be dry, sterile environments where students become separated from their peers by independent study projects. Technology can provide a means for turning classrooms into lively, challenging places where all students can thrive.

REFERENCES

Baldwin, A. (1994). The seven plus story: Developing hidden talents among students in socioeconomically disadvantaged environments. *Gifted Child Quarterly*, *38*(2), 80–84. doi:10.1177/001698629403800206

Brody, L. E., & Mills, C. J. (1997). Gifted children with learning disabilities: A review of the issues. *Journal of Learning Disabilities*, *30*(3), 282–286. doi:10.1177/002221949703000304 PMID:9146095

Center for Disease Control and Prevention. (2014). *Attention-deficit and hyperactivity disorder*. Retrieved from http://www.cdc.gov/ncbddd/adhd/facts.html

Center for Disease Control and Prevention. (2014). *Injury center: Suicide prevention; youth suicide*. Retrieved from http://www.cdc.gov/violenceprevention

Colangelo, N., Assouline, S. G., & Gross, M. U. M. (2004). A nation deceived: How schools hold back America's brightest students: Vol. 1. Belin: Blank International Center on Gifted Education and Talent Development.

Cross, T. (2013). *Suicide among gifted children and adolescents: Understanding the suicidal Mind*. Waco, TX: Prufrock Press.

Crothers, L., Field, J., & Kolbert, J. (2005). Navigating power, control, and being nice: Aggression in adolescent girls' friendships. *Journal of Counseling and Development*, *83*(3), 349–420. doi:10.1002/j.1556-6678.2005.tb00354.x

Dabrowski, K., & Piechowski, M. M. (1977). *Theory of levels of emotional development*. Oceanside, NY: Dabor Science.

Davis, G. (2003). Identifying creative students, teaching for creative growth. In N. Colangelo, & G. A. Davis (Eds.), *Handbook of Gifted Education* (3rd ed., pp. 309–324). New York: Pearson Education, Inc.

Delisle, J. R. (1990). The gifted adolescent at risk: Strategies and resources for suicide prevention among gifted youth. *Journal for the Education of the Gifted, 13*, 212–228.

Evans, K. (2000). Multicultural counseling. In L. K. Silverman (Ed.), *Counseling the Gifted and Talented* (pp. 277–290). Denver, CO: Love Publishing Company.

Ford, D. Y. (2003). Equity and excellence: culturally diverse students in gifted education. In N. Colangelo, & G. A. Davis (Eds.), *Handbook of Gifted Education* (3rd ed., pp. 493–505). New York: Pearson Education, Inc.

Freed, J. N. (1990). Tutoring techniques for the gifted. *Understanding our Gifted, 2*(6), 11-13.

Johnson, S. K. (2011). *Identifying gifted students* (2nd ed.). Waco, TX: Prufrock Press, Inc.

Lovecky, D. (1994). Exceptionally gifted children: Different minds. *Roeper Review, 17*(2), 116–120. doi:10.1080/02783199409553637

Meckstroth, E. (1991, December). *Coping with the sensitivities of gifted children.* Paper presented at the Illinois Gifted Education Conference. Chicago, IL.

Moon, T. R., & Brighton, C. M. (2008). Primary teachers' conceptions of giftedness. *Journal for the Education of the Gifted, 31*, 447–480.

Myers, I. B., & McCaulley, M. H. (1985). *Manual: A guide to the development and use of the Myers-Briggs Type Indicator.* Palo Alto, CA: Consulting Psychologists Press.

National Association for Gifted Children & Council of State Directors of Programs for the Gifted. (2011). *State of the states in gifted education 2010–2011.* Washington, DC: NAGC.

National Association for Gifted Children. (2014). *Frequently asked questions: Question 2.* Retrieved from http//:www.nagc.org/index2.aspx?id=548

National Institute of Mental Health. (March, 2014). *Attention deficit hyperactivity disorder.* Retrieved from http://www.nimh.nih.gov/health/publications/attention-deficit- hyperactivity-disorder-easy-to-read/index.shtml

Neihart, M., Reis, S. M., Robinson, N. M., & Moon, S. M. (2002). *The social and emotional development of gifted children: What do we know?* Waco, TX: L Prufrock Press.

Neumeister, K. S., Adams, C. M., Pierce, R. L., Cassady, J. C., & Dixon, F. A. (2007). Fourth- grade teachers' perceptions of giftedness: Implications for identifying and serving diverse gifted students. *Journal for the Education of the Gifted, 30,* 479–499.

Ogbu, J. U. (1992). Understanding cultural diversity and learning. *Educational Researcher, 21*(8), 5–14. doi:10.3102/0013189X021008005

Piechoswki, M. M. (1991). Emotional development and emotional giftedness. In N. Colangelo, & G. Davis (Eds.), *Handbook for Gifted Education* (pp. 285–306). Needham Heights, MA: Allyn & Bacon.

Project Bright Horizon. (February, 2014). *Gifted characteristics checklist for under-represented populations.* Retrieved from http://www.cfsd16.org/public/_century/pdf/ProjectBrightHorizonGiftedCharacteristicsChecklist.pdf

Reis, S. M., & McCoach, B. D. (2002). Underachievement in gifted students. In M. Neihart, S. M. Reis, N. M. Robinson, & S. M. Moon (Eds.), *The social and emotional development of gifted children: What do we know?* (pp. 81–91). Waco, TX: Prufrock Press.

Renzulli, J. S. (1982). Myth: The gifted constitute 3-5% of the population. *Gifted Child Quarterly, 26*(1), 11–14. doi:10.1177/001698628202600103

Renzulli, J. S., & Park, S. (2000). Gifted dropouts: The who and the why. *Gifted Child Quarterly, 44*(4), 261–271. doi:10.1177/001698620004400407

Renzulli, J. S., & Reis, S. M. (1991). The reform movement and the quiet crisis in gifted education. *Gifted Child Quarterly, 35*(1), 26–35. doi:10.1177/001698629103500104

Robinson, N. M. (2008). The social world of gifted children and youth. In S. Pfeiffer (Ed.), *Handbook of giftedness in children* (pp. 33–52). New York, NY: Springer. doi:10.1007/978-0-387-74401-8_3

Sak, U. (2004). Synthesis of research on psychological types of gifted adolescents. *Journal of Secondary Gifted Education, 15*(2), 70–79.

Schultz, R. A., & Delisle, J. R. (2003). Gifted adolescents. In N. Colangelo, & G. A. Davis (Eds.), *Handbook of Gifted Education* (3rd ed., pp. 483–492). New York: Pearson Education, Inc.

Shetky, D. H. (1981). A psychiatrist looks at giftedness: The emotional and social development of the gifted child. *Gifted Child Today*, *18*, 2–4.

Silverman, L. K. (1986). Parenting young gifted children. *Journal of Children in Contemporary Society*, *18*(3-4), 73–87. doi:10.1300/J274v18n03_08

Silverman, L. K. (1989). Invisible gifts, invisible handicaps. *Roeper Review*, *12*(1), 37–42. doi:10.1080/02783198909553228

Silverman, L. K. (2000). The gifted individual. In L. K. Silverman (Ed.), *Counseling the Gifted and Talented* (pp. 3–28). Denver, CO: Love Publishing Company.

Silverman, L. K. (2014). Characteristics of Giftedness. *Gifted Development Center*. Retrieved from http://www.gifteddevelopment.com/What_is_Gifted/characgt.htm

Steele, C. M. (1997). A threat in the air: How stereotypes shape intellectual identity and performance. *The American Psychologist*, *52*(6), 613–629. doi:10.1037/0003-066X.52.6.613 PMID:9174398

Steele, C. M. (2010). *Whistling Vivaldi and other clues to how stereotypes affect us*. New York, NY: Norton.

U.S. Department of Education. (1993). *National excellence: A case for developing America's talent*. Washington, DC: U.S. Government Printing Office.

Van Tassel-Baska, J. L. (Ed.). (2008). *Alternative assessments with gifted and talented students*. Waco, TX: Prufrock Press.

VanTassel-Baska, J., & Stambaugh, T. (2007). *Overlooked gems: A national perspective on low- income promising learners*. Retrieved from http://www.nagc.org/index.aspx?id=17194

ADDITIONAL READING

Daniels, S., & Piechowski, M. M. (Eds.). (2009). *Living with intensity: Understanding the sensitivity, excitability, and the emotional development of gifted children, adolescents, and adults*. Scottsdale, AZ: Great Potential Press.

Fonesca, C. (2011). *Emotional intensity in gifted students: Helping kids cope with explosive feelings*. Waco, TX: Profrock Press, Inc.

Lovecky, D. V. (2004). *Different minds: Gifted children with Ad/Hd, Asperger Syndrome, and other learning deficits*. London: Jessica Kingsley Publishers.

Renzulli, J. S. (Ed.). (2004). Identification of students for gifted and talented programs. In S. M. Reis (Ed.), Essential Readings in Gifted Education Series (pp. 34-56). Thousand Oaks, CA: Sage.

Silverman, L. K. (2002). *Upside down brilliance: The visual spatial learner*. Glendale, CO: DeLeon Publishing, Inc.

KEY TERMS AND DEFINITIONS

Creative: Pairing of original ideas with ingenuity, and inventiveness.

Identification: Classification; determining if criteria has been met.

Instructional Technology (IT): Any technology, electric or otherwise, used to aid instruction.

Leadership: Skill for management or providing direction.

Over-Excitability: Impulsive, easily stimulated emotions.

Twice Exceptional: Term used to describe individuals who are both gifted and have an exceptionality or learning disability.

Visual and Performing Arts: Category of Giftedness that encompasses art, dance, theater, music, and other categories of the Arts.

Chapter 2
Historical Overview of Adult Gifted Education in the United States

Judith Bazler
Monmouth University, USA

Letitia Graybill
Monmouth University, USA

Meta Van Sickle
College of Charleston, USA

EXECUTIVE SUMMARY

Giftedness is not present only in childhood. It persists for a lifetime. However, even though most colleges/universities provide special needs services for appropriate students, most if not all college faculty might not believe it necessary to provide any accommodations for gifted/talented students either at undergraduate or at the graduate level. In order to accommodate one or more gifted/talented students in a class, faculty need to rethink their pedagogy and assessment strategies. At the college/university level accommodations are usually absent because faculty do not perceive a need to do so in their courses. In courses for pre-service teachers, some instructors provide practices in courses including how to teach gifted and talented students in basic education settings for K-12 grades. This chapter presents a brief overview of gifted and talented education in the United States focusing more specifically on gifted and talented at the university (or adult) level.

DOI: 10.4018/978-1-4666-6489-0.ch002

SETTING THE STAGE

When college faculty design syllabi, the varied interests and abilities of the students enrolled must be considered providing an assortment of assessment choices that meet the requirements of the curricula and that give all levels of students an opportunity to develop their products according to their interests, abilities and relevance to the students that they are planning to teach. A universal design for instruction is one way to provide differentiation of instruction in each class. Differentiated instruction is accomplished through assessments and activities that are relevant to varied learning styles and interests within the course outcomes. At the university level, students are completing, or have completed diplomas, from accredited pK-12 schools followed by two-four years of content specific coursework at the college/ university. Hopefully students then arrive in their education courses, either during their undergraduate education or following at the graduate level, with a fairly good set of skills and content in a discipline explicit manner. Because giftedness is not always apparent during the first meeting of a course the instructor must consider differing ability levels when designing assessments and assessing material that students develop on an ongoing schedule during the course and begin the process of determining which students possess gifted and talented characteristics. From the first day of class, faculty may begin to identify gifted students during assessment of products and dialogue in the classroom. Faculty note that the gifted students in a college classroom are usually not afraid to take risks and to explore areas in which they feel they lack knowledge. They actively attack the material and show a level of interest beyond what the more conventional students show. They take these risks by selecting more challenging topics for research and by attempting in their own research to explore areas that have not been dealt with sufficiently in the past. They actively examine the material presented and show a level of interest beyond what the more conventional students show. This is as true on the undergraduate level as it is on the graduate level. It is in curriculum and assessment design that the needs of the students are considered. It is the job of the professor to provide the inspiration and direction of the products that is critical to meeting the needs of the gifted students.

ORGANIZATION BACKGROUND

There is an abundant amount of research focusing on gifted students at the K-12 level. Those of us working with gifted students in university settings face many of the same challenges faced by our colleagues in the elementary and secondary schools. There is, however, insufficient research on giftedness at the collegiate level (Rinn & Plucker, 2004) or beyond (Perrone, Perrone, Ksiazak, Wright, &

Jackson, 2007). Additional research is needed to focus on these collegiate popula-tions and beyond the college classroom. While much attention has been given to the education of gifted children and adolescents, very little work has been done on the teaching of gifted adults, especially those in teacher education. Kristin, Stephen, Tracy, Amy, & Vannatter, 2010) questioned gifted adult participants who enrolled in honors courses in college about their experiences in these courses (both positive and negative). They found that one fourth of the adults reported honors classes to be challenging and rewarding (Kristin et al., 2010). A small percentage of students (12-16%) liked the small class size, and enjoyed the social interaction but found the coursework overwhelming (Kristin et al., 2010). A few of the honors programs (5.9%) that were studied (Kristen et al., 2010) revealed that gifted and talented stu-dents had provided for an earlier graduation date, a faster paced learning experience, and a sense of accomplishment. The study also showed that the students found that programs could be disappointing when they were not designed for specific fields of study (Kristen et al., 2010).

A prior study by Hébert & McBee (2007), examined how involvement in college honors programs influenced the intellectual, social, and emotional development of seven gifted university students. The original study found the students had experi-enced a sense of isolation as adolescents, resulting from differences between their abilities, interests, life goals, and religious value systems and those of the com-munities in which they lived. Within the university honors program, the students discovered an intellectual and social network with gifted individuals like themselves. Together, they were able to recognize their strong desire for self-actualization. In advanced level courses, they found intellectual stimulation and academic challenge. Several components of the honors program allowed them to experience significant psychosocial growth. Throughout their experiences, the honors program director became a mentor and played an important role in facilitating experiences designed to address the diverse -needs of these gifted young adults.

In this review, we examine how gifted adults were identified historically, what attributes were identified for the gifted, how gifted education evolved and how gifted practices have been applied in the university.

Development in Educating the Gifted in the United States

The beginning of the 20th Century saw major developments in our knowledge of how people learn. It was during these early years in the last century that the research-based field, science of psychology and education, began to develop. The researcher and practitioners in education began to work on observed variations in intelligence, measurements of ability and the possible inheritance of such characteristics. The Table 1 summarizes the major developments in the field of gifted education from

Table 1. Key dates in the development of gifted and talented education

Year	Development	Effect
1868	First attempt at systematic efforts in public schools to educate the gifted.	Recognition that some children learn more rapidly and more effectively than others. Early attempts to separate these children from so called normal or average children
1869	Publication of Francis Galton's seminal work, *Hereditary Genius*. This book summarized his research of more than four hundred British men. Through the study of these men and the application of statistical methods, he concluded that intelligence was hereditary and therefore immutable.	Generated the idea that biology is destiny and that intelligence is a characteristic that is inherited and which cannot be changed. Gifted children and adults were special.
1901	First school for gifted children opened in Worcester, Massachusetts.	Recognized that more able children needed to be together and to be challenged by education.
1905	Alfred Binet and Theodore Simon began their work on the measurement of intelligence through the development of specialized testing tools. The notion of mental age that arose from their work revolutionized the study of intelligence and provided a basis for the intelligence levels as used in education.	Application of measurement techniques and the development of testing materials that enabled the gifted to be identified through statistical analysis. Attempt at a scientifically produced number as an identifier. Their work stimulates worldwide reaction.
1908	Henry Goddard joins Binet in France to learn about the development of testing instruments. He brings these ideas back to the United States.	American psychologists who are just beginning to apply statistical analyses to traits take ideas of Binet very seriously. An understanding of the characteristics of intelligence and its measurement now are seen as within grasp.
1916	Lewis Terman, considered "the father of gifted education," published the Stanford Binet test of intelligence. Some believe that this test changed American education forever.	Children were tested with this new instrument which many felt was rooted in scientific principles that could not be refuted or changed.
1917	The US enters Word War I. The mobilization of so many men resulted in the application of The Army Alpha and Beta tests that were created and administered to over one million recruits	This action legitimatized intelligence testing in both academia and the general public.
1918	Lulu Stedman establishes an "opportunity room" for gifted students within the southern branch of the University of California.	Again, this action further reinforcing the idea that gifted children deserved specialized education because now they had an instrument that "measured" intelligence.
1921	Lewis Terman begins what has remained the longest running longitudinal study of gifted children with an original sample of 1,500 gifted children who were identified through these new testing instruments	Helped to determine the characteristics of the gifted person and showed that no single characteristic accounted for exceptional scholastic ability.
1922	A Special Opportunity Class at P. S. 165 in New York City is established by Leta S. Hollingsworth for gifted students. This class provided rich resources for the publication of work on gifted education. Over 40 research articles, a textbook and blueprints for the future were spawned from Hollingsworth's work in this school.	Effect on the New York City Public Schools suggested that the necessity of special schools for those identified as being gifted intellectually was worth investigating further.
1925	Publication of Terman's *Genetic Studies of Genius*. This work concluded that gifted students were: a) Qualitatively different in school. b) Slightly better physically in comparison to normal students. c) Superior in academic subjects in comparison to the average students. d) Emotionally stable. e) Most successful when education and family values were held in high regard by the family	Actual identification and listing of the characteristics of the children Terman studied. They did not consider giftedness in other areas. This was in the first of five volumes describing his research on giftedness. It had wide appeal in psychology as well as education. Infinite variability among these possible trait combinations was established among those included in the study.

continued on following page

Table 1. Continued

Year	Development	Effect
1926	Leta Hollingsworth publishes the *Gifted Child: Their Nature and Nurture*	This was the first textbook published on the education of the gifted.
1936	Establishment of the Speyer 500 school in New York City by Leta Hollingsworth. This school was planned for children 7-9 years old and was the result of the blueprints developed from the PS 165 experiment from 1922.	Hollingsworth's work had concrete effects on New York City's public education system.
1944	Post World War II GI Bill of Rights gives unprecedented opportunity to soldiers returning home from the war. Such opportunity had never before opened up higher education to such a wide range of adults.	Opening up of higher education to returning soldiers who for the most part had not been tested. Colleges and universities all over the United States had an influx of students- soldiers who had all levels of academic prowess.
1950	Passage of the National Science Foundation Act provided support for research in STEM curricula.	Recognized the importance of science, mathematics and engineering concepts for the economic growth of the United States. We were entering a global economy with great competition.
1954	The National Association for Gifted Children is founded.	National organization devoted to issues important to the education and understanding of giftedness in children.
1954	The Supreme Court issues, in Brown vs. the Board of Education, a decision that separate education is not equal education in the US.	This had an effected on the education of the gifted. Should there be separate education for these children? And who could be deemed as gifted.
1957	The Soviet Union launches Sputnik and causes a sharp reaction to the lack of quality in American education.	Spurred strong feelings of jealousy and competition between the USSR and the US. How could a repressive society such as that in the Soviet Union exceed the accomplishment of the United states in science mathematics, and engineering? As a result substantial amounts of funding become available for gifted and talented education especially in the STEM areas.
1964	Passage of the Civil Rights Act.	Resulted in the mandate that there should be equality for all regardless of race, ethnicity, religious or socioeconomic status. This significant legislation began a movement in the United States for equality in all areas of life. This movement continues to the present day.
1972	Publication of the Marland report. This produced a formal definition and description of giftedness that added to the previously written Terman definition. These additional characteristics included, leadership ability., visual and performing arts ability, creative or productive thinking, and psychomotor ability.	Broadening of the concept of giftedness. There are many ways in which individuals can be considered gifted. Academic performance is not the only measure. This report also stated that gifted and talented children –*"can suffer psychological damage and permanent impairment of their abilities to function well which is equal to or greater than the similar deprivation suffered by any other population with special needs served by the Office of Education. (pp. xi-xii)."*
1974	Establishment of the Office of Gifted and Talented. This office is housed within the US Department of Education.	Legitimized the necessity of special education considerations for gifted and/or talented individuals.
1975	Passage of PL-142. This Act establishes a federal mandate to serve children with special education needs, but does not include children with gifted and talented characteristics.	This controversial law concentrated on the needs of special students but gifted and talented individuals were not included in this population.

continued on following page

Table 1. Continued

Year	Development	Effect
1983	Publication of *A Nation at Risk the Imperative for Educational Reform.* This document compared the scores of America's students with their international counterparts and noted even then the failure of American students to compete globally.	The report included policies and practices in gifted education, raising academic standards, and promoting appropriate curriculum for gifted learners. This report had a galvanizing affect on educational practices in the United States and marked the beginning of a national effort towards improved education in America. This report had a galvanizing affect on the public schools in that the United States education system was now regarded as mediocre by society.
1988	Congress passes the Jacob Javits Gifted and Talented Students Education Act as part of the Reauthorization of the Elementary and Secondary Education Act.	Special funds were set aside solely for classes for those identified as gifted and talented. Schools responded by establishing special classes and hiring teachers trained to work with exceptional academic students.
1990	National Research Center on the Gifted and Talented established at the University of Connecticut. This Center included researchers at the University of Virginia, Yale University, and the University of Georgia.	Research centers established devoted to the study of gifted children.
1993	Publication of *National Excellence: The Case for Developing America's Talent.* This report was issued by the United States Department of Education outlining how America neglects its most talented youth.	The report makes a number of recommendations influenced by the research record of the preceding years in the field of gifted education. It indicated that academically gifted children are not challenged and that the continued neglect of these children will "make it impossible for Americans to compete in a global economy."
1993	Publication of Howard Gardner's Multiple Intelligences: Theory In Practice	Further developed our understanding of giftedness and suggested a new way to conceptualize the many forms of giftedness. He further defined it and showed through his research that giftedness can occur in all content areas not just math and science.
1998	The national Association for Gifted Education publishes Pre-K-12 Gifted Program Standards to provide guidance in seven key areas for programs serving gifted and talented students. The standards were revised in 2010.	Development of curricula specifically designed for gifted and talented children.
2002	The No Child Left Behind Act (NCLB) is passed as the reauthorization of the Elementary and Secondary Education Act. The Javits program is included in NCLB, and expanded to offer competitive statewide grants. The definition of gifted and talented students is modified again.	Applied to all children/students, children, or youth who give evidence of high achievement capability in areas such as intellectual, creative, artistic, or leadership capacity, or in specific academic fields, and who need services and activities not ordinarily provided by the school in order to fully develop those capabilities.
2003	Robert Sternberg's triarchicle theory of intelligence begins to influence educators	Further defined intelligence as consisting of three components. These components include: acquisition of knowledge, experiential contributions and adaptability within the context of experience.

the late 19th through the 21st Centuries and also summarizes the developments resulting from research completed on characteristics of the gifted and methods of educating them.

Examination of the timeline above illustrates swings and changes in educational practice that were brought about by political and social action groups as well as by educational theorists and psychologists. These struggles between certain elite factions in our society and those seeking a more democratic system are illustrated by Congressional Acts and court cases that ruled in favor of groups of people from differing race, class and gender backgrounds being granted an opportunity for education. There continue to be ambivalent feelings about testing and practices used to teach and define what is meant-by giftedness in children and adults. Finally, multiple theories have evolved that have identified and described various features of giftedness. Thus, the socio-political terrain for teaching the gifted and talented was constructed by political, social, theoretical and research interests across the mid 1800's to today. Even with this legislation, research and information identifying gifted students is limited. Using educational practices to support and enhance research has not transferred to future teachers and the practices for use in their own classrooms. Worse, there is a public perception that teachers are not among the gifted and talented population in this country.

In a study by VanTassel-Baska (2010), the author notes that, "Not only is there little pre-service training in gifted education, but there also is lack of funding for teacher development" (p. 222). Thus, because the research notes the lack of teaching initial teacher certification candidates about the gifted and talented program; the lack of funding to support such teaching; and lack of knowledge about gifted and talented students who plan to teach, it is imperative to enter into dialog to generate the knowledge to interact in positive ways with these students who enter our science methods courses.

General Characteristics of the Gifted

Gifted individuals have been defined as people with outstanding talent who perform or show the potential for performing at remarkably high levels of accomplishment when compared with others of their age, experience, or environment.

We have observed, in our university experiences, that gifted students exhibit one or more of the following characteristics:

- Intense devotion to personal interests. They have well defined areas of interest and show a willingness to pursue their interests in all possible directions
- Independence. They do not have to rely on others to complete their tasks they have independent work habits.
- Boredom when not engaged in the activity presented. These students can show lack of interest when there is little or no challenge to the tasks assigned.
- Ability to see to the root of problems. They often see possibilities in a task that others do not at first recognize.

- Tendency to be a maverick and a rapid learner. They can present a challenge to the instructor sometimes seeing aspects of a problem that were not readily apparent.
- Ability to anticipate outcomes. Can foresee future ramification of problems solved.
- Capable of abstract thinking and learning skills. Show unusual ability in abstraction and inference.
- Have talent in creative or leadership abilities. Often act as natural leaders in classroom. Other students can look to them for help.

Gifted students who enroll as adults in our science methods classes possess these characteristics. These students actively accept the responsibilities of the requirements, work independently to produce excellent materials are not afraid to challenge the professor when opinions and techniques differ.

Gifted education and adult students may be viewed as driven with perfectionist tendencies aiming at high standards. They can also be overly sensitive and perhaps exhibit odd or intimidating behaviors and are prone to question authority. Psychologists who work with gifted adults find them to be independent, original, curious and open to changes. Thus, it becomes the task of the science educator to work with these gifted students so that they become excellent science teachers capable of utilizing these same characteristics when they become teachers. Gifted students who want to become science teachers can be challenging to work with but the products that they generate are noteworthy both in terms of content and form.

Theories of Intelligence

It is, perhaps, relevant here to further discuss the work of the three of the major theorists presented in Table 2 below who have been influential in defining intelligence in general and who have also influenced the instructional methods described in our chapter on Designing Instruction For Gifted Science Teachers. These theorists have done much to elucidate our conception of what it means to be *intelligent* and to help us to recognize the gifted adults with whom we work. Their work has helped educators to develop some understanding of how we think and how we learn. They have helped us to design instruction beyond the "one size fits all" model of planning.

Contributions to our understanding of giftedness are summarized in Table 2.

The work of these three educational psychologists supports the concept of giftedness that we have developed through observation of the skills and attitudes exhibited in our adult classes. We have also observed that this giftedness can be expressed in multiple ways and therefore should be challenged in multiple ways.

Table 2. Influential theorists in gifted and talented education

Theorist	Major Conceptions	Description	Definition of Giftedness	Affect on Education
Robert Sternberg	Triarchic Model	Intelligent behavior can be expressed as a balance among analytical creative and practical abilities	Dismissed the psychometric definition of intelligence as a number. Intelligence can be described as adaptability to the context in which an individual lives	Lessened the use of IQ scores u in identifying intelligence in children.
Joseph Renzulli	Three Ring Concept	Characteristics of high ability learners Above average learning skills. High task commitment Creativity	Gifted individuals possess all three of these characteristics in an interlocking set.	Establishment of gifted and talented programs in K-12 schools. Gave schools a model for the identification of the gifted that did not rely solely on tests.
Howard Gardner	Multiple Intelligence Theory	Intelligence can be expressed in multiple ways. Identified nine "intelligences."	Most individual who reach higher levels of ability are in the middle of the continuum that he described, Gifted individuals fall in the upper areas of the spectrum that he developed.	Helped educators to understand that students come to us with multiple skills an multiple abilities and learning styles

QUESTIONS FOR FURTHER DISCUSSION

Having researched the history of adult gifted in universities, we find ourselves asking numerous questions.

1. Is it really important for college professors to strategize teaching practices in their classes to include gifted and talented students' needs? If yes, will these strategies transfer to practices they choose for their own classrooms?
2. Aren't all college students gifted?
3. Have these students that we identified also been identified in previous institutions and if not why not?
4. Does the academic giftedness that we have identified and characterized indicate success in the secondary science and mathematics classrooms in which they will teach? Will gifted and talented teachers adapt to the contexts of the classrooms better than other teachers?

5. If students were identified as gifted and talented in their pK-12 education, why does this identification not follow in the university?
6. If identification of gifted and talented does follow into the university, what curricula other than honors courses has been provided.

CONCLUSION

Gifted students who enroll as adults in science methods classes possess the characteristics described in this chapter. These students actively accept the responsibilities of the requirements, work independently to produce excellent materials, and are not afraid to challenge the professor when opinions and techniques differ. The historical information about gifted and talented students through social, political and education research helps understand the need for using appropriate teaching strategies in teaching the practices and content of education to our future teachers. The notions about the ability to adapt to a variety of situations/contexts are especially important to schooling in the U. S. today because of the varying populations in all of our schools.

REFERENCES

Audrey, C. R., Jean, S. S., Denise, A. T., & Highnam, D. (2012). Creativity and thinking skills integrated into a science enrichment unit on flooding. *Creative Education*, *3*(8), 1371–1379. doi:10.4236/ce.2012.38200

Baslanti, U., & McCoach, D. B. (2006). Factors related to the underachievement of university students in Turkey. *Roeper Review*, *28*(4), 210–215. doi:10.1080/02783190609554366

Binet, A. (1907). *The mind and the brain*. London: K. Paul, Trench, Trubner & Co. Ltd.

Binet, A., & Simon, T. (1916). *The development of intelligence in children: (The Binet-Simon scale)*. New York, NY: Williams & Wilkins.

Brown v. Board of Education, 347 US. 483 (1959).

Daniel, R. H., Matthew, T. M., & Thomas, P. H. (2007). Exploring the motivational trajectories of gifted university students. *Roeper Review*, *29*(3), 197–205. doi:10.1080/02783190709554409

Department of Education. (2001). *No Child Left Behind (NCLB) Act*. Retrieved from www.ed.gov/nclb

Education of the Gifted and Talented-Volume1: Report to the Congress of the United States by the U.S. Commissioner of Education. (1971, Aug.). ERIC ED 056243.

Gallagher, J. J. (1994). Current and historical thinking on education gifted and talented students. In P. O' Connell (Ed.), *National excellence: A case for developing America's talent. An anthology of readings* (pp. 303–213). Darby, PA: Diane Publishing Company.

Galton, F. (1989). *Hereditary genius: An inquiry into its laws and consequences.* New York, NY: McMillan and Co.

Gardner, D. P. (1983). *A nation at risk: The imperative for educational reform.* Washington, DC: National Commission for Excellence in Education.

Gardner, H. (1993). *Multiple intelligences: The theory in practice.* New York, NY: Basic Books.

Hebert, T. P., & McBee, M. T. (2007, Spring). The input of an undergraduate honors program on gifted university students. *Gifted Child Quarterly*, *51*(2), 136–151. doi:10.1177/0016986207299471

Hollingsworth, L. S. (1926). *Gifted children: Their nature and nurture.* New York, NY: MacMillan and Co.

House Energy and Commerce Committee. (2009). *H.R.2036-111th Congress: Jacob K. Javitz gifted and talented students education enhancement act.* Retrieved from http://www.govtrack.us/congress/bills/111/hr203

Klapp, J. (2000). Gifted grownups: The mixed blessings of extraordinary potential. *Roeper Review*, *23*(1), 47. doi:10.1080/02783190009554062

Kristin, M. P., Stephen, L. W., Tracy, M. K., Amy, L. C., & Vannatter, A. (2010). Looking back on lessons learned: Gifted adults reflect on their experiences in advanced classes. *Roeper Review*, *32*(2), 127–139. doi:10.1080/02783191003587918

Kristin, M. P., Tracy, M. K., Stephen, L. W., Vannatter, A., Claudine, C. H., Shepler, D., & Philip, A. P. (2011/2012). Major life decisions of gifted adults in relation to overall life satisfaction. *Journal for the Education of the Gifted*, *34*(6), 817–838. doi:10.1177/0162353211425101

Marland, S. P., Jr. (1972). Education of the gifted and talented: Report to the Congress of the United States by the U.S. Commissioner of Education and background papers submitted to the U.S. Office of Education. Washington, DC: U.S. Government Printing Office. (Government Documents Y4.L 11/2: G36)

National Commission on Excellence in Education. (1982). *A Nation at Risk: The Imperative for Educational Reform*. Retrieved from http://www.ed.gov/pubs/NatAtRisk/risk.html

Perrone, K. M., Perrone, P. A., Ksiazak, T. M., Wright, S. L., & Jackson, Z. V. (2007). Self-perception of gifts and talents among adults in a longitudinal study of academically talented high-school graduates. *Roeper Review, 29*(4), 259–264. doi:10.1080/02783190709554420

Renzulli, J. S. (1978). What makes giftedness? Re-examining a definition. *Phi Delta Kappan, 60*(1), 180–184, 261.

Renzulli, J. S. (1994). *Schools for talent development: A practical plan for total school improvement*. Mansfield Center, CT: Creative Learning Press.

Renzulli, J. S., & Reis, S. M. (1985). *The school wide enrichment model: A comprehensive plan for educational excellence*. Mansfield Center, CT: Creative Learning Press.

Rinn, A. N., & Plucker, J. A. (2004). We recruit them, but then what? The educational and psychological experience of academically talented undergraduates. *Gifted Child Quarterly, 48*(1), 54–67. doi:10.1177/001698620404800106

Ross, P. O. (1993, October). *National excellence: A case for developing America's talent*. Washington, DC: U.S. Government Printing Office.

Sternberg, R. J. (1985). *Beyond IQ: A triarchic theory of intelligence*. Cambridge, UK: Cambridge University Press.

Sternberg, R. J. (1997). A triarchic view of giftedness: Theory and practice. In N. Coleangelo, & G. A. Davis (Eds.), *Handbook of gifted education* (pp. 43–53). Boston, MA: Allyn and Bacon.

Sternberg, R. J., Nokes, C., Geissler, W., Prince, P., Okatcha, F., Bundy, D. A., & Grigorenke, E. L. (2001). The relationship between academic and practical intelligence: A case study in Kenya. *Intelligence, 29*(5), 401–418. doi:10.1016/S0160-2896(01)00065-4

Terman, L. M. (1959). *Genetic studies of genius* (Vol. 5). Stanford, CA: Stanford University Press.

VanTassel-Baska, J. (2010). *Patterns and profiles of low income gifted learners*. Waco, TX: Pufrock Press.

KEY TERMS AND DEFINITIONS

Differentiated Instruction: Providing appropriate instruction to gifted and/or talented students in a comparable manner to non-identified students.

Gifted: A student or adult identified as having characteristics conducive to extended, in-depth learning/ knowledge of topic(s).

Gifted Education: The overall body of work encompassing curriculum, pedagogy, assessment, and/or standards regarding gifted students.

Gifted/Talented: Students having been identified through either state standardized assessment or anecdotal assessment of an instructor.

Honors Programs: Curricular placements in P-16 which include more advanced study of topic(s).

Section 2
Science and the Gifted/ Talented Student

Chapter 3
Using Technology to Teach Gifted Students in a Heterogeneous Classroom

Edward L. Shaw Jr.
University of South Alabama, USA

Rebecca M. Giles
University of South Alabama, USA

EXECUTIVE SUMMARY

The answer to educating gifted and talented students in heterogeneous classrooms may lie, at least partially, in using instructional technology to motivate learning and enrich lessons. This case study explores one aspect of effective instruction for gifted second graders during lessons conducted in their general education classrooms. This chapter summarizes the development and delivery, students' performance and perceptions, and professional implications of an elementary science lesson utilizing interactive whiteboard technology to convey science content and elicit participation. It also emphasizes the importance of teacher educators' modeling the use of interactive whiteboards for the purpose of differentiating instruction in teacher training programs to better prepare future teachers for the diverse learners who will fill their classrooms.

DOI: 10.4018/978-1-4666-6489-0.ch003

ORGANIZATION BACKGROUND

Substantial reports over the past 15 years indicate that large numbers of teachers choose to leave the profession early in their careers (Darling-Hammond & Sykes, 2003; Hare & Heap, 2001; Johnson, 2001; Pipho, 1998). According to 2004-2005 data collected by the National Center for Education Statistics, nearly a quarter of public-school teachers leave the profession within the first three years (Boyd, Grossman, Lankford, Loeb, Wyckoff, & National Bureau of Economic Research, 2008; Marvel, 2007), and nearly half of all teachers leave the profession after five years of teaching (Ingersoll, 2007; Alliance for Excellent Education, 2005; National Commission on Teaching and America's Future, 2003). The percentages of attrition are greatest for teachers in math, science, and elementary special education (Ingersoll, 2007). Though there may be many reasons for teacher attrition, the short-comings of a traditional teacher preparation program have been cited as at least partly contributing to the continuous teacher turnover currently plaguing the profession (Haberman, 2005; Kent, Feldman, & Hayes, 2009).

Preservice teachers must experience a wide range of learning opportunities during their preparation program to avoid feeling underprepared when they begin teaching (Kuster, Bain, Milbrandt & Newton, 2010). Advocating a one-size-fits-all approach to teaching does not work (Stotsky, 2006) because a classroom full of "regular" students simply does not exist. The disparity between the abilities of students in a single classroom is greater than ever before, thus, today's elementary teachers must be able to deliver lessons that accommodate students' varied learning styles and wide range of abilities when they are heterogeneously grouped for instruction. The future success of educating students who have an array of learning skills, academic abilities, physical challenges, and cultural variations is contingent upon how well prepared educators are in the pedagogies of differentiating instruction (Kent & Giles, in press).

Preservice teachers must be well prepared to teach in an innovative manner, utilizing principles and practices for differentiating instruction advocated in quality teacher-preparation programs. Further, novice teachers must be prepared to sustain this kind of teaching when faced with the obstacles of an overwhelmingly diverse student population (Lloyd, & Sullivan, 2012). The situation becomes even more challenging when considered in light of ever changing federal, state, and local regulations and expectations for student performance, particularly in regard to the recent adoption of Common Core State Standards and an increased investment in science, technology, engineering, and mathematics (STEM) education. Unfortunately, the needs of high-achieving and academically advanced students may become overlooked by elementary educators in the mist of such demanding circumstances.

Differentiating instruction is too often associated with making accommodations and/or adjustments for individuals with disabilities, who have a federally mandated Individual Education Program (IEP) to ensure that their instructional needs are appropriately met. While students identified as gifted and talented often receive supplemental services through enrollment in a gifted program when funds and space are available, their curriculum and instruction in regular classrooms is often provided without differentiation from that of the general population. The answer to educating gifted and talented students in heterogeneous classrooms may lie, at least partially, in using instructional technology to motivate learning and enrich lessons.

It is imperative that preservice teachers have experiences with gifted and talented students to extend their ability to address the learning needs of these students. First, instruction on the characteristics of gifted and talented students in needed. Preservice teachers must have the knowledge necessary to identify these students, especially in the lower grades where formal identification and classification may not yet be an option in some school systems. Further, preservice teachers must be provided with experiences in designing, implementing, and assessing lessons that address the needs of gifted students using instructional technology. Incorporating technology into instruction to introduce, expand, bring closure, extend, and assess the success of the lesson is a huge challenge for many new teachers. Despite initial frustration and, at times the feelings of being overwhelmed, instructional technology enables both pre- and in-service teachers to address the educational needs of the gifted and talented students.

This case explores one aspect of effective instruction for elementary students of varying academic abilities during science lessons conducted in their general education classrooms. The development and delivery, students' performance and perceptions, and professional implications of student engagement in a second grade science lesson employing interactive whiteboard technology are summarized. The focus of this chapter includes both the delivery and student perceptions of SMART-Board® use as well as the importance of adequately preparing preservice teachers to employ this type of instructional technology in K-6 classrooms for the purpose of differentiating instruction to meet the needs of gifted learners.

SETTING THE STAGE

Interactive Whiteboard Instruction

Interactive whiteboards (i.e., SMARTBoard®, Promethean Boards, etc.) combine the functionality of a whiteboard, computer, and projector into a single system which uses touch control to perform all mouse and keyboard functions. The large size and touch-sensitive display allow for easy navigation and make it especially suited for group activity. Romiszowski and Ravitz (1997) indicated that computer technology has changed the traditional *instructional* model to an information-age *conversational* model of learning where the learner is actively engaged in co-creating meaning and knowledge with peers. Interactive whiteboards (IWBs) in particular seem to invite collaboration through social interaction and communication.

Emerging research on the pedagogical effectiveness of using interactive whiteboards (IWBs) with young learners seems promising. For example, Mercer, Warwick, Kershner and Staarman (2010) found that IWBs offer some useful amenities for supporting discussions during children's group-based science learning in English primary classrooms. The researchers (Kershner, Mercer, Warwick, & Staarman, 2010) concluded that IWBs can make identifiable contributions to children's productive communication and thinking, while also providing both a tool and environment that encourages co-constructed knowledge building. Preston and Mowbry (2008) praise IWBs as highly effective for whole group instruction, active discussion, and questioning by holding "students' attention much better than a traditional lecture-and-blackboard lesson ever could" (Vallas & Williamson, 2009, p. 18) while allowing material generated to be saved and revisited at a later date. In addition, IWBs offer a powerful facility for integrating media elements into teaching to enhance content by providing access to a wide range of digital resources (Murcia & Sheffiedl, 2010). Short, focused interactive segments can be incorporated before, during and/or after first-hand investigation to help explore and construct knowledge of key scientific concepts (Preston & Mowbray, 2008). Including such resources allows teachers to increase the lesson's pace to effectively engage and motivate students (Murcia & Sheffiedl, 2010).

While Vallas and Williamson (2009) credit interactive whiteboards for solving the problem of only having one computer for a large number of students by making it easy and enjoyable for both teachers and groups of students to interact with educational software, others have attacked this new fad. There has been criticism that in too many classrooms, IWBs are nothing more than fancy, expensive chalkboards, especially when their interactive features are ignored by teachers who do not know how or refuse to use them (Manzo, 2010). With proper teacher training, however, IWBs can be an effective means of augmenting typical teaching strategies to make science learning more motivational and meaningful for today's technologically advanced students (Giles & Shaw, 2011).

Interactive whiteboards can be an effective tool for facilitating a "minds on" approach to science set forth by the *National Science Education Standards* (National Research Council, 1996) where teachers provide many, varied opportunities for children to explore and experiment so that learning science is "an active enterprise" (Lind, 1999, p. 73). As students make discoveries through first-hand, investigative experiences, the IWBs enhance, rather than replace, hands-on explorations and other practical activities (Preston & Mowbray, 2008). They are ideal for introducing a lesson and determining children's prior knowledge (Preston & Mowbray, 2008) as well as summarizing instruction and assessing understanding once a knowledge base has been investigated and mastered (Giles & Shaw, 2011). While interacting with words and images on the IWBs can never take the place of knowledge acquired through direct contact with actual materials, it is posited these digital experiences are beneficial for science learning.

Addressing Student Differences

Historically, elementary schools have used a limited range of learning and teaching techniques and have mainly employed linguistic and logical teaching methods. Even today, many schools rely on book-based teaching for the majority of instruction. The emergence of numerous learning style models during recent years, however, has brought increasing attention to the concept that individuals differ in how they learn (James & Gardner, 1995). The idea of individualized learning styles, based on the notion that students learn in diverse ways and that one approach to teaching does not work for every student or even most students, originated in the 1970s and has greatly influenced education today (Pashler, McDaniel, Rohrer, & Bjork, 2008).

Learning Styles

One way to address the pedagogical needs of students with diverse abilities in a heterogeneous classroom is to implement instruction addressing different learning styles. Learning styles are simply different approaches or ways of learning. While it is generally recognized that each person prefers different learning modes and techniques, learning styles group and label common ways that people learn. An individual's preferred learning style(s), or mode(s) of learning, is identified by the characteristic cognitive and affective behaviors related to how a learner perceives, interacts with, and responds to the learning environment and can be influenced by intellectual preferences, family culture, psychological attributes, or sociological histories (Collins & O'Brien, 2003). There are many different ways of categorizing learning styles with an instrument correlated to each model (i.e., the Kolb Learning Style Indicator, the Gregorc Style Delineator, the Felder–Silverman Index of Learning Styles, the VARK Questionnaire, and the Dunn and Dunn Productivity Environmental Preference Survey, etc.) available for identifying a learner's preferred style. One of the most widely-used categorizations of the various types of learning styles is Neil Fleming's VARK model (Hawk & Shah, 2007). Developed in 1987, this model identifies visual learning, auditory learning, learning through reading and writing, and kinesthetic learning (Fleming, 2012). Fleming claimed that visual learners have a preference for seeing pictures, movies, and diagrams while auditory learners prefer listening to lectures or discussions. Reading and writing preference learners make lists, read textbooks, and take notes while tactile/kinesthetic learners prefer to learn via experience through moving, touching, and doing. Fleming's three most commonly known learning styles are visual, kinesthetic, and auditory. Hutenger (2001) stated "Visual children tend to learn by watching; motor/kinesthetic learners tend to be involved and active; and, auditory tend to learn by being told instructions" (par. 2). Over the years, the names of these styles have changed—from "visual" to "global" and from "auditory" to "analytic," and a host of different dimensions have been suggested—two dimensional/three-dimensional, simultaneous/sequential, connecting/compartmentalizing, inventing/reproducing, reflective/impulsive, or field dependent/field independent (Stahl, 1999). Applying any learning style model to pedagogy allows teachers to prepare lessons that address each area working under the assumption that students' educational experiences can be maximized by focusing on the learning style that benefits them the most. Although learning styles will inevitably differ among students in the classroom, Dunn and Dunn (1978) say that teachers should try to make changes in their classroom that will be beneficial to every learning style.

While the concept of learning styles remains extremely popular in psychology and education, critics suggest that personal learning preferences have no actual influence on learning results. Pashler, McDaniel, Rohrer, and Bjork (2008) believe teachers should not waste time or energy trying to determine the composition of learning styles in their classrooms advocating that teachers focus on matching their instruction to the content being taught instead. Considering learning styles, however, encourages teachers to examine what would be the best instructional methods for a particular lesson and make adjustments accordingly. Further, Sternberg, Grigorenko, Ferrari, and Clinkenbeard (1999) found that students who were strongly oriented toward "analytical," "creative," or "practical" intelligence did better if they were taught by instructors who matched their strength.

The challenge for classroom teachers is to move beyond the basic concepts and content in each discipline to provide additional or advanced experiences for the gifted and talented students. Each of these students must be challenged in an alternative, instructional technique. This could be done via the teacher, an additional instructional strategy, utilizing a mentor teacher, or through the use of appropriate technology. Where a mentor may not be available, the incorporation of technology offers the best alternative. The real challenge is to find appropriate software, podcast, websites, etc., that matches the learning style of the gifted and talented students.

Multiple Intelligences

Conceived by Howard Gardner, Multiple Intelligence (MI) theory advocates various ways to demonstrate intellectual ability. Using eight specific criteria, Gardner originally identified seven Multiple Intelligences -- musical-rhythmic, visual-spatial, verbal-linguistic, logical-mathematical, bodily-kinesthetic, interpersonal, and intrapersonal, later adding naturalistic. While spiritual and existential intelligence have been mentioned, Gardner is less sure about how to define and incorporate these abilities in regard to his set criteria, thus, admitting that they may not be worthy of inclusion. Gardner identifies the following misconceptions regarding his theory that have been perpetuated in educational literature: there should be a test per MI; intelligence equals a discipline; intelligence and learning styles are indistinguishable; a MI approach that schools can use exists; there is no empirical data to support MI; MI is not compatible with environmental accounts, and; the theory of intelligences is too broad (Gardner, 1996). He further believes that a person's intelligence cannot be determined by a test but that the test reflects the student's ability to master a particular task. Furthermore, Gardner cautions educators to be careful categorizing students' intelligences to fit certain profiles (Gardner, 1996).

Waterhouse (2006) points out that Gardner's selection and application of criteria for his "intelligences" is subjective and arbitrary, while others (Stahl, 1999) criticize Gardner's lack of empirical evidence for his theory. Gardner (1999), however, argues passionately that the narrow definition of intelligence as equal to scholastic performance is simply too constrictive, claiming that the nature of schooling gives privileges to the linguistic and logical-mathematical traditions and that other intelligences go largely unidentified and uneducated (Collins & O'Brien, 2003). Despite criticism from both psychologist and educators, Multiple Intelligence theory remains considerably popular among teachers, many of whom integrate the concept in their teaching philosophies and classroom instruction.

The experienced classroom teacher tries to incorporate learning strategies that match his/her students' intelligences and learning styles. In every classroom multiple intelligences exist in all students but may be more evident with gifted and talented students. No one teaching strategy matches all intellectual abilities of the students in a traditional classroom. Differentiated instruction offers a solution to address the identified intelligences of students in a classroom. Particularly in teaching science, students bring a vast amount of experiences or inexpediences to the lesson. Technologies such as The Magic School Bus® series or Brainpop® use an array of presentation methods to match the content with students' various intelligences.

Teaching the Gifted in Heterogeneous Groups

Gifted students have been defined as those who possess exceptional abilities in any area of learning that significantly exceeds age-level expectations (Winebrenner, 2001). Another popular definition for gifted and talented is provided by the United States Department of Education (2007) as students having outstanding talent or potential for performing at remarkably high levels of accomplishment when compared with others of their age, experience, or environment, often display behaviors and traits different from those of their peers. According to O'Connell- Ross (1993), these children and youth exhibit high performance capability in intellectual, creative, and/or artistic areas, possess an unusual leadership capacity, or excel in specific academic fields; thus, requiring services or activities not ordinarily provided by the schools. Children and youth from all cultural groups, across all economic strata, and in all areas of human endeavor exhibit the qualities of gifted identified in these various definitions.

In terms of the placement of students who are deemed to be gifted, there are a variety of grouping options that have been found to be beneficial for gifted students (Rogers, 1993). Examples include placement in special enriched or accelerated programs, regrouping for enriched instruction in specific subjects, cross-grade grouping for specific subjects, pull-out grouping for enrichment, cluster grouping within an otherwise heterogeneous classroom, and within-class ability grouping. Except for full-time placement in special enriched or accelerated programs, all of these options have gifted students spending some part of the school day in a classroom that contains both gifted and non-gifted students.

While some practitioners (Benson, 2002) may argue that typical classrooms lack the necessary resources to serve gifted students well, Renzulli (cited in Knobel & Shaunessey, 2002) believes that gifted students can be served in regular classrooms containing students of varying abilities when teachers have been adequately equipped. Tomlinson (2001) agrees that the uncommon needs of gifted learners can be met in regular classrooms through differentiated instruction, such as giving them advanced reading material and asking them to think at a deeper level of complexity. When teachers differentiate effectively, there is general improvement in overall achievement for the entire class (Saunders, 2005; Tomlinson, 1999; Winebrenner & Devlin, 2001). This suggests that when teachers learn how to provide what gifted students need and provide similar opportunities to others as well, expectations and the levels of learning are raised for all students (Gentry & Kielty, 2001).

Regardless of one's learning style, type of intelligence(s), ability or talent, students' learning will be enhanced or diminished by the classroom teacher. Robinson, Lanzi, Weinberg, Ramey, and Ramey (2002) attribute successful classroom learning for gifted and talented students to a challenging and content-rich curriculum that promotes both critical and creative thinking across all academic disciplines including reading, math, science, and the arts. Barbour and Shaklee (1998) contend that ample and varied materials including but not limited to technology, print material, and manipulative resources are necessary to ensure learning for students displaying all modalities and preferences.

Classroom teachers must keep gifted and talented students on task, address their learning styles and needs, and prevent boredom from occurring. In most schools, technology has become an integral part of the classroom. Sometimes this technology may be in an isolated room, such as a computer lab, or within the classroom itself. In either situation, available technology can be used to challenge gifted and talented students beyond minimum expectations. A lesson on rock types, as with this case study, can be extended by having gifted and talented students investigate rocks to a greater depth. For example they could determine 1) which rocks are appropriate to be used in various parts of constructing a building, locally, nationally, and internationally; 2) availability of rocks used in constructing foundations and coverings; and 3) what makes certain rocks more valuable than others. These are a few types of questions that could be used to challenge gifted and talented students beyond the basics covered in a typical classroom science lesson. Once the information is located the gifted and talented students could share their findings with classmates using various presentation modes, which would allow a variety of technologies to be used. Having gifted and talented students use technology to disseminate information would benefit them directly and classmates indirectly by exposing them to additional new science content not normally covered.

CASE DESCRIPTION

Pedagogical Concerns

The challenge for elementary teachers is how to effectively introduce science concepts, extend this initial introduction, and ensure mastery and retention of the concepts within a short amount of time with limited access to hands-on materials. The sophisticated nature of rock types and unfamiliar vocabulary, specifically sedimentary, metamorphic, and igneous, makes it a difficult science concept to teach young learners. Most students have had little contact with rock identification or classification. Teachers are further challenged by classrooms of learners with a wide range of abilities. While gifted and talented students may become easily frustrated with the slow-moving pace of traditional lessons, other students rely on repetition for successful mastery. In an attempt to determine the most effective instructional approach—instruction using an interactive whiteboard, hands-on experience with rocks, and a combination of interactive whiteboard and rocks, a research study was conducted with eight second grade classrooms. This research is described in the case study.

Technology Components

The technology employed was SMARTBoard® brand interactive whiteboard using Notebook 10 software. The SMARTBoard® was used to show a video that was downloaded from the internet. The video's appeal for visual and auditory learners was the opportunity to focus on the concepts being taught as they were presented in a preferred delivery format. For most learners, the video served as either an advance organizer while it possibly provided a review for some gifted learners. Following the video, students engaged in simulated activities relating to each rock type, which held particular appeal for motor/kinesthetic learners. As students were seated on the carpet, a Notebook 10 file available through SMART Exchange and adapted to emphasize the specific concepts being taught was used to introduce rock types and describe their formation. Students were able to visit the board to manipulate various rocks images. Since the images on the board can be instantly restored with a touch, the process could be quickly and easily repeated allowing all children the opportunity to participate. For example, students touched the screen to simulate an increase in pressure resulting in an altered image representative of metamorphic change. Additionally, each child participated in creating a fossil in sedimentary rock by dragging and dropping bones into place on the board. It must be noted that the SMARTBoard® is utilized extensively by the second grade teachers at this school so regardless of the discipline; these students interact with the SMARTBoard® every day. There was not a learning curve with the technology as with the different types of rocks.

Case Description

Participants were 103 second graders from eight different classrooms at a single suburban elementary school in southern Alabama. The school had an enrollment of 1036 students in kindergarten through fifth grade with approximately 4% of the students eligible for free or reduced price meals (2011, National Center for Educational Statistics). Sixty-two (60%) of the participants were male and 41 (40%) were female. Although most (83) participants were white, ethnicities also represented were African American (13), Asian (5), and Hispanic (1).

Intact classes were randomly assigned roles. Students, for whom parental consent had been obtained, were participants in the various groups. Two classes served as the comparison group (n=17), and two classes were assigned to each of the treatment groups – SMARTBoard® only (n=36), rocks only (n=23), and SMARTBoard® with rocks (n=27). Students in the SMARTBoard® and SMARTBoard® with rocks groups received instruction delivered via the interactive whiteboard. In addition, the SMARTBoard® with rocks and rocks only groups had access to a collection of rock samples containing examples of the three rock types being studied and hand lens.

Data were collected using an 8-item content quiz designed by the researchers (see Appendix A). The quiz, based on the content standards from the Alabama Course of Study – Science (2005), used 5 multiple choice and 3 matching items to measure students' knowledge gain and retention of concepts related to various rock types--igneous, sedimentary, and metamorphic. Students were awarded 1 point for each correct response for a highest possible score of 8 points. This quiz served as the pre-, post- and delayed posttest.

A quasi-experimental pretest-posttest-delayed post comparison group design with three treatment groups—SMARTBoard® only, rocks only, SMARTBoard® with rocks—was employed. The study was conducted over a two week period. The pretest was administered to all participants by their own classroom teachers on Monday. The SMARTBoard® only group received instruction on Tuesday. The SMARTBoard® with rocks treatment occurred on Wednesday. The characteristics of rock types introduced and discussed using the interactive whiteboard were reinforced with first-hand observations of real rocks. The rocks only treatment occurred on Thursday. Participants in this group rotated through stations to observe each type of rock using a small hand lens. The rocks chosen were typical rocks, with many easily observable characteristics, from each category--igneous, sedimentary, and metamorphic.

The instructional time for each treatment was approximately one hour. The first author delivered instruction to all three groups in an attempt to control for teacher affect. The posttest was administered to all participants by their own classroom teachers about 20 minutes after the students had received instruction. The delayed posttest was administered to all participants by their own classroom teachers one week from the following Monday, which was two weeks after the pretest. Following administration of the delayed post, the comparison group received instruction on rock types using the SMARTBoard® with rocks method of delivery.

Each participant was assigned a number and treatment group code which appeared on all three quizzes-pretest, posttest, and delayed posttest. Each group's mean score on each quiz is reported in Table 1. Scores from the three tests were analyzed using the Statistical Package for Social Sciences (SPSS).

The alpha value for comparison was set at .05 and 95% as the confidence level. A mixed model (3 times X 4 groups) between-within subjects analysis of variance (ANOVA) was conducted to assess the impact of four different interventions (SMARTBoards® only, rocks only, SMARTBoards® with rocks, and a comparison

Table 1. Pretest, posttest, and delayed posttest means by group

	SMARTBoard® Only	Rocks Only	SMARTBoard® with Rocks	Comparison
Pretest	2.03	2.22	3.15	2.00
Posttest	4.31	3.70	3.85	3.92
Delayed Post	4.00	3.22	3.85	3.56

group) on students' test scores across three time periods (pretest, posttest, and a delayed posttest). There was a statistically significant between subjects main effect of intervention (F [3, 99] = 2.99, p = .04, η_p^2 = .083), a statistically significant within subjects main effect of time (F [2, 198] = 24.68, p < .001, η_p^2 = .2) and a statistically significant interaction between time and intervention (F [6, 198] = 2.34, p = .03, η_p^2 = .07). Tests of the simple effects and pairwise comparisons were conducted to follow up the significant interaction. The simple effect of time was statistically significant for both the SMARTBoards only (F [2, 98] = 25.73, p < .001) and the rocks only (F [2, 98] = 5.91, p = .004) groups indicating that students' scores significantly improved from the pretest (SMARTBoards M = 2.03, rocks only M = 2.22) to the posttest (SMARTBoards® M = 4.31, rocks only M = 3.70) in these conditions. Also, the differences between the posttest scores and the delayed posttest scores for these groups were not statistically significant indicating that the effect of the interventions remained over time (delayed posttest SMARTBoards® M = 4.0, delayed posttest rocks M = 3.22). Tests of the simple effect of time for the SMARTBoard® plus rocks group and the control group were not statistically significant (p > .05) indicating that students' scores did not significantly improve after the SMARTBoard® and rocks intervention or, as expected, in the control group (see Table 1). This lack of improvement in the SMARTBoard® plus rocks group could be a result of the superior performance of students in this group at the pretest (i.e., students in the SMARTBoards® and rocks group (M = 3.15) performed better than the other three groups (SMARTBoards® only M = 2.03, rocks only M = 2.22, control M = 2.0), p < .05).

An analysis of covariance was used to compare group posttest scores controlling for pretest group differences. The ANCOVA was statistically significant (F [3, 98] = 3.07, p = .03, η^2 = .085) demonstrating that, after adjusting for pre-intervention scores, scores on the posttest were not equal for all groups. Specifically, students performed the best on the posttest after receiving SMARTBoards® only instruction ($M_{adjusted}$ = 4.34) followed by SMARTBoard plus rocks ($M_{adjusted}$ = 3.76), rocks only ($M_{adjusted}$ = 3.71) and the control group ($M_{adjusted}$ = 2.92) respectively. However, pairwise comparisons revealed that the only statistically significant difference was between the SMARTBoards® condition posttest scores and the control group posttest scores ($p = .003$). It is surprising that all three treatments did not do better than the control on the three tests. The increase between pre- and posttest mean for the control group could be attributed to two possible factors. The first of these being test threat, as taking a test generally affects subsequent testing by increasing participants' performance as a result of their familiarity with the test items rather than any actual treatment. Further, it is possible that the control group participants' knowledge of rock types increased between the time of the pre- and posttest as a result of extraneous learning (i.e., discussion of rock types with peers in other groups during snack, recess, lunch, etc.). The SMARTBoard® group and rocks only group scored better, while not significantly, than the group whose instruction involved a combination of SMARTBoard® technologies along with the examination of actual rock samples. One possible explanation for this could be that all three delivery types lasted the same amount of time. For the SMARTBoard® with rocks group, information was first presented using the SMARTBoard® followed by an opportunity to examine the rocks themselves. The limited time available for each experience may have prevented concepts related to the three different types of rocks to be fully developed in either format.

While it appears that interactive whiteboards can be an effective teaching tool regarding content in science, the researchers are not advocating that the use of hands-on experiences be abandoned. In contrast, results suggest that further investigation of instructional methods using both technological resources and manipulative materials should be conducted, as the proliferation of technology into all educational arenas continues. This will impact the type of instructional strategies aimed specifically at gifted and talented students. This will allow them to master the content and go beyond what the other students may do in the instructional strategy.

Management and Organizational Concerns

The key to successfully challenging students in an elementary classroom, especially those identified as gifted and talented or academically high-achieving, is the classroom teacher. Although the gifted and talented students may be spend some instructional time with a teacher certified in gifted education, most of their instructional time is usually spent with the regular classroom teacher. Cummings (2013) notes that gifted and talented students need interesting and independent activities to prevent boredom, can benefit from a mentor in the area the student shows the greatest interest, enjoy participating in academic competitions, and need materials that incorporate higher level thinking and/or problem solving abilities. At least two of these suggestions—independent activities and higher level thinking—can be encouraged and facilitated with the incorporation of instructional technology.

Additionally, the use of instructional technology can compliment current classroom practice and/or extend content to challenge all the students. This extension of the content is limited only by the creativity of the teacher, collaboration with colleagues, and professional in-services.

Different teaching strategies allow students with differing modalities and intelligences to master, retain, and apply concepts to future learning experiences in a variety of ways. This provides learning opportunities for students ranging from special needs to the gifted and talented that allows them to use their strengths while improving areas of weakness. For example, a gifted student confident in a particular intelligence such as linguistics can use his linguistic strength while working to become proficient in another area such as logical mathematical.

Further, teachers can provide additional experiences with technology or the gifted and talented students. These experiences could include technology, from blogging to making Instagram® programs or Google Docs®, or research of rock types and uses in the local, state, and national economies, or designing something, imaginary or for their school, involving rocks for the benefit of mankind or their school or community. These activities could be designed by the classroom or gifted teacher as well as planned jointly.

Teachers must be aware of the learning styles of the gifted and talented students as compared to those of other students in the classroom so that instruction can be designed and implemented to benefit all. For students to master content, it must be taught in the best way for them to have the opportunity to acquire and retain concepts. It is the job of the educational community to guarantee a proper and appropriate education for all our students so as to ensure the success of our students and ultimately our country. In this case study, rock types was presented in using several different instructional approaches, each address a range of learning styles, to provide every student an opportunity to learn the content in a way that complimented his learning style, ability, and interest.

CURRENT CHALLENGES

Current challenges of providing appropriate educational experiences for gifted students in heterogeneous classrooms include adequately preparing preservice teachers to 1) recognize and accommodate differences and 2) integrate technology for the purpose of differentiating instruction. Preservice teachers must be prepared to plan, implement, and assess content and technology to fit the needs of all their students. Interactive whiteboards are only one of many technologies is readily available to pre- and in-service teachers for developing and implementing challenging lessons that accommodate all students, whether gifted and talent, general education, or special needs students.

The challenges facing today's classroom teachers include rigorous content, politically mandated expectations for student performance, extremely diverse student population, and limited availability of classroom materials and resources, including access to appropriate instructional technology. The availability of instructional technology--number of computers in the classroom, availability of a computer laboratory, access to digital tools (i.e., interactive whiteboards, e-readers, laptops, etc.), the compatibility of the software/hardware with the curriculum, and ever changing technologies are all factors facing classroom teachers every day. If technology is limited, then student's educational experiences will be limited. Teachers, especially those entering the profession, must be prepared to use whatever instructional technology is available to maximum advantage for differentiating instruction so students, particularly those who are gifted, will not miss any learning opportunities.

SOLUTIONS AND RECOMMENDATIONS

The International Society for Technology Education (ISTE) developed their National Education Technology Standards (NETS) for learning, teaching, and leading in the digital age. Technology has and will change not only "what we need to learn, but the way we learn" (ISTE, NETS, 2013, par. 1).This affects all types of learners regardless of their age, abilities, or learning style. The NETS' benefits are: *improving higher-order thinking skills; preparing students for their future in a competitive global job market; designing student-centered, project-based, and online learning environments; guiding systematic change in our schools to create digital places of learning; and inspiring digital age professional models for working, collaborating, and decision making. ISTE NETS, 2013, par. 1-5)*

How to implement these standards for mastery in the elementary classroom is an essential question facing thousands of teachers daily. The building administrator must believe in the standards and lead the process of implementation by providing the necessary software, hardware, technical support, and professional development for their faculty to be successful. The classroom teacher is the cornerstone for successful implementation and assessment of technology proficiencies, and effective teachers model and apply the NETS's as they:

design, implement, and assess learning experiences to engage students (of all degrees of learning ability), and improve learning; enrich their professional practice; and provide positive models for students, colleagues, and the community. All teachers should meet the standards and performance indicators. These indicators are: facilitate and inspire student learning and creativity; design and develop digital age learning experiences and assessments. Model digital age work and learning promote and model digital citizenship and responsibility; and engage in professional growth and leadership. (ISTE, NETS-T, 2013, par. 1)

These standards and performance indicators are the future of the teaching profession. As such, they must be adopted by both teachers and teacher educators to avoid adversely affecting the productivity and competiveness of future graduates. These standards, although they may seem very basic, address teachers' need to develop new, challenging, digitally oriented instruction to meet the learning needs of all students in their classrooms. As with the case study in this chapter, required, often difficult, content can be taught in a way that address all learning styles and abilities found within a heterogeneous classroom when instructional technology is utilized. For the classroom teacher to be successful in their instruction, the National Association for Gifted Children (NAGC) believes all teachers should:

understand the definition and theories of gifted and talented students; recognize learning differences of gifted and talented students and identify their related academic and social-emotional needs, and understand, plan, implement a range of evidence-based strategies for assessment and to differentiate instruction, content, and assignments. (NAGC, 2013, par. 1-3)

The standards and mission statements from the ISTE and the NAGC reflect the standards found in the new Common Core and in the Science, Technology, Engineering, and Mathematics (STEM) as they relate to gifted and talented students. For the success of the gifted and talented students, their program of study, instruction, and classroom environment must be conducive for them to learn new skills and make continuous academic progress.

There are various ways to incorporate the ISTE NETs. STEM, Common Core into the teaching of gifted and talented students, which are only limited by the teacher's creativity, experience in planning and executing lessons, understanding of standards as they pertain to this group of students, familiarity with various forms of appropriate technology, and the learning styles and intellectual orientations of the gifted and talented students. Technology allows the flexibility in teaching these students by utilizing web quests, electronic journals, podcasts, and educational videos for researching and extending content that is required to be mastered. There is an array of ways for them to present their results such as PowerPoints, movies, blog postings, Instagram®, Twitter®, and other forms of social media. The classroom becomes an international learning community with limitless boundaries, multicultural content, and collaboration with other students.

Just as the complexity of the learning process is readily acknowledged, it must also be acknowledged that there is no simple solution to remedy the complex issues related to providing effective instruction for the wide range of diverse learners in today's classrooms. While better preparing future teachers to differentiate instruction and incorporate instructional technology may contribute to improved educational experiences for gifted students in heterogeneous classrooms, there are no easy answers to the questions raised here.

REFERENCES

Alliance for Excellent Education. (2005). *Teacher attrition: A costly loss to the Nation and to the States*. Washington, DC: Author.

Barbour, N. E., & Shaklee, B. D. (1998). Gifted education meets Reggio Emilia: Visions for curriculum in gifted education for young children. *Gifted Child Quarterly, 42*(4), 228–237. doi:10.1177/001698629804200406

Boyd, D., Grossman, P., Lankford, H., Loeb, S., & Wyckoff, J. & National Bureau of Economic research, CA. (2008). *Who leaves? Teacher attrition and student achievement* (NBER Working Paper No. 14022). National Bureau of Economic Research, (ERIC Document Reproduction Service No. ED501989).

Cummings, L. (2013). How to challenge gifted students. *eHow* Retrieved from http://www.ehow.com/how_6569900_challenge-gifted-students.html

Darling-Hammond, L., & Sykes, G. (2003). Wanted: A national teacher supply policy for education: The right way to meet the "Highly Qualified Teacher" challenge. *Education Policy Analysis Archives, 11*(33). Retrieved from http://epaa.asu.edu/epaa/v11n33/

Dunn, R., & Dunn, K. (1978). *Teaching students through their individual learning styles: A practical approach*. Reston, VA: Reston Publishing Company.

Fleming, N. (2012). *Introduction to VARK*. Retrieved from http://legacy.hazard.kctcs.edu/VARK/introduction.htm

Gardner, H. (1993). *Multiple intelligences*. New York: Basic Books.

Gardner, H. (1999a). *Intelligence reframed: Multiple intelligences for the 21st century*. New York: Basic Books.

Gentry, M., & Keilty, B. (2004). Rural and suburban cluster grouping: Reflections of staff development as a component of program success. *Roeper Review*, *26*(3), 147–155. doi:10.1080/02783190409554260

Giles, R. M., & Shaw, E. L. (2011). SMART Boards rock! Using technology to investigate geology with young children. *Science and Children*, *49*(4), 36–37.

Gilman, L. (2013). *The Theory of Multiple Intelligence*. Indiana University. Retrieved from http://www.intelltheory.com/mitheory.shtml

Haberman, M. (2005). Raising teachers' salaries: The funds are there. *Education*, *125*(3), 327–343.

Hare D., Heap, J. L., & North Central Regional Educational Lab. (2001). *Effective teacher recruitment and retention strategies in the Midwest: Who is making use of them?* Naperville, IL: North Central Regional Educational Lab. (Eric Document Reproduction Service No. ED477648).

Hawk, T. F., & Shah, A. J. (2007). Using learning style instruments to enhance student learning. *Decision Sciences Journal of Innovative Education*, *5*(1), 1–19. doi:10.1111/j.1540-4609.2007.00125.x

Hutinger, P., & Johanson, J. (2001). *Learning modalities: Pathways to effective learning*. Retrieved May 10, 2013 http://www.pbs.org/teachers/earlychildhood/articles/learningmodalities.html

Ingersoll, R. M. (2007). Is there really a teacher shortage? In A. R. Sadovnik (Ed.), *Sociology of education: A critical reader* (pp. 159–176). New York: Routledge Taylor and Francis Group.

International Society for Technology Education's National Education Technology Standards. (2013). Retrieved from https://www.iste.org/docs/pdfs/nets-t-standards.pdf?sfvrsn=2

James, W., & Gardner, D. (1995). Learning styles: Implications for distance learning. *New Directions for Adult and Continuing Education*, *1995*(67), 19–31. doi:10.1002/ace.36719956705

Johnson, H. R. (2001). Administrators and mentors: Keys in the success of beginning teachers. *Journal of Instructional Psychology*, *28*(1), 44–49.

Kent, A. M., Feldman, P., & Hayes, R. L. (2009). Mentoring and inducting new teachers into the profession: An innovative approach. *International Journal of Applied Educational Studies*, *5*(1), 73-95.

Kent, A. M., & Giles, R. M. (in press). The influential role of field experiences in a dual certification teacher preparation program. *The Field Experience Journal.*

Kershner, R., Mercer, N., Warwick, P., & Staarman, J. K. (2010). Can the interactive whiteboard support young children's collaborative communication and thinking in classroom science activities? *International Journal of Computer-Supported Collaborative Learning, 5*(4), 359–383. doi:10.1007/s11412-010-9096-2

Lloyd, M. E. R., & Sullivan, A. (2012). Leaving the profession: The context behind one quality teacher's professional burn out. *Teacher Education Quarterly, 39*(4), 139–162.

Manzo, K. K. (2010). Whiteboards' impact on teaching seen as uneven. *Education Week, 3*(2), 34.

Marvel, J. (2007). Teacher attrition and mobility [electronic resource: results from the 2004-05 teacher follow-up survey / John Marvel ... [et al.]. Washington, DC: National Center for Education Statistics, Institute of Education Sciences, U.S. Department of Education.

Murcia, K., & Sheffield, R. (2010). Talking about science in interactive whiteboard classrooms. *Journal of Educational Technology, 26*(4), 417–431.

National Association for Gifted Children Standards in Gifted and Talented Education. (2013). Retrieved from http://www.nagc.org/index2.aspx?id=8188

National Commission on Teaching and America's Future (NCTAF). (2003). *No dream denied: A pledge to America's children.* Washington, DC: Author.

O'Connell-Ross, P. (1993). *National excellence: A case for developing America's talent.* Washington, DC: U.S. Department of Education, Government Printing Office.

Pashler, H., McDaniel, M., Rohrer, D., & Bjork, R. (2008). Learning styles: Concepts and evidence. *Psychological Science in the Public Interest, 9*(3), 105–119.

Pipho, C. (1998). A "real" teacher shortage. *Phi Delta Kappan, 80*(3), 181–182.

Preston, C., & Mowbray, L. (2008). Use of SMART boards for teaching, learning and assessment in kindergarten science. *Teaching Science, 54*(2), 50–53.

Robinson, N. M., Lanzi, R. G., Weinberg, R. A., Ramey, S. L., & Ramey, C. T. (2002). Family factors associated with high academic competence in former Head Start children at third grade. *Gifted Child Quarterly, 46*(4), 278–290. doi:10.1177/001698620204600404

Rogers, K. B. (2002). Grouping the gifted and talented: Questions and answers. *Roeper Review, 24*(3), 103–107. doi:10.1080/02783190209554140

Saunders, R. (2005). *A comparison study of the academic effect of ability grouping versus heterogeneous grouping in mathematics instruction* (Doctoral dissertation). Arizona State University, Scottsdale, AZ.

Scarr, S. (1985). An author's frame of mind Review of *Frames of Mind: The Theory of Multiple Intelligences. New Ideas in Psychology, 3*(1), 95–100. doi:10.1016/0732-118X(85)90056-X

Stahl, S. A. (1999, Fall). Different strokes for different folks? A critique of leanring styles. *American Educator, 23*(3), 27–31.

Sternberg, R. J. (1994). Comments on Multiple Intelligences. *Theory into Practice, 95*(4), 561–569.

Sternberg, R. J., Grigorenko, E. L., Ferrari, M., & Clinkenbeard, P. (1999). A triarchic analysis of an aptitude-treatment interaction. *European Journal of Psychological Assessment, 15*(1), 3-13.

Stotsky, S. (2006). Who should be accountable for what beginning teachers need to know? *Journal of Teacher Education, 57*(3), 256–268. doi:10.1177/0022487105285561

Tomlinson, C. A. (1999). *The differentiated classroom: Responding to the needs of all learners*. Alexandria, VA: The Association for Supervision and Curriculum Development.

Vallis, K., & Williamson, P. (2009). Build your own board. *Learning and Leading with Technology, 36*(9), 18–20.

Warwick, P., Mercer, N., Kershner, R., & Staarman, J. K. (2010). In the mind and in the technology: The vicarious presence of the teacher in pupil's learning of science in collaborative group activity at the interactive whiteboard. *Computers & Education, 55*(1), 350–362. doi:10.1016/j.compedu.2010.02.001

Waterhouse, L. (2006). Multiple Intelligences, the Mozart Effect, and Emotional Intelligence: A critical review. *Educational Psychologist, 41*(4), 207–225. doi:10.1207/s15326985ep4104_1

Winebrenner, S. (2001). *Teaching Gifted Kids in the Regular Classroom*. Minneapolis, MN: Free Spirit Publishing.

Winebrenner, S., & Devlin, B. (2001). *Cluster grouping of gifted students: How to provide full- time services on a part-time budget*. Eric Digest E538. www.ericec.org

KEY TERMS AND DEFINITIONS

Differentiating Instruction: A way to reach students with different learning styles, abilities, and needs by adjusting one's teaching.

Gifted Students: Students that achieve *high levels of accomplishment compared with others of their age, experience, or environment.*

Instructional Technology: Developing, implementing, and evaluating instruction involving the use of technology.

Interactive Whiteboard: An interactive display that provides a platform to boost the interactivity of lessons.

Learning Styles: An individual's way of acquiring and processing information and often classified as visual, auditory, tactile or kinesthetic.

Multiple Intelligences: Howard Gardner's list of different intelligences teacher may encounter in a heterogeneous classroom. The list included musical–rhythmic, visual-spatial, verbal-linguistic, logical–mathematical, bodily–kinesthetic, interpersonal, and intrapersonal.

National Education Technology Standards: Standards for learning, teaching, and leading in the digital age established by the International Society for Technology in Education and adopted worldwide.

National Science Education Standards: Standards for students to become scientifically literate in the 21st century.

APPENDIX

Name:

Teacher:

Types of Rocks: Quiz

Multiple Choice: Circle the letter of the correct answer below.

1. Which of the following is <u>NOT</u> a type of rock?
    a. Igneous;
    b. Metamorphic;
    c. Mineral;
    d. Sedimentary.

2. Which of the following begins as molten, or liquid, rock matter?
    a. Igneous rock;
    b. Metamorphic rock;
    c. Sediments;
    d. Sedimentary rock

3. What is sedimentary rock made of?
    a. Igneous rock that has cooled and hardened;
    b. Particles of ground up rock, shell, and bone;
    c. Beach sand;
    d. Lava.

4. What do scientists call igneous rock that cools quickly and is found on the surface of the Earth?
    a. Extrusive;
    b. Exterior;
    c. Intrusive;
    d. None of the above.

5. What is needed to form metamorphic rock?
    a. A stream or river
    b. Fire
    c. Sediment
    d. High pressure or heat

Matching: Draw a line connecting the rock name with its description.

Metamorphic	Particles of rock, shell, and bone are deposited in layers and compressed.
Igneous	Molten rock cools and hardens.
Sedimentary	High heat or pressure transforms existing rocks.

Chapter 4

Integrating Educational Robotics to Enhance Learning for Gifted and Talented Students

Amy Eguchi
Bloomfield College, USA

EXECUTIVE SUMMARY

Using educational robotics as a learning tool fosters gifted and talented students' learning, helping to instill the qualities necessary for them to be successful 21st century citizens and innovators who can profoundly affect the future US economy. Educational robotics provides a stimulating hands-on learning environment in which students constantly encounter problems that trigger inquiries, inspiring them to develop new solutions, test them out using the physical robots, and reiterate the process until they successfully solve the problems. Although educational robotics is considered "the most perfect instructional approach currently available" (Gura, 2013, para. 2), just bringing the tool into a classroom does not necessarily create the learning transformation that we wish to witness. The chapter presents the theories behind ideal Robotics in Education (RiE) approaches, introducing tips to ensure effective student learning and to maximize the potential of able students to display giftedness.

DOI: 10.4018/978-1-4666-6489-0.ch004

INTRODUCTION

In recent years, efforts to encourage innovation through expanding STEM fields in education have been discussed as critical for strengthening the economy in the US. Wagner (2012) urges that there is a general agreement that the new economy has to be based on innovation:

We have to become the country that produces more ideas to solve more different kinds of problems. We have to become the country that leads the way in developing the new technologies for sustainable planet and affordable health care. We have to become the country that creates the new and better products, processes, and services that other countries want and need. ... We must out innovate our economic competitors. (p.3)

Wagner (2012) introduces the Seven Survival Skills in his book, *the Global Achievement Gap,* which includes:

1. Critical thinking and problem solving
2. Collaboration across networks and leading by influence
3. Agility and adaptability
4. Initiative and entrepreneurship
5. Accessing and analyzing information
6. Effective oral and written communication
7. Curiosity and imagination (p.12)

Wagner continues to argue that the Seven Survival Skills are not enough for becoming successful innovators. Through his interviews with innovators, Wagner's research suggests that the qualities of innovators also include perseverance, in particular a willingness to experiment, take calculated risks, and tolerate failure. Although those are not the kinds of qualities that are emphasized in schools because of the extensive focus on standardized testing, these qualities are included in the core of 21st century skills that have become the focus of education in recent years. Moreover, those are the qualities that can be well-fostered through Robotics in Education (RiE). Gura (2013) explains what educational robotics can bring into classroom:

I feel that robotics just may be the most perfect instructional approach currently available. It offers classroom activities that teach high-value STEM content as well as opportunities to powerfully address ELA Common Core Standards. In fact, there are connections to robotics across the full spectrum of the curriculum. Robotics is also a highly effective way to foster essential work skills like collaboration, problem solving and project management. It does all this while keeping kids so motivated and engaged that getting them to stop working and move on to the rest of the school day can be a challenge -- a good problem to have! (para 2)

This chapter introduces educational robotics as a learning tool used to enable student mastery (especially for the gifted and talented students) of the qualities and skills necessary to be the driving force for rebuilding the US economy in the future. In this chapter, 21st century skills, gifted- and talented-ness, and educational robotics as a learning tool, are introduced and discussed, as well as how robotics in education can foster the mastery of qualities necessary for students to be innovators and what educators need to do to ensure the success of their learning.

TWENTY FIRST CENTURY SKILLS

21st Century Skills have been the focus of educational reform in several countries including the U.S., Australia, Finland and Singapore. Especially in U.S., the focus on the 21st Century Skills has been highlighted as the core of the educational reform. The Partnership for 21st Century Skills, a national organization (http://www.p21. org/) advocating for 21st century readiness for every student, states:

In an economy driven by innovation and knowledge ... in marketplaces engaged in intense competition and constant renewal ... in a world of tremendous opportunities and risks ... in a society facing complex business, political, scientific, technological, health and environmental challenges ... and in diverse workplaces and communities that hinge on collaborative relationships and social networking ... the ingenuity, agility and skills of the American people are crucial to U.S. competitiveness. (Partnership for 21st Century Skills, 2008, p. 1)

The Partnership for 21st Century Skills focuses on the 21st Century Skill Framework, which identifies 21st Century student outcomes and skills:

- **Core Subjects and 21st Century Themes:**
  - **Core Subjects:** English, World languages, Arts, Mathematics, Economics, Science, Geography, History
  - **21st Century Themes:** Global awareness, Financial, economic, business and entrepreneurial literacy, Civic literacy, Health literacy
- **Learning and Innovation Skills:**
  - Creativity and innovation skills
  - Critical thinking and problem solving
  - Communication and collaboration skills

- **Information, Media and Technology Skills:**
  - Information literacy
  - Media literacy
  - ICT
- **Life and Career Skills:**
  - Flexibility and adaptability
  - Initiative and self-direction
  - Social and cross-cultural skills
  - Productivity and accountability
  - Leadership and responsibility (p.13)

Learning and Innovation Skills - 4Cs (Critical thinking and problem solving, Communication, Collaboration, and Creativity and innovation) are considered to be the most essential skills necessary for our students to be successful in the future. The Partnership for 21st Century Skills emphasizes the importance of the 4Cs as the core of the 21st century skills necessary for every student to obtain:

Beyond the assessment of reading, mathematics and science, the United States does not assess other essential skills that are in demand in the 21st century. All Americans, not just an elite few, need 21st century skills that will increase their marketability, employability and readiness for citizenship ... . (Partnership for 21st Century Skills, 2008, p. 10)

Assessment & Teaching of 21st Century Skills, a research project with international collaboration based in Australia (http://atc21s.org/), organizes the 21st Century Skills into four broad categories as follows:

- **Ways of Thinking:** Creativity, critical thinking, problem-solving, decision-making and learning.
- **Ways of Working:** Communication and collaboration.
- **Tools for Working:** Information and communications technology (ICT) and information literacy
- **Skills for Living in the World:** Citizenship, life and career, and personal and social responsibility (Assessment & Teaching of 21st Century Skills, n.a., para 2)

Both organizations emphasize the importance of creativity, critical thinking, communication and collaboration (4Cs) as key of success in the 21st century. Those skills are important for any students including gifted and talented students. But before we move on, who are the gifted and talented students? The next section introduces the definition of gifted and talented population of students who are referenced in this chapter.

WHO ARE GIFTED AND TALENTED STUDENTS?

The definition of gifted and talented students differs between states. For example, the State of New York defines gifted and talented students as:

pupils who show evidence of high performances capability and exceptional potential in area such as general intellectual ability, special academic aptitude and outstanding ability in visual and performing arts. Such definition shall include those pupils who require educational programs or services beyond those normally provided by the regular school program in order to realize their full potential. (State of New York Department of Education, 2009, para 1)

Whereas, the State of New Jersey defines gifted and talented students as:

[t]hose students who possess or demonstrate high levels of ability, in one or more content areas, when compared to their chronological peers in the local district and who require modification of their educational program if they are to achieve in accordance with their capabilities. (State of New Jersey Department of Education, 2005, para 2)

While the State of New York specifically includes visual and performing arts as areas where students demonstrate high capability and exceptional potential, the State of New Jersey focuses more on the core subject areas. In general, giftedness and talented-ness are defined as a student's ability and potential that requires additional resources in order to support their educational needs. A student may be considered gifted or talented if it is not easy to meet her learning in the ordinary classroom with her peers because she is achieving at a level equivalent to students who are a few years older than her (Goodhew, 2009). All gifted children have different needs, learning styles, personalities, likes and dislikes, capabilities, backgrounds, and experiences (Weber & Smith, 2010). Davis, Rimm, and Siegle describes some of the common characteristics of giftedness and talented-ness to be the ability to make connections, learn more quickly than others, express an advanced language development, and demonstrate an outstanding ability to manipulate symbol systems and advanced observation skills, etc. (as cited in Weber & Smith, 2010).

While gifted and talented students are a certain group of students with special needs, Goodhew introduces Renzulli's work as focusing on a wider group of students who have the potential to join the pool of gifted and talented students. Renzulli's work does not focus solely on the concept of human intelligence or 'schoolhouse giftedness'. Schoolhouse giftedness is the giftedness that can be readily measured by test-taking. This can also be referred to as 'lesson-learning giftedness'. Renzulli also focuses on 'creative-productive giftedness' (Renzulli, 1998). He argues that many children of above average ability (not necessarily exceptional ability) have a potential of exhibiting giftedness when they are given a task with which they can engage with commitment and creativity. Renzull makes the connection between gifted- and talented-ness with 1) the ability to be creative when generating many ideas (fluency), 2) dealing with a problem/issue from different and non-standard point of views (flexibility), 3) developing a new idea (elaboration) and 4) coming up with something new (originality) (Renzulli, 1998).

Renzulli suggests that student creativity and commitment can be enhanced through opportunities and stimuli (Renzulli, 1998). Three Ringed Concept of Giftedness, including above average ability, task commitments, and creativity, is the concept developed by Renzulli that shows how gifted behavior could be enhanced. The above average ability consists of two abilities – general and specific abilities. General ability is "the capacity to process information, to integrate experiences that result in appropriate and adaptive responses in new situations, and the capacity to engage in abstract thinking" including the abilities of verbal and numerical reasoning, spatial relations, memory, and word fluency (Renzulli, 1998, p. 8). The general ability can be usually measured by tests of intelligence and can be applied in the traditional learning settings. The specific ability is more specific to one or more areas and includes the capacity of acquiring knowledge, skills or the ability of performing activities of a specialized kind to express themselves in real-life situations. The task commitment is a type of motivation that "represents energy brought to bear on a particular problem (task) or specific performance area" which is found in creative-productive people (Renzulli, 1998, p10). Someone who shows the task commitment can be described as demonstrating perseverance, endurance, and persistence, in addition to hardworking, dedicated to her practice, self-confident, and someone who believes in her ability to carry out important tasks or work. Those are similar qualities to what Wagner suggests as necessary qualities of innovators. Renzulli conducted literature review of studies and reports that showed academic ability traditionally measured by tests or grade point averages has a limited relationship with creative-productive accomplishment and nonintellectual factors especially related to task commitment which plays such an important role in characterizing highly productive people (Renzulli, 1998).

Creativity is the ability to produce high quality work that is new and original (Perkins, 1981). Seltzer and Bentley (1999) define creativity as the ability to apply knowledge and skills learned in new ways to accomplish a valued goal. Seltzer and Bentley define four key qualities of creativity as follows:

- *The ability to identify new problems, rather than depending on others to define.*
- *The ability to transfer knowledge gained in one context to another in order to solve a problem.*
- *A belief in learning as an incremental process, in which repeated attempts will eventually lead to success.*
- *The capacity to focus attention in the pursuit of a goal, or set of goals. (p. viii)*

Goodhew (2009) emphasizes that, although what should be taught in school is defined in State and National curriculum and standards, what determines if students are engaged, excited, encouraged, and inspired, is *how* teachers/educators deliver the curriculum in classrooms. She suggests an ideal learning environment for able children. The modified version of Goodhew's ideal learning environment that uses educational robotics as a learning tool to enhance student learning is presented (modifications in italic):

- Where teachers are empathetic, *enthusiastic, flexible to meet students' needs, curious to student learning, and open to students' creative ideas;*
- In which it is safe to be highly able, *and try out new ideas;*
- Which recognize students' abilities;
- A wide variety of approaches are utilized in teaching and learning of the students;
- Where students are engaged by their learning;
- Where students are challenged, sometimes to the point of failure;
- Which provides opportunities to work with students with similar abilities, *as well as different abilities;*
- Which provides opportunities to enrich and extend students' learning;
- Which provides access to a wide range of appropriate resources including technology;
- Where teachers use effective and varied assessment for learning *to enhance student learning.*

Goodhew's vision for an ideal learning environment for able children can be effectively created using educational robotics as a learning tool. To ensure the success of student learning with educational robotics, more specifics are required to do it right. In the following sections, the introduction to robotics in education (RiE) as a tool for enhancing the learning experience of not only gifted and talented student populations but also students with diverse needs including a much wider sense of *able* students is presented.

WHAT IS ROBOTICS IN EDUCATION?

Robots are increasingly important in modern life, and increasingly fascinating to the kids whose play today will shape the world tomorrow. (Edwards, 2008, para 2)

Mataric (2004), a professor of University of Southern California and the director of Center for Robotics and Embedded Systems and Robotics Research Lab, stated that "Robotics has been a growing field with the potential to significantly impact the nature of engineering and science education at all levels, from K-12 to graduate school" (p.1). The popularity of educational robotics in K-12 settings has been increasing for the past decade both in the U.S. and around the world. To accelerate the popularity of robotics, more and more robotics kits are becoming accessible for students of all ages including LEGO Mindstorms kit which has released the 3rd generation, EV3, in summer of 2013 (robotics kits will be discussed in more detail in the following section). An increased number of robotics competitions available to school age children has also contributed to the growth in popularity of robotics as an educational tool. For example, FIRST (For Inspiration and Recognition of Science and Technology) provides robotics competitions for several different age groups, including Junior FIRST LEGO league, FIRST LEGO League, FIRST Tech Challenge and FIRST Robotics Competitions. In addition, RoboCupJunior, World Robot Olympiad, and BotBall competitions are receiving worldwide attention. Because of the popularity of the robotics in education, robotics has been gathering educators' attentions including educators in K-12 classrooms and after school clubs. There are many conferences and workshops on Robotics in Education (RiE) offered around the world. Some of the educational robotics competitions offer their own workshops and conferences concurrent to their annual international competitions. RoboCupJunior offers the Workshop on Educational Robotics (WEROB) at the International RoboCupJunior competition, which is a part of RoboCup Symposium. BotBall offers the Global Conference on Educational Robotics during the International BotBall Tournament. Various academic and professional organizations also focus on promoting robotics in education. For example, the Institute of Electrical and Electronics Engineers (IEEE) sponsors Robotics in Education (RiE) conference (4th conference was held in the fall of 2013 in Poland, and 5th conference in summer 2014 in Italy). William Patterson University in N.J. has organized the 4th Annual Educational Technology Conference for local educators and K-12 teachers focusing on robotics in education entitled "Learning by Doing with Educational Robotics" in the fall of 2013. Moreover, there are various online communities that provide support to K-12 teachers and educators interested in using educational robotics with their teaching practice. For example, the LEGO Engineering Google group organized and facilitated by Damien Kee, an independent educational robotics educator in

Australia, provides a massive support network for participating educators around the world. The topic of the discussion for the LEGO Engineering Google group concerns mainly questions and ideas about using LEGO Mindstorms in education. Arduino Teacher's listserve also provides a large network of educators using the arduino controller board with school-age children.

Introduction to Robotics in Education (RiE)

A funny thing is happening in the field of robotics. A revolution is occurring without being noticed by many in the robotics research community. The robotics journals and conferences have largely missed the fact that robots are starting to leave the laboratory and make it out into the world. (Hendler, 2000)

Within less than a decade after Hender noticed that robotics was gradually becoming visible in our everyday life, robotics has moved into classrooms and our houses, and become a very popular activity in the field of K-12 education. Educational Robotics or Robotics in Education (RiE) is the term that teachers and educators use to describe robotics activities for school age children. The aim of RiE is to engage students in learning concepts and solving problems that were not easily taught with traditional classroom tools. Using educational robotics as a learning tool helps students to learn abstract concepts because it makes the concepts *visible* to students.

The use of educational robotics in the classroom settings has been made possible by the development of more simplified controllers and sensors that lower the cost of robotics and "more importantly, make robotics far more accessible to the many programmers of the world – from professionals to grade-school hackers" (Hendler, 2000, p.3). Such low-cost educational robotics kits have less sophisticated sensors and controllers compared to the robotics technologies that roboticists use in factories and laboratories. However, since the graphic-based programing environment used to control robots has also become available and programming has become easier for young learners and beginners, non-professional users can also achieve complex behaviors and programming.

Robotics Construction

Robots can be constructed with a commercial robotics kit or using a controller, motors, sensors and different materials available on the market. Commercial robotics kits are ideal tools for beginners and young students since they provide everything you need to get started with robotics. A typical robotics kit includes a programmable brick or controller that functions as the brain of a robot, different types of sensors including touch sensor, light sensor, distance (ultrasonic) sensor, motors, wheels, and other parts necessary to construct a robot. The robotics kits available on the market for educational use range in price from a couple of hundred dollars to about a thousand dollars. The most common and easily accessible robotics kit, especially in the United States, is the LEGO Mindstorms kit (Figure 1). There are two versions currently available. LEGO Mindstorms NXT is the version that was introduced in the summer of 2006. The NXT contained a much more sophisticated controller, sensors and servomotors than the previous model, RCX. LEGO Mindstorms EV3 is the newest version to become available (summer of 2013). It has an even more powerful controller. LEGO Mindstorms has been widely used by educators for two reasons. First, most students are already familiar with LEGO products and are eager to construct robotic creations with LEGO parts. Since it is a LEGO product available in toy stores, it is easy for parents to purchase and bring the learning experience into their home. Second, but most importantly, it is easier for teachers to use in the classroom because of the large number of resources, both print materials and on-line websites and forums, available to help with developing engaging educational lessons. In addition, LEGO provides entry level robotics kit for younger children called WeDo, which comes with various sensors, motors, construction pieces (LEGO block pieces), and a piece that connects the sensors to a computer. With the WeDo kit, the computer directly receives inputs from the sensors and controls the motors. The WeDo kit is much easier for younger learners to use since children are familiar with the LEGO block pieces. NXT and EV3 require LEGO technic pieces, different from LEGO blocks that can be easily snapped together. TETRIX is another set that can be used as an expansion to the LEGO Mindstorms kit (NXT). TETRIX features heavy-duty, aircraft-grade aluminum elements for robot construction that are more solid and durable than LEGO robots. TETRIX can be remote controlled (radio control) or controlled with an NTX controller. The fischertechnik, a German-based company, provides a robotics set called ROBO (Figure 2) that is similar to the LEGO Mindstorms kit. The kit includes a controller, encoder motors, indicator lights, NTC resistor, photoresistor, ultrasonic distance sensor, optical color sensor, IR trail sensor, and plastic construction parts. Robotis, a Korean-based company that produces a humanoid robot called DARwIn-OP, also provides educational robotics kits for school age children. OLLO is for younger students (elementary school, Figure 3), and BIOLOID is for older students (upper elementary, middle school to high school, Figure 4). OLLO is also similar to LEGO Mindstorms in that it includes a controller, servomotors, touch and IR sensors, and plastic construction parts. BIOLOID is more advanced set than OLLO. It includes several servomotors, various sensors and building parts to construct different types of robots including a humanoid robot. The VEX Robotics is another company produces robotics kits and materials. VEX Robotics Design System, also for more advanced students, provides

Figure 1. LEGO Mindstorms NXT and RCX robots

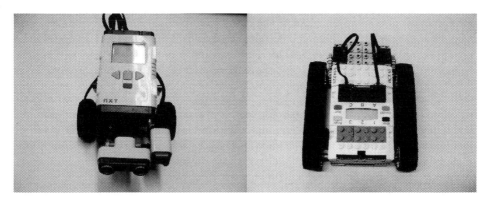

Figure 2. ROBO TX by fischertechnik (© fischertechnik. Used with permission)

metal parts and two types of controllers. On the other hand, VEX IQ is a robotics set with plastic parts, which is suitable for younger students.

In addition, there are many third party sensors and motors that can be controlled by controllers in robotics kits. Starting with a robotics kit is ideal for younger students who want to continue learning with robotics since a kit generally comes with various expansion options that will be helpful after they have learned the basics of robotics.

Advanced and older students may choose to construct a robot from scratch using a controller, motors, sensors, and other parts individually purchased. Since the introduction of Arduino, an open-source single board microcontroller that is less expensive than robotics kits and accessible for use because of many online resources

Figure 3. OLLO by Robotis (© Robotis. Used with permission)

Figure 4. BIOLOID by Robotis (© Robotis. Used with permission)

and publications, it has become easier for school age students to build do-it-yourself types of robotics creations. RaspberryPi and BeagleBone Black are credit-card size microprocessors that can also be used to control robots. Although a controller itself cannot be directly connected with other necessary parts to create a robot, using Arduino with breadboard and different shields to build a robotic creation is much easier than before. Moreover, Arduino sells an Arduino Robot (Figure 5), an Arduino with the necessary platform for a robot creation developed in collaboration with Complubot, a Spanish educational organization that offers a base for robotics with Arduino. BrickPi by Dexter Industries makes robotics with RaspberryPi easier. BrickPi allows RaspberryPi to communicate with LEGO Mindstorms NXT motors and sensors, which opens up a door for NXT users to advance their robotics learning to the next level.

Robotics Programming

LEGO WeDo, Mindstorms, fischertechnik kit, and Robotis's OLLO are suitable for younger students and beginners since they can be programmed using a graphic-based programming environment. For example, in WeDo graphic based programming environment, by simply dragging & dropping the programming icons, students, as young as those who can use a mouse to move blocks on a computer screen, can create programs that control the WeDo sensors and motors. The icons make it easy for younger students to program a simple task and execute it with the WeDo kit since the work does not require reading skills (Figure 6).

The next step for users of WeDo could be the LEGO Mindstorms kit because it also uses a graphic based programming environment. Although very little English reading skill is required, the student needs to be able to grasp a higher-level understanding of programming concepts and different functions (Figure 7).

The robotics kits not only provide specific graphic-based programming environments but also make it possible to expand the horizon of robotics learning by supporting text-coding language for more experienced users. For example, LEGO Mindstorms users can progress to learning C programming language by transitioning to the ROBOTC which is a C-based programming language developed by Carnegie Mellon Robotics Academy. LEGO Mindstorms can be also controlled with NCQ, C++, C#, JAVA etc. LEGO Mindstorms users can also move on to use LabView for controlling their robots since its graphic based programming environments are developed on LabView and the LabView for Mindstorms serves as an entry point for learning LabView based programming through robotics. The fischertechnik ROBO can be controlled with C languages, Visual Basic, Delphi etc. VEX uses a C-based language and can be programmed with easyC or ROBOTC.

Older and/or more advanced students who want to move on from kit robots to do-it-yourself type robotics can create robots using controllers such as Arduino, RaspberryPi, and BeagleBone Black. The robots created with those controllers require text-coding languages. For example, Arduino is controlled by Arduino IDE, a C-based programming language. RaspberryPi for robotics is usually programmed with Python. Because of the extensive levels, from novice to more advanced/professional, educational robotics has been used as a learning tool not only in K-12 settings but also in higher education classrooms.

Figure 5. Ardiuno Robot by Arduino and Complubot (© Complubot. Used with permission)

Figure 6. LEGO WeDo Program

THEORIES AND PRACTICES OF ROBOTICS IN EDUCATION

The concept of using robots as a learning tool was developed by Seymour Papert. He extended Piaget's *constructivism* theory when he developed his *constructionism* theory. With the constructivism theory, Piaget emphasizes that children need an *object to think with* and their learning involves constructing new knowledge out of prior knowledge when they manipulate artifacts and observe their behavior (Piaget, 1929, 1954). This notion of the manipulation of artifacts and observation of their behavior is also a fundamental part of Papert's constructionism theory. In addition

Figure 7. LEGO Mindstorms EV3 Program

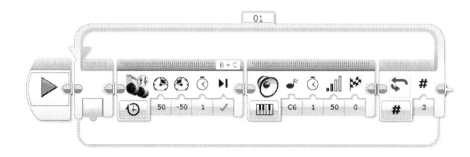

to manipulation and observation, what he thinks is fundamental for learning is also the *construction* of an object. Papert explains:

Constructionism – the N word as opposed to the V word – shares constructivism's connotation of learning as "building knowledge structures" irrespective of the circumstances of the learning. It then adds the idea that this happens especially felicitously in a context where the learner is consciously engaged in constructing a public entity, whether it's a sand castle on the beach or a theory of the universe. (Papert & Harel, 1991, p.1)

Since constructionism considers that it is important to have an object to think with, a successful constructionism learning environment requires tools with which children construct knowledge. Papert is the pioneer in considering the computer as the tool or the object to think with. In Papert's eyes, traditional computer-aided instruction in school simply means using the computer to teach or program children (Papert, 1993). He argues that children should be the ones who program computers rather than having a computer program children. By doing so, students acquire "a sense of mastery over a piece of the most modern and powerful technology" (p.5). He developed an idea of children using computers as tools for learning and for enhancing creativity. Papert developed the LOGO programming language based on his constructionism theory. LOGO is a computer language developed by Papert and his colleague in 1967 (Papert, 1993). With LOGO, children and nonmathematical beginners become programmers. LOGO is used to program *the Turtle,* which is a computer-controlled cybernetic animal (Papert, 1993). Papert calls the Turtle "an example of a constructed computational object to think with" (p. 11). In the early stage of development, LOGO was popularly used with *floor turtles* (Martin, Mikhak, Resnick, Silverman, & Berg, 2000). Later, LEGO Mindstorms robotics kit was developed based on LOGO with an effort to design tools that provide an environment where children can use computation for knowledge construction and recognize the learning opportunities afforded by this construction (Martin et al., 2000). By using such a robotics kit, educational robotics can create a learning environment in which children can interact with their surroundings (Danahy, Goswamy, & Rogers, 2008).

Educational Robotics as a Way to Translate Abstract to Tangible

Both constructivism and constructionism theories have their focus on the construction of knowledge, however, while Piaget's constructivism concentrates on the construction of knowledge in one's head, Papert's constructionism focuses more on "the role of constructions in the world as a support for those in the head" (Bers, 2008, p.13). Papert emphasizes the importance of having an object to think with in the real world. He suggests that the construction that takes place in the head often has been strengthened if its knowledge construction is supported by construction in the real world. In this way, the products can be shown, discussed, examined, probed and admired. In other words, the construction has to be *out there* in order for knowledge to be successfully constructed in the head, which will then stick with the child and bring more learning experiences that build upon previous learning experiences (Papert, 1993).

For many students, abstract concepts are difficult to fully understand without having the connection with ways to use the concept in real life situations. Because educational robotics provides a learning environment where students can construct the object to think with the real world, it becomes a tool that helps students to understand abstract concepts and ideas through tangible and concrete ways. With educational robotics, a robot is a manipulative that provides instant feedback to an abstract idea that students tested with it (Bers, 2008). Bers explains this with examples of students learning with educational robotics:

By adding gears to their machines, they explore the mathematical concept of ratio. By programming movement of these mechanical parts they start to explore the concepts of cause and effect, programming loops, and variables in a concrete and fun manner. By including sensors to detect input from the world, such as light or touch, they encounter the concept of feedback. (pp. 21-22)

For example, with educational robotics projects with LEGO Mindstorms, students need to use motors to control the movement of a robot. Motors are usually controlled by the power level, between 1-5 or 0-100, that a controller sends to the motors. To fine-tune the movement of a robot, students need to use a decimal number, i.e. 2.5 for the power level between 1-5, if motor power level 3 is too fast for the movement that students want a robot to make. If 2.5 does not move the motor(s) with the necessary power, they must test other decimal numbers, i.e. 2.3, 2.4, or 2.6 etc. Since a robot provides an immediate feedback by showing how it moves, it makes the abstract concept of decimal numbers visible to young students who may not have learned the concept yet. The experience helps students understand new concepts in a non-traditional learning environment. Through robotics projects using motor movements, even average ability 2nd and 3rd grade students can grasp the concept of decimal numbers and manipulate the numbers to make their robots do the specific movements that they planned.

Atmatzidou, Markelis, and Demitridis (2008) also report that educational robotics motivated and interested students to solve problems in basic programming concepts that they initially faced difficulty in comprehending, such as variables, conditions, and the loop structures, through computer programming. Robotics led to notably higher and better learning outcomes. Furthermore, their learning is reinforced because of the immediate feedback that a robot provides after testing a program that they created (Atmatzidou, Markelis, & Demitridis, 2008).

Educational robotics makes children's thinking in their head *visible* first through their development of the program, and then through the execution of the program on a robot that they constructed. The kit allows children to observe how physical aspects of their environment interact with robots and construct knowledge about that interaction. In this sense, educational robotics is a great tool for children to explore their interests in constructionist learning environment.

Because of the ability to make abstract concepts and ideas visible in the real world, educational robotics has been also integrated into curriculums at many higher education institutions around the world including MIT, Brown University, University of Maryland, Tufts University, University of Aarhus at Denmark, University of Utrecht in the Netherlands, Trinity College Dublin in Ireland, and University of Manchester in the UK, to name a few (Drew, Esposito, & Perakslis, 2004).

Student Driven Learning with Learner-Centered Approach

With the constructionism theory, a child becomes the central player of the construction of his own knowledge and the construction should be driven by the child's interest and initiative. In other words, providing a chance for a child to self-explore becomes an important part of his learning experience. Papert views children as naturally gifted learners since they acquire a vast quantity of knowledge through a process which he calls *Piagetian learning*, or *learning without being taught* even long before they start attending schools. He believes that technological tools become powerful learning tools when we use the tools to support Piagetian learning among our students, by encouraging the exploration of children's ideas and curiosity, while supporting the design and construction of personally meaningful projects (Papert, 1993). The personally meaningful learning experience helps children to establish an intimate relationship with in depth knowledge and ideas from science, mathematics, and the arts of intellectual model building. With this account, Papert sees children as "builders of their own intellectual structures"(Papert, 1993, p.7) when they take the lead as learners. To make students' learning experience successful and foster the Piagetian learning, we, as educators, need to encourage students to explore their ideas and curiosities. To provide a support for this type of learning experience where students are encouraged to explore rather than follow an instruction could be challenging in a traditional school environment where the teacher-centered approach is still a dominant teaching strategy. To support children's self-exploration, we need to let them reinvent and rediscover the wheel. The process of reinventing and rediscovering the wheel is a necessary process of learning for students, much more effective than simply following instructions given by a teacher. Constructionism theory emphasizes that effective learning happens when there is less direct instruction or teaching involved and more exploration driven by children. Papert further explains:

Constructionism is one of a family of educational philosophies that denies this "obvious truth [teach better]." It does not call in question the value of instruction as such. ... Constructionist attitude to teaching is not at all dismissive because it is minimalist – the goal is to teach in such a way as to produce the most learning for the least teaching. (Papert, 1993, p.139)

When children are encouraged and we value their interests, they are eager to work on a project because they are interested in it. The project, then, becomes personally meaningful to the students. For successful constructionism learning to take place, students need to be the center of a learning environment where their wonderful ideas are encouraged, shared and developed into personally meaningful projects.

Constructionism is both a theory of learning and a strategy for education (Bers, 2008). Bers emphasizes that the best learning environment is where making, creating, programming, discovering and designing their own object to think with are happening while students are engaged and having fun. Constructionism offers the framework for developing a learning environment that supports such meaningful learning by encouraging students to pursue their interests by exploring and making.

With educational robotics, after students learn basic skills about programming motors and sensors, they can start working on a project of their interest. The project requirements could be to use at least two motors and two sensors to develop a robotic creation that is useful in your everyday life, entertains children (robotic toy), or performs on a stage (Figure 8). As with any other project, first, they need to create their project plan with a drawing of their idea. Requiring them to keep a logbook or journal that documents their initial plan, problems that they face during the development, their solutions for the problems, all the programs that they developed, the iteration process with reflections on the process, will provide evidence of their learning through the project. Since the students are given the freedom to work on a project that they are interested in and is meaningful to them, the ideal constructionism learning environment have been created .If students are given ownership of the project, the degrees of complexity will vary depending on the level of students' mastery of robotics. Gifted and talented students can be challenged to apply more advanced skills and knowledge to their projects (Figure 9).

Educational Robotics as a Tool for Transdisciplinary Learning

Educational robotics is a learning tool that has a great impact on students' learning. Elkind (2008) suggests that educational robotics is opening a door for helping children learn about mathematics and scientific abstract concepts through concrete feedback given by robotic creations. In addition, it is a great tool to help students acquire the method of inquiry and develop technological fluency. Several studies show that educational robotics provides effective learning opportunities for students in the areas of STEM, such as physics, biology, geography, mathematics, science, electronics, and mechanical engineering, as well as in critical academic skills, such as writing, reading, and research skills (Eguchi, 2007c; Kolberg & Orlev, 2001; Oppliger, 2002; Sklar & Eguchi, 2004; Sklar, Eguchi, & Johnson, 2002a, 2002b, 2003). Those studies also emphasize that educational robotics provides a learning

Figure 8. Students getting ready for Robotics Dance performance (© RoboCup Federation. Used with permission)

Figure 9. Advanced students working on Soccer Robot (© RoboCup Federation. Used with permission)

experience that supports the development of the 4Cs of the 21ˢᵗ century skills including, critical thinking, decision making, problem solving, creativity, communication and collaboration.

The best learning environment for teaching 21ˢᵗ century skills is the transdisciplinary approach where students use various skills and knowledge across disciplines to solve a problem that they face. Educational robotics can be used as a learning tool to integrate many different subject areas and skills through project based learning. For example, robotics can be used for a project in which students study their community (social studies), interview people in the community and write their stories (language arts), and then, program their robots to retell the stories (robotics performance/storytelling). In order to make the robot do specific movements, students need to use mathematical and/or scientific concepts (math and science). Also, they can decorate their robots to represent the people living in the community and create the community by constructing houses, buildings and shops with robotics performers (art). The robots may move around the town accompanied by music/songs created by the students (music).

Robotics naturally excites and motivates students, inspiring them to enthusiastically become interested in science, technology, engineering and math (STEM). It has also been observed that educational robotics programs can increase retention rates among female students (Barr, Harrison, & Conery, 2011). Through educational robotics projects, the author has witnessed many examples of students who have difficulties in literacy and/or mathematics being transformed to enjoy learning in those subject areas. Working with robots inspires students to write about their robotic projects at length in order to share their experiences with others. Requiring journal writing (logbook) helps them enhance their writing skills through robotics activities. In addition, students can conduct a small research on the history of robotic developments as part of their project and include a summary of their findings. Robotics also inspires students to compute and learn mathematical concepts that they have not yet learned in the traditional classroom. In order to solve an interesting programming or robotic construction problem, students have to be able to manipulate different mathematical concepts freely. Having the goal to make their robotics creation work, students learn the mathematical concepts necessary for them to solve the problem that they face more enthusiastically. Moreover, because robotics can make abstract concept visible to students, it provides a learning environment that helps their acquisition of the concepts that they are trying to grasp. Educational robotics provides a *fun* learning environment because of its hands-on nature. With educational robotics, students are excited to tackle problems that they face. The engaging learning environment motivates students to learn whatever skills and knowledge is needed for them to accomplish their goals. Students are intrigued and engaged by the challenges of constructing and programming robots to make real what they have created and imagined in their head/mind.

Educational Robotics as a Tool for Promoting Collaboration

Educational robotics encourages students to learn collaboratively. In typical classrooms, each student works on one computer or in pairs where no collaboration is encouraged. Teacher instructions tend to focus on individual computer work. Learning through educational robotics encourages collaboration among students while working in groups. When students are excited and motivated to work on their robotic creations, they are eager to share their ideas, engage in collaborative decision-making and problem-solving, provide constructive criticism, and acquire the communication skills (Eguchi, 2007a, 2007b; Miller, Nourbakhsh, & Sigwart, 2008), which are part of the 4Cs of the 21st century skills. Since educational robotics is hands-on, a program virtually created can be tested with a physical entity in the real world, providing students with the opportunity to explore and solve real-world problems as a group. Miller et al. (2008) also point out that, while engaged in team-based/project-based robotics learning, students with low-esteem significantly improve their technology capacity, teamwork skills, and communication skills.

TIPS FOR CREATING SUCCESSFUL LEARNING ENVIRONMENTS WITH EDUCATIONAL ROBOTICS FOR GIFTED AND TALENTED STUDENTS

Although robotics in education (RiE) promises to enhance students' learning of 21st century skills (4C), abstract STEM concepts and other content knowledge in many subject areas, the actual results of RiE could vary if a learning environment that supports constructionist learning is not developed. Educational robotics is a perfect tool for children to construct knowledge in the classroom environment. The robotic tool enables students to observe how environmental aspects interact with robots and construct knowledge through their observation and interaction with the environment.

One of the prominent robotics educators describes the power of RiE, "Robots, like dinosaurs and space, arouse the curiosity and enthusiasm of most youngsters and robotics provides a hands-on introduction to technology" (Green, 2011, p.7). Educational robotics provides powerful learning experiences for students of all ages, levels, and gender (Alimisis & Kynigos, 2009; Mataric, 2004; C. Rogers, 2008; J. Rogers, Lisowski, & Rogers, 2006). However, just providing educational robotic tools in a classroom does not automatically guarantee that the kind of learning previously described will take place. Our society tends to focus and rely too much on technology, especially computers, as an agent of change in learning environments (Bers, 2008). However, simply bringing computers and robotics into a classroom does not in itself magically create the desired paradigm shift. Alimisis and Kynigos echo the view that a simple introduction of technological tools into a classroom cannot influence children's minds or leave an impact on their learning (Alimisis & Kynigos, 2009).

The key elements for successful constructionist learning experiences are 1) manipulatives (robotic tools), 2) students' interaction with their surroundings, 3) student observations of interactions with and feedback from the environment, and 4) students reflecting on their learning experiences in order to construct new knowledge. The educational philosophy, curriculum, pedagogical approach, and people involved in the teaching and learning are all important for creating a successful constructionist learning environment.

Critical Exploration for Understanding Students' Thinking

Constructionism theory values when teachers provide less direct instruction or teaching and, instead, encourage more exploration driven by children. The challenge for teachers is finding out how to encourage and understand the exploration of children's ideas without imposing our own agenda, especially when the exploration of children's ideas tends to be so often discouraged in classrooms. Without fully understanding how children construct their knowledge or understand a phenomenon, it is difficult to successfully facilitate further exploration of their knowledge. The pedagogy of critical exploration, developed by Eleanor Duckworth, another student of Piaget, invites children to express their thoughts and ideas. She emphasizes the importance of children's *having of wonderful ideas*. The pedagogy of critical exploration has a similar focus as the constructionist approach. It focuses on children's exploration of their knowledge construction. It also denies direct teaching by an adult or expert. However, the pedagogy of critical exploration focuses more on the importance of our understanding of children's construction of knowledge.

With critical exploration, the children's having of wonderful ideas is the essence of intellectual development (Duckworth, 2006). Duckworth emphasizes that educators need to develop skills in gaining insights into how children are really seeing a problem, by inquiring, listening and observing. This kind of teacher practice will "[lead] to a certain ability to raise questions that made sense to the children or to think of new orientations for the whole activity that might correspond better to their way of seeing things" (Duckworth, 2006, p.4). She emphasizes that one of the important lessons from Piaget is the basic idea of assimilation:

that a person takes any experience into her own previous understanding (schemes, structures); that we cannot assume that an experience whose meaning seems clear to us will have the same meaning to someone else. (p. 158).

In other words, it is dangerous for us, as educators, to expect all of our students to interpret the same experience in the way we do. Rather, our objective should be to understand the meaning that any particular experience holds for our students (Duckworth, 2005). With critical exploration, we encourage children to reflect on their experience and talk about what they think. Meanwhile, teachers aim to understand children's thinking and understanding of the experience. Duckworth points out that critical exploration has two levels of meaning – "exploration of the subject matter by the child (the subject or the learner) and exploration of the child's thinking by [the] adult (the researcher or the teacher)" (Duckworth, 2005, p. 259).

Duckworth also emphasizes the importance of children's having of wonderful ideas. Allowing and encouraging children to have their own wonderful ideas, raise questions for themselves, and then explore their questions is the key to supporting children's intellectual development (Duckworth, 2006). The more occasions for the having of wonderful ideas that children have, the better they develop the intellectual capacities that foster creativity and innovation in ways that are meaningful to them. Teachers need to develop a learning environment that is safe and welcoming for children to express and share their own ideas. Moreover, teachers should help children to deepen their understanding through inquiry and encourage them to explore their own questions. What is most important is to help them realize that their ideas are significant – important for them as well as for us, so that their interest, ability and self-confidence continue to grow. Educational robotics can spark children's curiosity and excite them to explore their ideas, reflect, and ask questions about their experience. RiE provides multiple ways for children to explore their wonderful ideas and construct their knowledge further through real world experiences with mechanical parts and programming. The instantaneous feedback that robotic tools provide inspires children to explore their ideas further.

For example, when students create different robot movements by controlling motors, there are several ways to make a robot turn 90 degrees. Students can control the motors by changing motor speed, time, amount of rotation of the motor, etc. When they have a perfect program that makes a robot make a 90 degree turn, depending on the condition of the floor or the amount of battery power (fully charged battery vs. 10% charged battery) the turn that a robot makes may vary. Here, students encounter a problem. Instead of the teacher explaining why the turns are all different with the same program, the students need to be expected to observe the situation, develop their own hypotheses, run several tests, reflect on what they observe, share their ideas, and come up with possible solutions. During the process, the teacher can ask questions to facilitate their understanding of the phenomena or encourage them to ask questions of themselves. When they arrive upon the solution, their excitement and joy of their success will help their new knowledge to endure.

Paradigm Shift with Teaching and Learning

With both constructionist and critical exploration pedagogical approaches, traditional ways of teaching – teacher providing information, knowledge, and instruction to students following inflexible curriculum, are not welcomed. The requirement for teachers to become successful is a paradigm shift – drop the notion of teaching and focus on facilitating students' learning. No more lengthy lecture-type instruction and the imposition of the teacher's agenda on the students. Rather, teachers need to flexibly provide technical and content knowledge on-demand by responding to the needs of the students. Housand and Housand report that, through their review of literatures, some degree of autonomy on student's choice on what to do and when to do it, has contributed to the increase of intrinsic motivation (Housand & Housand, 2012). Letting students have more control over their learning helps not only their construction of knowledge but also their motivation for learning.

The paradigm shift must happen with the students as well. They must be willing to explore and take responsibility for their learning. For successful constructionist and critical exploration learning to occur, it is necessary to develop a new type of learning community where peer interactions are encouraged and supported, and the role of students and teachers becomes more neutral.

The current state of education is casting a shadow on the development of constructionist learning among students. After more than a decade of experience teaching educational robotics, I have witnessed more and more students, especially at college level, whether able (gifted) or average, who come to class expecting the teacher to *teach* them by directly and specifically telling them what to do to get to the *right* answer. A growing number of students approach learning with the firm belief that they must have the *right* and the *only* answer. Typical questions that I receive during educational robotics lesson are "Is it right?" "Can you make sure this is correct?" and "You should tell me how to do it because you are the teacher!" before even testing their program on a robot. They have the fear of making mistakes because they have been educated through years of schooling intended to help them pass standardized tests rather than think for themselves. The years of experience with teachers expecting students to do the work *right* makes it very difficult for students to shift to a new way of learning. It is confusing for students that, with educational robotics as well as other hands-on, student-centered projects, there is usually no one right answer (C. Rogers & Portsmore, 2004).

It is also very confusing for many teachers that there are generally multiple ways to solve the same problem and no single *right* answer when it comes to educational robotics. Not many teachers are comfortable with knowing there are multiple ways of tackling a problem. They prefer the predictability of knowing there is one *right* answer. Usually, teachers employ a conventional teaching methodology in which they know all the answers prior to teaching a subject. Many teachers feel that they have to be able to tell if students are on the right track or not (C. Rogers, 2008). Within the educational robotics learning environment, it is common that teachers might not know the answer to the questions that students pose. I have heard many teachers express discomfort with this type of situation. During teacher training sessions, many teachers insist that they need to know all the answers so that they can provide their students with the right answers to their questions. This mirrors the expectation that students tend to have as previously explained. Not knowing the right answer makes both teachers and students very feel uncomfortable. However, this is a wonderful learning opportunity for both students and teachers. As Rogers and Portsmore point out, "most of the student learning comes from discussion and the teacher asking penetrating questions" (C. Rogers & Portsmore, 2004, p.23). With educational robotics, there could be many unknowns for teachers. What is more important than knowing all the answers to students' questions is to become good facilitators, thereby helping students find solutions and answers to their problems through their own explorations. It should be encouraged for teachers to learn from the experience together with their students. As previously stated, 21st century students are expected to be able to be good problem solvers and critical thinkers. For them, just knowing correct answers is not enough to be successful in the future. Furthermore, with critical exploration, teachers cannot be the ones providing all of the answers. Instead, they should be exploring with their students to more deeply understand their own thinking and learning processes – learning with students.

With learner-centered educational robotics, students are the center of their own learning. When work is driven by their inquiries, students are responsible for their own learning. A classroom where learning with educational robotics takes place probably makes many teachers uneasy since it tends to be a little chaotic. A typical robotics classroom has students moving around freely, interacting and talking with each other. Here, teachers are required to teach through chaos (C. Rogers, 2008). In this learning environment where students work in groups, they are encouraged to exchange their ideas, solve problems and come up with solutions together. Moreover, they are encouraged to teach each other. Teachers should be walking around the classroom, engaging in conversations with groups of students, and providing on-demand guidance or suggestions. They should continue to wander around in class so that they know what their students are working on, and understand their students learning processes. Through a teacher's active engagement with students' learning, the classroom environment feels more like controlled chaos.

In typical educational robotics classrooms, the levels or progress of groups start to be diverse after several sessions, which makes it hard for a teacher to provide help simultaneously to individual students and/or groups that need help. Different groups might require different supports or have different needs, such as a help with basic programming, some construction questions, a robot might have broken into pieces, a battery is dead and needs a replacement, or various other problems may arise. There is limit to what one teacher can provide. Here, another paradigm shift is required, both for the teacher and students. In learner-centered educational robotics classroom, more advanced students become teacher-aids to help other groups with solving problems. Students who are good at construction of robots can help solve a construction issue, while others who are advanced programmers can assist students who need help with programming. A mastery chart where each student checks off what they have completed (Figure 10) helps students who need help to find out who can be their teacher-aid. In learner-centered environment, everyone should be the learner, including the teacher. There are many occasions where a teacher can learn from students who are more savvy technology users or a programmer who can self-teach to advance her or his skills. Many gifted and able students could be the teacher-aids in a class where they can use their advanced skills to help other students and teachers. Providing this kind of support helps advance able students' learning since teaching is the most advanced form of learning. According to Phillips, people remember 10% of what we hear, 15% of what we see, 20% of what we hear and see, and 60% of what we do, 80% of what we do with active reflection, and 90% of what we teach (Phillips, 1984). To be able to teach, students need to have a strong foundation of established knowledge. In addition, the experience of teaching others helps students realize what they need to work on more to establish a much more solid foundation of knowledge. As constructivists and constructionists emphasize, students construct their knowledge through their experience. Teaching experience by helping peers can further student construction of knowledge.

Although learner-centered educational robotics classes may sometimes look chaotic to teachers who are more comfortable with a traditional teaching style, this learning environment benefits both teachers and students to learn from the learner-centered and hands-on experience.

Encourage Failures

What is failure in education? Robinson (2006) argues that traditional schooling is killing creativity in students because it discourages students to make and learn from mistakes. Schools have educated students to be fearful of making mistakes, leading them to avoid using their creative and original ideas for solutions, and taking risks in exchange of safe and right answers that teachers expect. Making a mistake will never show up on the list of goals that students and teachers put together at the beginning of an academic year (Tugend, 2011). Housand and Housand (2012) also add to the argument:

Figure 10. Sample mastery chart

The current climate focused on minimum competency standards, focused on rote learning with closed-ended, single answer questions instead of more open-ended questions, likely exacerbates a fear of being wrong among students. That is, children are more likely to be asked to merely name a simple machine in a picture than to turn it into an original and potentially useful innovation. (p.706)

Children who are afraid of mistakes are the *victims of excellence* (Tugend, 2011). They feel uncomfortable when they do not know something for even a few second. For them, making a mistake becomes a failure. Tugend emphasizes:

If students are afraid of mistakes, then they're afraid of trying something new, of being creative, of thinking in a different way. They're scared to raise their hands when they don't know the answer and their response to a difficult problem is to ask the teacher rather than try different solutions that might, gasp, be wrong. (Para. 4)

Learning with educational robotics requires students to analyze the problem they face, come up with their own solutions for construction and/or programming, and then test them out using a physical model – a robot. Students cannot be afraid of failure or making mistakes since their solution usually does not work on the first try. They need to go through several iterations until they arrive at a successful solution. This process is an important process for developing the best solution, and is how engineers and scientists work in real life. Educational robotics helps students to examine their ideas, observe and analyze how the idea works, take risks, and be persistent and keep trying until they get it right. The idea of learning through mistakes helps them to accept imperfection and become willing to face the uncertainty of not knowing (Tugend, 2011). Risk-taking helps students to be more creative and willing to use trial and error when they do not know how to proceed. They learn to view failure as an opportunity to learn (Brookhart, 2010). For successful educational robotics learning, teachers, again, have to change their view and acknowledge failure as a chance for learning. In the educational robotics-learning environment, taking a risk should be encouraged, creative and innovative ideas are welcomed, and failure or making mistakes is embraced. In the syllabus of my educational robotics course, one of the golden rules of the course states, "Make a mistake! Mistakes lead the way to successful learning." Making mistakes and/or failure should always be welcomed and encouraged, and never be discouraged or something that students are embarrassed with experiencing. As Samuel Beckett advised, we should encourage students, "Try again. Fail again. Fail better."

Keep It Challenging, but Not Too Challenging

Successful educational robotics learning occurs when students are challenged, sometime to the point of failure. But determining how much students need to be challenged to enhance their learning to the maximum point is always a challenge for teachers. Otta and Tavella (2010) describe that, when competence is at a high level, students gain the ability to autonomously complete a task, intrinsic engagement, and motivation. However, when competence is diminished, for example, by the student failing to successfully complete a learning task, engagement and motivation also diminish (Otta & Tavella, 2010). At the same time, if competence is high, but the task can be completed too easily, the level of satisfaction and continued engagement among students also decreases. How to keep students engaged in their learning is a challenge for any teacher.

Csíkszentmihályi studied an optimal experience where people feel both free from destructions, from their environment and/or their thoughts or mind and totally engaged at the moment. He calls the state of this intense concentration *flow* (Csíkszentmihályi, 2008). The flow state occurs when people's body or mind is stretched to its limits while voluntarily trying to accomplish something difficult or worthwhile. A chess player whom he studied explained that the state is similar to breathing, a behavior people never notice as a conscious act. In other words, it is not intentional. Rather, it happens naturally when people intensively focus on achieving something that they have voluntary chosen to pursue. Csíkszentmihályi further explains that people in the flow state are so engaged that it becomes enjoyable enough to make them feel that nothing else matters. Pernsky who studied game players explains how important it is for game designers to keep the flow state so that players continue playing games (Prensky, 2006). He explains:

Achieving a true "flow" experience, however, requires a second factor besides just "leveling up," a factor that complex games also provide. That factor is always being kept in a narrow zone between the game's being too hard ("I give up") and too easy ("I'm not challenged at all.") (p. 59).

Prensky also explains that people play games not for obvious rewards but because they are engaging and challenging, yet relaxing at the same time (Prensky, 2002). According to Prensky, the magical state of motivation is the flow state where the intrinsic motivation is so high nothing else matters for the player but to keep trying.

When my student teacher candidates interviewed 4th graders from a private school in New York City through Skype video, they explained their favorite teachers as the teachers who know when and how to challenge them. Gifted and able children would prefer more challenging tasks since they know that would help them learn.

However, as Otta & Tavella alert, too much challenge would lead to reducing their motivation. This balancing act of teachers who facilitate learning with educational robotics is a very important element of the success of students' learning. If the learner-centered classroom environment is successfully established, educational robotics is a great tool to balance the challenging situation for students. Educational robotics in learner-centered environments allows teachers to provide individualized learning experiences for students. With educational robotics, students conceive of their own solutions to the task or problems that they face. Because there is no one right answer with robotics projects, or engineering projects in general, there can be many different ways to develop a solution to a problem depending on their levels of skills and knowledge that they have previously acquired. Because there are so many diverse ways, teachers can facilitate and challenge some students whom they believe can take the challenge, while providing on-demand suggestions to those who are struggling to complete the task that they set for themselves. Managing this balance requires experience on teachers' part. Teachers need to walk around in class, while using critical exploration skills to observe and understand what students are working on and their understanding of what is going on with their robotics experiment, through engaging in conversations with them. Teachers need to learn to be able to judge if a student is too frustrated and needs on-demand direct assistance, or a student is loosing his motivation because of the task that he has set for himself is too easy, and he needs more advanced challenge(s). Teachers should help those who tend to set less challenging tasks for themselves by providing instructional scaffolding so that they can learn to challenge themselves and complete more challenging tasks without teachers' support in the future.

To continue providing different levels of additional tasks to keep students challenged and taking the initiative in their learning, Lisbeth Uribe, an experienced elementary school science and robotics teacher at The School at Columbia University, has created a system where students who complete the required tasks are encouraged to select an additional task to advance their robotics skills. She created 17 sets of extra programming challenge kits and 10 sets of extra building challenge kits for students who have completed the class required challenges. A system of optional challenges provides students with carefully crafted and scaffolded learning opportunities that allow students to learn additional important skills and knowledge that they can use for their final project. With this system, we can still allow students to take an initiative of their learning by selecting the extra challenge of their interest. Instead of letting able students wait till the whole class completes the required tasks, the system allows them to acquire more skills and knowledge that will help them to advance with mastery of additional robotics skills and learning of STEM concepts. Although the extra challenges are advanced and challenging for those able students, they are designed to provide enough instructional information to encourage independent learning. Since students are encouraged to work in pairs or a small group, they naturally help each other to accomplish the task in front of them, usually with enthusiastic excitement for doing extra work (Figure 11 and 12).

CONCLUSION

The following quote in a book titled "Creating Innovators – The Making of Young People Who Will Change the World" from a high school science teacher summarizes and well explains how students' learning should be:

To be a successful science teacher, you have to make it fun, and for kids that means making it theirs – so that they have ownership over what they are learning. It's what motivates them. The other problem is that teachers think that, in order to cover the

Figure 11. Extra programming challenge kits

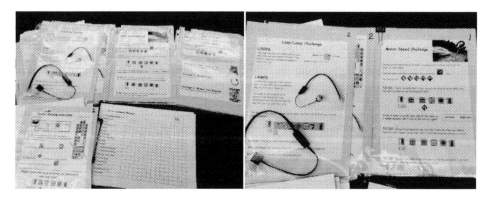

Figure 12. Extra building challenge kits

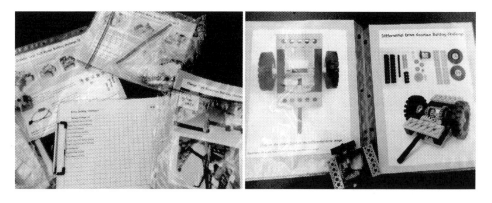

state standards, they have to give students all the answers, instead of having students discover the answers on their own. The most important thing is allowing students to ask questions and then give them the space to find the answers. They will actually retain more of the content by learning this way. (Wagner, 2012, P.148)

Educational robotics is an excellent learning tool for students with a wide range of abilities. RiE provides a learning environment where students are encouraged to test their curiosities, use their inquiries while taking risks to come up with innovative solutions to solve problems/tasks that they face while completing a project that they are interested in and find meaningful. RiE encourages students to think outside of the box – to be creative and innovative. It provides *hands-on, minds-on* learning experiences which benefit both able students and every student with their construction of knowledge through the experience that will remain in their mind while helping them to learn the necessary skills and qualities for them to become successful innovators. It is a learning tool that provides effective learning opportunities designed to enhance learning of any students. It is especially a great learning tool for helping children of above average ability to encourage developing giftedness. A Japanese educator, who has been teaching students in informal setting through the act of making while using various technologies including robotics, has shared his experience with students with various abilities working together. His students have been working together since they were in elementary school, for about 10 years, some students could be currently attending elite high schools where students with higher standardized test scores attend, and others could be in high schools which specialize in the learning of engineering and technology. He has observed that through the robotics activities of making, all the students are equally excited and enthusiastic and exchange their ideas equally among themselves. On some occasions, the students who do not attend the elite high schools have taught others and convinced others that their ideas could provide the best solution. They continuously work collaboratively while enjoying their act of making. Educational robotics is the tool that maximizes the potential of able students to display giftedness though the act of making.

REFERENCES

Alimisis, D., & Kynigos, C. (2009). Constructionism and Robotics in Education. In D. Alimisis (Ed.), *Teacher Education on Robotics-Enhanced Constructivist Pedagogical Methods*. Athens, Greece: School of Pedagogical and Technological Education.

Assessment & Teaching of 21st Century Skills. (n.d.). *What Are 21st-Century Skills?* Retrieved from http://atc21s.org/index.php/about/what-are-21st-century-skills/

Atmatzidou, S., Markelis, I., & Demitridis, S. (2008). *The Use of LEGO Mindstorms in Elementary and Secondary Education: Game as a way of triggering learning.* Paper presented at the International Conference of Simulation, Modeling and Programming for Autonomous Robots (SIMPAR). Venice, Italy.

Barr, D., Harrison, J., & Conery, L. (2011). Computational Thinking: A Digital Age Skill for Everyone. *Learning and Leading with Technology*, (March/April), 20–23.

Bers, M. U. (2008). *Blocks to Robots: Learning with Technology in the Early Childhood Classroom.* New York, NY: Teachers College Press.

Brookhart, S. M. (2010). *How to Assess Higher-Order Thinking Skills in Your Classroom.* Alexandria, VA: ASCD.

Csíkszentmihályi, M. (2008). *Flow: The Psychology of Optimal Experience.* New York, NY: HarperCollins Publishers.

Danahy, E. E., Goswamy, A., & Rogers, C. B. (2008). *Future of Robotics Education: The Designand Creation of Interactive Notebooks for Teaching Robotics Concepts.* Paper presented at the IEEE International Conference on Technologies for Practical Robot Applications. Woburn, MA. doi:10.1109/TEPRA.2008.4686687

Drew, J., Esposito, M., & Perakslis, C. (2004). *Utilization of Robotics in Higher Education.* Paper presented at the 21st Annual Information Systems Education Conference (ISECON 2004). Newport, RI.

Duckworth, E. (2005). Critical Exploration in the Classroom. *New Educator, 1*(4), 257–272. doi:10.1080/15476880500276728

Duckworth, E. (2006). *The Having of Wonderful Ideas: and Other Essays on Teaching and Learning* (3rd ed.). New York, NY: Teachers College Press.

Edwards, O. (2008). *Lego Mindstorms NXT Robots: Building Bonds with Bots - Learn science, technology, engineering, and math with robot-building projects.* Retrieved from http://www.edutopia.org/lego-mindstorms-robots-technology

Eguchi, A. (2007a). *Educational Robotics for Elementary School Classroom.* Paper presented at the Society for Information Technology and Education (SITE). San Antonio, TX.

Eguchi, A. (2007b). *Educational Robotics for Undergraduate Freshmen.* Paper presented at the Ed-Media Conference. Vancouver, Canada.

Eguchi, A. (2007c). *Educational Robotics for Undergraduate Freshmen*. Paper presented at the World Conference on Educational Multimedia, Hypermedia and Telecommunications. Vancouver, Canada.

Elkind, D. (2008). Forward. In M. U. Bers (Ed.), *Block to Robots* (pp. xi–xiv). New York, NY: Teachers College Press.

Goodhew, G. (2009). *Meeting the Needs of Gifted and Talented Students*. London, UK: Continuum International Publishing Group.

Green, A. (2011, February). Getting Started with LEGO Robotics. *D & T Practice,* 7-10.

Gura, M. (2013). *Student Robotics and the K-12 Curriculum*. Retrieved from http://www.edutopia.org/blog/student-robotics-k-12-curriculum-mark-gura

Hendler, J. (2000). Robots for the Rest of Us: Designing Systems "Out of the Box". In A. Druin, & J. Hendler (Eds.), *Robots for Kids: Exploring New Technologies for Learning* (pp. 2–7). San Diego, CA: Academic Press.

Housand, B. C., & Housand, A. M. (2012). The Role of Technology in Gifted Students' Motivation. *Psychology in the Schools, 49*(7), 706–715. doi:10.1002/pits.21629

Kolberg, E., & Orlev, N. (2001). *Robotics Learning as a Tool for Integrating Science-Technology Curriculum in K-12 Schools*. Paper presented at the 31st ASEE/IEEE Frontiers in Education Conference. Reno, NV. doi:10.1109/FIE.2001.963888

Martin, F., Mikhak, B., Resnick, M., Silverman, B., & Berg, R. (2000). To Mindstorms and Beyong: Evolution of a Construction Kit for Magical Machines. In A. Druin, & J. Hendler (Eds.), *Robots for Kids: Exploring New Technologies for Learning* (pp. 9–33). San Diego, CA: Academic Press.

Mataric, M. J. (2004). *Robotics Education for All Ages*. Paper presented at the American Association for Artificial Intelligence Spring Symposium on Accessible, Hands-on AI and Robotics Education. Retrieved from http://robotics.usc.edu/~maja/publications/aaaissymp04-edu.pdf

Miller, D. P., Nourbakhsh, I. R., & Sigwart, R. (2008). Robots for Education. In B. Siciliano & O. Khatib (Eds.), Springer Handbook of Rootics (pp. 1283 - 1301). New York, NY: Springer-Verlag New York, LLC.

Oppliger, D. (2002). *Using FIRST LEGO League to Enhance Engineering Education and to Increase the Pool of Future Engineering Students (Work in Progress)*. Paper presented at the 32nd ASEE/IEEE Frontiers in Education Conference. Boston, MA. doi:10.1109/FIE.2002.1158731

Otta, M., & Tavella, M. (2010). Motivation and Engagement in Computer-Based Learning Tasks: Investigating key contributing factors. *World Journal on Educational Technology*, *2*(1), 1–15.

Papert, S. (1993). *Mindstorms - Children, Computers, and Powreful Ideas* (2nd ed.). New York, NY: Basic Books.

Papert, S., & Harel, I. (1991). *Constructionism*. New York, NY: Ablex Publishing Corporation.

Partnership for 21st Century Skills. (2008). *21st Cenutry Skills, Education & Competitiveness Guide – A Resource and Policy Guide*. Retrieved from http://www.p21.org/storage/documents/21st_century_skills_education_and_competitiveness_guide.pdf

Perkins, D. N. (1981). *The Mind's Best Work*. Cambridge, MA: Harvard University Press.

Phillips, G. (1984). *Growing hope*. Minneapolis, MN: National Youth Leadership Council.

Piaget, J. (1929). *The Child's Conception of the World*. New York: Harcourt, Brace and Company.

Piaget, J. (1954). *The Construction of Reality in the Child*. New York: Basic Books. doi:10.1037/11168-000

Prensky, M. (2002). The Motivation of Gameplay or, the REAL 21st century learning revolution. *On the Horizon*, *10*(1), 5–11. doi:10.1108/10748120210431349

Prensky, M. (2006). *Don't Bother Me Mom - I'm Learning!* St. Paul, MN: Paragon House.

Renzulli, J. S. (1998). *Three Ringed Concept of Giftedness*. Retrieved from http://www.gifted.uconn.edu/sem/semart13.html

Robinson, K. (2006). Schools Kill Creativity. *TED Talk - Ideas worth spreading*. Retrieved from http://www.ted.com/speakers/sir_ken_robinson.html

Rogers, C. (2008). A Well-Kept Secret - Classroom Management with Robotics. In M. U. Bers (Ed.), *Blocks to Robots: Learning with Technology in the Early Childhood Classroom* (pp. 48–52). New York, NY: Teachers College Press.

Rogers, C., & Portsmore, M. (2004). Bringing Engineering to Elementary School. *Journal of STEM Education*, *5*(3&4), 17–28.

Rogers, J. J., Lisowski, M., & Rogers, A. A. (2006). Girls, Robots, and Science Education. *Science Scope*, *29*(6), 62–63.

Seltzer, K., & Bentley, T. (1999). *The Creative Age: Knowledge and Skills for the New Ecomony*. London, UK: Demos.

Sklar, E., & Eguchi, A. (2004). RoboCupJunior - Four Years Later. In *Proceedings of RoboCup-2004: Robot Soccer World Cup VIII*. Academic Press.

Sklar, E., Eguchi, A., & Johnson, J. (2002a). Children's learning from Team Robotics: RoboCupJunior 2001. In *Proceedings of RoboCup-2002: Robot Soccer World Cup VI*. Academic Press.

Sklar, E., Eguchi, A., & Johnson, J. (2002b). *Examining the Team Robotics through RoboCupJunior*. Paper presented at the the Annual Conference of Japan Society for Educational Technology. Nagaoka, Japan.

Sklar, E., Eguchi, A., & Johnson, J. (2003). Scientific Challenge Award: RoboCup-Junior - Learning with Educational Robotics. *AI Magazine*, *24*(2), 43–46.

State of New Jersey Department of Education. (2005). *Curriculum and Instruction - Gifted and Talented Requirements*. Retrieved from http://www.state.nj.us/education/aps/cccs/g_and_t_req.htm

State of New York Department of Education. (2009). *Curriculum and Instruction - Gifted and Talented*. Retrieved from http://www.p12.nysed.gov/ciai/gt/

Tugend, A. (2011). *The Role of Mistake in the Classroom*. Retrieved from http://www.edutopia.org/blog/benefits-mistakes-classroom-alina-tugend

Wagner, T. (2012). *Creating Innovators – The Making of Young People Who Will Change the World*. New York, NY: Scribner.

Weber, C. L., & Smith, D. (2010). Meeting the Needs of Gifted Students through Online Programs. *Distance Learning For Educators, Trainers, and Leaders*, *7*(2), 43–50.

KEY TERMS AND DEFINITIONS

Constructionism: Constructionism is a learning theory developed by Seymour Papert. He was inspired by Piaget's experimental learning theory and believes that children construct their new knowledge by constructing physical and manipulative materials, like blocks, beads, and robotics kits.

Educational Robotics: Educational robotics uses robotics kits, programming software and computer as hands-on learning tools. It can create a learning environment that can enhance collaboration and communication among students, problem-solving skills, critical thinking skills, and creativity.

Flow State: State of flow occurs when people are engaged in a task that is challenging but so meaningful that their focus on the task becomes impossible to be destructed by anything. People in the flow state are so engaged that it becomes enjoyable enough to make them feel that nothing else matters.

Giftedness and Talentedness: Giftedness and talented-ness in this chapter refer to the children who have above average ability (not necessarily exceptional ability) with a potential of exhibiting giftedness. They are called 'able children'. Their potential can reach higher when provided with a task with which they can engage with commitment and creativity.

Learner-Centered Approach: Learner-centered approach is a pedagogical approach that value learner's interest in learning. It considered that the learning needs to be driven by the curiosity and interest of students or learners. Learning happens when students or learners lead the learning activity by pursuing their curiosity and interests. With learner-centered approach, the role of educators changes to facilitators or mentors. Also it requires educators to take part in the learning experience with the learners.

Chapter 5
VoiceThread and iPad Apps Supporting Biological Change Concept

Emily Bodenlos
Morehead State University, USA

Lesia Lennex
Morehead State University, USA

EXECUTIVE SUMMARY

Kentucky science achievement data (KCCT, 2008-2011) for Biological Change indicated that middle grades students had little achievement compared to other concepts. The prior grade level for teaching this concept was fourth grade. A case study was designed to address the needs of three Fourth Grade classrooms. As part of No Child Left Behind (NCLB), language arts scores were supplemented with science and social studies. Objectives for the study were production of science and social studies curriculum using 3D instructional technologies for fourth grade in the following Kentucky Core Academic Standards (KCAS) Language Arts: Reading Standards for Informational Text K-5, Writing Standards K-5, Language Standards K-5, Range-Quality-and-Complexity of Student Reading; Core Content 4.1 Science Standard Biological Change; Core Content 4.1 Social Studies Standard Geography. Important findings for heterogeneous populations were made regarding the use of instructional technologies apps VoiceThread and Pangea Safari.

DOI: 10.4018/978-1-4666-6489-0.ch005

SETTING THE STAGE

In preparing research on science concept attainment for the National Science Foundation-Math Science Partnership (NSF-MSP) Start grant (2008-2010) and NSF-MSP Target Partnership (iSEEK, 2010-2014), it became apparent that middle grades teachers and specifically content in *Biological Change* needed further vertical content support. Students in middle grades showed the least amount of change in improvement with science concepts. One standard stood apart, *Biological Change*, because it had little achievement. Content area support, as of Spring 2011 from results of Kentucky Core Content Test (KCCT), continued to indicate need for support in learning and achievement. *Biological Change* involves learning about biological systems and the related geology and ecology. If middle grades were unsupported for achievement in *Biological Change*, the researchers wondered whether or not Elementary science also lacked support. Kentucky Core Academic Standards indicated that among Elementary grades, Fourth Grade addressed *Biological Change*.

Fall 2012 saw significant changes across Kentucky. NCLB testing was replaced in Elementary grades with Kentucky Performance Rating for Educational Progress (K-PREP) (KDE, 2012). Consistent with NCLB, science was specifically tested in Grades 4 and 7. The 2012-2013 academic year would serve as a baseline. This, of course, changed the focus of the unit from NCLB improvement to K-PREP criteria for baseline evaluation. Language arts components required Grade 5 to write with narrative and opinion stand-alone prompts as well as informative/ explanatory passage-based prompts. Science curriculum now contained 30% life sciences content and 20% geography (KDE, 2012). *Biological Change* was still important, but the degree to which it was measured had changed.

Also of concern to the researchers was the use of instructional technologies to support achievement for this curricular theme. 3D and iPad technologies hold great promise as an educational boost for learning and achievement with both heterogeneous and gifted and talented populations. Students who are considered Gifted or Talented may struggle to stay motivated in school due to lack of challenge or excitement, and the use of collaborative technology tools may give them the chance to obtain this (Crompton, 2013; Hubert & Ebner 2013; Zimlich, 2012). Renzulli (1995) found that independent study, mentorships, and electronic learning are top preferences for gifted learners. A curriculum unit addressing *Biological Change* was developed by Fourth Grade teachers in one Elementary school. Gifted and Talented students who were included in the general education classroom of each of the three Fourth Grade classrooms were able to use these apps during Biological Change instruction (Hur & Anderson 2013; Cumming, Rodriguez, & Strnadova, 2013). Within the three heterogeneous classrooms were approximately fifteen Gifted and Talented students. The unit was applied Fall 2012 with results in using apps VoiceThread and Pangea Safari.

It is important to note that Gifted and Talented students in this school had been identified and received targeted instruction one day per week for language arts and mathematics from a certified Gifted and Talented teacher. Other than this instruction, students receive no other specific supplement for Gifted and Talented identification.

Literature Review

One cannot have a discussion about use of iPad apps and neglect to mention m-learning, a cross of electronic and mobile learning. Crompton, Muilenberg, and Berge define m-learning as "learning across multiple contexts, through social and content interactions, using personal electronic devices" (Crompton, p. 4, 2013). M-learning can occur in multiple places with many kinds of electronic devices. The most common forms of electronic devices used in P-12 schools are cell phones, iPads, and Kindles or Nooks. Crompton (2013) provides a decent overview of m-learning, and all its iterations, from the early 1970's Discovery Learning to E-learning of the 2000's then finally M-learning. Crompton states that the "essence of m-learning is not in the learning or in the technology, but in the marriage between the two entities" (p. 10). Clearly, m-learning can be applied to research with iPads.

There are similarities between teaching technology courses and teaching gifted and talented students. Gifted and Talented educators and technology educators are being trained to teach in similar ways (Zimlich et al, 2012). Educators who teach gifted and talented students are realizing that using technology in their classrooms makes sense. Gifted and talented students can experience increased motivation when they have control over their studies. This is often easily implemented through use of technology (Zimlich et al, 2012). VoiceThread is a digital tool that can give them this control. Assignments can be given so that students work at their own pace. Each student can work independently, then receive collaborative feedback from others. Gifted and talented students would also enjoy the fact the VoiceThread gives them freedom of expression with choices as to what format of post and comment they would like to use. Differentiation of creativity is important to the gifted and talented student as well, and use of a digital, interactive presentation platform like Voice-Thread provides students with this outlet (Zimlich et al, 2012). Gifted and talented students enjoy collaboration based on mutual interests, as well as access to multiple levels of complexity (Zimlich et al, 2012). By differentiating the assignments that gifted and talented students post on VoiceThread, they are able to collaborate on a common topic but be challenged in a more complex way than their peers. Technology allows students to express themselves in unique ways and pursue independent investigations (Zimlich et al, 2012). According to Zimlich, the quality of feedback provided to students is an important component of technology use as well. Teachers should provide feedback to students that can help them to improve their assignments as well as challenge them to think further about a given topic. Enrichment activities can be implemented through collaborative experiences between teachers and students. It is evident that technology can be used to enhance instruction with Gifted and Talented populations through differentiation, and allowing students to express individual creativity.

Review of Apps

Many apps were reviewed for their use in a unit concerning *Biological Change*. Language arts, social studies, and science were to be blended together to support the school improvement plan as well as higher achievement with the science concept. This section addresses all apps that were considered for use in Fourth Grade. Apps were evaluated based on the following criteria: age appropriateness for all Fourth Grade students, interest of students in the apps, and applicability to the *Biological Change* unit.

Crazy Genetics (Creative Mobile Games, 2011) is an app that allows students to create new creatures by combining animals together. They must use different creatures to create new creatures by looking at specific traits that they have. This game can help students to see the relationship between traits and how they will be passed on to offspring. However, sometimes this game can be difficult for younger students because the traits do not always yield the expected result. Gifted and talented students may enjoy the challenge of creating new creatures in this app.

Gene Screen (Cold Spring Harbor Laboratory, 2011) is an app that could be used from elementary to high school in teaching genetics, and therefore would be easy to use as a differentiation tool. Many of the app components are too difficult for 4th grade, however there are a few which could be implemented. Gifted and Talented students may be able to use the more difficult features of this app as extension activities when learning about genetics. Under the "genetic traits" tab, widow's peak hairline is explained. Students can use the punnett square to predict what the children will look like after deciding if the parents have a peaked hairline or not. They then "mate" and show the babies as well as the different gene combinations, and predict randomly which hairline will occur in the offspring. There are also blank punnett squares/generators so that students can use the predictor to figure out what the chance is that a child will have any trait they are looking at. In the *Biological Change* unit developed by the Fourth Grade teachers, this app could have fit in with their lessons on traits passed from parents to offspring.

In Plant Tycoon (Last Day of Work, 2011), students grow different plants, provide them with the necessary requirements for life, and sell them to make a profit and purchase more plants. This game teaches students the specific conditions needed to grow a plant (water, light, etc.). Students also learn about money management. It takes a long time for the plants to grow, sometimes more than a day, which may cause students to become frustrated. This app would be good to use in a center where students use it daily for short periods of time.

Tiger Cam Lite (H. Rock Liao, 2011) is a fun way to help students understand adaptation. Students can use a picture of themselves or one of the demo pictures. They then camouflage the picture using various animal print backgrounds. This could be used in addition to a lesson about why a tiger has stripes, for example.

Puzzle Evolution HD (Wei Hong, 2010) shows the life cycle of a frog and a duck through a puzzle. Students put each layer of the puzzle together to see the entire life cycle unfold. This is a great way to help younger students visualize the different stages of the life cycle of a frog, but was too simple for use with Fourth Grade.

Life Cycle Lite (Rishi Chibber, 2011) is a very simple app that demonstrates the life cycle of a frog. The first screen is a picture of frog eggs, which you tap. These then become a tadpole. There is food on each screen that you drag to the frog in his various stages to "feed" him. He then changes into his next stage until he becomes a fully-grown adult frog. This would be a nice visual representation of the frog life cycle, especially for primary elementary grades that are just being introduced to this concept.

Singapore Zoo (Nanyang Polytechnic, 2012) teaches about the Zoo, specific animals, and includes quizzes and information on the animals. There are animal facts and pictures of each animal. While this is a fun learning and researching tool that may be used in the classroom, it is designed for those attending the Singapore Zoo. This app might be used as a virtual field trip or a research tool.

World of Animals Lite (World Book, Inc., 2012) was the best app that was found. This app has pictures and information about 15 different animals. It is a wonderful researching tool! Students can see pictures of the animal, hear the sounds it makes, watch videos that relate to that animal, etc. There are facts about each animal such as lifespan, habitat, predators, and more. Students are also able to compare 2 animals side by side and view all of these animals' information. There are quizzes that give an animal trait and students have to pick which animal it matches. There is also a portion of this app that ranks animals by multiple criteria such as lifespan, land speed, weight, etc. It is a great way to compare, contrast, and learn about these animals.

Virtual Manipulatives (ABCya.com, 2012) is an app that allows students to play with different fraction manipulatives. These virtual math tools are colorful, and can be made transparent for stacking to show part-whole relationships. iTooch Elementary (eduPad Inc., 2013) is an app that allows students to play games and quizzes at different grade levels. This is a great review tool with several content areas, games and quizzes involving different topics, and can be used for specified grade levels within the app. This app can be used for differentiation for Gifted and Talented students, because they have the opportunity to work with content at higher grade levels.

StoryLines for Schools (Root-One, Inc., 2013) is an app that takes the popular game of "Telephone" into education. "Telephone" is the beloved elementary school game in which students whisper the same phrase down a line of students, and see if the phrase changes as each individual repeats it. The first student using StoryLines writes a word or definition of a vocabulary word and passes the iPad onto the next student. That student then draws a picture of the word or phrase the previous student had created. The next student guesses what the drawing was, another student draws what the previous student guessed, and so on. This app is a great way to help students with vocabulary, sequencing, and collaboration with their peers. This app has phrases and elementary vocabulary words to choose from, or students can create their own. Once everyone has had a turn, students can watch the entire sequence of writing and drawing, and see how the original word changed as they played. Teachers can give students specific words to draw, or allow them to create their own. Gifted and Talented students may enjoy this app because they can vary the difficulty of words or the detail of their drawing, as well as review the information. They are also able to collaborate with peers while still having individual ideas. This app is a great addition to any classroom.

SparkleFish (Whoseagoodboy Partners, 2011) is a great game that teaches kids the different parts of speech. Much like the popular Mad Libs games, students are given a part of speech and asked to record a word that fits this category using the microphone. Examples are given so that students can learn the different parts of speech. These words then fill in the blanks of story. At the end of the game, the student's recordings are put into a story, which can often be hilarious! Students will love playing this game, and will be learning their parts of speech at the same time. Students will also learn how important word choice is within a story. This app would be a helpful tool for Gifted and Talented students to learn more about word choice and parts of speech.

A grammar app, called Using I and Me (Super Duper Publications, 2013), teaches students the different situations in which each of these pronouns is appropriate. A picture is shown with a sentence missing either "I" or "me", and students are asked to pick which one goes in the blank. The amount missed and the amount correct is recorded at the bottom of the screen, and students can see the percentage they got correct at the end. There is an unlimited amount of questions, so students can practice on the same game as long as they want. The "me" and "I" buttons switch sides randomly, making the students constantly think about what word they are selecting. This app will help students to better understand the different uses of I and me. Gifted and Talented students can use this app to strengthen their writing as well as deepen their understanding of the rules of when each of these pronouns is appropriate.

Stack the States (Dan Russell-Pinson, 2012) is an app that teaches students about different state facts. Students are asked to identify which state is which based on their shape, and answer trivia questions about the states, such as what is the capitol or which state is Mississippi. They then stack the states that they answered questions about correctly to reach the finish line. Every time the child reaches the finish line, they earn a new state for their map that marks their progress. Students only earn a state if they get a specific percentage of questions correct each round. When they earn a certain number of states, they unlock a mini game. This app helps students to learn information about the different states in an enjoyable way.

US States (EnsenSoft, 2012) teaches state names and locations, as well as state facts. There are multiple ways to play this app, including Learning, Game, and Test mode. This allows students to quiz themselves at different levels. A negative aspect of this app is that the Game and Test modes do not allow for process of elimination when finding the states because all states are always an answer option, which may make this app difficult for students who are just beginning to learn about the states.

SOFTWARE REVIEW

VoiceThread

Throughout their years at school, students are asked to record their thoughts and feelings in journals. These journals are used in virtually every subject from English to science to help students reflect. Students often are not engaged in the typical writing that is done in a journal, and long for a more exciting way to express their thoughts with their teachers and peers. VoiceThread can be used to help tech savvy kids get engaged in the reflective writing process (Boyle, Dyment, & O'Connell, n.d.) Gifted and Talented students may find VoiceThread to be a particularly engaging program due to its creative nature (Ducamp, 2010). By using VoiceThread, students are given a creative outlet that incorporates many different forms of expression into one easily shareable place. Students are often bored when writing typical paper and pencil journals, and do not dig deep to their true feelings and experiences (Boyle, Dyment, & O'Connell, n.d.) VoiceThread is a desirable program to incorporate into journal writing because it allows students to present their ideas and reflect using video, pictures, and recordings. Students can also view and comment on each other's VoiceThreads, making them a great collaborative tool (Boyle, Dyment, & O'Connell, n.d.). Students may be more excited to share their journals with their

97

teachers and classmates if the journal incorporates media such as videos, pictures, and audio commentary.

In her blog, Ddeubel discusses the benefits as well as the negative aspects of using VoiceThread in the classroom. VoiceThread can be used as a reflective tool for students. Students are able to share and explore their own beliefs and thoughts on various subjects in an engaging way (2010). The collaborative nature of VoiceThread, in which students can comment on their peers' posts as well as view VoiceThreads made by classmates, leads to a "social sharing" community within the classroom that has an educational design (Ddeubel, 2010). Gifted and Talented students may enjoy being able to communicate and collaborate with their peers, while still completing their own assignments (Hobgood & Ormsby, n.d.). Students are able to share their thoughts in an interesting and easy to use platform that they know other students, teachers, and even parents will be able to see. VoiceThread also allows students to construct presentations, which helps them with public speaking as well as writing for presentation (Ddeubel, 2010). This author believes that VoiceThread is a fun, interesting, educational way to get students sharing their ideas. She does, however, caution readers about a few negative aspects of VoiceThread. Some of the large VoiceThread files can take a while to download and run, which may be a hassle for teachers who are waiting for students to begin working (Ddeubel, 2010). The author also mentions that students must be carefully monitored when using VoiceThread so that they do not access any inappropriate content (Ddeubel, 2010). However, with the somewhat recent addition of VoiceThread Ed., only teachers, students, and administrators have access to the VoiceThreads, and teachers can restrict their students' work from being searchable.

English Learners/Special Education

VoiceThread is beneficial to the learning and comprehension of nontraditional students as well. Students who are learning English as a second language find this program helpful. There is a large range of levels of comprehension of English as well as academic readiness between different English language learners due to their differing backgrounds (Lopez, 2006). This can make instruction in the classroom setting difficult for the teacher as well as these students. Interactive White Boards that allow students to share their ideas are being used in these classrooms as an engaging way to help students understand the English language through sharing with each other (Lopez, 2006). VoiceThread can be used in this way as well, because students are able to comment on each other's work collaboratively as well as use pictures and videos to get their point across to their peers.

Students with special needs often have a decreased motivation when it comes to reading, either because they have struggled in the past or simply because they are not engaged in the material they are reading (Zorigian, 2009). Students must be motivated to read because it directly correlates to their progress. Students who struggle with reading in their early elementary years are likely to continue to struggle in their continued years of education as well (Zorigian, 2009). Motivation helps students in reading because they get excited and want to learn more, as well as share their ideas with their peers and teachers. Collaborative online tools such as VoiceThread are beneficial in motivating and engaging students in a way that excited students about the reading process. It was found that the use of VoiceThread increased student motivation in one specific study that was done with special education students (Zorigian, 2009). Students can use VoiceThread to discuss the books that they read, and learn about the books that their peers read. VoiceThread makes reading a social, collaborative task that is often more engaging for students than to read alone.

VoiceThread can be used to engage and assist all students in collaboration, both in special education and traditional classroom instruction. VoiceThread can be used across the curriculum in every grade level. One article has examples for several different subjects and ways to incorporate VoiceThread into the content lessons. In science curriculum, VoiceThread could be used to learn the life cycle of a butterfly, for example. Students could be asked to determine which stage the butterfly was going through in a picture or draw their own representation of the life cycle and comment on each other's work (Brunvand et al, 2011). In math, students can solve problems using the "doodle tool" available on VoiceThread, and then collaborate with peers about different ways that a problem could be solved (Brunvand, 2011). The possibilities of VoiceThread are endless. VoiceThread's ease of use and its ability to engage students make it a good choice for teachers in including students with special needs with traditional students. There are several examples given in the article regarding how students with special needs may have better academic experiences while using VoiceThread. For example, a Fourth Grade student with learning disabilities may use this program to have additional access to information about the book, in a simpler format (Brunvand, 2011). VoiceThread can be used to differentiate instruction because teachers can individualize instruction based on a student's specific needs.

Training Pre-Service Teachers/Professional Development

VoiceThread is not only being used in the K-12 classroom. It is also being used in teacher education programs. Teacher candidates were introduced to VoiceThread as a way to better formulate answers and a way for employers to understand their responses to interview questions. This program was also used as a reflective tool to use with a case study assignment and to look at a child's reading level (McCormack, 2010). Teacher candidates found that VoiceThread was easy to use and felt that the program allowed them to have a "more meaningful learning experience" than the traditional interview and case study review processes (McCormack, 2010, p. 162). These teacher candidates found that VoiceThread was a great tool to assess students as well as to share collaborative ideas with other teachers or employers (McCormack, 2010).

In another study, education graduate students used VoiceThread to improve their language arts instruction skills. With help from their IT assistants, these teachers were trained in using VoiceThread (Smith & Dobson, 2009). VoiceThread allowed students to create, comment, and collaborate via text, video, and pictures. These graduate students created language-arts themed projects for the purpose of integrating them into their elementary school classes during teaching experiences the following semester (Smith & Dobson, 2009). The students of this class were excited about the engaging software that VoiceThread is. Students who use VoiceThread have an audience for their projects that are more expansive that just the teacher, since peers and others can view their VoiceThreads on the Internet, and give feedback (Smith & Dobson, 2009). The author of this study points out that while Internet access is common and easy for university level students, this is not always the case for elementary students. Teachers must make sure that students are able to access VoiceThread in their particular school (Smith & Dobson, 2009). Using technology in the classroom is a wonderful creative way for students to express their ideas. "Students should be given few requirements when creating a VoiceThread for an assignment" because it encourages more creative thinking by students (Smith & Dobson, 2009).

VoiceThread is being used for professional development with in-service teachers as well. Probeware is often made available to science teachers but is rarely used to its full potential due to the lack of training that teachers receive (Nakagawa, 2010). Using VoiceThread for professional development solves many problems that previously hindered teachers from taking these workshops, such as the time that such workshops take up, distance to the place they are being held, and busy schedules (Nakagawa, 2010). By using an online collaborative tool such as VoiceThread, teachers are able to learn, comment, and create on their own time from their homes or during their planning periods. "Over eighty five percent of the participants rated VoiceThread as an excellent means of delivering online professional development" (Nakagawa, 2010). Because of this result, it is evident that VoiceThread may be a beneficial collaborative tool for teacher professional development.

Ferriter (2011) argues in this article that technology does not enhance the classroom experience alone, but that the teacher is the main factor in student success. However, technology can be integrated into the classroom with teacher instruction in order to help students learn better and be more engaged in the learning experience. An example of the technology that can be used for this purpose is VoiceThread. Ferriter uses VoiceThread as a continuation of his classroom by allowing students to continue conversations started in the classroom after they have already left school for the day (2011). VoiceThread can be used as a debating tool, allowing students to share their ideas on the VoiceThread about controversial topics without the nerve-wracking experience of talking face-to-face. This is a great tool for students beginning to debate. Students can use VoiceThread to view and respond to a political cartoon, for example, and then respond to the ideas of their peers (Ferriter, 2011). Because students have the option of thinking about their responses before sharing them, VoiceThread allows students to express themselves better in debates than they might have in the physical classroom, where comments may have been hastily shared (Ferriter, 2011). In addition to this, VoiceThread can help students who are absent from school. Because of the ability to look back at all the comments and follow the flow of the conversation, students are able to gain a better understanding of topics they may have missed in class (Ferriter, 2011). VoiceThread's integration into the classroom, as a debating platform is a great way to get students to express their thoughts on controversial matters, as well as a way to keep students up-to-date when they have missed a discussion.

Middle Grades

VoiceThread is a great way to engage students in school because it is similar to the social media sites that they already enjoy. A middle school in Salem, North Carolina introduced VoiceThread to its students in an attempt to engage them in this collaborative tool (Weir, 2008). Teachers found that students participated more on this online platform than they did in the physical classroom, as well as had more thoughtful contributions because they had time to think about their comments (Weir, 2008). Students are able to share their comments with their peers in an easy to use, online way that makes collaborating fun and less intimidating than standing up in front of the class giving a report.

High School

In one article, the use of VoiceThread as a pre-reading tool with a high school honors English class is discussed. The teachers and library specialist at this school realized that students despised reading the required novel *Death Comes for the Archbishop*. To help students find more pleasure when reading this book, they incorporated a pre-reading VoiceThread lesson to get students excited about reading this traditionally boring novel. Students were given prompts and guided through an exploration of the historical background, setting, etc. of this novel (Bomar, 2009). By using VoiceThread, students were able to collaborate from home and present cohesive group presentations to the class. The teachers found that VoiceThread was better suited to their needs than Power Point since multiple students could comment at a time, as well as include pictures and videos (Bomar, 2009). Students comprehended the novel better and enjoyed reading it more than students had in previous years. A majority of teenagers have experience using the Internet, and are often comfortable with using Web 2.0 programs such as VoiceThread in their free time. Students had no problems using the program, but struggled to have an academic focus on language in their work (Bomar, 2009). This may be due to the fact that students often use online collaborating tools for their social lives, not academic purposes. Teachers found that they struggled to use "academically sophisticated language" in their presentations, and plan to focus more on this when they implement VoiceThread into future projects (Bomar, 2009). It is evident from this project that VoiceThread can be used to engage students in typically difficult or boring assignments by adding an exciting, collaborative digital platform for sharing research and ideas.

Students can use VoiceThread to make history come alive and connect it to their lives in a relevant way. In a lesson plan example, students are asked to use Voice-Thread to create a virtual letter to their families, writing as if they were a soldier during World War II. Students use a variety of documents and resources to research what war conditions were like and what soldiers might say in a letter to their families (Nichols, 2010). Students receive support from their classroom teacher and library media specialist, and self-check their work to confirm that it contains all required aspects (Nichols, 2010). Students are then able to share their letters with the class, and comment using video, audio, or text to tell their peers what they liked about their letters. This VoiceThread project is a great way for students to share their creativity as well as historical knowledge about this interesting topic.

Library

Librarians are discovering the benefits of VoiceThread, too. Jane Lofton, a librarian at Lindero Canyon Middle School, has implemented VoiceThread as a way to share information between students as well as librarians across the country. Lofton (2008) has created book talks on her webpage using VoiceThread, in which librarians can describe books appropriate for young readers. She then encourages students to share their thoughts and ideas on the book by commenting on the VoiceThread. Lofton allows her students to create VoiceThreads to explain library procedures as well as tell about books they enjoyed, which gets the students involved and allows students to review information that they missed in class. She has found that by making her webpage more interactive, students are participating more in polls and other library related content (Lofton, 2008). VoiceThread is a great way for students to discuss books that they have enjoyed with their classmates, as well as provide feedback to their teachers.

Elementary Education

VoiceThread is a versatile program that can be used with children of all ages. Voice-Thread can be effectively used with children as young as five years of age with the proper guidance and support from adults. In the classroom discussed in this blog, VoiceThread was used to allow students to express their ideas about a topic. Serena Fan, an Early Childhood educator, feels that there are benefits to students, teachers, and even parents when using this program. Teachers are able to have one-on-one experiences with students while they are working, and guide them through the process of posting on VoiceThread (Fan, 2010). This is beneficial to the student-teacher relationship in that they are collaborating and learning together using this technology. Teachers are able to quickly see what concepts student's grasp and what they need extra assistance in. For students, there are many benefits. Students who used VoiceThread in this classroom had increased confidence after multiple uses of this program, evident in the way that they speak louder and speak longer (Fan, 2010). There are benefits for parents as well. Parents can collaborate on a VoiceThread, as well as learn what their children are doing in their classes (Fan, 2010). Due to the benefits that she observed in her Early Childhood classes, Fan recommends the use of VoiceThread in classrooms of all ages.

CASE DESCRIPTION

After reviewing the No Child Left Behind (NCLB) test scores for 2011-2012, it was evident that there was a need area in *Biological Change* for Fourth Grade. The instructional technology of choice was an iPad. The use of iPads and 3D apps were initially included based on literature review (Reitz, 2011; Truta, 2011; Ducamp, 2010; Lyall, 2010; Merchant, 2010) that achievement improved with these applications. The goals for the research, based on the school improvement plan for 2012-2013 were: Produce a viable science/social studies curriculum using 3D instructional technologies for Fourth Grade in the following Kentucky Core Academic Standards (KCAS) Language Arts: Reading Standards for Informational Text K-5, Writing Standards K-5, Language Standards K-5, Range-Quality-and Complexity of Student Reading; Core Content 4.1 Science Standard *Biological Change*; Core Content 4.1 Social Studies Standard Geography

Geography was minimally included by noting the different biomes and some adaptations within those biomes. Comparison between or among biomes was not addressed by students. Students did, however, focus on one biome and describe adaptations necessary for living in that biome. *Biological Change* was addressed as adaptation, but more specifically as physical characteristics responsive to biome. Teachers completed the unit in 10-15 days.

Four apps were found suitable for use in the Fourth Grade classroom to support instruction in this need area: World of Animals Lite, Life Cycle Lite, Gene Screen, and Tiger Cam Lite. However, the Fourth Grade teachers who were planning the unit found an app that they believed would work better: Pangea Safari. Pangea Safari is an app that allows students to add or remove different environmental factors, such as grasses and flowers, as well as add and remove animals. Students can add or remove gazelles, wildebeest, lions, and cheetahs. By introducing new animals and food sources to the environment, students are able to see how these new variables impact *Biological Change* within the safari environment.

VoiceThread was chosen to address language arts as well as science and social studies. Students were able to give virtual presentations on a specific biome and the adaptations necessary for animals that live there. Then, their peers were required to provide feedback on their presentations. VoiceThread was also used as a pre-assessment in which students responded to questions posed by the teacher. The initial findings on VoiceThread showed it to be a surprisingly versatile tool that students could use to communicate among a group and with others in a grade level. The researchers believed it could improve communications skills with oral presentation as well as provide skills with using iPad. The school improvement plan targeted improvement in the use of technology within each grade level. Using VoiceThread would improve the use of technology supporting curriculum.

Research Findings

Teacher records from 2011-2012 were compared to 2012-2013 performance to ensure comparability in delivery of instruction. An independent analysis of post-assessment for 2012-2013 is also included. In 2011-2012, this unit was presented over four separate activities. While the activity directions and rubrics were not provided to the researchers, it is possible to compare the overall conceptual under-standing based on theme of the assignment. Of the four activities comparing life cycles, animal adaptations, animal reproduction, and what appears to be a summative test on animal adaptations, two may be used for comparison to the pre and post-assessment in 2012-2013 (Appendix 3). The "comparing life cycles" activity cannot be studied because it asks for a comparison between two different life cycles. The post-assessment 2012-2013 requests the description of one life cycle. The "animal reproduction" activity cannot be studied because the specific contents of this title are not directly tied to any item on the post-assessment. Thus, the animal adapta-tion activities are the best comparisons. *Adapt* activity was valued at 3 points. 60% of students (N=20) achieved 2/3 points. 60% of students (N=20) achieved a score of 90/100 (90=A) on the *AAP* activity. An overall 95% achieved at least 85% and above on this activity. It would appear that nearly all students mastered the concept of animal adaptation according to *AAP* activity records.

The *Biological Change* unit contained two items that can be compared to data from the previous school year: of comparison- post-assessment item 4b (Describe the adaptations you listed above [2abc]) and 2 (Living in that biome, an animal may need certain adaptations. List three adaptations an animal may need to live in that biome- abc). Item 2 had several exceptions. Most notably, the teacher cited two students had 2/3 points and a third was incomplete. Independent research could not verify two other student submissions to VoiceThread at this time. It is possible that as many as four students (16%), discounting the incomplete student, did not list three correct environmental adaptations for a specific biome. Both the independent analysis and teacher analysis of successful concept achievement with 4b determined that 100% of students (N=23- there was one incomplete in a class of 24) success-fully completed the item. Keep in mind that item 2 was completed independently and item 4 was competed with at least one partner (Appendix 3).

In analyzing the differences in achievement VoiceThread and Pangea Safari contribute to learning about animal adaptation, one must rely on teacher anecdotal data. There is no significant difference in assignment scores between 2011-12 and 2012-13 for this concept.

An important detail within this unit of study is the acceptance and utilization of Pangea Safari for concept attainment. Each of the Fourth Grade teachers gave their students three questions relating to Pangea Safari and the unit on *Biological Change*. Mrs. Orange had thrown her class' responses away before copying them to researchers, causing students to re-answer the questions without having the op-portunity to review the apps.

The first question that each student in each class responded to was "What could you do to help the animals survive?" Students did not specify whether they were attempting to assist the herbivores or the carnivores. However, there were common threads of thought within each class.

In Mrs. Green's class, a majority of the students, nine out of twenty one, answered that they must add grass or flowers. Two students responded that you must "give them prey". Many students answered simply that you must "feed them" or "give them food", indicating that they too recognized that by manipulating the food sources in the environment, whether grasses or animals, the other animals and plants within the environment would react. One student had the misconception that they could "give them a spot to live", though shelter was not an aspect of this app.

In Mrs. Purple's class, almost every student referred to the necessity of feeding the animals, or presenting them with food to eat. Three students answered that the predator-prey relationship within the environment impacted the animals, either by giving an animal its prey to eat or removing predators so that the other animals did not get eaten.

In Mrs. Orange's class, the variety of answers was much greater. Once again, a majority of students responded that feeding their animals food or plants helped them to survive. The students in this class seemed to focus more on the fact that predators would eat the other animals, and that they should not put predators in the environment. One student in this class had the misconception that shelter was a factor within this game. Three students responded that reproduction was necessary. While the animals in this game did reproduce, this did not seem to be a theme in any other class' answers.

The second question presented to students was "What made the animals die?" In all classes, the answers were very similar. Students recognized that a lack of food or predator-prey relationships caused the animals to die. Common misconceptions were present among the classes as well.

In Mrs. Green's class, almost every student (all but 3) answered with a response that either referred to lack of food within the environment, or the relationship between predators and prey. One students mentioned reproduction, which while evident in this game, is not a cause of death. One student said that they did not save the animals. Another misconception that one student expressed was that people were killing the animals. There were not people in this game. They might have been simply answering what makes animals die in the wild, not within the game.

In Mrs. Purple's class, most students also answered either that a lack of food or predator-prey relationships caused the animals to die. However, one student in this class wrote, "they get show and there die", which is once again a misconception because there were no people in this app. Two students believed that an excess of food or plants would impact the animals negatively, though this was not the case within the app either. One student also said that the animals could die from running too much, but this is once again a misconception that they probably developed because animals would often die when a predator that had been chasing them caught up and killed them.

Mrs. Orange's class had the same majority of responses as the other two classes: a focus on lack of food and predator-prey relationships. One students mentioned reproduction as a cause of death, which is a misconception. Another student said, "people could killed them", though there were no people represented in this app. One student mentioned that decomposers made the animals die, though decomposers were not a part of this app, nor did the animals within the app decompose.

Question three asked, "How does an animal's environment affect its life expectancy?" Students seemed to answer this question about biomes in general, not relating their answers directly to the apps. However, some students made the connection between how the environment within Pangea Safari impacted the life expectancy of the animals within the app. Many students in every class said that lack of food and predators impact the life expectancy of the gazelles and wildebeest, but no students in any class discussed what impacts the life expectancy of the predators (lions and cheetahs).

In Mrs. Green's class, most students answered either that animals need food to survive, or that predators shorten the life expectancy of the wildebeest and gazelle. One student said that it was their fault that the animals died. One student mentioned the temperature of the environment, though this was not a variable within the app. One student said that the animals needed more space, though this was not a component of the app that they students' could change either.

In Mrs. Purple's class, there were not many common threads. Three students said that food impacts life expectancy, and three mentioned predators. Two students wrote that animals need to camouflage, though this was not an aspect of the app that the students could control, besides creating more plants for the animals to hide in. One student said that temperature matters. One student responded about Arctic Tundra, though the app was set in the savanna.

In Mrs. Orange's class, most students wrote about how predators cause the life expectancy of other animals to go down. One student mentioned that the temperature of an environment impacts the animals that live there. Three students mentioned that if animals do not mate, they would not survive, which is inaccurate. Several students clearly did not understand what the question was asking, and simple restated the question. 2 students told the definition of life expectancy, which is how long an animal lives.

In addition to the use of Pangea Safari, Fourth Grade teachers used VoiceThread as a pretest and posttest domain. VoiceThread allows students to create videos or presentations and then comment on their peers' work through text, video, or voice comments. In these classrooms, each teacher recorded herself asking several pretest questions. She then uploaded them onto her class' secure website. Each child and teacher had a username and password, and people outside of the group could not access their videos. Students commented their answers onto the video. VoiceThread was also used as a presentation tool for students. Students worked in pairs to create a presentation about a given biome, and the different animal adaptations that were needed to survive there. Students pre-scripted the presentation, then recorded it and posted it on VoiceThread. Then, each student was require to provide feedback to their peers via the commenting tools. VoiceThread was chosen to help support Language Arts and Social Studies curriculum, which were also identified, as need areas within Fourth Grade.

CURRENT CHALLENGES FACING THE ORGANIZATION

There are several motivators for using VoiceThread within the classroom. Students enjoy the use of it, and are engaged in their work. Students are able to respond via different formats, allowing students to express themselves in a way that makes them feel comfortable. Students are also able to answer questions or post videos at any time, whether at home or during the school day, allowing the teacher to have flexibility in assignments. VoiceThread can be accessed on a computer or iPad, giving diversity in the means of submitting responses. VoiceThread allows students to become increasingly confident with sharing their ideas with their peers, due to the non face-to-face interactions. VoiceThread can be used as a means to help students become more comfortable with expressing their ideas before engaging in a face-to-face presentation.

During this research, several flaws were discovered within VoiceThread. VoiceThread can be accessed via the VoiceThread website, or an app. While the app available is fairly simple to use, use of VoiceThread on the iPad requires wi-fi Internet access, which often ranges from minimal to nonexistent within elementary schools. In addition to this, the teachers experienced several occasions where students accidentally taped over each other's work. Sometimes the videos disappeared entirely. Students were tempted to copy peer responses when from video question responses because they could access the responses of their classmates. Grading was next to impossible when using VoiceThread as a pre-assessment, because there was no way to view all comments made by each child. The teacher must go through every comment on every video in the order in which they were uploaded. The comments often posted twice, leading to even more problems for the teacher as she tried to grade.

SOLUTIONS AND RECOMMENDATIONS

Of utmost concern to the researchers was the lack of time and consistency in teaching science to Elementary school students. The class was slated for thirty minutes each day, however, many days of either interruption to or abruption of teaching occurred due to school activities and time devotion to other subjects. The unit was originally supposed to occur simultaneously among three Fourth Grade teachers. None of the teachers delivered the unit simultaneously. The unit began nearly three weeks late and concluded much later than anticipated in fifteen days instead of seven. Also of concern was the change from KCAS to Next General Science Standards (NGSS) that was anticipated to occur 2013-14. Fortunately, NGSS (NGSS Lead States, 2013) includes Standard 3: Inheritance and Variation of Traits: Life Cycles and Traits and Standard 4: Interdependence Relationships in Ecosystems: Environmental

Impacts on Organisms (Appendix 2). At the time of writing this chapter, Kentucky has chosen to not support the NGSS. Many readers of this chapter will support the NGSS. Appendix 2 demonstrates the links between this unit and NGSS standards.

Biological Change in the Kentucky curriculum outlines change over time within genetic inheritance due to environmental impact. The delivered unit itself focused primarily on life cycles and heredity. Discussions of change in hereditary patterns over time resulting from adaptations to environment did not appear to specifically occur. Pangea Safari did not encourage further discussion. The app, while good for showing effects of scarcity and predator-prey relationships, did not demonstrate changes to the genetic inheritance of animals resulting from changes in their environment. A more appropriate app could have been Crazy Genetics (Creative Mobile Games, 2011). This app creates blended genetic animals but requires a working knowledge of biological terms not representative of higher-grade levels. It should be noted that the final project required students to identify animal environmental adaptations using VoiceThread. Students were given a random biome and asked to respond with an essay on VoiceThread with a partner. Anecdotal evidence suggests that students had better achievement in 2012-2013 than in 2011-2012 with this unit.

In remedying the most egregious of issues with using VoiceThread, the researchers recommend better fluency with the actual program and its related app prior to engaging students. Ferriter (n.d.) provides wonderful resources and a step-by-step guide for using VoiceThread. At the time of this research, only the company manual was available. To say the least, it is rather a dense reading. We further recommend turning off video viewing until all students have responded to unit queries. Not only was there difficulty with using the recording features, a primary motivator in capturing communications toward improving language arts achievement, there were also problems with erasing prior student work and even cheating because videos were available for viewing. The use of VoiceThread toward improved communications is well documented (Brunvand, 2011; Ddeubel, 2010; McCormack, 2010; Smith & Dobson, 2009; Zilmich, 2012). The researchers recommend students be evaluated on their delivery of the recordings rather than solely read from a prepared paper. This will enable achievement in language arts through the use of VoiceThread.

Of what utility were Pangea Safari and VoiceThread to gifted and talented students? Overall, the gifted and talented students were manipulating Pangea Safari to demonstrate predator-prey relationships. They were delighted to see that one could produce more plants, but not necessarily more gazelles. Gifted and talented students also reported better understanding of the gazelle and lion habitat geographic area needs. Gifted and talented students used more options on VoiceThread. They usually chose to illustrate their concepts as well as narrate their findings using the video or voice comment features.

ACKNOWLEDGMENT

This research was sponsored through Morehead State University.

REFERENCES

ABCya.com. (2012). *Virtual Manipulatives! (Version 1.2)*. Retrieved from Apple App Store.

Beecher, M., & Renzulli, J. (1995). *Developing the gifts and talents of all students in the regular classroom*. Mansfield Center, CT: Creative Learning Press.

Bomar, S. (2009). A pre-reading VoiceThread: Death comes for the archbishop. *Knowledge Quest, 37*(4), 26–27.

Boyle, I., Dyment, J. E., & O'Connell, T. S. (n.d.). The intersection of web 2.0 technologies and reflective journals: An investigation of possibilities, potential and pitfalls. *Independent.Academia.Edu*. Retrieved from: http://independent.academia.edu/IanBoyle/Papers/303036/The_intersection_of_Web_2.0_technologies_and_reflective_journals_An_investigation_of_possibilities_potential_and_pitfalls._in_press_

Brunvand, S., & Byr, S. (2011). Using VoiceThread to Promote Learning Engagement and Success for All Students. *The Council for Exceptional Children (CEC): TEACHING Exceptional Children*. Retrieved from: http://voicethread.com/media/misc/support/JTECVoiceThread.pdf

Chibber, R. (2011). *Life Cycles for Kids Lite (Version 1.0)*. Retrieved from Apple App Store.

Cold Spring Harbor Laboratory. (2011). *Gene Screen (Version 1.1)*. Retrieved from Apple App Store.

Creative Mobile Games. (2011). *Crazy Genetics (Version 1.1)*. Retrieved from Apple App Store.

Crompton, H. (2013). A historical overview of m-learning: toward learner-centered education. In Z. L. Berge, & L. Y. Muilenberg (Eds.), *Handbook of mobile learning* (pp. 3–14). Florence, KY: Routledge.

Crompton, H. (2013). New approach, new theory. In Z. L. Berge, & L. Y. Muilenberg (Eds.), *Handbook of mobile learning* (pp. 47–57). Florence, KY: Routledge.

Cumming, T., Rodriguez, C., & Strnadova, I. (2013). Aligning iPad applications with evidence-based practices in inclusive and special education. In J. Keengwe (Ed.), *Pedagogical applications and social effects of mobile technology integration* (pp. 55–78). Hershey, PA: IGI Global. doi:10.4018/978-1-4666-2985-1.ch004

Dan Russell-Pinson. (2012). *Stack the States Lite (Version 2.3)*. Retrieved from Apple App Store.

Ddeubel. (2010, Nov 8). *VoiceThread in education – empowering students* [Blog post]. Retrieved from http://ddeubel.edublogs.org/2008/11/08/voicethread-in-education-empowering-students/

Ducamp, G. (2010). *Technology and gifted learners, presented to NCAGT conference*. Retrieved from http://www.slideshare.net/gjducamp/technology-and-gifted-learners

eduPad Inc. (2013). *iTooch Elementary School (Version 4.6.1)*. Retrieved from Apple App Store.

EnsenaSoft. (2012). *US States (Match'Em Up History & Geography) (Version 1.0.12)*. Retrieved from Apple App Store.

Fan, S. (2010, April 8). *Why I'm falling in love with VoiceThread* [Blog post]. Retrieved from http://sinkorswim.posterous.com/why-im-falling-in-love-with-voicethread

Ferriter, B. (n.d.). *Using VoiceThread to communicate and collaborate.* Retrieved from http://www.learnnc.org/lp/pages/6538

Ferriter, W. M. (2011). Good teaching trumps good tools. *Educational Leadership*, *68*(5), 84.

Hobgood, B., & Ormsby, L. (n.d.). *Inclusion in the 21st century classroom: Differentiating with technology*. Retrieved from http://www.learnnc.org/lp/editions/every-learner/6776

Hong, W. (2010). *Puzzle Evolution HD (Version 2.0)*. Retrieved from Apple App Store.

Huber, S., & Ebner, M. (2013). iPad interface guidelines for m-learning. In Z. L. Berge & L. Y. Muilenberg (Eds.), Handbook of mobile learning (pp. 318-328). Florence, KY: Routledge.

Hur, J. W., & Anderson, A. (2013). iPad integration in an elementary classroom: lesson ideas, successes, and challenges. In J. Keengwe (Ed.), Pedagogical applications and social effects of mobile technology integration (pp. 42-54). Hershey, PA: IGI Global.

Last Day of Work. (2011). *Plant Tycoon (Verson 1.1.2)*. Retrieved from Apple App Store.

Lofton, J. (2008). New ideas take flight. *CSLA Journal, 31*(2), 14–15.

Lopez, O. (2006). *Lighting the Flame of Learning for English Language Learners Through the Use of Interactive Whiteboard Technology* (White Paper, Su-2006-01). The Corporation for Public School Education K16. Retrieved from http://extranet.mypromethean.com/us/upload/pdf/ELL_WhitePaper.pdf

Lyall, M. (2010, July 28). *First ever virtual iPad app for dissecting of frog*. Retrieved from http://www.knowabouthealth.com/first-ever-virtual-ipad-app-for-dissection-of-frog/4557/

McCormack, V. (2010). Increasing Teacher Candidate Responses through the Application of VoiceThread. *International Journal of Arts and Sciences, 3*(11), 160 – 165. Retrieved from http://openaccesslibrary.org/images/RLN147_Virginia_McCormack.pdf

Merchant, G. (2010). 3D virtual worlds as environments for literacy learning. *Educational Research, 52*(2), 135–150. doi:10.1080/00131881.2010.482739

Nakagawa, A. S. (2010, April 20). *Using Voicethread for professional development: Probeware training for science teachers*. Paper presented at the 15th Annual Technology, Colleges, and Community Worldwide Online Conference. New York, NY.

NGSS Lead States. (2013). *Next Generation Science Standards: For States, By States*. Washington, DC: The National Academies Press.

Nichols, A. (2010). VoiceThread and the World War II battle report. *School Library Monthly, 26*(6), 6.

Ostashewski, N., & Reid, D. (2013). The iPad in the classroom: three implementation cases highlighting pedagogical activities, integrating issues, and teacher professional development strategies. In J. Keengwe (Ed.), *Pedagogical applications and social effects of mobile technology integration* (pp. 25–41). Hershey, PA: IGI Global. doi:10.4018/978-1-4666-2985-1.ch002

Partners, W. (2011). *Sparklefish (Version 2.3)*. Retrieved from Apple App Store.

Polytechnic, N. (2012). *EducationZoo (Singapore Zoo) (Version 1.0.0)*. Retrieved from Apple App Store.

Reitz, S. (2011, Sept 3). *Many US schools adding iPads, trimming textbooks.* Retrieved from http://news.yahoo.com/many-us-schools-adding-ipads-trimming-textbooks-160839908.html

Renzulli, J. (1995). *Building a bridge between gifted education and total school improvement.* Storrs, CT: National Research Center on the Gifted and Talented.

Rock Liao, H. (2011). *Tiger Cam Lite (Version 1.3).* Retrieved from Apple App Store.

Root-One, Inc. (2013). *StoryLines (Version 5.6).* Retrieved from Apple App Store.

Smith, J., & Dobson, E. (2009). Beyond the book: Using VoiceThread in language arts instruction. In T. Bastiaens et al. (Eds.), *Proceedings of World Conference on E-Learning in Corporate, Government, Healthcare, and Higher Education 2009* (pp. 712-715). Chesapeake, VA: AACE.

Stern, R. (2014, February 19). *Look who's talking now: VoiceThreads are a novel way to spark "classroom" dialogue.* Retrieved from http://www.chicagonow.com/gifted-matters/2014/02/look-whos-talking-now-voicethreads-are-a-novel-way-to-spark-classroom-dialogue/

Super Duper Publications. (2013). *Using I and Me Fun Deck (Version 2.1).* Retrieved from Apple App Store.

Truta, F. (2011). *3D iPad 'textbooks' now available from Kno.* Retrieved from http://news.softpedia.com/news/3D-iPad-Textbooks-Now-Available-from-Kno-217950.shtml

Weir, L. (2008). VoiceThread extends the classroom with interactive multimedia albums. *Edutopia.* Retrieved from http://www.edutopia.org/voicethread-interactive-multimedia-albums

World Book, Inc. (2012). *World Book's World of Animals (FREE Lite Edition) (Version 1.1.2).* Retrieved from Apple App Store.

Zilmich, S. L., et al. (2012). *Using Technology in the Gifted and Talented Education Classrooms: The teacher's perspective.* (Doctoral dissertation). Retrieved from http://acumen.lib.ua.edu/content/u0015/0000001/0000903/u0015_0000001_0000903.pdf

Zorigian, K. A. (2009). *The effects of web-based publishing on students' reading motivation.* The University of North Carolina at Chapel Hill. ProQuest Dissertations and Theses. Retrieved from http://search.proquest.com/docview/304963123?accountid=12553

KEY TERMS AND DEFINITIONS

Apps: Programmed applications for an iPad or other internet device which allow students a self-contained supplement or extension to learning.

Biological Change: Concept theme within the Kentucky Core Academic Standards which addresses change over time of biological organisms. Includes genetic inheritance, life cycles, and geographic pressures to organisms.

iPad: An internet device.

Kentucky Core Academic Standards: The academic standards developed through Kentucky for all science courses P-12.

Next Generation Science Standards: The national curriculum standards for science P-12.

Pangea Safari: An app best demonstrative of predator-prey relationships. In this chapter, the app was used to demonstrate biological change.

VoiceThread: An app used for communications between and among students, teachers, and others. Please note that the app must be actively connected to the internet.

APPENDIX 1

Seven Day Learning Sequence (Unit) Plan for *Biological Change*

Day 1: Learning Target (LT)- I can activate prior knowledge. Students will use VoiceThread to answer questions posed by the teacher. Answer 4 of 7 questions. See the Pre-Assessment (Appendix 3)

Day 2: LT I can investigate and compare life cycles. Students will compare the life cycles they completed in the previous lesson. They will choose two, complete a Venn diagram, the write a short compare/contrast essay.

Day 3: I can understand that living things resemble their parents. Students will share family pictures and share the ways that they are similar to their family members. The class will discuss similarities to parents (body structure). The class will define genetics in their notebooks and use a Promethean flip chart.

Day 4: LT I can determine the difference between learned and inherited traits. Learned traits do not come from genetics and must be taught. Class discussion of those traits one has learned since early childhood.

Day 5: LT I can describe how some characteristics give certain animals advantages. Students will brainstorm a list of extinct or endangered animals. Class discussion of the reasons animals become extinct or endangered will lead to a discussion of adaptations. Students will be broken in to groups with a different habitat (arctic tundra, ocean, rainforest, desert, temperate forest, freshwater lake, or pond). Those group will use their textbooks, books from the library, and internet research to decide what [characteristics] animals in those habitats have that help them survive. Finally students will share with the class (powerpoint about animal adaptations: http://animals.pppst.com/adaptations.html).

Day 6: LT I can discuss life cycles and expectancies and draw conclusions about animals based on these. Students will use a variety of library books to research the life cycles and expectancies of animals in these books. They will then present what they've learned to the class. The class will use this information to decide what kind of climate and lifestyle these animals live. Students will experiment with Pangea Safari to theorize about life expectancies.

Day 7: LT I can show what I know. Students work in groups and will be assigned a biome. They will discuss the adaptations necessary for life in this biome. They will use VoiceThread to make presentations sharing information about their biome. Finally students will work independently to comment on other group's presentations on VoiceThread.

APPENDIX 2

Comparison of KCAS to NGSS Standards

KCAS Standards for Biological Change Fourth Grade

1. **SC-04-3.4.1:** Compare the different structures and functions of plants and animals that contribute to the growth, survival, and reproduction of the organisms.
2. **SC-4-UD-U-4:** Students will understand that offspring resemble their parents because the parents have a reliable way to transfer information to the next generation
3. **SC-4-UD-U-3:** Students will understand that organisms have different structures that are used for different functions. Observations of the structures of a certain organism can be used to predict how that organism functions or where it might live
4. **SC-4-UD-U-5:** Students will understand that some likenesses between parents and offspring are inherited (e.g. eye color) an some likenesses are learned (e.g. speech patterns).
5. **SC-4-UD-U-5:** Students will understand that some likenesses between parents and offspring are inherited (e.g. eye color) an some likenesses are learned (e.g. speech patterns).
6. **SC-04-3.4.4:** Students will identify some characteristics of organisms that are inherited from the parents and others that are learned from interactions with the environment.

NGSS Standards for Biology Fourth Grade

Inheritance and Variation of Traits: Life Cycles and Traits

Students who demonstrate understanding can:

3-LS1-1: Develop models to describe that organisms have unique and diverse life cycles but all have in common birth, growth, reproduction, and death. [Clarification Statement: Changes organisms go through during their life form a pattern.] [Assessment Boundary: Assessment of plant life cycles is limited to those of flowering plants. Assessment does not include details of human reproduction.]

3-LS3-1: Analyze and interpret data to provide evidence that plants and animals have traits inherited from parents and that variation of these traits exists in a group of similar organisms. [Clarification Statement: Patterns are the similarities and differences in traits shared between offspring and their parents, or among siblings. Emphasis is on organisms other than humans.] [Assessment Boundary: Assessment does not include genetic mechanisms of inheritance and prediction of traits. Assessment is limited to non-human examples.]

3-LS3-2: Use evidence to support the explanation that traits can be influenced by the environment. [Clarification Statement: Examples of the environment affecting a trait could include normally tall plants grown with insufficient water are stunted; and, a pet dog that is given too much food and little exercise may become overweight.]

3-LS4-2: Use evidence to construct an explanation for how the variations in characteristics among individuals of the same species may provide advantages in surviving, finding mates, and reproducing. [Clarification Statement: Examples of cause and effect relationships could be plants that have larger thorns than other plants may be less likely to be eaten by predators; and, animals that have better camouflage coloration than other animals may be more likely to survive and therefore more likely to leave offspring.]

Interdependent Relationships in Ecosystems: Environmental Impacts on Organisms

Students who demonstrate understanding can:

3-LS2-1: Construct an argument that some animals form groups that help members survive.

3-LS4-1: Analyze and interpret data from fossils to provide evidence of the organisms and the environments in which they lived long ago. [Clarification Statement: Examples of data could include type, size, and distributions of fossil organisms. Examples of fossils and environments could include marine fossils found on dry land, tropical plant fossils found in Arctic areas, and fossils of extinct organisms.] [Assessment Boundary: Assessment does not include identification of specific fossils or present plants and animals. Assessment is limited to major fossil types and relative ages.]

3-LS4-3: Construct an argument with evidence that in a particular habitat some organisms can survive well, some survive less well, and some cannot survive at all. [Clarification Statement: Examples of evidence could include needs and characteristics of the organisms and habitats involved. The organisms and their habitat make up a system in which the parts depend on each other.]

3-LS4-4: Make a claim about the merit of a solution to a problem caused when the environment changes and the types of plants and animals that live there may change.* [Clarification Statement: Examples of environmental changes could include changes in land characteristics, water distribution, temperature, food, and other organisms.] [Assessment Boundary: *Assessment is limited to a single environmental change. Assessment does not include the greenhouse effect of climate change.*]

APPENDIX 3

Pre- and Post-Assessments

The pre and post-assessments and KY core content standards for Fourth Grade science *Biological Change* follow. The unit is written in black text; the pre-assessment in underline text; the post-assessment in underline and bold text; the corresponding 4th grade curriculum in italics text

1. Choose any animal, describe that animal's life cycle.
2. Choose two animals. Think about their life cycles. Explain the differences between the life cycles of the two animals.
3. How might an animal's life cycle help determine their life expectancy? 4d. Choose one of those animals [from 4c that live in your biome]; 4e. Describe their life cycle and life expectancy. *SC-04-3.4.1: Compare the different structures and functions of plants and animals that contribute to the growth, survival, and reproduction of the organisms.*
4. Do you look more like your mom or your dad? Explain why you do or don't look like your parents. *SC-4-UD-U-4: Students will understand that offspring resemble their parents because the parents have a reliable way to transfer information to the next generation;*
5. Inherited traits are things an animal has or can do from birth. What are some examples of inherited traits? Living in that [assigned] biome, an animal may need certain adaptations. List three adaptations an animal may need to live in that biome. *SC-4-UD-U-3: Students will understand that organisms have different structures that are used for different functions. Observations of the structures of a certain organism can be used to predict how that organism functions or where it might live; SC-4-UD-U-5: Students will understand that some likenesses between parents and offspring are inherited (e.g. eye color) an some likenesses are learned (e.g. speech patterns).*
6. Learned traits are things an animal learns to do as it grows. What are some examples of learned traits? *SC-4-UD-U-5: Students will understand that some likenesses between parents and offspring are inherited (e.g. eye color) an some likenesses are learned (e.g. speech patterns).*

7.   Some animals live in extreme climates. How do they survive in these extreme climates? 4a. Describe your biome in detail; 4b. Describe the adaptations you listed above [2abc]; 4c. List some animals that may live in your biome; *SC-04-3.4.4: Students will identify some characteristics of organisms that are inherited from the parents and others that are learned from interactions with the environment.*

Students were assigned a biome in the post-assessment. They were required to work in a group to create a VoiceThread presentation. Students were also asked upon completion of their group work to comment on at least three different groups' VoiceThread presentations from within the class. They must (a) tell something you liked about the presentation, (b) explain something you agree or disagree with about their presentation, and (c) explain why you agree or disagree.

Chapter 6
To Boldly Go:
Instructional Technology and Environmental Science

Kimberely Fletcher Nettleton
Morehead State University, USA

EXECUTIVE SUMMARY

In an effort to help special needs students in the classroom, many teachers work very hard to differentiate curriculum for their struggling students. According to A Nation Deceived (Colangelo, Assouline, & Gross, 2004), the one group of students in American schools who make little or no yearly progress are the gifted students in the classroom. Enriching the curriculum for gifted students does not appear to be a high priority for teachers (Horne & Shaughnessy, 2013). Increasingly, teachers turn to the computer to provide independent work for students, relegating education to a solitary endeavor. Social skills and collaboration are traits encouraged in many classrooms. Instead of isolating gifted students, technology can be integrated into instructional strategies in order to enrich the curriculum for all students. Enrichment can become an integral part of instruction. Technology can create learning environments that challenge gifted students.

SETTING THE STAGE

"Captain, an incoming message has been received."
    "On Screen"
    The Admiral's face filled the large screen. "Attention"

DOI: 10.4018/978-1-4666-6489-0.ch006

The room immediately quieted. All eyes turned towards the screen as everyone snapped to attention and saluted the screen.

The Admiral glared round the room. "That's better," he snapped. He paused, and then continued, "At ease. Captain, StarPoint received your last report. You are about to enter a sector of space that has recently been explored by a scout ship. We would like you to divert your ship to the Galation Planetary system. The scout ship has compiled a data report of each of the five planets in this system. Your science crew is to review the data reports of each planet. Using the data, determine which planet would be best for colonization or mining. You will be arriving in the planetary system in two days. As you know, a decision to colonize in this system cannot be determined by data alone. StarPoint would like members of your science teams to shuttle to the planet's surface and explore. The recommendation of your team should be sent to StarPoint with available information and a variety of reasons to determine if it would be acceptable for colonization or mining. The data reports will be beamed to your ship computer. This is an important mission and StarPoint is looking forward to your Report.

"Aye, Aye, Admiral."

The Admiral's face faded from the screen.

The Captain pulled the Data reports folders off the desk, darkened the screen, turned to her crew, and dismissed them for recess.

"After recess", she reflected, "The students should be ready to look at the top secret reports."

BACKGROUND

What message does it send to a student to be assigned a project on the computer and sent to research independently while the teacher works with the rest of the class? How connected is the student to the rest of the students when engaged in solitary projects, reports, and online activities? Gifted students are often left to be solitary learners in social classrooms. Expected to teach themselves, with minimal guidance, learning can become an individualized experience in the classroom with distance education courses often providing a means for connecting and learning (University of Plymouth, 2006). Yet, although many gifted students are likely to be introverted (Silverman, 1986), students need social interaction.

Educational and Social Needs of Gifted Students

Gifted students are a unique group of students who have educational needs that are rarely being met in the classroom (Colangelo, Assouline, & Gross, 2004). Teachers (White. 1993) usually misunderstand divergent thinkers, whose instruction should be enriched beyond the general curriculum to meet their needs. Teachers are generally loathe to accelerate students in subjects due to preconceived notions of social and emotional maturity (Vialle, Ashton, Carlton, & Rankin, 2001). Teachers often site behavior or social problems as reasons to withhold accelerated lessons (Silverman, 2000).

In many classrooms, if enrichment or acceleration does occur, it is often a solitary experience (Latz, Speirs Neumeister, Adams, & Pierce, 2009). Students are given extra assignments or independent projects and as far as classmates are concerned, computer assisted learning or distance education is generally a solitary experience (Dykman & Davis, 2008; Siegle & Mitchell, 2011).

It is important that gifted students have the opportunity to learn through interactions with other students. Vygotsky's (1978) Zone of Proximal Development (ZPD) suggests that students move from one level to another and interaction with a teacher or peer supports the movement. . This zone is "the distance between the actual development as determined by independent problem solving and the level of potential development as determined through problem solving under adult guidance or in collaboration with more capable peers" (p. 86). In most American schools, the gifted student is rarely moved from one ZPD to another through interactions with lower level learners. Learning is generally through a teacher, book, or computer program (Siegle, 2004).

Social learning experiences for gifted students need to be a part of the educational process (Robinson, 2008). To address the social learning needs as well as the educational needs of gifted learners, teachers need a variety of resources beyond the textbook and computer based research projects. Problem based learning may be used to develop a learning community in the classroom where students at all levels can be part of the learning process. Students must take control for constructing their own meaning from the learning environment (Mergendoller, Markham, Ravitz, & Larmer, 2006). Problem based learning experiences may be solved at many levels, so all members of the group may contribute. English and Kitsantas (2013) describe a series of stages for carefully constructed learning environments that lead students from a teacher-directed unit to a student's self-directed unit. Divided into three phases, they are: Phase 1: Project/problem/launch; Phase 2: Guided Inquiry and Product/Solution Creation; and Phase 3: Project/Problem Conclusion. As students progress through these phases, they become more active in the learning process, while the teacher becomes less active. Problem based learning provides an approach to education that supports divergent thinking (Kumar, & Natarajan, 2007).

CASE DESCRIPTION

Project Tatibah, the environmental problem based learning (PBL) unit, was designed to integrate environmental education into the general curriculum. The unit utilized monthly visits to an outdoor classroom and ended with an integrated PBL activity. At the beginning of the school year, a supply list went out including such items as boots, 1 set of clothes that could get mucky, sun block, a waist pack, and a magnifying glass. Parent volunteers were recruited to help throughout the year. The teacher borrowed sets of walkie-talkies and GPS units for each pair of students during outdoor classroom visits. Parent volunteers were trained in safety procedures.

Using a case study methodology (Glesne, 2011), the teacher-researcher kept observational notes and used student field journals and reflections to document student growth. The students in this case were part of a split fifth and sixth grade classroom in a private school located in a rural town in eastern Kentucky. The class of 16 students was a curious mix. While many of the students had attended the school since Kindergarten, three of the students transferred to the private school when their public school teachers referred them for special education testing. These students were at the private school because their parents did not want them identified as needing special education. Of the nine fifth graders and seven sixth graders, six students were in the 99th percentile in at least one academic area on the *Terra Nova,* a standardized test administered each year at the school. Although the school was not large enough to have additional classes or pull out programs, Gentry's research (1999) suggests that all classroom students benefit from cluster grouping of gifted students within a classroom, and in this case, the level of overall student achievement was high due the pace set by the students.

While reading, language arts, and math were taught in small groups depending on student ability, science and social studies curriculum topics were taught to the whole class and rotated between two academic years. With the high number of gifted students in the classroom, the classroom teacher searched for ways to foster socialization and provide instruction at a level that would be challenging for all students in the classroom. Using Environmental Education (EE) as the basis of the unit, the teacher worked with the local county extension agent to create a unit of study. The EE curriculum was chosen because it offered a different location for learning. The instructional activities could be entered at a variety of learning levels. Additionally, this was an area that classroom K-8 students typically have a great deal of background knowledge, meaning that life experiences could enhance learning. The unit provided an enriched learning experience where every student, from the struggling student to the gifted student, could come together as equals. Classroom skills that separate students, such as reading levels or math skills, would not be an issue. With a wide variety of topics, students would learn through experience and interaction with the environment.

The yearlong unit had two broad cognitive goals:

1.   Teach EE curriculum in way that is meaningful to all students. Curriculum for gifted students should include teaching the discipline according to the discipline (Tomlinson, Kaplan, Renzulli, Purcell, Leppien, & Burns, 2002). By using the knowledge of experts, the curriculum would be accessible to students at many levels.
     a.   Change over time
     b.   Discipline-specific knowledge
     c.   Development of tools and technology
2.   Develop Social skills for all students

The important affective goals were:

1.   Appreciate the beauty and intricacy of the environment
2.   Recognize the survival difficulties of early people
3.   Appreciate and develop respect for members of the class
4.   Encourage curiosity

During the year of the case study, the teacher used a "Survival" theme and integrated it into the curriculum. Books portraying characters facing survival challenges were either read aloud to students or read by students, as part of language-arts instruction. *Hatchet* (Paulson, 1987), *Julie of the Wolves* (George, 1972), *Island of the Blue Dolphins* (O'Dell, 1960), and other survival novels became part of the classroom culture. Social studies units focused on how the many peoples populating North America have survived and prospered.

In the classroom, the science curriculum also supported the theme of survival. Each unit connected to the theme by helping students understand the fragile interconnectedness of life and science. The teacher taught two to three week units in variety of areas, but kept the survival thread throughout the year. The studies were the framework unit, Phase 1: Launching (English and Kitsantas, 2013) of an environmental study unit.

By using EE as the background, the teacher developed a yearlong EE curriculum, utilizing the county's outdoor classroom. The local community had arranged for several acres to be set aside to provide a countywide outdoor classroom. The outdoor classroom was equipped with outdoor facilities: an area for cooking, fire pit, outhouses, and an outdoor pavilion with several picnic tables. The grounds included

124

a large pond, hills and trees, a grassland, and a stream. The county extension agent for the community helped provide naturalists and specialized knowledge.

The teacher enlisted the aid of various environmental experts various during the unit, which allowed all students the opportunity to ask questions from specialists. The gifted students, were able to take advantage of the relaxed atmosphere and pursue their own line of questions while other students were engaged in activities. Gifted students are often identified by their divergent thinking skills (White, 1993), ability to make connections, and learn at a deeper level than their peers. The access to experts is an important part of gifted education (Tomlinson, et al., 2002). Students who were not interested in delving deeper into a subject could find plenty to learn in the practical outdoor environment. The teacher fully expected that due to the diversity of students in the classroom, many students who struggled in the classroom would find themselves resident experts in many of the outdoor learning experiences. Throughout the ten-month unit, students became more and more self-directed.

The teacher planned to use instructional technology whenever possible. One of the instructional goals was for students to understand that ancient technologies were created as tools to be used for environmental interaction. As people's needs changed or as technologies were improved, people learned to interact with the environment more safely. Successful interactions with technology depend on the user, the context, and the activity (Kuutti, 1996; Nardi, 1996; Zurita & Nussbaum, 2007). Student interactions with technology are improved when teachers have a solid understanding and familiarity with the technology (Lennex & Nettleton, 2010). In addition to students successfully using technology in the outdoor environment,, the teacher wanted students to use computer-based research more effectively and purposefully. Most of the fifth and sixth grade students appeared to think that if they Googled a topic and printed off whatever site came up, they had completed a well-researched report. Using questions students raised while at the outdoor classroom for follow-up research, the teacher planned to facilitate Phase 2: Guided Inquiry (English and Kitsantas, 2013) student learning through research based on students' interests.

Each month, students left the school and spent a full day in the outdoor classroom. The first month, students learned about the different areas in the outdoor classroom. In teams of two, with a parent volunteer keeping a close eye on safety, students were charged with the task of finding a *place*, somewhere in the outdoor classroom that would become *their spot* for the year. Once at their sites, students opened their field journals and made notes of what they saw, smelled, and heard. Students took pictures to put into their journals to document their particular site. This activity was part of every subsequent visit. Recording the change over time, students learned to document the effects of seasonal change and climate. Using the camera to help document changes was the first use of technology in the outdoor adventure.

As the year progressed, students used their pictures to predict what changes were likely to occur in the environment. The quiet time provided everyone with moments of reflection. All students used the field journals to document observations and thoughts. The teacher talked with student pairs concerning their spots at some point during the day. Often the teacher posed questions for students to research after returning to the classroom.

Although each month students visited the outdoor classroom, the focus of each visit was different. The days were packed with many activities. An overview of the year's learning activities provided. The final outdoor classroom learning experience pulled everything together.

August

During the first visit, students were told to wear mucky clothes and be prepared to get their feet wet. The teacher put rubber boots on the school supply list, although they were considered an optional supply. Sack lunches were stored on the picnic tables. After finding and documenting their quiet spots, students went to the most alluring place in the outdoor classroom: the stream. There is something about seeing the sun sparkle on water and following the swirl of fallen leaves as they ride the rush of water as it dances downstream, that drew the children's attention. This first visit set the tone for the year.

At the stream, students were guided through water quality testing experiments. In random pairs, students went into the stream, caught insects and indigenous life forms, and determined if the stream was a healthy environment. After the macro-invertebrates were returned to their habitats, students collected water samples and tested for oxygen and pH levels. Calculators and a laptop were part of the technology used at the site to record data and identify insects and fish in the stream. The laptop also provided information about several of the insects and organisms in the water through pre-saved pages. Follow-up in the classroom consisted of studying the problem of Whirling Disease in trout in freshwater streams.

September

Before going to the outdoor classroom, the teacher showed a small video clip from the Disney movie, *Honey, I Shrunk the Kids* (Naha, Schulman, Cox, Johnston, Moranis, Frewer, & Strassman, 2002). The video clip, which showed children riding an ant and eating a large oatmeal cream cookie, helped students focus on scale. Once at the outdoor classroom, magnifying glasses were used throughout the day as students examined teeny-tiny life forms. Students drew insects and their habitats as seen through the magnifying glasses. They examined the interaction of the insects with leaves and wildflowers. Although the hand lens is a simple technology, it provided an understanding of size and scale. Students used the laptop as a research station. Informational books concerning a variety of life forms were also available at the research station.

October

After updating the field data concerning their sites, student learning focused on plant life. The outdoor classroom had a large tree stump preserved for visitors and labeled with events from history: the walk on the moon, World War II, and the sinking of the Titanic. Students counted rings and determined the age of the tree. They were then challenged to examine the stump with their magnifying lenses, and by the width between lines, make predictions of weather in the area. When they returned to their classroom, the students used the computer lab to verify their historical weather predictions.

During the rest of the day, students used their hand lenses to explore leaves, bark, and other woodland plants. The hand lens provided a good introduction to the intricacy of plant life. Students drew pictures of their observations in their field journals.

November/December

The outdoor classroom was sprinkled with snow and the visit to document change at the sites was finished much more quickly than usual. While the main lesson centered on cooking in the outdoors, several pieces of old farm/home technologies were available. Students examined the tools and guessed their purpose. Once the item was identified, students were shown how to use the old technology. The old tools demonstrated to students that very often innovative technologies were designed for to complete tasks more efficiently.

The care of the campfire (and its heat) drew students' attention. Each student wanted to add sticks or leaves to the fire, poke at it, and drink hot cocoa as they watched it blaze. The campfire was one of the most popular spots that day. After eating pies, bread, and stew cooked over the fire, the day ended early as the class headed back to the warmth of the school.

January

During their January visit, students built bat houses and learned about nocturnal animals. This was not a month where any technology (except the timeless hammer) was part of the lesson. The unseasonable warmth made the day very enjoyable, but the activity was chosen because it would keep students moving. As several weeks had passed since students last visited their place, changes were much more obvious. Students used the laptop research station to find out more about bats and other nocturnal animals.

February

February was another warm month and after documenting change at their sites with photos, students spent the day learning about weather and soil. The outdoor classroom had a recycled, old, satellite dish to serve as a water gauge. An anemometer, barometer, and thermometer, attached to a portable stand, measured wind speed, temperature, and barometric pressure. Students chose several sites around the outdoor classroom to collect data: the woods, the open plain, the wetland area, the streams, and their own special sites. Information from the portable weather station was uploaded into a laptop computer and analyzed.

Students also collected soil samples from their weather station sites. The soil samples had to dry before analysis, so the actual testing was conducted later in the week at the classrooms. In small, mixed groups, students used handheld GPS units to record the exact longitude and latitude of their weather stations and soil sample sites.

March

This month, the outdoor classroom came alive with students investigating animal activity through tracks and scat. The boys seemed to be especially interested in scat. Plaster of Paris casts were made of the tracks. Students used the laptop research station, identifying animals by the clues they left behind.

April

During the last scheduled day at the outdoor classroom, students created a final record of their sites. They used their binoculars to watch for birds and learn about bird habitats. The tapping of hammers filled the air as small bird houses were constructed and then hung from tree limbs in copses of pines and maples.

As part of their final visit, the students also shared the changes over time they had observed in their sites. While students knew about changes that occurred due to seasons and weather, documenting the changes was an eye opening experience for many. Students spoke of variations in the stream, noting that it appeared much smaller in the hot month of August, compared to March, when it rose between the banks, swollen with rainwater.

Several students mentioned the change in some bushes. Several wild blackberry bushes grew in some sites and the students had noticed animal tracks crisscrossing the land around the bushes. Other observations included the sounds, the color, and the size of leaves. Altogether, the written and pictorial data caused the learners to appreciate the changes wrought in the environment over the year.

May: Problem Based Learning in Phase 3

As a culminating activity, the teacher planned an overnight camping trip with the class. Instead of going to the outdoor classroom, a totally unfamiliar site was chosen. Parent volunteers were photographed for an informational power point and briefed on their roles. One parent volunteer made foil dinners for the campers and volunteers. A foil wrapped dinner is composed of hamburger, cheese, and hash brown potatoes. Preparations were made at the exploratory camp for the student explorers. The stage was set.

The class was completing a science unit on Earth and Space when the teacher gathered the students in the library for some research. Suddenly, the large screen television came on and a man dressed in an Admiral's suit began speaking, telling the students that they were about to go on a mission. As the teacher interacted with the video, the students snapped to attention and entered into the roleplaying experience with enthusiasm.

According to the Admiral, they were no longer in the school library, but aboard an exploratory StarPoint space ship. The ship's crew was directed to send a survey team to one of the planets in the nearest sector. Their mission was to determine if the planet could be used as a mining operation, a colony, or if it should be interdicted. Information concerning the planets was sent for the spacers to review (See Table 1). With only enough fuel for one planet to be explored, the crew was asked to decide which planet to investigate.

At this point, the teacher/Captain passed out information concerning several planets in the sector. Looking at the information provided, there appeared to be several good choices, but several planets had some issues that required the applica-

Table 1. Planetary system data for the star, Kimisu

PLANET	Rotation	Revolution	Current Season	Water: Land Ratio	Atmosphere Primary gas
BRULY	15 hrs	40 days	Summer	3:1	Nitrogen and Oxygen based
TOPHER	5 hrs	60 Days	Winter	4:1	Nitrogen and Oxygen based
SCOVID	21 hrs	100 Days	Summer	3:1	Methane
MICDOM	200 hrs	600 Days	Summer	1:3	Carbon Dioxide
NIELBRU	6 hours	900 days	Spring	1:10	Chlorine and Ammonia based
TATIBAH	30 hours	1200 Days	Fall	3:1	Nitrogen and Oxygen based

tion of critical thinking skills. The teacher placed students in groups of four. The six gifted students were split into two groups. Another high achieving student rounded out the two teams which were primarily composed of gifted students. These teams were A and B. Two more teams, C and D, were composed of a mix of the rest of the students. These teams would remain together throughout the PBL culminating activity. The teacher monitored the discussions and the participation of all the students. Throughout the year, there had never been a time when a student was not involved in learning.

Each planet had some problems that made the choice for exploration difficult. One planet might have four seasons, but with a 60-day revolution, winter would last 15 days. However, the days were 5 hours long, which meant that the season would change every 15 hours. As teams looked at the data, the teacher asked questions at a variety of higher order thinking levels. The gifted teams understood that data analysis was essential and worked together to determine the best choice. After due deliberation, each team chose a planet to colonize and justified their reasoning. After listening to each team, the whole class voted on the planet they believed would be best for exploration: *Planet Tatibah.*

The Teacher/Captain sent a probe to the planet. The next day, the small teams looked at top-secret pictures beamed back by the probe. Thick fog enveloped the pictures and only one body part was visible in each picture: A long tail with jagged protuberances, an eye on a long stalk resembling an elephant's trunk, and a large talon or claw. In small groups, space teams examined only one of the probe pictures and extrapolated what the life form might look like, its habitat, and its habits. Students compared their ideas with each other and refined their ideas after seeing the other probe pictures. This was an old planet environmental study activity that the teacher updated for the unit.

In preparation for landing on the planet, the teacher showed a briefing PowerPoint and divided the students in to the four exploratory teams: A, B, C, and D. Each team had a parent volunteer "android", easily identified through photographs, attached attached as a safety officer. The android was to provide information concerning safety procedures, but was not knowledgeable about the planet and scientific tests that would need to be conducted. Teams were discouraged from asking their android for any help beyond a Band-Aids or sunscreen.

Teams prepared for the exploration of Tatibah by packing backpacks filled with the technology needed for each team. Each team was given one GPS unit and a Walkie-talkie. While this technology would work well, probes had already determined that due to an unexpected anomaly, cellphones and game devices were unable to work in Tatibah's atmosphere. Each team carried a field microscope, extra slides, binoculars, pH testing kits, butterfly/ water nets, rock hardness test kit, water collection bottles, and enough magnifying lenses for each person. Once the teams were checked out, they were ready to load their shuttle plane, cleverly camouflaged as a van.

After landing on the planet, the explorers were to study the land, water, rocks, plants, weather, insects, and other life forms on Tatibah. The Teams had logbooks to record information and baggies for collecting soil and artifact samples. The log-books contained specific GPS latitude and longitude coordinates of vital sites based on the probe data that the Captain had already identified as vital for exploration. Teams rotated through sites in different orders based on their logbook directions.

The outdoor area was prepared before the explorers arrive. The GPS trail list included sites that had been planted with unexpected artifacts. At one site, the space travelers would find food beamed from the ship for the exploratory teams in StarPoint Coolers. Bright purple aquarium rocks were scattered along a muddy trail. Students were expected to conduct pH tests on large puddles along the pathway into which white vinegar had been added. Tracks of animals never seen on the home planet, crisscrossed the muddy trails. Students would find strangely colored soil samples mixed with a bright, pink, chalk and glittery substance to collect for testing. Pond algae and macro-invertebrates could be investigated while the portable weather station would churn out data for the intrepid explorers.

The students quickly set up camp and departed with their androids to explore. Meanwhile, the Captain and additional androids prepared a temporary science lab for teams to use. Included were a laptop computer with preprogrammed research materials in it and rock, water and soil testing kits. Plaster of Paris was available for making casts of tracks. The rain gauge on the portable weather station was filled with very pale green water with just a little vinegar mixed in so that teams could test what fell from the skies. A camp-based safety officer monitored the communication system while teams set out to explore.

The logbooks stated the criteria for establishing a colony or a mining camp. The criterion for colonization was not based on healthy human parameters. Instead, the conditions for colonization were purposely designed so an environment unhealthy to earth-dwelling humans would be very comfortable for an alien exploratory group. By using different criteria, student teams would be forced to think about their rec-ommendations. Students were expected to analyze data they collected during the exploratory mission and problem-solve to determine if Tatibah could be colonized.

Although teams were encouraged to wade into the pond, the heavy layer of algae kept students from purposely jumping in. The water was teaming with tiny one-celled organisms, easily spotted with the magnifying lenses and field microscope. The discovery of the one-celled organisms on Tatibah surprised teams. After re-cording their finds, teams used the research station for identification purposes. At the research station, a notice popped up, warning that any water containing rotifers, an invertebrate, was inimical to the Explorers. While rotifers area found in nearly all fresh water sites, for the purpose of the PBL activity, rotifers were one of the criteria for deciding on colonization or mining. Luckily, none of the teams found a rotifer in their samples.

Throughout the day, teams crisscrossed the wilderness, collecting samples, testing rocks and soil, and viewing the outdoors in a different way. Because of their year-long association with the outdoors, students were confident as they travelled and were respectful of the safety procedures. Even though the environment was new, the students knew what to expect. They were more observant at the end of the year than they had been in August.

At the end of the day, the four exploratory teams met to evaluate their samples and findings. Each team put together everything they had collected to create a presentation about the planet and its life forms. As Environmental Scientists, they determined if Tatibah was a suitable habitat for colonists or mining operations, using the guidelines provided.

While each team was able to present their findings, the gifted students had been able to pull together the disparate samples strewn throughout their pathways into the most cohesive, inferred narrative of the planet. Team C pointed to the purple rocks they collected and stated, "Tatibah has purple rocks." Team D did not pick up any rocks.

In contrast, one of the gifted teams, Team A, declared the hard purple objects to be unhatched Dragon eggs, removed from nests in order to be eaten by the one-eyed creature the probes had photographed. The animal tracks were really dragon tracks and the pink, chalky soil was evidence that after chewing rocks to create flame, they regurgitated the pink substance. The glitter found in the pink substance was dragon hide scales sloughed off during regurgitation. Every sample the team subsequently shared supported the dragon's existence.

In the same way, the second gifted group, Team B, developed a completely different scenario of Tatibah, based on their research. This team described a world dependent on acid that had the strength of vinegar-laced water. The team gravely explained that instead of salt and fresh water, this planet had two types of water. The first was acidic, which the indigenous animals used for drinking. The second was pure water, which was unhealthy for the inhabitants to drink. The pink, chalky soil was indicative of soft rocks that had slowly been worn away by the acid rain. The glitter found mixed into the pink chalk was the remains of the rock that had not yet eroded. The green rain found at the weather station was green because both plants and animals used chlorophyll for photosynthesis to provide food and energy. Even the animals had developed this adaptation because the worldwide winter lasted for three years.

INTEGRATION OF TECHNOLOGY IN ENVIRONMENTAL EDUCATION

For both gifted and special education students, technology can be a positive tool in education (Nettleton & Lennex, 2010). Orienteering courses have long been part of outdoor learning (Shaunessy & Page, 2006). With a pre-plotted course, orienteers are taught to use compasses and with coordinates and maps, set out through meadows, woods, and moors, to plot courses and find their way through the wilderness. With the rise of handheld Global Positioning Satellite (GPS) units, GEO Casheing, became a worldwide activity. Gifted students often learn to use GPS units in a variety of ways to enrich their learning (Shaunessy & Page, 2006).

People who Geocashe receive a set of coordinates and, using their GPS units, hike to the coordinates. Once there, they search for a hidden box, filled with small, inexpensive treasures and exchange one they have brought for one in the box. Building on the Geocasheing concept, the teacher taught orienteering skills during the outdoor classroom visits and made it an integral part of the final outdoor experience for students. Interestingly, the GPS units and the walkie-talkie communication system were two of the students' favorite technologies. It was through the GPS units that the students found the sites the teacher had previously arranged for exploration.

Another technology that was especially useful was the handheld microscope. These portable devices could be used as a magnifying glass. They came equipped with small slides that students easily prepared to check soil and water samples. While the gifted students had learned to use them quickly and easily, by the end of the year, all the students were proficient with them.

Although soil and water testing did not require technological devices, the teacher had prepared research pages for the laptop that would set parameters for successful colonization tolerances of the soil and water. The rocks found along the pathways and by the water were also tested and the research pages offered advice as to what minerals were valuable to the StarPoint world.

Even though the use of fire is an old, old, skill, for the students, learning to cook on a campfire is an exciting event. Students built up the fire, cooked their meals over its embers, and used its flames for evening light. Just like the children of Earth, these planetary explorers enjoyed roasting marshmallows and slipping them between crackers and chocolate. Fire building and fire safety were best handled by students who had spent a great deal out of doors, either in scout programs or camping with their families. This was not always the gifted students and was another example how the students learned from each other during this unit.

In the end, each Exploratory team shared their recommendations for either colonization, mining, or ignoring the planet. While teams shared their decisions with a few supportive reasons, the gifted teams, A & B, demonstrated critical thinking skills beyond the rest of the class when making their decisions. They considered the temperature, climate, water, and soil before coming to a conclusion. This is not to say that Teams C & D did not consider these factors. Teams A & B however, delved deeper into the relationship of the environment and future inhabitants.

FINDINGS: THE EFFECT ON GIFTED STUDENTS

Teacher training on the use of small groups recommends carefully constructing learning groups of one high student, two average students, and one low student. In this way, teachers believe they are providing a peer leader for the group, someone who will help bring along the slower student. Using Vygotsky's (1978) ZPD as the underpinning of this decision, the gifted student often takes the place of the teacher in the collaborative group. Although collaborative in nature, in reality, the gifted student rarely learns much from the collaborative group unless the group is composed of students near their same learning level or higher. The gifted students assume a leadership role in many collaborative groups because they are able to understand directions and create a vision more quickly than the rest of the students.

At the beginning of the year, any teams composed entirely of gifted students in this classroom were often unable to come to agreement or work together. Used to making the decisions for their small groups, the gifted students initially had trouble listening to each other or knowing how to negotiate. In September, these groups wasted a good deal of time arguing. The gifted students had to be prompted to compromise and initiate a plan. Research stresses the need for gifted children to have the opportunity to interact with other gifted students. Patrick, Bangel, and Jeon (2005) found that collaborative learning can be beneficial to gifted students. By the end of the year, the students were able to work together, reach agreement, develop a plan, and implement it without engaging in lengthy arguments.

Gifted students do not only need to interact with each other, they need to learn to socialize with their peers. The unit emphasized cooperation and collaboration with everyone throughout the year. A totally unexpected outcome to the unit was the change it the dynamics of the classroom. Each month, as students traipsed through the fields and learned about flora and fauna, student strengths and interests had an impact on learning. One of the students, a struggling reader, happened to know a great deal about trees, birds, and wildflowers. He became the resident expert when the class hit the trails together. Another student, who hunted with his Dad, knew a great deal about animal tracks. All students became more accepting of each other, as evidenced in the ways in which they cooperated in the classroom. Throughout the year, the teacher continually reassigned student partners or small groups so that all students would work learn to work together. In addition, the teacher made sure that the gifted students were also provided with opportunities to work together. By the end of the year, the change of groups and the outdoor experience helped alter how the gifted students interacted with their classmates

The gifted students acknowledged other students as experts and often asked them to explain what they knew. One of the characteristics displayed by some gifted students was an increase in sensitivity. By taking the time to understand and appreciate the talents of others, the gifted students changed the ways in which they interacted. Their innate sensitivity and quick understanding encouraged them to change the ways they thought of and spoke to the other students.

This is not to say that these students were not usually kind to each other at the start of the year. What changed was the impatience the gifted students sometimes expressed with the students who were slower at understanding. The rest of the class stopped expecting the gifted students to provide answers and leadership. Once relieved of the expectation of shouldering the burden for the learning of their fellow students, the gifted students proved more willing to help and listen to others. At the end of the year, it was not unusual to see teams of students collaboratively working together, with all members respected for their contributions.

Gifted students learn faster and at deeper levels and the EE unit provided them with the chance to learn unfamiliar curriculum from experts. Students followed up on their interests. The relaxed environment allowed for private or small group conversations with guest speakers. These meaningful interactions helped students ask questions and dig deeper into subject matter to assuage their interest and curiosity without feeling as if they were boring other students.

There are many ways to use technology when providing instruction to gifted students. Often, the technology can be a cause for isolating gifted students. Differentiation does not need to be another area of separation between students. Gifted students need to be part of both the classroom and society. Using technology, teachers can use problem-solving curriculum that enhances education for all students, not just the gifted. Curriculum that may be learned at many levels provides positive benefits for all students. Teachers who have high expectations should use curriculum that supports their expectations.

While curriculum for gifted students may be more enriching, there is a loneliness that can emerge when students are not socializing with their peers. Interaction with intellectual peers is important, but the incidences of underachievement or hiding skills to fit in with peers, is high (Coleman, 1985). By the time they reach middle school, many gifted students refuse to be involved in gifted programs because of being stigmatized by their peers (Cross, Coleman, & Terhaar-Yonkers, 2014). It is important for teachers to be responsive to the needs of their gifted charges. By creating a learning environment that allows students to enter at different levels of expertise, the gifted students developed socially throughout the year.

FUTURE RESEARCH

The role of the teacher is critical in establishing the classroom culture. Further research should be conducted to determine the characteristics of effective classroom teachers for the gifted student. To understand the needs of the gifted student, does the teacher need to be gifted? Creative? What sort of training does an effective teacher need to provide a sustained enriched environment for gifted students?

Beyond the question of teacher training lies the issue of curriculum. Environmental education studies offer an open curriculum for students. It also offers a relaxed and engaging atmosphere. One question that should be examined is the relationship between content areas and learning environments. Are different disciplines more conducive to developing a comfortable learning environment for all students and especially the gifted student? How does the classroom environment effect the socialization of gifted students?

Another area of research for gifted education is the use of technologies during instruction. During the course of the year, the students utilized several low-level technologies. What level of technology is most effective for gifted students to use within the confines of a regular classroom? Had the teacher used higher level, more intricate technologies, would the gifted students have been set apart from the others? Do the ways in which technologies are used in the classroom have a separation factor built into them? The environmental science unit required low-level technologies simply because the location would not support tools that were more complex. However, investigation into the ways in which technologies cause separation in the classroom may be important to understanding student interaction on all levels.

Research into the day-to-day education of gifted students in classrooms is often focused on educational deficits due to a nondescript learning environment (Little, 2012). However, more research should be conducted on the best practices for engaging gifted students in the classroom. Gifted students can't explore the future if they don't learn in the present.

REFERENCES

Colangelo, N., Assouline, S. G., & Gross, M. U. M. (2004). A nation deceived: How schools hold back America's brightest students: Vol. 1. Belin: Blank International Center on Gifted Education and Talent Development.

Coleman, L. (1985). *Schooling the gifted*. Menlo Park: Addison-Wesley.

Cross, T. L., Coleman, L. J., & Terhaar-Yonkers, M. (2014). The Social Cognition of Gifted Adolescents in Schools: Managing the Stigma of Giftedness. *Journal for the Education of the Gifted*, *37*(1), 30–39. doi:10.1177/0162353214521492

Dykman, C. A., & Davis, C. K. (2008). Online education forum: Part two–Teaching online versus teaching conventionally. *Journal of Information Systems Education*, *19*, 156–163.

English, M., & Kitsantas, A. (2013). Supporting Student Self-Regulated Learning in Problem- and Project-Based Learning. *Interdisciplinary Journal Of Problem-Based Learning*, *7*(2), 127–150. doi:10.7771/1541-5015.1339

Gentry, M. L. (1999). *Promoting student achievement and exemplary classroom practices through cluster grouping: A research-based alternative to heterogeneous elementary education. Research Monograph for Educational Research and Instruction*. Washington, DC: OERI.

George, J. C. (1972). *Julie of the Wolves*. New York: Harper-Collins.

Glesne, C. (2011). *Becoming qualitative researchers: An introduction*. Boston, MA: Pearson.

Horne, J., & Shaughnessy, M. F. (2013). The response to intervention program and gifted students: How can it facilitate and expedite educational excellence for gifted students in the regular education setting? *International Journal of Academic Research*, *5*(3), 319–324. doi:10.7813/2075-4124.2013/5-3/B.48

Kumar, M., & Natarajan, U. (2007). A problem-based learning model: Showcasing an educational paradigm shift. *Curriculum Journal*, *18*(1), 89–102. doi:10.1080/09585170701292216

Kuutti, K. (1996). Activity theory as a potential framework for human-computer interaction research. In B. Nardi (Ed.), *Context and consciousness: Activity theory and human- computer interaction* (pp. 17–44). Cambridge, MA: MIT Press.

Latz, A. O., Speirs Neumeister, K. L., Adams, C. M., & Pierce, R. L. (2009). Peer coaching to improve classroom differentiation: Perspectives from Project CLUE. *Roeper Review*, *31*(1), 27–39. doi:10.1080/02783190802527356

Lennex, L., & Nettleton, K. F. (2010). The Golden Apple: A Quest toward Achievement. In J. Yamamoto, J. Kush, R. Lombard, & C. Hertzog (Eds.), Technology Implementation and Teacher Education: Reflective Models (pp. 124-145). Academic Press. doi:10.4018/978-1-61520-897-5.ch008

Little, C. A. (2012). Curriculum as motivation for gifted students. *Psychology in the Schools, 49*(7), 695–705. doi:10.1002/pits.21621

Mergendoller, J., Markham, T., Ravitz, J., & Larmer, J. (2006). Pervasive management of project based learning. In C. Evertson, & S. Weinstein (Eds.), *Handbook of classroom management: Research, practice, and contemporary issues* (pp. 583–615). Mahwah, NJ: Lawrence Erlbaum.

Naha, E., Schulman, T., Cox, P. F., Johnston, J., Moranis, R., Frewer, M., & Strassman, M. Buena Vista Home Entertainment (Firm). (2002). Honey, I shrunk the kids. Burbank, CA: Disney DVD.

Nardi, B. A. (1996). Activity theory and human-computer interaction. In B. A. Nardi (Ed.), *Context and Consciousness* (pp. 7–16). Cambridge, MA: The MIT Press.

Nettleton, K. F., & Lennex, L. (2010). Technodiversity: Lessons learned from a diversity exchange. In N. A. Alias, & S. Hashim (Eds.), *Technology Leadership in Teacher Education: Integrated Solutions and Experiences* (pp. 69–84). Hershey, PA: IGI Publications.

O'Dell, S. (1960). *Island of the Blue Dolphins*. New York: Houghton-Mifflin.

Patrick, H., Bangel, N. J., & Jeon, K. (2005). Reconsidering the issue of cooperative learning with gifted students. *Journal for the Education of the Gifted, 29*(1), 90–108.

Paulson, G. (1987). *Hatchet*. New York: Simon & Shuster.

Robinson, N. M. (2008). The social world of gifted children and youth. In S. Pfeiffer (Ed.), *Handbook of giftedness in children* (pp. 33–52). New York, NY: Springer. doi:10.1007/978-0-387-74401-8_3

Shaunessy, E., & Page, C. (2006). Promoting inquiry in the gifted classroom through GPS and GIS technologies. *Gifted Child Today*. doi:10.4219/gct-2006-11

Siegle, D. (2004). The merging of literacy and technology in the 21st century: A bonus for gifted education. *Gifted Child Today, 27*(2), 32–34.

Siegle, D., & Mitchell, M. S. (2011). Learning from and learning with technology. In J. VanTassel-Baska, & C. A. Little (Eds.), *Content-based curriculum for high-ability learners* (2nd ed., pp. 347–373). Waco, TX: Prufrock Press.

Silverman, L. K. (1989). Invisible gifts, invisible handicaps. *Roeper Review, 12*(1), 37–42. doi:10.1080/02783198909553228

Silverman, L. K. (2000). The gifted individual. In L.K. Silverman (Ed.), Counseling the Gifted and Talented (pp. 3-28). Denver, CO: Love Publishing Company.

Tomlinson, C. A., Kaplan, S. N., Renzulli, J. S., Purcell, J., Leppien, J., & Burns, D. (2002). *The parallel curriculum*. Thousand Oaks, CA: Corwin Press, Inc.

University of Plymouth. (2006). *Distance education: Why distance learning?* Retrieved from http://www.plymouth.ac.uk/distancelearning

Vialle, W., Ashton, T., Carlton, G., & Rankin, F. (2001). Acceleration: A coat of many colours. *Roeper Review, 24*(1), 14–19. doi:10.1080/02783190109554119

Vygotsky, L. S. (1978). *Mind in society: The development of higher psychological processes* (M. Cole, V. John-Steiner, S. Scribner, & E. Souberman, Eds.). Cambridge, MA: Harvard University Press.

White, W. F. (1990). Divergent thinking vs. convergent thinking—a GT anomaly. *Education, 111*, 208–213.

Zurita, G., & Nussbaum, M. (2007). A conceptual framework based on activity theory for mobile CSCL. *British Journal of Educational Technology, 38*(2), 211–235. doi:10.1111/j.1467-8535.2006.00580.x

ADDITIONAL READING

American Forest. (2007). *Pre K -8 environmental education activity guide*. Washington, D.C.: Project Learning Tree.

Ditchfield, C. (2002). *Soil*. New York: Children's Press.

Evslin, B. (1969). *The adventure of Ulysses*. New York: Scholastic, Inc.

George, J. C. (1988). *My side of the mountain*. New York: Puffin Books.

Headstom, R. (1977). *Adventures with a microscope*. New York, Dover.

Headstrom, R. (1976). *Adventures with a hand lens*. New York: Dover.

Johnson, S. K. (2012). *Gifted education programming standards*. Waco, TX: Prufrock Press.

Kelly, N. (2012). *Orienteering made simple and GPS technology*. Bloomington, IN: Authorhouse.

Magana, S., & Marzano, R. J. (2014). *Enhancing the art & science of teaching with technology*. Bloomington, IN: Marzano Research Laboratory.

McKenzie, W. (2005). *Multiple intelligences and instructional technology* (2nd ed.). Eugene, OR: ISTE.

Park, L. S. (2010). *A long walk to water*. New York: Clarion Books.

Robinson, A., Shore, B. M., & Enerson, D. L. (2007). *Best practices in gifted education*. Waco, TX: Prufrock Press.

Rogers, K. B. (2006). *A menu of options for grouping gifted students*. Waco, TX: Prufrock Press.

Sobel, D. (2005). *Place-based education: Connecting classrooms & communities. Great Barrington, MA: The Orion Society Stanley, T. (2011). Project-Based learning for gifted students: A handbook for the 21st-century classroom*. Waco, TX: Prufrock Press.

Speare, E. G. (2011). *The sign of the beaver*. New York: Sandpiper.

Stevenson, R. L. (2004). *Kidnapped. Abridgement by T. Mels*. New York: Atheneum Books.

Taylor, T. (1969). *The cay*. New York: Dell Laurel-Leaf.

Wyss, J. D. (2014). *The Swiss family Robinson*. New York: Harper Perennial Classics.

KEY TERMS AND DEFINITIONS

Environmental Education: The study of the environment.

Gifted Students: Students who have skills and talents above the norm for their age group. Gifted students may have a higher IQ, leadership or visual or performing art skills, specific knowledge of a specific discipline, or demonstrate creative and original thought. Gifted students may have asynchronous development, demonstrate over-excitability, or be more sensitive to issues of social justice. Gifted students often pair their ability with commitment.

Instructional Technology: Any technology that is used to facilitate learning. Instructional technology does not have to be electronic.

Problem Based Learning: An instructional strategy that provides the learner with a problem to be solved. After the problem is posed, the teacher allows students to initiate learning to facilitate solving the problems.

Chapter 7

Showcasing the Creative Talents in Science of the Academically Less-Inclined Students through a Values-Driven Toy Storytelling Project

Nazir Amir
Greenview Secondary School, Singapore

EXECUTIVE SUMMARY

It has been mentioned that gifted students may not necessarily just be the ones who have high IQ and perform consistently well in their examinations but also those who are able to showcase their creative talents through content and skills gained in their academic subjects. This chapter highlights how a class of academically less-inclined students in Singapore has been able to showcase their creative talents in science and other subjects through a values-driven toy storytelling project that serves a community need. Results from this study show that the project has provided an avenue for the students' creative talents in science and other subjects to be recognized by members of the community. The positive recognition through the students' work instilled a sense of pride and self-worthiness amongst them.

DOI: 10.4018/978-1-4666-6489-0.ch007

BACKGROUND INFORMATION OF NT STUDENTS IN SINGAPORE

In Singapore, students who do not perform well in the national Primary School Leaving Examination (PSLE) to qualify for the traditional academic streams are placed in the Normal Technical (NT) stream in secondary schools. The NT stream was established in 1994 and comprises about 15% of the students in each cohort in Singapore (Albright, Heng & Harris, 2008; Ismail & Tan, 2004; Ser, 2004a). The number of students that enter the secondary one NT stream ranges from 7795 in 2000 to 6491 in 2010 (Singapore Department of Statistics, 2011). In 2010, there are about 26,010 NT students across the neighbourhood schools in Singapore (Singapore Department of Statistics, 2011).

Many of the students in NT stream are predominantly kinesthetic learners with short attention spans and seem to exhibit a disinterest in studying when the subject content is not set in contexts that appeal to them and teaching approaches that are not matched to their learning styles (Chang, 1997; Ismail & Tan, 2004). Ser (2004b) stated that having already been relegated to the bottom stream, these students lose interest in their studies very quickly. Many students in this stream have also been identified as ones that have difficulties reading, understanding and answering questions across subjects because of their weak proficiency in the English language (Albright et al., 2008; Ismail & Tan, 2004; Kramer-Dahl & Kwek, 2011; Lee & Bathmaker, 2007). Several students in this stream have been diagnosed with dyslexia and exhibit ADHD-symptoms, and a few have been reported to have mild autism (Ho, Lim & Ho, 2005). Most of these students also come from low-income family backgrounds (Ng, 1993 as cited by Lee & Bathmaker, 2007) and are deemed to be the ones who are less academically inclined because of their poor performance in English, mathematics and science (Moo, 1997 as cited by Lee & Bathmaker, 2007). Ng (2004) reported that most teachers see these pupils as poor, coming from dysfunctional homes or having parents who do not care enough. Because of these, the pupils are then seen not to be coping well in school.

Reports have shown that teachers, parents and non-NT students (who are more academically-inclined) seem to have negative perception of students in the NT stream (Albright et al., 2008). Ser (2004a) mentioned from her interviews with parents and non-NT students that at their best, normal tech students are perceived to be unmotivated and lazy, and at their worst, an ill-disciplined and disruptive bunch generally beyond redemption.

Ser (2004a) also reported from her interviews with teachers that they felt there is only so much a teacher can do to help NT students, because not all of them are willing to be helped. Ser (2004b) mentioned that teachers and school councilors told her that many of these students also have a greater propensity for delinquency.

Ser (2004b) also stated that according to the Singapore Children's Society, one-third of kids who land up in (the juvenile) court are from this stream. Ser's (2004b) interview with teachers revealed that several teachers emphasise the need to look into the social issues of these students. A teacher mentioned that a lot of these NT students tend to come from the lower income families and face difficulties at home. He also mentioned that these students are very sensitive and while they can be loyalist and do a lot of things for their friends, they can also be easily influenced by the other students in a negative way. In this regard, it is very important to teach them how to manage their lives. The teacher also mentioned that these students often feel de-motivated once they realize that they are not able to achieve the same things when compared to the more academically-inclined students. Ser's (2004b) interview with several NT students revealed that while they acknowledge that they are slow learners, they wish for teachers and society to respect them and look up at them in a positive manner. When this happens, they too will act in a positive way. Ser (2004b) mentioned that perhaps what NT students need is a change in the way these students are guided in school in meeting up to such expectations.

SETTING THE STAGE

Giftedness and Creativity amongst Academically Less-Inclined Students

Fostering creativity amongst our students has become ever-increasingly important to prepare them for the complex work environments of the 21st century. Raviv (2002) mentioned that many schools seem to focus on getting students to acquire knowledge but neglect in getting students to be trained in creative thinking. This will lead to a considerable number of students losing the basic skills for defining, understanding and solving problems. These traits would be valuable in getting students to contribute to their personal, social, and technological achievements which could contribute to the economy (Haigh, 2007; Lee, 2001; Metz, 2010). Furthermore, Metz (2010) and Washton (1971) highlighted how students may perform very well in theoretical examinations but 'suffer' when they are out in the working world as they are insufficiently equipped with problem-solving skills to prepare them for the increasingly complex work environments of the 21st century. Job security for students today are not only dependent on just a high level of academic content and skill-sets that are instilled in them from schools and institutions of higher learning but also through their creative capabilities to contribute to a productive and innovative workforce (Metz, 2010).

Because routine work can be outsourced or automated, successful workers will be those who can imagine and create —Metz (2010) p 6

It has been mentioned that gifted students may not necessarily just be the ones who have high IQ and perform consistently well in their examinations but also those who are able to showcase their creative talents through content and skills gained in their academic subjects (Gilbert, 2005; Gilbert & Newberry, 2007; SingTeach, 2010). Stouffer, Russel & Olivia (2004) highlighted that the 'Torrance Tests of Creative Thinking' used in 1966 and 1974 (Torrance, 1966; Torrance, 1974), *'debunked the common assumption that IQ alone determined creativity'*. Torrance (1987) mentioned that he was spurred to come up with the creativity tests as he saw that students who were deemed as those who were 'unable to think' were actually showing traits of creativity.

I have seen children who had seemed previously to be "non-thinkers" learn to think creatively, and I have seen them continuing for years thereafter to think creatively. I have seen, heard, and otherwise experienced their creativity. Their parents have told me that they saw it happening. Many of the children, now adults, say that it happened. I also know that these things would not have happened by chance because I have seen them "not happening" to multitude of their peers —Torrance (1987) p 189

Palaniappan (2007) made use of the 'Torrance Tests of Creative Thinking' and did a study with 497 Form Four Malaysian students to explore the academic achievement of students based on creativity and intelligence. The results of his study showed no significant difference in academic achievement between students who were deemed intelligent (having high IQ and yet low in creativity) and students who were deemed less intelligent (having low IQ but high in creativity). He highlighted a need to push for fostering creativity among students who were less-academically inclined as this could enhance their academic achievement and put them on par with students who were more academically inclined. Earlier studies carried out by Guilford (1959) have also shown that that there is little correlation between academic performance and creativity.

These discussion points highlight the importance on the need to come up with classroom instructional approaches to foster the creativity of not just academically-abled students, but also NT students through content and skills gained in their academic subjects. As a classroom teacher of NT students over the last 11 years, I have observed that there are programmes in place to nurture NT students to showcase their creative talents in music and the arts (for example, showcasing their creativity in art through displaying paintings and sculptures done in art lessons, and showcasing their creativity in music and aesthetics through hip-hop dance and band performances in front of the school). Little however has been discussed on feasible classroom in-structional approaches in getting NT students gain science content while at the same time showcasing their creative abilities through knowledge from science. Many of the experiments in science activity books published for NT students, while allowing them to be engaged in learning science through a hands-on approach, seem to lack instructional elements that would allow teachers to guide them to showcase their creative talents in science (Abrahams, 2009; Abrahams & Millar, 2008; Amir & Subramaniam, 2012). As such, I find that while is important to push for instructional approaches to get NT students to be inquisitive and find out how science plays a role in the real world, what is equally important is to equip these NT students with the knowledge and skills to solve problems through knowledge from science, and guide them to showcase their creative talents in science.

Fostering Creativity in Science amongst NT Students During Science Lessons

Wardle (2009) highlights that 'creativity' can be perceived with a variety of mean-ings. According to Puccio (2011), Rhodes (1961) attempted to find one unifying definition of creativity. Rhodes's (1961) review of more than 50 studies led to him finding more than 40 different definitions of creativity. Rhodes (1961) found that traits of creativity are dependent and, can be grouped, around four themes. He called this the four P's of creativity. Based on Rhodes (1961) 4P's of creativity, Fox (2011) elaborated on how each of these themes such as the characteristics of a 'person', the components of a 'process', aspects of a 'product' and qualities of an environment (or 'press') all play a part in fostering creativity.

A common thread across the definitions of creativity based on the works of Barlex (2007), Christensen, (1988), Guilford (1959), Robinson (2006), Spendlove (2005) and Torrance (1966; 1974) is that creativity has to do with producing something original or novel and of value (product). The works of Amabile (1996), Besemer (2010), Craft (2001), Cropley & Cropley (2010), Cziksentmihalyi (1998), Dacey & Lennon (2000), Feldman, Csikszentmihalyi, & Gardner, (1994), Ryhammer & Brolin (1999), and Vernon (1989) suggest that the term 'fostering creativity' has equivalent meaning to 'encouraging' or 'promoting' creativity. A common ap-proach to foster creativity through problem solving activities is to equip students with divergent thinking skills during problem solving activities (process) (Gardner, 1997; Garret, 1987; McCormack, 1971; Moravcsik, 1981; Pereira, 1999; Plucker & Runco, 1999; Pizzini, Shepardson & Abell, 1989; Washton, 1971; West, 1981; and Williams, 1972). Based on the work of these educators, if we merge the 'process' and 'product' themes of creativity together, we can say that creativity in science can be looked upon as the *process* of solving problems through the use of science knowledge, in coming up with solutions that are original or novel and of value (product). In this regard, fostering creativity in science can be perceived as the process of guiding students to come up with original and valuable ideas that draws knowledge from science in the course of solving problems. Encouraging science teachers to foster creativity in science amongst NT students can provide a way for these students to exhibit the core components of creativity (*fluency*, *flexibility*, *originality* and *elaboration*) through scientific reasoning. This could be a way for them to showcase of their creative talents in science.

Instructional Approaches for NT Students to Showcase Their Creative Talents in Science

The work of Norman (1993), Sidawi (2009), and West (1997) suggest that a way to engage academically less-inclined students in science is through design-based science projects. Attempts to show how educators have presented science content and foster creativity in science through design-based science projects have been described in the literature (Childress, 1996; Fortus, Krajcikb, Dershimerb, Marx, & Mamlok-Naamand, 2004; 2005; Lewis, Barlex & Colin, 2007; Zubrowski, 2002). Furthermore, teachers who adopt design-based projects can stir students' interest in learning if the projects appeal to students (Hoang, 2007) such as toy projects that work on scientific principles (Featonby, 2005; Güémez, Fiolhais, & Fiolhais, 2009; Sarquis, Sarquis, & Williams, 1995). Such an approach taps on the kinaesthetic learning styles of the students and appeal factors that are in the toys to generate the NT students' interest in learning science. Being predominantly visual-spatial rather than visual-linguistic learners (Ramadas, 2009), a suitable way teachers can guide NT students to record their learning of science through design-based projects would be through the use of use of sketches and annotations in design sheets instead of getting them to write in full sentences (Austin & Shore, 1995; Barak & Doppelt, 2000; Mackin, 1996; Slater, 1996; Trumbo, 2006; Wiebe, Clark & Hasse, 2001).

While design-based toy projects may seem to offer a favourable approach in presenting science content to the academically less-inclined students, I find that little has been reported on how science-based toy projects can be extended to other subjects that these students study in school in view of making learning content within these other subjects relevant for them, and in offering support for these students to showcase their creative talents through these subjects. The work of Caine & Caine (1991), Fogarty (1991), Jarvis (2009) and Lee (2007) suggest that design-based science projects can be linked to other subjects so that NT students can find a sense of purpose in learning content in these other subjects. Showcasing the creative work of NT students through their projects to educational stakeholders and the community could lead to these students feeling proud of their efforts and develop heightened self-esteems (Anandan & Kan, 2008; Thuraisingam, 2007).

The points brought about in the previous sections highlight the possibility of crafting a multi-disciplinary science-based toy project that would allow NT students to pick up academic content across a number of subjects that they study in school, after which showcasing the work of these students to members of the community. Findings from a study by Lee, Goh, Chia, & Wan. (2006) revealed that from a pragmatic viewpoint of teachers, if there is a need to craft out approaches to foster creativity during curricula hours in school, then these approaches cannot be at the expense of presenting academic content that is in the subject syllabuses. As such, I was in search of feasible classroom teaching approaches that would allow NT students to gain science content and showcase their creative talents through knowledge from science, at the same time through a design-based science toy project.

CASE DESCRIPTION

Inspiration to Start the Toy Story: Telling Project

I was motivated to carry out a toy story-telling project for my NT students because I noticed that several teachers in special schools (teaching children who are intellectually disabled) struggle at engaging their young students to pay attention to them when it comes to teaching fairy tale stories through verbal modes, often accompanied by picture cards. I was unable to find toys that worked on science principles that could be suitable as aids for these teachers in telling stories to these intellectually disabled children or even to young children in nursery schools (three to four years of age). Currently, many of the toy story-telling teaching aids available are in the form of picture cards, puppets, cartoons available in CD/DVDs, and the internet. While these teaching aids may be colourful and attractive, they very much only tap on the visual and auditory senses of three to four year old children and intellectually disabled children in learning. These teaching aids lack the mechanics that a science toy may offer and do not seem to carry much elements of surprise in them. I feel that these are crucial factors that trigger the kinaesthetic senses of young children and get them curious and inquisitive to think about the mechanical operations of a toy.

Many of the science concepts that lower secondary NT students (13 – 14 years) study in school lie in physics. With this in mind, I came up with the idea of getting my class of 37 secondary two NT students (14 girls and 23 boys, averaging 14 years of age) to design and fabricate toys that work on physics principles, which would be suitable to be used as story-telling aids for the young children (three to six years of age) who may be less fortunate than them. This ties in nicely with the topics of 'forces' and 'simple machines' that has to be covered in the secondary two NT science syllabus (MOE, 2007). This toy story-telling project also created an opportunity for me to link with other subject teachers so that these students would be able to pick up knowledge and skills from other subjects to pursue the design requirements given to them. Apart from reaching out on the cognitive learning domains of my NT students, having such a project would also reach out on their affective domains, by promoting in them a consciousness of community needs. Feedback on the views of the young children and their teachers on the efforts of my NT students on being able to showcase their creative talents in science for a good cause could contribute to a sense of self-worth and heightened self-esteem amongst them.

This led me to the formation of three research questions in the interest of this action-research study:

1.   Are lower secondary NT students able to showcase their creativity in science through a multi-disciplinary toy story-telling project?
2.   What are some of the views of these students on acquiring academic content and showcasing their creative talents in science through this project?
3.   What are some of the views of these students on the use of this project as an avenue for them to contribute to the community and instill a sense of self-worthiness amongst them?

Capturing the Performance Task of NT Students through the Toy Story-Telling Project

In crafting a way to gather data to address the first research question, the works of Balchin (2005), Barak & Doppelt (2000), Childress (1996), Doppelt (2005), Fortus et al. (2004; 2005), Johnsey (1999), Lim, Lim & Atencio (2013), McCormick (1997), Sage & Steeg (1993), Sharkawy, Barlex, Welch, McDuff, & Craig (2009), Sidawi (2009), Welch & Barlex (2004), and Zubrowski (2002) suggest that the NT students' creative talents in science through their design-based toy story-telling project can be captured through scans of their sketches taken off from their design sheets, and photographs of their physical artefacts. Ideas gathered from Besemer (1998), Cross (2007), Davidson, Evens, & McCormick (1998), Hansen (2009), and Zubrowski (2002) suggest that a way to analyse creativity from the students' projects would be to sieve out the clever use of science in the students' projects through their design sheets, and look into the functionality of their artefacts through the contexts which they are placed in. As such, samples of the NT students' work will be presented in the form of scans of the students' design sheets, and photographs of their artefacts, which will be accompanied with descriptive commentaries on how science contributes to the functionality of their toy designs.

Capturing the Views of NT Students at the End of the Toy Story-Telling Project

In crafting a way to gather data to address the second research question, articles on subject interaction through the works of Amir & Subramaniam (2012), Brodie & Thompson (2009), Caine & Caine (1991), Davidson et al. (1998), Fogarty (1991), Höhn & Harsch (2009), Jarvis (2009), Klein & Shragai (2001), Lee (2007), and Nickerson (2009) suggest that it could be useful to come up with an instrument to capture the views of NT students on how they were able to acquire academic content and showcase their creative talents in science through the multi-disciplinary toy story-telling project.

In crafting a way to gather data to address the third research question, the works of Amir & Subramaniam (2012), Balchin (2005), and Lim et al. (2013) suggest that my students can be encouraged to reflect their views on the use of the toy story-telling project as an avenue for them to contribute to the community after going through the entire activity. The works of Stake (1995) and Yin (1989) suggest that the sentences written down by students can be broken down to sieve out key phrases to interpret their views. It seems plausible then that I can analyse the written views of my students to find out if this project has provided an avenue to instil a sense of self-worthiness amongst them.

The works of Baxter & Jack (2008), Brymen (2001), Denzin (1970), Guion, Diehl, & McDonald (2011), Jick (1983), Knafl & Breitmayer (1989) and Stainback & Stainback (1988) suggest that I could triangulate the results from the three research questions in finding out if the toy story-telling project adopted in this action research study would be a useful instructional approach in getting NT students to showcase their creative talents in science, and in getting them to acquire academic content through the various subjects, and also in instilling a sense of self-worthiness amongst them.

PROCEDURES

Staring Out the Project

Prior to the start of the project, arrangements were made with a special school such that I would be able to carry out a Community Involvement Program (CIP) with them through the toy story-telling project. Staff members from the special school welcomed the idea. I then invited the English and Computer Applications (CPA) teachers of my NT students to discuss the possibility of linking up the toy story-telling project to their subjects. This was done over a simple hour-long coffee session in the school canteen. In making the subject interaction approach feasible for all three of us, it was agreed that I (the science teacher) would present the design challenge to the students and guide them to make their toys through the use of scientific principles. This would be carried out over six weeks after which both the other teachers would guide the students to gather language, narration and some aspects of dramatization skills (in English lessons) and apply graphic and animation skills in MS-PowerPoint (in CPA lessons) into their project over two weeks. It was also decided that each story should be presented to the young children in a time span of five to ten minutes.

Guiding Students in Science Lessons (6 Weeks)

I first brought my NT students to the special school to let them have a feel of where they would be telling their stories. Here, they had a chance to talk to several teachers teaching these young children and see the children themselves to have an idea of how these children might best learn from their stories.

In the first science lesson back in school, my students were told to group themselves up into three to four students per group. Each group was then required to list out no less than five fairy tale stories. They were then made to narrow down to three stories they think the younger children will enjoy. Having done that, the students had to discuss about how physics principles, particularly from the topic of 'forces' and 'simple machines' can be incorporated into the functionality of some toy designs that would be suitable as teaching aids in the presentation of these stories. As not many toy demonstration models were available in the market, the students had to rely entirely on their experience of playing with toys and synergizing with their group-mates to look out for ideas on how physics can play a part in the functionality of their toy designs. As an aid to trigger their thinking, I guided them to look into the details of several simple everyday items that work on mechanical principles such as a cloth peg, pulley on a flag pole and a see-saw amongst a few others. The students were discouraged from buying anything that costs more than two dollars for each project.

The students used their science books as reference books and were observed to flip through all pages of the book (and not only the topics that they have been taught to them) as they brainstormed for ideas. I moved around from group to group facilitating the use of physics in their designs and provided ideas on how some of their designs can be improved. I encouraged them to come up with designs that would get the young children curious to find out how physics contributes to a toy's functionality. I also had to ensure that each group chooses to present a different story so that there will not be an overlap in the stories that will be told to the younger children. Along the way in facilitating my students, I constantly reminded them on the design context at hand – that is, why there is a need to make these toys, how and where they will be used and who are these toys are made for. These reminders kept the students in-check. They were able to realize that it is important that the stories be kept simple and suitable to be used as an aid in telling fairy tale stories to special children. As such, there should not be any complicated mechanisms or steps to operate their toys.

The students took about two weeks during curriculum time (about six hours) to finalize their ideas. Each group was made to present their finalized ideas to the other groups and explain how they plan to make their toys through the use of simple and recycled materials, and how their toys would function through the use of physics principles. As each group presented their design plans to their classmates, I noticed how other groups contributed more ideas to further improve each others' toy designs. I also observed how the different groups were able to tap on ideas on the use of physics principles from one toy design to another. A total of four weeks science curriculum time (about ten hours) was spent fabricating their toys which included experimentation with different materials, trying out principles of forces and making simple machines through ideas gathered from the internet. They also spent some part of this time colouring their toys. At the end of the four weeks, each group was made to submit their work which includes their prototype, their design sheets which describes how physics has been incorporated in the context of their fairy tale toy designs, and also the designs of three other groups. Doing this led to each group gaining the physics concepts that are also in their friends' designs.

Creative Use of Physics in Students' Fairy Tale Toys

As a whole, the efforts made by these students to incorporate physics into their toy designs are commendable. Figures 1-14 present samples of how the NT students were able to showcase their creative talents in science through their toy designs.

Design 1: Rapunzel

In the design to support the story of Rapunzel, a group of students made use of a cardboard roll (from a kitchen towel) to represent the tower of the castle. Extract from their design page in Figure 1 highlights the reason the group made use of the cardboard roll - *'This is the Rapunzel tower. We used kitchen towel because it is hard, stable and attractive'*, which is indicative of the students being able to reason out material properties of stiffness for their choice of design.

In terms of mechanical operations of the toy, the group made a pulley system to bring the prince up to Rapunzel. The group first made use of a small wheel (with a thin bamboo stick protruding in it's middle) that rest on an opening at the top of the cardboard roll. For Rapunzel's hair, the group wove two white strings and attached

Figure 1. Design page showcasing the scientific principles in the Rapunzel story

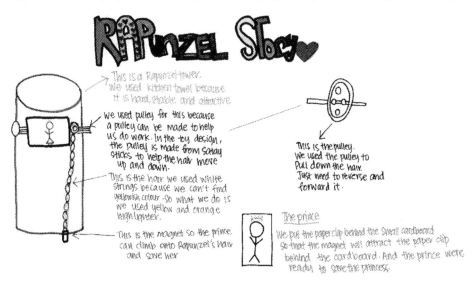

them to the small wheel through the use of adhesive tape. They then attached the small wheel to a bigger wheel(placed at the bottom of the tower), through the use of rubber band, which is affixed to an 'Allan' key that acts as a crank, as shown in Figure 2. In this configuration, users of the toy will only need to turn the crank a few rounds in order to get Rapunzel's hair to move up and down. This is possible because of the mechanical advantage of the pulley since different diameters of wheels are used. The group mentions in their design page that *'We use the pulley to pull down the hair. Just need to reverse and forward it'*. The word *just* suggests the simplicity of the mechanical operation of this toy.

Figure 2. Pulley system offers mechanical advantage

In the experimental stages of coming up with this toy, the group attached a small piece of magnet to the free-end of Rapunzel's hair through the use of a knot. The group decided to make the prince from a piece of cardboard since it is a light material. They decided to attach a paper clip to the back of the cardboard. Paperclip, being a magnetic material easily attaches itself to the magnet on Rapunzel's hair. The group mentions in their design page that *'We put the paperclip behind the small cardboard so that the magnet will attract the paper clip behind the cardboard and the prince will be ready to save the princess'*. When the crank is turned, users of the toy will be able to see the prince 'climbing up' to Rapunzel to 'rescue her'. Figure 3 shows how the group experimented with the mechanical operations of the toy through the combination of pulley, magnet and paper clip.

After successfully getting the mechanical operations of the toy to function well, the group then coloured the toy. The group convinced me that through their research on the internet, they found Rapunzel to be blonde. At that point in time, I only had limited paint colour tubes available in the physics laboratory. The group showed how resourceful they were by overcoming the problem through the use of coloured highlighters (which were easily available). The group mentions in their design page that *'we can't find yellowish colour, so what we do is we used yellow and orange highlighter'*. Figure 4 shows the coloured Rapunzel toy.

Figure 3. Experimenting with the mechanical operations of the toy

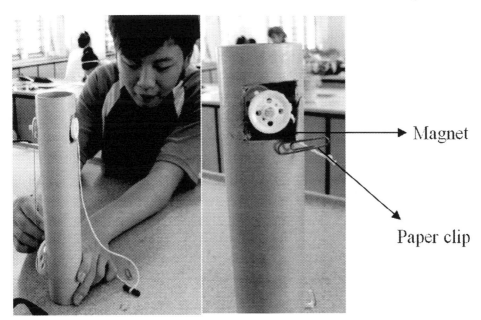

Magnet

Paper clip

Figure 4. Coloured Rapunzel toy (front view on the left and back view on the right)

Design 2: Hare and Tortoise

In the design to support the story of the Hare and Tortoise, a group of students made use of a rectangular piece of Styrofoam to represent the race track. The track is divided into two sections – one for the movement of the Hare and the other for the Tortoise. Both the Hare and Tortoise have strings attached to them in a way that allows the user to pull the two from the start to the finish line. The Hare is made from white corrugated board and cotton wool, while the Tortoise was already available as a toy from one of the students in the group.

In terms of scientific operations of the toy, the group decided that a way to get the Hare to 'stop and sleep' just before the finish line is through the principle of magnetic attraction. They decided to hide a metal piece in the body of the Hare, somewhere near it's base. On the race track, the students cut a rectangular slot in the Styrofoam board just wide enough to insert a bar magnet as shown in Figure 5.

After inserting the bar magnet into the slot, the group then used a piece of rectangular cardboard to cover the top of the Styrofoam. They painted the cardboard

Figure 5. Slot to insert a bar magnet

with green and black colour to make it look like a track in the woods. A tree was placed at a location where the magnet was hidden in the Styrofoam board, as shown in Figure 6.

Figure 6. Hidden magnet is below the tree

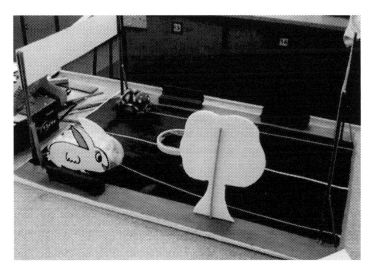

The group's idea is to invite two children from the audience to be volunteers in helping them tell this story to their classmates (in the special school). The children will not know about the hidden magnet. One child will focus on pulling the string attached to the Hare and the other child will pull the string that is attached to the Tortoise. At the start of the race, the child pulling the Hare will be told to exert a larger force as compared to the child pulling the Tortoise. The Hare, being subjected to the larger pulling force will move faster along the race track and be ahead of the Tortoise. However, when the Hare reaches the location of the tree, the hidden magnet in the Styrofoam board will attract the piece of metal in the body of the Hare causing it to stop. This depicts the Hare 'having it's nap'. The child who is applying a lesser amount of force on the Tortoise will inevitably cause it to move slower but there is nothing to stop the Tortoise till it reaches the finishing line. As the Tortoise passes through the finishing line, the group of NT students will encourage the child (pulling the Hare) to pull the string with a force large enough to overcome the magnetic attraction. By the time this is done, the Tortoise would have finished the race. The group hopes that such an interactive toy will entertain the young children as they watch their friends battle it out on the racetrack. They convinced me that such a design would also inject curiosity in the young children to find out the scientific operations behind getting the Hare stuck under the tree.

Design 3: The 3 Little Pigs

In the design to support the story of 'The 3 Little Pigs', a group of students made use of their knowledge from strength of materials to come up with the different houses for each little pig. Each little pig was made from plasticine (a soft modeling material) fairly easily as shown in Figure 7.

Figure 7. Using plasticine to make the three pigs

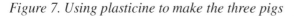

The challenge this group faced was in coming up with the different houses that would withstand a fair amount of wind energy that is produced by a hand-held motorized fan (depicting the huffs and puffs from the big bad wolf). In the experimental stages of coming up with this toy, the group first made several structures out of different simple materials. These include newspapers, printing papers, straws, ice cream sticks, bamboo sticks, dried leaves, Styrofoam boards and cardboards. They then made use of a hand-held motorized fan to blow on these structures to find out the time taken for each of these structures to collapse as shown in Figure 8. Care was taken to ensure that the distance from the motorized fan to each structure was the same throughout this part of the experiment.

The results from the group's experiment showed that the structure formed by interlocking printing papers will cause it to collapse within just a few seconds after it is subjected to wind energy coming from the hand-held motorized fan. It takes a longer time for the motorized fan to bring down a structure made from straws that are interlocked together. The motorized fan will not be able to bring down a structure made from ice cream sticks. These results led them to build the houses for the three little pigs as shown in Figure 9.

According to their story, the youngest pig would be placed under the structure made from printing papers. When this 'house' collapses, the pig will be shifted (by hand action) to the structure made from straws where the second pig will already be in. When this second house collapses, both the pigs will be shifted (again by hand action) to the house made from ice cream sticks, where all three pigs will unite. The rest of the story will be told through the use of PowerPoint slides.

Figure 8. Testing the structural strength of different materials with a motorized fan

Figure 9. Knowledge of material strength used in making the houses for the 3 little pigs

Design 4: Goldilocks and the 3 Bears

In the design to support the story of 'Goldilocks and The 3 Bears', another group of students also made use of their knowledge from properties of materials to come up with the different beds for each bear.

According to the story, papa bear sleeps on a very hard mattress on his bed, while mama bear sleeps on a softer mattress, and baby bear sleeps on an even softer mattress. In meeting up to this part of the story through their toy design, the group experimented with different materials that would be suitable to be used as mattresses for the three different beds. The group decided that the mattress for papa bear would be made from ice cream sticks as it is a hard material. Several ice cream sticks are joined together through the use of glue and attached to cardboard rolls that depict the legs of the bed. The headboard is made from a piece of cardboard. The bed designed for papa bear is shown in Figure 10.

Figure 10. Ice cream sticks depicting the hard mattress in papa bear's bed

The challenge this group faced was in coming up with two materials that had to be distinctively different in terms of hardness and yet suitable to be used as mattresses for mama bear and baby bear. The group eventually came up with the idea of using a sponge to be used as the mattress for baby bear's bed. They took several steps to try and convince me that baby bear would be comfortable on the mattress that was to be made from sponge. In doing so, the group first made the bed for baby bear by attaching a piece of sponge to the legs and headboard. They then made a figurine out of plasticine, and placed it on this bed. They convinced me that the sponge which was flat before the figurine is placed on it, would bend slightly and follow the contour of the body of the figurine as shown in Figure 11. This proves that baby bear will not be sleeping on a very hard or very soft mattress but rather a comfortable one.

A member of this group had a collection of old erasers (the ones that has the country flags on each of them). This sparked an idea in them to make use of erasers for mama bear's bed. The group told to me that erasers are made from rubber, and rubber is not too hard but yet not as soft as sponge, which would make it suitable for the mattress for mama bear's bed. I agreed to their justification and told them to go ahead in making the bed for mama bear. Each of the three bears was made from cardboard, which was coloured and attached to ice cream sticks to be handheld by the students when they tell this story. Figure 12 shows the bears resting on their respective beds.

The group took further steps to make the house for the three bears as shown in Figure 13. Similar to the three bears, Goldilocks was also made from cardboard, which was coloured and attached to an ice cream stick. The group's idea is to first show the audience Goldilocks coming into the house (through hand action), and then sitting down on each of the three chairs in the living room, after which she will taste the soup in three bowls, before going up the stairs to the bedrooms.

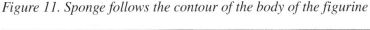

Figure 11. Sponge follows the contour of the body of the figurine

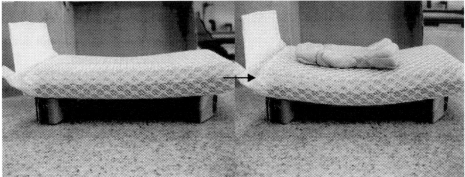

Figure 12. The three bears on their beds made from different materials

Figure 13. House of the three bears

Figure 14 shows the chairs made for the three bears. The group has made bigger chairs for papa bear and mama bear than for baby bear. Apart from the size of the chairs, another main difference is in the way the seats of the chairs (made from Styrofoam boards) are joined to the legs and the backrest (made from ice cream sticks).

For baby bear's chair, the group has made use of glue to firmly join the Styrofoam board to the legs and the backrest. However, for papa bear and mama bears' chairs, the group has glued the seat only to the backrest of each chair. The front legs of each of these two chairs are joined to the seat by just a little adhesive tape.

Figure 14. Chairs made for the three bears

This makes the chair collapsible when there is sufficient force applied on it. The group's idea is to show the audience that the chair designs for papa bear and mama bear will collapse when Goldilocks sits on them. This would be done by the hand action of pressing Goldilocks (attached to the ice cream stick) down on both these chairs. However when Goldilocks sits on the baby chair, it will not collapse. This corresponds to the part of the story that states the baby bear's chair being 'just the right' chair for Goldilocks to sit on.

Applying Knowledge and Skills from CPA and English Lessons into Their Projects (2 Weeks)

Two weeks before their presentation to children in the special school, the students prepared animation slides in their CPA lessons and practiced their language and narration skills in English lessons.

In CPA lessons, this part of the project provided them a chance to explore the graphic and animation tools available in MS-PowerPoint. When I visited them in these lessons, I noticed how the use of Information-Communication Technology (ICT) has helped them in expressing their creative ideas. Having in mind a known storyline helped them focus to come up with their slides. Having made their toys also helped them narrow down certain aspects of the stories that they would want the audience to focus more (or less) on. For example, the group that was came up with the 'Rapunzel' toy did not want much animation to be included in the slides showing the prince climbing up the castle tower as they wanted the audience to pay attention to mechanical operations of their toy. They however used more animation in the other slides (for example, the part where Rapunzel was locked up in the tower by the witch).

As a whole, a minimum of four hours was spent in coming up with the colourful slides and animations to capture the attention of the young children. As I walked around the computer terminals asking the students why they added so much colour into their slides, I was pleased to hear a common answer – *"to make the young children happy"* or *"so that they (the young children) will enjoy our story"*. A number of students even brought their self-made toys to the computer labs so that they can create a similar graphical model on their slides. This would help the young children relate the story they see on the screen to the physical toys. One example is a toy boat that is used to support a Singapore folk story entitled 'Sang Nila Utama'. This boat works on a mechanical principle in that it rocks vigorously during a thunderstorm and remains calm during sunny weather. The boat that almost depicts the physical toy is shown in Figure 15.

In one of the English lessons, the English teacher provided the students with an opportunity to be exposed to learn skills in dramatization. The teacher believes that this could help the students create an impact in the audience when they tell their stories. Groups of students were made to draft out aspects worthy of being dramatized in front of the young children. This included acting out as the hungry and eventually angry big bad wolf, or little Goldilocks jumping from one bed to another. Figure 16 shows students gaining skills in the dramatization lesson.

In the subsequent English lessons, groups had to present their stories in front of their classmates and teachers, who acted out as the mock-up audiences shown in Figure 17. Doing this allowed the groups to rehearse their language and narration skills, and familiarize themselves with the way the stories had to be told in front of

Figure 15. The toy boat (left) and its corresponding graphical form in MS-PowerPoint (right)

Figure 16. Dramatization lessons

Figure 17. Rehearsing in front of an audience

an audience. Prior to presenting their stories, members of each group had to distribute their roles - namely one or two students to operate the toy, one student to narrate the story and another student at the computer to click the buttons for slide transition. I observed how the students improved their presentation skills and gained confidence through these lessons.

Presenting the Stories to Younger Children

On the actual day of presentation, my students were enthusiastic to present their stories to the young children in the special school. It did not take long for us to set up a laptop to a portable projector in the school's library. Eight stories were presented in total to two classes of about 20 children, ranging from three to six years of age.

Figure 18 shows two groups of students presenting their stories. Several of the stories were made interactive for the young children. For example, at the end of presenting the story of Red Riding Hood, the group of girls posed several questions to the young children that required them to come up to the screen to select an answer. The image on the right of Figure 18 shows a young boy coming up to answer the question posed by the group – "Which picture represents the wolf in grandma's clothing?" The boy who answered the question correctly was rewarded with sweets. This is indicative that in the planning stages of coming up with the slides for their presentation, this group of students did not merely just think of presenting their stories through the slides and toys but has also carefully thought through of making their presentation enjoyable and interactive for the young children.

The efforts of my students paid off when the young children and their teachers gave loud applauses to each group at the end of each story presentation. I observed how my students beamed with pride as the teachers shook their hands and thanked them for engaging and entertaining all of them. Many teachers also congratulated my students on being able to come up with such creative work through knowledge that is acquired in their academic subjects.

In closing the CIP session, the teachers surprised my students by getting the children to present hand-made bookmarks as tokens of their appreciation to my students. Several teachers also invited my students back to the school to visit the children with more of their self-made toys.

ADMINISTRATION OF SURVEY INSTRUMENTS

I developed a simple survey instrument comprising six statements, placed on a 6-point Likert Scale (Strongly Disagree = 1 and Strongly Agree = 6) that aimed to

Figure 18. Presenting their stories to young children

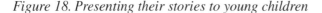
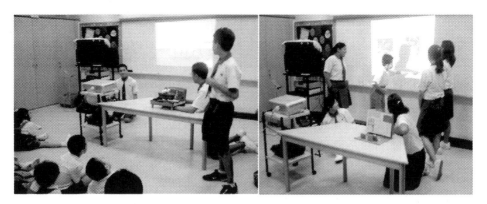

capture my students' responses in addressing the second research questions. The instrument has a section to allow students to reflect on their learning experience through the project and how the project was able to provide an avenue for them to contribute to the community. Students were guided by the statement:"How was your learning experience through the project and how do you feel about helping the young children through your project?"

I administered the instrument to my NT students the day after they presented their stories to the younger children in the special school. The students took about ten minutes to provide their feedback through the instrument. Table 1 shows the mean scores and standard deviations of the responses received from the 37 students.

Several of the student's comments that were written are presented as follows:

Speechless ☺ I think this is the brilliant idea to learn science because this is the fun way. We are able to show how creative we are through our toys. I feel proud that my toy is able to make the children happy (Female student)

Thank you teachers for helping us whenever we need help. I really enjoyed doing my portfolio and making the fun toys. Now I realized that I love science more and more! (Female student)

The science lessons are fun and make us more confident. Now this is the way to learn science! I wish to go back and help the little kids more next time! Thank you cher (teacher)! (Male student)

I'm very happy that I can use my science toy to make those nursery children smile. I just hope that all the NT students can learn science this way. This is amazing! (Male 14 Years Old)

Table 1. Views of students on the toy story-telling project

	Statements	Mean	SD
1.	I am able to show my creativity in science through the story telling project.	5.74	0.48
2.	I am able to understand several science concepts through the story telling project.	5.67	0.54
3.	I am able to make use of animation skills that I learnt in CPA lessons in the story telling project.	5.56	0.61
4.	I am able to make use of narration skills that I learnt in English lessons in the story telling project.	5.47	0.71
5.	As a whole, the story telling project has made learning fun for me.	5.80	0.69
6.	I am interested to do more CIP projects that allow me to showcase my creativity in science.	5.67	0.54

ANALYSIS OF RESULTS

Results from Table 1 suggest that the entire class of NT students gave positive response towards the toy story-telling project. The high mean scores for all six statements and small standard deviations indicated the consistency of students' responses. I triangulated the scores from the statements with several of their comments, and their performance through their toy projects in helping me find out if the toy story-telling project is a useful instructional approach in getting NT students to showcase their creative talents in science, and in getting them acquire academic content through the various subjects, and also in instilling a sense of self-worthiness amongst them.

Narrowing in to the different statements across the survey instrument, the mean score of the NT students through statement 1, which states that the students felt that they were able to show their creativity through the story telling project (score of 5.74 and standard deviation of 0.48), is closely aligned with the toy projects shown in Figures 1 to 14, which shows the commendable efforts made by these students to incorporate physics into their toy designs in clever ways. These results are further closely aligned with a student's comment "We are able to show how creative we are through our toys".

The mean score in statement 2, which states that the students felt that they were able to understand several science concepts through the story telling project (score of 5.67 and standard deviation of 0.54), and in statement 5, which states that the students felt that the story telling project has made learning fun for them (score of 5.80 and standard deviation of 0.69) are closely aligned with the scientific concepts of pulleys, magnets, and material science that they are exposed to in the projects through the context of a toy, as evident in Figures 1 to 14. These results are further closely aligned with students' comments such as "I think this is the brilliant idea to learn science because this is the fun way" and "Now I realized that I love science more and more" and "The science lessons are fun and make us more confident. Now this is the way to learn science!"

The mean score in statement 3, which states that the students felt that they were able to make use of animation skills that they learnt in CPA lessons through the story telling project (score of 5.56 and standard deviation of 0.61), and in statement 4, which states that the students felt that they were able to make use of narration skills that they learnt in English lessons through the story telling project (score of 5.47 and standard deviation of 0.71), are closely aligned with the students being able to explore the graphic and animation tools available in MS-PowerPoint for use in their slides, and in rehearsing their oral presentation skills and gaining confidence to speak in front of an audience. These results are further closely aligned to how each group was able to present their stories well to the young children and their teachers. A young child was also able to identify the character of the 'wolf in grandma's clothing', which is indicative of the graphic proficiency of the students picked up in the CPA lessons. This is also indicative that the groups have carefully thought through of making their presentation enjoyable for the young children.

The mean score in statement 6, which states that the students felt that they were interested to do more CIP projects that would allow them to showcase their creativity in science (score of 5.67 and standard deviation of 0.54), is closely aligned with the a student's comment "I wish to go back and help the little kids more next time!" This is further aligned to the invitation by the by teachers of the special students for these students to visit the children with more of their self-made toys.

The act of gesture by the young children and their teachers through the bookmarks given to the NT students is indicative of the appreciation they have on the efforts of the NT students to the community. This is closely aligned to students' comments such as "I'm very happy that I can use my science toy to make those nursery children smile" and "I feel proud that my toy is able to make the children happy". The terms 'happy' and 'feel proud' in the contexts of these statements suggest that the NT students feel a sense of self-worth after going through the project. This is also closely aligned to two students who mentioned *"thank you teacher"*, which could be indicative of them being appreciative to the teachers for paving a way to contribute their worth to the community through knowledge that is acquired in their academic subjects.

Findings from this action research study suggest that, as a whole, the responses of the NT students through the statements in the survey instrument are closely aligned with their comments, which are also closely aligned with their performance through their toy projects. Data from triangulating the results that came out of this study suggests that the toy story-telling project is a useful instructional approach in getting NT students to showcase their creative talents in science, and in getting them acquire academic content through the various subjects, and also in instilling a sense of self-worthiness amongst them.

FURTHER WORK

To show that the instructional approach presented in this study could work for the gifted and talented population of students across streams (and not just those who are academically less-inclined), more data could be collected by carrying out this similar study with average and high ability students. High ability students may lose interest through teaching approaches that do not stretch their potentials (Purcell, 1993; Vaughn, Feldhusen, & Asher, 1991; Viadero, 1995). The toy story telling project could provide the 'stretch' for this population of students by challenging their creative thinking skills through knowledge from science. In particular, it would be interesting to see how average and high ability students would respond to the same three research questions, and if there are similarities in their performance tasks and responses to the survey instrument. As mentioned earlier, the work of Stouffer, Russel & Olivia (2004); Palaniappan (2007) has shown how the 'Torrance Tests of Creative Thinking' (Torrance, 1966; 1974; 1987) does not show a correlation between IQ and creativity. Carrying out the toy story telling project with average and high ability students, and then comparing their performance tasks and responses to the survey instrument with that of results from NT students could be a way to show this.

CONCLUSION

The results that came out of this study should not be under-valued. There are currently more than 20,000 NT students in Singapore secondary schools, and similar type of academically less-inclined students all over the world. Many of them could be struggling at understanding academic content across several subjects, particularly in science and mathematics, because of the way they are presented (Albright et al., 2008; Ismail & Tan, 2004; Kramer-Dahl & Kwek, 2011; Lee & Bathmaker, 2007). The background of these students and their consistent under-performance in traditional paper-and-pen modes of assessment may lead to several members in our society adopting a view that these students as 'impossible to teach, disruptive in the classroom, insubordinate and defiant' (Favre, 2009). Ser (2004b) mentioned that what these students need is a change in the way they are guided in school and a change in the way society views them.

Up till now, little has been discussed on instructional approaches that are feasible enough to be carried out in schools in view of getting NT students to find learning academic content relevant and meaningful and at the same time, be guided to showcase their creative talents in science, which can be used to benefit society. There has also been little discussion on how avenues can be created for members of the community to recognize the creative talents of these students in science. The toy story-telling project addresses these gaps to a certain extent. In response to the first research question, findings from this study suggest that it is possible for NT students to showcase their creativity through toy story-telling project. Extracts from the NT students' design sheets and toys, as shown in Figures 1 to 14, show how the NT students made clever use physics principles in coming up with their toys. They were also able to come up with creative use of graphics and animations in their slides and made use of language and narration skills in their presentation of the stories. In response to the second research question, findings from the students' work suggest that they are able to acquire academic content in science, English and CPA lessons through this project. The high mean scores and low standard deviations evidence this through the instrument shown in Table 1. In response to the third research question, students' comments such as "I feel proud that my toy is able to make the children happy" and "I'm very happy that I can use my science toy to make those nursery children smile" suggest that this project provides an avenue for them to contribute to the community and instill a sense of self-worthiness amongst them.

In fostering creativity in science through a values-driven science toy project, what could be necessary, as shown through the science, CPA and English lessons is in keeping the students in-check of the design requirements - that is, why there is a need to make these toys, how and where they will be used and who these toys are made for. This kept students focused on their projects and on tasks with their assignments. The prior visit to the special school was important as it got the students to have an idea of how these children might best learn from their stories. In addition to fostering creativity, the school values are consciously reinforced through the toy story-telling project: students learnt to respect each other by working in groups; they are trained to be resourceful by making use of simple and recycled materials to fabricate their toys; they are taught to be responsible for the care of their own design sheets and toys; and they learnt important lessons about resilience. There are many occasions when they would not be able to get their toys working well in the initial stages, but were encouraged not to give up easily.

The general public perception that NT students in Singapore are not 'cut-out' to do well through their academic abilities (Ser, 2004a) needs to be challenged. The NT students' creative display of their knowledge in physics through their self-made toys as shown in this study may contribute to a positive change in the way society may view them - from students that are looked upon as unmotivated in school to ones that have the potential to be developed as future inventors. Students involved in this study were on-task in their science, CPA and English lessons. I observed how these students exhibited a much higher level of enthusiasm and engagement in acquiring content in these subjects through the project when compared to teaching them through just theoretical modes and stepped-through experiments. Teachers in my school are also happy to see how the use of the science-based toy story-telling project can be extended to other subjects in view of making learning content across subjects relevant and meaningful for our NT students. We truly believe that immersing our students in such a problem-solving process that requires a merger of content knowledge and skills across subjects to pursue a design task depicts a real-world setting.

REFERENCES

Abrahams, A., & Millar, R. (2008). Does Practical Work Really Work? A study of the effectiveness of practical work as a teaching and learning method in school science. *International Journal of Science Education, 30*(14), 1945–1969. doi:10.1080/09500690701749305

Abrahams, I. (2009). Does practical work really motivate? A study of the affective value of practical work in secondary school science. *International Journal of Science Education, 31*(17), 2335–2353. doi:10.1080/09500690802342836

Albright, J., Heng, M. A., & Harris, K. (2008). *Pedagogical Change in the Normal Technical Classroom, Final Research Report*. Centre for Research in Perdagogy and Practice, National Institute of Education, Singapore. Retrieved January 1, 2013, from: http://repository.nie.edu.sg/jspui/bitstream/10497/4157/3/CRP26_05JA_FinalResRpt.pdf

Amabile, T. M. (1996). Creativity and innovation in organizations. Harvard Business School.

Amir, N., & Subramaniam, R. (2012). Fostering inquiry in science among kinaesthetic learners through Design & Technology. In L. C. Lennex, & K. F. Nettleton (Eds.), *Cases on Inquiry Through Instructional Technology in Math and Science: Systemic Approaches* (pp. 221–257). Hershey, PA: IGI Global Publishing. doi:10.4018/978-1-4666-0068-3.ch009

Anandan, K., & Kan, V. (2008).*Enthusing NT students, start from scratch*. Paper presented at NT Science Professional Sharing Day 2008 - Teachers' Best Practices. Singapore.

Austin, L. B., & Shore, B. M. (1995). Using concept mapping for assessment in physics. *Physics Education, 30*(1), 41–45. doi:10.1088/0031-9120/30/1/009

Balchin, T. (2005). A creativity feedback package for teachers and students of design and technology (in the UK). *Design and Technology Education: An International Journal., 10*(2), 31–43.

Barak, M., & Doppelt, Y. (2000). Using portfolios to enhance creative thinking. *Journal-of-Technology-Studies, 26*(2), 16–25.

Barlex, D. (2007). Creativity in school design and technology in England: A discussion of Influences. *International Journal of Technology and Design Education, 17*(2), 149–162. doi:10.1007/s10798-006-0006-x

Baxter, P., & Jack, S. (2008). Qualitative Case Study Methodology: Study Design and Implementation for Novice Researchers. *Qualitative Report, 13*(4), 544–559. Retrieved September 1, 2013, from http://www.nova.edu/ssss/QR/QR13-4/baxter.pdf

Besemer, S. P. (1998). Creative product analysis matrix: Testing the model structure and a comparison among products – three novel chairs. *Creativity Research Journal, 11*(4), 333–346. doi:10.1207/s15326934crj1104_7

Besemer, S. P. (2010). Review of fostering creativity by Arthur and David Cropley. *Creativity Research Journal, 22*(2), 236–237. doi:10.1080/10400419.2010.481543

Brodie, E., & Thompson, M. (2009). Double crossed: Exploring science and history through cross-curricular teaching. *The School Science Review, 90*(332), 47–52.

Bryman, A. (2001). *Social Research Methods*. Oxford, UK: Oxford University Press.

Caine, R. N., & Caine, G. (1991). *Making connections: teaching and the human brain*. Alexandria, VA: Association for Supervision and Curriculum Development.

Chang, A. (1997). *The motivation, self-esteem, study habits and problems of Normal Technical students*. Singapore: Centre for Educational Research, National Institute of Education.

Childress, V. (1996). Does integrating technology, science and mathematics improve technological problem solving? A quasi-experiment. *Journal of Technology Education, 8*(1), 16–26.

Christensen, J. J. (1988). Reflections on teaching creativity. *Chemical Engineering Education, 22*(4), 170–176.

Craft, A. (2001). *An analysis of research and literature on creativity in education*. Qualifications and Curriculum Authority. Retrieved September 1, 2013, from http://www.euvonal.hu/images/creativity_report.pdf

Cropley, D. H., & Cropley, A. J. (2000). Fostering creativity in engineering undergraduates. *High Ability Studies, 11*(2), 207–219. doi:10.1080/13598130020001223

Cross, N. (2007). *Designerly ways of knowing*. London, U.K.: Springer- Verlag.

Csikszentmihalyi, M. (1998). Society, culture and person: a systems view of creativity. In R. J. Sternberg (Ed.), *The nature of creativity* (pp. 325–339). Cambridge, UK: Cambridge University Press.

Dacey, J., & Lennon, K. (2000). *Understanding creativity: the interplay of biological, psychological and social factors*. Buffalo, NY: Creative Education Foundation.

Davidson, M., Evens, H., & McCormick, R. (1998). *Bridging the gap: the use of concepts from science and mathematics in design and technology at KS 3*. International Design and Technology Education Research and Curriculum Development (IDATER), Loughborough University of Technology. Retrieved January 1, 2013, from https://dspace.lboro.ac.uk/dspace-jspui/handle/2134/1419

Denzin, N. K. (1970). *The Research Act in Sociology*. Chicago: Aldine.

Doppelt, Y. (2005). Assessment of project-based learning in a mechatronics context. *Journal of Technology Education*, *16*(2), 7–24.

Favre, L. R. (2009). Kinesthetic Instructional Strategies: Moving At-Risk Learners to Higher Levels. *Insights on Learning Disabilities*, *6*(1), 29–35.

Featonby, D. (2005). Toys and physics. *Physics Education*, *40*(6), 537–543. doi:10.1088/0031-9120/40/6/005

Feldman, D., Csikszentmihalyi, M., & Gardner, H. (1994). *Changing the World: A Framework for the Study of Creativity*. West Point, CT: Praeger.

Fogarty, R. (1991). Ten ways to integrate curriculum. *Educational Leadership*, *49*(2), 61–65.

Fortus, D., Krajcikb, J., Dershimerb, R. C., Marxc, R. W., & Mamlok-Naamand, R. (2004). Design-based science and student learning. *Journal of Research in Science Teaching*, *41*(10), 1081–1110. doi:10.1002/tea.20040

Fortus, D., Krajcikb, J., Dershimerb, R. C., Marxc, R. W., & Mamlok-Naamand, R. (2005). Design-based science and real-world problem-solving. *International Journal of Science Education*, *27*(7), 855–879. doi:10.1080/09500690500038165

Fox, J. M. (2011). *Creativity 101: 4Ps of Creativity. Creativity Series 101*. International Center for Studies in Creativity, Buffalo State, University of New York. Retrieved January 1, 2013, from http://www.youtube.com/watch?v=UDy5eTqot1M

Gardner, P. L. (1997). The roots of technology and science: A philosophical and historical view. *International Journal of Technology and Design Education*, *7*(1-2), 13–20. doi:10.1023/A:1008892400827

Garrett, R. M. (1987). Issues in science education: Problem-solving, creativity and originality. *International Journal of Science Education*, *9*(2), 125–137. doi:10.1080/0950069870090201

Gilbert, J. K. (2005). *Constructing worlds through science education*. London: Routledge.

Gilbert, J. K., & Newberry, M. (2007). The characteristics of the gifted and exceptionally able in science. In K. S. Taber (Ed.), *Science education for gifted learners* (pp. 15–31). London: Routledge.

Güémez, J., Fiolhais, C., & Fiolhais, M. (2009). Toys in physics lectures and demonstrations - A brief review. *Physics Education, 44*(1), 53–64. doi:10.1088/0031-9120/44/1/008

Guildford, J. P. (1959). The three faces of intellect. *The American Psychologist, 14*(8), 469–479. doi:10.1037/h0046827

Guion, L. A., Diehl, D. C., & McDonald, D. (2011). *Triangulation: Establishing the Validity of Qualitative Studies*. Retrieved September 1, 2013, from http://edis.ifas.ufl.edu/pdffiles/FY/FY39400.pdf

Haigh, M. (2007). Can investigative practical work in high school biology foster creativity? *Research in Science Education, 37*(2), 123–140. doi:10.1007/s11165-006-9018-5

Hansen, P. J. K. (2009). Analysing cases in technology and design education: How could designing and making technological products be a vehicle for enhancing understanding of natural science principles? *Design and Technology Education: An International Journal, 14*(2), 45–52.

Ho, Y. L. R., Lim, S. H., & Ho, B. T. (2005). *Differentiated Approach In Teaching Science To Normal (Technical) students*. Paper presented at CRPP International Conference on Education on 1stJune 2005 in The National Institute of Education. Singapore.

Hoang, T. (2007). Creativity: A motivational tool for interest and conceptual understanding in science education. *International Journal of Humanities and Social Science, 2*, 477–483.

Höhn, L., & Harsch, G. (2009). Indigo and creativity: A cross-curricular approach linking art and chemistry. *The School Science Review, 90*(332), 73–81.

Ismail, M., & Tan, A. L. (2004). *Voices from the Normal Technical World – An ethnographic study of low-track students in Singapore*. Retrieved January 1, 2013, from http://conference.nie.edu.sg/paper/new%20converted/ab00565.pdf

Jarvis, T. (2009). Promoting creative science cross-curricular work through an in-service programme. *The School Science Review, 90*(332), 39–46.

Jick, T. D. (1983). Mixing Qualitative and Quantitative Methods: Triangulation in Action. In J. Van Maanen (Ed.), *Qualitative Methodology* (pp. 135–148). Beverly Hills, CA: Sage Publications.

Johnsey, R. (1999). *An examination of a mode of curriculum delivery in which science is integrated with design and technology in the primary school.* International Design And Technology Education Research and Curriculum Development (IDATER), Loughborough University. Retrieved from https://dspace.lboro.ac.uk/dspace-jspui/handle/2134/1394

Klein, N., & Shragai, Y. (2001). *Creativity and the design approach: a proposed module.* International Design and Technology Education Research and Curriculum Development (IDATER), Loughborough University of Technology. Retrieved from https://dspace.lboro.ac.uk/dspace-jspui/bitstream/2134/1337/1/klein01.pdf

Knafl, K., & Breitmayer, B. J. (1989). Triangulation in qualitative research: Issues of conceptual clarity and purpose. In J. Morse (Ed.), *Qualitative nursing research: A contemporary dialogue,* (pp. 193–203). Aspen.

Kramer-Dahl, A., & Kwek, D. (2011). 'Reading' the Home and Reading in School: Framing Deficit Constructions as Learning Difficulties in Singapore English Classrooms. In C. Watt-Smith, J. Elkins, & S. Gunn (Eds.), *Multiple Perspectives on Difficulties in Learning Literacy and Numeracy* (pp. 159–178). Australia: Springer. doi:10.1007/978-1-4020-8864-3_7

Lee, K. W. L. (2001). Fostering Creativity in Science Education. *Review of Educational Research and Advances for Classroom Teachers, 20*(2), 27–31.

Lee, K. W. L., Goh, N. K., Chia, L. S., & Wan, Y. K. (2006). Report on Creativity in Science Education. National Institute of Education, Nanyang Technological University.

Lee, M. (2007). Spark up the American revolution with math, science, and more: An example of an integrative curriculum unit. *Social Studies, 98*(4), 159–164. doi:10.3200/TSSS.98.4.159-164

Lee, R. N. F., & Bathmaker, A. M. (2007). The use of English textbooks for teaching English to 'Vocational' students in Singapore secondary schools - a survey of teachers' beliefs. *RELC Journal, 38*(3), 350–374. doi:10.1177/0033688207085852

Lewis, T., Barlex, D., & Colin, C. (2007). Investigating interaction between science and design and technology (DandT) in the secondary school - a case study approach. *Research in Science & Technological Education, 25*(1), 37–58. doi:10.1080/02635140601053443

Lim, S. H. S., Lim, C., & Atencio, M. (2013). Understanding the processes behind student designing: Cases from Singapore. *Design and Technology Education: an International Journal, 18*(1), 20–29.

Mackin, J. (1996). A creative approach to physics teaching. *Physics Education, 31*(4), 199–202. doi:10.1088/0031-9120/31/4/014

McCormack, A. J. (1971). Effects of selected teaching methods on creative thinking, self- evaluation, and achievement of studies enrolled in an elementary science education methods course. *Science Education, 55*(3), 301–307. doi:10.1002/sce.3730550309

McCormick, R. (1997). Conceptual and procedural knowledge. *International Journal of Technology and Design Education, 7*(1-2), 141–159. doi:10.1023/A:1008819912213

Metz, S. (2010). Create and Innovate! *Science Teacher (Normal, Ill.), 77*(6), 6.

Ministry of Education Singapore. (2007). *Website, Science Lower Secondary NT syllabus.* Retrieved January 1, 2013, from http://www.moe.gov.sg/education/syllabuses/sciences/files/science-lower-secondary-nt-2008.pdf

Moo, S. N. (1997). Teachers' Perceptions of Normal (Technical) Students' Motivation and Classroom Behaviour. In A.S.C., Chang, S. C. Goh, S.N. Moo & A.Y. Chen (Eds.), Report on Motivation and Classroom Behaviour of Normal Technical Students. Singapore: National Institute of Education, Centre for Educational Research.

Moravcsik, M. (1981). Creativity in science education. *Science Education, 65*(2), 221–227. doi:10.1002/sce.3730650212

Ng, I. S. P. (2004). Perspectives on streaming, EM3 pupils and literacy: views of participants. (Unpublished B.A. thesis). National Institute of Education, Nanyang Technological University, Singapore. Retrieved from http://hdl.handle.net/10497/2225

Ng, M. (1993). *The Normal (Technical) course.Videorecording. Singapore: Curriculum Development Institute of Singapore.* Singapore: Ministry of Education.

Nickerson, L. (2009). Science Drama. *The School Science Review, 90*(332), 83–89.

Norman, E. (1993). Science for design. *Physics Education, 28*(5), 301–306. doi:10.1088/0031-9120/28/5/010

Palaniappan, A. K. (2007). Academic Achievement of Groups Formed Based on Creativity and Intelligence. In *Proceedings of the 13th International Conference on Thinking.* Retrieved January 1, 2013, from www.ep.liu.se/ecp/021/vol1/020/exp2107020.pdf

Pereira, L. Q. (1999). Divergent thinking and the design process. In P. H. Roberts & E. W. L. Norman (Eds.), Proceedings of the International Conference on Design and Technology Educational Research and Curriculum Development (pp. 224–229). Loughborough: Department of Design and Technology, Loughborough University. Retrieved from https://dspace.lboro.ac.uk/dspace-jspui/handle/2134/1403

Pizzini, E. L., Shepardson, D. P., & Abell, S. K. (1989). A rationale for and the development of a problem solving model of instruction in science education. *Science Education, 73*(5), 523–534. doi:10.1002/sce.3730730502

Plucker, J., & Runco, M. A. (1999). Deviance. In Encyclopedia of Creativity. San Diego, CA: Academic.

Puccio, G. (2011). *What is Creativity? Creativity Series 101*. International Center for Studies in Creativity, Buffalo State, University of New York. Retrieved January 1, 2013, from http://www.youtube.com/watch?v=coJ2T0iI0tQ

Purcell, J. H. (1993). The effects of the elimination of gifted and talented programs on participating students and their parents. *Gifted Child Quarterly, 37*(4), 177–178. doi:10.1177/001698629303700407

Ramadas, J. (2009). Visual and spatial modes in science learning. *International Journal of Science Education, 31*(3), 301–318. doi:10.1080/09500690802595763

Raviv, D. (2002). Do We Teach Them How to Think? In *Proceedings of the 2002 American Society for Engineering Education Annual Conference and Exposition*. American Society for Engineering Education Session 2630.

Rhodes, M. (1961). An analysis of creativity. *Phi Delta Kappan, 42*(7), 305–310.

Robinson, K. (2006). *Do schools kill creativity?* Paper presented at the Technology, Entertainment and Design (TED) Conference 2006. Retrieved January 1, 2013, from http://www.youtube.com/watch?v=iG9CE55wbtY

Ryhammar, L., & Brolin, C. (1999). Creativity research: Historical considerations and main lines of development. *Scandinavian Journal of Educational Research, 43*(3), 259–273. doi:10.1080/0031383990430303

Sage, J., & Steeg, T. (1993). Linking the learning of mathematics, science and technology within key stage 4 of the national curriculum, In *Proceedings of International Conference on Design and Technology Educational Research and Curriculum Development*. Loughborough University of Technology. Retrieved January 1, 2013, from https://dspace.lboro.ac.uk/dspace-jspui/bitstream/2134/1579/3/sage93.pdf

Sarquis, J., Sarquis, M., & Williams, J. P. (1995). *Teaching chemistry with TOYS: activities for grades K-9. McGraw-Hill.* Learning Triangle Press.

Ser, D. (2004a). *I really not stupid (Part 1).* NewsAsia, MediaCorp News. Retrieved January 1, 2013, from http://www.youtube.com/watch?v=HtfomNNKcmI

Ser, D. (2004b). *I really not stupid (Part 2).* NewsAsia, MediaCorp News. Retrieved January 1, 2013, from: http://www.youtube.com/watch?v=GDx6WbOgKxM

Sharkawy, A., Barlex, D., Welch, M., McDuff, J., & Craig, N. (2009). Adapting a Curriculum Unit to Facilitate Interaction Between Technology, Mathematics and Science in the Elementary Classroom: Identifying Relevant Criteria. *Design and Technology Education: An International Journal, 14*(1), 7–20.

Sidawi, M. (2009). Teaching science through designing technology. *International Journal of Technology and Design Education, 19*(3), 269–287. doi:10.1007/s10798-007-9045-1

Singapore Department of Statistics. (2011). *Education.* Retrieved January 1, 2013, from http://www.singstat.gov.sg/pubn/reference/yos11/statsT-education.pdf

SingTeach. (2010). *Science Education for Gifted Learners.* Retrieved from http://singteach.nie.edu.sg/issue24-scienceed/

Slater, T. F. (1996). Portfolio assessment strategies for grading first-year university physics students in the USA. *Physics Education, 31*(5), 329–333. doi:10.1088/0031-9120/31/5/024

Spendlove, D. (2005). Creativity in education: A review. *Design and Technology Education: An International Journal, 10*(2), 9–18.

Stainback, S., & Stainback, W. (1988). *Conducting a Qualitative Research Study. Understanding and conducting qualitative research.* Reston, VA: Council for Exceptional Children.

Stake, R. E. (1978). The case study method in Social Inquiry. *Educational Researcher, 7*(2), 5–8. doi:10.3102/0013189X007002005

Stouffer, W. B., Russell, J. S., & Oliva, M. G. (2004). Making the strange familiar: Creativity and the future of engineering education. In *Proceedings of the American Society for Engineering Education Annual Conference and Exposition, Engineering Education Researches New Heights* (pp. 9315-9327). Retrieved January 1, 2013, from: http://www.engr.wisc.edu/cee/faculty/russell_jeffrey/004.pdf

Thuraisingam, P. (2007). *Engaging the Normal Technical Stream Learner in the English language classroom*. Paper presented at the Redesigning Pedagogy Conference. Singapore.

Torrance, E. P. (1966). *The Torrance Tests of Creative Thinking-Norms-Technical Manual Research Edition-Verbal Tests, Forms A and B-Figural Tests, Forms A and B*. Princeton, NJ: Personnel Press.

Torrance, E. P. (1974). *The Torrance Tests of Creative Thinking-Norms-Technical Manual Research Edition-Verbal Tests, Forms A and B- Figural Tests, Forms A and B*. Princeton, NJ: Personnel Press.

Torrance, E. P. (1987). Teaching for Creativity. In S. Isaksen (Ed.), *Frontiers of Creativity Research: Beyond the Basics* (pp. 189–215). Buffalo, NY: Bearly Limited.

Trumbo, J. (2006). Making science visible: Visual literacy in science communication. In L. Pauwels (Ed.), *Visual culture of science: Re-thinking representational practices in knowledge building and science communication*. Dartmouth College Press, University Press of New England.

Vaughn, V. L., Feldhusen, J. F., & Asher, J. W. (1991). Meta-analysis and review of research on pull-out programs in gifted education. *Gifted Child Quarterly, 35*(2), 92–98. doi:10.1177/001698629103500208

Vernon, P. E. (1989). The nature-nurture problem in creativity. In J.A. Glover, R.R. Ronning, & C.R. Reynolds (Eds.), Handbook of creativity: Perspectives on individual differences. Plenum Press.

Viadero, D. (1995). Special Programs Found to Benefit Gifted Students. *Education Week*. Retrieved from http://www.edweek.org/ew/articles/1995/04/05/28gift.h14.html

Wardle. (2009). Creativity in science. *School Science Review, 90*, 332.

Washton, N. S. (1971). Creativity in science teaching. *Science Education, 55*(2), 147–150. doi:10.1002/sce.3730550208

Welch, M., & Barlex, D. (2004). *Portfolios in design and technology education: investigating differing views*. Paper presented in DATA International Research Conference 2004. Retrieved from https://dspace.lboro.ac.uk/dspace-jspui/handle/2134/2864

West, R. W. (1981). A case against the core. *The School Science Review, 63*(223), 226–236.

West, T. (1997). *In the Mind's Eye: Visual Thinkers, Gifted People with Dyslexia and Other Learning Difficulties, Computer Images and the Ironies of Creativity*. Amherst, NY: Prometheus Books.

Wiebe, E. N., Clark, A. C., & Hasse, E. V. (2001). Scientific Visualization: Linking science and technology education through graphic communications. *The Journal of Design and Technology Education*, 6(1), 40–47.

Williams, F. (1972). *Identifying and measuring creative potential* (Vol. 1). Educational Publications.

Yin, R. K. (1989). *Case study research: Design and methods*. Beverly Hills, CA: Sage.

Zubrowski, B. (2002). Integrating science into Design Technology projects: Using a standard model in the design process. *Journal of Technology Education*, *13*(2), 48–67.

KEY TERMS AND DEFINITIONS

Appealing Contexts: Contexts that are able to attract interest, draw favorable attention or deemed pleasing by a group of audience.

Creativity: A term used to describe the process of coming up with original and valuable ideas in the course of solving problems.

Design Sheet/ Design Page: A sheet showing a student's thinking process in linking science to the design of his/her product.

Normal Technical (NT) Stream: It is a system of education offered in secondary schools in Singapore to students who did not perform well in their primary school leaving examinations to qualify for the more academic streams.

Toy: A product created by students through the design-based learning approach.

Section 3
Arts and Humanities and the Gifted/Talented Student

Chapter 8
Creating Our World:
An Art Program for Alternative School Students

Jeanne Petsch
Morehead State University, USA

EXECUTIVE SUMMARY

A partnership between the Morehead State University Art Education Program and the Lake County Alternative School (LCAS) (pseudonyms are used for the school name and county where the school is located) was established in Fall 2011. This ongoing collaboration provides opportunities for Art Education students to teach art and work with at-risk middle and high school students. It also allows LCAS students, who otherwise have no coursework in art, the opportunity to work creatively with visual art media. In addition, Art Education students work toward meeting the Kentucky State Teacher Education field experience hour requirement of 200 contact hours in schools prior to clinical practice. LCAS students apply this art experience toward earning humanities credit.

CASE STUDY

Setting

The Lake County Alternative School is a public alternative middle (grades 6-8) and high school (grades 9-12) serving students in Lake County, which is located in the Appalachian region of Eastern Kentucky. Lake County is largely rural and thirty percent of the population lives below the poverty line (U.S. Department of Com-

DOI: 10.4018/978-1-4666-6489-0.ch008

merce Census Bureau, 2014). Typically, there are approximately fifteen students in the middle school class and fifteen students in the high school class. Even though some students attend the LCAS long term, much of the student population shifts frequently as students are transitioned back into the mainstream student population at the high school or the middle school. Some students also drop out. The LCAS is located in a decommissioned middle school building, which lacks amenities such as up-to-date, reliable technology and classrooms equipped for experiential study in many required subjects including the arts and sciences. One advantage to working in this building is the extraordinary amount of available space to make art and store it. There is a designated classroom to store art, a designated room for art with the high school students, and the middle school students can be moved from their classroom to the hallways and cafeteria for projects that require more space. Art supplies are purchased with funding from the Morehead State University Center for Regional Engagement and Department of Art and Design.

LCAS Students

Alternative schools can be "last chance" teaching and learning environments for students (Morrissette, 2011) and are typically viewed as, "places for students whose behaviors are disruptive, deviant, and dysfunctional" (Kim, 2011, p. 78). This is an apt description for LCAS students. This school serves students who have experienced a variety of difficulties in school and in their lives outside of school. Students are placed in this setting because they are at-risk of dropping out for issues including truancy, teenage parenthood, involvement in the criminal justice system and lack of motivation. Male students consistently outnumber female students. For instance, there are currently two female students and ten male students in the middle school group. There are five female students and eleven male students in the high school group. While keeping exact statistics is difficult with a shifting student population, the LCAS lead teacher reports only one student currently attending does not qualify for free or reduced meals.

Intentions and Goals

The goals for this program are two-fold because they address the learning experiences of both pre-service art teachers (referred to as student-teachers) and students who attend the LCAS. Relationship building is foundational for both groups.

The primary goals for student-teachers include the development of empathic and inclusive teaching, receptivity and responsiveness to the individual experiences and needs of LCAS students, and the creation of meaningful art experiences that take these needs into account. Student-teachers work in teams of 2-5. Each team works with either the middle school or high school class. Typically, student-teachers work at the LCAS for two semesters. Each semester a 12-week art program is developed, and 90-minute art classes are offered on Thursday afternoons. Experienced supervising teachers are present in both classrooms.

Without the benefit of important relationships, students can become disenfranchised (O'Brien and Curry, 2009). However, through positive relationships and explorations in art, they can see themselves as part of a school and community, rather than set apart. Goals for LCAS students include the development of self-confidence and self-motivation. This can be achieved when students experience a sense of belonging and inclusion, and through the experience of creative expression in art. Using her "species – centered" view, Dissanayake (1992) looks at art as a behavior that is a predisposition of all humans. She claims that underlying all of the reasoning about why art is necessary is the fact that our experiences with art feel good physically, emotionally, and spiritually. It is worth noting that LCAS students look forward to art class, anticipating the start of the program each semester and weekly classes. On the rare occasion when an art class has to be cancelled, students are disappointed.

Approach

Art invites hands-on, mindful participation with media and materials, where the objects created can be shaped and formed according to individual ideas and explorations (see students' individualized approaches to acrylic self-portrait paintings in Figures 1, 2 & 3). The art objects students create, and the experiences they have while creating and reflecting, provide openings where they can be engaged through thoughtful and receptive interactions, which can further development and understanding.

"The teacher who wants to help the pupil to realize his best potentialities must intend him as this particular person, both in his potentiality and in his actuality" (Buber, 1970, p. 178). When teaching art at LCAS student-teachers and students focus on the art lesson, while also building relationships. This occurs in two ways. First, student-teachers work as individuals with other individuals, allowing students to see that teachers make art and genuinely care about the practice of art making. In this way, students can see the teacher as an exemplar of one who teaches, yet also seriously practices the subject being taught. While doing so, teachers can exhibit their expertise and experience as artists, giving them credibility in the classroom, while also working alongside students, as helpful fellow artists.

Another way student-teachers work with students is by working in collaboration. When this practice began, it seemed to arise as a natural transition from presenting the lesson to working on projects. Low motivation is typical for LCAS students, and helping students find ways to start was an immediate challenge. Assisting

Figure 1. High school student self-portrait, 2' x 2,' acrylic on hardboard

Figure 2. Middle school student self-portrait, 2' x 2,' acrylic on hardboard

Figure 3. Middle school student self-portrait, 2' x 2,' acrylic on hardboard

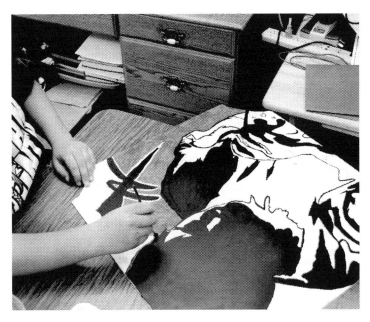

quickly turned into collaboration, where both the students and the student-teachers created projects together. In the continuing use of this practice student-teachers help individuals find places to start by talking about their interests and ideas, then together they strategize about approaches and move toward students taking over the decision-making and the work. To clarify, when working collaboratively, teachers are not doing the students' work *for* them, but *with* them, while gradually moving students toward working independently and gaining confidence in making their own decisions. Keeping in mind that "the longing for relationship is primary" (Buber, 1970, p. 78), working collaboratively also creates a place where students can share their experiences and ideas with a receptive and caring work partner.

Strategies for working with LCAS students are deemed as successful because students become increasingly responsive, less resistant, more self-motivated, more resilient in working through frustration, excited about participating in art, and are able to develop ideas and maintain involvement in art making independently. The following excerpts from student-teacher journals illustrate this growth. Pseudonyms are used for student names.

Timothy's clay project fell apart the other day. He was a little upset about it. He asked if I would come in Friday afternoon and help him finish it. I was so excited that he was excited. So on Friday we got to make a small clay pitcher. He is so proud!

He couldn't stop talking about how awesome it was and how he would protect it with his life. We did more than just build a pot. We built a relationship, established some pride, and made Timothy's day. I feel like I was reminded of why I want to be an art teacher, and Timothy is why. (student-teacher journal,...see clay pitcher with lid, Figure 4)

Watching Josh the past couple of classes I have noticed he has been much more enthusiastic and confident jumping straight into projects. He made a print and gave it to Rachel. Josh's attitude has changed. Last semester he was very hesitant, sometimes even reluctant to start on projects. (student-teacher journal)
We had to basically take the ink away from Mark because he worked until the last minute, which is a good thing. (student-teacher journal)

Working with alternative school students expands the abilities of pre-service art teachers to work with *all* students and create inclusive classrooms, preparing them for student-teaching and beyond. As they see the "...unique and particular bent of each personal expression" (Hammer, 1984, p. 183) they become adept at being mindfully present and attentive to individual propensities, experiences and development. The following student-teacher journal excerpts provide examples of the development of their perceptiveness:

I knew Tom was in a bad mood when he came in with his shirt over his head. He's done this before but I always let him have some time and space. He'll come around when he wants to, but if we immediately tackle him with commands, we won't get anything out of him. (student-teacher journal)

Justin seems like a fairly average high school boy most of the time. I have just recently started working one-on-one with him, and I believe he is very talented. At first I was wary because he seems to have a lot of anger issues, but he is very mature in some ways. When I was helping him work on his mask, which required a great many dreadlocks, each braided from 9 strands of yarn, I offered to take a few home and braid them for him. He didn't answer immediately, and he didn't quite look at me when he said it, but very respectfully and quietly he said, "But then it wouldn't be mine." I believe it was that point when I knew he was functioning beyond many of the other high school students. I didn't mean it as a demeaning gesture, I simply thought he might need help, but braiding the dreadlocks crossed the line between "help" and "do for you," and he was having none of that. (student-teacher journal, see mask with braids, Figure 5)

Figure 4. Middle school student clay pitcher with lid, approximately 7" x 4" x 4"

Figure 5. High school student plaster mask with braids, 12" x 7" x 7"

Many of the Art Education students are frequent visitors at the LCAS and surpass their field experience hour requirement of twenty-four hours for one semester and sixty-four hours for the second semester. They assist LCAS students when working on other subjects. They also eat lunch together and play basketball, which furthers relationship-building and expands their insights about LCAS students' experiences throughout their school day.

Advanced Artistic Abilities in the Alternative School Environment

No students at the LCAS have been identified as gifted or talented in art or any other subject area. Students mainly follow an online curriculum as they work toward graduating. Behavioral issues determine their placement in this alternative setting, and the students are acutely aware of their identity as "bad kids" and their separation from the mainstream schools. Most of the students have had little or no previous experience in art. Yet, in the midst of this context, the advanced artistic and creative abilities of individual students are apparent.

According to Csikszentmihalyi (1990) when one is involved and integrated in an activity such as art making he or she is creating purpose and meaning. Beittel (1991) saw art making as a means for self-formation and the development of consciousness, and May (1975) felt that we "express our being by creating" (p. 8). These ideals are worked toward with LCAS students, with the understanding that working creatively and forming identity in the alternative school environment can be difficult.

For many LCAS students school is less important than other concerns in their lives such as having enough food when they go home, or maintaining a tough exterior to counter ridicule or bullying by peers, or the need to respond to felt injustices perpetrated by those in authority. The challenge of teaching art with students who have learned to be self-protective in a classroom where bantering and bickering among students is common, is to help them find the courage to work creatively.

Given the day-to-day challenges of being a LCAS student and the courage required to working creatively among peers, some students develop and exhibit creative abilities. In some instances these students become known as being "good" at art and enjoy the admiration of their peers. The following student-teacher journal entries are attentive to advanced student work:

Someone that truly surprised me and left me speechless was Sam. He didn't have anything to glaze so we found him a small cup to glaze and he did. Then he started drawing with some markers. He was so nice, respectful, and worked hard on everything he did. I didn't really look at what he was drawing until the end of class and when I did I was stopped in my tracks. He was drawing such a colorful and detailed fish, and it all came from his head. He was talking to Emily and I about perspective, background, foreground and other things like colors and color schemes. He is such a smart kid and really does know art and enjoys it. He has some amazing talent. I would love it if we could get him and all the others sketchbooks. I could have sat there all day and watched Sam draw with those markers making truly beautiful drawings. (student-teacher journal, see Sam's marker drawing, Figures 6 & 7)

Figure 6. Middle school student colorful fish drawing in progress, approximately 8" x 10"

Figure 7. Middle school student colorful fish drawing completed, approximately 8" x 10"

Ben works easily and quickly with drawing- when he wants. He often gets bored with our lessons. The lessons aren't really advanced, especially for high school, but while some students at the LCAS struggle, he is generally one of the first done. He doesn't seem to like three-dimensional work, but his ability to draw realistically and the quality of lines he produces is far beyond many typical high school students. Ben does have talent, and I believe he is gifted in art. I also believe that he has an image to maintain. If he was not in an alternative school with such a badass image to uphold (can't art be badass, too?) things may be different and he may pursue art. (student-teacher journal)

Justin may not be 'designated' as gifted and talented, but I feel that it is just because he has been pushed away and denied to do what he wants to do, and through the school system discouraging his artistic creativity, he has acted out and not done what is expected of him. When he works on a project with the class as a whole, when they are all doing virtually the same thing, he does not find it stimulating and does not feel like he is making his own art, instead he is just doing something for someone else, but when you give him a project where he gets to choose what he is going to make, he will blow it out of the water. You give him plaster, and he will try and make an entire body with it, and it will look spot on. He is extremely dedicated when it comes to working on a project that he really wants to, and he often creates his own projects and wants to work outside of the classroom as well. One thing that really strikes me as talented about him, is that he can draw/paint/sculpt nude or partially nude figures, and have them look tasteful and artistic, not vulgar, and for someone his age I find that incredible, and instead of encouraging this creativity in this student, the schools that he has gone to kicked him out of art classes for making art - meaningful art. He is talented, and after looking at his art and watching him in class, those who can't see it are blind. (student-teacher journal)

It is easy to miss or discount the abilities alternative school students have when emphasis is placed on their behavior. Even though behavioral issues must be addressed, in art emphasis is placed on empathic understanding, building connections and working creatively with media and materials, while realizing that students' experiences and abilities are interwoven.

CONCLUSION

"The shaping of one's worldly identity is a central task of adolescent individuation" (Frankel, 1998, p. 129), and it is necessary for students to be come self-confident and self-motivated. For a student to be herself, to be creating identity in a place where "others determine 'exactly' what 'you are' and used fixed names" (Greene, 1995, p. 20) is a difficult struggle. "Those who are labeled as deficient, fixed in that category as firmly as flies in amber, have little chance to feel they can be yet otherwise than what they have become" (Greene, 1995, p. 39). In order for students to "discover a sense of self that feels real in the world" (Frankel, 1998, p. 214) teachers can encourage them to trust in themselves, to be intuitive and self-determined, developing identity through positive interactions and creative experiences in art.

In the alternative school setting student-teachers practice their abilities to enliven students by valuing and responding to each student as an individual. They become aware of how easily a vulnerable spirit can be crushed or how it can be sensitively lifted up. An empathic, accepting approach to teaching is especially important when students are experiencing struggles outside of school such as poverty and neglect, and struggles inside of school such as being cast out of the mainstream school culture. When working with alternative school students, who are described by the lead teacher at the LCAS as "the most difficult students in Lake County," student-teachers understand the need to create an inclusive environment where individual learner needs can be addressed through thoughtful interactions and meaningful experiences in art. They become receptive, responsive and flexible when working in an unpredictable classroom environment where behavioral issues are a constant challenge. They also see how their presence and thoughtful interactions can change a student's attitude and outlook. Student-teachers, who participate in field work at the LCAS, are well-prepared for clinical practice and to begin their teaching careers because they have developed these abilities and understandings.

Emphasizing abilities rather than behaviors can make a difference in the trajectory of students' growth and in their lives. "To place a person in a system takes less energy than to know him in his own right" (Maslow, 1968, p. 126). Students, such as the LCAS students who are marginalized by this system, are many times excluded and isolated. However, we can recognize that these excluded students have potential and ability, and focus on their potentialities by providing enriching experiences in art and other subject areas. Further study may include observing the progress of students who receive empathic, attentive interactions from teachers and experiential learning opportunities, especially when their needs are recognized and tended to early in their P-12 education. Also, exceptional creative and intellectual advancement could be determined by further analysis of students' artwork including adeptness and experimentation in the use of media and materials, depth and breadth of creative exploration and invention, and rate of artistic growth.

"Art offers life; it offers hope; it offers the prospect of discovery; it offers light" (Greene, 1995, p. 133). Art teachers can provide students a place where they are invited, accepted and engaged, and where they are free to experience their own expression among others doing the same. Students can be asked to "tell their stories, to pose their own questions, to be present – from their own perspectives – to the common world" (Green, 1995, p. 34). We must realize "the curriculum is not comprised of subjects, but of Subjects, of subjectivity" (Pinar, 1994, p. 220).

When the foundation of learning in art lies in each individual's creative and expressive experiencing students are allowed and encouraged to be originators of their own experiences (Zurmuehlen, 1990) and become self-formative (Beittel, 1991). Each student is called upon to apply "an initiating, constructing mind or consciousness to the world" (Greene, 1995, p. 23), experiencing an opening awareness and the power to create. As students see their creative expressions take form through their own actions in art, realizing their power to determine their own identity and affect others and the world, they can be inspired to take initiative and find meaning in their lives. Subsequently, they can envision themselves in the future and pilot themselves accordingly.

ACKNOWLEDGMENT

This program is supported by Morehead State University Center for Regional Engagement, Morehead State University Department of Art and Design and the Lake County Schools.

REFERENCES

Beittel, K. (1991). *A celebration of art and consciousness*. State College, PA: Happy Valley Healing Arts.

Buber, M. (1970). *I and thou*. New York: Simon and Schuster.

Csikszentmihalyi, M. (1990). *Flow: The psychology of optimal experience*. New York: Harper & Row Publishers, Inc.

Dissanayake, E. (1995). *Homo aestheticus: Where art comes from and why*. New York: Free Press.

Frankel, R. (1998). *The adolescent psyche: Jungian and Winnicottian perspectives*. New York: Routledge.

Greene, M. (1995). *Releasing the imagination: Essays on education, the arts, and social change*. San Francisco: Jossey-Bass.

Hammer, B. (1984). The artist as teacher: Problems and experiments. *Journal of Education, 166*(2), 181–187.

Kim, J. (2011). Narrative inquiry into (re)imagining alternative schools: A case study of Kevin Gonzales. *International Journal of Qualitative Studies in Education, 24*(1), 77–96. doi:10.1080/09518390903468321

Maslow, A. (1968). *Toward a psychology of being.* New York: Van Nostrand Reinhold.

May, R. (1975). *The courage to create.* New York: Norton & Co., Inc.

Morrisette, P. J. (2011). Exploring Student Experiences within the Alternative High School Context. *Canadian Journal of Education, 34*(2), 169–188.

O'Brien, E. R., & Curry, J. R. (2009). Systemic Interventions with Alternative School Students: Engaging the Omega Children. *Journal of School Counseling, 7*(24), 1–32.

Pinar, W. F. (1994). *Autobiography, politics and sexuality.* New York: Peter Lang Publishing, Inc.

U.S. Department of Commerce Census Bureau. (2014). *(Lake) County, Kentucky State and County QuickFacts* [Data file]. Retrieved from http://quickfacts.census.gov/qfd/states/21/21205.html

Zurmuehlen, M. (1990). *Studio art: Praxis, symbol, presence.* Reston, VA: National Art Education Association.

KEY TERMS AND DEFINITIONS

Alternative School: A school that utilizes alternative school structures and teaching techniques in place of regular curricular programs with a separate administrator or lead teacher in charge. Alternative schools typically serve between 30 and 250 pupils, who are placed in this setting because they are at risk of not graduating from high school.

Art: The creation of imagery or objects using visual art media including painting, drawing, sculpture, printmaking, photography, film, and any other media and/or combination of mediums.

Creativity: In visual art, the act of bringing new ideas and images into being. The ability to work outside of existing paradigms and concepts and use inventive and innovative approaches.

Empathy: The capacity to vicariously experience the emotions, thoughts and experiences of another through receptivity, awareness, and sensitive interaction.

Experiential: Learning from direct experience and involvement. Includes subsequent in-depth reflection and discussion.

Field Experience: Supervised pre-service teaching experience in school settings prior to clinical practice.

Identity: The distinct character or personality of an individual. The intrinsic qualities that make a person unique. Who someone is.

Relationship: Human connection through shared experience and understanding.

Student-Teacher: A university student who practices teaching under the supervision of an experienced, certified teacher in a P-12 school setting.

Chapter 9

From Student to Author:
Engaging Gifted Learners in the National Novel Writing Month Young Writers Program

Nancye Blair Black
Teachers College, Columbia University, USA

EXECUTIVE SUMMARY

Students develop and compose a long narrative story each November in a challenge called the National Novel Writing Month Young Writers Program (NaNoWriMo YWP). In Fall 2011, 16 gifted fourth and fifth graders participated through their twice-weekly pull-out gifted programming. Through use of a three-phase program implementation, NaNoWriMo YWP resources and online community, dynamic technology tools, and extended blocks of uninterrupted writing time, these students engaged in advanced writing instruction and practices in order to meet/surpass a personal narrative writing goal. Each of the participating gifted students met the school's learning objectives by identifying and applying advanced writing skills and improving knowledge and application of a personal goal-setting process. This chapter outlines the program's alignment with best practices in gifted education, the program implementation's educational goals/objectives, the specific strategies and practices used in implementing the program, the outcomes to student learning, and recommendations for gifted educators.

DOI: 10.4018/978-1-4666-6489-0.ch009

ORGANIZATION BACKGROUND

McKeel Elementary Academy (MEA) is a public charter elementary school in central Florida, which provides a technology-infused education for 348 students. The diversity of the student body includes 75.1% Caucasians, 13% Black or African American, 8.4% Hispanic or Latino, 1.4% Asian, 0.3% American Indian or Alaskan Native, and 1.7% with more than 1 race. Regarding socio-economic diversity, 22% of the students are on the free lunch program and 6% receive reduced-priced lunches. The 348 students are divided into three classes of each grade, with 18 students composing kindergarten through third grade classes and 22 students composing fourth and fifth grade classes. Generally, a similarly diverse make-up characterizes each of the classes. Since its establishment in 2003, McKeel Elementary Academy has demonstrated high student achievement and learning gains, gaining recognition as an "A" school.

SETTING THE STAGE

McKeel Elementary Academy provides a special instruction program to its students who are gifted. The state of Florida defines the gifted as "one who has superior intellectual development and is capable of high performance" ("6A-6.03019," 2002). According to *Florida's Plan for K-12 Gifted Education*, in order to be eligible for gifted services in the state of Florida, generally speaking, a student's evaluation must demonstrate a "need for a special instructional program, evidence of charac-teristics of the gifted, and [an] evaluation documenting intellectual development," including a score of 130 or higher on a qualifying IQ measure (Florida Department of Education (FL DOE), 2013b).

At the time of this program implementation, once students at MEA were identi-fied as gifted, they were typically staffed into the school's gifted pull-out classes (FL DOE, 2013b, p. 42). The classes took place in the school's computer lab twice weekly, each for one hour. During this time, students engaged in a variety of inde-pendent and cooperative learning activities aimed at mastering critical and creative thinking skills, extending learning beyond the general education curriculum, and working toward other goals or skills identified in the students' Educational Plans (EP). During the 2011-2012 school year in the course of these pull-out classes, sixteen fourth and fifth grade gifted students participated in the National Novel Writing Month Young Writers Program.

As the Technology and Gifted Specialist for the school, I taught the gifted students, both during their general education classes' weekly technology classes, as well as for the two weekly homogenous gifted pull-out classes. My educational certifications included both Elementary Education (K-6) and a Gifted Endorsement (K-12). While I served as the lead teacher for the National Novel Writing Month implementation, feedback regarding the students' attitudes and proficiencies in writing and task completion was additionally garnered from their general education teachers.

CASE DESCRIPTION

Program Background

The National Novel Writing Month Young Writers Program (NaNoWriMo YWP, ywp.nanowrimo.org) was launched in 2005 as an expansion to the adult National Novel Writing Month program, which was created by the Office of Letters and Light in 1999 (Office of Letters and Light, 2012a). The Young Writers Program was founded "in response to the countless teachers who wrote in wanting to bring noveling to the classroom" (Office of Letters and Light, 2012a). Within both programs, participants are challenged to write a novel (a long narrative story) that meets a word-count goal, starting no earlier than November 1 and finishing no later than midnight on November 30. While adult novel writing word-count goals in the NaNoWriMo program are automatically set at 50,000 words, students in the Young Writers Program are able to set their own personalized, age-appropriate word-count goals. The Young Writers Program provides many tools and resources to aid participants in reaching their goals. A web-based program platform allows students and teachers to register their goals and track their progress independently and as a class. Moreover, the program provides a student workbook with engaging curriculum for developing, planning, writing, and editing a novel, as well as classroom kits that include a tracking poster and pin-back buttons for students who "win" by achieving their personal goal (Office of Letters and Light Young Writers Program, 2010). Inspiration and motivation is additionally provided to participants throughout the month via emails and web-hosted "pep talks" by published authors. In 2011, over 51,000 students from over 2,000 classrooms worldwide participated in the program; 16,334 of the students met their word-count goals by the conclusion of the month (National Novel Writing Month, 2012).

At this time, there is a notable lack of published quantitative and qualitative research regarding the outcomes of student participation, gifted or otherwise, in National Novel Writing Month or the Young Writers Program. Nevertheless, research regarding general participation in National Novel Writing Month demonstrates that the program fosters an increased interest and motivation to write (Barack, 2009; Burton, 2009; Jones, 2013; Watson, 2012), provides a structure conducive to developing discipline to write regularly and achieve time-sensitive writing goals

(Burton, 2009; Donnelly, 2007; Jones, 2013; Olthouse, 2012), establishes a community that provides support, motivation and feedback (Barack, 2009; Jones, 2013; Olthouse & Miller, 2012), and cultivates a desire to improve writing abilities (Donnelly, 2007). Additionally, there is scholarly evidence to suggest that students in elementary, middle and high school have successfully participated in the National Novel Writing Month programs and completed up to 50,000 word-count goals ("A Novel Way," 2006; Barack, 2009; Donnelly, 2007; Olthouse, 2012). Olthouse and Miller (2012) also suggest that the National Novel Writing Month Young Writers Program provides an appropriate level of challenge for gifted and talented students. Clearly, further research opportunities exist to expand the literature concerning the effectiveness of these programs in both gifted and general education environments.

Despite the limited available research literature, the National Novel Writing Month Young Writers Program was chosen for implementation because many principles and components of the program had the potential to address the unique learning needs of gifted students in the area of writing. First, the program integrates the use of a three-phase writing process – in this case, planning, writing, and editing/publishing. According to Collins and Cross (1993), use of such a three-phase process can increase writing skills, engagement, and understanding in gifted students. Furthermore, the creation of a high quality product for authentic audiences through this phased process can increase gifted students' perception of work as meaningful and relevant (Olthouse & Miller, 2012; Renzulli, 2012), engaging them in the writing process at a level often unobserved in the general education classroom.

Second, the Young Writers Program had the potential to provide students with interconnected and process-oriented writing instruction while allowing for significant opportunities for choice and self-directed work. Research has shown that the curriculum and learning environment used with gifted students should include characteristics of differentiation, continuity, flexibility, and independence (Clark, 2002; National Association for Gifted Children (NAGC), 2010; Nugent, 2001). Due to the specific elements of this implementation during the students' planning, writing, and editing phases, the program could differentiate learning for the gifted students by allowing for an accelerated and/or individualized pace of learning (Clark, 2002; Colangelo, Assouline, & Gross, 2005; Kulik & Kulik, 1984; Rogers, 2007; VanTassel-Baska, 2005; Vialle, Ashton, & Carlton, 2001); the mastery of advanced, complex, and individualized lessons (Clark, 2002; Colangelo, Assouline, & Gross, 2005; Kulik & Kulik, 1984; VanTassel-Baska, 2005; Vialle, Ashton, & Carlton, 2001); novelty in intellectual challenge (Clark, 2002, Little, 2012; Rogers, 2007); and a platform for personal expression (Thompson, 2011).

Third, through the use of personal goal-setting in the novel writing process, gifted students could benefit from exercising choice in a more individualized learning environment (Clark, 2002). By allowing the gifted students to set personal goals with an appropriate degree of challenge (Little, 2012; Morisano & Shore, 2010; Schunk, 1991) and receive progress feedback throughout the program (Schunk & Swartz, 1993), they are more likely to improve in both their efficacy and achievement. To further promote achievement through the goal-setting process, research suggests that goals for gifted students should focus on mastery goal oriented practices like "effort, task, and improvement" and maximizing student buy-in to the value of the task at hand (Albaili, 2003, p. 116; Little, 2012; Siegle & McCoach, 2003). Moreover, research shows that a scaffolded approach to reaching an educational goal, such as the establishment of the where, when, and how in the YWP implementation, improves success at meeting those goals (Oettingen, Honig, & Gollwitzer, 2000).

Finally, the infused use of technology in the planned program implementation could further serve to support the creation of an appropriate gifted curriculum and learning environment. Technology in the gifted classroom should be used to engage students, individualize learning, develop communication skills, expand access to robust resources, and enable creative productivity (NAGC, 2010; Olthouse & Miller, 2012; Periathiruvadi & Rinn, 2012; VanTassel-Baska, 2005). For example, in practice, participation in digital writing and e-publishing has been shown to benefit achievement in gifted learners across curricular disciplines (Gentry, 2008). The use of technology for writing has also been shown to increase the writing production of gifted boys (Dixon, Cassady, Cross & Williams, 2005), although my anecdotal observations suggest that this benefit may cross gender lines as well. The use of various dynamic technology tools in this program implementation could enhance both the writing process and the implementation of an appropriate and differentiated gifted learning environment.

The alignment of the aforementioned principles and strategies of the program with the general best practices and learning needs of gifted and talented education made the National Novel Writing Month Young Writers Program a suitable choice for implementation in the McKeel Elementary Academy gifted program.

Goals and Objectives of the Program at McKeel Elementary Academy

The goal of the National Novel Writing Month Young Writers Program implementation with the gifted and talented students at McKeel Elementary Academy was to harness the benefits of real-world project-based learning, global project participation, and technology-infusion in order to increase learning. More specifically, the goal of the program implementation aimed towards two learning objectives, each of which aligned with the goals of *Florida's Frameworks for K-12 Gifted Learners* (FL DOE, 2013a).

The first learning objective was for gifted students to identify and apply advanced writing skills, including:

- Demonstrating increased understanding and proficient application of the writing process through planning/pre-writing, writing, and editing/publishing; and
- Demonstrating increased proficiency beyond grade level curriculum and benchmarks in establishing focus, using an organizational style, developing support, and properly using writing conventions.

This objective supports the *Frameworks'* Student Outcome Program Goal Seven, which states, "By graduation, the student identified as gifted will be able to develop and deliver a variety of authentic products/performances that demonstrate understanding in multiple fields/disciplines" (FL DOE, 2013a, p. 8). The development of a novel as an authentic product to demonstrate learning in the discipline of writing directly addresses this goal. Supplementary *Frameworks* objectives of Goal Seven (FL DOE, 2013a), like the broad synthesis of knowledge and skills from multiple fields or the communication of expertise to authentic audiences, could be met through the successful composition of a narrative story or the subsequent publication of the novel in digital and print formats for authentic student and adult audiences.

The second learning objective of the implementation was to improve knowledge and application of a personal goal-setting process, including setting an appropriate goal, developing and implementing an action plan, monitoring progress, and reflecting on personal achievement. This learning objective supports the *Frameworks'* Student Outcomes Program Goal Six, which states, "By graduation, the student identified as gifted will be able to set and achieve personal, academic, and career goals" (FL DOE, 2013a, p. 8). Program Goal Six names three subordinate objectives:

1. The identification and acceptance of challenges within one's areas of strength and weakness,
2. Personal ownership of learning, including setting appropriate goals, and
3. Construction of action plans for pursuing personal goals and for overcoming obstacles during pursuit (FL, DOE, 2013a).

In the course of improving knowledge and application of a personal goal-setting process, participation in the Young Writers Program can help students strategically work on each of these subordinate objectives from the *Frameworks*.

Prior to the onset of the program, the general education instruction and expectations in these two learning objective areas did not fully meet the needs of the participating gifted students. For example, in the general education classroom, demands for student achievement in writing at grade level did not address the writing potential of this group of gifted students. The standard requirement for narrative writing for these third through fifth graders was the completion of a five paragraph narrative essay, which was to include an introductory paragraph, three supporting action/event paragraphs, and a conclusion paragraph. This grade level instruction for organizational planning, limited to a sequential beginning, middle, and end, did not explore the application of flashbacks, stories within stories, in media res, or other more advanced uses of organizational structures for plot. Moreover, the use of an essay formatting for the narrative restricted instruction of more advanced techniques in formatting and conventions (Olthouse, 2012), like the proper use of new paragraphs for conversational dialogue. In contrast, writing instruction for gifted learners should require the use of imagination and higher-level thinking (Olthouse, 2012; Smutny, 2001). These examples of more complex structures mirror the organizational styles used in the novels these students were reading and more aptly meet the students' needs for intellectual challenge.

In addition to limited writing instruction in organization, content, and conventions, the length – and therefore, depth – of narrative development within the general education classroom curriculum lacked the intellectual demand needed by the gifted students. The approximate expected word-count length for standard narratives of the fourth and fifth graders in the school were about 250-350 and 300-400 words respectively. As is demonstrated by the outcomes of this program, the potential of the participating gifted students far exceeded the assignments given to them in the general education classroom. As a collective result of previous instruction, at the onset of the program, the quality of the gifted students' writing varied from adequate to masterful, yet all within the expected parameters of their grade level.

Beyond the varying levels of writing achievement, student attitudes toward writing and goal-setting were also diverse within the group. With regards to writing, student attitudes varied with two students expressing negative attitudes toward writing, seven students expressing neutral attitudes toward writing, four students expressing positive attitudes toward writing, and three students expressing strong positive attitudes. In many cases, the quality of student writing generally correlated with the participating students' attitudes toward writing.

Similarly, prior to the program implementation, participating gifted students had limited opportunities to set and pursue personally established academic goals in the general education classroom. As such, most students had little to no experience in choosing appropriate personal goals or developing the attitudes necessary to persevere in achieving them.

Given this background, through pursuit of each of the stated goals and objectives, the implementation of the Young Writers Program had the potential to benefit the gifted students' development both academically and affectively.

The Implementation

The implementation of the National Novel Writing Month Young Writers Program at McKeel Elementary Academy involved three phases: the planning phase prior to November 1, the writing phase between November 1 and 30, and the editing and publishing phase between November 30 and the end of the school year.

The Planning Phase

Beginning approximately four weeks before the November 1 novel-writing phase, the participating gifted students began their goal-setting and planning for their novel. In order to set an appropriate, yet challenging, word-count goal, the students considered several factors: time, type-based writing speed, grade-based recommendations, personal ability, and motivation. Using an interactive Word-Count Goal Calculator on the Young Writers Program website, students factored in their type-based writing speed and the amount of time they estimated could be spent writing their novel to calculate the approximate number of words they would be able to write during the month. Next, students referenced the YWP's grade level recommendation table (http://ywp.nanowrimo.org/wordcount), which provided a range of goals for each grade level. The fourth grade word-count goal recommendations ranged from 500 to 1,200 words; the fifth grade recommendations ranged from 800 to 2,000 words. By comparing their calculated estimate of words with the grade level recommendations and their personal assessment of their own writing abilities and motivation, students chose and committed to a word-count goal for their novel. The word-count goals set by the participating students ranged from 2,500 words to 18,000 words. Each of these self-established student goals represented an aspirational benchmark above even the highest grade level recommendations. Students signed commitment contracts, which were posted on a bulletin board alongside the classes' tracking poster.

While the students could not begin writing their novels until November 1, the program does allow for pre-planning and development of the characters, plot and other story elements. The *National Novel Writing Month's Young Novelist Workbook: Elementary School* includes a robust framework for brainstorming and plotting out the novel before writing (Office of Letters and Light Young Writers Program, 2010). While not using every part of the *Workbook*'s curriculum, the students did draw from and participate in a variety of the included activities in order to develop their story concept and characteristics of the main characters as well as construct a detailed plot outline "rollercoaster." In the planning stage, the use of graphic organizers as scaffolding (Price & Harkins, 2011), such as the character and "rollercoaster" activities provided in the *Young Novelist Workbook*, has the potential to significantly improve student achievement in writing. Additionally, consistent with a *knowledge transformation model* of composition appropriate for gifted learners (Smith, 2008), the students focused on depth of characterization, setting, and detailed plot as a means to guiding their novel development. Throughout planning, students shared their novel concepts with the class to obtain peer feedback and identify holes in the character development or plot outlines. The time spent focused on planning and development was critical to the students' ability to begin extensive writing on November 1.

The Writing Phase

With detailed planning and development behind them, the sixteen gifted students began the writing phase of the program on November 1. Our implementation of the writing phase of the program included several diverse elements.

1. *Cloud-based word processing for personal and collaborative document access during writing, editing, and peer-review:* The primary technological platform for the students' novel writing was the Google Docs word processor. At the onset of the program, all of the participating students had basic technological proficiency in word processing, email, and web navigation, which was easily transferred to the Google Docs platform. Plus, by creating a cloud-hosted Google document as the format for their novel draft, the students benefitted in three ways.

First, the digital platform allowed students to type their stories instead of hand-writing them, which had several advantages. For example, based on anecdotal observations during previous digital storytelling activities, students at MEA demonstrated longer task commitment and increased composition length when typing stories than when hand-writing them. Also, reflective of research regarding the use of technology in gifted education (Periathiruvadi & Rinn, 2012), the participating students expressed more enjoyment when using the technological platform than when writing with traditional tools like pencil and paper. Moreover, the typed stories were easier to edit and re-format as the students composed their novels, whereas handwritten compositions would have required being fully rewritten to accomplish any major editorial changes.

Second, the cloud-based platform provided around-the-clock student access to the composition. Whether using personal devices outside of school, using netbooks in the general education classroom, or using desktop computers in the computer lab during their gifted pull-out classes, the students could access their Google document. Confirmed in observations by their general education teachers, this ease of access prompted students to make more effective use of their personal downtime (frequently caused by finishing work at a faster pace than general education students) during the school day. Moreover, the students were able to immediately add to their novels when motivated or inspired despite their location or time of day.

Third, by hosting their compositions as a cloud-based Google document, the students could easily share their novel in a live document format with parents, teachers or other students. Sharing the documents provided students with the ability to garner real-time feedback and comments even while the novels were still in progress.

2. *A daylong Write-a-thon kick-off, including a videoconferenced interview with an author:* On November 3, what would have been the first gifted pull-out class day of the month, all of the participating gifted students engaged a full-day Write-a-thon to kick off the writing phase of the program. The Write-a-thon took place in a large multipurpose room at the school for approximately six hours with regularly scheduled breaks throughout the day. The size of the room allowed the students to create a preferred personal working environment whether near or far from other students, on the floor or at a table, et cetera. Students used netbook computers and the school's Wi-Fi network to access their cloud-based Google documents during the duration of the Write-a-thon.

During the last hour of the Write-a-thon event, the students collectively used Skype to videoconference with Fred Koehler, a local children's book author. The use of videoconferencing can allow students to connect with experts and mentor figures, despite distance and time limitations (Howland, Jonassen, & Marra, 2012). In alignment with NAGC's Gifted Programming Standards (2010), this particular videoconference interaction with a successful author connected the gifted students with a local expert and role model, demonstrating to them that reaching their ambitious writing goals was a realistic possibility (Pleiss & Feldhusen, 1995). The videoconference consisted of Koehler's presentation from his own experiences in writing his first novel, followed by a showcase of his writing and illustrations for children's picture books. Following the presentation, the students were able to ask questions of Koehler regarding his planning and writing process, his process for conquering writer's block, and other topics of interest.

3. *Extended blocks of uninterrupted writing time:* In addition to the long blocks of extended writing time established during the Write-a-thon, students continued to engage in extended blocks of uninterrupted work time throughout the month-long writing phase. The purpose of this element of the implementation was to promote the development of concentration and task commitment in the gifted students throughout the program. Joseph Renzulli portrays task commitment as a cluster of traits, including determination and will power, which are vital

to creative productivity (2012). Renzulli further stated, "one of the primary ingredients for success among persons who have made important contributions to their respective performance areas is their ability to immerse themselves fully in a problem or area for an extended period of time and to persevere even in the face of obstacles that would inhibit others" (p. 153, 2012). Other research of high-performing student creative writers suggests that the provision of structured writing time and deadlines is critical to sustained creative writing success (Olthouse, 2012). In a typical gifted pull-out class period during the program, students would have 45-60 minutes of time to work on their compositions. By having these long blocks of uninterrupted work time, the students' speed of writing and ability to focus noticeably increased throughout the month. Four of the students who had significantly struggled to focus on independent tasks prior to the NaNoWriMo program improved in their length of continuous attention to their work during the month. Moreover, all of the students learned and adapted new strategies that allowed them to take personal breaks as needed during these blocks without interrupting the other learners.

4. *Mini-lessons, including use of the robust National Novel Writing Month's Young Novelist Workbook:* Elementary School *(Office of Letters and Light Young Writers Program, 2010).* In addition to the extended blocks of dedicated writing time, during gifted pull-out classes, students engaged mini-lessons on a variety of writing strategies. The topics for both corporate and personalized mini-lessons were selected in response to students' self-identified needs and formative assessment via ongoing teacher observations. These topics included the use of various organizational strategies, such as the inclusion of a flashback or letter, as well as strategies for using content and conventions like narrator's point of view, figurative language, sensory-based descriptions, or the proper use of dialogue. Many of these mini-lessons drew from examples and activities within the *Young Novelist Workbook*, while others were taught through observation, inference, and discussion of published youth novels from the classroom or school library (Olthouse, 2012). The use of these strategic mini-lessons created an inductive learning environment that insured all students were making individualized progress toward the intended learning objectives and that opportunities for just-in-time learning were maximized (Renzulli, 2012).

While students were encouraged to immediately incorporate their new learning into their writing and continue use throughout the remainder of their compositions, students were discouraged from going back to edit or change what they had already written until the editing phase of the program. This practice served two purposes. First, it allowed students to focus on completing their stories without self-judging their in-process piece. Second, it allowed the novel composition itself to serve as a living and evolving documentation of their improvements in the use of various writing elements. For some students, a story that began as a single two-page paragraph suddenly emerged into separated paragraphs; for others, a "telling-style" story told by a third person narrator suddenly began to "show" the story through included dialogue and action. Use of grammar, punctuation, and more complex writing strategies and conventions noticeably improved for all students. Moreover, the students were able to observe, identify, and describe the changes and improvements they were making. This empowered them to continue putting effort into this academic growth throughout the program, as well as guided their action during the editing phase of the program.

5. *Technology-based research and resources to enhance content, word choice, spelling, and grammar:* As an added benefit to using a technology-based platform for writing, students had access to robust online resources for use in content research and writing support. During the course of the implementation, all of the students used online resources like digital dictionaries and thesauruses to improve the quality and precision of their word choices. Moreover, many of the students used online research to inform the accuracy of their descriptions of geographic places, behaviors and characteristics of various animals, and even the workings of machinery or scientific concepts relevant to their stories. In addition to online resources, students were able to harness the capabilities of the Google Docs word processor's spelling and grammar check in order to identify and correct errors in conventional use. Students used these editing features at various times during the program. Some students used them to improve their writing during the composition process while others found the digital notifications of errors to be a distraction to the writing process and chose to disable the features until the editing phase of the program. In both cases, access to these features enabled students to correctly transfer more advanced words from their verbal vocabulary into their written vocabulary, as well as to experiment with more complex sentence structures.

6. *Access to the online NaNoWriMo class environment and global online community as means of motivation, self-directed monitoring and goal-setting:* One of the most powerful elements of participating in the National Novel Writing Month Young Writers Program was the connection to both the virtual class and YWP environments on the NaNoWriMo YWP website (http://ywp. nanowrimo.org). Like those in many other virtual learning spaces (Burke & Settles, 2011; Gee, 2004; Howland, Jonassen, & Marra, 2012), participants in the Young Writers Program benefit from the use of Internet-based interactive and networking technologies in enabling powerful communication and collaboration within the virtual class environment and global YWP community.

First, the virtual class environment enabled a sense of camaraderie between the students both during and beyond the school day. Within the virtual class environment, the participating gifted students posted and shared their personal word-count goals, creating accountability to themselves and each other. Then, throughout the duration of the program, students monitored their writing progress using an online word-count tracking tool, which displayed their percentage of completion to the group. This proved to be a very motivating aspect to the virtual class site. Students could determine whether they were on track for completion by comparing their percentage of writing completion to the percent of the days in the month that had passed. Seeing their progress in this way developed self-direction and responsibility for each student's own success. Furthermore, students gained inspiration by seeing their peers succeeding at meeting their goals. As one student would post their progress, other students would be reminded that attaining their goal was possible and push to reach their next word-count benchmark.

Second, the students found great motivational value in being connected to the Young Writers Program online community. From that community, students could see that they were part of a global writing movement including tens of thousands of students from over two thousand schools in countries around the world (National Novel Writing Month, 2012). Participation in such online writing communities can benefit gifted students through the mirroring of common practices by published authors, such as writing, critiquing or publishing compositions (Olthouse & Miller, 2012). Moreover, participation in the social aspects of online communities like that of National Novel Writing Month, which support the attainment of challenging goals, has been shown to increase performance in achieving those goals (Barack, 2009; Burke & Settles, 2011). Based on comments made by students during the implementation, involvement in the program created a sense of belonging and connectedness to something greater than themselves. Furthermore, the online community included a variety of resources for the students. Whether from a writing tip, a daily idea to include in their stories, or a "pep talk" from a published author, the students were regularly drawing inspiration and ideas from their participation in the online community.

Each of these six elements worked together to promote the growth and success of each of the students. As the month drew to an end, nearly half of the participating students exhibited such commitment to their goal and the program that they voluntarily came to the gifted classroom before and after school to access and work on their novels. By the end of the month, both during and outside of class, the students rarely required redirection as they felt ownership and dedication to the writing task at hand.

Throughout the last week of the month, as students completed their novels and achieved their writing goals, they posted their final numbers to the virtual classroom on the NaNoWriMo YWP website. On December 1, during their gifted pull-out class, the students celebrated their accomplishments during the program. Those students who met their personal word-count goals received a certificate and a pin-back button. All students who participated took time to reflect on the program as a whole and to share with the group, not only about the length and content of their stories, but also about their personal struggles and successes in their aim to reach their personal goal. In addition to serving as a recognition of the students' accomplishments, this time of reflection and celebration was also a valuable reprieve for the students between the writing and editing phases of the program.

The Editing and Publishing Phase

Following the writing phase, students engaged in a series of editing activities in preparation for publishing their novels for authentic audiences. First, having finally completed the entire story, the students returned to the beginning of their novel. As they worked through the composition, students:

- Read the entire novel in order to identify typos and errors, as well as areas needing improvement,
- Corrected errors identified by the word processor's spelling and grammar check,
- Improved consistency in formatting and organizational style throughout the novel, and
- Improved the writing at the beginning of the novel to reflect their writing growth throughout the novel writing process.

Next, the students printed out two copies of their novel to share for feedback (Olthouse, 2012). One copy was shared with a parent or other adult that could give honest notes and feedback on the novel. The other copy was exchanged with a classmate for peer review. During the peer review, students "marked up" the copy they received, helping each other to identify areas of the novel needing improvement such as passages that were unclear, formatting needing to be corrected, and even spelling errors. Upon reception of both sets of notes and recommendations, students went back to their cloud-based digital document to make needed improvements and edits to their novels. Finally, the students shared the digital copy of the novel with me to garner recommendations on final edits before publication.

As an important element to the authentic learning of writing, the students further prepared their edited novels for digital and/or print publication and distribution to real audiences. This element is not only an important conclusion to the full writing process, but serves as the communication of expertise through presented products to authentic audiences, meeting a primary student objective for demonstration of mastery across disciplines in Goal Seven of the *Florida Framework's for K-12 Gifted Learners* (FL DOE, 2013a). Using the desktop publishing features of the word processor and available published novels as models, students created the title and introductory pages of their book; established appropriate margins, page sizes, and chapter breaks; and drafted their cover design. Once formatting was completed, students' novels were saved in portable document format (pdf) for digital publication to the school's website in order to grant access to the school's student body. In addition, the first page of each composition was published in the school's annual literary anthology with an accompanying link to the full digital novel.

In addition to digital publication within the school, students who met their personal word-count goals by the November 30th deadline were granted five free printed copies of their novel via the National Novel Writing Month Young Writers Program's partnership with Amazon's Createspace (www.createspace.com). The site allowed students to upload their properly formatted digital novel document and to create a professional looking cover. While other parts of this program were primarily completed through the gifted class, due to the requirement for detailed personal information in Createspace's publishing process, students choosing to print paperback copies of their novels instead received a redemption code, which they used with their parents in ordering their printed books. Upon delivery, the students who chose to print their books were extremely pleased and several of them donated a paperback copy to the school's library collection.

Outcomes

Participation in the National Novel Writing Month Young Writers Program was an exceptionally successful experience for the sixteen participating gifted students at McKeel Elementary Academy. All students participating in the program demonstrated increased learning gains as a result of the real-world project-based learning, global project participation, and technology-infusion included in the program implementation. In terms of the first learning objective, 100% of the students were able to identify and apply advanced writing skills as a result of the program. Each of the students learned and successfully applied new strategies for use in the writing process, including increased depth of character development, more detailed plot diagraming during planning, suspension of editing during the writing/drafting phase, and improved approaches for editing and peer feedback. Moreover, 100% of students demonstrated proficiency beyond grade-level curriculum and benchmarks in establishing focus, using an organizational style, developing support, and properly using writing conventions. Specific writing element improvements and achievements observed during the program included the increased proper use of paragraph breaks and conventions for dialogue, improved use of consistent or strategic narrative voice, and increased inclusion of advanced writing elements such as metaphor, simile, onomatopoeia, and varied or complex sentence structures. Moreover, fifteen of the sixteen students (94%) completed the composition a long narrative story of greater length, detail and support than both general education grade level requirements and the highest NaNoWriMo YWP grade level word-count recommendations.

In addition to improvements in writing achievement during the novel writing process, another particularly interesting result regarding their writing emerged: the students' individual and collective attitudes toward writing became more positive. In fact, during the program itself, the two students who previously demonstrated the most negative attitudes toward writing surpassed their personal word-count goals in order to properly complete the telling of their story, writing 3,546 words for a 2,500 word-count goal and 14,375 words for a 12,000 word-count goal. Moreover, once the participating students both developed the concentration and discipline needed to write for extended blocks of time and accomplished the completion of a significant written composition, the students subsequently tackled new required writing tasks with increased optimism and ease. For example, during a blogging activity, even the students previously negative and unmotivated toward writing assignments began working quickly and without complaint upon realizing they would be writing a mere one or two paragraphs. In fact, due to their personal observations and reflection on their growth as writers, all fifteen of the students who achieved their word-count goals before and after the deadline demonstrated increased confidence in their own writing abilities and a more positive attitude toward written assignments following the program. Whereas they had previously seen themselves as *students* of writing before the program, many of the students noted that they instead saw themselves as young *authors* who were learning to improve their writing (Black, 2011).

In regard to the second learning objective, students demonstrated various degrees of success within the engagement of the personal goal-setting process, which included setting an appropriate goal, developing an action plan, monitoring progress, and reflecting on personal achievement. As a result of this program, thirteen out of the sixteen participating students achieved their ambitious personal word-count goals (ranging from 2,500 – 18,000 words) by the November 30 deadline. While the National Novel Writing Month program reported that 16,334 out of approximately 51,000 participating young writers, or about 32%, met their word-count goals in 2011 (2012), about 81% of the participating gifted students at McKeel Elementary Academy met their word-count goals as a result of this implementation. Of the thirteen students who completed their writing goals by the NaNoWriMo deadline, eleven students completed the editing and publishing phase by the deadline for publication in the school's literary anthology and website. Additionally, despite not reaching their proposed word-count goals by the deadline, two of the three other students demonstrated personal ownership and application of the goal-setting and learning process as a result of this program. Without any external incentive, these two students pushed on to complete their personal writing goals in December even after the deadline. Moreover, both of these students completed the editing and publishing process in time to have their novels published in the school's literary anthology and on the school website.

In terms of the four components of an effective goal-setting process specific to the learning objectives of the program (setting an appropriate goal, developing an action plan, monitoring progress, and reflecting on personal achievement), student outcomes were as follows. Based on teacher observations, reflective interviews with the students, and the completion outcomes of the program, it was determined that fifteen of the sixteen students originally set an appropriate, yet challenging, personal goal for the month-long program. In the case of the sixteenth student, while the exceptionally high word-count goal was generally attainable by this student, it was not attainable for this student given his specific time restraints during these thirty days. Although this student's goal was not obtained during the given timeframe, this student was one of the students who continued writing and completed their novel during the following month. Moreover, during reflection, this student noted that he had learned about balancing a desire for challenge with realistic factors in setting goals, as well as a need for increased discipline and progress monitoring when attempting a more challenging long-term goal. Even given the unique outcome and reflection of this student, evidence demonstrated that, despite whether the goals were attained, all participating students successfully and reflectively engaged the concept of setting appropriate personal goals.

Furthermore, each of the students learned and successfully applied methodology for developing an action plan and monitoring their progress. While not all students implemented the same action planning and progress monitoring process, successful practices included creating task lists, mapping out a writing schedule on a calendar, dividing the word-count goal into 10 portions in order to schedule and track intermediate benchmarks, and using the embedded progress monitoring application within the NaNoWriMo website. Likewise, all of the students, regardless of success in meeting their word-count goals, participated fully in the reflection portion of the program. Each student identified areas in which they recognized personal strengths and areas in which they struggled throughout the program. While some of these reflections regarded academic achievement, many of the noted areas regarded self-discipline, time-management, peer-support, self-esteem and other affective characteristics. Based on teacher observations and student interviews, 100% of the students demonstrated improved knowledge and application of an effective personal goal-setting process as a result of the program.

Additionally, two unintentional outcomes of the program were observed. Based on teacher observations, the participating gifted students developed an expanded sense of interest and empathy in their fellow students, marked by increased interpersonal questioning and affirmation during and after the program. This improvement correlates with the desired student outcomes of the National Association for Gifted Children's Gifted Programming Standards, encouraging affective growth that includes the ability to "demonstrate understanding of and respect for similarities and differences between themselves and their peer group" and to engage in beneficial "social interactions with others having similar interests and abilities or experiences, including same-age peers and mentors or experts" (NAGC, 2010, p. 1). An increase in empathy, a core aspect of emotional intelligence, is beneficial not only to the overall development of the gifted child, but has also been linked to overall increases in academic achievement (Clark, 2002; Goleman, 1995; Goleman, 2006; Renzulli, 2012). Therefore, while this emotional growth was not a program objective, this result added to the comprehensive success of the school's implementation.

Moreover, the second unintentional outcome was the initiative taken by several students who went on to independently self-publish their novels. Using the Createspace platform, these students professionally published their novels via a "print on demand" agreement with Amazon. Although advertising and selling their books primarily to family and friends, the students were encouraged, seeing that their novels were garnering an authentic audience and authentic feedback. In the months following professional publication, one fourth grader even reached number seven on the Amazon bestsellers list for Sci-fi/Fantasy (Large Print). When this student made the bestsellers list, and subsequently received her first royalty check for the novel, it impressed upon all of the students that they need not wait until they are adults to make an important contribution to the world. They recognized that, even while they were elementary students, their voices and contributions were valuable to each other and to the world. Furthermore, the self-motivation, effort and achievement displayed in the professional publication of these novels demonstrated advanced achievement by these students in the program's two correlating Student Outcome Program Goals from *Florida's Frameworks for K-12 Gifted Learners*: the ability "to set and achieve personal, academic, and career goals" and the ability "to develop and deliver a variety of authentic products/performances that demonstrate understanding in multiple fields/disciplines" (FL DOE, 2013a, p. 8).

CONCLUSION

The implementation of the National Novel Writing Month Young Writers Program with the gifted and talented students at McKeel Elementary Academy was successful at harnessing the benefits of real-world project-based learning, global project participation, and technology-infusion in order to increase learning. All of the sixteen participating fourth and fifth grade gifted students demonstrated gains in both of the stated learning objectives of the program. First, they successfully identified and applied advanced writing skills, including demonstrating increased understanding and proficient application of the writing process through planning/pre-writing, writing, and editing as well as demonstrated increased proficiency beyond grade level curriculum and benchmarks in establishing focus, using an organizational style, developing support, and properly using writing conventions Second, they improved knowledge and application of a personal goal-setting process, including setting an appropriate goal, developing an action plan, monitoring progress, and reflecting on personal achievement. Two additional outcomes were observed. The participating gifted students demonstrated an expanded sense of interest and empathy in their fellow students as a result of the program, and several students independently took the initiative to self-publish their novels, leading one student to obtain Amazon best-seller status. Based on these outcomes and their alignment with research-based best practices for gifted and talented education, it is likely that the replication of this technology-infused implementation of the National Novel Writing Month Young Writers Program would benefit other gifted and talented learners as well.

Furthermore, in light of these outcomes, further research into the use of the National Novel Writing Month Young Writers Program is warranted. Research opportunities exist to investigate the quantitative and qualitative results of the program with larger samples of gifted elementary students, to explore the outcomes of use of the program and curriculum with gifted middle and high school students, to compare the outcomes of the program in use with gifted and general education populations, and to track the long term effects on participating students.

Challenges Facing the Organization

There were two challenges to the implementation of the National Novel Writing Month Young Writers Program. First, garnering the support of the participating students' parents was crucial to supporting the students in the pursuit of such ambitious, advanced goals that would take place both in and out of the school day. During the implementation, misunderstandings about the nature of and best practices for the gifted had to be addressed in order to acquire this support. For example, upon hearing of their student's self-chosen word-count goals, several parents felt that the goals may have been too high and that their student should chosen a lesser goal. Fortunately, through one-on-one conversations with these parents about the program goals, relevant research and best practices of gifted education, they were able to see how this program could provide their child with a low-risk opportunity to explore the reaches of their own potential. At the conclusion of the program, these parents were pleasantly surprised to see what their child had accomplished, which built trust, confidence and an openness for conversations about the nature of their child's giftedness and the scope of opportunities that might benefit them in the future. Many of the parents even remarked that this was one of the best projects in which their child had ever participated.

The second challenge to this and similar projects is managing the curriculum and classroom environment while students are learning and completing work at differing paces. While this was not as much of an issue during the planning and writing phases (as all students were able to use the entirety of the class time offered despite widely varying word-count goals), during the editing and publishing phase, the varying length of the novels significantly affected the amount of time needed for peer review, personal editing, and digital formatting. In order to respectfully use each of the student's time during this phase, we found it important to have other problem solving and creativity activities prepared for early finishers. While some of these activities were related to the writing process, others were not. Nevertheless, all activities available to early finishing students provided them with the chance to begin new work independently and at their own pace. By strategically planning ahead of time to have these resources prepared and accessible, all students were able to engage in meaningful work during all stages of the National Novel Writing Month Young Writers Program implementation.

Solutions and Recommendations

Based on the high levels of success in student writing achievement and goal-setting by the gifted students in this program, several recommendations for best practices can be made for future implementations of the National Novel Writing Month Young Writers Program by other teachers of the gifted and talented. First, educators should implement the program with as much fidelity to the provided curriculum as possible. This curriculum provides a Common Core aligned framework for instructing and facilitating students through the planning, writing, and editing processes (Office of Letters and Light, 2012b). According to Chris Angotti, the Director of Programs for National Novel Writing Month, anecdotal evidence suggests that "commitment to the model (using the lesson plans, "gamifying" the month, and frequently celebrating milestones) seems to be the most effective" in facilitating successful outcomes in the Young Writers Program (personal communication, November 19,

2013). During our implementation, the use of the NaNoWriMo YWP curriculum for full-length and mini writing lessons, as well as for developing a novel writing action plan and monitoring progress, provided a strong standards-based foundation for writing and goal-setting development that we believe was a significant factor toward student success.

Second, educators should schedule a substantial amount of class time for the program during which students would not merely work through the program's curriculum, but also have access to extended blocks of uninterrupted writing time. Based on program observations, the development of task commitment over the course of the month was crucial in assisting students with the stamina and determination needed to reach these ambitious word-count goals as the deadline approached. Furthermore, the obtainment and sharing of word-count benchmarks or milestones during progress monitoring was essential to sustaining steady motivation throughout the month. When ample time was provided during class time for students to make noticeable progress, they were more likely to regularly reach their benchmarks and continue working on their compositions outside of the gifted classroom. Likewise, the initial Write-a-thon provides an ideal example of how allotting a substantial amount of class time for the program can ensure early success - and consequent motivation - for the new novelists.

Third, if at all possible, the teacher of the gifted should also participate in writing a novel as part of the program. As the teacher of the gifted during our implementation, I committed to full adult NaNoWriMo word-count goal of 50,000 in order to model both the writing and goal-setting process for the students. In addition to the advantages of authentic modeling during the program's lessons, this practice had the added benefit of transforming the student perception of the "teacher" role into the additional roles of writing collaborator, role model and mentor for the program (Armstrong, 1994). Moreover, this shared participation developed a greater sense of camaraderie and trust within the learning environment of the gifted program. Since our implementation in 2011, the Young Writers Program adjusted the virtual class environment's word-count goal settings to allow the teacher to adjust their word-count goal to less than 50,000, making participation more feasible for the typical educator's time limitations.

Finally, educators should aim to harness the capabilities of technology to maximize the potential of a National Novel Writing Month Young Writers Program implementation in positively effecting learning for gifted and talented students. The use of a cloud-based application like Google Docs can provide students with the ubiquitous access to the live composition document needed to facilitate dedicated work within gifted and general education classes, as well as outside of school. The ability to type the novel within a word processor can aid in the speed of writing over time, enable the ability to garner feedback and make extensive edits with greater ease, and provide a dynamic desktop publishing platform. Access to technology-based research and tools can provide the resources necessary for students to improve content, precision of word choice, spelling, and grammar. Participation in the online YWP environment can provide students with digital progress monitoring tools, as well as support and encouragement from the NaNoWriMo YWP and the global online community of participants. Opportunities for videoconferencing with authors or writers can expand student access to impactful role models and mentors. Lastly, web-based systems like Createspace and Amazon can facilitate the culminating act of professionally printing or publishing student writing. As technology resources continue to emerge and evolve, technology-enriched benefits to writing instruction and learning will continue to grow, offering gifted and talented students increasingly powerful opportunities to successfully engage authentic learning experiences like the National Novel Writing Month Young Writers Program.

REFERENCES

6A-6.03019 Special instructional programs for students who are gifted. (2002). *Florida Administrative Code*. Retrieved from https://www.flrules.org/gateway/ruleNo.asp?ID=6A-6.03019

A novel way to hook teens on writing fiction. (2006). *Curriculum Review, 46*(3), 6-7.

Albaili, M. A. (2003). Motivational goal orientations of intellectually gifted achieving and underachieving students in the United Arab Emirates. *Social Behavior & Personality: An International Journal, 31*(2), 107–120. doi:10.2224/sbp.2003.31.2.107

Armstrong, D. C. (1994). A gifted child's education requires real dialogue: The use of interactive writing for collaborative education. *Gifted Child Quarterly, 38*(3), 136–145. doi:10.1177/001698629403800307

Barack, L. (2009). Penultimate. *School Library Journal, 55*(9), 40–41.

Black, N. B. (2011). *This is why I teach: NaNoWriMo* [blog]. Retrieved from http://www.engagingeducation.net/wordpress/this-is-why-i-teach-nanowrimo/

Burke, M., & Settles, B. (2011). Plugged in to the community: Social motivators in online goal setting groups. In *Proceedings of the 5th International Conference on Communities and Technologies*. ACM Digital Library. doi:10.1145/2103354.2103356

Burton, L. D. (2009). Lessons from NaNoWriMo. *Journal of Research on Christian Education, 18*(1), 1–10. doi:10.1080/10656210902752006

Clark, B. (2002). *Growing up gifted: Developing the potential of children at home and at school* (6th ed.). Upper Saddle River, NJ: Pearson/Merrill Prentice Hall.

Colangelo, N., Assouline, S. G., & Gross, M. U. M. (Eds.). (2005). *A nation deceived: How schools hold back America's brightest students.* Belin: Blank Center for Talent Development.

Collins, N. D., & Cross, T. L. (1993). Teaching the writing process to gifted and talented students. *Gifted Child Today, 16*(3), 22.

Dixon, F., Cassady, J., Cross, T., & Williams, D. (2005). Effects of technology on critical thinking and essay writing among gifted adolescents. *Journal of Secondary Gifted Education, 16*(4), 180.

Donnelly, L. (2007, January 1). Write away. *Teacher Magazine, 18*(04), 48.

Florida Department of Education (FL DOE). (2013a). *Florida's frameworks for K-12 gifted learners.* Retrieved from http://www.fldoe.org/bii/Gifted_Ed/

Florida Department of Education (FL DOE). (2013b). *Florida's plan for K-12 gifted education.* Retrieved from http://www.fldoe.org/bii/Gifted_Ed/pdf/StateGiftedPlan.pdf

Gee, J. P. (2004). *Situated language and learning: A critique of traditional schooling.* New York, NY: Routledge.

Gentry, J. (2008). E-publishing's impact on learning in an inclusive sixth grade social studies classroom. *Journal of Interactive Learning Research, 19*, 455–467.

Goleman, D. (1995). *Emotional intelligence.* New York, NY: Bantam.

Goleman, D. (2006). *Emotional intelligence: Why it can matter more than IQ.* New York, NY: Bantam Press.

Howland, J., Jonassen, D., & Marra, R. (2012). *Meaningful learning with technology* (4th ed.). Boston, MA: Pearson.

Jones, K. L. (2013). *Wonks, marathoners, and storytellers: Describing the participatory culture of NaNoWriMo.* (Order No. 3573433, Mercer University). ProQuest Dissertations and Theses, 262.

Kulik, J. A., & Kulik, C. C. (1984). Synthesis of research on effects of accelerated instruction. *Educational Leadership, 42*, 84–89.

Little, C. A. (2012). Curriculum as motivation for gifted students. *Psychology in the Schools, 49*(7), 695–705. doi:10.1002/pits.21621

Morisano, D. M., & Shore, B. M. (2010). Can personal goal setting tap the potential of the gifted underachiever? *Roeper Review*, *32*(4), 249–258. doi:10.1080/027831 93.2010.508156

National Association for Gifted Children (NAGC). (2010). *Pre-K-Grade 12 gifted programming standards*. Retrieved from http://www.nagc.org/index.aspx?id=546

National Novel Writing Month. (2012). *Year thirteen: A lucky number in our book*. Retrieved from http://nanowrimo.org/history#year-thirteen

Nugent, S. A. (2001). Technology and the gifted: Focus, facets, and the future. *Gifted Child Today*, *24*(4), 38–45.

Oettingen, G., Honig, G., & Gollwitzer, P. M. (2000). Effective self-regulation of goal attainment. *International Journal of Educational Research*, *33*(7-8), 705–732. doi:10.1016/S0883-0355(00)00046-X

Office of Letters and Light. (2012a). *For the press*. Retrieved from http://ywp. nanowrimo.org/press

Office of Letters and Light. (2012b). *Lesson plans*. Retrieved from http://ywp. nanowrimo.org/lesson-plans

Office of Letters and Light Young Writers Program. (2010). *National novel writing month's young novelist workbook: Elementary school* (3rd ed.). Berkeley, CA: Office of Letters and Light.

Olthouse, J., & Miller, M. T. (2012). Teaching talented writers with web 2.0 tools. *Teaching Exceptional Children*, *45*(2), 6–14.

Olthouse, J. M. (2012). Why I write: What talented creative writers need their teachers to know. *Gifted Child Today*, *35*(2), 116–121. doi:10.1177/1076217512437732

Periathiruvadi, S., & Rinn, A. (2012). Technology in gifted education: A review of best practices and empirical research. *Journal of Research on Technology in Education*, *45*(2), 153–169. doi:10.1080/15391523.2012.10782601

Pleiss, M. K., & Feldhusen, J. F. (1995). Mentors, role models, and heroes in the lives of gifted children. *Educational Psychologist*, *30*(3), 159–169. doi:10.1207/ s15326985ep3003_6

Price, E. A. & Harkins, M. (2011). Scaffolding student writing. *Language & Literacy: A Canadian Educational E-Journal, 13*(1), 14-38.

Renzulli, J. S. (2012). Reexamining the role of gifted education and talent development for the 21st century: A four-part theoretical approach. *Gifted Child Quarterly, 56*(3), 150–159. doi:10.1177/0016986212444901

Rogers, K. B. (2007). Lessons learned about educating the gifted and talented: A synthesis of the research on educational practice. *Gifted Child Quarterly, 51*(4), 382–396. doi:10.1177/0016986207306324

Schunk, D. H. (1991). Goal setting and self-evaluation: A social cognitive perspective on self-regulation. In M. L. Maehr & P. R. Pintrich (Eds.), Advances in motivation and achievement, (vol. 7, pp. 85-113). Greenwich, CT: JAI Press.

Schunk, D. H., & Swartz, C. W. (1993). Writing strategy instruction with gifted students: Effects of goals and feedback on self-efficacy and skills. *Roeper Review, 15*(4), 225–230. doi:10.1080/02783199309553512

Siegle, D., & McCoach, D. B. (2003). Factors that differentiate underachieving gifted students from high-achieving gifted students. *Gifted Child Quarterly, 47*(2), 144–154. doi:10.1177/001698620304700205

Smith, K. (2008). Teaching talented writers in the regular classroom. *Gifted Child Today, 31*(2), 19–26.

Smutny, J. F. (2001). Creative strategies for teaching language arts to gifted students (K-8) (ERIC Digest E612). Arlington, VA: ERIC Clearinghouse on Disabilities and Gifted Education. Retrieved from http://www.hoagiesgifted.org/eric/e612.html

Thompson, C. (2011). A dose of writing reality: Helping students become better writers. *Phi Delta Kappan, 92*(7), 57–61. doi:10.1177/003172171109200712

VanTassel-Baska, J. (2005). Gifted programs and services: What are the nonnegotiables? *Theory into Practice, 44*(2), 90–97. doi:10.1207/s15430421tip4402_3

Vialle, W., Ashton, T., & Carlton, G. (2001). Acceleration: A coat of many colors. *Roeper Review, 24*(1), 14–19. doi:10.1080/02783190109554119

Watson, A. (2012). NaNoWriMo in the AcadLib: A case study of national novel writing month activities in an academic library. *Public Services Quarterly, 8*(2), 136–145. doi:10.1080/15228959.2012.675273

KEY TERMS AND DEFINITIONS

Cloud-Based Software: A computer program or file system hosted on remote servers such that a user can access it from multiple devices via the Internet.

Goal-Setting: The process by which students set and achieve their own goals, which may include: setting an appropriate goal, developing and implementing an action plan, monitoring progress, and reflecting on personal achievement.

National Novel Writing Month Young Writers Program (NaNoWriMo YWP): A month-long, high-intensity writing program established in 2005 by the Office of Letters and Light in order to support educational efforts to teach novel writing to students.

Online Community: A shared virtual learning space that is established via a web-based platform and promotes communication and collaboration amongst its users.

Pull-Out Program: A gifted program delivery model in which gifted students are removed from their general education classes for a portion of each school day or week in order to participate in separate class activities with gifted peers.

Videoconference: A visual and auditory conversation, facilitated via a digital platform like Skype, which allows users to communicate with people at a remote location or locations.

Writing Process: The process by which students prepare and execute the development of a written composition, which may include planning/pre-writing, writing, editing, and publishing.

Chapter 10
Culturally Relevant Applications of Digital Audio Workstations in the Heterogeneous GT Classroom

Chris Deason
Full Sail University, USA

EXECUTIVE SUMMARY

The purpose of this chapter is to discuss, explain, and share how the author has used culturally relevant instructional methods (i.e., hip-hop pedagogy) and Digital Audio Workstations (DAWs) in K-12 classroom environments to impact learning motivation and learner achievement from 2005 to 2012. Emphasis is placed on the elements of hip-hop culture (i.e., rapping, graffiti art, beat making, and break dancing) combined with DAWs to impact learning motivation and learner achievement in the heterogeneous Gifted and Talented (GT) classroom. Recommended hardware and software is discussed. Examples include audio interfaces, cables and microphones required, recommended audio recording software, and classroom environment preparations. Photographs and illustrations are included to make the chapter applicable to practitioners in classroom environments and educational researchers.

DOI: 10.4018/978-1-4666-6489-0.ch010

ORGANIZATION BACKGROUND

Prior uses of DAWs combined with hip-hop culture include the following:

1. Applications of DAWs to generate social studies-based hip-hop audio CDs for high school age adolescents in the Upward Bound program at Texas Tech University.
2. Applications of DAWs and hip-hop pedagogy to impact reading motivation in an after school program for 4th and 5th Grade children at Oakwood Elementary.
3. Applications of DAWs to impact writing achievement via rap pedagogy at Midway Elementary.

The applications of DAWs to generate social studies-based hip-hop audio CDs for high school age adolescents first took place in the Upward Bound program at Texas Tech University in Lubbock, Texas in 2005. Olthouse (2013) claimed that multi-literacies like writing, rapping, art production, audio production, and other seldom-employed authentic assessments are essential to gifted and talented education. The Upward Bound program provides opportunities for participants to succeed in their pre-college performance and ultimately in their higher education pursuits. The Upward Bound program often serves *gifted and talented* (GT) high school students starting in the 10th grade. Warne, Anderson, and Johnson (2013) warn that many gifted education experts have found that Black, Latino, and Native American students are less likely to be identified for gifted programs than Asian American and White students. The goal of Upward Bound is to recognize GT students, often from minority and underprivileged socio-economic classes, and increase the rate at which these participants enroll in and graduate from institutions of postsecondary education. Most of the learners in Texas Tech's Upward Bound program were Latino and African American learners. Ramos (2010) reminds us that Latinos are underrepresented in gifted and talented programs.

Implementation of DAWs and hip-hop pedagogy to impact reading motivation for gifted and talented 4th and 5th Grade children also took place in Oakwood Elementary school in the West Texas Panhandle in 2008. This particular mixed-method case explored urban elementary children's motivation to read via a culturally relevant computer environment based on results of the Motivation to Read Profile (MRP) questionnaire, Culturally Relevant Pedagogy (CRP) theory Interview Protocol, and several ethnographic data collection methods. CRP theory framed the case and addressed the problem of cultural discontinuity between home culture and school culture.

Lastly, applications of DAWs to impact writing achievement took place at Midway Elementary in Central Florida between 2011 and 2012. Both quantitative and qualitative data were collected. Quantitative data included district assessment scores and summative Florida Comprehensive Assessment Test (FCAT) scores. Qualitative data included two open-ended question video interviews. Emergent codes will be reported. Implications of the data to support 21st Century digital literacy will be discussed.

Setting the Stage

In all three cases discussed herein culturally relevant pedagogy framed and guided the processes of each DAW-based hip-hop program case. The primary goal of each case was to generate learning artifacts including an audio compact disk (CD) of educational and content-based rap songs created entirely by the learners. This included all original beats, all original lyrics, and all original CD jewel case art using Graffiti Art created at the Graffiti Creator website (http://www.graffiticreator.net/).

Ladson-Billings (1995) claimed that culturally relevant pedagogy (CRP) must provide students with cultural integrity while helping them succeed academically. Ladson-Billing's (1995) data suggested that culturally relevant teachers *should raise expectancy and value for classroom academic success* in all domains to its highest potential. Culturally relevant teachers (Ladson-Billings, 1995) should leverage a *community of learners* (Lave & Wenger, 1991) in a collaborative classroom atmosphere rather than promote a competitive environment. Finally, culturally relevant teachers should leverage *assessments and learning tasks that are authentic* in nature (Shank, 1999). DAWs offer this potential to address all three factors of CRP theory.

REVIEW OF RELEVANT LITERATURE

Cultural heterogeneity is the norm within many urban K-12 public schools within the United States today. Protheroe (2003) stated, "Children grow up within culturally situated environments that influence how they present themselves, interpret experiences, and understand the world" (p. 1). Because of this fact, cultural discontinuity can take place between schools, communities, and home cultures. Dimitiradis (2001) argued that a schism has grown between in-school and out-of-school culture, with unofficial curricula (e.g., rap music, hip-hop culture, Black and Latino American film, and music videos) and traditional learning settings (e.g., schools, community centers, churches, and the like). Gay (2002) claimed that misconceptions about culturally situated environments are often due to teachers, schools, and communities lacking knowledge of social contributions made by minority ethnic groups and subgroups. Pewewardy (1993) argued that schools have tried to insert culture into education rather than inserting education into culture.

This case study reported herein was grounded in culturally relevant pedagogy (CRP) theory, which theorized that minority children's self-perception and value for schoolwork would increase in a learning context that was collaborative, authentically assessed and culturally sensitive. Participants claimed that the use of hip-hop culture during the intervention made reading fun, authentic, and collaborative. Comparably, the University of California Berkeley's (UCB's) Youth Hip-Hop Digital Music Production Project integrated hip-hop culture in diverse after-school settings with gifted and talented secondary learners. This project looked to integrate the cultivation and production of music and the arts as a sphere in which gifted and talented urban youth were actively engaged in as producers of hip-hop culture, rap, audio production and video production. UCB's research illustrated that today's youth are coming of age and struggling for their identity amid new potentials for communication, friendship, play, and self-expression. The project summaries and research reports offer practitioners and teachers creative ideas for addressing youth popular culture with gifted and talented urban youth. The uniform resource locator (URL) to download a two-page summary of the findings of the Youth Hip-Hop Digital Music Production project is the following (http://digitalyouth.ischool.berkeley.edu/report.html).

Morgan (2011) reported how ten Black male K-12 teachers used the organizing principles of hip-hop culture for pedagogical purposes and the implications of using popular culture and hip-hop for creating teaching environments that attract and support Black male teachers. Rodriguez (2009) explored cultural capital and student engagement via hip-hop pedagogy in the high school and university classrooms. Darius (2012) noted how hip-hop artists constructed a sense of democratic education and pedagogy with transformative possibilities in their schools and communities.

However, little attention has been paid to the impact of embedding instructional technology into distinct ethnic and cultural value systems (exceptions include Cole, 1998; Deason & Zhang, 2012; Gutierrez, Baquedano-Lopez, & Tejada, 1999; Pinkard, 2001; Serpell & Boykin, 1994). Lee (2003) argued that many computer tools are used under the banner of constructivism assuming homogenous learning structures apply to all students. This efficiency model is limited in that it does not address the social, cultural, and historical values of GT learners. There is little evidence that educational technologies are serving heterogeneous gifted and talented classrooms. Desbottes & Nicholls (2004) argued that GT learners need cross-curricular projects focused on independent learning to explore their hidden talents in unique social settings.

Computer technology and culturally relevant pedagogy should be used as complementary tools for learning and achievement motivation for GT learners. Dede's (2006) research suggested that schools and teachers should capitalize on learners' digital based tool knowledge, especially in an age of ubiquitous technology use and learner diversity. Mahri (2000) posited that Twenty-First Century popular culture pedagogies have the potential to engage people in technologically mediated processes for making meaning and giving meaning to people's lives. Henry Giroux views popular culture such as the hip-hop culture as a legitimate aspect of the everyday lives of students. Pop culture includes ubiquitous digital tools like microcomputers, MP3 players, portable digital assistants (PDAs) and wireless technologies as well as the associated media that includes popular music, text messaging, movies, games, and music videos. Giroux (1997) argued that pop culture becomes a primary force in shaping the various and contradictory positions adolescent students take up and bring to our nation's classrooms. Zyngie (2004) insisted that we should put young people's experiences at the center of any discussion of pedagogy and make learning relevant to children's lives.

Rap music, as pedagogy can be very effective, Lock & Lock (1993) stated, "By getting student's to write their own rap songs, they are obliged to construct their own meanings in verse" (p.244). Mahiri (2000) noted that pop-culture pedagogies dynamically engaged people in technology-mediated processes for constructing meaning. Gifted and talented learners need independent opportunities to construct meaning regarding their learning. Computers may be used as mind-tools (Jonassen, 2003) in which learners can immerse themselves in cognitive flow (Csikszentmihalyi, 1996) and orchestrated immersion. Rap music naturally uses a superimposed meaningful structure and flow (Ormrod, 1999) in the forms of storytelling, poetry, and rhyming, which can lead to improved student learning and long-term memory retention. Hellweg (2005) discussed a successful renovation of the English program through the integration of hip-hop culture and rap lyrics to literature and poetry, and another case with local hip-hop artists in language learning classrooms. Such efforts turned a 70% failure rate into only 2 out of 150 failing her class that year.

McHugh (2005) proposed that educators must work to motivate a new kind of digital learner who interprets the world via computing devices. Shneiderman (2003) claimed that computers are becoming extensions of human creativity. In a well-designed, culturally sensitive multimedia-learning environment, students may learn various knowledge and skills through creation of their own musical representations of the instructional content delivered by their teachers.

Case Descriptions

In the three cases described earlier (i.e., Upward Bound program at Texas Tech University, Oakwood Elementary, and Midway Elementary) digital audio workstations, hip-hop pedagogy and Internet resources were leveraged for teaching, learning, motivation and play. Beisser, Gillespie and Thacker (2013) reported that play is an essential factor in the academic and intellectual growth of gifted and talented learners. Currently, Digital audio workstations (DAWs) have little notoriety as pedagogical tools used for the Social Sciences, reading motivation, and the development of writing skills; exceptions include (Deason & Zhang, 2012) who used hip-hop pedagogy and digital audio workstations to impact motivation for studying United States History. DAWs have little to no references in peer-reviewed literature in general when used for K-12 instructional content acquisition and academic motivation. Code (2007) noted that it is exciting to imagine the effect of the Internet and other emerging technologies on the intellectual and social development of gifted and talented youngsters, as well as on the pursuit of their interests and passions. The remainder of the chapter below will report technology concerns and learning impacts details regarding all three cases.

Technology Concerns

Figure 1 below is photograph taken from Oakwood Elementary and illustrates a typical DAW setup that includes the desktop computer loaded with audio recording software, a USB or Firewire interface, tuned reference studio speakers or headphones, a condenser microphone, and a midi controller.

A typical DAW experience is illustrated in Figure 1 showing a learner from the Oakwood Elementary School producing her song. Technology included a Midi Controller for original music creation, a USB sound interface to plug an allowing condenser microphone input to the desktop computer, and tuned reference monitors for monitoring the quality of recordings.

Figure 1. Photograph of a typical DAW setup

Teachers can transform any desktop computer into a DAW using these components. A midi controller is optional although useful to leverage virtual instruments available in audio software like Ableton Live.

The primary constraints of a classroom-based culturally relevant DAW for GT learners are funding and creative teachers interested in sound engineering. The primary costs are the actual laptop or desktop computer and the audio software required for multitrack recording. Educators can leverage an existing desktop computer or laptop computer to develop a DAW environment for a very low cost. Desktop computers are superior as audio workstations as their harddrives spin at 7200 revolutions per minute (rpm) versus a laptop harddrive, which often spins only at a 5400-rpm rate. Audio recording software can be expensive but there are free sources. For example, the Audacity multitrack recording software for free (http://audacity.sourceforge.net/) could be utilized. Audacity runs on both IBM PC operating systems and Macintosh operating systems, and is easy to master with a little practice. Online support and help materials are free. Audacity exports several file formats like .wav and .MP3 files.

Next, one will need a USB audio interface or an IEEE 1394 Firewire interface cabled to a computer of one's choice. Firewire interfaces have superior data bus rates and appear to have much less audio latency when learners are capturing their vocals for their rap songs. Latency, in this case, refers to the speed at which the audio input reaches the audio output. If the audio latency is too large the learner will hear the audio output from his or her vocal recordings too late, which can throw off the timing of the raps when monitoring with headphones. Condenser microphones used for recording can be very expensive. However, the Audio Technica 20/20 (AT2020) condenser microphone and the M-Audio Nova microphone are both priced at under $100; both of these condenser microphones well for young learners' raps, vocals and when recording instruments of any type. Condenser microphones like the AT2020 require 48-volt phantom power to work properly. Phantom power, in the context of professional audio equipment, is a method for transmitting DC electrical power through microphone cables to operate microphones that contain active electronic circuitry. Almost all USB and Firewire audio interfaces provide the 48-volts of Phantom Power required when recording with condenser microphones. Next, one will need balanced XLR male-to-female microphone cables, which will transfer the learner's audio signal from the microphone into the audio interface. Microphone stands are also essential. A high quality microphone stand with a telescoping boom is highly recommended and will cost under $50. Telescoping boom microphone stands offer more vocal and instrument recording flexibility than a purely vertical stage microphone.

Having a midi controller for utilizing virtual instruments inside of programs like Ableton Live can transform a typical DAW setup into much more than a recording studio. The DAW now becomes a music production center allowing learners to create their own beats and music prior to their vocal recordings. Studio quality tuned reference audio monitor speaker pairs vary greatly in price. Genelec and Tannoy make the best studio monitors. However, for classroom purposes these reference monitor speakers are too costly given most schools' budgetary constraints. M-Audio AV40s cost $149 for the pair and provide very transparent audio clarity for listening to a final mix containing beats and vocals in a classroom based DAW. Both teachers and learners will be amazed at the quality of your vocal recording renderings. Reyes (2010) noted that although all speakers are biased, studio monitors offer a *truer* sound since they offer a wider and flatter frequency response compared to home stereos and car stereo systems. This audio clarity and flatter frequency combined with the low cost of audio software has the potential to offer educators and gifted and talented learners professional tools for audio-based learning artifacts like beat productions and raps.

Sadly, many teachers will not have time to capture learner's original beats using recorded drums and electronic drum machines. Pre-quantized beat loops like Pro-Sessions M-Audio Hella Bumps save time and are helpful when implementing DAW-based hip-hop pedagogy. Quantized beats results in notes being set on beats and on exact fractions of beats allowing the learner to drag and loop the beat seamlessly the entire length of his or her song. Quantized beats offer the teacher and learner rapid hip-hop beat production allowing the instructional focus to revolve around researching, writing and recording the learner's academic raps.

Finally, one will want to set up a proper acoustic recording space by mounting acoustic foam, blankets or anything else that will hang on walls to prevent sound from reflecting within the acoustic recording space. Audio reflections from flat hard walls often create harsh sounds and detrimental feedback that can ruin quality recordings from learners. Combining DAWs with hip-hop pedagogy offers teachers and learners a way to leverage professional tools and culturally relevant pedagogy for gifted and talented learners today.

Technology Components and Learning Impacts of the Upward Bound Program

The Upward Bound program provided a total of $3,700 in funding. This was a four-week summer program. Fifteen learners in the Upward Bound (UB) program at Texas Tech University in the Summer of 2005 were provided with five pre-acquisitioned laptop computers, three CDs of pre-quantized beats to create infinite song loops, five M-audio USB audio interfaces, five AT2020 condenser microphones, five microphone stands, two Denon DNS1000 digital turntables, one two-channel digital USB mixer, five copies of Ableton Live Software, and one wireless inkjet printer. Eric Strong of the UB program leveraged his laptop computers used in his prior projects for the needs of this particular DAW-based hip-hop social studies project; he was a brilliant leader of the Upward Bound program on the campus of Texas Tech University. It is important to leverage all available resources to increase impact and keep costs low. As mentioned prior, finding motivated teachers to support a program of this nature is imperative. Luckily, two talented teachers from the Lubbock Independent School District (LISD) Shirley Green and Gladys Hardaway taught and supported Ubward Bound's DAW based hip-hop pedagogy throughout the summer. The high school participants used the laptops daily for research, word processing, and Web-based writing resources like Rhymezone.com to support their use of rhyming couplets in their rap songs. The laptops were shared among the participants. The Denon DNS1000 digital turntables and USB mixer allowed the learners to practice turntable and deejay skills; turntabilism is a large component of hip-hop culture. The two-channel USB mixer allowed learners to remix their original beats and raps into the Ableton software tracks.

It took an additional two weeks time to compile all the songs, burn multiple copies of the audio CDs, print CD labels, print and insert jewel case inserts, and Xerox multiple copies of the song lyrics for the learners. Figure 2 is a photograph of learners working on the final processes prior to distribution.

Figure 2. Photograph of learners working on final album art and CD jewel case inserts

The three components of Ladson-Billing's (1995) culturally relevant pedagogy (CRP) theory guided the development of the program and the evaluation of the program. The three tenets of CRP theory include the following:

1. High learner expectations.
2. Authenticity of instructional tasks.
3. Creation of a collaborative community of learners.

Learners were given *high expectations for achievement.* Learners were given the *authentic task* of transforming a 500-page high school United States History book into a double compact disc (CD) that included a song book with all songs typed professionally and organized into a 3-ring binder. The goal was to create a Rap music United States History audio CD that might support classroom teachers and secondary student's preparations for the 11ᵗʰ grade social studies Texas Assessment of Knowledge and Skills (TAKS) standardized test. The following URL hosted on the Internet Archive is an example of one learner's final raps regarding Tecumseh's views of the White Man destroying Native American culture and traditions (https://archive.org/details/Virus_583).

Learners were allowed to work together as a *community of learners* in a non-competitive environment to develop and record the CD. Finally, during weeks two and three of the summer program, twenty young children from the Mentoring Activities for Children (MAC) joined our 15 class members for two weeks. The MAC program served children from 6 - 18 having at least one parent incarcerated in a state or federal prison. The following URL provides a video captured by Fox34 in Lubbock, Texas regarding the DAW-driven hip-hop based program from the Upward Bound program (http://tinyurl.com/hiphoppedagogy).

Eight of the fifteen Upward Bound high school learners were female and eleven students were in the eleventh grade. Four learners were seniors in high school. Half of the participants lived with both parents and half lived with just their single mothers or other family relatives. A majority of the learners claimed a middle class family socio-economic status.

There was no statistical significance found between pretest and posttest observations on the United States' History exam administered. However, five learners scored slightly better on the posttest observation than on the pretest observation. In addition, one of the learners that scored better on the posttest had no prior post Civil War U.S. History knowledge. A 66-item Likert-type questionnaire to measure self-esteem and motivation pre and post yielded no statistically significant results. Post- intervention focus group interviews revealed that the learner's tasks in transforming academic content into rap songs was very challenging while also learning how to use the DAW hardware and software simultaneously; this result suggested that more pre-program technical training for the learners was needed allowing learners to focus more on the writing and recording. Positive impacts noted through open coding of post-interview transcriptions included the following:

1. Participants learned to work together on a team and mentor each other to accomplish the goal of producing the audio compact disk.
2. Participants claimed that the project taught them to set their own intrinsically motivated learning goals rather than prompted through external rewards and grades.
3. Participants claimed that recording lyrics took repeated practice, which helped them to memorize the United States history content.
4. Participants claimed that mentoring the Mentoring Activites for Children (MAC) participants gave them a sense of accomplishment while serving their community in a positive way.

Technology Components and Learning Impacts at Oakwood Elementary

Oakwood Elementary leveraged ten of its existing laptop computers for writing songs lyrics, and purchased one wireless laser printer for printing song lyrics, four AT2020 condenser microphones, five telescoping boom microphone stands, two Denon DNS1000 digital turntables, five CDs of pre-quantized beats for creating infinite beat loops in Ableton, one Peavey PA system for live performance opportunities, one Desktop-based PC computer with Ableton Live installed, two USB audio interfaces, and one digital USB mixer. Participants used Rhymezone.com to support their uses of rhyming couplets within their rap songs. Again, Shirley Green and Gladys Hardaway of the LISD supported and helped build the Oakwood Elementary hip-hop pedagogy program on this particular campus from the fall of 2005 until the fall of 2008. Their dedication and support made the program such a success on this particular campus. Technology like DAWs is worthless without creative and dedicated teachers guiding their pedagogical uses. The following URL captures a video from Nancy Sharp's local television show called *Out and About*, which highlights my after school DAW based hip-hop pedagogy program at Oakwood Elementary (http://tinyurl.com/digitalaudioworkstations).

The three components of Ladson-Billing's (1995) CRP theory were again employed. The GT learners were given *high expectations for achievement.* Learners were given the *authentic task* of transforming assigned books from the school library into a double-compact disc (CD) that included a songbook with all songs typed professionally and organized into a 3-ring binder. The goal was to create a Rap CD that the children could take home at the end of the summer program and share with their parents. In addition, the processes allowed the learners to deeply digest the reading content during the rap writing stages. Learners were allowed to work together as a *community of learners* in a collaborative classroom atmosphere rather than promoting a competitive environment. Figure 3 is a photograph of a small team of learners conducting research on their topic, writing their raps using MS Word, and preparing to print their document to the wireless printer.

Figure 4 is a photograph of one of a learner audio monitoring another learner recording her rap song into the Ableton software. The learner needs a headphone to monitor the beat while recording his or her vocals. The other learner needs a headphone to monitor the vocal input to make sure the vocals are not too loud and is staying on beat with the track during the vocal recording processes.

Oakwood Elementary purchased an Aiwata airbrush for graffiti art, and a break-dancing training DVD that was utilized during the 4-week six hours per day summer program. Due to ventilation concerns the airbrush required a dedicated teacher to work with the children in an outdoor setting at the back of the school. Breakdancing was promoted daily throughout the summer program allowing the children an opportunity to form breakdance crews, which promoted dance interpretation of their raps. Figure 5 is a photograph of airbrush work from students on a large sheet of watercolor paper. Learners then took a digital photo of this airbrush work, which ultimately became their album cover for the CD.

Figure 3. Learners working as writing teams on a shared laptop

Figure 4. Student audio monitoring another student's vocal track

Fifty-one fourth and fifth grade participants were involved. The general results are described below. Six guiding research questions were explored at Oakwood Elementary providing data to stakeholders, which included school administrators,

Figure 5. Learner's airbrushed album cover art

teachers at the school and parents of the young GT learners. A control group was used to test compare reading motivation differences with the intervention group. The questions and results included the following:

1. For the intervention group, did the mean difference between pretest and post-test scores on the Motivation to Read Profile (MRP) scales differ significantly from zero? Results using a paired samples t-test indicated that overall, the average difference between pretest and posttest means for the intervention group's pretest and posttest scores were not significantly different from zero. The null hypothesis was retained for the intervention group's *self-concept of reading* scales, *value of reading* scales, and the *full-scale* scores.

2. Between the intervention group and control group, was there a statistically significant mean difference between posttest and posttest scores on the Motivation to Read Profile (MRP) scales? Overall, there were no statistically significant differences found between the intervention group's posttest means and the control group's posttest means using an independent samples t-test.

3. Using the Culturally Relevant Pedagogy (CRP) theory interview protocol piloted and developed by the researcher, what percentage of intervention participants chose hip-hop culture, peer collaboration, or authentic assessment as their primary reading motivator? Overall, *addressing the cultural values of the learner* (i.e., hip-hop culture) was the most frequent choice among the gifted and talented participants. Twenty-five out of 44 participants chose hip-hop culture as their primary reading motivator during the intervention. Table 1 below shows the frequencies and the percentages of intervention participants choosing a particular component of CRP theory as their primary reading motivator.

Table 1. Frequencies and percentages of participant's who chose that particular component of CRP theory as their primary reading motivator

Element of CRP	Frequency	Percentage
Addressing the cultural values of learner	25	56.82
Authentic assessment	12	27.27
Collaborative learning context	7	15.91
Total	44	100.00

Note. Due to the ages of the respondents the words cultural values, authentic assessment and collaborative learning context were not used during the interview processes. Instead, the respondent's choices were hip-hop, making a real CD, and getting to work with peers and friends as a team.

In what ways did available technologies mediate task-engagement during the intervention based on daily participant and teacher 10-second video clips? Overall, five technologies impacted task engagement. The young participants used the digital camera for a myriad of diverse archival activities by learners; these included videos of their rap performances, videos of breakdancing routines, and videos of their airbrushed graffiti art. The DAW was used extensively during the 4-week reading motivation program to make beats and record vocal tracks. The laptops were used predominately for their wireless Internet capabilities and word processing allowing the learners to develop their rap songs based on the books they read during the four weeks. The deejay equipment was used extensively during the final week to remix participants' songs. Participants used the airbrush throughout the intervention to create their name with graffiti letters, and to airbrush t-shirts learners brought from home.

What were the intervention group's perceptions of what it learned during the class based on participant's learning journals they were required to write following each day of the four-week program? Overall, *hip-hop activities inspire reading* from the assigned books, and *new uses of audio technology* represented the primary learning categories claimed based on the emergent codes obtained via content analysis of the learners' journals.

Based on photo-elicited interviews of class activities, what were the intervention groups' perceptions of their primary reading motivators during the 4-week summer program? Each intervention participant shared the use of a digital camera during the four-week program time. Participants received a minimum 15-minute time period with the digital camera during the intervention timeframe for any given day. A kitchen timer was utilized to regulate and promote sharing among participants. At the end of each participant's time period a folder was created with their name and transferred their digital images and videos they captured to their laptop. Windows XP's slide show function was used to review photographs with participants. At the end of the summer program, participants were asked to pick the photograph that most represented the primary motivating factor(s) for reading and learning in the class. Once chosen, the photograph was renamed with the participant's first name and last initial. The interview then commenced. Participants were asked to explain *which* photograph they selected, and explain *why* they chose the particular photograph as representative of their reading motivation. Each interview lasted no more than 5 to 10 minutes. *Peer collaboration* represented 17 out of 50 or 34% of participants' reading motivation claims. Beisser, Gillespie, & Thacker (2013) reported that play is a way to increase attention, retention, and focus in learning and helps gifted and talented children to develop teamwork and problem-solving skills. *Hip-hop culture* represented 13 out of 50 or 26% of participants' reading motivation claims. *Teacher collaboration* represented 11 out of 50 or 22% of participants' reading motivation claims. Last, *authentic assessment* represented 9 out of 50 or 18% of participants' reading motivation claims. *Makes learning fun* was the primary explanation of *why* they chose peer collaboration, hip-hop culture, teacher collaboration, and authentic assessment.

Oakwood Elementary's DAW-based hip-hop pedagogy program continues in 2014 as a sustainable daily course option now entitled *Sound Engineering* for fourth and fifth grade learners. The program has continued for over 7 years now with the support of the school principal and a dedicated core group of teachers. Quality teachers make DAW-based hip-hop pedagogy programs sustainable.

Technology Components and Learning Impacts at Midway Elementary

The goal at Midway Elementary in central Florida was to improve writing and vocabulary skills for nineteen 4th and 5th grade GT participants. Midway did not provide funding; existing hardware and software were leveraged or donated. The learners named themselves the Midway Hip-Hop Writers. A volunteer teacher, Beth Pocious, and I leveraged the use of an available Macintosh desktop that had Garageband pre-installed as the primary DAW. Garageband is part of the iLife Suite of tools from Apple products. Garageband is very easy to use, and exports in AIFF, AAC, and MP3 formats. The primary researcher donated an external PreSonus Firewire sound card, and an M-audio Nova condenser microphone. The class took place from 10:30 am to Noon EST every Wednesday from the fall of 2011 through the spring of 2012. Midway leveraged a cart of iPads for word processing, research, and beat making. However, learners primarily composed their raps with pencils and ruled paper. Visual Thesaurus (www.visualthesaurus.com) and Wikirhymer (http://wikirhymer.com/) were leveraged on the iPads for lyric writing support. A private Edmodo-based learning management system class was leveraged to allow participants to share and upload their Mp3 exports from Garageband, and critique each other's songs. The Edmodo learning management system allowed sharing with parents and promoted Facebook-like discussions among the learners. The writing themes in the fall included *Favorite Foods, Holidays and Pets*. The writing theme in the spring was *My Hero*. Code (2007) argued that technologies such as web portals and digital audio are noteworthy technology resources allowing gifted and talented students opportunities for research, parent communication, and authentic sharing. Eckstein (2009) concurs with Code's sentiment that Web 2.0 tools offer gifted and talented educators and learners the potential to enrich learning with collaborative portals allowing students to share resources and ideas and complete authentic learning artifacts.

Again, the three components of Ladson-Billing's (1995) CRP theory framed the design of the case. Learners were given *high expectations for writing achievement.* Learners were given the *authentic task* of composing raps about their favorite foods, holidays, pets and their hero into a double compact disc (CD) that included a song-book with all songs printed and organized into a three-ring binder. Learners were allowed to work together as a *community of learners* in a collaborative classroom atmosphere rather than promoting a competitive environment. Many of the learners formed their own writing teams.

To address the hip-hop component of deejaying the primary researcher donated a CD of M-audio Hella Bumps quantized beats. Learners were taught how to preview the beats and then how to drag their quantized loop to track one in Garageband. Most learners rarely needed more than a two-minute beat loop to execute their rap. Learners would then record their rap into track two using the donated M-audio Nova condenser microphone and the Firewire interface. In the spring we installed the Idle drum sequencer application to all iPads, which allowed learners to create their own unique and personalized beats. The Idle drum sequence can be down-loaded from the following URL (https://itunes.apple.com/app/idle-drum-sequencer/id458037926?mt=8). The photograph in Figure 6 illustrates learners using the Idle Sequence App on the school's iPads. To transfer the beats from the Idle software on the iPad we used a 1/8 TRS to 1/4 TRS cable connecting the iPad to the PreSonus sound interface allowing the beats to be recorded by Garageband.

To address graffiti art we prompted the learners to create digital graffiti online using Graffiti Creator at (http://www.graffiticreator.net/). Learners developed their own album art that was turned into a graffiti book that complimented their final lyric book by the end of the school year.

Learning impacts were measured with quantitative data using two formative district writing assessments and the summative Florida Comprehensive Assessment Test (FCAT) for writing. The results are illustrated in Figure 7. District writing scores are on a 5-point scale from 1 to 5. Zero infers the learner did not take the assessment due to an absence the day the assessment was measured. Ten out of nineteen of the Hip-Hop Writers made improvements in their district writing scores as the year progressed.

Qualitative data involved two summative open-ended video interview questions prior to the summer break of 2012. Open coding using the constant comparative method was used to analyze these interview data.

Question One asked participants to explain how the technology applications impacted his or her writing motivation? The emergent themes from the twenty participant's responses included the following:

Figure 6. Learner's developing beats on the school's iPads

1. Edmodo allowed a writing community to emerge.
2. The goal of making an audio CD motivated writing.
3. Skills developed with the DAW supported future life goals.
4. DAW-based recording made writing fun.
5. Self-expression through raps increased writing motivation.

Question Two asked participants to explain what they learned about writing during the intervention processes. Emergent themes from the nineteen participants included the following:

Figure 7. District assessment gains for the hip-hop writers

Initials	DA #1	DA #2	FCAT 2012	Improvement
CA	3	4	4	+1
JA	3	4	3.5	-
RC	3	2	4	+1
LC	3	0	3	-
AF	2	2	3.5	+1.5
BH	3	3	3	-
TM	3	1	3.5	+.5
SM	2	4	3.5	+1
AM	3	3	3	-
BM	3	3	3	-
EN	3	1	3.5	+1
NO	3	2	4.5	+1.5
AP	3	5	4.0	+1
AR	3	3	3	-
ZS	3	3	3	-
TV	3	3	4	+1
KV	3	4	3.5	-
KW	3	3	2	-1
SW	3	3	4	+1

Hip Hop Writers
Writing Scores 2011-2012

10/18 demonstrated improvement

8/18 showed no growth

DA= District Assessment
FCAT= Florida Comprehensive Assessment Test

1. Writing takes lots of practice.
2. Writing takes lots of thought.
3. Stressing personal feelings through writing are important to learning how to write.
4. Writing improves vocabulary.
5. Shyness to share one's writing decreased.
6. Time is important to writing. Writing takes lots of time.
7. Rhyming and creative uses of vocabulary increased.

Broad implications of this particular DAW-based hop-hop pedagogy intervention included the following:

1. Learners enjoy becoming digital creators. Educators need to offer learners opportunities to create culture rather than only consume culture.
2. Creativity skills can improve motivation for writing and writing skills.
3. Social networking skills using platforms like Edmodo can be leveraged to motivate reluctant writers due to a child's natural tendency to share what they produce.
4. DAWs encourage 21st Century digital technology skills.

MANAGEMENT, ORGANIZATIONAL, AND PRACTICAL CONCERNS

Management, organizational, and practical concerns were analyzed by reflecting on videos and photographs from the three cases described herein. The categories that emerged include administrative responsibilities, unplanned events, encouraging culture, research and lyric writing, composing music, recording time, reviewing and editing, printing jewel case inserts and lyrics, performance, sharing, and recognition time. Administrative responsibilities are often require both hardware and software troubleshooting when managing a DAW-based learning environment. For example, arriving earlier than the learners to ensure that the hardware and software are working properly is essential. If not, frustration develops among the learners. The technical sequence often included the following:

1. Turn on the DAW computer and verify that the sound interface input drive is working properly. Verify that the Firewire or USB cable is plugged into its proper port if the driver is not working.
2. Check to see that phantom power is turned on if using condenser microphones, and turned off if using direct microphones.
3. Verify that the XLR cable(s) are plugged into the microphone(s) and sound interface.
4. Check the signal routing by running the recording software and making sure an input signal is showing audio levels in your recording track. Check the output by playing a previously recorded song. If there is no output verify the speakers are turned on and are connected to the sound interface. The best policy is to have both the input and output both come out of the sound interface device. This makes it easier to verify the input/output signal routings using the software preferences.
5. Set the input and outputs on your sound interface to proper levels to avoid audio clipping on the input side, and blasting on the output side. If working with headphones, verify the output level is not set too high for young learners to avoid harming their hearing.
6. Make sure the DAW studio area is clear and free of trash, liquids, debris, and is well organized. No food or drink should ever be allowed in a DAW environment.
7. Post the policies and procedures for recording in a visible spot for learners to read. Leverage the three-strike rule concerning hitting, screaming, abusing equipment, bringing food and drinks into the DAW environment and profanity.

It is always important to plan for the unplanned. Sometimes the best learning is unplanned. Allow the learners space and time to talk, discuss, and share their raps and songs. On some days children will be productive and other days they will be non-productive. This is a natural part of the workday in the real world and professional DAW studios.

Encourage the sharing of popular music and be tolerant of others values. At the high school level the researcher often discussed West Coast and Gangsta rap very openly with learners, but did not allow learners to use profanity in their raps on the school-based DAW. At the elementary level any discussions that were adult in nature were never entertained. It is probably best that one finds his or her tolerance level for sharing and playing popular music. In most situations, it is best to keep learners focused on researching, writing, recording, and mixing.

Research and lyric writing takes time. Composing rhyming couplets does not come easy to all learners. Synthesizing academic content and transforming this content into raps does not come naturally for all learners. If the raps require research, a library or Internet connection is a must. It is best to have a writing support team composed of at least two teachers if possible in a given DAW workspace. Eventually, teachers utilizing a DAW workspace can leverage learners that are more skilled at writing to assist and support other learners who require it.

Composing music with midi controllers or external midi keyboards requires that closed monitor headphones are available to the learners; else, a chaotic mess of sound emerges. In addition, hand written songs take extra time to record. If writing, research, and academic content are the primary concerns pre-quantized loops allows teachers to quickly drop beats and get learners rapping, recording, and producing quickly. Capturing percussion instrument recordings is a skill that comes with practice and many revisions. Be patient, practice, know the software, know the hardware, and learn how to control live instrument audio clipping, which can ruin learners' recordings if the input levels are too hot.

Recording sessions require a quiet setting. If other learners in the room continue to talk, laugh, and make noise, condenser microphones will capture these ambient sounds. Avoid this by setting a policy of stating "3, 2, 1 quiet in the studio". Encourage learners to have respect for their peers and classmates in this way. Let learners know that if they want respect during their recording session, they have to show respect for others.

One of the most rewarding processes is post editing following recording. Levels can be adjusted, compression added, reverb added, voices can be made to go backwards, pitch adjustments can be made to make girls sound like boys, boys sound like girls, and the like. Post editing, adding effects, adding additional sounds and final mastering for quality export is fun and rewarding but does take extra time. If the goal is primarily academic or writing, it is best for the teacher to control post editing without learners present so the final product is of a high quality. Not all learners are interested in the tedious work that must be applied to post editing and audio mastering.

Having a printer available is essential for printing song lyrics, and printing jewel case inserts for the final CD production. Wireless printers are preferable. Any color printer will do but printer cartridges can be costly. Do not allow learners to print using color everyday. Use a black and white laser printer for printing song lyrics. Reserve color printing for final CD productions. Nero, Roxio, or other software is needed for burning *Red Book* quality audio CDs, printing CD labels, and printing jewel case inserts. It is very rewarding for learners to leave with a professional product at the end of a semester, which can be shared with parents and their friends. In addition, social networking and video distribution platforms like YouTube make digital distribution much quicker and more cost effective than compact disc productions. However, it is the researcher's opinion that producing a physical archive like a compact disc is more rewarding. Plus, learners get to assist in developing the album art.

At some point learners deserve to deliver a public performance of their hard work. Planning a live show requires a public address (PA) system and direct microphones like Shure SM-58s; in addition, all songs and beats must be saved without lyrics to a digital device or played live using digital turntables. In addition, learners must practice often if they plan on memorizing their lyric content for a public venue. It is a very good idea to have learners to burn a copy of their work on a CD, and practice at home until they can perform their song from memory.

CURRENT CHALLENGES

There are three major challenges that must be overcome to promote and encourage DAW-based hip-hop pedagogy programs for gifted and talented learners. The first problem is the lack of intellectual challenges offered to GT learners by many public schools. Berman, Schultz, & Weber (2012) argued that GT learners in most classroom settings endure unchallenging curriculum, a slow pace of instruction, and a state of ignorance by many of their general education teachers. They admit their words are harsh, but claim in the current educational (financial) crisis, GT learners deserve respect.

The second problem is the negative attitudes that rap and hip-hop conjure in the minds of school administrators and teachers. Hip-hop and rap are often at odds with the culture of K-12 schooling in the United States due to the genre's reputation for vulgarities and adult content contained within its lyric content. Hart (2009) posited that the culture industry, the hip-hop artist, and the music consumer often perpetuate and reinforce the historical and negative attitudes towards Blackness. In the early

1990's hip-hop music became associated with materialism, violence, hypersexual lyrics, and misogyny. Hart (2009) claimed that the purpose of this one-dimensional view of Black culture was packaged by the culture industry for a predominately middle class White consumer.

The third problem is locating and training teachers to administer and maintain the program once the hardware and software is acquired. These teachers must be dedicated and be willing to troubleshoot hardware and software often. To illustrate this point, only Oakwood Elementary in the West Texas Panhandle discussed herein has followed up on the researcher's efforts and continues to support and sustain its DAW-based hip-hop pedagogy program as of 2014. Without strong administrative and teacher support DAW-based hip-hop pedagogy programs are not sustainable. In addition, a DAW requires dedicated space, dedicated hardware, dedicated software and dedicated technical expertise.

SOLUTIONS AND RECOMMENDATIONS

Berman, Schultz, & Weber (2012) recommend more focus be placed on the recognition of Gifted and Talented learners in teacher pre-service training programs. In addition, classrooms for gifted students would provide a space for their needs to be met with more challenging and rewarding work. In an appropriate setting, GT students experience a curriculum modified in pace, breadth and expected outcomes. GT students should be given an opportunity to experience independence, self-direction and challenging activities.

A practical solution to countering the culture industry's negative portrayal of African American culture through *gangsta rap* is to promote DAW-driven hip-hop pedagogy to administrators and teachers as a contested cultural ground in which academics, core content and critical thinking can be leveraged by schools to benefit learning. Pitching a new DAW-driven hip-hop program to schools can provide administrators and teachers with prior student lyrics, prior audio recordings, prior media coverage, thus creating an atmosphere that allows discussion of the benefits of sound engineering for the development of 21st Century skills.

DAWs have math and science benefits that are untapped by most schools. The physics underlying acoustic space and sound engineering are complex instructional topics that can challenge gifted and talented learners. Giroux (1997) pointed out that popular culture such as hip-hop culture is a legitimate aspect of the everyday lives of students. Pop culture also includes ubiquitous digital tools like microcomputers, MP3 players, portable digital assistants (PDAs), popular music, text messaging, movies, games, and music videos. Zyngier (2004) argued that we should put young people's experiences at the center of any discussion of pedagogy and make learning relevant to children's lives.

The solution to sustainability of a DAW-based hip-hop pedagogy is proper training and continued contact with a key member(s) of the teaching faculty that continues once the program is initially developed. Social networking via Facebook and instant messaging software such as Skype, Messages, and Google Hangouts offer live follow-up support to foster program sustainability. DAWs and culturally relevant pedagogy should be used as complementary tools for learning and achievement motivation. Dede's (2006) research suggested that schools and teachers should capitalize on learners' digital based tool knowledge, especially in an age of ubiquitous technology use and learner diversity. Mahiri (2000) emphasized that 21st Century pop culture pedagogies have the potential to engage people in technologically mediated processes for making meaning and giving meaning to people's lives. Mayer (1999) concurs that these technology-mediated pedagogies create a potential for constructivist learning in which learners actively create his or her own knowledge. Bailey, Pearce, Smith, Sutherland, Stack, Winstanley, & Dickenson (2012) found in their recent review of GT literature that social interaction and the development of new skills and learning strategies were paramount to effective learning for GT students. DAW-based hip-hop pedagogy requires social interaction among learners and the development of complex sound engineering and computer skills.

Petraglia (1998) contended that constructivist-learning scenarios persuade and convince the learners of their authenticity rather than promote environments with pre-authenticated problems. Pagares (1996) argued that interventions should be designed with authentic mastery experience in mind. Jonassen (1991) acknowledged that instruction should focus on providing tools and environments for engaging learners in contexts of *negotiated meaning* within a socially constructed reality. DAW-based hip-hop pedagogy promotes a negotiated meaning between popular culture, music, and academic content. These teaching and learning spaces of negotiated meaning offer GT learners an opportunity to express their own unique worldviews. Schneiderman (2003) insisted that technology should allow one to interpret the world, creating, and sharing one's creations with others. Culturally situated computer activities like DAW-based hip-hop pedagogy can have a positive impact on digital skill acquisition, negative classroom behaviors, and might strengthen cultural connections between school and home.

York (1991) declared that projects which affirm cultural identity and give children a strong sense of self-worth support healthy child development. Ladson-Billings (1995) argued that educators often undervalue literacy skills include storytelling in the African American oral traditions. Meadows & Murphy (2004) reasoned that children need digital tools to help them develop a clear sense of who they are and where they fit into family, community and their peer groups. DAWs offer teachers and learners tools for personal expression and creativity involving writing practice and computer skills. Olthouse (2013) argued that multiliteracy theory frames education for GT learners since literacy is situated, multimodal, and social. DAW-based hip-hop pedagogy offer teachers and learners situated learning scenarios that involve collaboration, teamwork, and critical thinking. Multiliteracies theory includes attention to varied forms of communication in addition to text including gestural, audio, visual, spatial and multimodal (i.e., a mix of the other modes) forms of communication. In the cases contained herein, some learners expressed that they could understand academic content better by using narrative raps than through a traditional essay. In addition, learners can personal what they learned to a greater extent using narrative raps.

Sociocultural mediations were essential factors in learning (Brown, Collins, & Duguid 1989). Lave & Wenger (1991) asserted that it is through situated social activity that human cognition and consciousness emerge. Vygotsky (1981) declared that knowledge is distributed within and between human sociocultural populations. Pransky & Bailey (2003) noted that research has shown that attention to cultural mismatch between home and school may be a key to equitable school achievement. DAW-based hip-hop pedagogy can mitigate this mismatch between home and school. Jonassen (August, 2003) concurred that learning is distributed among knowledge-building communities based on their beliefs and values. Research grounded in the dualistic theoretical constructs of field-dependent/field independent learning styles has shown that African American and Latino learning styles differ from Asian and Caucasian learning styles; the research illustrates that Asians and Caucasians have field-independent learning styles in which abstract learning, at first inert, is seen as necessary preparation for future work and tasks. On the other hand, African Americans and Latino learners prefer to respond to the whole rather than isolated parts (i.e., field-dependent), focusing on people, knowledge, and skills in contextually situated activities. Latino American learners prefer *collaborative* learning and *learning by doing* (Anderson, 1988; Banks, 1988; Gilbert and Gay, 1985). DAW-based hip-hop pedagogy might allow teachers to address field-dependent learning styles to a greater extent than traditional direct instruction. Neuroscience research by (Hung, 2003) revealed that strong cultural support assisted learners with reading, writing, and complex problem solving. Evelyn (2008) exclaimed that you have to meet the students where they are. That's the nature of education. That's pedagogy.

REFERENCES

Anderson, J. A. (1988). Cognitive styles and multicultural populations. *Journal of Teacher Education, 39*(1), 2–9. doi:10.1177/002248718803900102

Bailey, R., Pearce, G., Smith, C., Sutherland, M., Stack, N., Winstanley, C., & Dickenson, M. (2012). Improving the educational achievement of gifted and talented students: A Systematic review. *Talent Development & Excellence, 4*(1), 33–48.

Banks, J. A. (1988). Ethnicity, class, cognitive, and motivational styles: Research and teaching implications. *The Journal of Negro Education, 57*(4), 452–466. doi:10.2307/2295689

Beisser, S., Gillespie, C., & Thacker, V. (2013). An investigation of play: From the voices of fifth- and sixth-rade talented and gifted students. *Gifted Child Quarterly, 57*(1), 25–38. doi:10.1177/0016986212450070

Berman, K. M., Schultz, R. A., & Weber, C. L. (2012). A Lack of awareness and emphasis in preservice teacher training: Preconceived beliefs about the gifted and talented. *Gifted Child Today, 35*(1), 18–26. doi:10.1177/1076217511428307

Bridges, T. (2011). Towards a pedagogy of hip-hop in urban teacher education. *The Journal of Negro Education, 80*(3), 325–338.

Brown, J., Collins, A., & Duguid, P. (1989). Situated cognition and the culture of learning. *Educational Researcher, 18*(1), 32–42. doi:10.3102/0013189X018001032

Code, K. P. (2007). Developing student gifts and talents using web-based resources. *Understanding Our Gifted, 19*(4), 10–12.

Cole, M. (1998). Can cultural psychology help us think about diversity? *Mind, Culture, and Activity, 5*(4), 291–304. doi:10.1207/s15327884mca0504_4

Csikszentmihalyi, M. (1996). *Creativity: flow and the psychology of discovery and invention.* New York: Harper Perennial.

Darius, P. D. (2012). *Culturally relevant teaching: Hip-hop pedagogy in urban schools.* New York: Peter Lang.

Deason, C., & Zhang, K. (2012) Technology-enhanced rap music pedagogy for history learning at an alternative school: impacts of a culturally-sensitive computer environment on at-risk teenagers. *Asian-Pacific Collaborative Education Journal, 8*(1), 39-58. Available at http://www.acecjournal.org/2009/Journal_Data/Vol8No1/201203.pdf

Dede, C. (2006, Spring). Virtual reality of learning. *Interactive Educator, 2*(1), 40–41.

Desbottes, A., & Nicholls, T. (2004). What is the impact of cross-phase, cross-curricular learning on gifted and talented pupils? *Educational Review, 18*(1), 79–84.

Dimitriadis, G. (2001). *Performing identity/Performing culture: Hip-hop as text, pedagogy, and lived practice*. New York: Peter Lang.

Eckstein, M. (2009). Enrichment 2.0 gifted and talented education for the 21st Century. *Gifted Child Today, 32*(1), 59–63.

Evelyn, J. (2008). The Miseducation of hip-hop discrimination in education. In *Pop Perspectives-Readings To Critique Contemporary Culture* (pp. 559–565). New York: McGraw-Hill.

Gay, G. (2002). Preparing for culturally responsive teaching. *Journal of Teacher Education, 53*(2), 106–116. doi:10.1177/0022487102053002003

Gilbert, S. E., & Gay, G. (1985). Improving the success in school of poor black children. *Phi Delta Kappan, 67*(2), 133–137.

Giroux, H. A. (1997). *Pedagogy and the politics of hope: Theory, culture, and schooling*. Boulder, CO: Westview.

Gutiérrez, K., Baquedaño-López, P., & Tejeda, C. (1999). Rethinking diversity: Hybridity and hybrid language practices in the Third Space. *Mind, Culture, and Activity, 6*(4), 286–303. doi:10.1080/10749039909524733

Hart, W. E. (2009). *The culture industry, hip-hop music and the white perspective: How one-dimensional representation of hip-hop music has influenced white racial attitudes*. (Unpublished Masters Thesis). The University of Texas in Arlington, Arlington, TX.

Hellweg, E. (2005). Hip-hop high the musical language of the street has new fans: Teachers, who are using it as a classroom tool. *Edutopia, 1*(6), 4-7.

Hung, D. (2003). Supporting current pedagogical approaches with neuroscience research. *Journal of Interactive Learning Research, 14*(2), 129–155.

Jonassen, D. H. (1991). Objectivism vs. constructivism: Do we need a new paradigm? *ETR&D, 39*(3), 5–14. doi:10.1007/BF02296434

Jonassen, D. H. (2003, August). The vain quest for a unified theory of learning. *Educational Technology, 43*(4), 5–8.

Ladson-Billings, G. (1995). Toward a theory of culturally relevant pedagogy. *American Educational Research Journal, 32*(3), 465–491. doi:10.3102/00028312032003465

Laffey, J. M., Espinosa, L., Moore, J., & Lodree, A. (2003, Summer). Supporting learning and behavior of at-risk young children: Computers in urban education. *Journal of Research on Technology in Education, 35*(4), 441–458. doi:10.1080/15 391523.2003.10782394

Lave, J., & Wenger, E. (1991). *Situated learning: Legitimate peripheral participation.* Cambridge, UK: Cambridge University Press. doi:10.1017/CBO9780511815355

Lee, C. D. (2003). Toward a framework for culturally responsive design in multimedia computer environments: Cultural modeling as a case. *Mind, Culture, and Activity, 10*(1), 42–61. doi:10.1207/S15327884MCA1001_05

Lock, J., & Lock, R. (1993). Revision raps: Elect this musical route to ease the pain in passin' GCSEs! *Journal of Biological Education, 27*(4), 2p. doi:10.1080/0021 9266.1993.9655342

Mahiri, J. (2000). Pop culture pedagogy and the end of school. *Journal of Adolescent & Adult Literacy, 44*(4), 382–394.

Mayer, R. E. (1999). Designing instruction for constructivist learning. In C. M. Reigeluth (Ed.), *Instructional-design theories and models: A new paradigm of instructional technology* (Vol. 2). Mahwah, NJ: Lawrence Erlbaum.

Mchugh, R. (2005, October). Synching up with the iKid. *Edutopia, 1*(7), 33-35.

Meadows, M., & Murphy, F. (2004). Using technology in early childhood environments to strengthen cultural connections. *Information Technology in Childhood Education Annual,* 39–47.

Morgan, T. (2011). Towards a pedagogy of hip-hop in urban teacher education. *The Journal of Negro Education, 80*(3), 325–338.

Olthouse, J. M. (2013). Multiliteracies theory and gifted education. *Gifted Child Today, 36*(4), 246–253. doi:10.1177/1076217513497575

Ormrod, J. E. (1999). *Human Learning* (3rd ed.). Upper Saddle River, NJ: Prentice Hall.

Pajares, F. (1996, Winter). Self-efficacy beliefs in academic settings. *Review of Educational Research, 66*(4), 543–578. doi:10.3102/00346543066004543

Petraglia, J. (1998). The real world on a short leash: The (mis)application of constructivism to the design of educational technology. *ET R&D, 46*(3), 53–65. doi:10.1007/BF02299761

Pewewardy, C. (1993). Culturally responsible pedagogy in action: An American Indian magnet school. In E. Hollins, J. King, & W. Hayman (Eds.), *Teaching diverse populations: Formulating a knowledge base* (pp. 77–92). Albany, NY: State University of New York Press.

Pinkard, N. (2001). *Lyric reader: Creating intrinsically motivating and culturally responsive reading environments.* Center from the Improvement of Early Reading Achievement (CIERA). Report #1- 013.

Pransky, K., & Bailey, F. (2003, January). To meet your students where they are, first you have to find them: Working with culturally and linguistically diverse at-risk students. *The Reading Teacher, 56*(4), 370–383. doi:10.1598/RT.56.4.3

Protheroe, N. (2003). Culturally sensitive instruction. Educational Research Service, 1-11.

Ramos, E. (2010). Let us in: Latino underrepresented in gifted and talented programs. *Journal of Cultural Diversity, 17*(4), 151–153. PMID:22303650

Reyes, I. (2010). To Know beyond listening monitoring digital music. *Senses & Society, 5*(3), 322–338. doi:10.2752/174589210X12753842356043

Rodriguez, L. F. (2009). Dialoguing, cultural capital, and student engagement: Toward a hip-hop pedagogy in the high school and university classroom. *Equity & Excellence in Education, 42*(1), 20–35. doi:10.1080/10665680802584023

Serpell, R., & Boykin, A. (1994). Cultural dimensions of cognition: A multiplex, dynamic system of constraints and possibilities. In R. J. Sternberg (Ed.), *Thinking and problem solving* (pp. 369–408). San Diego, CA: Academic Press. doi:10.1016/B978-0-08-057299-4.50018-9

Shank, R. C. (1999). Learning by doing. In C. M. Reigeluth (Ed.), *Instructional-design theories and models: A new paradigm of instructional theory* (Vol. 2, pp. 161–181). Malwah, NJ: Lawrence Erlbaum.

Shneiderman, B. (2003). *Leonardo's laptop: Human needs and the new computing technologies.* Cambridge, MA: MIT Press.

Vygotsky, L. S. (1981). The genesis of higher mental functions. In J. V. Wertsch (Ed.), *The concept of activity in Soviet psychology.* White Plains, NY: M. Sharpe.

Warne, W. T., Anderson, B., & Johnson, A. O. (2013, December 01). The impact of race and ethnicity on the identification processes for giftedness in Utah. *Journal for the Education of the Gifted, 36*(4), 487–508. doi:10.1177/0162353213506065

York, S. (1991). *Roots and wings: Affirming culture in early childhood programs.* St. Paul, MN: Redleaf Press.

Zyngier, D. (2004, August). Putting young people at the center of the discussion: A review. *Primary and Middle Years Educator, 2*(2), 3–11.

KEY TERMS AND DEFINITIONS

Ableton Live: Relative to other software digital audio recording software, Live is designed around the notion of being as much an instrument for live performances as a tool for real-time composing and arranging. Elementary age children can learn the basic interface quickly. All processing is performed in real time rather than having to process and then play back to hear the results. It's basic functionality for audio recording and its interface is easy to use for gifted and talented K-12 environments. Its major drawback is the need for a 7200-rpm harddrive, and at minimum 2-4 Gigabytes of RAM. It's exports both .wav and .aiff formats. I personally recommend Ableton if working in a Windows or Macintosh OS environments.

Culturally Relevant Pedagogy: A theoretical construct Dr. Gloria-Ladson Billings suggests that *culturally relevant pedagogy* (CRP) is a pedagogy providing students with cultural integrity while helping them succeed academically. Dr. Billing's research suggests that culturally relevant teachers should raise the *expectancy and value* for classroom academic success in all domains to its highest potential, leverage a *community* of learners in a collaborative classroom atmosphere rather than promote a competitive environment, and leverage assessments and learning tasks that are *authentic* in nature. The concept of culturally relevant teaching often deals specifically with instruction of African American students in the United States but has been show to be an effective form of pedagogy for students of many ethnic backgrounds.

Digital Audio Workstation (DAW): A DAW is a PC or Macintosh-based computer used for audio recording, editing, mixing, and processing. DAWs necessitate the use of an external USB or Firewire soundcard, and professional condenser microphones or direct microphones. In addition, multitrack recording software is required that might include Ableton, Acid Pro, Cubase, ProTools, Garageband, Audacity, Magix Studio, and the like.

Garageband: Garageband is a Macintosh only digital audio recording sequencer. Its interface is easy to use and it exports aiff, aac and mp3 formats. I personally recommend Garageband if working in a Macintosh OS environment.

Hip-Hop Culture: Hip-hop culture describes the independent collective consciousness of a specific group of inner-city people. Ever growing, it is commonly expressed through such elements as breakin' (breakdancing), emceein' (rap), graffiti (stylized aerosol art), deejayin', beatboxin', street fashion, street knowledge, and street entrepreneurialism. Emerging in early 1970s, hip-hop is an independent and unique community, an empowering behavior, and an international culture particularly among African American, Latino American youth, and many youth cultures worldwide.

Hip-Hop Pedagogy: Hip-hop pedagogy is a teaching method that leverages breakin' (breakdancing), emceein' (raping), graffiti (stylized aerosol art), deejayin', beatboxin', street fashion, street knowledge, and street entrepreneurialism with instructional content of any type. Common examples include writing, reading, science, and History.

Quantization: The process results in notes being set on beats and on exact fractions of beats allowing one to drag and loop a hip-hop beat seamlessly throughout the entire length of a rap or song to infinity. Quantized beats allow the learner to make a full song very quickly allowing the vocalist to execute his or her rap with no music development or background in music theory to create a professional audio production.

Section 4
Voices from the Schools

Chapter 11
iMovies and Gifted Grouping

Cletus Turner
Morehead State University, USA

EXECUTIVE SUMMARY

Grouping of gifted and talented students in conjunction with how students interact with technology is the focus of this case study. Groups were created and observed while a lesson utilizing the program iMovie and utilizing iPads for research was taught. Findings are discussed and possible future actions are explained.

CASE SETTING

Working with gifted students in middle school can be stimulating, but because students are generally placed in heterogeneous classes, there are several barriers to delivering enriched content. Providing differentiation within a 50-minute class period requires a great deal of planning. With a wide range of student levels of skills and abilities, teachers struggle to reach everyone. Teachers must look for ways to create lessons that teach all their students and cover the curriculum. Developing units of study that promote student learning at all levels is a challenge.

In a middle school in a rural eastern Kentucky county, the students in a Social Studies/ World Geography content course were the focus of a study on curriculum, instructional technology, and gifted student content enrichment. The class was composed of 6th from a school of 500 students. The class had twenty-three students, who

DOI: 10.4018/978-1-4666-6489-0.ch011

averaged of twelve years old, with a composition of fifteen males and eight females. Among these students were six gifted students and two special needs students.

The unit of study dealt with Central and South America. Students were assigned a country to research and then create an iMovie to demonstrate what they learned. The iMovie was the culminating event. The students were expected to present their movies to their peers. The lesson was meant to have the students delve deeper into a specific country. To make the assignment more challenging, students were required to include pictures, music, and voiceovers. Moreover, by allowing creativity, the creation of the movie allowed all students the opportunity to show demonstrate what they could do.

For this social studies unit, the ideas from the Parallel Curriculum (Tomlinson, 2009) provided the basis for development. During the unit, the science teacher was covering a unit on the rain forests with an emphasis on Central and South America. At the same time, the language arts teacher was covering a short story writing unit that emphasized the Aztec and Incan civilizations. By having the curriculum connect across disciplines, it was hoped that students will see the connections made through differing lessons and differing classes. In many ways, this type of planning can be beneficial to not only gifted and talented students but also to middle and lower level students. This unit of study was taught over four days. As well, the grouping of students, identified as gifted and talented, was utilized. Gifted and talented students were partnered with each other, and middle level students and lower level learners were partnered. Rogers (2006) and Tomlinson (2009) both advocate using grouping to facilitate gifted and talented student learning. As a teacher, I was able to observe my students interacting with one another, the technology, and the curriculum.

The technology used for research during the lesson was an iPad. Students also used iMac computers for the creation of the iMovie *(see Appendix A, Rubric)*. Luckily, some of the students had used the iMovie program before and were able to show each other some of the finer details, such as how to use transitions and sound. As a middle school social studies teacher of ten years, I have used iMovie before, so I was familiar with its use, and that made it easier to use. Students learn better when teachers are very familiar with technology (Lennex & Nettleton, 2010).

The research portion of the lesson required a great deal of direct instruction. The students were shown how to use google.com to look for websites and information, then it was discussed how to tell if the source is a reliable one or if it is one the students should not trust. For instance, Wikipedia was an example of a source that can be changed and so students were told not to use it. However, they could scroll down to the reference portion of the website and look at those sources. This was one of the hardest concepts for my students to understand.

BARRIERS/OBSTACLES

As well, the classroom usually has fourteen computers in it, which would have been enough to accommodate all the groups in the class; however, because of school testing, which is completed via the internet, only had eight computers were available. Since six of the computers were needed in another classroom, I was told I would not be receiving them back after the testing. The lack of easily accessible technology caused some delay in the creation of the iMovies. The reason this lesson was created was because the students love using technology. This unit allowed students to connect something they liked to do to a creative project that also integrated social studies content and English/Language Arts (ELA) standards designed by the Common Core Standards Initiative. These standards were adopted by my state. The unit allowed the students to teach each other.

In the winter, school days in eastern Kentucky are often cancelled due to snow days. A snow day occurs when the mountain roads become too icy or snow covered to safely transport students to school. The unit was launched during a time when my school had several snow days, which disrupts the smooth flow of lessons. With the school year nearing its end, tests looming, and students having to catch up, the iMovies were not only a teaching tool for students, but they provided a way for students to teach each other about the countries they had researched. I knew the lesson would be enhanced by the technology since students would interact with the information in a meaningful way. Also, any students who were gifted and talented could research more in depth and look for extra information they might find interesting.

As for the grouping, I decided to group them in several ways. Group A and B were all gifted and talented students. This grouping was part of an action research project which I developed to determine optimal grouping and to analyze the kind of end product which would be produced from a group of gifted and talented students when compared with the other groups. Group C consisted of one gifted and talented student and the rest were middle level learners. Group D contained one gifted and talented and the rest of the group members were lower level learners. Gender was not considered for this exercise; however, each group had at least one female. The boys in the class greatly outnumbered the girls.

To begin the lesson, students were able to choose a country in Central or South America to research. Once they had chosen, the students divided amongst themselves who would research the history, government, culture, economy, and geography of their country. The students utilized iPads for the research portion and moved to the computers to begin creating their iMovies as soon as they had their information. I served as a facilitator, and if students had a problem finding information, I was available to help them. However, I made sure the students understood they were responsible for finding their information and assuring it was accurate.

FINDINGS

As the students worked on their projects, it seemed that Group A argued about the project – what to include, what was not important, and what was important. Intervention was needed to stop the arguments before the situation escalated. It was frustrating for the students; however, by having them work together, it was hoped that much needed social skills would be developed. The final project was not of high quality and the fact that the individuals had to rush to complete the project was obvious.

Group B was able to work together without many problems and the arguments that did occur were not of any consequence. By observation, it was noticed that the group had a higher level of social skills than Group A and this facilitated a more pleaser encounter for this group. The final product was not of high quality, but showed great promise. This probably came from the fact that we had only completed one iMovie project before and that was at the beginning of the year.

Group C did not have as much of a problem. The gifted students took control of the project and led the other students through the process. This leadership status seemed to please them and they were able to complete the iMovie project quickly. My fear that the gifted student would be made to do all the work materialized in less than one fourth of the groups. Mostly, this was alleviated when students were told they must "share the computer." In this manner, the gifted students could advise their partners on how to do something, but the partners had to complete their parts of the project themselves. The final product here was not high quality, but showed growth from the first movies made at the beginning of the year.

Observing Group C complete the assignment was an eye-opener for me as a teacher. By focusing on how the groups interacted with each other and with the technology, the outcome for this group was very disappointing. The gifted students ended up having to compensate for the lower performing students and it was frustrating for them. The gifted student had to be literally hands-on during the entire process. This included reading for the other student, spelling words for the student when they were looking for pictures to include, and helping the student write the storyboard. The gifted student had to complete twice the work for the same result the other two types of groups were achieving.

During the whole process, the gifted students were achieving at a high level with their movie making skills as well as towards the completion of the movie. For instance, they were using transitions, themes, and other aspects of the iMovie while at the same time, they were showing other students how to utilize those features. The gifted students also enhanced their iMovies by using colors, fonts, and other features to ensure the viewer could see all aspects of the movie. Most of their movies were organized and clear. The storyboards, the backbone of the iMovies, were explicit. The storyboards organized the information that made the iMovie flow.

256

The other groups in the classroom, those that did not have gifted students in them, achieved mixed success. In some cases, excellent iMovies were created. However, a vast majority did not have much content and were populated mostly with pictures and very little information.

The research portion of the unit had to be turned in separately. For the gifted student Groups, A and B. it was detailed and showed a great deal of effort. While the other student groups turned in research that contained some content, there was very little attention to detail and the work tended to be perfunctory. Overall, the general goals of the unit were met. Students were able to complete the movies, although the overall quality of the movies left something to be desired. I believe this is because the students were still learning how to use the technology. They will improve over time.

As the class watched each movie, the students were alternately amazed and commented on the ones that were of medium quality. However, the ones that were thrown together haphazardly were obvious and the students commented on those as well. I made sure to keep the comments to constructive criticism. I asked, "What could have be done to make this better?" of all the products and we used this to discuss more ideas for a future project.

Technology Problems

Problems arose when two of the eight computers began having technical issues. Whenever the students would try to type information onto slides, iMovie would shut down and the students would have to restart the application. Strangely, this problem only occurred in one one class. The technology coordinator, the person in charge of implementing and fixing technology in the building, was called in and he was able to discover that a missing file was causing the problem. This is the sort of problem that most classroom teachers would not know how to fix on their own, so having someone to call when technological glitches occur is essential. Naturally, the normal problems that are often associated with using technology in the classroom, such as absence of the person who logged onto the computer caused groups to lose time while the user name and password were found, occurred during the unit.

Before beginning this type of lesson, students should have interaction with technology that is less arduous. For instance, perhaps teachers should introduce their students to a program such as Plasq's *ComicLife*, which requires two to four frames and conveys less information. From there, Microsoft's *PowerPoint* would add more dimensions and complexity for the student. By starting simple and working toward a more complex program, the students can slowly learn how to use each program and build on their understanding.

FUTURE RESEARCH

This lesson was certainly a learning experience. Perhaps the biggest eye-opener was the interaction between the participants. The intense arguing was a surprise. The participants of the arguments were usually very quiet students. They tended to complete their classwork quickly and then begin their enrichment activities. During this lesson, they quickly fell behind and eventually had to be separated because of the amount of arguing which occurred. Their frustration from the first lesson carried over into the next day, when it was decided that the next time technology was assigned, it would be an individual assignment. This was determined because the students lacked the social skills to be able to interact well. After a time, the students will be part of project that will utilize partners rather that groups of three to four. At that time, we will work on social skills as a class and how to deal with problems more constructively. Teachers need to be aware of the level of socialization between students when using collaborative learning models.

If this lesson were taught again, the technology would be used in the same way; however, the arguments have led me to rethink the groupings and how I use groups. First, instead of jumping into groups of three to four people, I think I should build group learning and interaction gradually. Start off with partners and build from there. Any social skills and interactions can be taught and constructively dissected to help the students learn. The students seemed to enjoy researching on the iPads and really loved creating the iMovies. However, I would have an example so students could understand what is expected, since several of the students' work went off in unexpected paths. An example of what is expected would help the students keep on path toward the expected outcome.

FUTURE USE OF CLASSROOM TECHNOLOGY

As I observed the students interact with the technology, I noticed that my students asked about PowerPoint and other programs on the iPads. As a teacher, I would like to continue to grow in my applications of technology. Since this unit was completed, I have discovered several applications for the iPad that I would like to use to see if they could be helpful to use with students in the future. Several programs will allow me to quiz my students to see if they understand content material. One application allows the teacher to ask a question, push a button to bring up the multiple choice menu, and the students answer the question. The program then tallies the answers and the teacher has immediate formative information. Technology that teachers can readily adapt for classroom use is becoming more available. As teachers become more adept at using the new technologies, they will be better able to meet the needs of their gifted students by differentiating instruction at a variety of learning levels.

REFERENCES

Lennex, L., & Nettleton, K. F. (2010). The Golden Apple: A Quest toward Achievement. In J. Yamamoto, J. Kush, R. Lombard, & C. Hertzog (Eds.), Technology Implementation and Teacher Education: Reflective Models (pp. 124-145). doi:10.4018/978-1-61520-897-5.ch008

Rogers, K. B. (2006). *A Menu of options for grouping gifted students*. Waco, TX: Prufrock Press.

Tomlinson, C., Kaplan, S. N., Renzulli, J. S., Purcell, J., Leppien, J., & Burns, D. (2002). *The Parallel Curriculum*. Thousand Sands, CA: Corwin Press, Inc.

KEY TERMS AND DEFINITIONS

ComicLife: A program owned by Plasq, Inc. which has been included on many Apple, Inc. products, but is now a purchasable download. The program allows the user to create short posters or boards using speech bubbles and pictures. It can also be used to create a type of digital storytelling.

iMovie: A program owned by Apple, Inc. which is included on many products produced by the company. This software allows the user to create movies which then can be used to educate or entertain.

PowerPoint: A program owned by Microsoft and was included on many personal computers, but is now a purchasable download. It is a presentation software where slides are created and then shown in a slide show format. The software has many uses in education and business.

APPENDIX

Table 1. iMovie rubric

Names:						
Objectives	4 – Distinguished	3 – Proficient	2 – Apprentice	1 – Novice	0 – No Work	Earned Scores
Storyboard	Completed and approved	Completed some detail	Completed with little detail	Incomplete		
Music	Fits the information	Is close to the information	Does not fit the information	Is left out		
Images	Pictures are clear and fit the information	Pictures are clear and most fit the information	Pictures are unclear or are close to the information	Pictures are unclear or do not pertain to the topic		
Effects, Transitions and Titles	Are used effectively, no spelling or grammar errors	Are used effectively with little spelling or grammar errors	Are not effective – some errors in spelling and grammar	Are not effective with many errors in spelling and grammar		
Bibliography	Is complete and is in APA format	Is mostly complete and is in APA format	Is not complete and is in APA format	Is not complete and is not in APA format		
						Overall Score: _____

Chapter 12
Motivational Video for State Testing

Kristen Renee Waller
Morehead State University, USA

EXECUTIVE SUMMARY

The following vignette describes a way to use different types of technology with gifted students. The students' grades ranged from three through six in a school district. Gifted students used a variety of skills—leadership, creativity, performing arts, and technology—to develop a motivational video. The video was designed to be used to generate excitement for upcoming state assessment. The building administrator suggested the project, and the gifted students were engaged in almost all stages of production. From development to the final production, the students were engaged. Students used iPhones, iMovie, and a MAC computer to develop their product and produced a video to motivate fellow students.

SETTING THE STAGE

It was getting close to the time of the year, when teachers and building administrators are starting to think of ways to really motivate students for state testing, and my school in eastern Kentucky was no different. In hopes to inspire the faculty and staff, the principal emailed everyone a few You Tube videos. The videos were created by schools in order to pump up their students for their testing. They were all very well put together and as a teacher, I was impressed with the videos. While some of the videos were extremely over the top, others kept it simple. All in all, I

DOI: 10.4018/978-1-4666-6489-0.ch012

was impressed with all of them. I was then shocked the next day when I was surprised with a request from the principal. After watching the videos multiple times, the principal had been inspired to have a motivational video made for our students to pump up the excitement and enthusiasm for our yearly state test. The catch, my gifted and talented kids are in charge of creating the video. Watch out Hollywood, this gifted teacher is headed your way.

We are a small, independent school district in what is a semi-rural part of eastern Kentucky. Approximately forty percent of our students are on Free or Reduced lunch. The district is divided into three buildings; K-3rd, 4th-6th, and 7th-12th. As the newly appointed gifted and talented teacher in the district, I provide instruction for the 4th, 5th, and 6th graders every Tuesday, Thursday, and Friday. This is a pull-out program, meaning students are taken from their regular classroom and brought to my classroom for enriched instruction. There are approximately 222 students in the 4th-6th grade building. Each week I work with thirty-eight of those students.

These thirty-eight students have been identified as gifted in at least one of five areas: leadership, creative thought, visual and performing arts, specific academic area, and/or overall intellectual ability. In Kentucky, students are formally identified as gifted in the fourth grade. To be placed in our district gifted program, students must be in the 98th percentile and be given a Distinguished on their yearly state test. They must also have the recommendation of their teachers. Students who have been identified for general intelligence scored within the 98th percentile on the Raven Intelligence Test and have been recommended for the gifted program by their classroom teacher. To identify students for music, art, dance, or drama, students must bring in documentation of their skills from a studio teacher or instructor. They need a recommendations from someone who is skilled in the area of visual or performing arts. If it appears that a student might be gifted in this area, I can contact professionals to request a recommendation for the student.

Prior to fourth grade, students who appear to have high potential for giftedness are placed in the primary talent pool. Approximately twenty five percent of the kindergarten through third grade students is expected to be in the talent pool. However, due to uneven developmental stages, at the end of third grade or beginning of fourth grade, Kentucky schools formally identify students as gifted and talented. In Kentucky, a Gifted Student Service Plan (GSSP) is created for students. This plan outlines how the school system will address the needs of the gifted student in the classroom. Not every child in the talent pool will qualify for the gifted program.

In my school system, my role as a gifted teacher means that I work with a large number of students. It was the fourth through sixth graders in one of my gifted pull out classes that was requested to create the motivational video for our school. Within this group, eight of the students were in fourth grade, twenty-two were in fifth grade, and eight were sixth graders. The gender composition was skewed towards girls.

This group was composed of eleven are boys and twenty-seven girls. Only one student was identified as a twice-exceptional child, meaning that this student needed special education services in addition to gifted services. The student worked with a specialist to overcome specific problems.

CASE DESCRIPTION

The next time I pulled out the students after my principal made his request, instead of separating the students by grade level, I brought all three grades together. The students were clearly wondering what was going on because of the change in routine. The principal showed the students a variety of motivational videos; the ones he had previously emailed out to the staff. These videos were all found on YouTube. The principal challenged the students to create one of their own.to share with the school.

The students began cheering and "Whoo-hooing" as I asked myself, "What have I just gotten myself into?"

As the principal left the room, the students began buzzing. My job was to pull them together into a collaborative group. This is not always easy to do with gifted students, as they are often used to being leaders in the classroom and not collaborators. However, one of the goals of pullout programs is to provide gifted kids to learn with students who are at their intellectual level. The socialization is important and learning to effectively collaborate with each other is one of the goals that I had set for my students.

As a group, the students generated general ideas for the video. They began discussing what song they might want to use. I expected the students would want to use one of the example songs they just seen on the You Tube videos…not a chance. They wanted to pick their own song and re-write the lyrics.

After class, I took the list of suggested songs to one of the classroom teachers and explained to her what was taking place. She teaches 4th and 5th grade, but she is the go-to person when anyone needs creative guidance. This project had her name written all over it and she was very eager to help get it going. Together we listened to all of the songs the students suggested and the teacher said she would work on a few of the songs over the weekend.

The next time I was in the building, I came back to the teacher to find she had changed the lyrics to the catchy little song, *What Does the Fox Say?* by Ylvis (2013). Our school mascot is a ram, so the song would now be known as, *What Do the Rams Do?* She and I sang the song together with the music and re-written lyrics.

I prepared song sheets for the students. As I met with students, I broke them into grade level groups. The students practiced signing the song and tried to learn the words. The excitement really started to build once they heard the new lyrics about the *Rams*.

The students really got caught up with the creation of the video. They made notes and changed a few lines here and there as they practiced singing. They sounded amazing. But the video was not going to rest on signing alone. We needed to put create a dynamic video.

The next step was to examine the lyrics and decide what we could film for different portions of the lyrics. As the ideas flew, the students took over the production. Students kept track of the props they needed, the people in the district they wanted to include in the videos, and what video clips they would use for each part of the lyrics. Once the students really knew the words, I made a tape of all the students while they sang in order to have an audio track available. The audio track would later be matched to the video clips they were planning on filming. We were planning on using the iMovie program to create our masterpiece.

After the students had their list of all of the props and all of the clips they needed, they began deciding how to create the props. The students compiled a materials list and started collecting brushes, paint, and pencils. I was instructed by the students to find large pieces of cardboard. Lucky for me, my husband works at a local store and could save large boxes for me. The students used a projector to trace letters and breakfast foods onto cutout pieces of cardboard. They also put letters on an apron for our principal. Students painted and created each prop themselves. I was really just there to facilitate material procurement if they needed something not already available. I did, however, do all of the cutting of the cardboard; I wasn't comfortable with elementary students using a box cutter.

Now that the groups had all of their props finished; it was time to start filming. Originally I had planned on allowing the students to use my Sony HandyCam to film everything but once I thought about using our Principal's Mac computer, it was clear that an iPhone was a much better idea for a camera. Plus, the majority of my students had iPhones already. The download would be much easier and filming could be more versatile with the iPhone.

I compiled a master check off sheet with all of the clips the students wanted included in the video and divided the list among groups.. Some of the students requested to be allowed to video certain things, because they had already visualized the storyboard, but it all worked smoothly and I was able to accommodate those requests.

During filming, I walked the halls to make sure my students were staying on-task and not being too disruptive. Each filming day, students would compile all of the videos onto the Mac computer and place them in the correct order according to the lyrics of the song on the iMovie program. The students quickly taught me about detaching audio and speeding things up or slowing them down to make the clips fit with the words of the song. Once the filming was complete for the day, students would come back together and check off the things they completed and update the master list of what was left to do. Our class time together was completely devoted to the video and they continued this until all of the filming was completed.

The students did much of the editing during the uploading process so there wasn't much editing left to do once all of the filming was completed. The students created clips of the faculty and staff that made it appear they were the ones asking, *"What Do the Rams Do?"* The students worked with our principal, who was adept at the iMovie program, to add written lyrics the movie so to the other students in the school could sing along.

The technology my students used in this project was a Mac computer, their iPhones, my iPhone, my principal's iPhone, and the iMovie program. These Apple based products seemed to be the best choices because they were synchronized with each other. It made it easier to work with the iMovie program and create the video. Almost all of my students had background knowledge with using iPhones, since most of them either have one or an iPod. Only a handful of students had used the iMovie program previously, but the program was very user friendly. Once students were exposed to its features, they quickly picked up on how to use iMovie. Having the Apple devices made the uploading process and video transfer go much quicker and smoother. Not all of my students have an iPhone but that didn't cause too much of a problem as students shared their phones.

I expected all of my students to know how to record videos because they use the video feature on their own personal devices all the time. My surprise came when students actually started putting things into the iMovie program. Our school has a few Macs but they are typically only used to get on the Internet or maybe type a paper of some sort. I had never heard one of our teachers say their students were creating an iMovie for a project. However, they were much more knowledgeable than I expected. The students were definitely teaching me something about the program every time we used it.

I would say, "Man, I wish we could…"

And they would reply, "Oh, that's easy, you just need to…"

Their knowledge of the program, which is NEVER used for assignments, was uncanny. It was fascinating to watch as they pulled the film together. The students not only taught me, but they pooled their knowledge and taught each other.

When the video was debuted at our Distinguished and Proficient Awards Ceremony, it was a great hit with all of the students, faculty, staff, and parents. I have a feeling that next year, we will be creating a sequel.

FINDINGS

After completing this task, I thought about all that I had learned as a result of the project. I would say that I would definitely be willing to try it again. I don't think the gifted and talented students are going to let me out of it for next year, anyway. Since all of my students are gifted, I was not able to compare their progress to non-gifted students. However, I did observe some of the students shining in the areas of leadership and creativity. While we were working on props and the video clip list, the creative students were throwing ideas out left and right, which gave a great starting point for my not-so-creative students. I discovered unidentified areas of giftedness in some students and I will be recommending to our school committee that we add leadership to their identified areas. These students really stepped up and organized things in a natural way that didn't appear like they were trying to be "bossy" with their peers. It reminded me that teachers need to observe students engaged in enriching activities in order to help identify gifted students.

It is not always easy for teachers to identify students in leadership or creative thought, so projects such as this one, really help teachers identify students for some of the more elusive areas of giftedness. It also provides those students with the opportunity to have their area of giftedness addressed.

All of the students worked very cooperatively with each other during this process. They are all high-level students and they relate to this specific group of peers because they are all thinking and processing skills at a higher level. They could bounce ideas off each other without the other students looking at them and saying, "Huh?" I could actually see that the students truly understood each other.

As this was my first year as a gifted and talented teacher, this project provided me with greater insight into the needs of my gifted students. As a former classroom teacher, I was not as aware of how much enrichment my students needed each day. Gifted students need enrichment. They must be provided with opportunities to be engaged in learning at a higher level than most students. Regular classroom teachers need to be more proactive in providing appropriate education to their gifted students. Teachers need to be just as focused on the educational needs of their gifted and talented students as they are on the kids who are struggling.

If I had to point out some drawbacks of the program, it would be not having enough computers. I would really like to let each student, or a small group of students, be in charge of one specific area of the video. If we could save the video on the cloud, it would allow them to work on it from multiple computers during their free time.

Another drawback was the amount of time spent out of the classroom. The regular classroom teachers were very concerned that the gifted students were missing test review time. For many, high stakes assessment does not allow for time spent away from drill and practice. Some of the teachers saw this activity as merely playtime and resented the time the students were away from their classroom. Instead, these students were really were creating something amazing for our school and learning valuable skills in the process.

FUTURE DIRECTIONS

After completing this activity with the gifted students, I feel I might need to purchase a Mac computer. Coming from the world of a PC and a Windows based operating system, I feel like I need to be savvy using both types of computers because my students are clearly using both types. I would really like to use this experience to encourage other teachers in the building to use iMovie. The presentations of knowledge the students could create would be an amazing asset to any classroom. Students could use a student-created video in a presentation or project. The teachers could save them for many activities in the future. It would be a great way to provide differentiated instruction in the general education classroom. I will be offering iMovie as a choice to my students when it comes time to create a presentation.

REFERENCES

Ylvis. (2013). What Does the Fox Say?. *The Fox*. Parlophone Music.

KEY TERMS AND DEFINITIONS

Differentiated Instruction: A way to reach students with different learning styles, different abilities to absorb information and different ways of expressing what they have learned.

iMovie: A video editing software application sold by Apple Inc for the Mac and iOS (iPhone, iPad, iPad mini, and iPod Touch).

iPhone: An Internet-enabled smartphone developed by Apple.

MAC (MAC OS): The official name of the Macintosh operating system developed by Apple.

You Tube: A video-sharing website, created by three former PayPal employees in February 2005 and owned by Google since late 2006. Users can upload, view and share short videos.

Section 5
Teacher Training

Chapter 13
Differentiating through Technology for Gifted Students

Debra R. Sprague
George Mason University, USA

Beverly Shaklee
George Mason University, USA

EXECUTIVE SUMMARY

Challenging gifted students in regular classroom settings can be effectively accomplished through the use of innovative technology. This chapter explores the case of pre-service teachers addressing the needs of gifted students by differentiating curriculum using sophisticated technologies. Also considered are the technological tools that go beyond simple reporting and move toward authentic real-life experiences. Further, in review, the case specifically addresses attributes of the gifted learner along with the skill of the classroom teacher to promote differentiation through technology. Finally, recommendations for practice are discussed along with the need for teacher preparation programs to prepare teachers more effectively to use technology in complex and challenging ways for gifted students.

CASE BACKGROUND

There is no doubt that many gifted students have access either at home or through school to instructional technologies. However, as evidenced in school-based practice often the focus of the use of instructional technologies in gifted child education is

DOI: 10.4018/978-1-4666-6489-0.ch013

on research or as aptly described by Siegle (2004) the Phase II stage of technology development in the schools where students use technology to "collect data; analyze and organize it and create multimedia presentations that demonstrated their understanding"(p 33). A review of state and local guidelines on technology competencies for students (not just gifted students) primarily focus on collaboration and communication, creativity and innovation, and critical thinking skills. It is no longer enough for students to master technology skills. They now need to be able to use technology to analyze, explore, and learn

A number of scholars in the field of gifted child education (Siegle, 2013; Renzulli & Reis, 2007; Shaunessy & Page, 2006) have called for more sophisticated use of instructional technologies in gifted education classrooms. Focusing on critical thinking skills in geography, Shaunessy and Page (2006) make a clear case for the use of GPS and GIS devices to enhance social studies education in a gifted middle school classroom. Students in this program developed a community atlas of significant places in the community's development, focused on developing a holistic understanding of both the cultural and physical attributes of their community through the use of GPS and GIS. Further, they report increased academic gains including their inquiry and critical thinking skills (p 50). Siegle (2013) shares his insights into using *iPads* with young gifted and talented students to give them opportunities now that the touch and swipe gestures are very easy for young children to master as opposed to the older keyboard or mouse approaches. Further, he notes the wide variety of uses for teaching and learning including but not limited to: general production of information (which in some cases a young gifted child could not produce in written form); creating graphics, text, line drawings and voice recordings; video recordings and an ability to edit; electronic books both intact and created by the child; dictation capability to further assist with writing and spelling; and multiple content domains such as astronomy, geography, and the arts can all be available for the young gifted child. Not only does Siegle note the types of technology available he also describes the reasoning behind using technology with gifted students, "many gifted and talented students enjoy learning through exploration and experimentation…Technology allows the freedom to investigate various paths to multiple solutions…technology transforms students from receptacles of knowledge to active producers who direct their own learning" (2013).

Today's technologies allow students to not only access knowledge, but also to create it. These technologies enable students to participate in a culture of learning that can expand their understanding of the world around them. By drawing on students' interests and learning styles, teachers can create engaging and challenging lessons. Having worked with technology and differentiation for some ten years, the authors will use authentic examples to demonstrate how to go beyond traditional uses of technology with gifted students. This case study will explore some of these technologies and how they can be used to differentiate instruction for gifted and talented students within the regular classroom environment.

Gifted Students and Learning

As teachers and scholars in gifted child education we have long sought a specific and clear definition of what is giftedness and such a discussion could fill a chapter alone. For the purposes of this chapter giftedness is defined in a simple manner, a child who demonstrates developmentally advanced skills and abilities including but not limited to cognitive, artistic or physical traits. In this instance we will focus on primarily the use of cognitive and artistic skills in relationship to classroom practices which utilize technology. Along with the definition of giftedness there are identifiable traits of many gifted students that can be found in the literature of the field. These include: curiosity, inventiveness, inquiry orientation, proficiency in some but often not all academic skills, as well as evidence of strong areas of interest. The intersection of giftedness and learning is often most apparent when the child reaches school age and the relationship becomes a triad – the parent, child and teacher interaction. What the parent has supported in the growth and development of their gifted child is now mitigated by what the school and teacher can provide.

At a recent conference a young man by the name of Michael Furdyk spoke on, "Imagining Future Friendly Schools: Technology, Global Citizenship and Student Voice," (Association for the Advancement of International Education, 2014). During his talk Michael described his childhood and receiving his first computer at age 2, by high school he had started a technology magazine with friends, selling that company at age 17 earning him recognition as one of "20 teens that will change the world" (Teen People's). He has since taken his interests in technology and youth development to become co-founder with Jennifer Corriero of TakingITGlobal, a non-governmental organization, focused on global youth entrepreneurship through digital engagement, global education and social innovation. He described the usefulness of technology in terms of connecting with mentors, developing new skills and collaborating on an idea – the work they are doing is available online in 12 languages fostering engagement across countries. Finally, Michael described their newest initiative, Taking IT Global for Educators (TIGed), designed to assist schools and teachers to "understand and act on the world's greatest challenges" (www.tigweb.org/tiged/). Michael also commented briefly on what school/teachers did for him, in fifth grade his classroom teacher taught him how to write programs for the computer so he could make it do what he wanted to accomplish. Whether or not Michael was identified as gifted he certainly demonstrates the traits associated with giftedness. The point in sharing the example of Michael Furdyk is to focus our attention on what kind of learning support he found to pursue his passion and his interest in technology. He was not sent online to do yet one more research report, give a presentation or create a power point, he was encouraged to use the technology in an authentic and purposeful manner, connecting with mentors, learning new skills and creating a business plan and finally publishing a highly successful online magazine for the review of new technologies all before he left high school.

When we look at best practices in teaching and learning we find some commonalities with Michael's experiences and with the ways in which effective and engaging teaching and learning should look with or without technological tools. Carol Ann Tomlinson (1997) has provided guidelines through her work with the National Association for Gifted Children (www.nagc.org) on how to teach gifted learners. Her recommendations include:

1. Rich deep curriculum that is focused on key concepts and principles, utilizing important ideas, that are meaningful and authentic;
2. Teaching that is paced to the student's individual needs but that also includes time for deep study in content of both breadth and depth;
3. Challenging curriculum that is at a higher 'level of difficulty' and offered at a higher level of sophistication; multifaceted, more ambiguous, less teacher directed and for those who are able, more independent;
4. High challenging tasks with 'supported risk' that allows gifted students to take a risk with a teacher who provides support, nudges, insists while scaffolding their learning in new and more difficult areas.

If we combine Tomlinson's principles with technological tools what kind of teaching and learning would we see?

ORGANIZATION BACKGROUND

We teach in a college of education at a university located in a suburb of a major city on the East Coast. The area is very diverse in terms of languages spoken in the local schools, cultures represented, and readiness levels of the student body. Teachers face the challenge of trying to meet the learning needs of students who have not yet developed phonetic awareness being in the same class as students who are reading two grade levels above their class placement. The Elementary Education Program prepares preservice teacher interns to meet these challenges by placing them in the classroom four days a week while taking their classes at the university one day a week. As part of their teacher preparation the interns take a course titled Assessment and Differentiation.

The Assessment and Differentiation course provides a research-based introduction to differentiated instruction for children in grades K-6. The emphasis in this course is on the assessment of learners and differentiation of instruction to meet the needs of all learners, including those who are gifted. The interns often struggle to meet the needs of the gifted students. They are not sure how to create challenging opportunities for these students. Their differentiation often focuses on providing more work ("those who finish early will have an enrichment worksheet to complete") as opposed to providing an activity that would further the students' understanding of the concepts. Seldom do the interns consider technology as a way to meet the needs of the gifted students; despite the fact the interns have completed a series of one- credit hour technology courses prior to enrolling in the Assessment and Differentiation course. One of the authors on this chapter teaches the assessment and differentiation course and the technology courses. It is clear that the interns need more experience with looking at ways to use technology to differentiate instruction for gifted students.

In our state the guidelines for the identification of a gifted student are focused on school district identification of students who "demonstrate high levels of accomplishment or show the potential for higher levels of accomplishment when compared to others of the same age, experience or environment" (8 VA-20.20.40: Definitions). Further, students can be identified in any one or combination of the following areas: general intellectual aptitude; specific academic aptitude; career and technical aptitude; and visual and performing arts aptitude. Identification must be a multi-stage process using multiple sources of evidence to determine if student aptitudes and learning needs should be served by the district's gifted education program. Finally, in the specific district in which most interns teach, the model for the program is based on levels of service beginning within the regular classroom and extending through Level IV or gifted education programming that is a self-contained assignment. Therefore all of our interns are actively involved in teaching gifted children within the regular classroom in Levels 1-3. Furthermore, the school districts and classrooms within our region are considered to be technologically sound (sophisticated) in terms of the availability of technology although the level of use in classrooms is questionable.

SETTING THE STAGE

Today's technologies have the ability to impact learning in a way not previously envisioned. Mobile devices allow learning to occur anywhere at any time on an individual basis. Schools that once banned cell phones are now embracing these devices. At the 2011 Fairfax Education Summit, the superintendent of Fairfax County

Public Schools in Virginia announced that mobile devices were no longer banned from the schools (Dale, 2011). He called it "BYOD: Bring Your Own Devices." Students were now encouraged to bring their cell phone, *iTouch*, *iPad*, and other tablets to school and hook into the district's network, allowing them instant access to the Internet and its vast resources. What prompted such a switch in policy was the realization that mobile technologies could help to meet the learning needs of individual students, allowing for more individualized instruction and differentiation (Dede and Bjerede, 2011).

Through the use of *iTunes* and *iTunes U*, students have access to podcasts on a variety of topics. In addition, students can access *Ted Talks* and videos from the Khan Academy (see Appendix for a description of programs and technologies discussed in this chapter). For gifted children who are ready to explore topics at a much deeper level than their peers, these resources enable teachers to differentiate instruction around the students' interests and readiness level.

These mobile devices provide more than just access to the Internet and to resources. They provide students the opportunity to problem-solve, create new knowledge and communicate with others. Using the applications (or apps) developed for these devices (many of which are free or require a small amount of money to purchase) students are able to create their own electronic books (using *iBooks* from Apple), comic strips (using the *Make Beliefs Comix* app), or movies (*iMovie* from Apple, *Toontastic*). Students are even able to create their own apps. Once created, these various artifacts can be shared with others through the app networks. Sharing these artifacts enables students to receive feedback from users of their product, thereby helping them to think critically about what they are creating.

Researchers have found that mobile technologies can engage students and have an impact on their attitudes and behaviors towards learning (McCombs & Liu, 2010). However, it is not the technology alone that will impact the learning of gifted children, but how teachers choose to use these technologies. Milrad and Spikol (2007) found that mobile technology is most useful when it is incorporated into course content and call for a balance between the pedagogical practice and device capabilities.

AUGMENTED REALITY

Augmented reality (AR) refers to the blending of the physical world with the virtual world. As people interact with the physical world, they are also engaged with the virtual world through the use of cell phones, tablets, and other mobile devices. The virtual world provides the person with information through videos, text files, and web resources. In addition, the person can interact with virtual avatars that reveal additional information and clues. The purpose of AR is to supplement the physical world, not replace it (Wu, Lee, Chang, & Liang, 2013).

What makes AR an interesting technology is not the fact that the virtual world can superimpose itself over the physical world, thereby allowing users to learn about an area, but the storylines that can be created that will engage students and motivate them to explore both the physical and the virtual world. These stories allow history to come alive, science to move out of the classroom and into the physical world, and users to step into the lives of their favorite fictional characters. These storylines are often presented in a game-like environment "played out in the world, in real space, centered on compelling, contemporary, and complex real-world problems; as such, they invite students to bring in what they know (and can find) about their worlds around them" (Squire, 2010, p. 2568). For an example of AR, check out Moon Walking, an augmented reality app that transforms your backyard to Tranquility Base, the site of the first moon landing (see Appendix for URL).

According to Dunleavy & Dede (in press) the most frequently reported affordance of AR is the ability to present multiple incomplete perspectives to a group of users. This means that users have to work together to create a complete problem and solution. This ability for multiple perspectives could allow gifted students to experience an issue through the eyes of different characters. It is said that history is written by the victor, but with AR history could also be seen through the experience of the conquered. This will enable gifted students to gain new insights and to develop a deeper understanding of historical events.

AR games are being created for use in K-12 classrooms, around a variety of topics. Dikkers, Martin, and Coulter (2012) published an e-book in which they discussed several AR projects currently being used in education. They also discuss some of the tools used to develop these games. Although many readers might feel intimated about creating AR games, the tools under development require little to no programming skills.

ARIS is a free user-friendly development tool that allows one to create narratives, games, and tours. Once created the game is hosted on the *ARIS* website so anyone can access it. Games are developed in a web-based tool. Once developed, *ARIS* games run on the iOS platform.

FreshAir is a web-based editor that allows one to create AR games for the Android and iOS platforms. *FreshAir* includes the ability to create in-app assessments using multiple choice questions. One can create AR games for free for personal use. However, if one wants to share the games with other people or have students access them then a monthly fee is required.

Because of the ease in which these tools can be used, gifted students could create their own AR games. These games can then be used by other students in the class. For example, gifted students could collaborate and create a mystery based on local history. Other students in the class would have to engage in the AR game and use their historical knowledge to solve the mystery.

Web 2.0

Perhaps one of the greatest affordances of Web 2.0 technology is the ability to create content and get feedback from others. Learning no longer occurs in isolation as the technology allows students to engage in participatory learning. Through blogs, wikis, digital stories, video sites, and fan fiction sites, students are able to share their thoughts and understandings about the world around them. For gifted students this allows them to move beyond their comfort zone and to have their ideas challenged. They have the opportunity to engage in rich conversations with like-minded individuals.

One interesting website is taking the idea of participatory learning to a new level. Brilliant (http://brilliant.org) is a website designed for gifted students around the world to learn from each other. Students are able to propose Computer Science, Math and Science problems and then interact with other users who solve the problems and propose solutions. The goal of Brilliant is to go beyond the standard curriculum and help gifted students to reach their full potential so they can achieve breakthroughs that move the world forward (Brilliant, 2013).

Another Web 2.0 tool is fan fiction. Our preservice teacher interns are exploring fan fiction as a tool to promote literacy skills. "Fan fiction involves taking characters already developed by someone else and placing them into a new adventure. Instead of having to create the entire story from scratch, students use predefined characters and settings and focus more on the action and dialog" (Sprague, 2012, p. 28). We are building a fan fiction site for elementary students, where they can post stories and receive feedback (Where the Story Never Ends). The preservice interns, as part of their coursework, can either write their own fan fiction story and post it to the website or they can conduct a lesson and have their students write stories to post.

Multi-User Virtual Environments

Another Web 2.0 tool that has potential for engaging gifted students is multi-user virtual environments or MUVEs. There are multiple types of MUVEs, but they all allow people to interact while engaging in a task. People create avatars, computer representations of themselves. These representations can be made to look like the person or could be cartoon characters. The avatars can gather in the MUVE, create artifacts, and interact with each other. The avatars can recreate real spaces, such as the Sistine Chapel, fantasy worlds, or places based on literature, such as Hogwarts from the Harry Potter series (Lamb & Johnson, 2009).

Although not specifically designed for gifted students there are some interesting MUVES that can be used to differentiate instruction and challenge these students. Atlantis Remixed is a 3D virtual environment which immersive students in educational tasks. Designed for children ages 9-16, Atlantis Remixed supports teachers and students in inquiry-based projects.

Kidz Connect has students creating live shows with students from another country. "Guided by artists and educators from theatre and digital arts, students learned skills like playback theatre, digital storytelling, and 3D modeling" (Vega, Pereira, Carvalho, Raposo, & Fuks, 2009, p. 168). Students collaborate with each other to write, create, and perform the show in a virtual world within Second Life.

Eduweb is a company that works with museums and educational organizations to create interactive simulations and virtual environments. Many of their projects are free and available on the Internet or as apps for mobile tablets. One of their projects is Wolf Quest in which students learn about wolf behavior by becoming part of a wolf pack. Another of their project is moon walking discussed earlier in this chapter.

Dictation Programs

How do you differentiate for a student who is clearly gifted and can think and understand at a very high level but who also has difficulty expressing his thoughts?

This question was posed by one of the interns in her class journal. It led to a discussion about twice exceptional children, those who are gifted, but also have a learning disability. The intern expressed concern about helping this child be successful and challenged when he had difficulty communicating. The student had terrible hand writing and would become frustrated when trying to write. Dictating the work to a teacher was a slow process and kept him from participating in other lessons. This led to frustration and the student would become upset if he missed out on other activities. Furthermore, it prevented the teacher from helping other students who need to dictate as well, such as English-As-A-Second-Language (ESL) students.

Two technologies could be used to meet the needs of children who are twice-exceptional. First, the use of a word processor has proven to be successful for students who struggle with the physical act of writing. Many children with disabilities, such as those with Attention Deficit Disorder (ADD) or learning disabilities (LD) struggle to write letters and words. Their writing is sloppy and they spend such an enormous amount of time trying to write the letters accurately that the message they are trying to convey gets lost. Allowing these students to use a word processor has proven to be successful. Once the physical act of writing is removed teachers have discovered that these children have a lot to say.

Second, dictation software allows the student to convey his ideas through talking and the software program types the words. This frees up the teacher to work with other students. Dictation software has been around for some time, but it has not been easy to use. It takes a while to train the program to recognize the voice and accent of the user. Because the voice recognition is not always accurate, the user needs to go through the document and correct any errors. This can be frustrating for students. However, the level of voice recognition is improving. An app available for the *iPad*, *Dragon Dictation*, is pretty accurate and does not require any training. Immediately after downloading this app (available for free), students can use it to dictate their assignments. The program types what is said and saves the file. The file can then be emailed as an attachment and imported into a word processing document.

CASE DESCRIPTION

Although the preservice teacher interns are exposed to the technologies mentioned previously and are provided opportunities to use these technologies, they seldom consider using them with their students once placed in their internships. Furthermore, they often fail to consider how to differentiate for gifted students, focusing more on the students who need additional learning support to accomplish educational objectives.

During the fan fiction assignment several interns chose to teach their students about fan fiction and have them write stories to place on the website, *Where the Story Never Ends.* One of the preservice interns, Ms. Overberg, had a gifted student in her class who was not being challenged by the traditional curriculum. Ms. Overberg wanted to find a way to challenge the young lady (Erin) and approached her with the concept of writing a fan fiction story. Erin was interested in the idea. Because the story would be published on the website, Ms. Overberg contacted Erin's mother to explain the project. The mother indicated that Erin was frustrated that she was not being challenged in school. Like many gifted students, Erin felt the schoolwork was too easy. Ms. Overberg challenged Erin to write a fan fiction story that could be posted to the website. She provided Erin with the opportunity to explore the stories on the site so she would become familiar with the concept of fan fiction.

Erin was excited about having her own "unique" project and was not afraid to take a risk. She worked on her story every day and shared it with her family to get feedback. Erin's grandmother was a former English teacher and provided Erin with advice throughout the project. Unlike many of the other students who chose to write fan fiction stories based on popular children's books, such as *If You Give a Mouse a*

Cookie or the Harry Potter books, Erin chose a difficult story to base her fan fiction on (*Jane Eyre* by Charlotte Bronte).

The result of this project was that Erin succeeded in producing a story worthy of the original. The intern, Ms. Overberg, was in awe of the results, as were we. The story was told from the point of view of a supporting character. It is rich with details that draw the reader in. Even Erin's parents expressed their surprise at her writing talent. Erin's mother stated in an email to Ms. Overberg, "Thank you again for this opportunity! Erin was really needing a creative outlet and this came about at a perfect time." Erin's story can be found at https://kidfanfiction.pbworks.com/w/page/76462142/Jane%20Eyre%20by%20Erin%20Bailey.

In her reflection paper, Ms. Overberg wrote "As a pre-service teacher, this is the most gratifying response possible: Erin was excited to have her own project, she took on a challenge, she shared her writing with her family, and she persisted until she had a top-notch piece" (Overberg, 2014). At the end of the project Erin's mother contacted us and asked if Erin could have access to the fan fiction site so she could post additional stories. We happily obliged and look forward to reading Erin's next story.

The story of Erin and Ms. Overberg demonstrates one way technology can be used to differentiate for gifted children. Erin needed a creative outlet that would challenge her. Fan fiction provided that outlet and the website gave her an authentic audience that went beyond her teacher and parents. Furthermore, this assignment met two of Tomlinson's (1997) criteria for differentiation for gifted students: a) Challenging curriculum that is at a higher 'level of difficulty' and offered at a higher level of sophistication; multifaceted, more ambiguous, less teacher directed and for those who are able, more independent; b) High challenging tasks with 'supported risk' that allows gifted students to take a risk with a teacher who provides support, nudges, insists while scaffolding their learning in new and more difficult areas.

CURRENT CHALLENGES

There are two challenges currently faced by the Elementary Education Program. First, there is a lack of technology available to explore some of the technologies discussed in this chapter. Although the university has multiple computer labs, the Elementary Education courses are not usually assigned to these labs. These courses usually meet in a classroom that has an instructor's station connected to a SMARTboard. This makes it difficult to provide hands-on experiences with the technology. The instructor often has to present the app or website and hope the interns explore it on their own. In order to address this issue the Elementary Education faculty have agreed to use some funds to purchase *iPads* for use in the Elementary Education courses.

The second challenge is trying to help the preservice interns to be aware of the needs of the gifted students so they can find ways to differentiate for these students. How do we get our preservice interns to realize the learning needs of students like Erin? How do we get them to take a risk and think outside the box in the way Ms. Overberg did? This semester 27 students enrolled in the Assessment and Differentiation course submitted lesson plans right after completing a module on working with special needs students, including those who are gifted. Two students included strategies for differentiating for gifted students. The rest did not consider this population's learning needs and needed to be reminded by the instructor to address the needs of gifted students.

Of the two who did consider the needs of the gifted students, one wrote "Some students are already proficient based on pre-assessment data. They are invited to extend themselves to recall / apply aspects of the next lesson on their own." The second student wrote "With regard to product, students' journal groups [were] created based on pre-assessment data. The three groupings allow students to show their knowledge to the teacher in different ways and provide extensions for the higher-level students." Although not at the level we had hoped to see, these two students at least *thought* about the needs of the gifted students.

SOLUTIONS AND RECOMMENDATIONS

The challenges discussed in the previous section are probably faced by many teacher education programs. In an effort to address them, the following solutions have been proposed. In terms of the lack of technology, as previously mentioned, the program is purchasing five *iPads* to be used in the courses. Although not enough for all students to have one, it is the hope that some students will provide their own and there would be enough to pair students up.

A second proposal is to change the technology course and offer summer camps that combined technology and differentiation. These summer camps will provide the interns with the opportunity to design curriculum and to explore differentiation for unique learners outside of the confinement of school curriculum and standardized tests. The interns, under guidance of an instructor, will plan and teach the curriculum to students attending the camp.

A recommendation for the Assessment and Differentiation course is to separate out the Special Needs module and provide a separate module on gifted students. Due to the nature of high stakes testing and the need to ensure all students meet benchmarks, the interns tend to focus their attention on the students who need additional support. They do not consider the needs of the gifted students because they are already above the benchmark. It is important that the Assessment and Differentiation course helps the interns understand that the gifted students also need differentiation if they are to reach their full potential. In order to do this more emphasis needs to be placed on these students in the course.

Another recommendation would be to invite gifted students in to talk to the interns. This will help them to understand these unique learners and to appreciate the frustration they feel at not being challenged. Ms. Overberg was able to step out of the box because she took the time to know Erin and to make a personal connection with her. She saw how frustrated Erin was and how much she wanted to be challenged. This led to the technology based fan fiction project. Helping the interns connect with the gifted students may enable them to develop empathy for these students and lead the interns to come up with activities that will challenge the gifted students, that will take into account their unique needs, and that will allow them to take risks.

CONCLUSION

This chapter outlines ways to use technology to differentiate instruction for gifted students. However, we wish to reiterate that it is not the technology that will challenge the students, but the types of activities the teacher designs. Only by providing activities that meet Tomlinson's principles of differentiation, that allow for teaching that is paced to the student's individual needs and is challenging can we hope to engage gifted students. The technology tools discussed in this chapter can engage and motivate students, but if the activities designed by the teacher are not challenging, gifted students will soon become bored with these technologies.

REFERENCES

Dale, J. (2011, October 15). *Fairfax Education Summit*. Fairfax, VA: Fairfax Education Summit.

Dede, C., & Bjerede, M. (2011, February). *Mobile Learning for the 21ˢᵗ Century: Insights from the 2010 Wireless EdTech Conference*. San Diego, CA: Qualcomm. Retrieved from http://isites.harvard.edu/fs/docs/icb.topic1116077.files/!Wireless%20 EdTech%20Research%20Paper%20Final%20March%202011.pdf

Dikkers, S., Martin, J., & Coulter, B. et al. (2012). *Mobile media learning: Amazing uses of mobile devices for learning*. Pittsburgh, PA: ETC Press.

Dunleavy, M., & Dede, C. (in press). Augmented reality teaching and learning. In J. M. Spector, M. D. Merrill, J. Elen, & M. J. Bishop (Eds.), *The Handbook of Research for Educational Communications and Technology* (4th ed.). New York: Springer. doi:10.1007/978-1-4614-3185-5_59

Lamb, A., & Johnson, L. (2009). The potential, the pitfalls, and the promise of multi-user virtual environments: Getting a second life. *Teacher Librarian, 36*(4), 68–72.

McCombs, S., & Liu, Y. (2011). Channeling the channel: Can iPad meet the needs of today's m-learner. In M. Koehler & P. Mishra (Eds.), Proceedings of Society for Information Technology & Teacher Education International Conference 2011 (pp. 522–526). Chesapeake, VA: AACE. Retrieved from http://www.editlib.org/p/36322 on 10/28/11

Milrad, M., & Spikol, D. (2007). Anytime, anywhere learning supported by smart phones: Experiences and results from the MUSIS project. *Journal of Educational Technology & Society, 10*(4), 62–70.

Overberg, L. (2014). *Fan fiction reflection.* Course assignment. Used with permission.

Renzulli, J., & Reis, S. (2007). A technology based resource for challenging gifted and talented students. *Gifted Children, 2*(1), 14.

Seigle, D. (2010). *Gifted students & technology: An interview with Del Siegle.* Center for Talented Development. Retrieved from: http://www.ctd.northwestern.edu/resources/displayArticle/?id=158

Shaunessy, E., & Page, C. (2006). Promoting inquiry in the gifted classroom through GPS and GIS technologies. *Gifted Child Today.* doi:10.4219/gct-2006-11

Siegle, D. (2004). The merging of literacy and technology in the 21st century: A bonus for gifted education. *Gifted Child Today, 27*(2), 32–34.

Siegle, D. (2013). iPads: Intuitive technology for 21st century students. *Gifted Child Today, 36*(2), 146–150. doi:10.1177/1076217512474983

Sprague, D. (2012). Use fan fiction with elementary students. *Learning and Leading with Technology, 39*(7), 28–29.

Squire, K. (2010). From information to experience: Place-based augmented reality games as a model for learning in a globally networked society. *Teachers College Record, 112*(10), 2565–2602.

Tomlinson, C. A. (1997). *The dos and don'ts of instruction: What it means to teach gifted learners well.* Retrieved from http://www.nagc.org/index.aspx?id=659

Wu, H., Lee, S., Chang, H., & Liang, J. (2013). Current status, opportunities and challenges of augmented reality in education. *Computers & Education, 62,* 41–49. doi:10.1016/j.compedu.2012.10.024

KEY TERMS AND DEFINITIONS

Augmented Reality (AR): A technology that involves the blending of the physical world with the virtual world. Through the use of mobile devices, people are able to engage with the virtual world while immersed in the physical world.

Dictation: The act of saying words for the purpose of having them written, typed, or recorded. Dictation software will turn the spoken word into written text.

Differentiation: A framework for providing different students with different avenues for to learning.

Fan Fiction: Stories that make use of characters and settings from published works, written by fans of the original work.

iPads: Tablet computers produced by Apple Inc. The user interface is built around multi-touch screen.

Mobile Devices: Small, handheld computing devices that a user can carry around. These include smart phones, tablets, and personal digital assistants (PDA).

MUVE: Online multi-users virtual environment also referred to as virtual worlds. MUVEs allow people who are located in different places to interact synchronously.

APPENDIX

ARIS (http://arisgames.org/): A free user-friendly development tool that allows one to create narratives, games, and tours. Games are developed in a web-based tool. Once created the games are hosted on the *ARIS* website so anyone can access it. *ARIS* games run on the iOS (Apple) platform.

Atlantis Remixed (http://atlantisremixed.org/): Is a 3D virtual environment which immersive students in educational tasks. Designed for children ages 9-16, Atlantis Remixed supports teachers and students in inquiry-based projects. The project includes online and offline learning activities, with a storyline that leads to social action. The website indicates there are over 60,000 players, world-wide.

Brilliant (http://brilliant.org): A website designed for gifted students around the world to learn from each other. Students are able to propose Computer Science, Math and Science problems and then interact with other users who solve the problems and propose solutions. The goal of Brilliant is to connect exceptional students with each other in an effort to help them reach their full potential.

Dragon Dictation (https://itunes.apple.com/us/app/dragon-dictation/id341446764?mt=8): A free voice-recognition app available on *iTunes*. You speak into the built in microphone and you will see the program type your message. The file can them be sent as a text or via e-mail.

Eduweb (http://www.eduweb.com/): A company that works with museums and educational organizations to create interactive simulations and virtual environments. These simulations are provided free of charge and can be played on the web or through apps that can be downloaded for mobile tablets. Although some of the simulations focus on American history (George Washington's World for Kids, Texas Independence, and Building Detroit) others have a more global appeal (A Sailor's Life for Me, Into the Book, Wolf Quest, and The Renaissance Connection.

FreshAir (http://playfreshair.com/): A web-based editor that allows one to create augmented reality games for the Android and iOS platforms. *FreshAir* includes the ability to create in-app assessments using multiple choice questions. Open-ended and fill-in-the-blank questions are also supported.

iBooks Author (http://www.apple.com/ibooks-author/): Free program available from Apple that allows anyone to create and publish their own electronic books (called e-books). When completed, the e-book can be submitted to *iBooks* for purchase or free download so others may read it.

iMovie (http://www.apple.com/ios/imovie/?cid=wwa-us-kwg-features-com&siclientid=6381&sessguid=46bd9852-eaeb-41d7-a6f6-cc3c79b14c0e&userguid=46bd9852-eaeb-41d7-a6f6-cc3c79b14c0e&permguid=46bd9852-eaeb-41d7-a6f6-cc3c79b14c0e): A program that allows you to edit video clips and create movies. It is available for the Mac computer and for IOs devices (iPhone, iPad, ITouch).

iTunes (https://www.apple.com/itunes/): A program that allows you to organize your songs, podcasts, videos, and apps. You can also shop for these using iTunes. It is available for Mac and Windows platforms.

iTunes U (https://www.apple.com/apps/itunes-u/): Provides access to the world's largest catalog of free online education content for the world's leading institutions. Teachers are able to set up content for the students to access.

Khan Academy (https://www.khanacademy.org/): Provides access to free educational videos on a variety of topics.

Kidz Connect (http://www.kidzconnect.org/): Through the use of virtual worlds, youth in different countries collaborate to produce theatrical performances.

Make Beliefs Comix (http://www.makebeliefscomix.com/): An online program that allow students to create comic strips. The site supports the writing of comics in multiple languages (English, Spanish, French, German, Italian, Portuguese, and Latin. There is also an app that can be downloaded for iOS devices. In addition, the site offers e-books designed to support writing ideas.

Moon Walking (http://www.moon-walking.com/): An augmented reality app that recreates Tranquility Base, the site of the first Apollo moon landing. A large field, playground area or backyard is needed to fully appreciate Tranquility base.

Podcasts (http://www.apple.com/itunes/podcasts/): Audio and video files that can be played on the computer or mobile devices.

Second Life (http://secondlife.com/)**:** A virtual world where people interact and explore. It is used by Kidz Connect to perform their theoretical productions.

SMARTboard (https://smarttech.com/)**:** Interactive whiteboards that allow instructors and teachers to manipulate the data presented.

Ted Talks (https://www.ted.com/)**:** A platform for sharing ideas, the site provides video talks on a variety of topics in more than 100 languages. The videos are free to access and there is an app available for downloading to mobile devices.

Toontastic (http://www.launchpadtoys.com/toontastic/)**:** An app that allows students to create video cartoons.

Where the Story Never Ends (https://kidfanfiction.pbworks.com)**:** A fan fiction website designed for children to write stories based on their favorite books and characters. The site is free to access. In order to post a story or comments, authors will need an account (also free). The site is moderated so only stories appropriate for children are accepted. Erin's story can be found at this site. Click on explore our stories and then Jane Eyre to locate Erin's story.

Chapter 14

Differentiation 2.0:
Using the Tools of Technology to Meet the Needs of All Learners

Jennifer G. Beasley
University of Arkansas, USA

Marcia B. Imbeau
University of Arkansas, USA

EXECUTIVE SUMMARY

This case study highlights the essential components of differentiating instruction to meet the needs of all students, including those most advanced, and English Language Learners by using a variety of technologies. Many teachers in the study had access to technology, but few received limited professional development. Roadblocks that many teachers encountered are identified with possible solutions for addressing those concerns. The recommendations provided for addressing concerns that classroom teachers face are (1) how to differentiate instruction for all learners, (2) how to learn and sustain growth in using the tools of technology in lesson planning and implementation, and (3) how to manage all of the various components so that chaos does not ensue and every students' learning is maximized. A review of all of these issues can be beneficial to other teachers in heterogeneous classrooms who want to use technology as tool for differentiating instruction.

DOI: 10.4018/978-1-4666-6489-0.ch014

INTRODUCTION

Today our classrooms are a tapestry of diversity. Classroom teachers meet many challenges as they try to address the student needs. Classrooms are not only academically diverse, but culturally and linguistically as well (Sapon-Shevin, 2000/2001; U.S. Department of Education, 2012). In the district where this case study takes place, educators work very hard to collaborate and utilize the resources they have to meet the growing population of English Language Learners while continuing to balance equity and excellence when serving the needs of all students. During the school year, the authors spent time in the schools where teachers met to plan curriculum and instruction to implement the Common Core State Standards (NGA & CCSSO, 2010). Through these discussions, teachers collaborated and modified lessons as they tried to attend to the goals of the lessons while embedding technology into their classrooms. While the case study represents a common issue in the school, all names used in the case study are pseudonyms in order to ensure anonymity of the participants. This case study highlights the reality that there are many issues in meeting the needs of all students, but in concert with professional development, the tools of technology provide a promising resource for classroom teachers. The case study is organized to (1) present information about the organization, (2) introduce the scenario where the problem is defined, (3) outline problems and concerns, and (4) offer recommendations and solutions.

ORGANIZATION BACKGROUND

The district in which the school in this case study is located has a total number of 18,810 students in 25 schools. The district is culturally, linguistically, economically, and academically diverse. The student population ethnic breakdown for the school district is as follows: 8,062 White; 7,674 Hispanic; 1,563 Native Hawaiian/Pacific Islander; 621 two or more races; 438 Black; 352 Asian; and 100 Native American/ Native Alaskan. There are 10,351 students that receive free lunch and 1,681 students that receive lunch at a reduced rate. A total of 1,785 students are involved in the district's gifted and talented program, 1,818 students involved in the district's special education program, and 8,006 students classified as Limited-English Proficient in the district.

Elementary School

The elementary school itself has a population of 683 students. In terms of student population, 51% are Hispanic and 69% of the students receive free or reduced lunch. The elementary school serves kindergarten through fifth grade. All classroom teachers are highly qualified and many not only have their teaching certificate, but an endorsement in teaching English as a Second Language as well. This school is highly responsive to the needs of English language learners. All communication sent to students' home is done in English and Spanish. The school tries to involve parents in the school community in multiple ways. Students with other needs, such as students with disabilities and gifted and talented learners are also served in this school.

Gifted and Talented Services

Gifted and talented students are served through the district's program. The district states that gifted students need to participate in classes in which they receive instruction services different from those normally provided in the regular classroom. Approved or licensed teachers of the gifted are required to deliver direct instruction for 150 minutes by a designated teacher each week. In terms of gifted services, students meet with the gifted facilitator once a week to work on curriculum designed by the the program teachers. This district has received numerous awards from the department of education as the outstanding gifted program for large schools in the state, as well as, received curriculum awards from the state association for gifted education. The gifted curriculum does not currently include the use of technology.

Access to Technology

The case study school has access to a variety of tools of technology. Every teacher is given a netbook as well as an iPad for use in the classroom. Many teachers use both the netbooks and iPads with students during center time or special projects. Every classroom is equipped with three desktop computers and a desktop printer. All classrooms have interactive whiteboards (Promethean board) with access to a laptop computer. All classrooms visit the computer lab once a week for keyboard training as well as work on subject driven computer games.

SETTING THE STAGE

There are many characteristics used to describe the Robinwood School District that serves a growing diverse population. The most prominent characteristic is their motto *"Teach them All, Learning for All."* The district administration, faculty and staff firmly believe that is the standard by which their actions should be judged and develop action plans to implement all new initiatives with this important idea central to their planning.

The district recently received a substantial federal grant for innovative projects which includes a push for upgrading technology equipment. Additionally, the district has been working for the last two years to develop Common Core State Standards (CCSS) English/Language Arts Units of Study using the *Understanding by Design* curriculum development model (Wiggins and McTighe, 2011). This effort has included writing teams of 4-6 people from a grade level representing classroom teachers along with at least one instructional facilitator from every school in the district. These teams met during school hours (substitute teachers covered classrooms) several times throughout the school year as well as during the summer (for additional pay). The intent behind this initiative was to focus instruction on teaching and assessing for understanding and also encouraging teachers to differentiate the learning experiences to meet the needs of their students. In many ways, this curriculum effort was set up as an extension of the work that many teachers are accustomed to at their school. Elementary teachers routinely gather in weekly grade level meetings along with at least one instructional facilitator and frequently with building administrators in professional learning communities (PLCs). This structure allows time for collaboration, deliberation, problem-solving and planning for students in addition to dealing with issues pertinent to that grade level. PLCs are a stable professional development activity for teachers in this district.

Another focus for each school's PLC, is reviewing assessment data to determine each student's growth, identifying strengths and weaknesses and noting specific students who are ahead and behind. Determining the progress of each student frequently leads teachers to discuss ways that they might successfully address the varying needs of their students as they continue their study and implementation of differentiation throughout the district. At Sherwood Elementary, teachers believe that while there is certainly room for improvement, they have made much progress with their practice of differentiation.

This case study focuses on one teacher who is growing in his knowledge of technology and how it can be used to meet the needs of his students. Data for this case study was collected by the first author who works in a university partnership school where this teacher teaches. Observations and notes were collected over a school year during weekly meetings with participants and a descriptive case was developed from themes that arose from the data. All names used within the case study are pseudonyms.

Our case study teacher, Mr. Lewis, is a member of a PLC comprised of the 4th grade team which includes four classroom teachers, one instructional facilitator, and the school media specialist. The team groups students for reading/language arts instruction based on their students' reading readiness but otherwise have their own students for all other subjects. Three of the four teachers are experienced at teaching 4th grade while our case study teacher is new to this grade although not new to the school. One teacher on the team is more traditional in her delivery of instruction but is highly respected with two of her colleagues viewed as particularly good at classroom organization and management. Our case study teacher is not yet up to the same level of comfort and effectiveness as his colleagues as he has only been teaching for four years and this is his first year in fourth grade.

A recent team meeting discussion dealt with the issue of teaching more science content for this grade level. The team recognized that their attention had recently concentrated on implementing Common Core State Standards in Reading/Language Arts and Math and have paid less attention to the teaching of science and social studies. One source of evidence to support this conclusion was the result of a recent survey that was conducted in the building focusing on teachers from grades 3-5 who noted that they spent less than 70 minutes a week teaching science with the exception of 5th grade teachers who departmentalize instruction and their students change classrooms for different subject areas.

Lastly, while the use of technology in this school is growing, all teachers in this school believe they have more to do to meet the district's expectation for increasing technology-enriched instruction. All classrooms have an interactive whiteboard but typically use them as screens to view power point slides or videos. The interactive functions of these boards are underutilized. When asked about their use of technology in the classroom, many teachers reported that they felt they either didn't have the time to use the technology, or they didn't feel confident trying new things. Teachers admitted that they have received little professional development in how best to use the technology available to them. The district administrators are hoping for an increase in professional development when they receive the new grant money.

CASE DESCRIPTION

The fourth grade team is currently planning for an upcoming science unit on electricity. They estimate that it will probably take 10 days for the unit. Three of the four teachers on the team are very familiar with their science standards and based on those standards have decided that fourth graders need to be familiar with how to classify electrical conductors and insulators and be able to construct simple circuits from circuit diagrams. When the team originally met to discuss their unit, one of the teachers came in with a folder of activities that she has done in the past. She showed the team a worksheet that she has used that required students to label the parts of a simple circuit. She also told them that she has students complete a worksheet of definitions of conductors and insulators. In her class, the unit culminates with students making a light bulb light up by using wires and a battery to show a complete circuit. All students in her class are expected to do the same project at the end of the unit. The team looks over the materials and likes the ideas but a couple of the teachers aren't sure if their students could do all of the activities. One of the teachers reminds the group about a discussion from the last faculty meeting and how the school is being encouraged to utilize technology more in the classroom. They aren't sure how they are going to do this. They decide that they will bring their ideas to an upcoming Professional Learning Community (PLC) meeting with the instructional facilitator and media specialist to get their input.

Following the grade level meeting, Mr. Lewis, who is new to the fourth grade team, is wondering how this unit will work in his classroom. Of the 28 students in his classroom, 24 are English Language Learners (ELL) and primarily speak Spanish at home. He also has three identified gifted students in the classroom and five students who work with the learning specialist for reading. His students love to learn by doing, and many of the students would rather draw than spend their time doing anything else. He knows that differentiating instruction is important and something the school has talked about as a way to meet student needs. Mr. Lewis realizes that his lack of knowledge in science may impact the upcoming unit. Frankly, he is not sure why it is important for his students to learn about conductors and insulators. He thinks the circuit building activity sounds fun, but he has tried a few experiments in the past with the students and he thought that many of his students spent time playing with science materials and didn't really follow directions. When it comes to thinking about using technology, Mr. Lewis feels confident creating power points for his lessons. Beyond that, he is not certain.

On Monday, the PLC team meets to discuss the upcoming science unit. The fourth grade team shows the media specialist and instructional facilitator their ideas. Mr. Lewis also brings up some of his concerns about his class and his lack of knowledge in science. Each of the team members weigh in on the planning decisions and snapshots of their comments illustrates the various perspectives.

The Instructional Facilitator

"I love the idea that you are making sure to target the grade level standards for this unit on electricity. Have you thought about why students need to learn about electricity? If you have them simply do a worksheet for definitions and terms, it may not help them uncover why electricity is important and it also may be difficult for your ELLs to just focus on academic terms. One of the first places I go when planning a lesson is to the professional organizations for the subject I am teaching. It can help me with the content. I noticed that the National Science Teachers Association (NSTA) has a very good website that really talks about what fourth graders need to know (www.nsta.org). When I was looking up information for this unit I noticed that in science they really talk about how electricity as evidence that energy can be transferred from place to place. Do you know what your students already know about this? Perhaps you need to think about pre-assessing what they know before you begin. Maybe you could use your *Interactive Whiteboard* clickers to see what they already know---or you could create a *Poll Everywhere* (www.polleverywhere.com) survey that kids could take when they come to the computer lab. We also really need students to be able to gather information not only from relevant information from print sources, but digital as well. NSTA also suggests that students conduct short research projects that will help build knowledge. We know from our most recent data that it might be hard for some of our kids to do research projects without some scaffolding---but we have a group of students who really need to be challenged in this way. This seems quite different from some of the worksheets you are gathering here."

The Media Specialist

"I think that I can help you access a number of resources for this unit. We have e-books available on our *iPads* that can be checked out from the library. I can also make sure you have access to our computer lab to find some websites that might help you find more information on electricity. I have made a *Symbaloo* (www.symbaloo. com) website for you with a number of websites already marked for the students so that when they come into the lab the websites will be bookmarked for them. There are also some great podcasts on *iTunes University* that might be great for some students who want to dive into this topic even deeper. Have you thought about a project that might tie this unit together? I know some of you have made a simple light circuit, are there any others? Many museum websites, such as the Museum of Science and Industry in Chicago (www.msichicago.org) have lots of resources that help with providing virtual and in class experiments. Perhaps your students could have a choice in what experiment they do instead of everyone doing the same one. Those are just a few thoughts; let me know if you need anything else!"

Following the PLC meeting, Mr. Lewis goes back to his room to think through how he might design a unit that would best meet the needs of his students. Some questions he considers are:

- How will he locate sources for content needed to design lessons that challenge all students?
- How will he make sure that the content that he is sharing is accurate and getting at what is most important in the discipline?
- How will he know where students are in terms of the goals of his lesson?
- What should he do for ELLs? How can he help them access materials if they have difficulty reading?

- If students need extensions to challenge them, how will he manage students doing different things?
- What kinds of project options will be most relevant and engaging?
- How will he promote collaboration and sharing in his classroom?
- How will he manage the technology suggestions given by the Instructional Facilitator and the Media Specialist?

Mr. Lewis understands that this will not be an easy task but is eager to begin designing a unit that will meet the needs of all of his students.

Summary

It is clear from this PLC meeting, that many of the school team members are very knowledgeable about resources that the new teacher could incorporate into the classroom. Mr. Lewis has started to prioritize how he might follow up on many of the suggestions. When it comes to incorporating new technologies and resources, teachers need to start where they are most comfortable. Once clear goals are set, the next step is finding people and resources to help meet those goals.

Technology Concerns and Components

There are several technology concerns Mr. Lewis wants to consider as he thinks about differentiating instruction for his students. The concerns really center on (a) locating sources for content, (b) assessing and monitoring students' progress, (c) adjusting instruction to match the various learner needs of his students, (d) helping students apply what they have learned to the real world, (e) collaborating with others, and (f) managing classroom procedures.

Locating Sources for Content

Mr. Lewis and his team have been working on designing units that focus on the "big ideas" of the discipline. He knows that he needs to find content and resources that helps his students uncover the concepts in his unit while also providing challenge for his advanced learners and support for his ELLs. For his unit on electricity, Mr. Lewis has decided that he will help his students answer the essential questions: "How can electrical energy be transformed?" and "What impact does electricity have on our world?" For content resource, Mr. Lewis decides to start with the national professional organizations that the Instructional Facilitator suggested. Using NSTA will assure that the content collected is reliable. In addition, he has also selected two university podcasts on *iTunes University* for his academically advanced students to pursue. He also bookmarked an online professional journal on his personal *Symbaloo* site that will provide concepts and skills that most accurately align with the skills and dispositions in the discipline. He knows for academically advanced students, simulating how a practitioner in the field works and thinks provides the challenge students seek (Tomlinson, et al., 2009). In addition, he was able to find a few articles on electricity and copied them into the school's *Dragon Dictation* software in order to have the word document translated into an audio file for his ELLs to access the content.

Assessment

In a differentiated classroom it is important to gather data on where students are with the respect to the learning goals. It is also important to know what students' interests are and how students learn best. Mr. Lewis wonders if there are some technology resources to gather this information on his class in an efficient and effective way. He wants to know what his students already know about electricity transformation. He knows that he will need to include not only some multiple choice questions, but open-ended as well. For gifted learners, the questions need to be open-ended enough to know where students need support. He thinks that if he only gives multiple-choice questions through the school's Smart Board clicker system some of his students may get 100% and he won't know where to go next. For an assessment he decides to ask a series of questions through www.polleverywhere.com. He signs up to use the computer lab and includes some multiple-choice questions as well as one open-ended question. He is able to download the results in an Excel file. He realizes from this data that his ELLs also benefited from an open-ended question---it seemed that vocabulary on the multiple-choice questions was confusing.

Adjusting Instruction

Mr. Lewis knows from Tomlinson's work on differentiation (Tomlinson, 2001), that he needs to differentiate according to readiness levels, interest, as well as learning profile in order to meet the needs of his students. When planning tasks to meet the readiness levels of his class, he always starts with a task that would challenge his most advanced learner and then builds in scaffolds to help other students reach the task. He found that it helps him provide rich experiences to all students. He often uses a tool called The Equalizer to help him design his tasks (*Figure 1*).

He thinks about the activity or task that he wants to assign the class and then adjusts one or two of the "buttons" on the Equalizer in order to provide the "just right fit" for his students. Mr. Lewis found a website resource that adjusts the level of difficulty for his students (http://zunal.com/webquest.php?w=178995). He loads

Figure 1. The Equalizer (Adapted from Tomlinson, 2001)

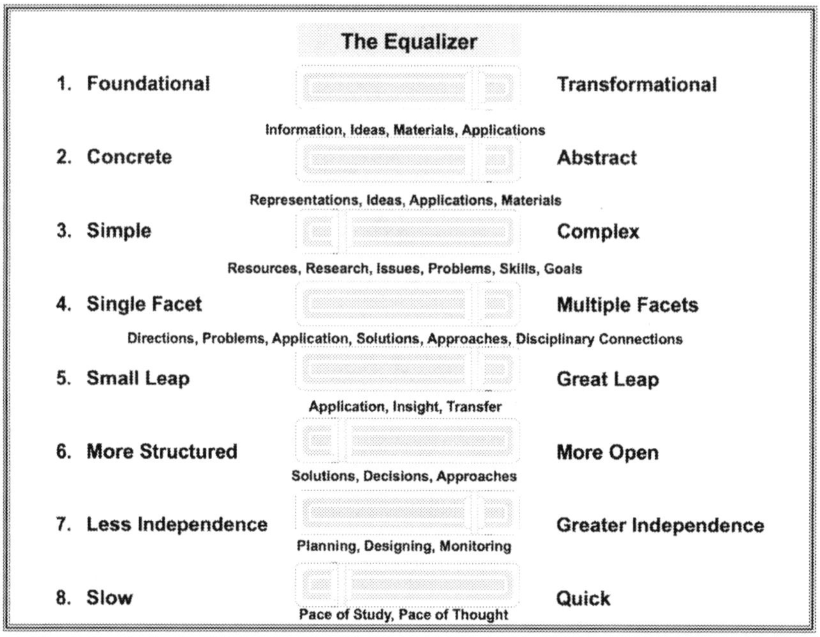

The Equalizer

1. Foundational		Transformational

Information, Ideas, Materials, Applications

2. Concrete		Abstract

Representations, Ideas, Applications, Materials

3. Simple		Complex

Resources, Research, Issues, Problems, Skills, Goals

4. Single Facet		Multiple Facets

Directions, Problems, Application, Solutions, Approaches, Disciplinary Connections

5. Small Leap		Great Leap

Application, Insight, Transfer

6. More Structured		More Open

Solutions, Decisions, Approaches

7. Less Independence		Greater Independence

Planning, Designing, Monitoring

8. Slow		Quick

Pace of Study, Pace of Thought

the Electricity and Circuits site on a few iPads and keeps them at his science station so that students can be challenged to make circuits beyond the standard light bulb circuit they usually create.

Mr. Lewis utilizes his pre-assessment to see where kids are in terms of the goals in his unit, but he also finds out how his kids like to learn best and some of their interests. For instance, from his Poll Everywhere pre-assessment he asked students to tell him one thing they like learning about in science. He found out that one of his gifted students is really interested in brain research. He should have known that because Lucia is always bringing in books to share. He thought that a great independent project that he could create in his unit might be for students to have a choice of learning how electricity is the key to our survival. He found an article on brain synapses and a website about the brain through the American Museum of Natural History (www.amnh.org/explore/ology/brain). During the unit, Lucia chose to pursue the question "How is electricity tied to our survival?" and was able to use the resources given to explore the answer.

Application to the Real World

In Robinwood School District, teachers have been learning how to design experiences that are engaging to students. They have discussed that one way they might engage their students is to design tasks that are connected to the real world. Mr. Lewis wonders if using technology will help simulate a real world experience and how much guidance will be needed for the activity? Might the task help connect with how real scientist solve problems? For his academically advanced students, he wanted to provide a task that was open enough to allow them to pursue questions they were passionate about answering. For the independent project associated with this unit, Mr. Lewis wanted his students to get at the goals of his unit in deeper ways. He decided to look into questions that scientists currently are asking about electricity. He found a website called "Science Questions with Surprising Answers" (www.sciencequestionswithchris.wordpress.com). He asked his students to find one question that scientists are trying to answer about electricity and to create a video or digital story about their journey in trying to find the answer to that question. Some of his students used the classroom iPads to videotape themselves or to take pictures for their digital story. Mr. Lewis had no idea where students might go with this project but he was pleased with the results. At the end of the unit he asked a nearby university science professor to come in and speak about his research and the types of questions he is trying to answer.

Collaboration

In a recent faculty meeting, Mr. Lewis' principal discussed the need for developing 21st Century skills in order to be college and career ready. One skill that his principal highlighted was collaboration. Mr. Lewis thought that this idea tied nicely with what he knew about differentiation since creating community in the classroom is the foundation for differentiation (Tomlinson & Imbeau, 2010). Providing experiences where students work together for a common purpose not only gives students a chance to share with one another but also gives the teacher one more peek into students' lives. After meeting with the Media Specialist, Mr. Lewis found a WebQuest that students could complete as a group and share with one another. He learned that a WebQuest is an inquiry-oriented lesson format in which learners work together to gather information from the web. Many require teams to work together to gather information to complete a task. Each WebQuest is designed with a rubric-scoring guide for educators to assess student work. He found one on a WebQuest library site (http://zunal.com/webquest.php?w=178995). His students worked in teams of four to create a report that culminated in each group talking about why it is important to conserve energy.

Managing Classroom Procedures

Mr. Lewis wants his students to work in small groups. He also knows he will need to think about procedures for moving from one group to the next, how to pass out materials, and how to give multiple sets of directions. For his gifted students, technology can hold promise for answering many of their questions, but without direction it may lead to wasted learning time.

Mr. Lewis is concerned about how students will share computers as well as how he will manage the iPad laptop cart when it is brought in the room. He met with the Media Specialist and she gave him the idea of assigning one person each day to take on the role of "Set-up Manager." He decided to let this student help pass out the iPads as well as pick up them up at the end of class. Many students still needed to wait, but at least he had another person helping him.

Management and Organizational Concerns

Differentiating instruction involves proactive planning on the part of a teacher. When it comes to preparing lessons to meet the readiness, interest, and learning profiles of students, it helps to have support. In the Robinwood School District, they stand by the philosophy of differentiation. Mr. Lewis and his fourth grade team meet weekly in their PLCs to plan units and give each other feedback on their lessons. They regularly look at student data to see where their students are with the standards. For this school district, technology has not been their focus. Mr. Lewis is excited about including technology, but doesn't feel confident with how to manage the equipment as well as how to best utilize the technology. Like many of his colleagues, he just hasn't had enough experience to feel confident. In order for teachers to develop ways for technology to be meaningfully incorporated into the curriculum so that it impacts student learning, they must first become competent with the new technology to the point where they are no longer merely trying to master the hardware or software. As discovered through the Apple Classrooms of Tomorrow (ACOT) research (Dwyer, Ringstaff, & Sandholtz, 1990) building efficacy with new technology takes time. Professional development to address technology skills will need to be coupled with Mr. Lewis' belief that the technology adds value to his students' learning experience.

CURRENT CHALLENGES FACING THE ORGANIZATION

There were several challenges that Mr. Lewis encountered as he planned a new unit of study and incorporated various technologies to meet the wide range of learning needs of his students. Among those challenges were his lack of knowledge and experience regarding specific resources that could help him with planning a unit of study on a topic in which he was unfamiliar and technology resources that could be helpful in differentiating instruction to meet the varied learning needs of his 4th graders. These challenges are likely familiar ones to many schools and districts especially when teachers try to plan curriculum and instruction that includes meeting the needs of their most abled learners and also increase their use of new technologies that might aid them in their efforts.

Professional development at Mr. Lewis' school primarily involved in-house leadership through the PLCs. The ultimate goal of any professional development is to improve student achievement, which can be accomplished through (1) increasing teacher content knowledge, (2) changing teachers' attitudes about their content areas, and (3) expanding the teacher's repertoire of instructional practices (Killion & NSDC, 2002). In one study (Lawless & Pellegrino, 2007), it was reported that only 7% of schools have teachers who are technologically advanced enough to integrate technology into their lessons. The same study found that 36% of schools provide no professional development for technology (Lawless & Pellegrino, 2007). If Mr. Lewis' school is similar to other schools, allowing the teachers to provide their own training in technology may be problematic if not provided access to professional development. In this case study, the most pressing challenge to the Robinwood School District and the Sherwood Elementary School is making sure that all teachers have both information and support for implementing differentiation and the use of technology to enhance instruction for all the learners they serve.

SOLUTIONS AND RECOMMENDATIONS

Understanding the Principles of Differentiation

It is difficult to implement ideas that are not fully understood. While Mr. Lewis appears to be familiar with some techniques for unit planning and differentiation, it is likely that they are not topics that he has reviewed recently so implementation may not have incorporated important components that would improve his and his students' success. He appears to have a good start on the process but he may need to review the principles of differentiation and connect those to the learners he currently has in his classroom to ensure that he has carefully instituted them all in his practice.

Recommendation 1

Teachers and leaders may need to review the principles of differentiation and determine why they matter to the learners in his classroom. *Figure 2* illustrates a flowchart of differentiation as a system with interdependent parts and how they relate to one another (Tomlinson and Moon, 2013, p. 2). Reviewing these elements may improve teachers understanding of differentiation making it more likely that teaching with this approach becomes more automatic thereby positively affecting the learning outcomes of all of their students.

Another resource that might be helpful to Mr. Lewis and his colleagues regarding understanding differentiation is an observation tool, *Differentiated Instruction Observation Look-Fors,* developed by Tomlinson and her colleagues that translates each of the principles highlighted in *Figure 2* to specific actions one might see evidence of in the classroom. Initially the tool could be used by teachers to self- assess their own practice and note areas of weakness and growth then perhaps over time could be used by colleagues and/or leaders to provide additional feedback (see Appendix A).

Understanding the Technology

In the case study, Mr. Lewis was unclear about various technology resources that might be helpful to him and his students and of the ones he was aware of, he lacked some practical knowledge. Knowing some key starting places generally helps ef-

Figure 2. Differentiation flowchart (with permission from Carol Tomlinson, 2013)

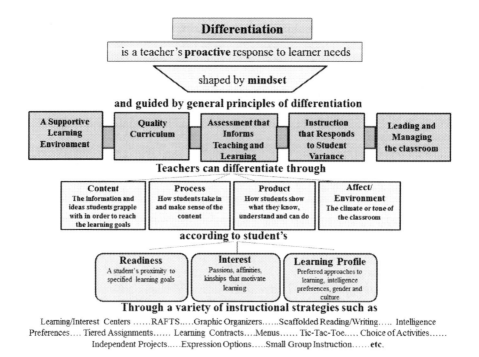

fective teachers believe they are staying current in what technology is available and are typically open to suggestions for how best to use the technology to enhance the learning of their students.

Recommendation 2

In today's classrooms, teachers are educating students who, through their everyday activities outside of school, are completely immersed in technology and are comfortable when utilizing it in almost any setting, particularly as a tool for communication. In the Robinwood school district, teachers face the challenge of engaging a student audience that is accustomed to having information at their fingertips in the form of a Google web search or instant communication with family and friends via tablet or computer. Most teachers, however, were not born into the digital age (Prensky, 2010) and thus are not innately familiar with these technologies. Helping teachers to feel comfortable utilizing these new instructional tools in a manner that both improves the effectiveness of instruction and keeps 21st century students fully engaged in the learning process is a challenge that school administrators continue to face.

Research on promising practices for professional development suggest that teachers need to see two things for transformational change to take place: (1) A clear connection to the curriculum, and (2) time and training to put the skills of technology into practice.

To make a clear connection to the curriculum, teachers need to be clear about their content and the students they serve. A key characteristic of gifted learners is that they tend to learn at a faster pace than their nongifted peers (Colangelo et al., 2004). Technology can provide more autonomy and flexibility when it comes to instructional pace. All learners, including academically advanced, need to have opportunities for in-depth problem-solving (Ravitz, 2009). Teachers can provide many Web 2.0 technology tools to help students simulate real world problem solving. Each of these ideas support content as well as individual needs of students, but it can be challenging for a classroom teacher. It is the case that teachers generally begin with technology uses to support existing practices (Ottenbreit-Leftwich, Glazewski, Newby, & Ertmer, 2010). In order for teachers to move beyond existing practices and provide more student-centered approaches, professional development in technology to be tied directly into the needs of students.

The second issue in helping teachers incorporate new technologies into the classroom is lack of time and training. Time is often not available for teachers to plan together or experiment with new technologies. To help teachers move from more comfortable uses of technology to more transformational uses, they need to have the time to practice and build increase efficacy for using various tools. In this case study, many teachers underutilized the interactive whiteboard technology. In a study by Marzano (2009) using interactive whiteboards were associated with a 16 percentile point gain in student achievement. Even though interactive whiteboards hold promise for increasing student achievement, the study went on to find that in 23 percent of the classrooms, teachers had better results without the interactive whiteboards. These results were attributed to a misuse of the technology such as too many visuals on the screen, or not capitalizing on the interactive nature of the device and using it merely as a whiteboard or screen. In order to give the time and training needed to implement new technologies, the literature suggests providing mentors for teachers. Another suggestion is to provide vicarious learning practices, such as watching a colleague teach a lesson using technology, or to practice the new practice in front of others (Besnoy, Dantzler, & Siders, 2012). One innovative outlet for this is available through online communities. The online resource *The Teaching Channel* (www.teachingchannel.org) has created a way for teams of teachers to watch each other teach as well as give feedback. They have created *Teaching Channel Teams* (www.teachingchannel.org/teams). *Teaching Channel Teams* is a private collaboration platform for schools, districts, and organizations that enables teachers and teacher leaders to work together.

In response to the time and training needed for new technologies to be integrated into the classrooms, many professional development models rely on a single or short series of face-to-face sessions that have a negligible impact on classroom practice (Anderson & Henderson, 2004). Studies have supported the use of blended professional development that includes face-to-face as well as online components (U.S. Department of Education, 2010). Currently there are social networking sites dedicated to the blended learning model. One of note is *Sanderling* (www.sanderling. io). Sanderling is a social platform for professional development that empowers educators to authentically curate and share their personal learning and professional development projects. Through this blended learning network and others like it, it can help create communities that are both face-to-face and online that is customizable and empowering.

No one argues the benefit that technology can bring into any classroom, but finding the connection to the curriculum and the time to put new ideas into practice needs to be addressed if we can expect change to take place. In the Robinwood School District, teachers need to find ways to support each other and be given time to implement technology with support. As a way to save some time, teachers can watch classroom videos asynchronously and provide feedback. They can join blended learning communities to further their growth. Truly, there are many efficient and effective ways for teachers to collaborate; it is a matter of Robinwood School District choosing what fits best for them.

Understanding Classroom Management

One area of classroom practice that continues to be an issue for Mr. Lewis and many teachers who want to become accomplished in meeting the needs of all their learners is determining how they can effectively implement differentiation and technology in their classroom. While managing a classroom was noted as one of the key elements of a differentiated classroom in *Figure 2* and included in the *Differentiated Instruction Observation Look-Fors* in Appendix A, it continues to be an area of teaching practice that can either "make" or "break" a great unit of study or lesson. LePage, Darling-Hammond, and Akar (2005) found that there was a strong relationship between a teacher's ability to manage a "complex set of activities in the classroom and his or her ability to teach intellectually challenging material" (Tomlinson & Imbeau, 2010, p.76). In other words, two outcomes are likely to result when teachers do not have a good grasp on how to organize the classroom and prepare their students for the high level learning they are aiming for. The first outcome is limiting the number activities because they have little confidence for how they would implement various tasks for diverse learners. The second outcome is limiting the scope of the tasks which may help students avoid the challenge designed to stretch their thinking. This last outcome is problematic since it is very often an issue for a teacher's most advanced learners who sometimes do not realize that they have not been challenged until they are in college or graduate school which can be quite upsetting because they have had little practice for how to persevere and may not have developed a mindset or strategies for doing so.

Recommendation 3

Lastly, studying key components of leading and managing a differentiated classroom could be very beneficial to Mr. Lewis by improving his effectiveness in promoting his students' skills of self-directedness and independence as well as improving achievement. Tomlinson and Imbeau (2010) suggests that effective teachers are systematic in their approach to organizing and setting-up a differentiated classroom in order to be respectful of the learners they teach and flexible enough to make doing so possible. "Leading in a differentiated classroom suggests that a teacher has a vision of a classroom where the welfare of each student is paramount, where members come together as a team to achievement important goals—a community designed to support the maximum development of each individual and the group as a whole" (Tomlinson and Imbeau, 2010, p. 14). They further suggest that this approach is a growth mindset (Dweck, 2006) way of working with students that balances structure and flexibility to match the variety of learners likely to be found in all classrooms.

While leading one's students in a differentiated classroom should come first in the process of implementation, there is no denying that there are many important routines and procedures that a teacher needs to manage. Tomlinson and Imbeau (2010) suggest the following are important for flexible classrooms:

- Arranging the classroom so materials that students need are easily accessible
- Giving directions for tasks in which not all students will do the same work
- Keeping conversational noise at a reasonable level when students work together
- Providing ways for students to get help when the teacher is working with individuals or small groups
- Providing guidelines for what a student should do (and how) when an assigned task is completed
- Sharing expectations for moving around the classroom
- Ensuring that students know how and when to help peers who need assistance
- Ensuring that students know where to put completed work
- Having expectations for keeping materials and supplies in order (p. 15).

Mr. Lewis had begun to think of some of these ideas for his *Electricity Unit* but he could be much more efficient and effective by thinking about how he could maximize student use of the technology. Building time into the schedule to teach students how to properly use various technologies is extremely important and can ultimately lessen class eruptions maximizing time on tasks. Also, having students take on various jobs associated with logging-on and off computers, distributing laptops or iPads, ensuring that the printer has ink and paper and/or electronically monitoring task completion sends the message to students that the teacher believes they are capable and promotes his students' independence. He may also want to design some tips for what to do when the technology is not working properly and he is working with a small group of students and is not available at that precise moment to offer assistance. Some of these tips could be shared in a mini-workshop he holds for the entire class prior to the full implementation of a specific technology and could also become a job that students would have over the course of a week or marking period.

In order to promote equity of access to the content and technology, Mr. Lewis may also need to think about how he will ensure that everyone has access to the in-class computers by developing a schedule that shows when particular students are assigned to the station and how "open" times can be handled so that no one student is viewed as having an unfair advantage. It may also be possible that with the teacher's consent some students who are ready for more computer time work at another location (perhaps in the library or open computer labs) and not in the classroom. This kind of arrangement works well, however, only when the expectations for student work and conduct have been clearly established prior to implementation.

Many teachers frequently find that it is difficult to design learning experiences that meet the target learning goals and the varied learners in a classroom and also have everyone stop and start the lessons at the same time. A routine that addresses this issue of "ragged time" is necessary to ensure that there is a clear expectation for what to do when students finish before others and is called an anchoring activity. Tomlinson and Imbeau (2010) offer the following as characteristics of high-quality anchor activities:

- Activities are focused on essential learning goals (not tangential or trivial).
- Activities are engaging (not rote practice).
- Activities address a broad range of student interests and help make content relevant for students from a variety of backgrounds
- Activities address a broad range of readiness needs and vary from concrete to abstract, structured to open-ended, and simple to complex (see *Figure 1. The Equalizer*).
- Activities allow for a variety of ways of taking in and expressing ideas that address a broad range of learning profile needs.
- Activities are presented with clear directions so students know what to do, what the final product should be, how they will know when they are finished, and what to do with the work they generate.
- Activities incorporate a monitoring system so the teacher and students can recognize the level of quality produced and any need for adjustment (p. 127).

If Mr. Lewis had already implemented such a routine in his classroom, there would be much more opportunity for on-task behavior, time spent on completing tasks, and less interrupted small group instruction. Additionally, anchor options provide a wonderful opportunity to use technology for students who are advanced to explore areas of interests, gain access to advanced materials and resources, work on independent projects or move ahead with programs that have self-paced materials.

These suggestions and recommendations are first and foremost doable but only to the degree that a teacher is willing to accept the responsibility for the success of all his/her learners. To some extent all classrooms, even those that have designations of gifted, honors, advanced, etc. are heterogeneous so teachers making adjustments to be more flexible and responsive to the array of learners is critical in every classroom if we want every student to maximize their learning. Smart use of technology may make this journey a little more enjoyable as well as effective for teachers and students and is one more way for this district to truly live their motto *"Teach them All, Learning for All."*

REFERENCES

Anderson, N., & Henderson, M. (2004). e-PD: Blended models of sustaining teacher professional development in digital literacies. *E-learning, 1*(3), 383–394. doi:10.2304/elea.2004.1.3.4

Besnoy, K., Dantzler, J., & Siders, J. (2012). Creating a digital ecosystem for the gifted education classroom. *Journal of Advanced Academics, 23*(4), 305–325. doi:10.1177/1932202X12461005

Colangelo, N., Assouline, S. G., & Gross, M. (2004). *A nation deceived: How schools hold back America's brightest students* (Vol. 1). Iowa City, IA: University of Iowa, The Connie Belin & Jacqueline N. Blank International Center for Gifted Education and Talent Development.

Dweck, C. (2006). *Mindset: The new psychology of success*. New York: Random House.

Dwyer, D. C., Ringstaff, C., & Sandholz, J. H. (1990). *Teacher beliefs and practices part II: Support for change. ACOT Report #9: Apple Classrooms of Tomorrow*. Advanced Technology Group, Apple Computer.

Frey, N., Fisher, D., & Gonzalez, A. (2013). *Teaching with tablets: How do I integrate tablets with effective instruction?* Alexandria, VA: ASCD.

Gardner, H., & Veenema, S. (1996). Multimedia and multiple intelligences. *The American Prospect, 7*(29), 75–84.

Killion, J. (2002). *Assessing impact: Evaluating staff development*. Oxford, OH: National Staff Development Council.

Lawless, K. A., & Pellegrino, J. W. (2007). Professional development in integrating technology into teaching and: Knowns, unknowns, and ways to pursue better questions and answers. *Review of Educational Research, 77*(4), 575–614. doi:10.3102/0034654307309921

LePage, P., Darling-Hammond, L., & Askar, H. (2005). Classroom management. In L. Darling-Hammond, & J. Bransford (Eds.), *Preparing teachers for a changing world: What teachers should learn and be able to do* (pp. 327–357). San Francisco: Jossey-Bass.

Marzano, R. J. (2009). The art and science of teaching/teaching with interactive whiteboards. *Educational Leadership, 67*(3), 80–82.

National Governors Association Center for Best Practices & Council of Chief State School Officers. (2010). *Common Core State Standards for English language arts and literacy in history/social studies, science, and technical subjects*. Washington, DC: Authors.

Ottenbreit-Leftwich, A., Glazewski, K., Newby, T., & Ertmer, P. (2010). Teacher value beliefs associated with using technology: Addressing professional and student needs. *Computers & Education, 55*(3), 1321–1335. doi:10.1016/j.compedu.2010.06.002

Prensky, M. (2010). *Teaching digital natives: Partnering for real learning*. Thousand Oaks, CA: Corwin Press.

Ravitz, J. (2009). Summarizing the findings and looking ahead to a new generation of PBL research. *The Interdisciplinary Journal of Problem-Based Learning, 3*(1), 4–11. doi:10.7771/1541-5015.1088

Sapon-Shevin, M. (2000/2001). Schools fit for all. *Educational Leadership, 58*(4), 34–39.

Tomlinson, C. A. (2001). *How to differentiate instruction in mixed-ability classrooms* (2nd ed.). Alexandria, VA: ASCD.

Tomlinson, C. A. (2005). Quality curriculum and instruction for highly able students. *Theory into Practice, 44*(2), 160–166. doi:10.1207/s15430421tip4402_10

Tomlinson, C. A., & Imbeau, M. B. (2010). *Leading and managing the differentiated classroom*. Alexandria, VA: ASCD.

Tomlinson, C. A., Kaplan, S. N., Renzulli, J. S., Purcell, J. H., Leppien, J. H., Burns, D. E., et al. (2009). The parallel curriculum: A design to develop learner potential and challenge advanced learners (2nd ed.). Thousand Oaks, CA: Corwin Press.

Tomlinson, C. A., & Moon, T. R. (2013). *Assessment and student success in a differentiated classroom*. Alexandria, VA: ASCD.

U. S. Department of Education, National Center for Education Statistics. (2012). *The condition of education 2012 (NCES 2012-071)*. Washington, DC: U. S. Government Printing Office.

U.S. Department of Education, Office of Planning, Evaluation, and Policy Development. (2010). *Evaluation of evidence-based practices in online learning: A meta-analysis and review of online learning studies (ED-04-0040)*. Washington, DC: U. S. Government Printing Office.

KEY TERMS AND DEFINITIONS

Common Core State Standards: A common set of standards created by the National Governors Association Center for Best Practices and the Council of Chief State School Officers that communicates what is expected of students at each grade level.

Differentiation: A teaching philosophy based on the premise that teachers should adapt instruction to student differences. Teachers modify their instruction to meet students' varying readiness levels, learning preferences, and interests in order to meet the goals of the lesson.

English Language Learners: A person who is learning English in addition to their native language.

Learning Profile: Learning Profile encompasses learning styles, intelligence profiles, and cultural and/or gender preferences and can be one way to meet a student's need in a differentiated classroom.

Professional Learning Community: Professional Learning Community or PLC is an extended learning opportunity to foster collaborative learning among colleagues in a working environment. It is often used in education to organize teachers into collaborative groups.

Readiness: One way to meet a student's need in a differentiated classroom. Readiness refers to adjusting a task to meet a student's level of difficulty as assessed prior to the lesson or unit of instruction.

WebQuest: An inquiry-oriented lesson format in which most or all the information that learners work with comes from the web.

APPENDIX

Differentiated Instruction Observation Look-Fors

Drawn from observation tools created by Tomlinson & Hockett (2007), Tomlinson & McTighe (2008), and Hockett (2010)

Table 1. Background: This is a tool for gathering evidence of certain sights and sounds that are hallmarks of responsive classrooms environments. Neither differentiation nor good teaching in general is a "checklist," and no classroom, teacher, or lesson manifests all of these look-fors during a single observation. Directions: Check a box if there is evidence of the "look-for" during the observation.

Learning Environment	☐ The teacher and students respect one another.
	☐ The teacher shows interest in students as individuals.
	☐ There is active participation by a broad range of students.
	☐ Students seem comfortable with one another.
	☐ The teacher creates collaborative learning experiences.
	☐ There is an emphasis on *student growth* toward important goals versus on *student competition*.
	☐ There are routines and rituals in place that help students feel they belong and are valued.
Comments:	
Learning Goals	☐ There is clarity about what students should know, understand, and be able to do.
	☐ Students examine big ideas, essential questions, concepts, and/or principles.
	☐ Students explore knowledge (e.g., facts, terms) and skills in context (e.g., of ideas, of real-world situations).
	☐ The teacher connects learning goals to students' interests and experiences.
	☐ All students are working toward common learning goals.
Comments:	
Learning Goals	☐ There is clarity about what students should know, understand, and be able to do.
	☐ Students examine big ideas, essential questions, concepts, and/or principles.
	☐ Students explore knowledge (e.g., facts, terms) and skills in context (e.g., of ideas, of real-world situations).
	☐ The teacher connects learning goals to students' interests and experiences.
	☐ All students are working toward common learning goals.

continued on following page

Table 1. Continued

Comments:	
Ongoing Assessment	☐ The teacher has used pre-assessment of student readiness, interest, and learning profile to gauge students' points of entry into the unit or lesson.
	☐ On-going/formative assessment of student readiness, interest, and learning profile has informed the teacher's instructional planning.
	☐ Multiple assessments (including self-assessments) and/or multiple forms of assessment are used during the lesson.
	☐ The teacher uses assessment to gauge what students have learned.
	☐ The teacher uses assessment to help students understand their achievement and progress.
	☐ Significant class time is spent on inquiry and reflection.
Comments:	
Adjustment for Student Needs	☐ The lesson/tasks make appropriate provisions for a range of student needs.
	☐ The teacher proactively planned for differing specific student readiness, interest, and/or learning profile needs.
	☐ There is differentiation of content *(how students access essential knowledge, understanding, and skill).*
	☐ There is differentiation of process (how students *make sense of* essential knowledge, understanding, and skill).
	☐ There is differentiation of product/performance (how students demonstrate what they have come to know, understand, and be able to do).
	☐ The teacher uses instructional strategies that are appropriate to the lesson goals.
	☐ The teacher uses a range of instructional strategies to support student engagement and understanding.
Comments:	
Tasks	☐ Tasks require high levels of thinking.
	☐ Tasks are appealing from a student perspective.
	☐ Tasks represent a wise use of students' time and allow each student to work efficiently.
	☐ Tasks approximate the thinking and/or "doing" of people who do similar work in the real world.
	☐ Tasks are aligned with common learning goals, and with one another.
	☐ Tasks provide appropriate challenge and/or scaffolding in anticipation of individual student needs.
Comments:	
Grouping and Management	☐ Students work in a variety of groups within a relatively short time span.
	☐ Students know how to get and give help appropriately as needed.
	☐ There is differentiation of content *(how students access essential knowledge, understanding, and skill).*
	☐ The teacher uses space, time, and materials flexibly to address varied learning needs.
	☐ The teacher and students share responsibility for making the classroom work smoothly.
	☐ The teacher acts as a coach or facilitator of learning for individuals and the group.
	☐ There are clear guidelines/expectations for how students should work individually and as a group.
Comments:	

Chapter 15
School Activities with New Dot Code Handling Multimedia

Shigeru Ikuta
Otsuma Women's University, Japan

Fumio Nemoto
University of Tsukuba, Japan

Diane Morton
University of Saint Joseph, USA

Masaki Ohtaka
Takashima Special Needs Education School, Japan

Mikiko Kasai
Hirosaki University, Japan

Mieko Horiguchi
Otsuma Women's University, Japan

EXECUTIVE SUMMARY

The authors use a new communication aid in conducting many activities at preschools, special needs schools, and general schools. They use dot codes printed on paper and linked with multimedia such as voices, sounds, movies, Web pages, html files, and PowerPoint files. More than one audio file can be linked with a single dot code, and other multimedia files can be further linked to the same dot code in addition to the audios. Just touching the dot code with sound pens (Speaking Pen and G-Talk) can produce the original voices and sounds clearly. If a G1-Scanner pen is connected to a tablet or a personal computer, the multimedia can be replayed on its screen. This chapter reports recent advancements in software used to create handmade teaching materials as well as several case studies from preschools, special needs schools, and general schools.

DOI: 10.4018/978-1-4666-6489-0.ch015

ORGANIZATION BACKGROUND

One of the authors (S. I.) organized the dot code research project (now involving nearly 20 school teachers) in 2005, when he was on the faculty of the Education Bureau of Laboratory Schools, University of Tsukuba. The Education Bureau has 11 laboratory schools, of which six are general and five are special needs schools. He started the research project to help laboratory school teachers promote fruitful school activities by creating *original handmade teaching materials* with sounds and voices. He was also the leader of a regional research community of teachers in the Hachioji and Tama cities of Tokyo, unifying two groups into one skillful, competent group. Researchers from outside the Tokyo area have now joined the project. Teachers from the School for Young Children at the University of Saint Joseph in Connecticut are actively co-researching with their Japanese counterparts. After S. I. moved to Otsuma Women's University, the students there also became involved in creating original handmade teaching materials and conducting school activities at both the special needs and general schools.

To support the individual needs and desires of each student, creating *original teaching materials* is essential. The authors have been developing *original handmade* teaching materials that can pronounce voices and sounds by "reading" and interpreting the dot codes printed on paper, and have been conducting many school activities for students with various challenges and abilities at special needs and general schools.

The authors have held workshops three or four times a year, as well as a symposium to present research progress to the public at the annual conference of the Japanese Association of Special Education.

Financial support was given to one of the authors (S. I.) by the Japanese Ministry of Education, Culture, Sports, Science, and Technology and by the Institute of Human Culture Studies at Otsuma Women's University. Software and hardware for this project are developed with these funds. Continuous support by the developer, venture business company Gridmark Inc., has been essential.

This chapter describes recent advancements in software and hardware of a new dot code system (GridOnput) that can handle multimedia such as movies, web pages, html files, and PowerPoint files in addition to audios. It also offers insight into the development of original handmade teaching materials and reports on recent interesting activities utilizing this new communication aid at preschools, special needs schools, and general schools.

SETTING THE STAGE

Several companies have developed "sound pens" that use dot code technologies in which touching printed matter with dot codes can reproduce original sounds and audios. One such business, Afaya Co. Inc. (Afaya Co. Inc., 2005), offers various types of sound pens (Afaya Co. Inc., 2005); with its business partners, Afaya creates and publishes contents using dot codes. The company recently produced label sheets with dot codes that can be linked with the recorded voices in a sound pen that has a voice-recording functionality.

Franklin Electronic Publishers, Inc. developed AnyBook (Franklin Electronic Publishing, Inc., 2013), a "magic" reading pen that enables words and pictures to "talk" using vocal recordings with any book. The company sells sound pens and unique reusable stickers that users can link with their recorded sounds. The most sophisticated sound pen, DPR-5100, holds up to 200 hours of recorded audio. Unfortunately, these systems can link only one audio to each dot code printed on the paper or sticker.

The present authors first used the Scan Talk code developed by Olympus Corporation (1999), which can be printed on ordinary paper; tracing the dot codes with the Sound Reader tool reproduces the original voices and sounds clearly. However, some students in lower grades at general schools and with severe hand/finger challenges at special needs schools could not trace the Scan Talk codes correctly, and therefore could not join their classmates in all activities. These initial-stage research works were described in detail in a recently published book (Ikuta et al., 2013).

The new dot code system that can handle multimedia, presented in this chapter, has proven very useful for students with various needs and abilities, including gifted and talented students who desire and can benefit from independent study (National Society for Gifted and Talented, 2003). For such students, teachers and/or parents can create *handmade original* contents according to the degree of individual advancement.

New Dot Codes That Can Handle Multimedia

One of the authors (S. I.) has been collaborating since 2010 with a venture business company, Gridmark Inc., which developed a new dot code system, GridOnput (Gridmark, 2009). We conduct "smart" school activities and develop original handmade teaching materials for students with individual needs and desires. These materials are then shared with Gridmark Inc. along with a request for the company to develop them further.

Figure 1. Speaking Pen with contents (left), G-Talk pen (center), and G1-Scanner (right)

Touching the printed dot codes with specially designed sound pens (Speaking Pen and G-Talk) reproduces original voices and sounds (Figure 1, left and center). The GridOnput system has another attractive characteristic; in addition to the audio files, more than one multimedia file – such as movies, web pages, html files, and PowerPoint files – can be linked to the same dot code (Kaneko et al., 2011).

The dot codes, which are nearly invisible to the naked eye, do not spoil the printed design and pictures; therefore, characters and illustrations can become buttons. GridOnput is utilized in various information services as an inter-media interface linking paper and digital contents. The E-pencil released in October 2010 for Kumon Educational Japan Co., Ltd. (Kumon, 2010) became a great success with this technology, and its use is expanding in various educational fields; of course, only the commercial contents with sound pens are packed and sold.

Software and Hardware

The software that overlaps the dot codes on the target positions of the sheet, Grid Layouter (Oki Data, 2010), is shown in Figure 2, left. Three frames are visible: a thumbnail frame on the left, a main frame in the center, and a property frame on

Figure 2. Grid Layouter (left) and Grid Contents Studio (right)

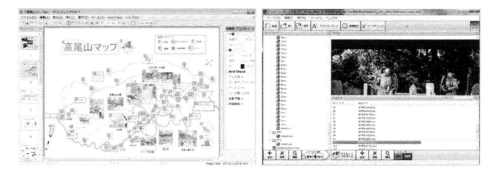

the right. One of the pages of a PDF file, published in the previous procedure, is selected and shown in the main view panel, where the positions linked to voice and sound are marked with a square or circle. The marked positions (printed as dot codes on the paper) are numbered by turns in the right property panel; some of the numbers are kept unused for special purposes as noted later on.

Gridmark Inc. recently developed a new program (NANA.exe) that produces a content folder available for the new sound pen G-Talk. A specially designed new file (filelist.csv) that can be edited with a Microsoft Excel spreadsheet is used to easily link each dot code to the corresponding audio file. The produced content folder can be copied into the Micro SD card of a sound pen or its internal memory and used. Touching the sound pen to the invisible dot codes printed into the paper plays back clearly the original voices and sounds.

In the GridOnput system, more than one audio file can be linked to each dot code; thus, advanced content such as a bilingual (or trilingual, etc.) supplementary reader can be loaded. The authors can easily link four audios to a single dot code, and the symbol icons to switch such audios can be printed on the sheet. Unique dot code numbers are assigned for such switching dot code icons. Advanced coding using an assembly program, instead of the filelist.csv file, can connect even more than four audios to just one dot code.

To link dot codes with multimedia such as movies, the Grid Contents Studio (Figure 2, right) is used. It also has three panels: a content-list panel on the left, a preview panel on the upper right, and a link-list panel on the lower right. All multimedia files linked to the dot codes are first dragged and dropped into the content-list panel, and then assigned to the corresponding dot code number one by one in the link-list panel. Such linking can be verified in the preview panel and finally saved to produce an executable file. The executable file with the corresponding media and its linkage table are installed into the memory of the tablet or personal computer. Touching the dot codes with a G1-Scanner (Figure 1, right) connected to the tablet or personal computer displays the multimedia on the screen. Linked multimedia, such as movies, can be easily added or replaced without the need to use the Grid Contents Studio again. Audios and movies used in the contents are edited with software such as Audacity and iMovie, respectively.

The biggest limitation of the GridOnput system might be the cost associated with printing the dot codes, which can only be accomplished using a pricey model (Oki Data C841dn). To overcome this deficiency, the authors can prepare a specially designed sheet, where the order for each dot code is imprinted on each symbol icon in advance using a Grid Layouter. Each icon printed on the sheet can then be cut, pasted onto the target object, and touched with the sound and scanner pens; this "magical sheet" enables us to use the costly GridOnput system at any school at a low cost.

CASE DESCRIPTION

Handmade Contents and School Activities with New Dot Codes

The present authors have been developing *original handmade* teaching materials with new dot codes for preschool, general school, and special needs school students, and conducting many school activities. For the newly required subject "Foreign Language Activity" in the fifth and sixth grades at all elementary schools in Japan, several contents with native speakers' voices were handmade and used with classes in general schools in the Hachioji and Tama cities of Tokyo. One of the authors (S. I.) and his university students created "Let's Play Tama Zoo!" and "Let's Learn Mt. Takao!" Each has more than 200 audios and 60 movies. They also conducted many activities at both general and special needs schools before, during, and after school excursions. These school activities clearly indicate that new, handmade contents with dot codes are especially helpful in improving learning in "English as a Second Language" and "Integrated Study and Extracurricular Activities" classes. In this chapter, we discuss only a few of the many school activities conducted at preschools, special needs schools, and general schools.

The School for Young Children at the University of Saint Joseph

The sound pen (G-Talk) assistive technology can be utilized in the classroom to support young children's success in a preschool setting. One of the authors (D. M.) employed the assistive technology in four different classrooms (Rooms 2, 3, 5, and 6) with an average of 16 children, ages three and four, in each room. Children independently utilized the sound pen throughout the day when viewing charts for the daily schedule, snack routine, classroom rules, and steps for dressing for the outdoors. Children with a special need also utilized the G-Talk with prompt cards for such tasks/activities as transitioning to school, going to the bathroom, washing hands, and getting in line.

The School for Young Children serves approximately 140 three- and four-year-old children in a part-day preschool environment with extended-day programming for working families. The classrooms are mixed age, with three- and four-year-olds participating in a class at the same time. Each classroom is staffed with two teachers. English is the primary language, with eight other languages represented in the school community. Seventy-five percent of the population is Caucasian. The other 25% includes 3% African American, 7% Asian American, 4% Hispanic or Latino, and 11% other ethnicities. Approximately 6% of the families experience economic disadvantages. Children attend the school two, three, or five days per week in the half-day or full-day program; 70% of the children attend half day and 30% attend full day.

About half of the total school population participated in using the sound pen assistive technology. Each week, 10 of those children attended two half days, 35 attended three half days, 15 attended five half days, and 15 attended five full days.

All children who used the G-Talk did so at the encouragement of their classroom teachers. Five of those children speak a home language different from that of the classroom, and three other children are bilingual. The children who used the G-Talk were in classrooms in which the teacher implemented the assistive technology voluntarily. The teachers were given complete freedom to incorporate the G-Talk technology into any aspect of their classroom environment.

A typical school day consists of structured teacher-led group time as well as unstructured play time. Weather permitting, children engage in play and other outdoor activities every day. As part of their experiences, children develop the ability to maneuver independently through many routines and transitions during their school day. These include mealtime routines, toileting routines, dressing tasks, and care for their personal belongings.

The children showed great skill and comfort in utilizing the G-Talk independently. Children with unique needs benefited when they separated from their loved ones at the onset of the day, as well as during daily routines and tasks. Benefits were also discovered for children whose home languages were different from the one spoken in the classroom.

Audio sounds for the G-Talk were created using the language of the classroom (English) and, in some cases, the various home languages present in the school community. English, German, Mandarin, and Spanish were used for the sound bites. Voices of school staff members, teachers, and family members were used for the recordings. Each sound bite was matched to a dot code printed into a symbol; the school logo was used as the common symbol for all materials. When children touch the sound pen to the symbol, it reads the dot code and plays the matching prerecorded audios. Each dot code has the capacity to represent more than one audio, thus allowing for each symbol to correspond to multiple (up to four) languages.

The audio content created for the G-Talk supplements visual charts located in the classrooms (Figure 3). The charts are teacher-made posters that provide children with a visual support system as they manage typical school routines and transitions. Symbols for the G-Talk were added to the charts for items such as the daily schedule, snack routines, classroom rules, and getting dressed for the outdoors. A typical daily schedule chart is formatted chronologically to relate to the progression of the school day. Such headings include Morning Meeting, Snack Time, Free Play, Small Group Time, Outdoor Time, Lunch, and Dismissal. A Snack Routine chart lists sequential steps for children to help them partake in snacks. This chart has such phrases as "Wash your hands," "Lay out your mat," and "Clean up your trash." The Classroom Rules chart gives children a visual reference for the rules of their particular classroom. The chart consists of phrases and images for rules such as "Be nice to your classmates," "Walk in the classroom," and "Keep your hands to yourself." Visual charts are also used to support children when they dress for outdoor play in the snowy season. A chart for getting dressed for the outdoors contains photographs and phrases that prompt children to take off their shoes, put on their snow pants, put on their boots, put on their hats, and put on their gloves.

Audio content was also created for use with individual children who need additional support, such as second-language learners and students struggling to transition from home to school. Prompt cards for tasks such as going to the bathroom, washing hands, getting in line, and sitting down for lunch contain the coded symbols for use with the sound pen. A family photo with a coded symbol was created for one child at the morning drop-off time.

The G-Talk provided children with support in developing self-help and independence skills, as well as the opportunity to reinforce concepts of print and word recognition. The recurring review of the various classroom visual charts with accompanying audio resulted in the children having more familiarity with classroom routines and expectations. The sound pen also provided teachers access to a different strategy to support children whose primary language differed from that of the classroom.

The G-Talk was utilized in Room 3 to support independence for children when engaging in their daily snack routine and for reminders of the classroom rules. Vi-

Figure 3. Handmade original materials for daily routines

sual classroom charts for the Snack Routine and Room 3 Rules incorporated audio sounds that corresponded to each step in the snack sequence and to each rule.

In Rooms 2 and 5, the G-Talk was utilized to supplement the classroom Daily Schedule chart. Though each classroom's daily schedule differs, the concept is similar: First we do this, then that, and so on. At any time during the day, a child could be seen viewing the Daily Schedule. Room 5 created audio sounds in the language of the classroom (English). Room 2's audio was recorded in both Spanish and English.

In Rooms 2 and 6, the G-Talk was utilized to supplement a visual chart guiding children through the sequential steps for dressing for the outdoors in the winter. The steps for putting on snow gear are very specific; for example, it is necessary to put on snow pants before snow boots. In Room 2, English and Spanish were used to create the sound bites with the voices of a staff member and a family member. In Room 6, three languages were used: English, German, and Mandarin. As with the other classrooms, the audio was recorded by a school staff member and by family members.

The sound pen assistive technology was used to support English as a second language for two three-year-old boys. A German-speaking boy in Room 5 was supported during the arrival routine and throughout the bathroom routine by using the G-Talk. A symbol with embedded sounds recorded by the child's mother was affixed to a family photo that hung in the child's cubby. (A cubby is an area for each child to place his or her personal belongings, such as lunches and outside garments.) Upon arrival, the teachers in Room 5 could be observed greeting this young German-speaking boy, who hid behind his mother. The boy's mother showed her son that the family picture posted inside his cubby had a special symbol affixed to it that would allow him, with the use of the G-Talk, to hear his mother's voice by holding the sound pen to the symbol. When the boy became sad and cried for his mother, he was guided to his cubby and encouraged to use the G-Talk.

Prompt cards were used to support a Mandarin-speaking three-year-old boy in Room 6. The cards included pictures of typical classroom routines or tasks, with accompanying written phrases such as "Go to the bathroom," "Wash your hands," and "Line up at the door." The written phrases reflected the classroom language, and the audios coded into the symbols were recorded in Mandarin by a family member. Teachers utilized the sound pen themselves at times when these prompts were necessary to guide the child through classroom routines. The prompt cards were made accessible to the child during free play, where he was observed viewing them and using the G-Talk.

Use of the G-Talk assistive technology had some interesting outcomes in the preschool classrooms. In general, the author found that children gained a sense of familiarity with the daily schedule, classroom routines, and behavioral expectations more quickly when the assistive technology was incorporated into their classroom, particularly among children new to the educational setting. This may have occurred because the G-Talk technology offered an additional modality for children to access the information provided by the classroom visual charts and prompt cards. In addition to visual information in the form of photographs and print, the G-Talk provided auditory information (Figure 4).

An exciting result of the use of the G-Talk is a connection between the sound pen and a concept in early childhood education whereby the environment is known as the "third teacher." Visual cues, such as charts and prompt cards with information about classroom rules and procedures, are strategically designed to support children's success in the classroom. Crafted just right, these visual cues help children function more independently at school, as if there were a third teacher in the classroom. In our classrooms, the G-Talk offered teachers a new dimension to this concept.

Teachers in both Rooms 2 and 3 noticed that children learned the sequential steps for classroom routines such as snack time and outdoor dressing more quickly than what was observed in previous years. Teachers in Room 3 were excited to observe the effect the G-Talk had in assisting children to learn the classroom rules. The children's regular use of the sound pen to listen to the classroom rules made it possible for teachers to merely mention the number of the rule ("Remember rule number four") as a means to redirect a child's behavior. This is an exciting finding, because the life of a preschool teacher is very hectic, as children compete for teacher attention and assistance often throughout the day.

Figure 4. Handling handmade content with the G-Talk pen

Outdoor dressing routines during the snowy season also create busy times for teachers. Room 2 teachers found that the sound pen provided a productive diversion for children waiting for teacher assistance with dressing tasks such as zippering. Room 3 teachers made a similar observation with a specific child who was easily distracted. The teacher was successful in keeping the child engaged in the snack routine by encouraging her to use the G-Talk. As a result, the sound pen reinforced the steps of the routine, leading to less need for direct teacher support. This was an unexpected positive outcome for a child who typically needed a greater degree of teacher support for regular classroom routines and tasks.

It is interesting to note that a child's age seemed to impact the decision to use the G-Talk. The younger children appeared to use the sound pen more regularly than the older children for the Daily Schedule chart. The teachers in Room 2 reported that their children used the G-Talk more regularly for the Daily Schedule chart than was reported by the teachers in Room 5. It is worth noting that Room 2 had an even balance of three- and four-year-old children in the classroom, while the roster in Room 5 consisted of 12 four-year-old children and just five three-year-olds. The limited participation with the sound pen assistive technology in Room 5 could be explained by the age configurations in the classroom, as the older children were already familiar with the daily schedule without need for the chart or the G-Talk. Teachers in Room 6, where the sound pen was used to support their outdoor dressing chart, observed participation with the G-Talk similar to that in Room 5. The children in Room 6 included 14 four-year-olds and just two three-year-olds.

Another possible explanation for the differences in the use of the G-Talk was accessibility. Teachers in Room 2 made the sound pen available to children throughout the day. Teachers in Rooms 5 and 6 reported that they did not make the G-Talk readily available to children for independent use during the course of the day, but rather only when children showed an interest or a need for the assistive technology. Those two teachers were also more focused on supporting the single child in each of their classrooms who had limited speaking abilities with the language of the classroom.

Teachers in two of the classrooms discovered that their children who experienced separation anxiety appeared to benefit from using the G-Talk. Separation anxiety is a common phenomenon in the preschool setting, where children can experience stress when saying goodbye to a loved one at the door of a new classroom. Children with separation anxiety were observed to use the sound pen more regularly than other children, and they seemed comforted by the assistive technology. It is important to note that in one classroom, the G-Talk was accessible at all times, and in the other classroom, the G-Talk was offered to children when needed; yet each child appeared to be comforted by the sound pen to ease separation anxiety. It is also interesting to note that these children were three years old, which seems to support our observation that younger students tend to use the G-Talk more readily than older children.

Furthermore, one of the children spoke a home language different from that of the classroom. The sound pen appeared to comfort the children, despite their varying language abilities.

The G-Talk had some appealing outcomes for teachers as well. The teachers in Rooms 5 and 6 felt that the sound pen assistive technology offered them a means to initiate interactions with second-language learners, whereas previously they did not have such an option. They were able to offer second-language learners access to their home language in the classroom through the use of the G-Talk. Both teachers had a child who began the school year with no speaking abilities in the language of the classroom. The teacher in Room 5 felt successful in comforting the German-speaking child who experienced separation anxiety; he appeared to benefit as noted above. The teacher in Room 6 felt successful in supporting the Mandarin-speaking child during the various classroom routines. Furthermore, the first phrase this child spoke in the classroom language was from one of the prompt cards.

Teachers had the freedom to create the assistive technology content for any of the many possible charts or other visuals that currently existed in their classrooms. We found that this led to a greater motivation for implementation of the G-Talk. Each teacher incorporated the sound pen in unique ways. The personal connection that the assistive technology offered children through the use of teacher and family voices for the audio may have had some impact on a child's use of the G-Talk. Children appeared to be highly motivated to listen to the sound pen when the recordings were voices they recognized. Both of these factors – teachers' freedom in creating content and familiar voices used – may have contributed to the positive outcomes we observed.

SCHOOL FOR SPECIAL NEEDS EDUCATION, FACULTY OF EDUCATION, HIROSAKI UNIVERSITY

Looking-Back Activities with Movies

This activity was performed for all students (grades 1 through 6) at the elementary division of the School for Special Needs Education, Hirosaki University. Of 10 boys and five girls, three are mentally challenged (IQ = 35–46), eight have Down syndrome (IQ = 33–52), and four are autistic (IQ = 40–98). The intelligence quotient (IQ) was tested by using the Tanaka-Binet Intelligence Scale (TAKEN Publishing, 2003). Although they have a very wide intelligence quotient range, most of the students have cheerful dispositions. They are given opportunities to learn music and physical education as a group, and often play together between class periods and during lunch breaks. Some students enjoy quietly playing cards and computer games using iPads.

About 80% of the students have difficulty in composing Japanese words and phrases and communicating with others. Some of them do not speak on their own initiative. Some can indicate their desires, such as likes and dislikes, with actions or gestures, but for others it is problematic even to select their likes from among many and express them to others. They sometimes act violently, raise their voices in strange ways, and lose their tempers. Most students cannot remember and recount to others what they have learned in the classroom and at school events; they need visual assistance such as pictures and photos.

Previously, teachers created PowerPoint slides and DVD movies for such students to help in recalling their school activities. However, each of the students wanted to "look back" at different activities. Teachers realized that passive activities prepared by them were not effective, but active exercises in which students could select their own favorite movie from images or photos printed on a paper would be more helpful.

The team leader (head teacher) first met with each classroom teacher, and then selected suitable pictures and movies for each student. Children were actively involved and highly motivated in selecting what they wanted to see. Teachers edited the students' favorite movies with a title, comments, and background music; these movies were linked with the corresponding photos placed on a large sheet of imitation Japanese vellum. The symbol icon imprinted with the dot code numbers was pasted on the target photo.

Many students were able to select their favorite movie by saying, "This is it! This is my favorite!" After touching the picture with a G1-Scanner pen connected to a personal computer, the selected movie was projected onto a large screen. At the beginning of the activity, some students were unable to touch the photo of their favorite movie, because they focused on looking at *several* favorites instead of selecting *one* photo and touching it. After they learned how to do it, they were able to easily touch the symbol with dot codes placed on the photo and view their favorite movie. Students calmly waited for their turn to use the G1-Scanner pen (Figure 5, left).

A first-grade student with autism likes reading picture books, playing with toys in the classroom, and spending time alone. Although he cares about his classmates, generally he chooses not to interact with them. He selected a movie titled "Wonderful Time," in which he and his close friend were filmed in a thrilling game that involved picking up a French fried potato from blocks. Both he and his friend roared with laughter while looking at the movie. The student really wanted to look back at that wonderful memory shared with his friend.

A third-grade boy with Down syndrome is always pleasant. He speaks often to his homeroom teacher, though his pronunciation is inarticulate. He uses a personal computer at home and eagerly participates in learning with an iPad at school. During

Figure 5. Looking-back activity with G1-Scanner (left) and two-day school excursion with handmade booklet and G-Talk pen on the train (right)

the looking-back activity, the teacher noticed that he was the first to want to touch a photo pasted onto the vellum and sat hopefully on his chair. When his name was called, he struck a victory pose and stood up. The movie he selected was "Learning through Overnight Staying." He watched this movie with his classmates and said, "I put my mattress down and felt very scared, but it tested my courage." The overnight stay with his classmates and teachers was a first for him; he felt a bit independent and the experience resulted in an impressive memory.

A sixth-grade girl with Down syndrome selected a photo for the movie "Parlor Trick Festival," in which she danced with her friends. The student was a leader of the dance team and practiced many times with her friends for the festival. She was thrilled that her team was awarded the "Teamwork Prize" at the competition, just before she graduated from the elementary division. While watching the movie, she said with a smile, "My friends danced very well and my mother said to me that it's very nice dancing!"

The large imitation Japanese vellum showing many photos with the dot code symbol is a very convenient way for students to look back at their favorite activities; simply touching the G1-Scanner pen to the symbol on the paper plays back the original movies. All the students could share their significant memories with their friends, and individuals could connect with many wonderful memories in their minds.

Two-Day School Excursion: Grades 5 and 6

Every other year, students in grades 5 and 6 take a two-day school excursion. Last October, the school excursion to Hakodate, Hokkaido included five students – three with Down syndrome and two with mental challenges. Five teachers, including the principal and a school nurse, accompanied the party. It took more than three hours by train from Hirosaki to Hakodate. Although most students obscure the vowels in their pronunciation, they can explain their needs and desires to their parents and teachers in their own ways. The levels of their mental disabilities are medium to serious, but they can understand images through photos and pictures and can read simple texts. However, they have difficulty in imagining the future, and thus often feel a bit afraid of the next step in their daily routines. The *visual contents* of photos and pictures and the *leads and prompts* usually help students to describe their needs and desires to their teachers and families.

The students left the Hirosaki train station early in the morning, and arrived at Hakodate city around noon, eating lunch at the Hakodate Market. In the afternoon, they visited a milk factory and Hakodate Mountain, noted for its scenic beauty. They arrived at the hotel in the evening, bought some souvenirs for their families, and had dinner. In the morning of the second day, they visited Goryokaku Historical Park by streetcar. They admired the scenery overlooking Hakodate from the tower in the park. Then they visited Hakodate Meiji Memorial House, which was constructed as a post office in 1911 (during the Meiji era in Japan), and were challenged to make a music box. After having Japanese ramen noodles for lunch, they visited Daimon Kids Stadium (an amusement park) and then returned to Hirosaki by train.

In preparing the unit "Let's Go on a School Excursion," the teachers initially considered it important to use both PowerPoint files and a videotape recorder to introduce the contents to the students. The students, however, often focused only on the photos and movies and had difficulty grasping the meanings of the teachers' explanations.

Therefore, the teachers used a handmade tour booklet with a G-Talk pen to help students grasp the itinerary for the school excursion, both individually and with their friends. The head teacher first discussed with the homeroom teachers any uneasy feelings they thought the students might experience. The homeroom teachers then collected suitable messages to be added to each page of the booklet for the two-day excursion. The head teacher recorded the corresponding voices and sounds; edited them with Audacity software; linked them to the symbols imprinted with the dot code numbers using a specially designed file (filelist.csv) and program (NANA.exe); and saved the content folder for installation into the internal memory of a G-Talk pen or a Micro SD card. Touching the sound pen to the dot code symbols placed on each page played back clearly the itinerary of the two-day trip and various explanations of the places to be visited.

Before going on the trip, students had a chance to see photos and movies of various places they would visit, facilities for travel, and the hotel, all of which were taken during the previous excursion. The teachers wanted the students to become excited about the trip. First they learned how to use the G-Talk pen, and attached their respective favorite colored straps to their own pens. They were surprised that they could hear the voice saying "Let's go on a school excursion" just by touching the G-Talk pen to the small symbol with dot codes pasted in the booklet. Turning over the page, they could check and listen to "when," "where," "with whom," "the day's activities," and so on by using the G-Talk pen. They could also follow the itinerary by checking various photos, reading texts, and answering the questions written in the tour booklet. At breaks, students took turns using the booklet with their sound pens.

In the early morning of the first day of the trip, they gathered at the Hirosaki station with their parents, exchanged greetings with teachers and friends, and had an individual health check. Then they reviewed the first day's program by using the booklet with a G-Talk pen. They carried the booklet and pen throughout the day to check the names of the trains and buses they would take, the current and next destinations, and explanations of historic and scenic places (Figure 5, right). The booklet and G-Talk pen were essential tools for the excursion. For students who have a hard time waiting for their turns to board a train or bus and listening to explanations of the places to be visited, touching the symbol icon placed at the corner of the booklet and listening to the audio of "I can wait" calmed them down.

Returning home from the excursion, the students recounted for their parents exciting memories and answered the parents' questions by using the booklet and sound pen. Parents said to the teachers, "We could really understand what our children experienced and how happy they felt." During the looking-back activity, while the teachers presented the various events from the trip with photos and video movies, students touched the booklet with the G-Talk pen to verify the names and explanations of the various places they had visited.

These cases show that it is very important for teachers to understand the status and characteristics of individual students and create original handmade contents suitable for them. By using original contents with a G-Talk pen, students can easily solve problems that happen to occur. This type of advance learning, tailored to an individual's needs and personality, helps the student with a disability to understand and look forward to new experiences. Repeated learning using handmade teaching materials with a sound pen along with communication with friends, teachers, and parents improves the ability of students to understand words and phrases and express their needs and desires to others.

TAKASHIMA SPECIAL NEEDS EDUCATION SCHOOL

Acquiring Daily Routines with Audio Box

The teacher at Takashima Special Needs Education School in Tokyo has conducted a wealth of activities by adding voices and sounds to the handmade teaching aids that have been used for a long time. This activity was performed with two autistic students in grade 6. A cognitive assessment using the Kyoto Scale of Psychological Development 2001 (Nakashika, 2010) showed that one student had the ability of a two-and-half-year-old and the other of a five-year-old. While there is a fairly wide gap in the perception abilities of the two, both are poor at group projects, refuse to do various exercises, and often leave the class. Therefore, the teacher decided to place them together in a class of their own.

The teacher added dot codes to the existing teaching aids (wooden blocks prepared to learn word meaning and pronunciation), and also made a specially designed box (Audio Box I) to use with the blocks. A Speaking Pen was installed in the wooden audio box, and handmade wooden blocks can be slid along the guide rail (Figure 6, left).

For half a year prior to performing the activity, the students had been learning the school's daily routines and Japanese Hirakana characters during the first class period, which is called "Instruction in Daily Life." For this activity, the teacher put the dot codes on the backs of the wooden blocks, and the students were encouraged to slide the blocks along the guide rail of the specially designed wooden audio box and listen to the corresponding voices.

The student with higher ability, who was very much interested in this system, tried to listen to the voices repeatedly and left the classroom less often. But the other student, afraid of the voices coming from the wooden blocks that were previously used without audio, rejected the activity. The teacher realized that this kind of activity should be carefully prepared and begun by using audio with the wooden blocks from the beginning of the academic year. The teacher also discovered that not all students with a disability like "smart" teaching aids, and that individual aid should be prepared for each student.

Learning the Weather and the Date

This activity was done with four students in grade 5: two girls and two boys. Using the Kyoto Scale of Psychological Development, the students' expressive language abilities were determined to be four years, two years, and one year (two students). Although there is a wide range in developmental age among the students, they are all serene and eagerly take part in the classes. Three students have higher linguistic

Figure 6. Audio Box I with Speaking Pen (left), Audio Box II with wooden block overlapped with dot codes (center), and Audio Box III (right)

and social skills than recognition and adaptation skills. Because they work well in a group, their adaptation ability appears to be higher than it actually is. However, each student has many different and complicated issues.

The teacher modified an audio box and put dot codes on the wooden blocks to teach the weather. This activity was also performed during every day's first period class in "Instruction in Daily Life." The students push the wooden block corresponding to the weather horizontally into the modified audio box (Audio Box II) and listen to the voice (Figure 6, center). The teacher made two types of blocks – the picture relating to the weather and the corresponding Hirakana word – with dot codes on them. The teacher asked the students first to put the picture block into the audio box, and then to insert the Hirakana word block. Finally, the students were asked about the relationship between the two.

With a further modified box (Audio Box III), the homeroom teacher also helped the students learn the date (month and day). (See Figure 6, right.) By sliding the bar to the left and right, students can hear voices saying the month and the day, respectively. This activity was also performed during every day's first period in "Instruction in Daily Life." The teacher first asked the students to select a wooden block by saying, for example, "Which block is appropriate for today's date?" Then the teacher helped the students to slide the bar, focus on listening to the voice from the audio box, and verify whether or not the selected block was correct.

In these activities, the teachers always asked the students to pick up the appropriate block first, put it in the box, and slide the bar of the audio box by themselves. The students' own handling promoted concentration and careful listening to the voices. All the students progressed in reading ability by using such blocks with dot codes; their own handling of the blocks and listening to the audio box, rather than having the teacher read, facilitated their learning.

Learning Japanese Hirakana Characters and Words

In the second class period of each day, "Japanese and Math," the two grade 5 students tackled the learning of Japanese Hirakana characters and words. Testing with the Kyoto Scale of Psychological Development showed one student to be at about four years and the other at two-and-a-half years. The teacher considered students at these developmental ages capable of learning Hirakana characters. It is very important for students with disabilities to recognize the direction of the lines and their cross-ings that constitute the Hirakana characters; visual recognition and sense of touch promote understanding of the characters.

The teacher had been using small magnetic dots that can compose Hirakana characters. In the present activity, the teacher further wanted the students to develop hearing ability and acquire the meaning of words consisting of several Hirakana characters (Figure 7). The teacher encouraged the students to pronounce such char-acters and words voluntarily.

Before using the Audio Box, when the students encountered words they could not read, they simply asked the teacher; without mastering reading and understand-ing the word, they proceeded to the next word. During the present activity, how-ever, they began to realize whether or not their readings were correct. The students made serious efforts and eventually mastered the reading of all Hirakana characters. They also tried to pronounce several words necessary for daily living. From this activity, the teacher learned that mastering characters and words is not restricted to writing and reading; various audio aids like the Audio Box might be very effective and helpful for students with severe handicaps.

Figure 7. Speaking Pen with words (left) and with all Hirakana characters (right)

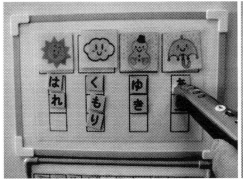 

SCHOOL FOR THE MENTALLY CHALLENGED
AT OTSUKA, UNIVERSITY OF TSUKUBA

Extracurricular Activities: One-Day Trip to Mt. Takao

One of the authors (S. I.), with his university students and the teachers at the School for the Mentally Challenged at Otsuka, created an original booklet with dot codes titled "Let's Learn Mt. Takao." The booklet was prepared for an extracurricular activity, a field trip to Mt. Takao, regularly taken by junior high students at the Otsuka School. Mt. Takao is a popular recreation area for both Japanese residents and foreign visitors, as it is fairly close to downtown Tokyo and rich in scenic beauty.

The 12-page GridOnput booklet contains 152 audios and 35 movie clips that provide information on the history of Mt. Takao and the Takao-san Yakuo-in temple, as well as oral descriptions of the famous scenic mountain views. The booklet also includes several mountain roads to the top of Mt. Takao, the railway map with the time required to reach various stations from Shinjuku terminal, and quizzes on Mt. Takao. The handmade booklet was laminated and held together with two rings that could be handled easily. Students accessed the booklet prior to their outing by simply touching the dot codes with G-Talk and G1-Scanner pens (Figure 8, left). During the field trip in June, the university students recorded video clips for the younger students and placed them into the booklet so that students could look back on their trip later.

Just before the field trip in December, the junior high students learned the history of Mt. Takao. The university students joined in the learning activities and introduced their handmade booklet to the younger students, who could easily handle the booklet. Touching the dot codes – which overlapped the figures, photos, and texts – with G-Talk or G1-Scanner pens reproduced the voices and sounds and played the video clips on the screen of a tablet or personal computer, respectively. They enjoyed hearing the sounds of a wooden gong, a triton, a cable car, and songbirds.

Figure 8. School activities with Speaking Pen (left) and G1-Scanner pen (center), and photo from a field trip to Mt. Takao (right)

They were surprised that touching the railway stations on the route map to Mt. Takao could tell them the travel time from the Shinjuku terminal. The younger students were able to work with their classmates to find correct answers to the quiz questions using a G-Talk pen.

The junior high students also viewed and enjoyed the video clips of various scenic and historic spots, taken during the field trip to Mt. Takao the previous June (Figure 8, center and right). The screen of a personal computer connected with a G1-Scanner pen was projected onto a large screen (Figure 8, center). The junior high students who had participated in the earlier trip shouted with pleasure, "It's me!" Some of the students tried to read the texts added to the video clip.

The handmade booklet helped the younger students to climb Mt. Takao with great interest, and provided them with learning activities before and after the trip. The variety of voices, sounds, and video clips helped to increase the students' pleasure, and they gained confidence through their looking-back activity.

ACTIVITIES AT A GENERAL SCHOOL AND REGIONAL EVENTS

Showcase at Renkoji Elementary School

A day-long activity was conducted in the library of Renkoji Elementary School in Tama, Tokyo (December 13, 2012) by Otsuma Women's University students and one of the present authors (S. I.). At Renkoji School, the lower-grade students have a weekly lesson in the library called "Time for Reading." The average number of books read by each student last year was 68. About 20 parent volunteers often come to the school to mend books and provide support to the librarians.

This activity, held during the "Time for Reading" lessons, showcased seven original handmade contents developed through co-research with the principal, vice principal, and librarians of Renkoji School. Six contents with new dot codes were displayed: "Let's Play Tama Zoo!" "Let's Learn World Greetings!" "Let's Learn Mt. Takao!" "Let's Learn English with Flash Cards!" "Let's Read More Books!" and "Emi and Alex with Sound Reader!" Two of the contents ("Let's Play Tama Zoo!" and "Let's Learn Mt. Takao!") included many movies in addition to audios.

In one of the contents ("Let's Play Tama Zoo!"), three audios, two hints, and its answer were linked to just one dot code each for 60 different animals. The voices of second grade students at Renkoji School provided the answers to the quiz. An electronic book with audios for iPads/iBooks was also presented.

On the day of the showcase, even the youngest students easily handled the G-Talk pen and excitedly joined the activity (Figure 9, left). All the students were surprised at first that *the paper could speak,* and then they listened to the audios by sharing earphones with friends. They especially enjoyed the movies embedded in "Let's Play Tama Zoo!" and "Let's Learn Mt. Takao!"

In the middle of this activity, some parents who were present expressed interest in working with the university students to create handmade content. Following the showcase, the university students gave questionnaires to the elementary students; all the materials received very high scores. The university students were pleased with the positive response to their handmade contents from the elementary students, teachers, and parents. As they left the school, they were surrounded by children waving goodbye.

Showcase at Regional Events Such as a Food and Nutrition Education Festival

One of the authors (M. H.), along with her university students who are studying to become nutritionists, organized a group of volunteers who participate in many regional events to promote food and nutrition education for children and their parents. In addition to conducting a live cooking lesson, if possible, they exhibit many handmade teaching aids created from natural materials to resemble fish, cakes, vegetables, fruits, and so on. They also display original quiz content that includes handmade sheets with dot codes that produce the sounds of cutting cucumber, sweet potatoes, and Chinese cabbage; grating Japanese radish; frying an egg; pouring a carbonated drink into the ice in a cup; and so on.

At the Food Education Festival in Tokyo (October 6-7, 2012), the volunteers exhibited their handmade quiz content, and children tried to guess the sounds reproduced with a G-Talk pen. They were very surprised to hear the "real" sounds of food preparation reproduced with the pen, and listened repeatedly to the sounds

Figure 9. Photos from activity at Renkoji Elementary School (left) and from quiz content displayed at a food education festival (right)

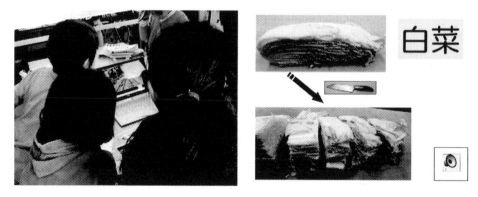

in responding to the quiz. This event was especially fun for children who did not normally help their mothers with cooking; after hearing the sounds, they were eager to know the various sounds in an actual kitchen.

Similar activities were conducted at the Otsuma Women's University Cultural Festival (October 22, 2012) and the Food Education Festival hosted by Kita Ward in Tokyo (January 27, 2013). An elderly person attending the Food Education Festival listened to the sounds with pens over and over and said, "Amazing! A wonderful era has arrived!"

The voices and sounds reproduced with the G-Talk pen drew many attendees to the showcase, and they engaged in lively conversations. The university students who prepared the contents with dot codes were able to expand their technical skills and enjoy communicating with people across a wide age span.

Activities for Gifted and Talented Students

The present GridOnput system is very useful for gifted and talented students who want independent study; for such students, the teachers and/or parents can create *handmade original* contents according to the degree of individual advancement.

Bilingual handmade supplementary readers with native narrations (for example, English and Japanese) are effectively used to learn English as a second language at several general schools in Tokyo. Textbooks and picture books with narrations, providing the students with opportunities to read aloud, help them to acquire reading abilities and deepen the meanings of the books.

To promote the "Reading More Books" activity, teachers and volunteers at several elementary schools create handmade books with narrations. The teachers have also achieved success through preparing homework sheets with hints in their own voices to encourage voluntary activities at home. Handmade illustrated books of animals and vegetables, including explanations in teachers' voices, are helpful in the lower grades in cultivating gifted students' abilities in natural science.

These examples illustrate teachers' applications of the easy-to-handle software and hardware presented in this paper with gifted, talented, and other students.

CURRENT CHALLENGES FACING THE ORGANIZATION

The GridOnput developer, Gridmark Inc., has not publicly distributed the commercial software that enables people to create *original handmade* contents. They only develop the contents in cooperation with companies and organizations. However, the software to create original handmade contents and "magical sheets" imprinted with dots may be obtained from one of the present authors (S. I.).

The following challenges are essential for us to continue and expand creating original handmade contents and conducting school activities.

1. Results should be classified both qualitatively and quantitatively, and deliberated theoretically (using the basic terms of pedagogy, special education, and psychology) by continuously accumulating school activities with original handmade contents.
2. One of the present authors (S. I.) has been doing co-research with Gridmark Inc., and the company constantly provides him with newly developed software that allows him to create original handmade contents. The authors continue to develop such materials, conduct "smart" school activities, and introduce them to the company with requests to promote further development. The continuing good relationship between the authors and Gridmark Inc. is essential to advance our research project.
3. Continually acquiring funds is another essential requirement to promote this project, since most Japanese schools do not have the means to purchase commercial teaching materials.
4. School activities with *original handmade contents with audios* have led to many rewarding outcomes that help students to communicate with their families and classmates, experience the pleasures and satisfactions of everyday life, gain confidence, and improve their ability to perform tasks necessary for daily life. These fruitful results, however, are not widely distributed even in Japan. The authors now want to introduce these "smart" school activities worldwide to researchers and teachers, and to begin collaborative projects.
5. Teachers should create *original handmade teaching materials* for individual students in their classes and conduct productive school activities. University students should be asked and encouraged to help teachers, whose time is so limited, to develop their handmade contents.

SOLUTIONS AND RECOMMENDATIONS

Original handmade teaching materials with dot codes help students to improve their daily lives and learning at preschools, special needs schools, and general schools. These handmade materials should be created for the individual needs and desires of each student, including the gifted and talented. Touching the sound and scanner pens to the invisible dot codes printed into the materials plays back the linked audios clearly, repeatedly, anywhere, and anytime; the linked multimedia, such as movies, are also reproduced on the screen of a tablet or personal computer connected with a G1-Scanner pen. Although the creative contents and school activities rely on teachers' careful consideration of their individual students, the following examples may help many people to improve their daily lives and learning.

1. Those who want to learn another language: Original contents with native speakers' voices and narrative movies are vital. The handmade contents with G-Talk pens are quite helpful for teachers of the required subject "Foreign Languages" in all Japanese elementary schools. Handmade contents with dot codes linked to the corresponding audio and/or movie are also quite useful to promote and deepen the learning of "Integrated Study" in extracurricular school activities.

2. Gifted and talented students: The new dot code technology gives thoughtful teachers and parents the ability to create original handmade teaching materials for exceptionally bright and talented individuals and conduct fruitful activities with such contents, tailored to the unique motivations and interests of each student. Their intellectual gifts and special talents can be encouraged and nurtured in ways that appeal to their natural learning styles.

3. Students with expressive language disabilities and mental challenges: Constant long-term activities with sound pens may help to promote listening to words and phrases and pronouncing them. The authors have been reporting productive long-term activities in which students acquire the pronunciation of several key words in their daily lives (Nemoto & Ikuta 2010; Ishitobi, Ezoe, & Ikuta, 2010; Ikuta et al., 2013).

4. Students with no verbal skills: Telling their needs and desires to others is essential in their daily lives. The contents with dot codes help such students to join in various school activities. At the start of the school day, they can even call the class roll merely by touching their classmates' photos with a sound pen.

5. Students with a stammer and disability in composing words and phrases: The contents with dot codes are very useful in listening carefully and repeating the audios, thus improving their own voices through repetition. The GridOnput system is helpful in distinguishing the relationships among photos (figures), words, and their pronunciations.

6. Non-native speaking students: Hearing contents in their native tongue using dot codes is very beneficial in grasping their daily routines and reducing anxiety.

7. Students who learn better through auditory than visual means: The contents with dot codes help them to acquire information on the daily routines and learning in their classes.

8. Extracurricular activities such as day trips and overnight excursions: The booklets with audios help students, especially those with disabilities, to grasp daily schedules, become calm, and obtain information on scenic and historic spots.

9. Looking-back activities: The contents with dot codes linked to movies help students to remember activities and events. Handmade picture books and dictionaries with dot codes linked to multimedia (such as audios, movies, web pages, html files, and PowerPoint files) also help students to learn the basic skills of reading, writing, and arithmetic.

10. Preschool and general school students: The contents with dot codes help preschool students to acquire reading comprehension and to understand sentence construction. The books with dot codes that enable students to hear content read aloud help them to acquire hearing and reading ability. Homework sheets with dot codes including hints and answers using teachers' voices are very helpful for the self-learning of lower-grade students.

11. Elderly persons with linguistic problems: The sheets with dot codes assist them in recovering their pronunciation ability. The dot codes could also be attached to medicine prescribed at a pharmacy; such audios could help people who cannot read or write and who are visually impaired.

ACKNOWLEDGMENT

The authors thank all the teachers and students at the School for Young Children, University of Saint Joseph; the School for Special Needs Education, Hirosaki University; Takashima Special Needs Education School; the School for the Mentally Challenged at Otsuka, University of Tsukuba; and Renkoji Elementary School. This work was supported both by Grants-in-Aid for Scientific Research (JSPS KAKENHI (C) Grant Numbers 20653068 and 22530992) and the Institute of Human Culture Studies, Otsuma Women's University. The authors would like to express their sincere gratitude to Gridmark Inc. for continuous support. The authors would like to thank Lise Greene for the English language review and valuable comments.

REFERENCES

Afaya Co. Inc. (2005). *Afaya*. Retrieved from http://www.afaya.co.jp/afayapen.html

Franklin Electronic Publishers, Inc. (2013). *AnyBook*. Retrieved from http://www.anybookreader.com

Gridmark Inc. (2009). *GridOnput*. Retrieved from http://www.gridmark.co.jp/english/gridonput.html

Ikuta, S., Nemoto, F., Endo, E., Kaiami, S., & Ezoe, T. (2013). School activities using handmade teaching materials with dot codes. In D. G. Barres, Z. C. Carrion, & R. L.-C. Delgado (Eds.), *Technologies for inclusive education: Beyond traditional integration approaches* (pp. 220–243). Hershey, PA: IGI Global.

Ishitobi, R., Ezoe, T., & Ikuta, S. (2010). "Tracing" is "speaking": Communicating and learning using supportive sound books [in Japanese]. *Computers & Education*, *29*, 64–67.

Kaneko, S., Ohshima, M., Takei, K., Yamamoto, L., Ezoe, T., Ueyama, S., & Ikuta, S. (2011). School activities with voices and sounds: Handmade teaching materials and sound pens [in Japanese]. *Computers & Education*, *30*, 48–51.

Kumon Educational Japan Co. Ltd. (2010). *E-Pencil*. Retrieved from http://www.kumon.ne.jp/eigo/index.html?lid=eigo_002

Nakashika, A. (2010). *Kyoto Scale of Psychological Development 2001*. Retrieved from http://www.prccs.otemon.ac.jp/item/clinic/clinic03_nakashika.pdf

National Society for the Gifted and Talented (NSGT). (2003). Retrieved from http://www.nsgt.org

Nemoto, F., & Ikuta, S. (2010). "Tracing" is "speaking": A student acquiring the happiness of communication using "Sound Pronunciation System" [in Japanese]. *Computers & Education*, *28*, 57–60.

Oki Data Corporation. (2010). *Grid Layouter and Grid Contents Studio*. Retrieved from http://www.okidata.co.jp/solution/gridmark

Olympus Corporation. (1999). *Scan talk*. Retrieved from http://www.olympus.co.jp/jp/news/1999b/nr990823r300j.cfm

TAKEN Publishing. (2003). *Tanaka-Binet Intelligence Scale V*. Retrieved from http://www.taken.co.jp/contents/vinet/vinet_top.htm

KEY TERMS AND DEFINITIONS

Audio Box: A Speaking Pen is installed in a handmade wooden box. Wooden blocks with dot codes can be slid along the various types of guide rails, producing voices very clearly.

Dot Code: Invisible dot codes developed by Gridmark Inc. are a novel two-dimensional code technology consisting of extremely small dots. Simple touch by the sound and scanner pens on printed dot codes enables the linking between paper and digital contents.

Extracurricular Activity: In the "Period of Integrated Study," a required subject in Japan, no textbooks or curricula are used. The handmade original contents with dot codes may help to make such classes more interesting and enjoyable.

Handmade Content: *Handmade original* teaching contents play a key role in learning; individual content suitable for each student should be prepared and used, especially in preschool and special needs classrooms.

Intelligence Test: Many intelligence tests have been developed to assess abilities, using a great variety of tasks including skills or behaviors. The authors used the Tanaka-Binet Intelligence Scale or Kyoto Scale of Psychological Development.

"Magical Sheet": On this specially designed sheet, the order for each dot code is imprinted on each symbol icon. The icons can then be cut, pasted onto the target object, and touched with the sound and scanner pens. The "magical sheet" enables the costly GridOnput system to be used at any school at a low cost.

Scanner Pen: The G1-Scanner pen can read the dot codes printed on the paper and play back multimedia (such as movies) on the screen of a G1-Scanner connected to a tablet or personal computer.

Sound Pen: The G-Talk and Speaking Pen can reproduce original voices and sounds by simply touching dot codes printed on the paper. In the present GridOnput system, more than one audio can be linked to each dot code symbol.

Chapter 16
Designing Instruction for Future Gifted Science Teachers

Judith Bazler
Monmouth University, USA

Letitia Graybill
Monmouth University, USA

Meta Van Sickle
College of Charleston, USA

EXECUTIVE SUMMARY

Honors programs are designed to provide talented students the opportunity to excel with a group of peers having a similar level of ability, motivation, and prior academic achievement. A problem that results is Honors Programs and education programs rarely interface, and thus, current models do not optimally serve the gifted adult who will become a science teacher. Gifted students are not easily identified in the science methods class. Notices about involvement from Honors Programs are often not forwarded to people in teacher education programs. Such lack of information means that science methods instructors must identify the students without benefit of Honors Program insight. This chapter discusses identification and curriculum for gifted adults.

DOI: 10.4018/978-1-4666-6489-0.ch016

SETTING THE STAGE

There are many factors that potentially influence the motivational trajectories of university among gifted students. The challenge, however, lies in the identification of the gifted among a selection of students who have met university entrance requirements on the undergraduate level and that have degrees granted by accredited colleges and universities especially if the education program is not informed about the honors designation of the teacher candidate. Consequently, science methods and other education faculty must learn to identify and then differentiate instruction for this population. So some key questions are, how do we challenge the gifted among an already select group of teacher education candidates? What differentiation of teaching methods needs to occur, and what products should the instructor expect from the gifted and talented teacher education candidate? These questions must be answered because the general characteristics that all future teachers hold is a desire for autonomy, a desire to study a topic in depth and the ability to be creative with lesson planning and classroom implementation, and projects that motivate future teachers and include integrated curricula and activities in either solo or group work that also meet the social needs of the gifted student.

Gifted students exhibit one or more of the following characteristics:

- Intense devotion to personal interests.
- Independence.
- Boredom when not engaged in the activity presented.
- Ability to see to the root of problems.
- Tendency be a maverick and a rapid learner.
- Ability to anticipate outcomes.
- Capable of abstract thinking and learning skills.
- Have talent in creative or leadership abilities.

Gifted students who enroll as adults in science methods classes may possess these characteristics. These students actively accept the responsibilities of the requirements, work independently to produce excellent materials and are not afraid to challenge the professor when opinions and techniques differ.

Gifted adult students may be viewed as driven with perfectionist tendencies aiming at high standards. They can also be overly sensitive and perhaps exhibit odd or intimidating behaviors and are prone to question authority. Psychologists who work with gifted adults find them to be independent, original, curious and open to changes. Thus, it becomes the task of the science educator to work with these gifted students so that they become excellent science teachers who are capable of utilizing these same characteristics when they become teachers. Gifted students who want to become science teachers can be challenging to work with but the products that they generate are noteworthy both in terms of content and form.

ORGANIZATION BACKGROUND

Gifted individuals are defined as people with outstanding talent who perform or show the potential for performing at remarkably high levels of accomplishment when compared with others of their age, experience, or environment.

All of the students that enroll in graduate and undergraduate teacher preparation programs have been successful in achieving the level of education prescribed by their career goals. The graduate students have all received baccalaureate degrees from accredited undergraduate institutions and the undergraduate students have reached the third year of their teacher preparation programs. They are not typically able to accept that the educational practices that they have endured in their content major prior to taking teacher education courses may not constitute best teaching practice. We, as science educators, are challenged by these students because:

- We want to provide the best preparation for future teachers of future children.
- We understand and accept a need for accountability for ourselves as well as for our students.
- We want to make our courses challenging as well as useful.
- We want to model the type of teaching that has shown success with gifted children and adults.

To meet our goal to explore teaching tactics that support the gifted and talented future teacher, each professor employed Project Based Learning strategy. Project Based Learning focuses on allowing individuals to select a topic for a project and to choose which aspects of the problem they will work on each day.

Our experience indicates that Project Based Learning generates motivation and results in the gifted adults in our classes becoming stimulated to further develop personal interest in a topic related to public school curricula and their subject area expertise. Providing an opportunity for choosing their own topics generates an interest and a level of motivation beyond what is usually seen in these courses. Thus, such projects provide the time and the framework for differentiated education. The gifted can be challenged to learn advanced content, exercise higher process or thinking skills, and develop more complex products (Gallagher & Gallagher, 1994). At the same time this allows other students to complete the same task to the best of their ability and meet the state and accreditation standards.

The academic challenge is created for gifted future teachers by the fact that the course instructor generated an assessment that requires a content and teaching design that will stimulate interest and motivation in their future students. The assessment of the product(s) include; a motivational aspect that causes children to ask more questions and find more resources and a design with plans that will challenge themselves as well as their future students to deeply study a topic.

Each student is supported and challenged at her or his individual academic levels because teachers work within small groups or among individuals throughout project time. Decision making skills, design strategies, testing and engineering skills empower all students and especially supports gifted adults in their natural curiosity and their need to deeply explore a topic or topics. The process for Project Based Learning begins with selecting a topic of interest perhaps often based on questions provided by the science educator. Questions may include, what type of car is the most energy efficient? Or, what is resonance? And how can resonance be illustrated? Such questions may be proposed to provide guidance and to spur ideas. Once a topic is chosen, students work on the topic either in a group or alone. In this way, students are encouraged to choose their social interaction level. Students then are given time to research as much information as possible through use of Internet, print, and other resources. They may develop a model and may design and create a real-world product in addition to a lesson and implementation plan for their future classroom. This work needs to be completed with the understanding that they must eventually share their project with an audience. Thus these projects are student directed, connected to the real world, informed by multiple resources, research based, embedded with knowledge and skills, and conducted over time. Teachers in Project Based classrooms use varied teaching strategies to increase student learning and depth of concept understanding on the topic being studied. The flexibility of project work allows individualization and the ability to modify the skills that are taught to the gifted. This flexibility makes it relatively easy to meet the different levels of skills and ability demonstrated by all students in the class. (Diffily, 2002).

An additional strategy used in the science methods courses involves use of inquiry methods of teaching. The information and products from this instruction allowing us to collect data were derived to write the case studies for our national accreditation reports. This teaching practice was chosen in addition to project based learning because few professors express their visions, philosophies and strategies for finding and nurturing giftedness and making gifted learning blossom (Patricia, 2001). Schillereff (2001) shared an inquiry process used in the elementary science classroom for gifted students in grades 3-5 during a professional development event. This process provided a guide for other teachers to reflect upon and perhaps use to help with the redesign of lessons for their classes. According to Schillereff (2001) the development of varied questioning skills is the first step towards self-directed inquiry. This skill aids the students' ability to create questions that focus on content, process, product, presentation, audience, and assessment.

Because self-directed learners may have a strong sense of achievement, the beginning of each unit is spent building rubrics with the future teacher. This aids the process by having them take responsibility for the content, the outcomes, the assessment and the strategies used. By including this process, the future teachers are able to reflect on prior knowledge and then design a plan to achieve their goals. Time is then provided in order for them to investigate their questions and to reflect on their experiences in their journals.

The authors of this study considered the nature of their students, future teachers, the motivational level of curriculum and the opportunity afforded for individual work on a topic of personal choice, interest and expertise. We hoped that this method would motivate the gifted as well as the more traditional student.

In this study, we examine the experience of a sample of gifted high-achieving university students wishing to become science and mathematics teachers in all levels of basic education by:

1. Identifying and describing factors and influences that were exhibited in the college methods classroom so that others can more easily identify such students in their own courses and
2. Identifying and describing methods that are compatible with their development as science teachers and
3. Designing and describing projects that did not add only to the work load of the gifted students. Rather, the projects designed were planned to capitalize on the unique learning styles and interests of these students.

This paper will describe our observations of gifted and talented students in our classrooms. It will also suggest methods of capitalizing on giftedness in the preparation of future science and mathematics teachers.

PROBLEM BASED LEARNING UNITS

Problem Based Unit 1

In order to provide an assessment designed to focus on engineering and design stressed in the Next Generation Standards, an open-ended project assignment in a graduate level elementary science methods class was developed and implemented over time. The Project was to be accomplished in two weeks not in a group but individually at home. Many other projects completed in education courses are assigned as group work. This assignment was to be one completed individually in order to encourage each student to be creative and to excel. The open-ended directions were for each student to design and build and bring to class to show a measuring tool for length that could be used by a sight impaired person. Each student was told to document the process used for designing the measurement device including any library research completed with appropriate references, all designs (used and those that were discarded) and procedures used for testing the product and any redesign necessary. The only other information given was to show them a simple example of a meter stick with dots made with glue at each centimeter. This was passed around for all students to feel and for them to begin their thoughts on possibilities. The rubrics developed for this project included research process, design process, creativeness, testing and redesign. One of the purposes for this assignment was to provide an opportunity for students to create, design and build establishing an opportunity for students to use their engineering skills and to learn the engineering process.

Most future teacher designs to meet the project requirements were extremely simple from including adding a glue dot at every centimeter on a meter stick or using a string, and tying a knot at every centimeter. Over 4 years, this assignment resulted in two products that were developed by extremely gifted students who embraced the challenge and exceled in their engineering skills. The designs to be discussed in the chapter will be the T.A.M.A.L.E. and the Electronic Ruler. Both projects went well beyond the assignment and the T.A.M.A.L.E project was then field tested and finally patented for distribution. The Electronic Ruler is currently being developed into an article for other teachers to use.

Products from This Case

The Electronic Ruler

This device was developed for people who are visually impaired for use to complete length measurements. It can be used in any subject; however, it was designed for use in a science/math class.

The student first decided that a stationary device that objects could be placed onto for measurement would allow a sight impaired student the capability of measuring small, portable objects. A diagram of the device was then developed including suggested measurements of the device and the materials needed to build the device. The electronic ruler was built using plywood, basso wood, metal pins and conductive metal. The ruler consisted of a solid platform with a slider component enabling the user to place the object to be measured between the slider and adjust the slider to the object in order to obtain an exact reading measurement. Because the device was built for a user who had visual impairments, the student determined that the device needed to be connected to a computer with software development allowing the measurement to be orally given to the user. The student built the device, wrote the software program and determined and established the links necessary for the device to be connected to a computer for voice activation.

The T.A.M.A.L.E. Project

This device focused on using a measuring tool for higher-level mathematical operations like circumference and tangent determination. The student modeled the device on the typical meter stick. An initial diagram of the device included the model size and tactile components with suggested incremental designs. The tool was to measure the length of a meter with notches on one edge at raised centimeter increments. Holes were to be drilled in order to attach strings for circular and angular measurements. The device was to be made out of plastic in order for safety. After the tool was designed and built, readjustments to the design were made and curricula were written for specific topics in a 3rd grade mathematics class focusing on measurement. The device and curricula were tested and then revised in two schools with over 300 students. The student then researched the process for patenting the device and after two years successfully packaged the device under a patent.

Problem Based Unit 2

There were six future teachers who created or adapted their cases as part of an NCATE requirement, for a methods course for middle level learners. All submitted cases included standards based content and designed for the unique interests and motivational strategies needed for middle level learners. The students created or adapted their cases based on curriculum standards appropriate for their content specialties and certifications sought. The cases created then provided opportunities for these candidates to develop interactive, problem based lessons that sought to determine research-based solutions to a dilemma created by them in their case studies. The cases required interdisciplinary approaches and the candidates worked in teams to prepare their products. Although all students submitted acceptable products, there were two cases created by what I consider gifted teaching candidates. I reached this conclusion based on descriptions of gifted in the literature and through personal experience developed through many years of teaching gifted students. Several of the lessons associated with the cases were field tested in a practicum experience required of these students.

Teaching methods developed by the university professor modeled what was expected. Sample cases were presented to the students. These cases were then discussed in class. Students in the class presented a challenge to the professor in that their majors included a variety of subject backgrounds and specialized knowledge. An integrated team approach was used to follow the motivational needs of the middle level learners that they were preparing to teach and which provided a reasonable integration of material. Integrated case study units were prepared in science, mathematics, English, and social studies. Standards were examined to select those that the students would address in designing lessons and in developing cases.

Characteristics of middle level learners were considered because of the unique needs of these students. Questions of motivation and class management of problem based learning methodology were considered. How can the science and math instructors generate interest in solving the problem presented by the case? These students are just beginning to be able to think formally. Many of them are still in concrete stages of cognitive development. Inclusion classes could contain students who have special instructional needs. Instruction must be geared to motivate all of these children. Many of the teaching candidates in the classes that my undergraduate and graduate students were assigned to for their practicums were inclusion classes. They can also expect to teach such classes when they begin their own professional careers. The prevailing approach was one that stressed the need for middle level learners to be presented with a case that was related to their own experiences and which also presented an opportunity to research for resolutions. The ideas always related to the concept that when children are interested in a problem they will be self-motivated to find answers. Much class discussion re: these ideas took place so that students would understand the environment in which the problem based case study method would be used

It was clear from this stage that certain students in the class were highly motivated to develop their own ideas. It was these two groups of students who exhibited the characteristics of gifted individuals and who continued this interest through to the completion of the course and the development of the two excellent problem based case study units that are described below The role of the professor in this process was to provide resources and, encouragement to support this interest and to allow the students free reign in developing their ideas.

Products from This Case

Rock n Ride Project

This is an original case study developed to capitalize on the natural interest of middle level learners in riding roller coasters and to learn some math and science in the process. There is a popular theme park in our area that many of the children in local schools visit. The roller coaster is one of the most popular attractions. The unit was designed to integrate mathematical and scientific principles in discovering how a roller coaster operates.

The unit was planned for use as a supplement to the mathematical and scientific curricula at grade 8. These curricula include study of kinetic and potential energy, force, motion, acceleration, and velocity as well as such concepts as slope, angle, and mass. This study provided an ideal integration of STEM concepts. The authors of the unit created two characters, Jack and Sally, who debate the relative importance of math and science in building and operating a roller coaster. Each thinks his/her own content area is the more important in this process. This is the basis of the case study and the development of lessons and research needed to solve the dilemma--which is more important science or mathematics in building and operating roller coasters?

Each of the lessons contained differentiated outcomes and activities designed for the diversity of the children in the classrooms. Assessment plans followed the philosophy of unit planning.

Sea Otter Decline in Population in Alaska Project

This case was adapted from those examined on the National Center for Case Study Teaching in Science website (http://sciencecases.lib.buffalo.edu/cs/) The authors considered the interests of middle school students in preservation of the environment and in animal populations. These gifted authors applied much of what they had previously studied about teaching effectiveness in planning this unit. Questions asked in this case involved examining the possible causes of sea otter population decline, how one species affects another in the balance of life and the use of graphic analysis in examining correlations in populations of organism.

This unit was crafted carefully with integrated science, mathematics and social studies lessons designed to answer the questions asked. The assessment plan for this unit again followed the inquiry methodology of teaching'

Problem Based Unit 3

The case of the gifted science student in a secondary science/mathematics methods courses using apps to solve problems and create a product. This is about a gifted mathematics college senior in a mathematics methods course. Standing in the center of a college classroom with senior mathematics majors who want to become high school teachers is a huge responsibility especially in this age of accountability. This feeling is especially noticeable when the future teachers will be working with high school students with backgrounds that typically do not do well in public schools. In the session to be described, the college students were talking, moving, and working to solve a problem that included the use of iPad apps that assist with data collection and analysis. However, they did not turn in laboratory reports, or answer questions. They did solve problems and defend their answers. The case described below is the result of such a problem-based lesson that reveals the gifted future high school mathematics teacher.

During this three-hour class session, the students were able to analyze commercial tops (yes those toy spinning things) as well as maple tree seeds for science concepts related to spinning objects. The problem was to study these materials to discern the properties that mattered, how these properties interacted and then to create a top of their own that could spin longer than the commercial products available. They needed to control for energy input and cost. The problem was to create a top that did not cost more in materials than the commercial tops available but would be a superior product. The students were encouraged to use their iPads to collect their data, identify and describe the features important to a top spinning and then development models to test via a different app before building their own top.

The students were very methodical in their testing and were able to collect data about torque, mass, center of gravity and other properties of tops or spinning things that made them "work". They appeared to be engaged in the mathematics and science activities they were supposed to be doing. The truth is—they were engaged, but not necessarily getting to the depth needed to develop a model top that worked. One student began to explore the app for collecting data more effectively than the others. She learned how to use the app more quickly, with more acumen and thus was able to identify and describe the properties (physics/mathematics) of the top more quickly than the other students. Thus, her ability to move to the design phase of the project occurred more quickly than her peers. To her credit, she did show others in the class ways to use the data collection apps and then how to analyze the data they collected.

Fortunately, the design phase was next and this student was able to proceed with something productive to do. She proceeded to an app that allowed her to design and test models of tops to see how long and evenly (non-wobbling) her models would be. Again, this is her process. Upon completion of testing her models she began to build her own top from a very sparse set of materials (golf pencils, masking tape and paper plates). She had the use of tools such as rulers, protractors, mass scales, and exacto knives.

Product from This Case

Measurement Project

She created a top that spun using those materials for over 90 seconds because of her data analysis and testing of models. No one else in the class was able to complete the task to the same degree in the three-hour timeframe as this student. Her ability to create this top was then noted by her classmates. This gifted student then guided her classmates through the modeling and testing processes. All the students took the project home and returned the following week with tops that were worthy of competition. More importantly all the students now knew both some of physics content/concepts, properties, associated with spinning objects and a method to teach their future students.

Next, the group debriefed about the use of iPads and how their peers were engaged, explored the topic, identified and explained the variables that made the top work, developed models and finally tested the constructed products. The future teachers noticed that one student was "far ahead" of the others in her ability to use a new app and develop the science concepts and create a product. This allowed the group to dialogue about characteristics of gifted students like they will have in their classrooms and ways to work with them so that everyone remains productive, but no person's abilities are thwarted, stymied or otherwise reduced.

ANALYSIS OF THE CASES, RESPONSIBILITIES OF PROFESSORS, AND CHARACTERISTICS AND PERFORMANCE OF THE GIFTED STUDENTS

Giftedness in These Adult Future Teachers

An examination of attitudes towards this project brought out the difference between gifted adults and the more conventional teaching candidates.

The future science teachers:

1. Almost immediately recognized the value of project based and case study techniques in motivating themselves and their future students.
2. Actively sought out ideas that would be challenging as well as interesting to their future students.
3. Recognized the importance of collaboration in further development of their ideas.
4. Worked cooperatively to develop cases and to apply valid teaching methods to develop outcomes and assessment.
5. Revealed their ability to express depth in the required content knowledge.
6. Recognized when they needed additional content and actively researched material necessary to fill in the gaps that they uncovered.
7. Developed exemplary concept maps that showed the integration of their lessons. The sequence of their lessons and formal and informal assessments recommended.

The science education professor:

1. Provided a variety of resources to pique the interests of the candidates.
2. Remained enthusiastic about the value of the technique suggested.
3. Allowed freedom for the candidates to develop their own ideas.
4. Provided the basis for the characteristics of middle level learners through readings and class discussion.
5. Allowed candidates autonomy in the production their product and teaching plans.
6. Acted as a support and sounding board for the production of these specific methods.
7. Provided guidance of candidates in presenting and explaining their ideas to their colleagues.
8. Remained open to suggestions made by the students and considered these suggestions seriously in light of the whole project.

Table 1 summarizes observations made during the process of using this methodology with gifted as well as conventional teaching Candidates.

The identification of gifted adults is possible after the professor explains and identifies the projects that fulfill the outcomes of the course taught. The professor must be capable of identifying those who actively begin to attack solutions for the challenges. All candidates in the class might not receive the same attention from the professor but those who are more capable and creative will need less attention throughout the development of the projects but more attention with interacting with their peers and in support of their innovation.

SOLUTIONS AND RECOMMENDATIONS

The case studies described in the previous sections show the depth and degree to which project based and case study teaching methods are successful in motivating, stimulating and generating topics of interest for all of our students. The cross analysis of the case studies also revealed that special opportunities for gifted students to work individually as well as collaboratively on topics was useful. The future science teachers were especially interested in learning more about each topic and how their future students would respond. They easily discerned which problems and inquiries related to their expertise in content knowledge. These methods gave these students confidence in choosing and adapting or creating cases/projects on which they could base a motivating curriculum for their future students.

The authors took into account the science and mathematics standards that would need to be supported in their future classrooms. There have been major developments in updating standards in mathematics and science and students need to be aware of how these standards will impact their future teaching. The standards provided the

Table 1. Comparison of performance based on characteristics of gifted identified above

Characteristics	Teaching Candidates Identified as gifted	Teaching Candidates Capable but not showing all characteristics of gifted
Intense devotion to personal interests	Reacted quickly and positively to the specified teaching method Recognized creative aspect of assignment and did not need additional direction.	Slower response to the specified teaching method Demonstrated lesser understanding of methodology. Needed much explanation of procedure
Independence	Readily accepted challenges presented by a methodology with which they were not familiar. Worked collaboratively to research and develop case study. Immediately began research to develop content relevant to the solution of the dilemma presented in their case. Worked to relate content to state specific Core Content Standards in Mathematics, Science, and Technology. Developed their own case or adapted a case that would relate to the cognitive levels of the school children that they were designing case based lessons for.	Students needed more direction from the professor. Conference between groups were needed to discuss methodology and rationale. There were more questions on the validity of the approach suggested.
Boredom when not engaged in the activity presented.	Boredom was not apparent. These students talked excitedly of their plan and submitted updates on schedule.	Boredom was not apparent but these students were not as excited about the possibility of the assignment. They did not readily see the assignment as a challenge.
Ability to see to the root of problems	Identified early on the essential questions developed for the unit Saw the possibility and importance of curriculum integration at the specified school level.	Needed almost constant support and guidance from the professor to develop a rationale and essential questions for their plan.
Tendency to be a maverick and a rapid learner	Questioned and challenged the professor about methods of using such an approach at the specified school level. Challenged the professor on integration of math and science standards. Responded positively to suggestions and took advice willingly but with reservations until proven valuable in further developing their own ideas.	Had to be prodded to challenge the ideas of the professor. Seemed to accept without question what needed to be done even though they claimed to lack of understanding of what was needed.

continued on following page

Table 1. Continued

Characteristics	Teaching Candidates Identified as gifted	Teaching Candidates Capable but not showing all characteristics of gifted
Ability to anticipate outcomes	Developed an exemplary concept map outlining lesson outcomes relevant to content standards. Developed assessment plan relevant to inquiry methods for math and science instruction.	Had difficulty seeing the whole picture. Needed much help in developing a rational plan for the whole project.
Capable of abstract thinking and learning skills	Rapidly identified concepts of math and science for integration throughout the teaching plan. Saw the possibilities of developing curricula that were challenging and interesting for middle level learners.	Needed more time to identify related concepts and significantly more time to integrate the concepts into their teaching plan.
Have talent in creative or leadership abilities	Acted in a leadership role in the class in discussing their work and explaining their plan and methodology.	Were not secure in discussing progress made on assignment.
Quality of product produced	Excellent teaching unit produced. The unit was professional in content and rationale. Lessons were related to possible answers to essential questions asked	Acceptable teaching unit was submitted but needed considerable revision and suggestion needed before final acceptance by the professor.

groundwork for the development of lessons because of the future science teachers' ability to identify a problem or an inquiry and develop them.

The candidates found that the standards and technology available in the classroom would be critical in motivating their future students. We also found as professors of these candidates that the use of technology would be essential in developing quality products.

Technology

Classrooms using a problem based or case study inquiry method for gifted students should have the ready availability of computers, IPad (and/or other hand held devices), and projection capability with full access to the Internet. Teaching candidates must have access to resources that help them in creating or adapting their own cases for use in their problem based units. Many students have their own notebook computers but there should be computer stations available for use in the classroom for collaborative use. Time should be provided for in class discussions and collaboration. The professor must remain diligent in observation of the future teachers as possible to ensure that appropriate content and teaching methods will be used in the future high school classroom (Figure 1).

Figure 1. Helpful internet based resources for case study teaching

```
Active Learning in Higher Education

 Sage. http://alh.sagepub.com/

Center for Case Study Teaching in Science

http://www.sciencecases.lib.buffalo.edu

Center for Teaching. Vanderbilt University

 http://cft.vanderbilt.edu/teaching-guides/

Case Based-Teaching and Problem-Based Learnin

http://www.crlt.umich.edu

National Research Center for Gifted Education and Talent Development University of Connecticut

http://www.gifted.uconn.edu/

National Academies Press. Next generation science standards by state. http://www.nap.edu/NGSS

Problem Based Learning

http://www.questia.com/library/education/
```

CONCLUSION

The academic challenge is created for gifted future teachers by the fact that the course instructor generated an assessment that requires subject area content and teaching design that will stimulate interest and motivation in their future students. The assessment of the product(s) include; a motivational aspect that causes children to ask more questions and find more resources and a design with plans that will challenge themselves as well as their future students to deeply study a topic.

Questions for Further Research

While we have found this methodology to be successful in motivating the gifted teaching candidates that we encounter in our classes, there is still much work to be done in this area. Future researchers could replicate this study or utilize quantitative methods (e.g., structural equations modeling) to examine gifted adults' academic and interpersonal experiences in science methods courses (Kristin, Stephen, Tracy, Amy, & Vannatter 2010).

Questions remaining to be answered include:

1. What traits and behaviors made these teacher education candidates stand out from their peers?
2. How can we generate curricula that are motivational to all students and stimulating to the more able candidates?
3. How can we relate what we do in the university classroom to the real world of the schools in which these candidates will work?

REFERENCES

Aldridge, B. G. (1989). *Essential changes in secondary school science: Scope, sequence and coordination*. Washington, DC: National Science Teachers Association. American Association for the Advancement of Science.

American Association for the Advancement of Science. (2010). *Project 2061: Science for All Americans*. Washington, DC: AAAS.

Association for Middle Level Education Columbus Ohio. (n.d.). *This I believe: Developmentally responsive middle level schools*. Retrieved from http://www.amle.org

Audrey, C. R., Jean, S. S., Denise, A. T., & Highnam, D. (2012). Creativity and thinking skills integrated into a science enrichment unit on flooding. *Creative Education, 3*(8), 1371–1379. doi:10.4236/ce.2012.38200

Baslanti, U., & McCoach, D. B. (2006). Factors related to the underachievement of university students in turkey. *Roeper Review, 28*(4), 210–215. doi:10.1080/02783190609554366

Bazler, J. A., & Charles, M. (1993). Project 2061: A university model. *Journal of Science Teacher Education, 4*(4), 104–108. doi:10.1007/BF02614562

Daniel, R. H., Matthew, T. M., & Thomas, P. H. (2007). Exploring the motivational trajectories of gifted university students. *Roeper Review, 29*(3), 197–205. doi:10.1080/02783190709554409

Diffily, D. (2002). Project-based learning: Meeting social studies standards and the needs of gifted learners. *Gifted Child Today, 25*(3), 40–43.

Doyle, A. E. (1999). Dishing the personal narrative: Its present classroom ignominy, its classroom potential. *Bridgewater Review, 18*(1), 20–23.

Ertmer, P. T., Newby, T. J., & MacDougall, M. (1996). Students' responses and approaches to case based instruction: The role of reflective self-regulation. *American Educational Research Journal, 33*(3), 719–752. doi:10.3102/00028312033003719

Freeman, C. (2008). *Science stories: Using case studies in teaching critical thinking*. Washington, DC: National Science Teachers Association.

Gallagher, J. J. (1994). Current and historical thinking on education gifted and talented students. In P. O' Connell (Ed.), *National excellence: A case for developing America's talent. An anthology of readings* (pp. 303–213). Darby, PA: Diane Publishing Company.

Gardner, D. P. (1983). *A nation at risk: The imperative for educational reform.* Washington, DC: National Commission for Excellence in Education.

Klapp, J. (2000). Gifted grownups: The mixed blessings of extraordinary potential. *Roeper Review, 23*(1), 47. doi:10.1080/02783190009554062

Koch, J. (2005). Science stories: Science methods for elementary and middle school teachers (3rd ed.). New York, NY: Houghton Mifflin Company.

Kristin, M. P., Stephen, L. W., Tracy, M. K., Amy, L. C., & Vannatter, A. (2010). Looking back on lessons learned: Gifted adults reflect on their experiences in advanced classes. *Roeper Review, 32*(2), 127–139. doi:10.1080/02783191003587918

Kristin, M. P., Tracy, M. K., Stephen, L. W., Vannatter, A., Claudine, C. H., Shepler, D., & Philip, A. P. (2011/2012). Major life decisions of gifted adults in relation to overall life satisfaction. *Journal for the Education of the Gifted, 34*(6), 817–838. doi:10.1177/0162353211425101

Marland, S. P., Jr. (1972). Education of the gifted and talented: Report to the Congress of the United States by the U.S. Commissioner of Education and background papers submitted to the U.S. Office of Education (2 vols.). Washington, DC: U.S. Government Printing Office. (Government Documents Y4.L 11/2: G36)

National Commission on Excellence in Education. (1982). *A Nation at Risk: The Imperative for Educational Reform.* Retrieved from http://www.ed.gov/pubs/NatAtRisk/risk.html

National Research Council. (2012). *A Framework For K-12 Science Education Practices, Crosscutting Concepts, and Core Ideas.* Washington, DC: National Research Council.

National Science Education Standards. (1996). Washington, DC: The National Academies Press.

O'Brien, T. (2011). *Even more brain-powered science; Teaching and learning with discrepant events.* Arlington, VA: National Science Teachers Association.

Patricia, A. H. (2001). Gifted teachers: Facilitators of becoming. *Roeper Review, 23*(4), 189. doi:10.1080/02783190109554096

Schillereff, M. (2001). Using inquiry-based science to help gifted students become more self-directed. *Primary Voices K-6, 10*(1), 28-32.

Speece, S. (1993). National Science Education Standards: How You Can Make a Difference. *The American Biology Teacher, 55*(5), 265–267. doi:10.2307/4449657

KEY TERMS AND DEFINITIONS

Next Generation Standards: Next Generation Science Standards (NGSS).

NCATE: National Council for the Accreditation of Teacher Education.

Gifted Adults: Teacher education candidates that display gifted qualities.

Science Teachers: Teacher candidates in a course of study to become certified teachers.

Project-Based Learning: Focuses on allowing individuals to select a topic for a project and to choose which aspects of the problem they will work on each day.

Section 6
Teacher Education

Chapter 17
A Case Study of Distance Education for Informatics Gifted Students

JeongWon Choi
Korea National University of Education, Korea

SangJin An
Korea National University of Education, Korea

YoungJun Lee
Korea National University of Education, Korea

EXECUTIVE SUMMARY

This chapter analyzes cases in which programming was developed via e-learning in informatics gifted classes in Korea. The gifted class, which aimed to improve computational thinking and problem-solving ability, received the algorithm and programming education and experienced the design and implementation process of a programming project entitled "Interactive Movie Production through Scratch Programming" through the creation of a learning group. The learners received gifted education via e-learning systems, such as video lecturing, video conferencing, and smart phones. However, there was much difficulty in providing appropriate feedback and scaffolding to resolve the trial-and-error issues experienced during the programming learning process, which involved learning flow interruptions of the learners, which in some cases caused them to give up on the learning process. To overcome this difficulty, the selection of educational content appropriate for distance learning was regarded as important, and algorithm learning utilizing puzzles was proposed as an alternative. Puzzles can encompass learning content using texts and

DOI: 10.4018/978-1-4666-6489-0.ch017

images while also providing feedback and scaffolding appropriate for learners via suitable learning document compositions and descriptions of the problem solving process while also evaluating the learner's ability in detail.

ORGANIZATION BACKGROUND

Traditionally, Korea has considered promoting gifted students as one of the most important roles that a nation can fulfill, expending great effort to discover and educate the gifted students who will lead the future society in a variety of areas. In particular, gifted education has concentrated on mathematics, science, informatics and inventions by focusing on the science and engineering sectors, which can affect the advancement of state-of-the-art technologies and industries.

Terms and Definitions

'Informatics education' usually regarded as computing education in Korea. In the past, 'computer education' and 'ICT education' are used to mean computing education. In the 2007-revised national curriculum, the name of the subject related ICT and computer science changed to 'informatics', so informatics encompasses computer education, ICT literacy education, and computer science education. Though, the focus of informatics has changed to computer science now, informatics education has a comprehensive meaning that includes education for all computing-related contents. 'Informatics gifted education' also means the education for the gifted and talented students in computer science.

Educational System for Gifted Students

The main parties that operate gifted education programs in Korea are the Offices of Education in metropolitan areas and provinces around Korea and universities. Gifted students are selected via a selection process and are assigned to gifted classes operated by a school or are assigned to a regional collaborative gifted class operated by affiliated schools in that region. Furthermore, these students can attend institutes for gifted education operated by the local Offices of Education or other institutes for gifted education operated by science high schools, schools for the gifted, or education and science research institutes to take a high level of gifted education. The gifted education courses operated by 25 universities around Korea are managed by the Science Gifted Education Institution supported by the Korea Foundation for the Advancement of Science & Creativity. There are also gifted education courses in many other universities supported by regional Offices of Education. The types of gifted education institutions in Korea are summarized in Table 1.

The number of students receiving gifted education in gifted classes, gifted education institutes, and at the Institute of Science Education for the Gifted and Talented is 105,000 in 2012, which accounts for 1.56% of the total student population (6,721,176 students) in Korea (Lee, Kim, Lee & Kim, 2012).

Because gifted classes are managed by Offices of Education and aim to find gifted and talented students within schools, they run basic levels of gifted education courses. Each gifted class recruits its learners from schools or through collaboration with nearby schools. If a school principal would like to offer a gifted class, the corresponding Office of Education grants the right to operate the class, or classes, after taking the number of students in the school, the assigned hours for education, and the abilities of the teachers who would be responsible for the class into consideration. In 2012, 64,283 students in a total of 3,521 classes were in a gifted class (Lee et al. 2012). In gifted class education, various subjects such as mathematics, informatics, biology, foreign languages, creativity, arts, music and dance are taught. Because gifted classes target students who attend nearby schools, recruiting students is convenient. Most classes are taught after the students' regular school, and a camp for the gifted is operated during the school holidays for concentrated education.

The Institute for Gifted Education has two parts. One is directly operated by the Office of Education and the other is commissioned by the Office of Education and operated by science high school, gifted schools and the Education & Science Research Institute. Generally, institutes for gifted education operated by the Offices of Education provide an intermediate level of education to heighten the talents of the

Table 1. Types of educational institutes

Operating Party	Operating Mode	Operating Institution	Details
Office of Education	Gifted class	A school	Each school manages their classes.
		Regional collaborated schools	Class consisting of students who live close the the schools
	Institute for Gifted Education	Office of Education	Operated by the Office of Education
		Science High School, Gifted School, Education & Science Research Institute etc.	Operated by Science High School and Education & Science Research Institute and commissioned by the Office of Education
Universities	Science Education Institute for The Gifted	Ministry of Education, Science and Technology	Operated by 25 universities around Korea and supported by Korea Foundation for the Advancement of Science & Creativity
		Office of Education	Supported by regional Offices of Education

students by selecting students from among those who have already completed gifted education in gifted classes, but some institutions provide a basic level of education for the purpose of finding gifted students to select students identical to those in gifted classes. Institutes for gifted education under the Offices of Education select teachers from among those who belong to the Office and who have completed a gifted education course as a major or who have excellent capability in their major subjects to provide the education. In 2012, institutes for gifted education had 2,122 classes and 34,474 students around Korea. The curricula are identical to those in gifted classes but are concentrated on science, mathematics, and informatics subjects. Institutes for gifted education target students who attend schools that belong to their Office of Education. This often causes many students to have to commute long distances to attend these classes. Hence, most classes operate on weekends, while concentrated education and camps are provided during the school holidays (Lee et al. 2012).

There are two types of university-affiliated institutes for gifted education: science education institutes for the gifted supported by the Korea Foundation for the Advancement of Science & Creativity and institutes for gifted education supported by the Offices of Education. University-affiliated science education institutes for the gifted, which are supported by the Korea Foundation for the Advancement of Science & Creativity with accreditation by the Ministry of Education (MOE), are currently operated at 25 universities nationally. Science education institutes for the gifted are operated for the purpose of providing educational opportunities for students selected from those who have already completed gifted education in a gifted class or at an institute for gifted education to grow their outstanding potential, leading them to achieve their goals and career paths. The subjects of the education are mainly mathematics, science (physics, chemistry, earth science and biology) as well as informatics subjects, and the teaching method is based on the mentorship education model in which a team consisting of university professors and teachers assists the students with various research activities and learning (Hwang, Choi, Lee, & Lee, 2013). 520 classes and 6,243 students are currently attending university-affiliated science education institutes for the gifted around Korea. Science education institutes for the gifted also provide the classes on the weekend as well as concentrated education and camps during school holidays as the constituent students live in all corners of cities or provinces, similar to those in the institutes for gifted education operated by the Office of Education. University-affiliated institutes for gifted education supported by the MOE operate in the same manner as the institutes for gifted education operated by the Offices of Education.

Curriculum and Assessment of Informatics Gifted Education

Informatics gifted education is a part of gifted education. In this section, we explain the education content of informatics gifted education only, as its student selection process and assessment methods are identical, as described in earlier sections. The education contents are collected from 30 institutions around nine cities and provinces out of 17 in Korea. The overall content area is divided into six major areas. These are a programming language area to improve logical thinking and problem solving abilities as a core tool in computer science; an application program utilization area that teaches students how to utilize computer programs practically; a communication area including security, network and encryption related subjects; a computer science principle area that teaches classes on the representation of information, data structures, and algorithms; classes that teach computer assembly or how to prepare for an Olympiad competition; as well as other areas such as databases, media art, robots and puzzles. Not all gifted education institution provides education in all of the above areas, but the education curriculum is selected at the discretion of the school principal such that some of institutions concentrate on the three main subjects of programming languages, algorithms and data structures while other institutions teach the nine subjects of robotics, application programs, data structures, puzzles, research and discussion, security, databases, computer assembly and networking. Still other institutions concentrate on only application program utilization, showing that there is great variation in terms of the education content between gifted education institutions.

Regarding programming education, programming languages for education such as web programming or Scratch, based on C language and considered as a basic programming language, are taught, and robot programming for robots using NXT MINDSTORMS and ROBOROBO is used to improve the students' problem solving ability and logical thinking ability. The goal of the content for computer science is for students to learn computer operation principles through algorithms, data structures and data representation. In addition, Hangul, PowerPoint or Prezi, and spreadsheet applications for basic document editing or image, video and animation editing programs for promoting the ability to handle various types of data are used to improve the students' computer utilization ability. Other institutions provide education on databases, communication, network security, and computer assembly depending on their needs.The assessment method for gifted education is similar from institution to institution, but it can differ slightly depending on the education circumstances of each institution. The assessment is mostly completed according to the deliverables submitted by students as they receive their education.

Assessments are scored by teacher evaluations and colleague evaluations and in terms of the class attitude of the students, the degree of creativity, the research abilities and thinking abilities shown in class and by portfolio assignments. Other than these methods, interest in the classes, satisfaction, and student ideas through surveys can be evaluated. Some institutes utilize multifaceted evaluations through consultations between teachers, interviews and self-assessments. Very few institutes use a paper-based test.

Target Students

The target students for gifted education are selected starting from their fourth year of primary school. Because primary to middle school students receive gifted education from gifted classes, institutes for gifted education, or university-affiliated institutes for gifted education, the number of available classes is sufficient. On the other hand, high school students receive gifted education from science high schools or gifted high schools, and there are much fewer of these compared to the number of schools available for primary and middle school students. The assigned number of hours for a gifted class is set to around 100 per year, and the main subjects are science, mathematics, and informatics, as well as a range of other subjects such as music, art, creative writing, foreign languages and inventions, although the subjects provided differ from institution to institution.

The selection process for gifted students is different between institutions operated by the Office of Education and by universities. Gifted classes and institutes for gifted education operated by the Office of Education have a four-step selection process consisting of 1) a recommendation by the student's school principal, 2) a gifted test, 3) an academic aptitude test, and 4) an in-depth interview. In contrast, university-affiliated science education institutes for the gifted have a two-step selection process consisting of 1) a recommendation by a teacher from a gifted education institution, and 2) an in-depth interview, as the purpose is to provide a type of mentorship education for those who have experienced gifted education in the past.

SETTING THE STAGE

The present study presents a case study in which distance education was provided for a regional collaborative gifted class from among the many gifted education institutions. The regional collaborative gifted class is set up by several schools in proximity in the same region for students from a wide range of distributed schools who have difficulty gathering at one place for offline classes. Thus, the need for distance education has long been an issue. The target students were in their fourth, fifth and sixth years of primary school, and the education content was programming via Scratch. Programming is a core content area in computer science and is suitable for the development of various high-level thinking abilities in students. This is why programming was applied to our case study.

Legal Grounds for Providing Cyber Gifted Education

The comprehensive promotion planning activities associated with gifted education presented the need for cyber gifted education and its foundation. In the First Comprehensive Measure for Gifted Education, remote education was described as a means to complement the class attendance type of gifted education. However, its characteristics have gradually changed and now encompass target students and the goal of resolving the education gap due to students in marginalized groups (MOE, 2002; MOE, 2004; MOE, 2007). Table 2 summarizes the legal basis to support the operation of cyber gifted education (Lee & Hong, 2009).

Table 2. Regulations for cyber gifted education

Basis		Details
First Gifted Education Comprehensive Measure (2002)	5. Detailed driving plan	Strengthening of a research support function for gifted education Remote gifted education systems are developed to complement the class attendance type of gifted education. It operates as it targets long-distance commuting students who lack access opportunities for gifted education and gifted classes that limit the education time as well as students in institutes for gifted education.
Excellence in Education Comprehensive plan (2004)	4-2. Driving strategy	Gradual expansion of target students and regions for excellence in education Cyber gifted education institutions operated by the Offices of Education are expanded for students in marginalized groups such as those in rural and fishing areas and on remote islands.
	5. Main driving tasks	Operation of cyber gifted education institutions Increase of accessibility to gifted education through links with e-learning support systems on the basis of the Office of Education Increase of efficiency through cyber education and class attendance
Second Gifted Education Comprehensive Measure (2007)	2. Gifted class specialization	Specialization of gifted class operation according to specific regions Regional Offices of Education recommend the opening and operation of cyber gifted classes for schools located in rural and mountainous areas, fishing areas, and remote islands.
	Strategy 2. Strengthening of social integration	Expansion of the foundation of gifted education for marginalized groups The operation of gifted education program such as cyber education that match the characteristics of marginalized groups

Technical Infrastructure for Distance Learning

Korea has steadily carried out e-learning and mobile learning, utilizing state-of-the-art devices through an education informatization process. The "Education Informatization" project started in late 1990s. It was an initiative with the goal of introducing the latest information and communication devices into education fields in parallel with the national trend toward informatization. As a result of this project, more computers were put in place in the education fields and a high-speed broadband communication network was constructed to link school environments, thereby providing an education environment in which e-learning could be applied. Along with these information communication infrastructure developments, many services that provide various types of distance education content, such as the 'Edunet', cyber home learning system and EBS were established, while e-learning became one of the major education forms on the university entrance test and in lifelong education. Thus, most learners in Korea are now used to various forms of e-learning, and content providers are providing reliable e-learning services through the continuous research and development of content.

E-Learning for Gifted Education

The education method at the initial stage of gifted education was mostly the face-to-face method in which students attending classes in person, while no consideration of the education environment was given for students who were geographically remote (Cho et al. 2002). Moreover, although many training courses to sharpen teachers' areas of specialty were provided, 82.8% of teachers who were responsible for gifted education did not participate in the training due to their geographical and temporal conditions, which created concern over whether expertise in gifted education is adequately provided (Cho et al. 2002). Because the gifted education curriculum is determined at the discretion of school principals, teachers who are responsible for delivering the gifted education developed their own curricula without consultation with experts in gifted education. Also, although there were learning materials that had been developed previously, no sharing system was put in place between gifted education institutions, resulting in a lack of education content that could be utilized. Therefore, an urgent need for measures that can overcome geographical and temporal disadvantages and provide a rich education environment while also facilitating teacher training arose as well as a need for an online learning systems.

Considering the educational characteristics of e-learning, the following areas that require funding most in public education were chosen: resolution of education gaps between learners, support for a selection-oriented curriculum, and gifted education. These chosen areas were identified through the convergence of consultations from related experts based on reviews of credible government periodicals and various policy documents such as the Education Informatization White Paper. In particular, gifted education was selected as an area that requires its scope of education to be widened via the e-learning system, thereby opening distance education to a wider audience (KERIS, 2003).

As one of the measures for the expansion of gifted education established in 2007, the currently 0.6% of gifted education students was expanded to 1% of all students by 2010 through e-learning and a system that shares various learning materials developed individually in gifted education institutions. Moreover, research information and best practices will be developed to provide gifted students with suitable e-learning content (MOE, 2007). Thus, a new paradigm of education has been introduced to gifted education through an increase in motivation levels and learning appetites via a virtual space and the activation of interaction between learners and between learners and teachers, overcoming both spatial and temporal limitations (Lee, 2003). This introduction was necessary because it provides practical help for gifted students and teachers while also helping to secure core human resources for national development ultimately through the promotion of gifted education (Kang, 1997). Initially, e-learning was used as a means to complement the problem of face-to-face education, delivering additional education content that could be learned at times other than regular class times, presenting assignments or providing a means for question-and-answer sessions online. Subsequently, associated systems were developed to introduce online gifted education and a pilot program was established considering the characteristics of gifted students. The result of the pilot program showed that learners can study whenever and wherever they want regardless of spatial and temporal limitations, resulting in high satisfaction, while they enjoy in-depth search-oriented gifted education. All of these findings indicate the introduction of online gifted education was positive (Kang, Cho & Kum, 2000).

The typical characteristics of gifted students are a high level of task commitment and intelligent curiosity. A rich material supply and learning possibilities that overcome spatiotemporal limitations, which are regarded as advantages of the e-learning system could match the characteristics of gifted students, which can be especially appropriate for gifted education (Davis & Rimm, 2004). The cyber gifted education currently provided is now departing from the existing e-learning system which served as a secondary function of offline learning, and a new education model of cyber gifted education is under discussion. The education method is also moving into the m-learning paradigm as the social paradigm is changing to a mobile terminal-utilized environment. The gifted education provided mainly during every second weekend or during school holidays outside of the regular curriculum has used online education fully. In the distance education environment in this smart society, beyond the lecture-style e-learning education system of one-sided knowledge transfer and instead in an environment tailored to individual learners, both a face-to-face educa-tion environment as in regular school education and active interaction are possible is now provided. In particular, the m-learning environment can help with the active utilization of rich materials, providing an education environment that overcomes spatiotemporal limitations, thereby taking the characteristic of gifted students into consideration fully. This m-learning environment can also help to design education, which is linked to practical daily living or stories familiar to learners, to learners' interests based on problem-oriented learning and project-based learning online, as is currently done offline, providing an opportunity to realize self-directed learning while also collecting and analyzing various pieces of information and the data required for the learning process themselves by providing themes with which gifted students can experience problem-realization and design solution processes by themselves. The m-learning environment is designed to provide all education content online except for experimental practice, field trips or camps, which are provided offline during school holidays. In particular, due to the proliferation of wireless terminals such as smart phones and smart pads, more convenient learning is now possible to suit learners' needs compared to conventional e-learning systems. In particular, the development of web sites that can be accessed via mobile environments can support more education activities for gifted students freely and actively. Such an environment can provide a video chat function, a video lecture function and an immediate texting transmission function, thereby creating the optimal education environment, as the advantages of online and offline education methods can be combined.

CASE DESCRIPTION

Organizational Concerns

The informatics gifted education presented in this study was conducted in a regional collaborating class operated by the Office of Education. The subjects were 20 stu-dents in their fourth year, 20 students in their fifth year, and 20 students in their sixth year of a primary school located in G city in Korea. The selection of the students was done via a four-stage process: 1) recommendation of the classroom teacher and principal, 2) a gifted test and an information thinking ability test, 3) a four-week ob-servation type of class, and 4) an academic test and a final delivery presentation and interview. In particular, a notable point during the selection process was that during the third stage, five teachers who were responsible for gifted education provided a project-based learning process using a team teaching method for four weeks. The learners has to solve the given problems by themselves during this period and then submit the deliverable while the teachers observed their learning process to check their characteristics, aptitudes and interest levels closely, thereby selecting the gifted students. Furthermore, during the selection process, a session that explained gifted education was held twice for parents of the candidate students regarding a sufficient overview of the gifted education program and how the education is provided and managed, including the selection process, thereby ensuring sufficient exchanges among teachers, students and parents while the education is given.

E-Learning Environment

The e-learning environment was constructed for remote lecturing to provide primary online education while a camp for gifted or gifted day festival, a leadership camp and overseas service experience were conducted as offline activities. A website was operated via an independent server in order to ensure a reliable distance education service. The web server supported streaming services for video lectures and provided a web board for each group to facilitate project learning. Furthermore, teachers and learners could exchange questions and feedback regarding the learning process by direct chatting through the web browser, with video chatting and video lecturing provided as parts of the service. The network lines for the server were dedicated lines such that no problems arose even if all members of the gifted student group were connected at the same time.

Course Management

The number of yearly class hours for the gifted class was set to 110 hours of curriculum-related content and 60 hours of extracurricular activities, for a total of 170 hours per year to complete the course. The curriculum employed in the gifted class was developed by field teachers who have master's degrees in informatics gifted education as well as university professors who are experts in related subjects to meet the education objectives according to the level of the learners. The education objective of the gifted class was "to promote a leader of future society through improvements of computation thinking and problem-solving abilities," which are the essential abilities required to solve complex problems which arise in everyday life efficiently and which can be improved by learning and utilizing the principles of computer science (Wing, 2006). The most effective way to improve the students' computational thinking using the principles of computer science is to learn algorithms or programming. The process to create an algorithm can help students to concentrate on abstraction, which is a core factor of computational thinking, and this builds the ability to model a problem by extracting the required factors for problem solving after grasping the core problem. On the other hand, programming, i.e., coding executed by a computers using the created algorithm, helps students to concentrate on automation among their computational thinking by understanding computing devices and learning their operating processes (Wing, 2006). Therefore, algorithms and programming was selected as the educational content with which to achieve the educational objectives of the gifted class.

The detailed education process started with the theme "Interactive Movie Production via Scratch Programming." The project implements, per group, the theme by Scratch via the combination and reconfiguration of a variety of fairy tales creatively and creates relevant characters, thereby making a movie in which the created characters are moving. The created movie is not one that is simply played after the program is produced. Instead, while playing the movie, each story can be selected, akin to a game. That is, someone watching the movie can change the movie story through a selection or quiz, as it involves participation and an interactive setting.

The interactive movie production exercise via Scratch follows the project-type collaboration model among the gifted education learning models. However, because learners did not have any lessons on programming as part of their school curriculum, a simple class was given to the learners on the Scratch programming language at an early stage of learning. Even during this coarse, basic block use is learnt via video lecturing online while the programming language is self-learnt individually through a self-practice process. Once the Scratch programming language is learnt, teachers present themes for the movie production for each group as the learners create their own groups. The learners set a plan of how to proceed with the project with members of other groups and configure the move scenario through various discussions, finally completing the deliverable themselves via sharing and collaboration as regards character development and programming implementation. The completed project result is presented in front of their parents as well as their colleagues at a festival called Gifted Day as an offline activity in an effort to allow them to enjoy their work. During this process, a weekly report was created regarding how the learning progressed according to the weekly plan, thereby preventing a possible side effect such as students giving up in the middle of the project or delaying the work.

Operation of Lecturing

The "Interactive Movie Production via Scratch Programming" course consisted of 36 hours in total, three hours per week for 12 weeks out of 110 hours of total class hours. First, an algorithm for movie production was designed and the self-learning of information collection was done to understand the algorithm in order to code the computer programming according to the designed algorithm, thereby providing an opportunity to express the algorithm sequentially (Table 3).

The role of the teacher in this curriculum began with guidance on each function of the Scratch blocks for the learners to have them to produce the movie by them-

Table 3. Lesson plans for scratch programming

Week	Main Theme	Detailed Education Contents	Teaching and Learning Method
1	Algorithms in everyday life	• Understanding the meaning of algorithms • Flowcharting	Information collection type of exploration learning
2-4	Scratch as an expression tool	• Scratch lecturing video watch • Simple work production to become familiarized with Scratch	Lecturing class, hand-on practice
5	Scenario contest	• Telling a story and composing the story to produce a scenario	Project-type collaboration learning
6-7	Movie production team configuration and design	• Through group division, movie and story board produced	Project-type collaboration learning
8-9	Mentoring per group for movie production	• Movie production activities per group	Project-type collaboration learning/Teacher team teaching
10-12	Individual mentoring for movie production	• Individual Scratch programming	Project-type collaboration learning/Teacher team teaching

selves as well as an assistance role in the movie scenario creation, character development, and role sharing steps between group members. Furthermore, the teachers were responsible for learning management tasks such as learning progress checks, notice board read confirmations, encouraging regular attendance to the class and encouraging students to leave comments on the web board to promote interaction between learners. Moreover, due to the lack of distinguished grades among the fourth-, fifth- and sixth-year students, the use of polite words was encouraged between colleagues to minimize any ethical problems which could arise given the online format.

Depending on the learning circumstances, the effects of learning were maximized by utilizing single-teacher classes, team teaching classes, and team mentoring schemes by the teachers. For real-time education for team mentoring, it was planned to send an SMS text message to a responsible mentor teacher whenever a learner leaves a comment on the web board. Furthermore, volunteer students to assist with the leering of junior students were recruited from among those who had experienced and knew well the procedures associated with online gifted education. These volunteers helped with student activities, created a learning atmosphere and better relationships between students in each group, and helped alienated students, if any, to restore their relationships through teacher intervention, thereby providing advice on how to cope with difficulties as well as how to utilize the web site (Figure 1).

Figure 1. Project steps

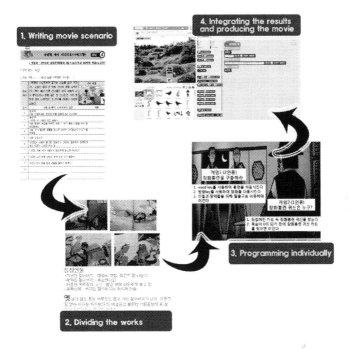

Learning Process

The learners started their learning activities via video chatting initially. Although some awkwardness was felt among them as they were only slightly acquainted, the learners gradually became familiarized with one another. The video chatting served as a means of interaction akin to offline face-to-face classes and overcame the limitations of online education. Accordingly, learners recognized that the video chat facility helped then to share their stories about their lives via the web board and while also helping them make new friends. While the learners recognized that communication, which may occur naturally in an offline environment, should be initiated consciously in an online environment, they realized the importance of communication such that contact by means of video conferences or smart phones occurred naturally along with consideration of how to use language appropriately and express themselves effectively.

A web board was assigned to each individual group for project activities, on which the members of each group could share their tasks, receiving feedback from one another and discussing the difficulties experienced during the problem-solving process, thereby improving the deliverables. If facing difficulties that could not be resolved within the group, requests for a teacher's assistance through the web board or video chatting with teachers were made possible in an effort to solve the problem in real time. Video chatting can be used for video lecturing or for blackboard demonstrations by teachers as well as for chatting with other learners, thus facilitating real-time face-to-face education that includes video chatting between learners.

The learners were satisfied when they understood that a well-designed algorithm is necessary to process a task effectively and efficiently and when they learned how algorithms could be used in real life. They also showed considerable enthusiasm toward the tasks of the project.

Examples of Actual Class

The classes during the tenth and twelfth weeks, in which Scratch programming was conducted according to the scenario created per group, had the most frequent question-and-answer sessions by the learners. The questions and answers generated during this period were needed to implement each individual story, controlling the sprites and background in the Scratch programming steps and finalizing the program developed by the members of each group. In particular, the final program needed to retain the order of the introduction of characters with a background implemented through the sharing of roles between members while also controlling it so that they could understand the entire program and could control the flow according to the entire program clearly. The teachers were responsible for appropriate feedback to be given to the learners. Therefore, they should study the code produced by the learners and understand the reasoning process of the learners to provide appropriate feedback and scaffolding. Overall, the learners did not utilize the Scratch blocks properly, in which the characters and backgrounds appeared in the proper order initially with the addition of all of the sub-programs made by the group members. Thus, feedback and scaffolding regarding the use of the blocks should be provided sufficiently.

The feedback pattern during the Scratch programming course proceeded in the following order: colleague feedback via the group board between members, the utilization of the Q&A web board with messages to/from teachers, feedback via telephone conversations with teachers, and feedback via remote connections and telephone conversations.

Consensus between members was well positioned while creating the scenarios and producing the characters and backgrounds for the movies, as were the frequent interactions between the members. Thus, learners liked to receive feedback from their closest colleagues. Until the scenario creation and development of the characters and the background were completed, feedback between colleagues was also actively given. However, once the Scratch programming started, feedback was considerably reduced, with only a small number of examples given. Initially, the feedback from colleagues allowed members to realize their misunderstandings, but after some time, the colleagues corrected the misunderstandings by themselves.

I need to merge the program files. If anybody knows how to merge the program files, upload a captured image along with some comments. Or, send me a text message. I am in hurry. Please send it to me by tonight.

However, no student responded to the above post in the group web board. Therefore, the student started to utilize the web board function of Q&A to/from the teacher.

Please explain to us how to merge the Scratch files made by us easily.

Once a teacher found that significant posts were made regarding how to merge Scratch files implemented by each student and understood that this was a common difficulty faced by most learners, he/she tried to provide feedback to solve this problem via the web board. However, the utilization of a web board is a one-way communication method which cannot guarantee real-time and immediate feedback. Thus, students tried to call the teacher if they required more explanation from them. Telephone calls had an advantage that the learners could gain immediate feedback regarding an explanation of something that did not understand clearly. However, a telephone call cannot replace accurate feedback regarding the coding parts, as this type of feedback required visual interaction.

Finally, we chose a method of remote control with a telephone call at the same time. Nonetheless, such a method required an environment in which the learner and teacher have available computers at the same time, thereby requiring the both of them to communicate at the same time. The reasoning process behind the programming procedure could not be recorded either. Therefore, it was difficult to provide the best feedback in this situation.

CURRENT CHALLENGES FACING THE ORGANIZATION

Problems of the Learning Process

The learning activity processes such as scenario creation, the selection and development of characters, and the creation of an interactive environment went well, but the students have trouble with programming process. The more complicated the plan of the program structure was, the larger the programming data size became, along with the programming level of difficulty. Thus, many trial-and-error steps were required during the coding process. This problem acted as an obstacle to efficient learning. To provide appropriate feedback from colleagues and teachers, many programs coded by many students needed to be understood clearly. However, this required much time, especially for checking block by block. Moreover, during the communication process with the learners, the use of ambiguous terms and a lack of clear definitions caused misunderstandings when seeking to grasp the logical reasoning process for the listing of the blocks selected by the students. This misunderstanding interrupted the learning flow, and some students even gave up on the project at this stage.

Problems of the Course Operation

We considered that a curriculum utilizing the Internet and mobile devices had an advantage in that a learner could access education content whenever and wherever needed, thus resolving a limitation pertaining to temporal and spatial differences. Most curriculum operations were conducted through the web boards of home pages, and learners could access home pages to achieve their learning and record their learning results and comments. During this procedure, we found some problems with the operation.

The most frequently occurring request from the learners was for immediate feedback. An e-learning environment was considered to give immediate feedback conveniently regarding the learning result or questions. However, we found that providing immediate feedback in our study was not simple because the learning times of the leaners differed in each case, and an analysis of each program took much time.

The roles of teachers during the learning of the programming tasks are very important, as the teacher will observe the logical flow of the programs and help the students to modify the program in the right directions to obtain an appropriate learning deliverable. Thus, a lack of immediate feedback could interrupt the learning flow quite often. We found that if a learner who concentrated on learning experienced a situation in which appropriate scaffolding was lacking, he/she tried to continue learning by either interrupting their learning temporarily, asking for some advice from the class teacher via telephone, or receiving advice from available experts. These attempts may be thought of as a part of the learning process, but in the end we found that these cases did not have a positive effect on the overall learning flow if appropriate scaffolding was not given to learners when they needed assistance. In particular, when all of the learners continued their learning in parallel, an interruption of learning by a single learner could result in a delay of the project for other learners, having a negative effect on the overall learning process. From the viewpoint of the class teachers, understanding the current status of learners was difficult and much time was needed to give appropriate feedback to learners.

Problems with Assessments

More importantly, we would like to know whether this type of distance education course can have a positive effect on achieving the objectives of the gifted education. The current education objective of the gifted class is to develop a variety of higher thinking skills through an appropriate learning process. Furthermore, it seeks to observe when giftedness is found in a learner and to continue individual observations of the learner as they receive a higher level of education. For a face-to-face class, this observation of a learner can be accomplished through learner questions, answers to teachers' questions, and the observation of changes in thinking during the deliverable production process. However, for distance education as described in this study, it is difficult to observe the learning process of a learner. Because most classes are conducted remotely and questions and answers are posted on an Internet bulletin board, mainly being in the form of simple questions that cannot be solved without help and without representing the thinking process of the learner, it becomes very difficult to measure the inner-thinking process of a learner. This is far from the objective of our gifted education program, where a learner with true giftedness is discovered through the gifted education curriculum.

SOLUTIONS AND RECOMMENDATIONS

Although distance education has many advantages in terms of overcoming the spatiotemporal limitations and accessibility of education content, it is also true that there are some complementary areas that must be considered in order to accomplish the objectives of gifted education. In particular, because informatics gifted education is based on the understanding and utilization of information and communication devices, the design of distance education should be very carefully done. The programming education via distance education method has several implications. First, an informatics curriculum requires much immediate feedback because it involves activities that utilize information and communication devices primarily. Nonetheless, with distance education, it takes much time to identify where this feedback is required and then to provide appropriate feedback. Furthermore, the ability of a teacher to identify the learning condition of a learner, giftedness, and creativeness while observing a programming course only is limited. And because of the programming outcome evaluation, learners' attention was focused on the program layout rather than program algorithm or thinking process. Considering this problematic situation, we concluded that the programming education with the distance learning system is unsuitable to the informatics gifted education. The foremost task is to select appropriate education content for distance education in order to accomplish two objectives of the gifted education: improvement of the variety of thinking skills and the discovery of giftedness through the observation of the learning process.

We suggest puzzle-based education as an alternative to the programming education. Puzzles can be an appropriate form of content for distance education in informatics gifted education. Puzzles can be utilized for distance education appropriately except for tangram, pentomino, and jigsaw puzzles where physical tools are required, as education content can be created using only text and image materials. The following advantages can be realized if puzzles are utilized for distance education.

- *Learning free from spatiotemporal limitation and learning tools*
- *Immediate and appropriate feedback*
- *Analysis of the reasoning process of a learner*

The programming learning as presented above as an example can be done only using personal computers. Programming itself requires the use of a computer; thus, access to the learning content is difficult when relying on a variety of environments. However, puzzle-based algorithm learning utilizes text-based learning content, making free of physical media to some extent. Taking advantage of this strength, a learner can study whenever and wherever desired by developing an education environment. And there is no burden of producing result, learners can focus on their thinking process with puzzles rather than producing visual output.

From the viewpoint of providing feedback, appropriate feedback and scaffolding could not be given due to the great amount of coding analysis time required for a teacher to solve trial-and-error issues which arose during the coding process and the reasoning process, which is difficult to understand. For these reasons, it had a negative effect on the learning progress. However, with puzzle-based algorithm learning, an activity sheet which is designed appropriately to solve a given puzzle is provided to induce clues for the problem solution, and parts that are not solved during the problem-solving process can be solved by educating a learner to describe the solution in detail. As shown in the figure below on the right, a learner here describes their understanding of the problem, the main elements of the problem, and solution measures regarding the given puzzle problem so that the teacher can infer what type of reasoning the learner used, how the learner developed this reasoning, and how the learner solved the problem and their specific ideas. Furthermore, a framework such as that shown in the figure below required for the problem-solving process is presented, thereby enabling a demonstration of how the learner solved the problem and experienced the trial-and-error process. Through this activity sheet, a teacher can identify which parts a learner felt were difficult and provide the proper feedback during the problem-solving stage, as the teacher can clearly understand what the learner essentially needs (Figure 2).

Finally, the learning sheet itself, which describes the solution process of a puzzle, can be an important type of material that shows the reasoning process of a learner. If a learner describes their understanding of a problem, the identification of the main elements for the problem solution, and the configuration process of an appropriate strategy and algorithms by themselves and a teacher evaluates their reasoning process, the teacher can identify the current learning status of the learner clearly. This will be a good basis on which to discover the achievement and giftedness of a learner.

Other than such advantages for distance education, puzzles have also various possibilities which can be utilized in informatics gifted education. The general puzzle problem-solving process consists of three steps: understanding the core elements of the puzzle, the exclusion of intuition, and modeling. The first step is to identify terms and objective that can be helpful when attempting to solve the puzzle, while the second step is to search for a measure that can solve the puzzle clearly by excluding intuition, by which a human may guess. The final step is to devise a modeling step to find a solution by taking various variables and constraints related to the solution into consideration. This type of puzzle problem-solving process is

Figure 2. A mobile system for puzzle-based learning and a puzzle activity sheet

equivalent to the abstraction process of computational thinking, which is one of the objectives of informatics gifted education. Thus, it is suitable for achieving the objectives of informatics gifted education (Choi & Lee, 2013). Moreover, various puzzles can be developed and applied according to the level of the learners, and situational problems in relation to daily living can be presented in such a way as to attract the interest of a learner and have the learner become committed to learning.

In the future, puzzles that will be utilized in distance education are those related to the concepts of constraint, optimization, statistics, pattern recognition, and strategy, all of which are solved via computer science principles. Five to six problems per category will be produced and taught. While solving the problems posed by the puzzles based on setting up an appropriate strategy and creating a model of an algorithm, various computer science principles, such as backtracking, divide-and-conquer, and recursion will be utilized and learnt.

The combination of the appropriate selection of education content and effective teaching and learning methods will increase the effect of learning for learners. In particular, the need of various types of distance education in an education environment where spatiotemporal limitations exist is becoming ever greater. From the viewpoint of a specific education target to realize informatics gifted education and an education type that involves regional collaborative gifted classes, puzzles which utilize algorithms as a form of education can be expected to contribute to learning in the form of distance education.

REFERENCES

Cho, S. H., Kim, H. W., Park, S. I., & Jeong, H. C. (2002). The study of promotion of comprehensive planning for gifted education, Korea Education and Research Information Service (KERIS). *CR (East Lansing, Mich.)*, 2002–2056.

Davis, G. A., & Rimm, S. B. (2004). *Education of the gifted and talented* (5th ed.). Pearson Education.

Hwang, S. J., Choi, J. W., Lee, E. K., & Lee, Y. J. (2013). Analyzing curriculums of university affiliated institutions for informatics gifted in Korea. In *Proceedings from IADIS International Conference ICT, Society, and Human Beings 2013*. Prague: IADIS.

Kang, S. H. (1997). Use of new media as constructivism-oriented learning environments. *Journal of Educational Technology*, *13*(1), 117–131.

Kang, S. H., Cho, S. H., & Kum, M. R. (2000). The plausibility of cyber gifted education: A case study. *Korean Association for Educational Information and Broadcasting, 6*(1), 49–70.

Korea Education and Research Information Service (KERIS). (2003). *The plans for building cyber home learning system: The 6th educational research and development related systems.* KERIS.

Lee, G. Y. (2003). *A study of community-centered cyber education for the gifted children of information science.* (Master's thesis). Gyeongin National University of Education.

Lee, J., & Lee, K. S. (2004). A study of e-Learning utilization to support elementary & secondary education. *The Journal of Korean Association of Computer Education, 7*(5), 71-82.

Lee, J. H., & Hong, C. E. (2009). Development and validation of teaching-learning model for cyber education of giftedness. *Journal of Gifted/Talented Education, 19*(1), 116-137.

Lee, Y. J., Kim, Y. S., Lee, E. K., & Kim, J. S. (2012). The evaluation research on gifted education continuity. *Korea Foundation for the Advancement of science & Creativity Report 2011-06.*

Ministry of Education and Science Technology (MEST), Korea Education and Research Information Service(KERIS). (2013). 2012 Adapting Education to the Information Age. Seoul, Korea: Author.

Ministry of Education (MOE). (2002). *The 1st comprehensive plan for gifted education promotion.* Seoul: Korea Government Printing Office.

Ministry of Education (MOE). (2004). *The master plan of education for excellence.* Author.

Ministry of Education (MOE). (2007). *The 2nd comprehensive plan for gifted education promotion.* Seoul: Korea Government Printing Office.

Ministry of Trade, Industry, and Energy (MOTIE), National IT Industry Promotion Agency (NIPA), Korea Association of Consilience Education (KAOCE). (2013). *2011-2012 e-Learning White Paper.* Author.

KEY TERMS AND DEFINITIONS

Algorithms: Algorithms mean procedures to solve problem. Algorithm education helps students solve complex problem effectively and efficiently.

Cyber Gifted Education: Gifted education using various types of distance learning system, such as e-learning or m-learning system.

Distance Learning: Learning systems that can help students attend classes remotely, instead of attending face-to-face classes.

E-Learning: E-learning generally means the education using electronic media. In this article, e-learning means a kind of distance learning system using a web server and a homepage. It offers many services such as a video chatting, community boards, and a video lecturing system.

Informatics Education: 'Informatics' is the name of a subject related to computing education in Korea. So 'informatics education' generally has a comprehensive meaning that includes education for all computing-related contents. But nowadays, its focus gradually changed to the computer science.

Informatics Gifted Education: Gifted education for the students who have giftedness and talent on informatics.

Feedback: Feedback means the information about the results of students.

Programming: Programming means a process that make a computer executes given orders. Programming education includes knowledge for programming language, problem-solving, algorithms, coding, testing, and debugging.

Puzzle-Based Education: Education of logical thinking, problem-solving skills, and computational thinking using puzzles.

Chapter 18
Gifted Education and One Case Solution through E-Learning in Japan

Masahiro Nagai
Tokyo Metropolitan University, Japan

Noriyuki Matsunami
Nishi-Tokyo Shi Sakae Elementary School, Japan

EXECUTIVE SUMMARY

Japanese parents are genuinely concerned about their children's education, especially if the latter display exceptional abilities. Such parents also believe that the public education system insufficiently nurtures their gifted children's potential. Consequently, parents frequently enroll their children in private schools and afterschool programs at cram schools (juku), which feature accelerated, condensed curriculums. Juku have subsequently prospered, with approximately 37.8% of Japanese sixth grade students attending one (Ministry of Education, Culture, Sports, Science, & Technology in Japan, 2008). Public schools have noted juku students' excellent examination results and begun hiring juku instructors (Kuroishi, 2009). Unfortunately, equally gifted, but poor, students cannot afford to enroll in these institutions (Mimiduka, 2009). Therefore, the authors propose implementing an e-learning system, granting students affordable access to supplemental learning opportunities. Herein, they discuss the state of Japanese gifted education before highlighting e-learning's effectiveness in this context based on practical educational research at a Tokyo elementary school.

DOI: 10.4018/978-1-4666-6489-0.ch018

Figure 1. International comparison of compulsory education years (Central Council for Education, 2006)

age	2	3	4	5	6	7	8	9	10	11	12	13	14	**15**	16	17	18	19

Japan — Kindergarten — Elementary school(6) — Junior High school(3) — High school(3) — Compulsory education 9years

USA — kindergarten — Elementary school(5) — Middle school(3) — High school(4) — Compulsory education 9years

UK — Childcare — Elementary school(6) — Secondary school(5) — 6th Form(2) — Compulsory education 11years

France — kindergarten — Elementary school(5) — Junior high school(4) — High school(2~4) — Compulsory education 10years

Germany — kindergarten — Elementary school(4) — Secondary school(5~9) — Compulsory education 9years

China — kindergarten — Elementary school(6) — Junior High school(3) — High school(3) — Compulsory education 9years

Korea — kindergarten — Elementary school(6) — Junior High school(3) — High school(3) — Compulsory education 9years

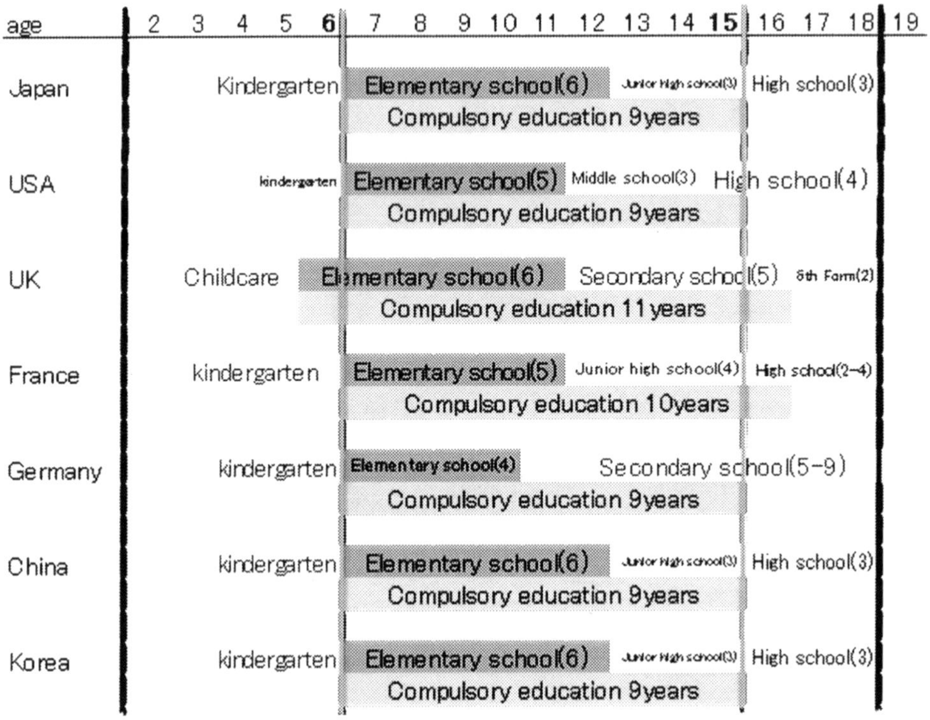

ORGANIZATION BACKGROUND

As is shown in Figure 1, Japan has adopted a nine-year compulsory educational system, during which time students attend public schools free of charge. From an international perspective, many countries likewise have compulsory education for children aged from 6 to 15 years, and in this respect, Japan is no different from many other countries (Central Council for Education, 2006) (Figure 1).

Unlike other countries, Japan has not adopted a grade-skipping system within the framework of compulsory education nor does it have a system adapted to the special needs of gifted students. On the completion of compulsory education, for the most part, Japanese students sit a selective examination to continue to high school. High schools provide general and specialist education for students who have completed compulsory education, and students must complete three years of education to graduate from high school (Ministry of Education, Culture, Sports, Science and Technology [MEXT], 2005) (Figure 2). The percentage of students continuing their education in high school exceeded 90% in the 1970s and a similarly high percentage is maintained today.

In addition, higher education in Japan is mainly conducted by universities and junior colleges. At these higher education institutes, students can receive an advanced, specialized education in four years at universities and two years at junior colleges. The percentage of students attending universities is currently around 50%, which is below the Organization for Economic Cooperation and Development (OECD) average.

It is important to understand how the parents and guardians of school-age children evaluate the education provided in Japan, particularly compulsory education. A survey of 6,831 parents and guardians with children attending public and private schools throughout Japan was recently conducted by the Benesse Educational Research and Development Institute (2013), which is a private-sector educational research institute. This research institute is considered to be one of the most reliable in Japan, as, for example, it conducts studies on behalf of MEXT. As is shown in Figures 3 and 4, the results of this survey revealed that approximately 80% of parents and guardians with children attending elementary schools, and around 70% with children attending junior high schools were satisfied with the education being provided.

Another nationwide survey was conducted by MEXT to assess the satisfaction levels of Japanese school-age children. The results of this survey involving 7,067 elementary and junior high school students are shown in Figure 5. When these survey results on student satisfaction levels are viewed in conjunction with the findings from the parent and guardian survey, we may ascertain that on the whole, Japan's educational system is seen in a positive light.

Taking a closer look at the reasons given by school-age students regarding their levels of satisfaction, we see that while the items, "School life is fun" (p. 3) and "Playing with friends and meeting people," were selected by 93.6% and 94.1% of elementary and junior high school students, respectively, the item, "Studying and learning," was only chosen by 40.9% and 14.3%, respectively. Conversely, in the section entitled "Aspects of school life with which you are dissatisfied" (p. 4), the students selected the following items: "Lesson contents and the way they are conducted and progress" (54.8% and 37.2% for elementary and junior high school students, respectively) and "Grades" (37.1% and 44.9%, respectively). From these results, we observe that students' satisfaction levels with their studies are an issue. Moreover, regarding the item, "Level of understanding school lessons" (p. 10, Figure 6), we see that few students claim to "fully understand" the lesson contents, with only 22.8% and 7.8% of elementary and junior high school students, respectively giving this response.

As shown, currently in Japan, many students do not fully understand the content of their lessons, and so we can anticipate that they will experience difficulties in

Figure 2. School educational system in Japan (MEXT)

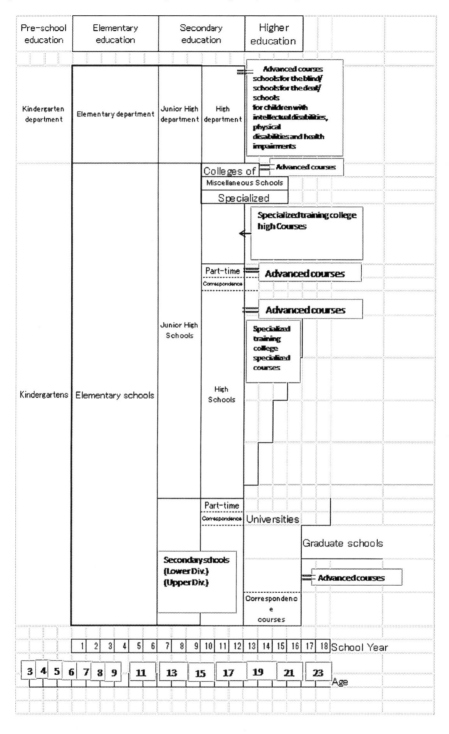

Figure 3. Overall satisfaction levels with elementary schools (Benesse, 2013)

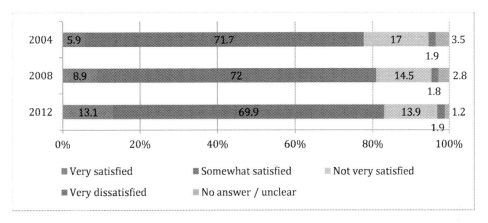

Figure 4. Overall satisfaction levels with junior high schools (Benesse, 2013)

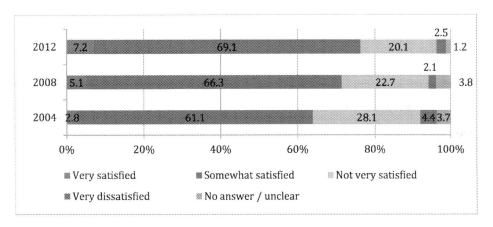

their subsequent studies, which will in turn affect their low opinions about the lessons.

In addition, Benesse (2005) conducted a survey on students' opinions about class lessons (Figures 7 and 8) and clarified the views of elementary and junior high school students regarding the level of difficulty of lessons and the speed at which lessons progress. Examining the results of this survey, it emerges that the percentage of students who consider lesson contents to be difficult or cannot understand the content increases with student age; in other words, older students find lessons more difficult to understand. In contrast, approximately 10% of the younger elementary school students find that the lessons progress slowly and are "boring" (p. 28).

Therefore, from the above data, we may conclude that the lesson programs prepared by schools in Japan are not necessarily adapted for children who do not fully

Figure 5. Satisfaction with school life among elementary and junior high school students (based on MEXT data)

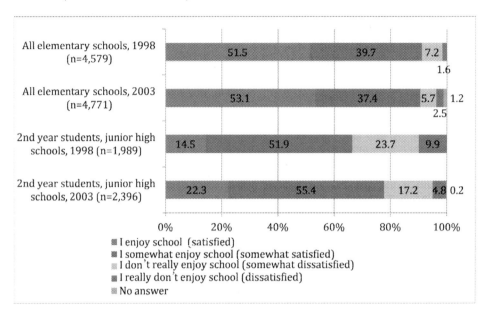

Figure 6. Level of understanding school lessons (MEXT)

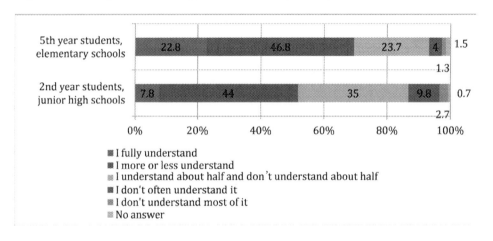

understand the lesson contents as well as for those who do understand it. In other words, we considered that the lesson programs were only effective for ordinary students in Japan.

In this context, we should consider the question as to the type of school education that Japan should aim for in the framework of the Fundamental Law of Education.

Figure 7. Opinions of elementary school students regarding lessons (data extracted from Benesse, 2005)

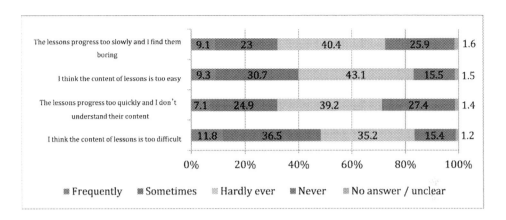

Figure 8. Opinions and feelings of junior high school students regarding lessons (data extracted from Benesse, 2005)

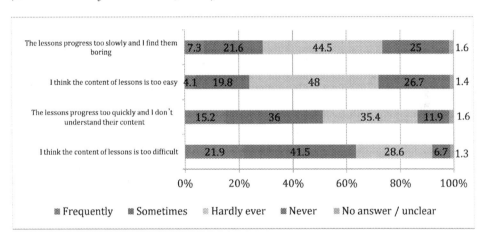

The Fundamental Law of Education is the highest law in Japan for school education. The educational activities in all Japanese schools providing compulsory education are conducted in accordance with this law as well as related laws and ordinances. In Europe and the USA, educational ideals and principles are rarely provided at a national level in the same way as they are specified in Japan through this law. The Fundamental Law of Education stipulates that "The people shall all be given equal opportunities of receiving education according to their ability, and they shall not be subject to educational discrimination on account of race, creed, sex, social status, economic position, or family origin." However, within this statement, it is uncertain what the terms "equal" and "according to their ability" actually mean. To respond to this issue, MEXT clarified that "equal" and "according to their ability" do not mean "that all younger and older students shall receive an identical education, but that they will be provided with an education according to their individual differences" (MEXT website (a), retrieved August 28, 2013). In other words, all Japanese elementary and junior high school students should be given equal educational opportunities according to their abilities, with educational content being developed to take into account the differences between individual students. In other words, it can be interpreted as meaning that the most capable students should be provided with special education designed for gifted students, and in this context, the previously described levels of understanding lesson contents and students' opinions about lessons may be seen to represent problems. Further, all students will be satisfied with the lessons at school, meaning that we can help promote the leaders of the future.

THE CURRENT STATE OF SPECIAL EDUCATION FOR GIFTED STUDENTS IN JAPAN'S PUBLIC EDUCATION

Regarding the current state of special education for gifted students in Japan, we see that schools adopt a social-promotion system. Iwanaga and Matsumura (2010) note that this formal egalitarianism is expressed regardless of whether the children are elementary school students aged over six years, junior high school student aged over 12 years, or high school students aged over 15 years. As seen in the previous section, students who are gifted relative to the average student in their class are not given any special consideration. In this section, we will thus consider the special education system for these types of gifted students.

Early Entrance to University

Since the end of the Second World War, public schools in Japan have provided minimal special education for gifted students. However, through systems adopted by a limited number of institutions since 1998, it has become possible for younger students to enter university as a regular student even if aged less than 18 years. However, such treatment is applied only as an exceptional measure. Allowing students to enter a higher-level school by skipping a grade was addressed in a 1971 report by the Central Council for Education, which proposed that "this exceptional measure of advancing a grade or attending to a higher-level school is to be permitted according to students' abilities and at an advanced stage in their education after they have achieved a certain level of maturity (the Central Council for Education (1971) website, retrieved August 28, 2013)." Following this report, grade skipping came to be formally introduced in the Central Council for Education's 1997 report entitled "Exceptional Educational Measures (the Central Council for Education (1997) website, retrieved August 28, 2013)." Yamamoto (1997) ridiculed this introduction after so many years, stating that, "the leisurely pace of educational reforms in Japan is amazing, as this was a measure that was described a quarter of a century ago" (p. 116). In the context of the various approaches adopted in other countries, he concluded that "'Appropriate education' according to ability does not necessarily represent 'inequality'" (p. 117).

Japan has thus, over the course of many years, introduced a system of grade skipping allowing students to enter university prematurely. However, this system is far from widespread. According to data from MEXT (website (b), retrieved August 28, 2013), as summarized in Table 1, in the university entrance exam for the 2013 academic year, only six universities nationwide adopted the early entrance system. Considering that there are 780 universities in Japan, (Statistical Research and Training Institute, Ministry of Internal Affairs and Communications, 2013), these six universities constitute an extremely small number of universities or just 0.8%. In addition, only a limited number of students opt for the system. The Asahi newspaper (2012) reported that nationwide, only 11 students in 2006 entered university at an earlier age, while in 2012 only four people did so. This system is thus limited in its capacity.

Various reasons were proposed as to why this system is not widespread in Japan. Saito (2007) noted that "there is no clear definition as to what 'gifted' is," meaning that "it is difficult to identify students who are gifted within a specific field." He also observed that "as universities do not have sufficient staff to provide guidance or structure for them, they are cautious about accepting these students." Matsumura (2008) describes the situation in detail:

Table 1. Universities implementing the grade-skipping system for university entrance

University Name	Implementing Faculty or School	Year Introduced
Chiba University (national)	Faculties of Arts, Science, and Engineering	1998
Meijo University (private)	Faculty of Science and Technology	2001
Showa Women's University (private)	Faculties of Arts, Human and Social Sciences, and Human Life and Environmental Sciences	2005
Seijo University (private)	Faculty of Arts and Literature	2005
Elizabeth University of Music (private)	Faculty of Music	2005
University of Aizu (public)	School of Computer Science and Engineering	2006

As the universities implementing this system are not the top schools, its implementation is welcomed by neither students nor high school teachers, and there is little merit or appeal to attend these universities one year earlier than normal. Instead, there are grave concerns about the demerits of interrupting studies and school life by leaving high school one year early. Frankly speaking, the system of grade skipping for university entrance can be considered as a failure in terms of its original intention. One factor behind its failure may be that the University of Tokyo does not participate. For gifted students ranked among the best nationwide for math and physics, it is more attractive to wait until the following year, graduate from high school, and then try to enter the University of Tokyo (p. 189).

In addition, the Asahi Shimbun Digital (2013) recently reported that Showa Women's University, as shown in Table 1, will discontinue the university entrance exam for students "who have skipped a grade" from the 2014 academic year onwards. The article summarized the situation as follows:

There are six universities in Japan that allow a student to skip a grade for university entrance, but withdrawals from the system have already begun. This is because since the introduction of the system in the 2005 academic year, Showa Women's University has only had one applicant. But it has stated that if an environment is in place, such as the systemic aspects, it is possible that it will restart it in the future.

In this article, a person responsible for conducting a university entrance exam was quoted as saying that "should a student skip a grade and enter university, but then quit university before graduating, ultimately their schools records will show that they have only graduated from junior high school. This is a factor influencing the lack of applicants."

Other than grade skipping for university entrance, it is necessary to enquire whether Japan provides other kinds of special education for gifted students. Matsumura (2008) proposed the following as techniques for individualized study: "flexibly forming study groups within each school and school year, selective learning, guidance for individuals and groups, learning according to scholastic proficiency, repeated learning, supplemental learning, and developmental learning" (p. 194).

Elective Subjects and Differentiated Guidance

We shall now consider the issues of elective subjects and differentiated guidance according to scholastic proficiency, which have been positioned as educational systems in Japan. Regarding elective subjects, in elementary, junior high, and high schools, the legally binding guidelines from MEXT known as the Guidelines for the Course of Study are provided to all schools for each subject. These are the national standards and in 2006 (MEXT, 2006, p. 23), for example, a report addressed to the Deputy Minister of MEXT detailed the following reasons for the use of these standards:

In elementary and junior high schools, students do not possess the ability to critique the lesson contents, and it is also necessary to ensure they have equal educational opportunities and levels of education. In this context, teachers cannot be allowed complete freedom in carrying out lessons. For these reasons, the State defines the standards for curriculums, such as through the Guidelines for the Course of Study, and teachers provide students with an education based on these standards (p. 23).

The Guidelines for the Course of Study for junior high schools are revised about once every 10 years. In the 1998 revision, the number of elective subjects was significantly expanded with an attempt to make them available in every school year and for every subject. Moreover, the number of classroom hours per elective subject was increased from 35 annual hours per subject (1 hour per week) to 70 annual hours per subject (2 hours per week). However, despite this expansion, a reform policy was proposed by the Central Council for Education (2008). The reason was that "in addition to elective subjects, time periods allocated to integrated study are being introduced, and as a result, the curriculum has become overly complicated" (p. 37). This points to a situation in which schools are unable to respond to the demands required of them. Further, among the classroom hours spent on elective subjects, more than 60% of this total was allotted to Japanese, society, mathematics, science, and foreign languages, and a high percentage of elective subject hours were being incorporated into supplementary learning. From this perspective, it was reported that "as the classroom hours of elective subjects are decreasing and the educational content and classroom hours of compulsory subjects are increasing, there is a need to increase the commonality of the curriculum. It is therefore appropriate for each school to establish elective subjects outside the framework for the benchmark number of classroom hours" (p. 37). In other words, the goal was for a substantive reduction in elective subjects.

In terms of the differentiated guidance according to scholastic proficiency, this expression was first used in the context of the formation of classes according to scholastic proficiency in the 1978 notification of the Guidelines for the Course of Study for high schools. This system is currently nationwide among the schools providing compulsory education, and according to MEXT, in the 2009 academic year, it was implemented by 70.5% of elementary schools and 66.3% of junior high schools. In elementary schools, it is primarily used for arithmetic. Regarding the benefits of this system, MEXT (2008) conducted an analysis of the results of its national scholarship surveys, remarking that "small-group guidance for groups with different levels of ability is related to an increase in the level of scholastic proficiency of younger and older students (Web, retrieved August 28, 2013)." It additionally claimed that "developmental guidance for groups that demonstrate abilities at an early age is related to an increase in scholastic proficiency among younger and older students."

Implementation in Tokyo

Let us now consider the actual implementation conditions of this system in Tokyo. Every year in Tokyo, school principals apply to implement a differentiated guidance according to scholastic proficiency of students and then reports on it; the Board of Education must then inspect and report on this implementation. These reports are known as the "Report on Implementation Conditions of Lesson Improvement Guidance Methods," but this system tends only to be adopted in schools with the goal of improving guidance methods. At many schools, one additional teacher is employed and is mainly responsible for developing arithmetic and mathematic lessons according to the students' levels of scholastic proficiency. On examining these reports from the Board of Education, we find comments such as, "As many children must be dealt with on a one-to-one basis, the time required also increases. It is possible to deal with children with different levels of understanding by using the same teaching materials, but changing the level." Another comment relates to children with difficulties: "The system can be implemented by spending more time with children who are slower in understanding. It produces results in terms of learning and understanding." In short, it seems that differentiated guidance according to scholastic proficiency is producing results in schools and is welcomed by them. However, it is not always the case that schools find this system easy to manage since, for example, it is limited by the fact that the extra teachers deployed for this purpose cannot be used for team teaching and other types of teaching that have been previously implemented in schools. According to one school administrator, in the case of Tokyo, there is evidence of a tendency for schools to use extra teachers instead of teachers who are appointed to their first positions and cannot take charge of a class, those who cannot take charge of a class because of complaints from parents and guardians, or those who are about to go on maternity leave. In such cases, the authorities are likely to receive reports from the Board of Education demanding a decrease in the number of supplementary teachers for the next academic year.

One experimental approach attempted in recent years for high school students is the Super Science High Schools (SSH). The aims of this project are summarized in the guidelines from MEXT (2012) as follows: "The development and implementation of curriculum not covered by the Guidelines for the Course of Study, the promotion of task-orientated research, and support for experiential and problem-solving-type learning through observation and experiments (Web, retrieved September 1, 2013)."

However, Misono (2012) highlighted that evaluations of the SSH are not necessarily being carried out appropriately each year.

This section described some of the typical examples implemented for the special education of gifted students in public schools in Japan. However, even if such measures are introduced, they may not be widely utilized such as with the grade skipping for university entrance, or the authorities may attempt a policy reversal as with the elective subjects. Further, as is the case with the differentiated guidance according to scholastic proficiency and SSH, even when the approach appears to be correct and progressing relatively smoothly, there are still problems in terms of managing these systems or the lack of appropriate evaluation. Therefore, it would appear that special education for gifted students in Japan's public education system is still very much a work in progress.

SPECIAL EDUCATION FOR GIFTED STUDENTS IN PRIVATE EDUCATIONAL INSTITUTIONS IN JAPAN

We should now turn to the current situation in the special education of gifted students in private educational institutions. In terms of the approaches adopted by private educational institutions in Japan, the notions of special education for gifted students and early education are widely known and used. On this point, Mutou (2006) stated that "in order to select and develop talent, in addition to a general educational environment, early education and special education for gifted students are the same in terms of preparing a special and more stimulating environment and aiming to cultivate gifted students" (p. 21). On the other hand, he noted that early education and special education differ as "early education is the initial education in a student's life and refers to the early implementation of education that normally would be provided later. This includes from the time that it can be coordinated smoothly within the school education until the early discovery of the child's talents" (p. 21). Furthermore, he defines special education for gifted students as "providing a special education environment for children who are expected to be gifted and advancing them earlier to a higher level compared with other children of the same age" (p. 21).

Sony co-founder, Masaru Ibuka, is a well-known advocate of early education. His collection of sayings on education (Early Development Association, 1998) shows that one of his reasons for advocating early education relates to the notion of a "critical period." He explains this in the following words: "The critical period refers to the boundary line or period marking the end of when a child can easily remember things, but after which he cannot absorb things as well or has difficulty acquiring them" (p. 143). Ibuka also discusses the importance in prenatal care in "From Birth is Too Late" (p. 154). A boom in early education occurred in Japan in the 1980s, and Sato (1984), while commenting on this phenomenon at the time, collected the following comments below from newspaper ads and other sources.

- Recently, progress has been made in the field of cerebral physiology allowing us to better understand the growth and development processes in babies. We now know that "3 years old is too late." A child's nature and abilities are formed between the ages of 0 and 2 years old. We have come to understand that the earlier the education is provided, the more effective it is.
- A child-rearing method of allocating 10 minutes per day until the child is 3 years old produces wonderful parenting results.
- Failures in raising a child up to the age of 3 years will result in delinquent children. (p. 226)

In response to such comments, Matsumura (2008) pointed out that regarding the critical developmental period, while cases of problem children were often discussed in psychology in the past, the reality is that around half of these cases were fictional. Further, Hisada (1996) discussed the strangeness of the development of infant classrooms in cram schools throughout the country. He quotes one mother as saying,

Both the parent and child are constantly in tears. Anyway, the targets that we have heard about are for the child to remember 200 songs. The target for reading and listening to books is 10,000 times, which means the quota is a minimum of 20 books a day. ...In our house, we started when he was 2 years and 8 months, and as this was too late, we are now pressured. Once we get him to sit down, he must absolutely do the 10 sheets that we printed out. (p. 203)

Parents reported on bringing up their children in this kind of tumultuous environment. These cram schools were criticized by a number of researchers for their methods and claims. For example, Nakayama (1997) reported on a cram school that widely and repeatedly advertised false claims about their classes, which probably did more harm than good—for example, "equations for infants" and "calculus differentiation and integration for elementary school students"—while stating that the sooner a child's education is begun, the better. The cram school also admonished parents: "You can start your child's education early, so why are you waiting? The only problem is doing nothing" (p. 138). However, Nakayama criticized this approach as being a hoax based on the notion that "the more the thought process is omitted and memorization is relied on, the faster a child's progress will be in their studies" (p. 138). Despite early education gaining much attention in Japan, as the approaches adopted were based on vague educational theories, the momentum of the movement in its golden period gradually ceased.

In terms of special education for gifted students in private educational institutions, the weekly magazine *Shukan Bunshun* (2006) reported its "Survey of 1000 parents; although the best three are swimming, English, and the piano" (p. 146) in a special edition on children's learning through practice. From this survey, we can ascertain the conditions for special education for gifted students in Japan, even if termed "learning through practice." In addition to learning through practice, private educational institutions that focus on improving students' IQs have emerged, and many parents in Japan frequently take their children to these types of institutions. The flourishing popularity of this type of educational industry in Japan is thought to stem from the increasing desire of parents and guardians to provide their children with the best possible education. Therefore, one of the features of education in Japan is the high proportion of education expenses that are paid for privately. According to the OECD (2011), the percentage of privately paid educational expenses in Japan is 33.6%, which was the third highest among the 28 countries surveyed. Related to this, Murata (2013) surveyed parents and guardians regarding their perceptions about the educational expenses that they bear. The survey showed that, when including "Not sure" from both fathers and mothers in "It is a burden," (p. 9) over 60% of parents and guardians considered educational expenses to be a burden. On the other hand, for the item of "I don't begrudge having to pay my child's educational expenses," (p. 9) when combined with "Not sure," 70% of parents answered that they did not begrudge having to pay such expenses. This suggests that the Japanese believe that they must spend money on their children to provide them with a better education. Private educational institutions make use of these sorts of feelings, and based on various educational theories, they have enflamed the anxieties of parents, with children becoming caught up in these anxieties. However, while this sort of educational system is feasible for affluent households, less affluent households and children do not benefit from this type of system.

In terms of the evaluations of early education and special education for gifted students as provided by private educational institutions, Fujinaga (2006) is one of the few researchers to conduct follow-up surveys in this area. He carried out a follow-up survey of one male child attending a cram school, and using fixed validation criteria, he ascertained the form of his learning over time in conjunction with his development. However, no research to date has traced the development of a large number of children receiving instruction from a private educational institution. There are thus problems with this educational system in terms of evaluation. One important aspect in Fujinaga's survey was the interviews with the mothers of boys participating in the survey. The mothers said that they told their sons to be sure that they never said at school, "I have already done this" or "I already know this" (even if they had already studied it at cram school) (p. 10). These mothers said that "it is common knowledge that everyone at school really hates the children who say,

'I have already learnt this' and act superior because of it" (p. 10). Based on this, a reason why special education for gifted students is not supported in Japan may be that for the Japanese people, in terms of the abilities of others, they have a sense of equality and want to fit in.

Difficulties in Providing Special Education for Gifted Students in Japan

As described in the previous section, the Japanese have not developed a correct understanding of special education for gifted students due to a variety of factors, such as the damage caused by private educational institutions and Japanese people's innate sense of equality. Yamasaki (1980) made the following remark:

Reflecting on the situation in prewar education when many students were unable to continue their education due to economic reasons even if they were academically gifted, in postwar education, the priority was given to providing students with equal educational opportunities, and therefore, so-called special education for gifted students has continued to be viewed as a taboo. (p. 41)

It is considered that little progress has been made in providing special education for gifted students due to various misunderstandings of this sort. However, while discussing his own background, Tachibana (1980, p. 48) explained the need for special education for gifted students: "Since I was young, I loved to learn and I preferred studying to playing. But I was not at all able to satisfy my desire for knowledge in my school education" (p. 48). These comments probably reflect the feelings of many children with excellent powers of comprehension. Tachibana continues further, saying that "while discarding children who lack abilities is often perceived to be a problem in the educational world, it seems that able children are also discarded" (p. 48). Also, according to our experience as school teachers, the topic of conversation at schools often tends to concern children who lack abilities, while it is often said that capable children are left to their own devices at school; even if they study in their own way, they will still be fine.

When considering public education in Japan, educational support is provided for children with disabilities or those who lack powers of comprehension, but support is not provided to able children. As a result, there is a real need to build a similar structure to provide appropriate support for children with remarkably high powers of comprehension. Tachibana (1980) made many suggestions with regard to this situation:

When a child demonstrates talent in areas such as physical education, music, or drawing and handicrafts, they are given the chance to devote all their energies to their talent. However, when the child's talent is for learning knowledge, he or she will not necessarily be given the same chance to devote all their energies to their talent. (p. 48)

In other words, there is a need to provide a structure permitting all children with the opportunity to devote their energies to learning, regardless of the financial situation of their household.

Regarding the kind of structure that should be established, we may refer to the suggestions provided in the description of "free, high-quality education for all the people of the world" in *The One World Schoolhouse* (Khan, 2013, p. 9). In this book, Khan demonstrates how anyone can take video classes on the Internet for free and how children who lack powers of comprehension can use this framework to progress at their own pace and proceed while repeating their learning. Furthermore, children with high powers of comprehension can select and then watch the lesson content that interests them. Even in Japan, we can see examples of a similar approach with the introduction of so-called "flipped classrooms," which connect home learning and public education (Kyoiku Katei Shinbun, 2013).

In the next section on special education for gifted students, we look at e-learning systems and consider the kinds of results that they can produce regardless of the financial strength of the household.

The Potential Benefits of E-Learning Among Gifted Japanese Students

Three years ago, we introduced the Blackboard Learning System (BLS) in an elementary school for both in-class and at-home activities; BLS is e-learning software that still requires hardware such as a server and computer. We recognize that e-learning is not only needed at universities, but also in elementary, junior high, and high schools. However, it is difficult to find cases of the introduction of e-learning into Japanese schools because they lack an adequate budget to purchase the system. Therefore, we decided to implement an e-learning system in an elementary school in Tokyo for the purpose of an experimental case; in other words, we lent the software to the school without charge. The following screen shots and pictures indicate the various uses of e-learning system at the school; BLS was used. Figures 9 to 11 show an arithmetic, Japanese, and domestic science course, respectively. Numerous courses are integrated into the e-learning system, even physical education. Moreover,

Figure 9. Screenshot of the arithmetic course on the e-learning system: An arithmetic test with multiple-choice questions

schoolteachers use it as a dashboard to inform students, for example, about what items to bring to school tomorrow (Figure 12). In this way, students can use BLS in their ordinary classroom, although they mostly use it in the school's computer room (Figure 13).

Figure 10. Screenshot of the Japanese course on the e-learning system: A student's composition entitled "Relationship between me and books"

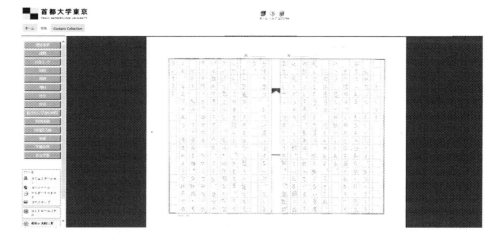

Figure 11. Screenshot of a domestic science course on the e-learning system: Learning to knit by watching a video on demand

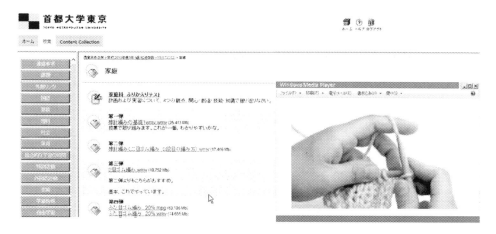

Figure 12. E-learning in a classroom

Figure 13. E-learning in the computer room

Methods 1

After allowing students to gain adequate educational practice using BLS, we surveyed participating students' attitudes toward the program and assessed their performance. Between February 21 and 22, 2013, a total of 40 students from one fifth and two sixth grade classes in a Tokyo public elementary school completed a questionnaire regarding their experience with BLS. Students' academic achievements were extracted from their records, as illustrated in Figures 14 to 16, using multiple regression analysis with stepwise selection.

Results and Discussion 1

The results of the analyses were as follows: (**$p<.01$, *$p<.05$, +$p<.10$).

In Figure 14, we observe that students' academic achievements were not only strengthened by *juku*, but also by BLS use at home. Moreover, by comparing Figures 15 and 16, we notice that the sample's top eight students displayed a greater improvement than the other students after using BLS. Therefore, we believe that using BLS at home is effective in improving gifted students' academic performance, especially due to its positive effect on pupils who have traditionally demonstrated the highest ability.

Figure 14. Influence of juku and e-learning on academic ability (40 students)

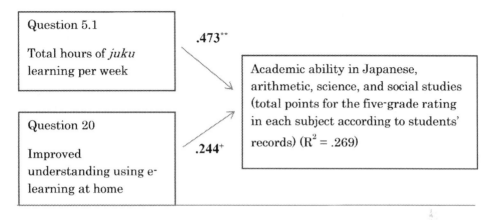

Figure 15. Influence of e-learning on academic ability (40 students)

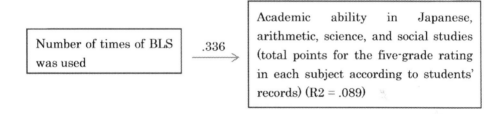

Figure 16. Influence of e-learning on academic ability (top eight students only)

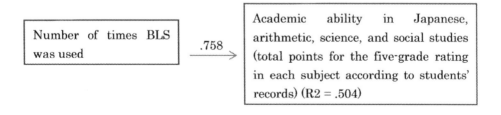

Methods 2

In our educational research, students discussed rice cultivation using a web bulletin board on the e-learning system. The outline of lessons on rice cultivation is as follows. In total, 29 fifth grade students studied the rice cultivation using rice plants in a bucket during the "Class for Integrated Study" between April 19 and October 10, 2012. In this exercise, students experienced the cultivation of rice plants by creating a small rice paddy in a bucket and sowing unhulled rice donated by Japan Agriculture (Figure 17).

Students wrote observation cards in every lesson (Figure 18) in addition to a learning activity report in their Japanese lesson between June 23 and July 4 while referring to the observation cards in the portfolio (Figure 19). The reports were subsequently uploaded onto the e-learning system. Students also wrote comments about what they had learned in a web bulletin board on the e-learning system (Figure 20). In other words, students identified benefits and avenues of future work through self-evaluating their own learning activity reports and referring to those of other students.

Subsequently, on July 29 and 31, 2013, nine students who had studied and experienced rice cultivation the previous year wrote about how to write the research report on Project-Based Learning by referring to students' comments on the web bulletin board. The time schedule was as follows: nine students looked at others' comments on web bulletin boards (30 min), wrote what they learned from them (60 min, Figure 20) and answered a questionnaire (30 min).

Figure 17. Rice cultivation using a bucket planted with rice plants

Figure 18. An observation card: A student's drawing of the planted rice plants and itemization of their discoveries

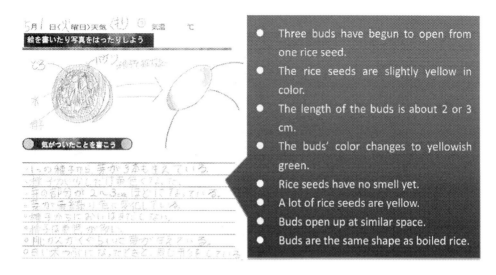

- Three buds have begun to open from one rice seed.
- The rice seeds are slightly yellow in color.
- The length of the buds is about 2 or 3 cm.
- The buds' color changes to yellowish green.
- Rice seeds have no smell yet.
- A lot of rice seeds are yellow.
- Buds open up at similar space.
- Buds are the same shape as boiled rice.

Figure 19. A learning activity report

Learning Activity Report about the rice farming using a bucket 2012

5th grade 1st class no.4 Name

Introduction

I cultivate the rice at the school and my home. The brand-name of rice at the school is "Nihonbare" and another one at my home is "Koshihikari". I wrote the growth of rice and results of experiments as follows.

[Activity Plan]

April: For sprouting

I poured water to submerge the seeds of rice in a shallow container and put it in a warm and dark room. Moreover, I changed the water every day so that the oxygen was absorbed enough.

May: Seeding

After I put the soil into a bucket, I poured water not to become a buddle. And, I sowed the seeds of rice making same spaces between each seed and push seeds into the soil at the depth of 6 mm or 7 mm and covered them with the soil.

June: Tillers of rice

July: Advancing of tillers of rice

I put 2 or 3 of well-grown young rice plants in the center of bucket when 3 or 4 leaves increasing and thinning out. And then, I poured water at the depth of 2 cm or 3 cm. After keeping this condition and proceeding the tillers of rice, I poured water at the depth of 5 cm.

[Activity Report]

April

Small and white buds have begun to grow from 1 mm to 3 mm. And I tried to compare "Nihonbare" and "Koshihikari". The tip of seeds of "Koshihikari" were colored with green although buds of "Nihonbare" were colored with white. 5 days later, 3 buds grew from rice seeds.

May

Mosses grew at "Koshihikari". But, they did not grow at "Nihonbare". Moreover the length of "Nihonbare" is only 10 cm although "Koshihakari" was 15 cm. These data indicate that there is

Fig.1 Rice at the school

difference of growth based on the degree of sunshine and the kind of rice.

June

I began an experiment to compare the difference of growth between with sunshine and not. 5 days later, the difference developed 7 cm. 10 days later, it was 12 cm. 20 days later, it was 21 cm. At last, the difference became 48 cm.

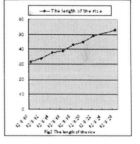

Fig.2 The length of the rice

Conclusion of the experiment

I understood that the sunshine was necessary for the growth of rice.

July

The difference of growth between "Nihonbare" and "Koshihikari" were only 6 cm in May. However, it developed 24 cm in July.

My thought for the learning activity

I got that there was the difference of growth by the kind and place of rice. Moreover, I knew that there was the rice which moss could grow or not depend on the kind of rice.

Fig.3 The rice at my home

Future work

I will conduct a different experiment in the next time because my experiment mentioned above was only focused on with sunshine of not. Moreover, I will write an obvious and clear report in the next time.

Figure 20. One student's comment on the web bulletin board on our e-learning system

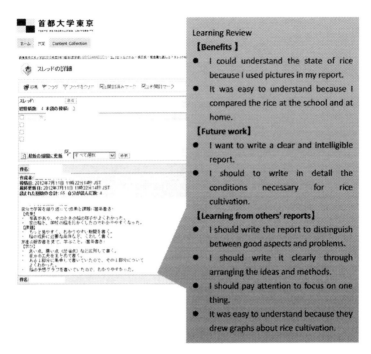

Results and Discussion 2

We analyzed the nine students' comments (text) on how to write a research report on Project-Based Learning. We calculated the number of characters and words in each student's longest comment, with the results shown in Table 2. The table also indicates the shortest and average length of the comments. Furthermore, we analyzed the total number of comments and the frequency of each part of speech. Trustia,[1] a text mining software, was used for the analysis.

The following results were thus obtained from Table 2 using correlation analysis. First, it appears that the length of comments tended to be shorter when students submitted a high number (total number of comments versus average number of words per comment, $r = -0.502$), while students tended to use more nouns in the shortest comments (number of words in the shortest comment versus number of nouns, $r = -0.632$). Moreover, comments tended to be shorter when students had higher scores in the four subjects under study (namely, Japanese, arithmetic, science, and social studies) (total score in four subjects versus number of words in the shortest comment), while students used more nouns and fewer verbs when they had higher scores in the four subjects (total points in four subjects versus number of nouns and verbs, $r = 0.365, -0.419$). Second, Trastia was used to extract the most

Table 2. Analysis of comments

No	Total Score in four subjects	Total Number of comments	Number of Characters per Comment			Number of Words per Comment			Number of Different Parts of Speech				
			Min	Ave	Max	Min	Ave	Max	Noun	Adjective	Adverb	Verb	Other
12	12	10	3	20	46	4	28	69	23	6	1	21	49
21	12	17	1	18	54	2	24	83	32	14	1	14	39
20	11	15	3	11	28	3	17	38	27	10	4	18	41
18	11	24	1	10	20	2	15	29	34	4	1	23	38
28	10	31	1	16	45	2	21	56	28	10	4	19	39
9	9	23	6	18	58	10	25	84	22	6	6	24	42
23	8	14	3	24	62	5	36	92	29	7	2	20	42
24	8	14	1	16	46	2	24	62	25	6	2	20	47
13	8	12	7	12	20	10	17	27	24	10	2	22	42

commonly used 10 words in the comments for every part of speech in their order of frequency. Table 3 shows the results which we counted the number of correspondence of nouns through comparing each ranking 10: one of them is a class students' comments on the web bulletin board and another one is comments written by 9 students. That is, we can understand how each student (9 students) refer other students' (a class students') comments.

By the way, we call students' comments on the web bulletin which the number of referring by other students are average and more and the number of replies are 2 and more "high value comments group." And, we called "low value group": the number of referring by other students are average and less and the number of replies is 0

Table 3. Total score in four subjects and referring other students' comments

Students' No.	Total Score in Four Subjects	Number of Correspondence of Nouns	
		High-Value Comments Group	Low-Value Comments Group
12	12	3	4
21	12	5	6
20	11	5	5
18	11	3	2
28	10	5	7
9	9	3	3
23	8	4	4
24	8	1	1
13	8	2	2

We conducted correlation analysis, with the correlation coefficient being 0.542 between the total score obtained in the four subjects and the number of correspondenceof nouns in the high-value group, compared with 0.513 in the low-value group. This indicated that nine students often referred to other students' nouns on the web bulletin board regardless of whether they were high-value or not. The students also used them in their comments when they had higher academic ability (score in four subjects).

As mentioned above, students with high academic abilities who are targets for gifted education were able to write comments about how to write reports using nouns, such as keywords from their classmates' comments on the web bulletin board. Furthermore, we considered that the method of using many nouns tended to make comments shorter. In addition, this method along with the shorter comments would decrease the number of phrases embellished with adjectives, adverbs, etc. The comments comprised brief, concrete sentences since nouns express knowledge, conceptions, object names, facts, and so forth. In addition, such comments would be clear because they did not contain verbiage or needless words. In other words, we assumed that students with high academic abilities could write comments concretely, clearly, and plainly using other students' keywords on the e-learning system. This therefore suggests the effectiveness of e-learning for gifted education.

Nevertheless, we need to understand above correlation coefficients as results of case study because of the limited data, and as a result, we could not determine their statistical significance.

Limitations

This research is an ongoing case study based on the experiences of a small number of students. In the future, we aim to improve our objectivity and validity by refining the study's methodology.

REFERENCES

Asahi Shimbun Digital. (2013). Retrieved from http://www.asahi.com/edu/articles/TKY201308220269.html

Benesse. (2005). *Attitude survey on compulsory education: Interim report*. Tokyo: Benesse Educational Research and Development Institute, pp. 28-29.

Central Council for Education. (2003). *Attitude survey on school education: Interim report* (pp. 1–10). Tokyo: Curriculum Section, Elementary and Secondary Education Bureau, MEXT.

Central Council for Education. (2006). Primary materials on elementary and secondary education (excerpts edition). *Subdivision on Elementary and Secondary Education (42ⁿᵈ meeting) meeting minutes, 7,* 10. Retrieved from http://www.mext.go.jp/b_menu/shingi/chukyo/chukyo3/siryo/06083007/001.pdf

Central Council for Education. (2008). *Regarding improvements to the Guidelines for the Course of Study for kindergartens, elementary schools, junior high schools, high schools, and special support schools (report).* Tokyo: MEXT.

Early Development Association (Ed.). (1998). *Collection of sayings on education by Masaru Ibuka.* Tokyo: Goma Shobo.

Fujinaga, T. (2006). Thoughts on early special education for gifted students. *Kyoiku to Igaku, 54*(10), 892–900.

Higuchi, T., Hashimoto, N., & Okabe, S. (2013). *Attitude survey of parents and guardians on school education, 2012 Digest.* Tokyo: Benesse Educational Research & Development Institute.

Hisada, M. (1996). Special education for gifted students is practically child abuse. *Gendai, 30*(7), 202–205.

Iwanaga, M., & Matsumura, N. (2010). *Talent and education: Toward a new horizon for individuality and talent.* Tokyo: NHK.

Katei Kyoiku Shimbun. (2013). *Flipped classrooms as an escape from homogenous classes.* Retrieved from http://www.kknews.co.jp/maruti/news/2013/0204_4c.html

Kuroishi, N., & Takahashi, M. (2009). A study on collaborations between the cram-school industry and public education: From present circumstances to future proposals. *Educational General Research. Bulletin of Japan Professional School of Education, 2,* 1–14.

Matsumura, N. (2008). Education to discover true "talent": Special education for gifted students that has damaged children. Tokyo: Minerva Shobo.

Mimiduka, H. (2009). Report on additional analyses regarding Japanese students' academic achievement and learning conditions from the 2007 and 2008 surveys. *Ministry of Education, Culture, Sports, Science & Technology in Japan.* Retrieved from http://www.nier.go.jp/07_08tsuikabunsekihoukoku/07_08_tsuikabunseki_houkokusho_3_1.pdf

Ministry of Education. (2005). Culture, Sports, Science and Technology. In Guidebook for Starting School. Author.

Ministry of Education, Culture, Sports, Science, and Technology. (2006). Main statement in the diet deliberation about the Fundamental Law of Education revision. Tokyo: MEXT.

Ministry of Education, Culture, Sports, Science, and Technology. (2007). Main report on Diet discussions on revisions to the Fundamental Law of Education. Tokyo: MEXT.

Ministry of Education, Culture, Sports, Science, & Technology in Japan. (2008). *Report on a survey of the actual conditions regarding children's learning activities outside of schools.* Retrieved from http://www.mext.go.jp/b_menu/houdou/20/08/__icsFiles/afieldfile/2009/03/23/1196664.pdf

Ministry of Education, Culture, Sports, Science, and Technology. (2008). *Results of the additional analysis of the 2007 nationwide scholarship and learning conditions survey.* Retrieved from http://www.mext.go.jp/a_menu/shotou/gakuryoku-chousa/zenkoku/08020513/001/003.htm

Ministry of Education, Culture, Sports, Science, and Technology. (2012). *Super science high schools reference 1.* Retrieved from http://www.mext.go.jp/b_menu/houdou/24/08/__icsFiles/afieldfile/2012/08/09/1324481_1_1.pdf

Ministry of Education, Culture, Sports, Science, and Technology. (n.d.b). *Universities implementing grade skipping for university entrance for the 2013 entrance exam.* Retrieved from http://www.mext.go.jp/a_menu/koutou/shikaku/07111318/001/002.htm

Ministry of Education, Culture, Sports, Science, and Technology. (n.d.a). *Welcome to the Fundamental Law of Education data room!* Retrieved from http://www.mext.go.jp/b_menu/kihon/about/004/a004_03.htm

Ministry of Internal Affairs and Communications Statistical Research and Training Institute. (2013). *Statistics of Japan.* Tokyo: Ministry of Internal Affairs and Communications Statistics Bureau.

Misono, M. (2012). Enhancing the evaluations of science education programs. *Japan Society for Science Education, Annual Meeting Collection of Papers, 36,* 263-264.

Murata, H. (2013). Preparing for a harsh future – parents who value study: "School lives of junior high and high school students and the 2012 attitude survey. *Hosoken-kyu to Chosa, 63*(2), 2–19.

Mutou, T. (2006). Differences between early education and special education for gifted students. *Kyoiku to Igaku, 54*(10), 909–915.

Nakayama, N. (1997). *Intellect, scholastic attainments, and people skills that only parents can develop: Early special education for gifted students so as not to fail in elementary school*. Tokyo: Yosensha.

Organization for Economic Cooperation and Development. (2011). *Education at a glance 2011: OECD indicators*. Retrieved from http://www.oecd.org/edu/eag2011

Saito, T. (2007). *"Grade skipping" not increasing for universities*. Retrieved from http://benesse.jp/blog/20071115/p3.html

Salman, K. (2013). *The one world schoolhouse: Innovation from "learning × technology"*. Tokyo: Diamond, Inc.

Sato, Y. (1984). Special education for gifted students from zero years? Solitary child rearing and the baby classroom. *Sekai, 466*, 225–235.

Shukan, B. (2006). Difficulties of special education for gifted students: Survey of 1000 parents; the top three being swimming, English, and piano. *Shukan Bunshun, 48*(34), 146–148.

Tachibana, T. (1980). The joys of learning for the capable child: Memory that becomes stimulated from being provided with intellectual challenges. *Gekkan Kyoiku no Mori, 5*(4), 48-51.

Terasaki, M., Kaifu, T., Muchaku, S., Matsuzaki, Y., & Ishii, K. (1980). What is required now for "special education for gifted students": Conditions for schools to improve "individuality and ability". *Gekkan Kyoiku no Mori, 5*(4), 24-39.

Yamamoto, N. (1997). Grade skipping, skipping a grade for university entrance, and special education for gifted students: Current conditions in eight countries (or how an increasing number of young Japanese mothers are educating "geniuses"). *Sapio, 9*(10), 116–117.

Yamasaki, H. (1980). "Special education for gifted students" beginning with Tanigaki's comments: Troubled feelings in the Ministry of Education with the Japanese teachers' union declaring its opposition. *Gekkan Kyoiku no Mori, 5*(4), 40-47.

KEY TERMS AND DEFINITIONS

Board of Education: This administrative board at local public bodies performs various tasks regarding the organization of schools, curriculums, textbooks, educational materials, and teachers' management of the schools belonging to the local public body.

Central Council for Education: This is most important council belonging to MEXT that takes a leading role in Japanese educational administration. Its mission is to discuss the policy of education, science, and culture and submit its findings and suggestions for review to the Minister of Education. The Guidelines for the Course of Study, revised about once a decade, is based on the Council's discussion and report.

Fundamental Law of Education: The Fundamental Law of Education is the highest law in Japan for school education. The educational activities in all Japanese schools providing compulsory education are conducted in accordance with this law. It comprises ten articles treating the aims, policies, and principles of education. Partial amendments were made in 2006 and 2012, with patriotism being emphasized and the importance of education being placed not only in schools, but also at home.

Guidelines for the Course of Study: The Guidelines are the national standards for the educational curriculum of elementary, junior high, and high schools, and considered to be the binding power of the law. The latest Guidelines highlight the development of students' thinking, decision-making, and expressive abilities as well as their acquisition of knowledge and skills based on the principle of promoting "Zest for living" by reviewing the present state of children.

Juku: These private schools and afterschool programs at cram schools teach subjects for examinations and give supplementary lessons. Jukus are notably in the position of being the second school in Japan and are recognized by the general public. Their problems include the quality of teachers and instructions, and the extreme examination-oriented instruction. However, MEXT recognized their function in contributing to learning at schools and thus changed the policy by which Jukus and schools coexist.

ENDNOTES

[1]   (C)2010 JustSystems Corporation

Chapter 19

The Role of Technology in Providing Effective Gifted Education Services in Clustered Classrooms

Geri Collins
Mercer University, USA

Jeffrey Hall
Mercer University, USA

Bridget Taylor
Mercer University, USA

EXECUTIVE SUMMARY

The purpose of this chapter is to examine the rationale of clustered classrooms and to explore methods of using technology to enhance the educational outcomes of gifted students in clustered classrooms. The need for this training is great because clustered classrooms can help teachers overcome the problems associated with mixed-ability groupings, tight budgets, and accusations of elitism that often plague gifted education services (Brulles & Winebrenner, 2012). The chapter includes research-based strategies for facilitating clustered classrooms, provides ideas for incorporating technology across multiple content areas, identifies what exemplary student products should look like, and offers a sample lesson plan that can be adapted to cultivate problem-solving skills, critical thinking, and collaboration in a clustered classroom. By highlighting and examining these issues, the authors hope that more teachers will utilize the clustered classroom model, providing outstanding educational opportunities that can benefit all students.

DOI: 10.4018/978-1-4666-6489-0.ch019

SETTING THE STAGE

In an era of constrained education budgets and high-stakes standardized testing, a vital pedagogical concern is ensuring that the unique needs of gifted students are still being addressed (Brulles & Winebrenner, 2012). Traditional approaches to offering gifted services, such as homogeneous classrooms or pull-out services, often fall victim to other needs when money is tight, due in part to the misguided belief that "gifted kids will make it on their own" and perform well enough on standardized tests (Brulles & Winebrenner, 2012, p. 42). In the face of these challenges, one potential solution is the "clustered classroom" model, which consists of multiple clusters of students in a single classroom who "are grouped according to their ability and achievement levels" (Brulles & Winebrenner, 2012, p. 42). Alternatively known as within-class ability grouping (Kulik & Kulik, 1992), this model provides a compelling option for teachers and other stakeholders who are interested in providing a curriculum that is differentiated and better suited for gifted learners compared to whole-class instruction in a heterogeneous classroom. Instead of concentrating gifted students in a homogenous gifted classroom (which generally costs more money and can lead to accusations of elitism) or having mixed-ability groupings of gifted and non-gifted students (which can lead to stunted academic growth and resentment from gifted students), the clustered classroom model enables gifted students to remain in heterogeneous classrooms that include multiple levels of learners. Students in clustered classroom are grouped according to ability level, which can enable teachers to provide gifted-level academic opportunities for those who need it while avoiding the aforementioned problems that are often associated with other models of gifted education (Brulles & Winebrenner, 2012). Although "little empirical evidence is available attesting to its effectiveness" (Brulles, Cohn, & Saunders, 2010, p. 327), the evidence that exists about the cluster grouping of gifted students is promising. As a result, it is important that teachers of gifted students learn more about clustered classrooms and consider applying this model in their own schools.

Cluster grouping may be "a cost-effective way to provide gifted services," (Brulles, Peters, & Saunders, 2012, p. 200), but providing effective instruction and differentiation across clusters of varying skill levels and cognitive capabilities in a single classroom can be challenging. Although ability grouping generally yields positive results for high-ability students (Fuligni, Eccles, & Barber, 1995; Gentry & Owen, 1999; Kulik & Kulik, 1992; Teno, 2000), research on cluster grouping has also highlighted "teachers' inability to appropriately challenge students due to the diverse levels of prior knowledge, aptitude and motivation common in today's heterogeneous classrooms" (Kanevsky & Keighley, 2003, p. 21). Therefore, increased and specialized training with clustered classrooms is necessary for teachers to differentiate instruction at the highest level for all students.

In order to provide effective gifted education services in a clustered classroom, the first requirement is for teachers to understand the unique learning needs and characteristics of gifted students. This knowledge and understanding is not widespread because the "basic principles of special education, including giftedness, are omitted from many initial teacher training programs" (Matthews & Foster, 2005, p. 223). Although teachers may not have received any specialized training in gifted education, they can become proficient in meeting the needs of gifted students by reading published research and learning from mentor teachers.

Research has indicated several factors that enhance learning among gifted students. Kanevsky and Keighley (2003) identified the five characteristics of effective learning tasks for gifted students, labeled the "five C's: control, choice, challenge, complexity and caring [of the teacher]" (p. 22). The five C's should always be considered when developing assignments for gifted students in order to promote their interest in course work. In a heterogeneous classroom, this is best accomplished by differentiating assignments as necessary to meet the needs of gifted students and non-gifted students alike. Brulles and Winebrenner (2012) found that "gifted students more readily take advantage of differentiated learning opportunities when others are working at advanced levels" (p. 44). Thus, clustering groups according to student ability level and then differentiating assignments accordingly is an excellent way to provide gifted services. This is a challenging task, however, and easier said than done.

Given the challenge of differentiating for gifted students in clustered classrooms, one effective strategy is to incorporate more technology (Eckstein, 2009; Siegle, 2004). As Periathiruvadi and Rinn (2012) note, "technology not only allows teachers to provide differentiated instruction for gifted children and adolescents, but also serves as an educational and creative outlet for some of the best and brightest minds in the world" (p. 153). It can also address the "five C's" previously mentioned, providing students with a world of possibilities (Kanevsky & Keighley, 2003). Given the vast array of technological options available today, teachers with the knowledge and training to effectively use these resources can begin to construct a viable curriculum that benefits all of their students in a clustered classroom.

For example, technology can be used to individualize instruction to a high degree, either by cluster or by individual student. While research about technology in gifted education is relatively rare, the National Mathematics Advisory Panel (2008) found that "a small number of studies suggest that individualized instruction, where the pace of learning is increased and often managed via computer instruction, produces gains in learning" for gifted students (p. 20). Another example is to enable gifted students to move past the confines of the classroom and open up the possibility of contacts across the world with technology. Students can have conversations with their peers in other nations, learning about international issues, discovering com-

413

monalities, and collaborating on assignments. With the aid of new technologies, collaboration can thus take on a global meaning. Another example is the creation of authentic products. Using the latest Web 2.0 tools and software, gifted student can utilize technology to create their own books, films, stories, news articles, and other forms of media to deal with far-reaching issues and academic subjects. These three examples highlight a variety of methods through which technology can help provide productive learning opportunities for gifted students.

Clustered classrooms can function smoothly if each ability group is able to work toward goals that are appropriate to their needs—challenging yet attainable. The key to this ideal situation is to have dedicated, effective teachers with proper training, adequate access to resources, an understanding of individual student needs, and administrative / community support. By adding technological awareness and prowess, teachers of clustered classrooms can provide differentiated instruction at an even higher level, an outcome that is especially beneficial to gifted students.

CASE DESCRIPTION

For clustered classrooms to work effectively across the various content areas, technology must necessarily be adapted to meet the needs of teachers and students. The following cases describe examples of technology-based clustered classrooms across four primary content areas: social studies, science, English/language arts, and mathematics. For the purposes of this chapter, the ideas presented here are focused on middle grade content standards, but clustered classrooms can be effective at other grade levels, too. Each case is supported by relevant research and provides suggested technological tools to achieve the unique aims and goals of their respective content areas. Most of the recommended software described in these cases are free or at least provide some free services along with premium options.

Social Studies

The school day begins. As a group of students moves into their social studies classroom, they will take their seats in clustered groups—two to four desks joined together to provide a working area separated from other groups. Each group will have access to tablets and laptops to use for research and to begin working on differentiated assignments that require an examination of the day's lesson: the Colonial period of American history.

For the gifted students who are grouped together in their own cluster, their unique assignment will be to analyze the events that are leading to the American Revolution and then develop a Web 2.0-based product to present their analysis.

The findings of the cluster's research may be presented in various ways that spark the creative nature of the gifted student. To challenge the gifted students to expand their technological skills and creativity, specialized tools such as timeline creators could be required. Examples include Tiki-Toki (www.tiki-toki.com), TimeGlider (www.timeglider.com), and myHistro (www.myhistro.com). Such programs often enable the use of multimedia resources to enrich presentations, empowering gifted students to supplement their work with pictures, videos, and music. Other, less specialized examples of presentation tools that could be used include Prezi (www. prezi.com) and Microsoft Movie Maker. An example: a Prezi presentation by a group of gifted eighth graders depicted a large Coke bottle with dates of the Progressive Era pouring out of it, punctuated with pictures and text added by each member of the group. Products can be created individually or with group collaboration, and can then be shared with the whole class or even published online to be shared with the world. The best products will be infused with accurate information as well as cogent analysis and evaluation, and present an appealing and thoughtful mix of multimedia resources.

Other groups, which were organized according to pre-assessed student ability levels, will also scrutinize the same time period, but will focus on appropriately differentiated learning tasks such as defining key terms, identifying and understanding main issues, and examining connections between the issues. These groups will also be responsible for developing products to present their work, but the tools used may be more generalized and common (such as Microsoft Word or PowerPoint) to meet the needs and abilities of students.

The differentiated tasks reflect an understanding of the revised Bloom's taxonomy (Krathwohl, 2002). The lower-performing students will focus on defining and understanding tasks, the average-performing students will focus on applying and analyzing tasks, and the high-performing and gifted students will focus on evaluating and creating tasks. There will be some overlap in tasks and expectations, but these guidelines can help teachers start the differentiation process in a clustered classroom. As students demonstrate their capability to learn more and produce more, the expectations can be increased to provide an ever-increasing yet still surmountable challenge. In addition, this method of grouping students together to discuss concepts and create authentic products using technology fits with the "distributed cognition" theory, which "emphasizes the distributed nature of cognitive phenomena across individuals, artefacts (sic) and internal and external representations in terms of a common language of 'representational states' and 'media'" (Rogers, 1997, pp. 1-2).

Another example of clustered classrooms in a social studies setting could occur during an economics study. Clustered once again with other gifted students, the economic issues that they will address will include the use of mercantilism for the economic basis of the English colonial period. Within the group, each member can solve different problems which arise as a result of colonial trade. Products that emerge can also incorporate mathematics by using graphs and calculations to depict profit and loss. The social aspect can be included as the slave trade becomes part of the trading that goes on between England, Africa, and the 13 colonies. This will appeal to another common characteristic of gifted students – their moral sensitivity – as they grapple with the issue of slavery.

As Silverman (1994) notes, gifted students often have a deeper awareness of ethical and social issues than their contemporaries. The sensitivity towards justice can be the catalyst for lessons that focus on the establishment of the American government and the reasons behind its formation. An excellent lesson idea that can be used with gifted eighth graders is a simulation of Supreme Court cases (www. springvillegi.org/webpages/cspan/supreme.cfm), which allows students to participate in a mock trial. Each group of students is given assigned parts which included witnesses, lawyers, judges, defendants, and plaintiffs. The ensuing simulation can cause students to question aspects of modern society. The court cases emphasize that proper procedures must be followed if students wish to pursue social changes.

Other significant social studies topics, such as issues of peace and war, civil rights, immigration, voters' rights, student rights, world hunger, child labor, pollution, and basic human rights, can also be used to engage gifted students in different activities. With the use of internet, these issues can be debated outside of the classroom with connections across the world. Using internet-connected tablets and laptops, students can either conduct or participate in surveys with students from other countries. The connections that are possible will give them a broad perspective of the world and allow them to grow in their knowledge of how the rest of the world views the same issues. By encouraging access to these arenas, students can produce debates, speeches, and advocacy letters, perhaps sparking more active involvement in organizations that address important social and ethical issues. As students build their knowledge, they can ultimately use their new understanding to more effectively address issues that are important to them.

A myriad of lessons can be created around these themes throughout the rest of the year. Each time period has events that can be analyzed, either in groups or individually, using the technological tools available. Economics is the corner stone of the establishment of any civilization; understanding how and why economies work is important to give gifted students the ability to analyze modern situations that erupt around the world with deeper understanding. After analyzing economics, the next logical topic of study becomes government. The connections between economics and government need to be addressed so that gifted students will understand the relationship between idealistic government goals and practical limitations imposed by economics. For example, gifted students in a classroom were once instructed to choose an issue that their national representative could help change. The students decided on the issue of raising the minimum wage. The students' ensuing research activities about this topic revealed arguments for both sides of the issue, giving them insight into the difficulties that elected representatives face when trying to serve two groups of constituents.

In summation, the study of social studies encourages students to explore different perspectives and develop realistic solutions to tackle problems of personal and community concern. As gifted students work together in clustered groups, they will learn to rely on their own intelligence while gaining encouragement from peers that understand how they think. In such cases, technology can help broaden the academic community in which gifted students participate, potentially providing a national or even global perspective that might otherwise be difficult to obtain.

English/Language Arts

Once social studies class has ended, the students move on to their next class: language arts. When students arrive to language arts, they set their belongings on their desks and move to computer stations to work on a project they are completing with partners. Most students in the class are still moving toward an understanding of adjective and adverb phrases, but those students who demonstrated mastery of the material through a pretest are working on a related project. These students are creating a menu for a restaurant, providing rich descriptions for each item by using adjective and adverb phrases. They have chosen Italian food as the theme for their restaurant, and they are using the internet to research authentic Italian dishes. Some students are using Microsoft Publisher to create menus that are well-organized, have a unified format and color-scheme, and include pictures to highlight their descriptions. Others are using Microsoft Word to create web pages. Before beginning the project, students looked at actual menus provided by the teacher as well as on-line menus that they found themselves to determine criteria for a professional-level product. They used those criteria to create a rubric to guide their work.

When the portion of class allocated for grammar instruction ends, the advanced students return to their desks to participate in a discussion about texts that the class has been reading. The class has been involved in a unit on heroes, and the teacher has been encouraging students to use online sources to locate articles about modern-day heroes. This has made the unit relevant for the students. Additionally, it has fostered differentiation of instruction, as students have been able to locate articles that are appropriate for both their reading ability and their interest level. The teacher has encouraged the gifted students to use databases such as ProQuest and EBSCOhost to locate articles. Students have also been encouraged to use the search feature on particular newspaper websites such as *The New York Times* to access articles with appropriate depth as well as text complexity. Using these online sources to access articles addresses an important element of building technology skills for students: knowing where to look and selecting information (Siegle, 2004).

The gifted cluster has been working together to create a wiki page that highlights the class's learning during the heroes unit. Carney-Strahler (2011) cited extensive research supporting the benefits of wikis for literacy development, particularly for collaborative writing. Siegle (2004) wrote that "education movements to promote student technology literacy will serve gifted children well since current technology literacy goals are very compatible with many gifted and talented students' learning preferences" (p. 32). Siegle noted that the benefits of assigning multimedia projects to gifted students are twofold: developing technology skills and exploring interests in depth. Another benefit of asking gifted students to create wikis is that these website-building tools encourage students to work collaboratively rather than in isolation (Carney-Strahler, 2011).

Wikis provide a shared space for students to respond to questions, post reflections, and offer feedback on one another's thoughts and work. Students can place links to files, web tools, and information sources on the wiki page, as well (Eckstein, 2009). For this unit, students post links to articles that they have located related to acts of heroism as well as to works of literature that are available through databases such as Bartleby.com and Project Gutenberg. Students have also embedded links to videos they created using Animoto (www.animoto.com), an online resource that allows users to combine images, music, and text to create original videos. Students have used Animoto to create video collages that visually represented their conceptions of heroism.

To build their wikis, the class uses PBworks (www.pbworks.com/education), which offers free wiki spaces for educators and the ability to offer limited access to the site, protecting students' privacy. The teacher has asked students to use this wiki-building site because it allows the teacher to track changes made by each student. This enables the teacher to monitor each student's contributions to the wiki and provide personalized feedback, in addition to the feedback that students receive from their peers. The teacher could have also chosen Wikispaces (www.wikispaces.com) or a variety of other sites.

The class wiki page is linked to both individual and class blogs. The teacher has chosen to use Weebly (www.weebly.com), a website builder that is free for educators, password protected, includes student accounts for developing web pages and blogs, and allows the teacher to monitor content before it is posted. A viable alternative is Edublogs (www.edublogs.org). Blogs have many uses for education as they essentially allow students to "create personal webpages of text, pictures, graphics, videos, and other multimedia with the same ease as creating a word processing document" (Boling, Castek, Zawilinski, Barton, & Nierlich, 2008, p. 504). Additionally, blogs provide a space for students to receive feedback from and engage in conversations with teachers and peers.

Individual blogs allow students to share their responses about what they are reading while providing a space for reflection following class and group discussions. Students' individual blogs also serve as electronic portfolios where they collect samples of the work they have completed throughout the year. In contrast, the class blog promotes collaborative writing and responses. For example, during the heroism unit, both the teacher and students are able to post quotes related to heroism to the class blog. Students then share their reactions to the quotes, including connections to real life and to the texts they have been reading. The blog format allows students to respond to one another's thoughts in their own time and after careful consideration of what they would like to share, something that is not possible during classroom or small group discussions. It also allows space for all students to participate in the discussion. Through blogs, "concepts or contexts are discussed and articulated in both a personalized and group exchange, and ideas are built on previous educational content" (Huffaker, 2005, p. 95).

In addition to individual blogs and the class blog, the gifted cluster also has a dedicated blog. Throughout the year, the blog has served as a forum for the students to share their experiences as gifted learners. Additionally, the teacher periodically posts excerpts from articles related to being gifted or links to websites related to giftedness for the students to read and respond to electronically. In this way, the students have a safe space for discussing issues that are unique to them as gifted learners and the teacher has a greater awareness of the issues and concerns that are affecting her students.

One thing the teacher observed through the blogs was that her students were often connecting the texts they were reading in class to other subject areas or personal interests. In response to this, the teacher began allocating time for students to engage in independent study to explore their interests. To organize tools and resources that they use during their investigations, each student uses Symbaloo (www.symbaloo.com). This web-based application allows students to organize links to each of the electronic resources that they use in class, as well as personal links. In this way, each student has created his or her own personal learning network (PLN). When working collaboratively, students in the class, or even in other classes, can connect to one another's Symbaloo pages to share resources.

Students could also have used Netvibes (www.netvibes.com), which allows them to construct personalized dashboards that are related to subjects that they choose to investigate. A personalized dashboard is a collection of resources that connect to the curriculum in ways that reflect each individual student's interests. Teachers can help students customize their dashboards to target specific skills, such as particular resources for students with advanced reading abilities or those with particular interest in heroes who have fought for human rights.

A PLN serves as one element of a student's personal learning environment (PLE). An individual's PLE is not a tool or a product that schools may purchase, though there are products such as Symbaloo and Netvibes that facilitate the creation and use of individual PLEs. Rather, PLEs are "an approach or process that is individualized by design, and thus different from person to person" (Johnson, Adams, & Cummins, 2012, p. 24). Personal learning environments encompass both the human resources and technological tools that students collect to support their learning (Drexler, 2010; EDUCAUSE Learning Initiative, 2009; Johnson, Adams, & Haywood, 2011). Thus, learning through PLEs is not an isolated process. Indeed, through technology, learners are able to collaborate not only with other learners who share their interests, but also experts in the field (EDUCAUSE Learning Initiative, 2009). The essential idea is that students are in charge of the process by which they learn with the freedom to make choices that reflect their individual needs and preferences (Johnson, Adams, & Cummins, 2012).

PLEs are not only personalized but also student-centered. Though teachers are an essential resource for supporting students (Drexler, 2010), students drive decisions regarding the tools they will use, the content they will access, and even the topics they will study. Textbooks and teacher-delivery are no longer the primary source of information. Through technology, learners access information through "learning communities, information management and communication tools, personal learning networks, . . . authoritative sources, online tutoring and guided sources tailored to their needs, knowledge-building tools, and peers with common interests" (Demski, 2012, para. 10). To develop their PLEs, students might incorporate blogs, *YouTube,* RSS feeds from news agencies, social media, Skype, wikis, and a variety of other resources (EDUCAUSE Learning Initiative, 2009; Johnson, Adams, & Cummins, 2012)

When used in formal educational settings, the use of PLEs requires a balance of student autonomy, predetermined lessons, and teacher facilitation (Johnson, Adams, & Haywood, 2011). Teachers typically provide some structure for student learning, including helping them to set goals for learning and guiding students to lessons and resources that are suited to their interests and abilities (Drexler, 2010). Implementing PLEs affords educators the opportunity to connect the learning that students engage in outside of school with what takes place in the classroom. Demski (2012), quoting Jayne James, who once served as ISTE's senior director of education leadership, emphasized that PLEs allow students and teachers to connect students' interests and natural curiosity with the curriculum and competencies that teachers want them to master. They also allow teachers to differentiate instruction, a practice that is difficult to implement through traditional methods of curricular and instructional development. When teachers collaborate with students to develop students' PLEs, teachers have the opportunity to provide both flexible and customized instruction. Differentiation is possible not only through teacher facilitation, but also through student control of their PLEs, which provide access to a wealth of online material that students can use to gain content knowledge as well as tools that they can use to transform that knowledge into a variety of products and applications. Students can control the style, pace, and direction of learning as they collect resources (Johnson, Adams, & Cummins, 2012). Greaves observed that students have the potential to personalize their learning more effectively and efficiently than teachers, who often lack time to individualize instruction for each student (Demski, 2012).

PLEs can also serve as electronic portfolios to document individual student learning (Johnson, Adams, & Cummins, 2012; U. S Department of Education, 2010).

In addition to sharing their Symbaloo accounts, each student is also connected through the social bookmarking site Diigo (www.diigo.com/education). Though many social bookmarking sites exist, Diigo has features that make it particularly useful for education. Teachers are able to create accounts for students without using email addresses, and there are privacy settings that limit access to students and teachers. Teachers can also create unlimited groups of students for the purposes of sharing resources. Once students begin using Diigo, they can bookmark pages, adding tags to indicate how pages are related to particular content or projects. Teachers and students can also highlight portions of webpages, create electronic sticky notes, and share comments. A teacher can create a group of gifted students, select a website specifically for that group, and attach a sticky note indicating the significance of the text or providing directions for a particular assignment. Additionally, students working collaboratively can easily share resources as well as comment on how they might be useful.

The purpose of these activities is not merely engagement; rather, the purpose is to create a digital ecosystem that capitalizes on technological resources to provide appropriate challenge for gifted students and opportunities to develop skills that will be essential for the 21st century. As Besnoy, Dantzler, and Siders (2012) have written, "An ecologically sound classroom brings together a multitude of cognitive processes that enables students to experience, create, and transform knowledge" (p. 306). The appropriate use of technology allows teachers of gifted students in the clustered language arts classroom to facilitate literacy development targeted to the specific needs of advanced learners, whether students are working independently or in collaboration with their peers.

Mathematics

Following language arts, it is time for math class to begin. As students enter the classroom, they notice that the teacher has arranged their desks into groups of two to four. Within each cluster, students have access to technologies such as graphing calculators, laptops, and/or tablets. For the gifted students' cluster, the teacher's goal will be to enhance both "schoolhouse giftedness" and "creative-productive giftedness" (Renzulli & Reis, 2002). This can be accomplished by encouraging the gifted students to deeply explore mathematical concepts and create authentic products demonstrating their knowledge and skills by using technologies such as Web 2.0 tools (Eckstein, 2009). One of the best ways to accomplish this is through problem-based learning, a constructivist approach that emphasizes authentic learning experiences, interesting and relevant problems, and student ownership of solutions (Savery & Duffy, 2002). Using this method, clusters can work independently to solve complex math problems and present their findings in a level-appropriate fashion. This enables the teacher to spend less time lecturing in front of the whole class and spend more time facilitating student problem solving skills. Differentiated successfully, problem-based learning can provide a level-appropriate challenge for all learners.

There are a variety of Web 2.0 tools that are useful for problem solving in a clustered mathematics classroom. One excellent tool is GeoGebra (www.geogebra. org), a free and open-source computer program which combines the capabilities of dynamic geometry software, computer algebra systems, and spreadsheets to enable deep explorations of mathematics in a digital environment (Hall & Chamblee, 2013). With this software, students can create their own mathematical models to visualize concepts, explore the creations of other GeoGebra users around the world, share their own creations, and participate in a global community of GeoGebra mathematicians. GeoGebra can be used to model and test mathematical relationships in order to solve complex problems in a relevant, real-world fashion.

Another teaching strategy is to task the gifted cluster students to develop math resources and assessments for the other clusters. For example, Quizlet (www.quizlet.com) could be used to create and share flashcards to help other students, both in class and around the world, study for math exams. With Formulator Tarsia, a downloadable program from www.mmlsoft.com, students can easily create their own jigsaw puzzles based on math problems, providing a fun way for others to accurately match math questions and answers as a review activity.

For the type of individualized, self-paced, computer-based instruction recommended by the National Mathematics Advisory Panel (2008), students can do practice problems based on Common Core State Standards using websites such as TenMarks (www.tenmarks.com) or IXL (www.ixl.com). These websites provide students with standards-based mathematics problems and are supplemented with hints, instant feedback, and other resources. Similarly, Khan Academy (www.khanacademy.org) provides a wealth of video tutorials that explain how to solve math problems and enables students to practice their skills with instant feedback. To achieve a flipped classroom (Tucker, 2012), Khan Academy videos and TenMarks practice problems can be assigned for homework, allowing more class time to be devoted to group work and more complex problem solving with the ready assistance of the teacher.

In addition to the tools mentioned above, the following mathematics education resources are also recommended for potential use by gifted students in clustered classrooms:

- **Problem Solving Decks:** mathlearnnc.sharpschool.com/cms/One.aspx?portalId=4507283&pageId=5856325
- **NRICH:** nrich.maths.org/frontpage
- **Wolfram Demonstrations Project:** demonstrations.wolfram.com/topic.html?topic=Mathematics&limit=20

These websites and tools provide excellent opportunities for meaningful and rich mathematical learning experiences that can be shared in a clustered classroom setting.

Research on cluster grouping and math achievement is limited, but the results so far are encouraging. In a study conducted with an Arizona elementary school district, the mathematics performance of 772 gifted students from clustered and non-clustered classes was analyzed (Brulles, Cohn, & Saunders, 2010). Based on pre-assessment and post-assessment data, the results indicated that "gifted students in the cluster-grouped classrooms achieved at higher rates in mathematics than those students of similar ability in regular heterogeneous classes" (Brulles, Cohn, & Saunders, 2010, p. 329). Further research is needed to more definitively state that cluster grouping improves mathematics performance among gifted students, but the available evidence is promising.

Science

The final academic course of the day is science. As a subject that is conducive to group work, the study of science can become very engaging when hands-on projects are employed. The very nature of science involves inquiry, research, and collaboration. The inquiry aspect of science, both in terms of content and method, is a fundamental part of national science standards (Lewis, 2006).

Once more, students enter the classroom and sit in clustered groups. The gifted students begin the process of finding solutions to theoretical questions. The content focuses on the nature of matter, forms of energy, force/mass, sound waves, and the characteristics of gravity, electricity and magnetism. Each topic can be approached collaboratively, using technology to enhance student engagement and learning. Wallace (2002) stated that technology can enable meaningful learning opportunities in science through four categories: Representation (displaying "ideas and processes that are difficult or impossible to represent without technology"), Information ("providing access to data and content"), Transformation ("changing the nature of the task in which students engage"), and Collaboration ("facilitating communication and collaboration with peers and experts") (p. 6).

Each of these affordances are readily on display as technology can be used by students to investigate and explore the relationship of over 100 elements and their physical or chemical properties. Simulations that have possible explosive or destructive outcomes can be virtually constructed and the results can be viewed safely on a computer screen. Students can use previous data to guide new constructions, adding variations and comparing the results to other virtual simulations. Using previously collected data can create collaborative connections between past experts and modern students. Student teams can then analyze their information, answering questions that require critical thinking skills and collaboration with peers.

Another fruitful topic for clustered classrooms is the study of energy. As before, Wallace's (2002) four categories can be employed to investigate the Law of Conservation of Energy as it applies to the use of energy around the world. Experiments in teams can be done regarding different kinds and forms of energy as questions of energy use are researched. Once an understanding of conduction and radiation are reached, students can analyze data on the use of energy by different countries. Analyzing the consumption of energy by different countries around the world can engage students in social studies-connected issues of economics, governance, and equity, once again encouraging gifted students to grapple with ethical issues.

The curriculum continues to revolve around mankind's ability to harness the earth's resources as students are asked to investigate the relationship between force, mass, and the motion of objects. Simple machines become the center of focus. Student teams can be challenged to make a simple machine that will accomplish predetermined tasks involving levers, incline planes, pulleys, wedges, screws, wheels, and axles. Technology plays a key part in giving students the information needed to design and build the required machine. Students can view simulations of such machines on-line and gain information to help them construct their own. In teams, students can be asked to conduct experiments that reveal the forces on objects in terms of gravity, inertia, and friction that will help them understand what makes simple machines work. Hoffman, Wu, Krajcik, and Soloway (2003) support this method of teaching by noting the "relationship between on-line resource quality and the construction of learners' content understanding," concluding that "sites that presented engaging easy-to-read information while combining it with other supports for learning fostered the construction of content understandings" (p. 341).

Other interesting topics that could be successfully explored in clustered class-rooms include the wave nature of sound, electromagnetic radiation, gravity, electricity, magnetism, and their relation to the forces in nature. For example, gifted students can be tasked with determining the everyday experiences of the properties of sound and the relationship of light waves to reflection, refraction, diffraction, and absorption. Students, working either individually or in a cluster group, can perform experiments to demonstrate these issues, while technological tools could aid in the presentation of results.

One unique way for gifted students to demonstrate their newly developed knowledge is through student-created games. Mayer (2012) describes how student-created games can be used:

[S]tudents are free to explore and construct their own designs, demonstrating their understanding through application of content. While the flexibility of this model easily fits into most curricular areas, the challenge for students is the development of a game space and mechanisms that reflect the curriculum in a thoughtful and meaningful way. This process helps students build and display mastery of the content being covered in the project because of the deeper understanding needed to create playable spaces capable of engaging the audience with the content. (para. 4)

By creating games based on their new scientific understanding, gifted students can reinforce their knowledge, exercise their creativity, and build fun activities that can be used by classmates.

There are many programs that support the use of technology that focus on specific areas of science. Two programs that are available that encourage students to perform experiments include Science Buddies (www.sciencebuddies.org) and Science Bob (www.sciencebob.com). Both sites allow teachers to choose from a list of topics that address specific areas of science. Gifted clusters can first complete the experiment presented in the program; then, they can do a variation of their own, which involves both creativity and critical thinking.

The use of games can also enhance the students' ability to understand the working of simple machines. The Fantastic Contraptions (www.fantasticcontraptions. net) game illustrates how simple machines work, encouraging student to learn how levers, incline planes, pulleys, wedges, screws, and wheels work together. When the game was recently assigned in an eighth grade classroom, the students began to help one another complete the tasks instead of competing with one another. As each student took a turn with the game, experienced classmates began to share tips to improve the construction of the simple machine. Collaboration can become a byproduct of the game and can lead to a group analysis of the underlying mechanics, helping all students to better understand the relationship between the working parts of simple machines.

When simulations are desired, students can explore PhET Interactive Simulations (phet.colorado.edu), a website which can lead to more inquiry-based research. Other research inquiries can be addressed using BioKIDS Kids' Inquiry of Diverse Species (www.biokids.umich.edu). Students can then use the same types of presentation technologies used in other disciplines (such as Prezi) to share what they have created, helping to enhance the learning of all the students in the classroom.

In summary, it is clear that technology must play a vital role in the science education of gifted students in clustered classrooms. Wallace's (2002) four categories encapsulate these benefits and affordances: unique representations of processes and ideas that are easily accessible using websites or software, the wealth of information available on-line that can be used to investigate concepts beyond the resources available inside school walls, transformation of tasks to help students deepen their understanding of science, and collaborative opportunities that connects students to peers and experts around the world.

Lesson Planning

When developing lesson plans for clustered classrooms, the teacher must be sure to include activities that meet the unique needs of gifted students. However, though the previous sections of this chapter detailed a variety of suggested technology-based activities for gifted learners across the academic subject areas, teachers must also develop lesson plans that account for the abilities of all students in any given classroom. What follows is a sample lesson plan template for clustered classrooms that can be adapted and used for any content concentration:

SAMPLE LESSON PLAN TEMPLATE

Standard

Identified by subject area and with all elements to be used for each lesson. For example, an assigned standard may be a Common Core State Standard or national organization standard (e.g., National Council for the Social Studies standard, etc.). Gifted students should be expected to explore assigned standards in greater depth and complexity. If necessary, gifted students can also be assigned more standards than their non-gifted peers.

Objectives

Observable/measurable objectives that help the assessment of the learning. It is important that the teacher starts with the intended curriculum and then determines how to implement it. Objectives help to build scaffolding from beginning to completion of the lesson. For example:

The student will be able to.....

- Define the vocabulary of the lesson.
- Identify the issues of the subject.
- Explain the connections of the different parts.
- Analyze the outcome of the issues.

Gifted students should be expected to demonstrate higher order objectives that require greater skill and knowledge, such as synthesizing multiple data points or evaluating diverse arguments.

Classroom Environment

The structure of the classroom must allow for differentiation in a clustered classroom. By assigning students to homogeneous ability groupings, the teacher can more effectively assign different activities that are uniquely challenging to each group. The class will generally be divided into groups of two to four students. Depending on the characteristics of the students in the classroom, most of the groups will be populated with non-gifted students based on their ability/knowledge levels: low, average, and high. The gifted students will compose the final group (or multiple groups, depending on the number of gifted students in the class).

Essential Question

A short, thought-provoking question that is related to the topic of the day's lesson can be used as an opening activity as students arrive in class. Open ended questions work well and give students a chance to think about what will be presented in the upcoming lesson. Examples include: Why did Shay rebel? How do atoms function? How can poetry be used to tell a story? Why are square roots important? Gifted students should be expected to provide more complex answers to these questions.

Instructional Procedures

The following can be used in a writing-focused classroom, and should be adjusted for content and pacing needs. This lesson is for approximately 55 minutes.

7 min: Students will enter class, go to their assigned seats and individually answer the Essential Question (posted on the front board) in writing. After all the members of a clustered group are present, the students can share and discuss their answers.

30 min: Each cluster group will be given their instructions for the day's work. Each group should have a computer and the textbook to use for assistance in completing the assignment.

Group One (Low-Performing): Define the lesson's vocabulary and prepare to share them with the class using appropriate technology.

Group Two (Average-Performing): Identify the main issues of the lesson and prepare to share them with the class using appropriate technology.

Group Three (High-Performing): Explain the connections of each part and prepare to share with the class using appropriate technology.

Group Four (Gifted Cluster): Analyze the connections of the different parts showing the relevance of the material to the topic. Prepare to share with the class using appropriate technology.

15 min: Each group will present their part of the lesson to the class. When not presenting, each student will takes notes with a graphic organizer as the presentations are being made.

3 min: At the end of the period, students will turn in their graphic organizers so the teacher can assess their work.

CURRENT CHALLENGES TO CLUSTERED CLASSROOMS

Technology-enabled clustered classrooms can be challenging to implement, but research indicates that the results are worth it for gifted students. While homogeneous classrooms of gifted students would likely yield better results, this option may not always be feasible. Therefore, the clustered classroom approach of grouping gifted students together in a heterogeneous classroom and differentiating lessons with technology is likely the next best option.

There are several logistical challenges that must be overcome in order to successfully conduct clustered classrooms. These include the challenges of differentiating lessons for diverse student abilities, adequately planning and preparing technology resources, communicating clear expectations, explaining how to use new technologies, monitoring student performance, managing physical classroom constraints, deploying appropriate technologies, and ensuring adequate access to technology. The following section will describe methods for overcoming these challenges.

SOLUTIONS AND RECOMMENDATIONS

Based on the experiences and research of the authors, the following are some lessons learned about using technology with gifted students in clustered classrooms and recommendations for classroom practice:

1. Successful cluster grouping requires differentiation. As Brulles, Cohn, and Saunders (2010) note, "differences in the achievement gains between the cluster and noncluster classroom may be primarily attributed to cluster teachers' awareness and acceptance of the fact that students begin the school year at varying academic levels, along with the assumption that instruction must be directed toward those varying levels" (p. 344). Without pre-planned, level-appropriate differentiation of lesson activities, cluster grouping will be far less effective. The time required to plan differentiated lessons is likely greater than planning whole-class lessons, but teachers may not meet the needs of all students, particularly gifted students, unless adequate differentiation is employed. Administrators must recognize this requirement and provide enough time for teachers to adequately plan and prepare their lessons.

Using technology to differentiate instruction for gifted students is an effective way to extend students' knowledge and skills and to increase gifted students' engagement in learning. Students who have been jaded by educational experiences that offer no new learning or challenge come alive when they are able to participate in differentiated learning experiences using technology. Students who had displayed apathy and disinterest during whole group instruction of concepts that they had already mastered blossomed when they were able to conduct research, access information from a variety of academic and real-world sources, learn new concepts, collaborate with their peers, and create products that demonstrated their learning.

2. Successfully differentiating instruction using technology requires careful planning on the teacher's part as well as a willingness to take risks and learn with students. It is not sufficient to place students in front of a computer and tell them to research something interesting. Students need lists of potential topics and products, models of excellent work, and training in how to use different technologies. They also need guidance in how and where to access the most

useful and credible information. Additionally, many technology resources, though free, require teachers to set up their own accounts as well as student accounts. Without careful planning, the time that gifted students have access to technology can be both frustrating and fruitless.

3. Students need clearly defined expectations for differentiated learning experiences. While it is tempting to think that gifted students just dive into learning and figure things out for themselves, they are still children who need guidance. They need clear expectations for how to spend their time, what they should accomplish as a result of their learning experiences, how to behave appropriately within their group, where to save and store materials, how to submit assignments, and how to transition from one activity to another. Communicating clear expectations eliminates confusion and allows students to focus on learning.

4. It is beneficial to have one or two students who have expertise with each technology so that they can assist other students. When students are attempting to use a new technology, much of a teacher's time can be absorbed with putting out fires: explaining simple steps (even if students already have written instructions), helping students get unstuck, and answering very basic questions. Having one or two students who are knowledgeable about the technology and available to answer other students' questions frees the teacher to focus on content questions rather than on technological questions.

5. Even when the work is engaging, students need to be monitored. There is a prevailing myth that when students are engaged in appropriately challenging and interesting learning experiences, they will stay focused on the learning task and there will be no behavior issues. This is not true. Students still have a tendency to engage in social talk with their peers, to access internet sites related to personal interests (such as new styles of tennis shoes or the class photo gallery), or to play computer games. A teacher's presence is important to encourage students to stay focused. If it is necessary for students to work somewhere other than the classroom, such as the library, it is important to communicate beforehand with adults supervising the students so that they know how students are supposed to be spending their time and can encourage them to stay on task.

6. Attention must be paid to the physical layout of the classroom. Desks and/or tables must be arranged so that there is adequate separation between groups while still providing ample working space within groups. Students should be able to comfortably interact with their partners while not be distracted by the activities of other groups.

7. Assuming there is enough technology to use for clustered classroom purposes, teachers must consider how to deploy technology for any given lesson. Each cluster group must have access to the technological tools necessary to complete

the lesson's requirements. Wi-Fi-enabled laptops and/or tablets are ideal for clustered groups since they provide mobility and require less space compared to desktop workstations. Beyond physical considerations, teachers must also consider which technological tools should be utilized for each lesson. The examples provided earlier in this chapter provide content-specific suggestions for getting started, but are by no means exhaustive. Teachers should strive to learn more about available technological resources, particularly Web 2.0 tools, since developments occur rapidly.

By anticipating and managing these pedagogical and logistical challenges, teachers will be better prepared to successfully cluster their classrooms. Planning time will likely increase, but the increased attention and service to all levels of students in a classroom is worth it. Without technology-enabled clustering, gifted students may not receive the academic challenge and authentic opportunities they need to improve their knowledge and skills.

In summary, technology-enabled clustered classrooms are an effective option for providing gifted education services. The following are the requirements which must be met to effectively implement technology-based lessons in clustered classrooms with gifted students:

- A teacher who is knowledgeable and trained in gifted education.
- A teacher who is knowledgeable and trained in the clustered classroom model.
- A teacher who is knowledgeable and trained in differentiating instruction that provides instruction tailored to meet diverse student needs.
- A teacher who is knowledgeable and trained in a variety of technological tools.
- Ready access to appropriate technological tools.
- Adequate planning time.
- Administrative and community support.

If each of these requirements is met, gifted students will be able to participate in worthwhile, technology-enriched academic activities while still remaining in heterogeneous-ability classrooms. Clustered classrooms enable teachers to address the needs of all levels of students in their classrooms. With the additional capabilities and opportunities that technology provides, teachers can ensure that gifted students in clustered classrooms can partake in the complex and compelling assignments that they so rightfully deserve.

REFERENCES

Besnoy, K. D., Dantzler, J. A., & Siders, J. A. (2012). Creating a digital ecosystem for the gifted education classroom. *Journal of Advanced Academics, 23*(4), 305–325. doi:10.1177/1932202X12461005

Boling, E., Castek, J., Zawilinski, L., Barton, K., & Nierlich, T. (2008). Collaborative literacy: Blogs and internet projects. *The Reading Teacher, 61*(6), 504–506. doi:10.1598/RT.61.6.10

Brulles, D., Cohn, S., & Saunders, R. (2010). Improving performance for gifted students in a cluster grouping model. *Journal for the Education of the Gifted, 34*(2), 327–350.

Brulles, D., Peters, S. J., & Saunders, R. (2012). Schoolwide mathematics achievement within the gifted cluster grouping model. *Journal of Advanced Academics, 23*(3), 200–216. doi:10.1177/1932202X12451439

Brulles, D., & Winebrenner, S. (2011, October). The schoolwide cluster grouping model: Restructuring gifted education services for the 21st century. *Gifted Child Today, 34*(4), 35–46.

Brulles, D., & Winebrenner, S. (2012). Clustered for success. *Educational Leadership, 69*(5), 41–45.

Carney-Strahler, B. (2011). Wikis: Promoting collaborative literacy through affordable technology in content-area classrooms. *Creative Education, 2*(2), 76–82. doi:10.4236/ce.2011.22011

Demski, J. (2012, January). This time it's personal. *T.H.E. Journal.* Retrieved from http://thejournal.com/articles/2012/01/04/personalized-learning.aspx

Drexler, W. (2010). The networked student model for construction of personal learning environments: Balancing teacher control and student autonomy. *Australasian Journal of Educational Technology, 26*(3), 369–385.

Eckstein, M. (2009). Enrichment 2.0: Gifted and talented education for the 21st century. *Gifted Child Today, 32*(1), 59–63.

EDUCAUSE Learning Initiative. (2009, May). *7 things you should know about... personal learning environments.* Retrieved from http://net.educause.edu/ir/library/pdf/ ELI7049.pdf

Fuligni, A. J., Eccles, J. S., & Barber, B. L. (1995). The long-term effects of seventh-grade ability grouping in mathematics. *The Journal of Early Adolescence, 15*(1), 58–89. doi:10.1177/0272431695015001005

Gentry, M., & Owen, S. V. (1999). An investigation of the effects of total school flexible cluster grouping on identification, achievement, and classroom practices. *Gifted Child Quarterly, 43*(4), 224–243. doi:10.1177/001698629904300402

Hall, J., & Chamblee, G. (2013). Teaching algebra and geometry with GeoGebra: Preparing pre-service teachers for middle grades/secondary mathematics classrooms. *Computers in the Schools, 30*(1-2), 12–29. doi:10.1080/07380569.2013.764276

Hoffman, J. L., Wu, H.-K., Krajcik, J. S., & Soloway, E. (2003). The nature of middle school learners' science content understandings with the use of on-line resources. *Journal of Research in Science Teaching, 40*(3), 323–346. doi:10.1002/tea.10079

Huffaker, D. (2005). The educated blogger: Using weblogs to promote literacy in the classroom. *AACE Journal, 13*(2), 91–98.

Johnson, L., Adams, S., & Cummins, M. (2012). *NMC Horizon Report: 2012 K-12 Edition*. Austin, TX: The New Media Consortium.

Johnson, L., Adams, S., & Haywood, K. (2011). *NMC Horizon Report: 2011 K-12 Edition*. Austin, TX: The New Media Consortium.

Kanevsky, L., & Keighley, T. (2003). To produce or not to produce? Understanding boredom and the honor in underachievement. *Roeper Review, 26*(1), 2–28. doi:10.1080/02783190309554235

Krathwohl, D. R. (2002). A revision of Bloom's taxonomy: An overview. *Theory into Practice, 41*(4), 212–218. doi:10.1207/s15430421tip4104_2

Kulik, J. A., & Kulik, C. L. C. (1992). Meta-analytic findings on grouping programs. *Gifted Child Quarterly, 36*(2), 73–77. doi:10.1177/001698629203600204

Lewis, T. (2006). Design and inquiry: Bases for an accommodation between science and teaching education in the curriculum? *Journal of Research in Science Teaching, 43*(3), 255–281. doi:10.1002/tea.20111

Matthews, D. J., & Foster, J. F. (2005). A dynamic scaffolding model of teacher development: The gifted education consultant as catalyst for change. *Gifted Child Quarterly, 49*(3), 222–230. doi:10.1177/001698620504900304

Mayer, B. (2012). Get kids designing with student-created games. *School Library Journal.* Retrieved from http://www.slj.com/2012/08/opinion/the-gaming-life/get-kids-designing-with-student-created-games-the-gaming-life/

National Mathematics Advisory Panel. (2008). *Chapter 6: Report of the task group on instructional practices.* Retrieved from http://www2.ed.gov/about/bdscomm/list/mathpanel/report/instructional-practices.pdf

Periathiruvadi, S., & Rinn, A. (2012). Technology in gifted education: A review of best practices and empirical research. *Journal of Research on Technology in Education, 45*(2), 153–169. doi:10.1080/15391523.2012.10782601

Renzulli, J. S., & Reis, S. M. (2002). *The schoolwide enrichment model: Executive summary.* Retrieved from http://www.gifted.uconn.edu/sem/semexec.html

Rogers, Y. (1997, August). *A brief introduction to distributed cognition.* Retrieved from http://mcs.open.ac.uk/yr258/papers/dcog/dcog-brief-intro.pdf

Savery, J. R., & Duffy, T. M. (1995). Problem based learning: An instructional model and its constructivist framework. *Educational Technology, 35*(5), 31–38.

Siegle, D. (2004). The merging of literacy and technology in the 21st century: A bonus for gifted education. *Gifted Child Today, 27*(2), 32–35.

Silverman, L. K. (1994). The moral sensitivity of gifted children and the evolution of society. *Roeper Review, 17*(2), 110–116. doi:10.1080/02783199409553636

Teno, K. M. (2000). Cluster grouping elementary gifted students in the regular classroom: A teacher's perspective. *Gifted Child Today, 23*(1), 44–53.

Tucker, B. (2012). The flipped classroom. *Education Next, 12*(1), 82–83.

U. S. Department of Education. (2010). *Transforming American education: Learning powered by technology.* Retrieved from http://www.ed.gov/sites/default/files/netp2010.pdf

Wallace, R. M. (2002, May). *Technology and science teaching: A new kind of knowledge.* Paper presented at the TIME conference. Battle Creek, MI. Retrieved from http://www.msu.edu/course/cep/953/readings/WallaceTimeFinal.pdf

KEY TERMS AND DEFINITIONS

Clustered Classrooms: Classrooms that have heterogeneous academic-leveled students including gifted students. In clustered classrooms, students work in groups of homogeneous ability levels.

Differentiation: Implementing strategies which meet the academic needs of diverse levels of students by addressing their unique learning characteristics.

Gifted Education: Specific teaching for those students who have been identified as "gifted." This includes four criteria: Mental Ability, Motivation, Creativity, and Achievement.

Lesson Plan: A guide for implementing a day's instruction that gives step-by-step procedures for conducting a class. Lesson plans should incorporate differentiation strategies such that students of all academic levels can receive developmentally appropriate instruction.

Technology: In the educational sense, technology includes any internet websites, computer programs (including games), or microprocessor-based hardware used by teachers and students in the classroom relating to content being taught.

Within-Class Ability Grouping: Arranging students into groups according their academic level within one classroom. Such arrangements allow teachers to provide instruction that meets each level of student's academic needs.

Chapter 20
Instructional Technology and the Nature of the Gifted and Talented

Jana Willis
University of Houston – Clear Lake, USA

Douglas J. Steel
University of Houston – Clear Lake, USA

Vanessa Dodo Seriki
Loyola University Maryland, USA

EXECUTIVE SUMMARY

This collective case study explores the use and impact of instructional technology on fourth grade Gifted and Talented (GT) students' engagement and motivation to learn. Through this exploration, the authors were able to modify their use of instructional technology to suit the needs of the heterogeneous group of GT learners. Although the level of use, purpose for use, and how students used the instructional technology varied between the courses, this case reveals that the heterogeneous nature of the GT students necessitated a flexible approach to instruction and use of IT in order to maintain high levels of engagement and motivation. While these findings are not novel, they add to the discourse regarding teachers' perceptions of GT students and how those perceptions inform instructional practices. This chapter intends to stimulate critical self-reflection regarding perceptions of GT students and the impact those perceptions have on instructional practices.

DOI: 10.4018/978-1-4666-6489-0.ch020

ORGANIZATION BACKGROUND

The gifted and talented education program (GATE-P) is the enrichment program for GT students in a local school district in the Southwest region of the United States. The program from which we drew our sample is a collaborative partnership between a local university and the public school district. Through this program fourth and fifth grade students, during different semesters, come to the university campus once per week, over 12 weeks, to engage in a self-selected enrichment course. These courses span a range of content and skills such as, principles of science, technology, engineering, and mathematics (STEM) using robotics, business and marketing principles through the development of products that are later sold, theatrical arts, visual art, computer programming, and science. Prior to enrollment in the program, students are provided a menu of course offerings from which to select. Typically, students are able to enroll in their first or second choice, which aligns well with the students' personal interest in the topic. Since this is a designated GT program, all students have already undergone assessment to determine if they are identified as GT.

The GT identification process and criteria are very diverse and broad thereby generating diversity among the participating GT population. Specifically, the school district's "gifted services are designed for students who demonstrate significantly above-average achievement or potential in the areas of general intellectual ability, specific subject matter aptitude, and creative/productive thinking skills. Criteria for selection include cognitive skill tests, professional recommendations, classroom performance and portfolio samples" (School District, 2013).

The subjects in the case were three classrooms of students identified as gifted by their school district. Student data provided by the district gave the instructors a minimal level of understanding of the giftedness of their students and their learning needs, but standardized test score data were available for 58 students. The data was heavily redacted, which prevented the authors from performing detailed analysis and matching standardized scores with individual student performance in class. Selected statistics are presented in Table 1.

The range of verbal and non-verbal results for the most-used standardized test is illustrated in Table 2. The available data suggests that the 4 students who scored poorly on the Cognitive Abilities Test (CogAT) managed to gain entry into the GT program based on excellent scores on other exams such as the Otis-Lennon School Ability Test (OLSAT) or Naglieri Nonverbal Ability Test (NNAT).

As expected with the sample population, the student test scores generally fell within the top percentiles. As illustrated in figure 1, the data was leptokurtic with only a small percentage of the scores below 85%. In this case, four scores fell below the 85th percentile.

Table 1. Median value of standardized test scores

	Verbal	Non-Verbal	Quant	Composite
CogAT (n=39)	92.0	97.0	93.5	96.0
WISC (n=5)	98.0	97.0	-	98.0
OLSAT (n=27)	97.0	97.5	92.0	98.0
NNAT (n=11)	-	99.0	-	99.0

Table 2. Descriptive statistics for the CogAT standardized test

	Verbal	Non-Verbal	Quant	Composite
Mean	85.8	93.2	90.1	94.1
Median	92.0	97.0	93.5	96.0
Std. Deviation	14.3	7.9	10.4	5.8
Minimum	38.0	57.0	55.0	73.0
Maximum	98.0	99.0	99.0	99.0
Count	39			

Figure 1. Standardized test scores of the subset of students with reported CogAt results (n=39)

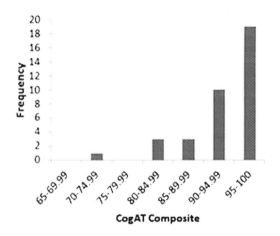

Setting the Stage

Three different instructional technology (IT) - utilizing courses were specifically designed for fourth grade GT students. In these courses, the authors either used IT as the focus of the curriculum or as an integrative tool. The two uses of technology allowed for the examination of the effect IT had on class dynamics related to student collaboration, self-efficacy, and confidence to use IT by students, and the resulting instructional decisions that supported student engagement and learning. Before delving into the case, it is important to note that while the implementation and use of IT varied, the three courses were linked because the sample came from the same population, and there were similarities in the findings despite the varying use of IT.

There is a wide range of diversity in the gifts and talents of students identified as Gifted and Talented (GT) (Johnsen, 2009). Methods of identification range from observations to testing. GT programs and associated curriculum are as varied as the students they serve. Programs structures include pullout sessions, in-class clusters, or enrichment curriculum. Addressing diversity in the GT classroom requires a flexible curriculum that offers a variety of experiences for the GT learner. Providing opportunities for creativity, problem solving, and exploration can offer new directions for learning, but attention to individualities and areas of giftedness should not be overlooked. Instruction that does not address the heterogeneous qualities of the GT population can negatively impact learning motivation and create barriers to learning (Treffinger, 1978; Wood, 2008).

There continues to be an increase in interest and awareness of the potential impact of IT in the GT curriculum. However, empirical research in this area is still in its infancy. Efforts to better inform teachers, practitioners, and researchers on best practices for IT use in the GT curriculum are necessary if programs are to effectively include IT in the GT classroom (Periathiruvadi & Rinn, 2012). While technology is often included in the classroom to extend and enrich learning experiences for the GT student, a closer examination of the student interactions with IT is necessary if we are to explore its potential. Studies, such as Blumen-Pardo (2010), have shown that GT students enjoy learning in experiential and exploratory ways, and IT can offer opportunities for students to independently find answers to questions and seek solutions to problems they are investigating. IT can help the GT student move from the role of knowledge receivers to knowledge producers who direct their own learning (Siegle, 2005).

GT students, who approach learning and knowledge acquisition from varying viewpoints, often challenge traditional instructional methods (Rogers, 2007). Teachers must differentiate their instructional strategies and IT initiatives to meet the unique needs of the GT student, recognizing that GT students are a heterogeneous group. In this chapter, IT use by GT students is explored in an effort to understand the potential impact on the efficacy, confidence, motivation, and collaboration among students in three different, yet similar, fourth grade GT classes.

George Betts and Maureen Neihart have developed profiles of gifted students, which are composed of six different types of GT students. The profiles offer a succinct view of different "types" of gifted learners that include the following types:

successful, challenging, underground, dropouts, double-labeled and autonomous. These profiles describe typical feelings, attitudes, behaviors, needs, adult & peers perceptions, identification, home and school support (2009) of the various types of GT learners. For this case study, the profiles serve as the framework for analysis of the impact IT had on the gifted students (see Appendix).

Instructional Technology as Curriculum

Two of the courses used IT as the main component of the curriculum and focused on the creative task of IT product development. The first course, *Webmaster of the Universe*, allowed the GT students to creatively design and build Internet web sites. The instructor requested the latest version of the popular Adobe Creative Suite web development software from the university in order to increase student enthusiasm towards the class. The software had enough flexibility to allow students to take multiple approaches to site development.

The second course, *Designer of the Online Universe*, focused on the design and development of video games. Not unlike the previously discussed course the GT students used a contemporary free video game software, Gamemaker Lite, which was found to be age appropriate and supported by substantial online documentation and user-friendly video tutorials. Multiple avenues to user support accommodated the GT students' wide variety of learning needs. The interactive, multi-modal nature of video games provided the motivational foundation of the course. Today an estimated 99% of boys and 94% of girls under the age of 18 report playing videogames regularly. They clock an estimated 10,000 hours of game play by the age of 21 "— or 24 hours less than they spend in a classroom for all of middle and high school if they have perfect attendance" (McGonigal, 2011, 1). The software product used in the course provided a basic step by step "getting started" game that allowed the user to build their first game in approximately 30 minutes.

Instructional Technology as an Integrated Tool

The third course, *Science through the Media,* was designed with the understanding that GT students required time and opportunity to explore science concepts in depth using hands-on inquiry-based instruction. Using input from the GATE-P director, teachers in the school district and the professors own assumptions the course was deliberately designed to integrate writing, technology, and popular culture. The decision to integrate writing was based on a need expressed by fourth grade teachers, as writing was a key assessment area for that particular grade. Technology was selected because it is often times used, simply, for research in the formal school setting (Kozma, 2003) thereby preventing students-particularly GT students-from using the technology in more nuanced or creative ways. Moreover, while most teacher preparation programs require at least one instructional technology course, the use of technology within the classroom varies according to teachers' comfort, knowledge, and level of use (Ley, 2000). Thus, the integration of technology was one way of generating excitement among the students since it is infrequently or inconsistently used in elementary classrooms (Alevizou, 2008; Ertmer, 2005).

Science Through the Media was designed to critique the accuracy of science portrayed by popular culture-specifically through television and film media. With an explicit intent to integrate writing, science and instructional technology, the instructor hoped that students would not only gain new science content but be introduced to and feel comfortable using a different form of instructional technology to demonstrate their learning. In connecting popular culture and science, specific age appropriate and relevant television shows and movies were selected for use in the course. This led to the introduction of science content that was familiar to most students, but required a deeper level of understanding in order to critique. Thus, depending on the depth of content knowledge needed to critique the science, the viewing of the movie would sometimes precede or follow engagement in associated science concepts. Additionally, the culminating project challenged students to select various science or science related concepts, research the topic, and develop an animated short video that portrayed the science content. This video was not to be a presentation of their topic, but rather a creative scene between 2-5 minutes that depicted the science either accurately or inaccurately. During the presentation of the animated shorts, parents and students were asked to critique only the accuracy of the science content. The enduring understanding for which students were to take from the course was the ability to question the portrayal of science through the media-specifically popular culture.

Case Description

This case study examined two different uses of IT, across three courses, with a heterogeneous group of GT students. Specifically, the authors sought to examine how IT influenced classroom dynamics. Using examples from the three courses and appropriate literature, the authors describe the ways in which the use of IT affected student collaboration, self-efficacy, and confidence, as well as how it influenced teaching methodology and integration strategies.

Technology and Student Collaboration

Active collaboration among the students was a fundamental strategy used through all of the courses. However, it was not mandatory across all three courses, and often there appeared to be a waxing and waning of collaborative effort among students.

The *Webmaster of the Universe* instructor did not observe that the technology impacted student collaboration. Students collaborated and helped others when a student had difficulties or asked a question. One reaction was to demonstrate a solution or edit another student's code in response to a problem. However, this is the same level of response one would expect even if the technology was absent from the classroom. That is, regarding collaboration, the students helped each other with their work while they happened to be completing computer-related assignments. Had the assignments been non-technical ones such as assembling puzzles, one would expect the same levels of collaboration observed at the computer workstations.

In the *Master of the Online Universe* (video game development), the class format was based on individual game development. This allowed students to develop games that met their own skill levels and topics of interest. However, throughout the semester approximately 15 minutes of daily class time was designated for peer play, review, and criticism. This instructor noted the student behavior during the interactions and assessments of peer game play. Finding that regardless of the level of expertise of the game designer or the peer reviewer the responses were predominantly positive with high levels of praise for the game developer. Unplanned collaboration occurred throughout the semester when more advanced students would voluntarily share their expertise with their classmates either one to one or by sharing their games with the entire class. Once the initial game techniques were explained by the instructor the students worked independently with the instructor assuming the role of facilitator. While the class encourages students to work independently on their individual games, each class session began with the instructor sharing a new technique to could be applied to each students' game development. The remainder of the class period was focused on independent game enhancement. The students were allowed to utilize online tutorials that were available in text and video formats to independently extend their skills. Working with GT students can be a revelation to the aspects of collaboration and cooperative interactions. In this classroom, you would often find GT students sitting 2-3 to a chair, sharing ideas, contributing, and never criticizing. This population is open to the views of their peers not only as partners but also as supporters or even leaders. In the *Master of the Online Universe* video game class, there were multiple opportunities for peer-review of the video games developed. This was a highly energized time in the classroom. Groups of students would often cluster around a game that caught their attention or that they found to be intriguing. It very refreshing to experience this level of mutual respect and openness. The students whose behaviors closely align to the profile of the "Autonomous Learner" offered their support to their classmates. It should be noted that these students had usually committed time outside the classroom setting to expand their skills and knowledge in game development. They pushed themselves further than their classmates and were eager to show their advancement. The instructor would allow these students to "student teach", where they would take the stage and lead their classmates through a particular component of the game development. They frequently volunteered to let other students test their game and were equally willing to test the games developed by their classmates. This proved to be one of the most rewarding times with this population. The high levels of interaction coupled with the non-existence of criticism helped to make collaboration a rewarding experience for all of the students in the class.

In *Science Through the Media,* students were seated in collaborative teams or groups, but were not obligated to work on their projects or assignments within these groups. The culminating project was designed to allow the students to work collaboratively or independently, but only six students, forming three groups of two, worked as a cohesive group. Another four students formed a group but worked individually on the project but collaborated to link their products into one coherent product. The remaining students worked independently. While the instructor did not assign explicit roles for the group members, certain students became the group leader and served as the representative who advocated on behalf of the group to the instructor. This hierarchy within the groups was not planned, but those groups that designed or had a de facto leader functioned in ways that were much more productive than those groups that did not. In this context the use of IT was important as it allow group members to continue working on their projects while their leader conferenced with the instructor about issues the group experienced; in this way technology offered flexibility in time management and productivity.

Technology Impact on Student Self-Efficacy and Confidence

In *Webmaster of the Universe,* the area in which IT had the largest impact on the learning population was computer self-efficacy. Early in the semester, students successfully replicated demonstrations of multi-step processes and this directly affected their efficacy and confidence levels. For example on the first day of the course, the students used a text editor to create a complete, working web page with a couple of advanced features like images and links that were covered in depth later in the course. Although some of their work was copied and pasted from an example (without a full understanding of how it worked), the exercise set a tone of success early in semester. Building a complete, working page on the first day of class, boosted each student's confidence and computer self-efficacy levels.

A lesson learned regarding this was to allow for "little victories" early in the semester to impact computer self-efficacy and self-confidence. To facilitate this experience, assignments were broken down into manageable chunks. This strategy paid off later in the semester as the difficulty of projects increased. In general, those who struggled with the easy assignments on day one (the "dropouts" and the "underground") did not demonstrate high levels of computer self-efficacy and required more instructor support throughout the semester. Even with extra coaching, it seemed that those who failed early in the semester did not recover well over time, especially as the difficulty of assignment increased. I attribute this, in part, to a lack of confidence and computer self-efficacy in those particular students.

In *Designer of the Online Universe*, all the students in the class possessed above average levels of proficiency in computer skills. In particular, an impressive knowledge base of both online and traditional video games (e.g. Nintendo, Xbox, PS3). Confidence levels were high from the beginning of the course but as the complexities of the video game development process increased some experience a drop in self-efficacy. The course software tutorials and step by step processes provided even the most timid user with a sense of instant gratification establishing a sound base of self-efficacy and personal accomplishment upon which to build in subsequent classes. The students who upon observation seemed to fit within the profiles of "Double Labeled" appeared to experience the highest levels of anxiety and reduced levels of self-efficacy. They required additional support from the instructor and their peers. They also tended to isolate themselves from the class and almost "tune out" the rest of the class during their times of frustration. One student responded emotionally during those periods of self-doubt, which is a documented concern of GT students (Reis, 2004). Another group of the class experienced a drop in confidence as their games became more complex however their responses were vocal or demonstrative. This group sought my help or the help of their peers to push their skills farther and later settle into the "Successful" profiles. They did not allow themselves to become frustrated but they did express disappointment that their games were not at the level they wanted. This group was found to fit most closely with the "Underground" profile. Once this group was able to master the skill and move their game forward their confidence levels increased as well. Those students who most closely aligned with the "Successful" and "Autonomous Learner" profiles exhibited consistent increases in self-efficacy throughout the semester.

In *Science Through the Media*, formal measures of self-efficacy and confidence were not used with the students, but observations of student interactions with their classmates, the content, technology, and the professor revealed that the design of the course provided opportunities for students to display their confidence levels. Student self-efficacy and confidence appeared to ebb and flow based on the teaching methodology employed as well as the student technology skills and levels of creativity For instance, during whole class discussion those students who possessed more self-confidence and efficacy about the given topic, quickly engaged in and directed class discussion. When an open-ended question, which allowed for creative expression, was posed the creative GT students came alive as they quickly provided ideas and brainstormed solutions. Another example is illustrated in the use of more open-ended or creative technology tools. The less creative GT students felt frustrated by the lack of structure or guidance often voicing their confusion or concern about their ability to succeed. However, their creative peers willingly assisted them which did not result in successful use of the IT to create their product.

Technology Impact on Teaching Methodology

Teaching courses that focus on technology skill acquisition or technology application often requires a pedagogical approach that follows a constructivist model inclusive of modeling, student-centered hands-on activities, and a significant amount of exploratory learning. Just as teachers' possess preferences for teaching methodology, students arrive in the classroom with a preferred style of learning. Student interest in obtaining new skills or knowledge, their motivation to learn, as well as their confidence in skill application influence their learning processes. Each of these factors directly affects the engagement levels of the students. Variability of the learner calls for variability and flexibility in pedagogical choices.

In *Webmaster of the Universe* the instructor used experiential and exploratory learning techniques. Having a network-connected computer with properly licensed professional-grade Adobe Creative Suite web design software installed and ready for use for each student enhanced this teaching methodology. The availability of the software also simplified the process of allowing students opportunities where they could immediately apply their knowledge. The instructor set up problems and then asked the students to implement solutions using the technology available in the room. Inevitably, problems and roadblocks occurred. Students who demonstrated traits of the "Autonomous Learner" tended to find a work-around and seek their own solutions while continuing to move forward. Others did require coaching and help in their journey toward mastery. For example, in one exercise, students were asked to build an image using a vector graphics program and then add the image to one of their existing web pages. A small group of students successfully replicated the demonstrated process and installed the image correct. However, many determined that they constructed an image too large to properly fit on a web page. A few of these students (The "Successful" and "Autonomous Learners") responded by exploring the web program menus, property pages, and other toolbars to figure out how to adjust the scaling in order to fix the problem. The remainder failed to resolve the problem until they received coaching or help from their neighbors.

There were various amounts of assistance required by the students as the weeks progressed during the semester. Those who for the most part seemed independent (i.e., the "Successful" and "Autonomous Learners") occasionally required individual assistance to solve problems encountered on particular challenges of exercises – generally after making multiple attempts to find their own solutions. In contrast, those that were bored or lacked confidence (the "Underground" and the "Challenging") remained fairly dependent the entire semester without having bouts of large, independently achieved successes.

The *Designer of the Online Universe* instructor entered the classroom with a "pedagogical toolbox" from prior experiences ready to teach video game development to 4th grade students. However, the individual needs of the GT learners required adaptations to traditional instructional methods by allowing for multiple levels of differentiated instruction; offering more opportunities for exploration and -Socratic conversations. In a single classroom, there could be students with a wide range of prior skills in technology, communication, reading comprehension, creativity, problem solving, and critical thinking. Whole class instruction was next to impossible; structured lesson plan cycles that required a linear process left too many bored and too few on task. To ensure success for all students it was time to revisit the "pedagogical Toolbox" and add new tools. A review of literature indicated that best practices relevant to Interactive Instruction models allowed for student to student interactions and increased levels of involvement with the materials; leaving the teacher to facilitate and guide the learning (Creemers, Kyriakides, Antoniou, 2013). Experiential Learning and Discovery models promoted active engagement and encouraged students to build their own understanding and meaning for their game development (Whale, Fisher, Valenzuela, 2012). Viewing this student population through the descriptors in the GT profiles as defined by Betts & Neihart (2009) highlighted the wide range of diverse needs in this classroom. In order to engage every student and allow him or her to explore video game development in directions of interest, adjustments in teaching methodology was needed. It would appear that teaching an entire class of GT students might take individualized instruction to an all new level.

In the *Designer of the Online Universe* the teaching methodology the independent development of the video game demanded that the instructor assume the role of facilitator or coach. Since the students could individualize their games both aesthetically and functionally no two sets of questions were the same. Providing the students with the tools to research and solve their own issues became a primary component of the classroom instruction. It was essential to their own skill development that they not be "handed" the answer to their questions but be presented with the path by which to seek solutions to their questions. For example, during one class period a student excited exclaimed that they had successfully been able to make their player jump up into the air. The next question of course was how they went about getting the player to come back down. Rather than simply providing the student with the coding sequence to resolve the situation, the instructor had the student get up from their desk, perform a small jump and then explain how that event had occurred. In the telling of the actions the student excitedly exclaimed it must have to do with gravity. The student then returned to their game development with the answer to their dilemma. Guiding and directing rather than dispensing answers became the methodology of the course.

The use of IT as an integrated tool provided flexibility to the teaching methodology, employed in *Science Through the Media* by allowing the professor to work one-on-one with students struggling with the scientific concepts while others continued to use the IT to create the culminating project. This level of flexibility also allowed the professor to assist those students who struggled to use the technology. However, unrelated to the use of technology but vital to the class dynamics is the fact that the students and instructor had built a learning community that allowed students to seek assistance and guidance from their peers. While technology, per se, did not create this environment, it certainly contributed to sustaining this collaborative community by stimulating a need for collaboration and offering flexibility in teaching methodology and interactions.

Technology Impact on Integration Strategies

In *Webmaster of the Universe* the differences among the students presented a challenge to integration of the technology into to the lessons. Having readily available technology helped reinforce the educational goals of the course, but simultaneously, it served as a distraction during lecture and exploratory components of the instructional time. For the majority of the class, the ability to immediately replicate a demonstration or work on a problem just covered in a lecture seemed to appropriately reinforce the concept and enhance learning. On the other hand, about 15 percent of the class (the "Dropouts") often ignored lectures and were distracted by the Internet while they were supposed to be following along during a demonstration in progress. Inevitably, these students failed to grasp some of the basic concepts covered during lecture and therefore struggled with application of the principles explained during lecture. It did not negatively affect achievement of the learning objectives because the students were still successful after receiving individual coaching during the application exercises. Overall, having the appropriate computers and software available for each individual student was advantageous and the benefits of asking students to immediately apply what they learned during lecture seemed to outweigh the drawbacks of distraction caused by the inclusion of technology and access to the Internet within the classroom.

In *Designer of the Online Universe* the integration strategies were restricted based on the course learning objectives. Technology was the primary focus of the course with integration being the expectation for the instructor. The course goal was to expose students to the art of video game development using a free software application. Students developed games based on their individual interest and ideas rather than on specific classroom content. Reflecting on the course during the writing of this case study, I have concerns about limiting or directing the content of the game development. In a previous class with this gifted population, that focused on digital tool development and use I found that projects that were too open-ended or too restrictive had a negative impact on engagement, motivation, and confidence. I believe that drawing upon the TPACK model students could identify a content area of their own choice on which to base their game while retaining a high level of creativity (Mishra & Koehler, 2006).

In *Science Through the* Media the intent of the course was to provide enrichment in not only science, but also the eight practices of science and engineering, as highlighted and described in the Framework for K-12 Science Education (NRC, 2012), and the use of technology. While the focus was neither engineering nor technology, both were integrated throughout the course, which rendered the course relevant to and interesting for participating students. Despite deliberate choices in designing the course, the diversity of learners required a flexible course design that could be easily and efficiently altered to meet the range of needs of the students. After meeting and interacting with students, on the first day of class, it was clear that students fit Betts & Neihart's (2009) profiles of GT students. Across the 22 students in the Science through the media course, three of the GT student profiles were observed in the group. These three include: The successful, creative, and autonomous learner all of which required the use of various instructional and integration strategies to meet the needs of the students.

CURRENT CHALLENGES FACING THE ORGANIZATION

One of the major challenges is the lack of student data provided to the instructors while planning the courses. The district provided minimal data, which did not include students' academic history, personal interests, or access to resources. Thus, instructors were at a disadvantage when planning their courses. This challenge, based on these case studies, was easily overcome by using a flexible course design. Just as in any other classroom setting, it is vital that instructors not make assumptions about students' abilities, interests, or level of need etc. Providing students with autonomy coupled with flexibility and moments of success opens the door to increased self-efficacy and confidence. The persistent challenge, in this regard, is helping other instructors recognize this need and being open to designing their courses in such a way.

It would appear that each of the three instructors had similar experiences with this population. Two of the instructors taught classes that had technology as the main component of the curriculum while the third utilized technology as an integrative tool. All three noted the motivation and engagement generated by the technology use in the classroom, which is not surprising, based on the extensive research in that area. The inquisitive nature of the GT population appears to be a natural fit to the exploratory qualities of technology tools. The three instructors reported instructional methodologies reflective of critical thinking, inquiry, exploratory, and experiential with this population. As with any group of learners, traditional lecture based formats did not provide the best learning outcomes and created more opportunities for distraction among the students. Instructors noted that when students were not engaged in the classroom experience they were often frustrated; resulting in low levels of confidence.

It continues to be a challenge to locate instructors, especially faculty who will commit to working with this population. Grouping such a large number of GT students into a single environment produces a setting that demands both high levels of motivating and engaged learning.

In *Webmaster of the Universe*, students responded better to short demonstrations of specific tasks rather than lengthy lectures describing multiple steps to complete a product. With the short demos, the majority of students retained knowledge of the required steps necessary for completing the assignment. This may be due in part to the students' ability to immediately reinforce their knowledge of a demonstrated process using the technology in the classroom. This seemed to work particularly well for the "autonomous learners," who enjoyed working independently on their web sites.

The students in the Webmaster course who showed low levels of computer self-efficacy often struggled with their assignments and required frequent coaching. The coaching did help the students build successful projects. Over time, the instructor learned that students benefited most from help that showed them how to break a task down into small, manageable chunks. Once tasks became small and manageable, these students demonstrated more confidence and success.

In the *Designer of the Online Universe* it was clear that allowing the students to engage in exploratory learning benefited them. The instructor found that free exploration was more effective in the application of knowledge. It was still expected that the students would be able to recall basic facts and concepts about the technology they were using. Having short quizzes about basic concepts laid a proper foundation for the self-directed application of what they learned. All the students responded well to individual feedback and coaching. Those who failed to pay close attention to a demonstration and those who did not recall the steps required to do an exercise benefited from the instructor's help solving problems encountered. Furthermore, the "successful" students occasionally pitched in and assisted other students with individual coaching. This contributed to classroom learning.

The *Science Through the Media* class noted that as with any set of characteristics or profiles attributed to people, there are always exceptions. So, while Betts and Neihart's (2009) profiles of GT learners is useful in explaining observable behavior among GT students, they do not necessarily apply to all GT students. While this is not a challenge, per se, it could be for those instructors who fail to recognize the heterogeneous nature of the GT learner.

SOLUTIONS AND RECOMMENDATIONS

In *Designer of the Online Universe* one of the surprises in the classroom was that traditional lecture with theory followed by examples demonstration was not effective. Only a small percentage of students retained enough knowledge to independently apply the knowledge to new contexts. In this case, the majority of the class was dependent on individual coaching and the help of their fellow students for understanding. The long lectures were replaced with short bursts of demos and explanation, followed by class exercises that supported application of the topic of interest. A plausible explanation for the failure of traditional lectures is tied to having the technology in the classroom. The students were either too excited about using the technology and could not wait to get started or they were distracted by the technology and did not fully listen to the lecture.

This instructor noted another take away from their experience in the GT classroom was that it should be recognized that GT students are a heterogeneous group. Having 24 GT students in the class illuminated the various types of students in terms of abilities and motivation. Clearly, what worked for one student did not necessarily work for another. The contrasts became apparent early in the semester. Classroom teachers with a small percentage of GT students in their classroom can support those students by taking the time to get to know the individual characteristics and learning needs of each GT student rather than applying a one-size-fits-all approach to GT student instruction.

The two instructors who used technology as the primary focus of their instruction found that tools that provided paths for both the creative and non-creative approach to be the most accommodating for the class. An example would be tools that included both templates as well as free form development options.

If instructors are to adequately address the learning needs of GT students in their classrooms more training and education is needed to guide their understanding of this population. GT students are as diverse as any student population and should not be grouped and addressed as a monolithic population with one size fits all instruction. Individual identities as noted in the Bett & Neihart (2009) profiles are clearly distinguishable and classroom instruction should accommodate those differences. Simply providing "more" or "accelerated" learning experiences will not meet the educational needs of this population. Additional research with this population is critical if as educators we are to provide classrooms that provide substantial environments that fulfill their learning needs and provide support for their individual giftedness.

REFERENCES

Alevizou, P. (2008). Beyond technology: Children's learning in the age of digital culture. *Children & Society*, *22*(1), 70–71. doi:10.1111/j.1099-0860.2007.00135.x

Bandura, A. (1994). Self-efficacy. In V. S. Ramachaudran (Ed.), *Encyclopedia of human behavior* (Vol. 4, pp. 71–81). New York: Academic Press.

Betts, G. T., & Neihart, M. (2008, October 31). *The revised profiles of the gifted and talented: A research-based approach*. Paper presented at the NAGC 55th Annual Convention & Exhibition. St. Louis, MO.

Blumen-Pardo, S. (2002). Effects of a teacher training workshop on creativity, cognition, and school achievement in gifted and non-gifted second-grade students in Lima, Peru. *High Ability Studies*, *13*(1), 47–58. doi:10.1080/13598130220132307

Bomia, L., Beluzo, L., Demeester, D., Elander, K., Johnson, M., & Sheldon, B. (1997). The Impact of Teaching Strategies on Intrinsic Motivation. Champaign, IL: ERIC Clearinghouse on Elementary and Early Childhood Education. (ERIC Document Reproduction Service No. ED 418 925).

Cohen, E. G., & Lotan, R. A. (1997). *Working for equity in heterogeneous classrooms: Sociological theory in practice*. Teachers College Press.

Creemers, B., Kyriakides, L., & Antoniou, P. (2013). *Different approaches to teaching which emerged from teacher effectiveness research. In Teacher Professional Development for Improving Quality of Teaching* (pp. 81–99). Springer Netherlands. doi:10.1007/978-94-007-5207-8_6

Dockstader, J. (1999). Teachers of the 21st century know the what, why, and how of technology integration. *T.H.E. Journal*, *26*(6), 73–74.

Ertmer, P. A. (2005). Teacher pedagogical beliefs: The final frontier in our quest for technology integration? *Educational Technology Research and Development, 53*(4), 25–39. doi:10.1007/BF02504683

Hall, G. E., Loucks, S. F., Rutherford, W. L., & Newlove, B. W. (1975). Levels of use of the innovation: A framework for analyzing innovation adoption. *Journal of Teacher Education, 26*(1), 52–56. doi:10.1177/002248717502600114

Harding-Smith, T. (1993). *Learning together: An introduction to collaborative learning*. New York, NY: HarperCollins College Publishers.

Johnsen, S. K. (2009). Best practices for identifying gifted students. *Principal, 88*(5), 8–14.

Kozma, R. B. (2003). Technology and classroom practices: An international study. *Journal of Research on Technology in Education, 36*(1), 1–14. doi:10.1080/15391 523.2003.10782399

Leh, A. S. C. (2000). Teachers' comfort level, confidence, and attitude toward technology at a technology course. In *Proceedings of Society for Information Technology & Teacher Education International Conference 2000*. AACE.

McGonigal, J. (2011). *Reality is broken: Why games make us better and how they can change the world*. New York: Penguin Press.

Mishra, P., & Koehler, M. J. (2006). Technological pedagogical content knowledge: A framework for teacher knowledge. *Teachers College Record, 108*(6), 1017–1054. doi:10.1111/j.1467-9620.2006.00684.x

National Research Council (U.S.). (2012). *A framework for K-12 science education: Practices, crosscutting concepts, and core ideas*. Washington, DC: The National Academies Press.

Periathiruvadi, S., & Rinn, A. N. (2012). Technology in gifted education: A review of best practices and empirical research. *Journal of Research on Technology in Education, 45*(2), 153–169. doi:10.1080/15391523.2012.10782601

Reis, S. M., & Renzulli, J. S. (2004). Current research on the social and emotional development of gifted and talented students: Good news and future possibilities. *Psychology in the Schools, 41*(1), 119–130. doi:10.1002/pits.10144

Rogers, K. B. (2007). Lessons learned about educating the gifted and talented: A synthesis of the research on educational practice. *Gifted Child Quarterly, 51*(4), 382–396. doi:10.1177/0016986207306324

Shulman, L. S. (1986). Those who understand: Knowledge growth in teaching. *Educational Researcher, 15*(2), 4–14. doi:10.3102/0013189X015002004

Siegle, D. (2010). *Gifted Students & Technology: An Interview with Del Siegle.* Retrieved from http://www.ctd.northwestern.edu/resources/displayArticle/?id=158

Treffinger, D. J. (1978). Guidelines for encouraging independence and self-direction among gifted students. *The Journal of Creative Behavior, 12*(1), 14–20. doi:10.1002/j.2162-6057.1978.tb00155.x

Whale, S., Fisher, J., & Valenzuela, F. R. (2012). Promoting engagement and interaction through a technology supported learning activity. In *Proceedings of Ascilite Conference.* ASCILITE.

Wood, P. F. (2008). Reading instruction with gifted and talented readers: A series of unfortunate events or a sequence of auspicious results? *Gifted Child Today, 31*(3), 16–25.

KEY TERMS AND DEFINITIONS

Collaboration: Students working together to search for understanding, meaning, or solutions or to create an artifact or product of their learning (Harding-Smith, 1993).

Gifted and Talented: "Students who perform or show the potential for performing at a remarkably high level of accomplishment when compared to others of the same age, experience, or environment and who exhibit high performance capability in an intellectual, creative, or artistic area, who possess an unusual capacity for leadership, or excel in a specific academic field" (School District, 2013).

Heterogeneous: Students with a wide range of previous academic achievement and varying levels of oral and written proficiency in the language of instruction (Cohen & Lotan, 1997).

Instructional Technology: "The theory and practice of design, development, utilization, management, and evaluation of processes and resources for learning," (Association for Educational Communications and Technology [AECT], 2003).

Integrated Technology: "Technology integration is using software supported by the business world for real-world applications so students learn to use computers flexibly, purposefully and creatively (Dockstader, 2008).

Motivation: A student's willingness, need, desire, and compulsion to participate in, and be successful in, the learning process" (Bomia, Beluzo, Demeester, Elander, Johnson, & Sheldon, 1997, p.1).

Self-Efficacy: "People's beliefs about their capabilities to produce designated levels of performance that exercise influence over events that affect their lives" (Bandura, 1994).

APPENDIX

Table 3. Analysis of the impact IT had on the gifted students (Betts, G.T. & Neihart, M., 2008)

Type	Feelings And Attitudes	Behaviors	Needs	Adults & Peers Perceptions of type	Identification	Home Support	School Support
The Successful	Boredom Dependent Positive self-concept Anxious Guilty about failure Extrinsic motivation Responsible for others Diminish feelings of self and rights to their emotion Self-critical	Perfectionist High Achiever Seeks teacher approval and structure Non-risk taking Does well academically Accepts & conforms Dependent	To see deficiencies To be challenged Assertiveness skills Autonomy Help with boredom Appropriate curriculum	Loved by teachers Admired by peers Loved and accepted by parents	Grade point average IQ Tests Teacher nominations	Independence Ownership Freedom to make choices Time for personal interests Risk taking experiences	Accelerated and enriched curriculum Time for personal interests Compacted learning experiences Opportunities to be with Intellectual peers Development of independent learning skills In-depth studies Mentorships College & career counseling
The Challenging	Boredom Frustration Low self-esteem Impatient Defensive Heightened sensitivity Uncertain about social roles	Corrects teacher Questions rules, policies Is honest, direct Has mood swings Demonstrates inconsistent work habits Has poor self-control Is creative Prefers highly active &questioning approach Stands up for convictions Is competitive	To be connected with others To learn tact, flexibility, self-awareness, self-control, acceptance Support for creativity Contractual systems	Find them irritating Rebellious Engaged in power struggle See them as creative Discipline problem Peers see them as entertaining Want to change them Don't view as gifted	Peer Recommendations Parent nomination Interviews Performance Recommendation from a significant, nonrelated adult Creativity Testing Teacher advocate	Acceptance and understanding Allow them to pursue interest Advocate for them at school Modeling appropriate behavior Family projects	Tolerance Placement with appropriate teacher Cognitive & social skill development Direct and clear Communication with child Give permission for feelings Studies in-depth Mentorships build self-esteem Behavioral Contracting

continued on following page

Table 3. Continued

Type	Feelings And Attitudes	Behaviors	Needs	Adults & Peers Perceptions of type	Identification	Home Support	School Support
The Underground	Unsure Pressured Confused Guilty Insecure Diminished feelings of self and right to their emotions	Denies talent Drops out of G/T and Advanced classes Resists challenges Wants to belong socially Changes friends	Freedom to make choices To be aware of conflicts Awareness of feelings Support for abilities Involvement with gifted peers Career/ college info Self-acceptance	Viewed as leaders or unrecognized Seen as average and successful Perceived to be compliant Seen as quiet/shy Adults see them as unwilling to risk Viewed as resistive	Gifted peer nomination Home nomination Community nomination Achievement testing IQ Tests Performance Teacher advocate	Acceptance of underground Provide college & career planning experiences Time to be with same age peers Provide gifted role models Model lifelong learning Give freedom to make choice	Recognize & properly place Give permission to take time out from G/T classes Provide same sex role models Continue to give college & career information
The Dropouts	Resentment Angry Depressed Explosive Poor self-concept Defensive Burnout	Has intermittent attendance Doesn't complete tasks Pursues outside interests "Spaced out" in class Is self-abusive Isolates self Is creative Criticizes self & others Does inconsistent work Is disruptive, acts out Seems average or below Is defensive	An individualized program Intense support Alternatives (separate, new opportunities) Counseling (individual, group, and family) Remedial help with skills	Adults are angry with them Peers are judgmental Seen as loners, dropouts, dopers, or air heads Reject them and ridicule Seen as dangerous and rebellious	Review cumulative folder Interview earlier teachers Discrepancy between IQ and demonstrated achievement incongruities and inconsistencies in performance Creativity testing Gifted peer recommendation Demonstrated performance in non-school areas	Seek counseling for family	Diagnostic testing Group counseling for Young students Nontraditional study skills In-depth studies Mentorships Alternative out of classroom learning experiences G.E.D.

continued on following page

Table 3. Continued

Type	Feelings And Attitudes	Behaviors	Needs	Adults & Peers Perceptions of type	Identification	Home Support	School Support
The Double-Labeled	Powerless Frustrated Low self-esteem Unaware Angry	Demonstrates Inconsistent work Seems average or below May be disruptive or acts out	Emphasis on strengths Coping skills G/T support group Counseling Skill development	Seen as "weird" Seen as "dumb" Viewed as helpless Avoided by peers Seen as average or below in ability Perceived to require a great deal of imposed structure Seen only for the disability	Scatter of 11 points or more on WISC or WAIS Recommendation of significant others Recommendation from informed special ed. teacher Interview Performance Teacher Advocate	Recognize gifted abilities Challenge them Provide risk taking opportunities Advocate for child at school Do family projects Seek counseling for family	Placement in gifted program Provide needed resources Provide alternative Learning experiences Begin investigations And explorations Give time to be with peers Give individual Counseling
The Autonomous Learner	Self-confident Self-accepting Enthusiastic Accepted by others Supported Desire to know & learn Accepts failure Intrinsic motivation Personal power Accepts others	Has appropriate social skill Works independently Develops own goals Follows through Works Without approval Follows strong areas of passion Is creative Stands up for convictions Takes risks	Advocacy Feedback Facilitation Support for risks Appropriate opportunities	Accepted by peers and adults Admired for abilities Seen as capable and responsible by parents Positive influences Successful Psychologically healthy	Grade point average Demonstrated performance Products Achievement Testing Interviews Teacher/Peer/Parent self-nominations IQ tests Creativity Testing	Advocate for child at school and in community Provide opportunities related to passions Allow friends of all ages Remove time and space restrictions Do family projects Include child in parent's passion	Allow development of long-term integrated plan of study Accelerated and enriched curriculum Remove time and space restrictions Compacted learning Experiences with pretesting In-depth studies Mentorships College & career Counseling and opportunities Dual enrollment or early admission Wave traditional school policy and regulations

457

Compilation of References

6A-6.03019 Special instructional programs for students who are gifted. (2002). *Florida Administrative Code*. Retrieved from https://www.flrules.org/gateway/ruleNo.asp?ID=6A-6.03019

A novel way to hook teens on writing fiction. (2006). *Curriculum Review, 46*(3), 6-7.

ABCya.com. (2012). *Virtual Manipulatives! (Version 1.2)*. Retrieved from Apple App Store.

Abrahams, A., & Millar, R. (2008). Does Practical Work Really Work? A study of the effectiveness of practical work as a teaching and learning method in school science. *International Journal of Science Education, 30*(14), 1945–1969. doi:10.1080/09500690701749305

Abrahams, I. (2009). Does practical work really motivate? A study of the affective value of practical work in secondary school science. *International Journal of Science Education, 31*(17), 2335–2353. doi:10.1080/09500690802342836

Afaya Co. Inc. (2005). *Afaya*. Retrieved from http://www.afaya.co.jp/afayapen.html

Albaili, M. A. (2003). Motivational goal orientations of intellectually gifted achieving and underachieving students in the United Arab Emirates. *Social Behavior & Personality: An International Journal, 31*(2), 107–120. doi:10.2224/sbp.2003.31.2.107

Albright, J., Heng, M. A., & Harris, K. (2008). *Pedagogical Change in the Normal Technical Classroom, Final Research Report*. Centre for Research in Perdagogy and Practice, National Institute of Education, Singapore. Retrieved January 1, 2013, from: http://repository.nie.edu.sg/jspui/bitstream/10497/4157/3/CRP26_05JA_FinalResRpt.pdf

Aldridge, B. G. (1989). *Essential changes in secondary school science: Scope, sequence and coordination*. Washington, DC: National Science Teachers Association. American Association for the Advancement of Science.

Alevizou, P. (2008). Beyond technology: Children's learning in the age of digital culture. *Children & Society, 22*(1), 70–71. doi:10.1111/j.1099-0860.2007.00135.x

Alimisis, D., & Kynigos, C. (2009). Constructionism and Robotics in Education. In D. Alimisis (Ed.), *Teacher Education on Robotics-Enhanced Constructivist Pedagogical Methods*. Athens, Greece: School of Pedagogical and Technological Education.

Alliance for Excellent Education. (2005). *Teacher attrition: A costly loss to the Nation and to the States.* Washington, DC: Author.

Amabile, T. M. (1996). Creativity and innovation in organizations. Harvard Business School.

American Association for the Advancement of Science. (2010). *Project 2061: Science for All Americans.* Washington, DC: AAAS.

Amir, N., & Subramaniam, R. (2012). Fostering inquiry in science among kinaesthetic learners through Design & Technology. In L. C. Lennex, & K. F. Nettleton (Eds.), *Cases on Inquiry Through Instructional Technology in Math and Science: Systemic Approaches* (pp. 221–257). Hershey, PA: IGI Global Publishing. doi:10.4018/978-1-4666-0068-3.ch009

Anandan, K., & Kan, V. (2008).*Enthusing NT students, start from scratch.* Paper presented at NT Science Professional Sharing Day 2008 - Teachers' Best Practices. Singapore.

Anderson, J. A. (1988). Cognitive styles and multicultural populations. *Journal of Teacher Education, 39*(1), 2–9. doi:10.1177/002248718803900102

Anderson, N., & Henderson, M. (2004). e-PD: Blended models of sustaining teacher professional development in digital literacies. *E-learning, 1*(3), 383–394. doi:10.2304/elea.2004.1.3.4

Armstrong, D. C. (1994). A gifted child's education requires real dialogue: The use of interactive writing for collaborative education. *Gifted Child Quarterly, 38*(3), 136–145. doi:10.1177/001698629403800307

Asahi Shimbun Digital. (2013). Retrieved from http://www.asahi.com/edu/articles/TKY201308220269.html

Assessment & Teaching of 21st Century Skills. (n.d.). *What Are 21st-Century Skills?* Retrieved from http://atc21s.org/index.php/about/what-are-21st-century-skills/

Association for Middle Level Education Columbus Ohio. (n.d.). *This I believe: Developmentally responsive middle level schools.* Retrieved from http://www.amle.org

Atmatzidou, S., Markelis, I., & Demitridis, S. (2008). *The Use of LEGO Mindstorms in Elementary and Secondary Education: Game as a way of triggering learning.* Paper presented at the International Conference of Simulation, Modeling and Programming for Autonomous Robots (SIMPAR). Venice, Italy.

Audrey, C. R., Jean, S. S., Denise, A. T., & Highnam, D. (2012). Creativity and thinking skills integrated into a science enrichment unit on flooding. *Creative Education, 3*(8), 1371–1379. doi:10.4236/ce.2012.38200

Austin, L. B., & Shore, B. M. (1995). Using concept mapping for assessment in physics. *Physics Education, 30*(1), 41–45. doi:10.1088/0031-9120/30/1/009

Bailey, R., Pearce, G., Smith, C., Sutherland, M., Stack, N., Winstanley, C., & Dickenson, M. (2012). Improving the educational achievement of gifted and talented students: A Systematic review. *Talent Development & Excellence, 4*(1), 33–48.

Balchin, T. (2005). A creativity feedback package for teachers and students of design and technology (in the UK). *Design and Technology Education: An International Journal., 10*(2), 31–43.

Baldwin, A. (1994). The seven plus story: Developing hidden talents among students in socioeconomically disadvantaged environments. *Gifted Child Quarterly, 38*(2), 80–84. doi:10.1177/001698629403800206

Bandura, A. (1994). Self-efficacy. In V. S. Ramachaudran (Ed.), *Encyclopedia of human behavior* (Vol. 4, pp. 71–81). New York: Academic Press.

Banks, J. A. (1988). Ethnicity, class, cognitive, and motivational styles: Research and teaching implications. *The Journal of Negro Education, 57*(4), 452–466. doi:10.2307/2295689

Barack, L. (2009). Penultimate. *School Library Journal, 55*(9), 40–41.

Barak, M., & Doppelt, Y. (2000). Using portfolios to enhance creative thinking. *Journal-of-Technology-Studies, 26*(2), 16–25.

Barbour, N. E., & Shaklee, B. D. (1998). Gifted education meets Reggio Emilia: Visions for curriculum in gifted education for young children. *Gifted Child Quarterly, 42*(4), 228–237. doi:10.1177/001698629804200406

Barlex, D. (2007). Creativity in school design and technology in England: A discussion of Influences. *International Journal of Technology and Design Education, 17*(2), 149–162. doi:10.1007/s10798-006-0006-x

Barr, D., Harrison, J., & Conery, L. (2011). Computational Thinking: A Digital Age Skill for Everyone. *Learning and Leading with Technology*, (March/April), 20–23.

Baslanti, U., & McCoach, D. B. (2006). Factors related to the underachievement of university students in Turkey. *Roeper Review, 28*(4), 210–215. doi:10.1080/02783190609554366

Baxter, P., & Jack, S. (2008). Qualitative Case Study Methodology: Study Design and Implementation for Novice Researchers. *Qualitative Report, 13*(4), 544–559. Retrieved September 1, 2013, from http://www.nova.edu/ssss/QR/QR13-4/baxter.pdf

Bazler, J. A., & Charles, M. (1993). Project 2061: A university model. *Journal of Science Teacher Education, 4*(4), 104–108. doi:10.1007/BF02614562

Beecher, M., & Renzulli, J. (1995). *Developing the gifts and talents of all students in the regular classroom.* Mansfield Center, CT: Creative Learning Press.

Beisser, S., Gillespie, C., & Thacker, V. (2013). An investigation of play: From the voices of fifth- and sixth-rade talented and gifted students. *Gifted Child Quarterly, 57*(1), 25–38. doi:10.1177/0016986212450070

Beittel, K. (1991). *A celebration of art and consciousness.* State College, PA: Happy Valley Healing Arts.

Benesse. (2005). *Attitude survey on compulsory education: Interim report.* Tokyo: Benesse Educational Research and Development Institute, pp. 28-29.

Berman, K. M., Schultz, R. A., & Weber, C. L. (2012). A Lack of awareness and emphasis in preservice teacher training: Preconceived beliefs about the gifted and talented. *Gifted Child Today, 35*(1), 18–26. doi:10.1177/1076217511428307

Bers, M. U. (2008). *Blocks to Robots: Learning with Technology in the Early Childhood Classroom.* New York, NY: Teachers College Press.

Besemer, S. P. (1998). Creative product analysis matrix: Testing the model structure and a comparison among products – three novel chairs. *Creativity Research Journal, 11*(4), 333–346. doi:10.1207/s15326934crj1104_7

Besemer, S. P. (2010). Review of fostering creativity by Arthur and David Cropley. *Creativity Research Journal, 22*(2), 236–237. doi:10.1080/10400419.2010.481543

Compilation of References

Besnoy, K., Dantzler, J., & Siders, J. (2012). Creating a digital ecosystem for the gifted education classroom. *Journal of Advanced Academics*, *23*(4), 305–325. doi:10.1177/1932202X12461005

Betts, G. T., & Neihart, M. (2008, October 31). *The revised profiles of the gifted and talented: A research-based approach.* Paper presented at the NAGC 55th Annual Convention & Exhibition. St. Louis, MO.

Binet, A. (1907). *The mind and the brain.* London: K. Paul, Trench, Trubner & Co. Ltd.

Binet, A., & Simon, T. (1916). *The development of intelligence in children: (The Binet-Simon scale).* New York, NY: Williams & Wilkins.

Black, N. B. (2011). *This is why I teach: NaNoWriMo* [blog]. Retrieved from http://www.engagingeducation.net/wordpress/this-is-why-i-teach-nanowrimo/

Blumen-Pardo, S. (2002). Effects of a teacher training workshop on creativity, cognition, and school achievement in gifted and non-gifted second-grade students in Lima, Peru. *High Ability Studies*, *13*(1), 47–58. doi:10.1080/13598130220132307

Boling, E., Castek, J., Zawilinski, L., Barton, K., & Nierlich, T. (2008). Collaborative literacy: Blogs and internet projects. *The Reading Teacher*, *61*(6), 504–506. doi:10.1598/RT.61.6.10

Bomar, S. (2009). A pre-reading VoiceThread: Death comes for the archbishop. *Knowledge Quest*, *37*(4), 26–27.

Bomia, L., Beluzo, L., Demeester, D., Elander, K., Johnson, M., & Sheldon, B. (1997). The Impact of Teaching Strategies on Intrinsic Motivation. Champaign, IL: ERIC Clearinghouse on Elementary and Early Childhood Education. (ERIC Document Reproduction Service No. ED 418 925).

Boyd, D., Grossman, P., Lankford, H., Loeb, S., & Wyckoff, J. & National Bureau of Economic research, CA. (2008). *Who leaves? Teacher attrition and student achievement* (NBER Working Paper No. 14022). National Bureau of Economic Research, (ERIC Document Reproduction Service No. ED501989).

Boyle, I., Dyment, J. E., & O'Connell, T. S. (n.d.). The intersection of web 2.0 technologies and reflective journals: An investigation of possibilities, potential and pitfalls. *Independent.Academia.Edu*. Retrieved from: http://independent.academia.edu/IanBoyle/Papers/303036/The_intersection_of_Web_2.0_technologies_and_reflective_journals_An_investigation_of_possibilities_potential_and_pitfalls._in_press_

Bridges, T. (2011). Towards a pedagogy of hip-hop in urban teacher education. *The Journal of Negro Education*, *80*(3), 325–338.

Brodie, E., & Thompson, M. (2009). Double crossed: Exploring science and history through cross-curricular teaching. *The School Science Review*, *90*(332), 47–52.

Brody, L. E., & Mills, C. J. (1997). Gifted children with learning disabilities: A review of the issues. *Journal of Learning Disabilities*, *30*(3), 282–286. doi:10.1177/002221949703000304 PMID:9146095

Brookhart, S. M. (2010). *How to Assess Higher-Order Thinking Skills in Your Classroom*. Alexandria, VA: ASCD.

Brown v. Board of Education, 347 US. 483 (1959).

Brown, J., Collins, A., & Duguid, P. (1989). Situated cognition and the culture of learning. *Educational Researcher, 18*(1), 32–42. doi:10.3102/0013189X018001032

Brulles, D., Cohn, S., & Saunders, R. (2010). Improving performance for gifted students in a cluster grouping model. *Journal for the Education of the Gifted, 34*(2), 327–350.

Brulles, D., Peters, S. J., & Saunders, R. (2012). Schoolwide mathematics achievement within the gifted cluster grouping model. *Journal of Advanced Academics, 23*(3), 200–216. doi:10.1177/1932202X12451439

Brulles, D., & Winebrenner, S. (2011, October). The schoolwide cluster grouping model: Restructuring gifted education services for the 21st century. *Gifted Child Today, 34*(4), 35–46.

Brulles, D., & Winebrenner, S. (2012). Clustered for success. *Educational Leadership, 69*(5), 41–45.

Brunvand, S., & Byr, S. (2011). Using VoiceThread to Promote Learning Engagement and Success for All Students. *The Council for Exceptional Children (CEC): TEACHING Exceptional Children*. Retrieved from: http://voicethread.com/media/misc/support/JTECVoiceThread.pdf

Bryman, A. (2001). *Social Research Methods*. Oxford, UK: Oxford University Press.

Buber, M. (1970). *I and thou*. New York: Simon and Schuster.

Burke, M., & Settles, B. (2011). Plugged in to the community: Social motivators in online goal setting groups. In *Proceedings of the 5th International Conference on Communities and Technologies*. ACM Digital Library. doi:10.1145/2103354.2103356

Burton, L. D. (2009). Lessons from NaNoWriMo. *Journal of Research on Christian Education, 18*(1), 1–10. doi:10.1080/10656210902752006

Caine, R. N., & Caine, G. (1991). *Making connections: teaching and the human brain*. Alexandria, VA: Association for Supervision and Curriculum Development.

Carney-Strahler, B. (2011). Wikis: Promoting collaborative literacy through affordable technology in content-area classrooms. *Creative Education, 2*(2), 76–82. doi:10.4236/ce.2011.22011

Center for Disease Control and Prevention. (2014). *Attention-deficit and hyperactivity disorder*. Retrieved from http://www.cdc.gov/ncbddd/adhd/facts.html

Center for Disease Control and Prevention. (2014). *Injury center: Suicide prevention; youth suicide*. Retrieved from http://www.cdc.gov/violenceprevention

Central Council for Education. (2003). *Attitude survey on school education: Interim report* (pp. 1–10). Tokyo: Curriculum Section, Elementary and Secondary Education Bureau, MEXT.

Central Council for Education. (2006). Primary materials on elementary and secondary education (excerpts edition). *Subdivision on Elementary and Secondary Education (42nd meeting) meeting minutes, 7,* 10. Retrieved from http://www.mext.go.jp/b_menu/shingi/chukyo/chukyo3/siryo/06083007/001.pdf

Central Council for Education. (2008). *Regarding improvements to the Guidelines for the Course of Study for kindergartens, elementary schools, junior high schools, high schools, and special support schools (report)*. Tokyo: MEXT.

Chang, A. (1997). *The motivation, self-esteem, study habits and problems of Normal Technical students*. Singapore: Centre for Educational Research, National Institute of Education.

Chibber, R. (2011). *Life Cycles for Kids Lite (Version 1.0)*. Retrieved from Apple App Store.

Childress, V. (1996). Does integrating technology, science and mathematics improve technological problem solving? A quasi-experiment. *Journal of Technology Education*, *8*(1), 16–26.

Cho, S. H., Kim, H. W., Park, S. I., & Jeong, H. C. (2002). The study of promotion of comprehensive planning for gifted education, Korea Education and Research Information Service (KERIS). *CR (East Lansing, Mich.)*, 2002–2056.

Christensen, J. J. (1988). Reflections on teaching creativity. *Chemical Engineering Education*, *22*(4), 170–176.

Clark, B. (2002). *Growing up gifted: Developing the potential of children at home and at school* (6th ed.). Upper Saddle River, NJ: Pearson/Merrill Prentice Hall.

Code, K. P. (2007). Developing student gifts and talents using web-based resources. *Understanding Our Gifted*, *19*(4), 10–12.

Cohen, E. G., & Lotan, R. A. (1997). *Working for equity in heterogeneous classrooms: Sociological theory in practice*. Teachers College Press.

Colangelo, N., Assouline, S. G., & Gross, M. (2004). *A nation deceived: How schools hold back America's brightest students* (Vol. 1). Iowa City, IA: University of Iowa, The Connie Belin & Jacqueline N. Blank International Center for Gifted Education and Talent Development.

Colangelo, N., Assouline, S. G., & Gross, M. U. M. (2004). A nation deceived: How schools hold back America's brightest students: Vol. 1. Belin: Blank International Center on Gifted Education and Talent Development.

Colangelo, N., Assouline, S. G., & Gross, M. U. M. (Eds.). (2005). *A nation deceived: How schools hold back America's brightest students*. Belin: Blank Center for Talent Development.

Cold Spring Harbor Laboratory. (2011). *Gene Screen (Version 1.1)*. Retrieved from Apple App Store.

Cole, M. (1998). Can cultural psychology help us think about diversity? *Mind, Culture, and Activity*, *5*(4), 291–304. doi:10.1207/s15327884mca0504_4

Coleman, L. (1985). *Schooling the gifted*. Menlo Park: Addison-Wesley.

Collins, N. D., & Cross, T. L. (1993). Teaching the writing process to gifted and talented students. *Gifted Child Today*, *16*(3), 22.

Craft, A. (2001). *An analysis of research and literature on creativity in education*. Qualifications and Curriculum Authority. Retrieved September 1, 2013, from http://www.euvonal.hu/images/creativity_report.pdf

Creative Mobile Games. (2011). *Crazy Genetics (Version 1.1)*. Retrieved from Apple App Store.

Creemers, B., Kyriakides, L., & Antoniou, P. (2013). *Different approaches to teaching which emerged from teacher effectiveness research.* In *Teacher Professional Development for Improving Quality of Teaching* (pp. 81–99). Springer Netherlands. doi:10.1007/978-94-007-5207-8_6

Crompton, H. (2013). A historical overview of m-learning: toward learner-centered education. In Z. L. Berge, & L. Y. Muilenberg (Eds.), *Handbook of mobile learning* (pp. 3–14). Florence, KY: Routledge.

Crompton, H. (2013). New approach, new theory. In Z. L. Berge, & L. Y. Muilenberg (Eds.), *Handbook of mobile learning* (pp. 47–57). Florence, KY: Routledge.

Cropley, D. H., & Cropley, A. J. (2000). Fostering creativity in engineering undergraduates. *High Ability Studies, 11*(2), 207–219. doi:10.1080/13598130020001223

Cross, N. (2007). *Designerly ways of knowing.* London, U.K.: Springer- Verlag.

Cross, T. (2013). *Suicide among gifted children and adolescents: Understanding the suicidal Mind.* Waco, TX: Prufrock Press.

Cross, T. L., Coleman, L. J., & Terhaar-Yonkers, M. (2014). The Social Cognition of Gifted Adolescents in Schools: Managing the Stigma of Giftedness. *Journal for the Education of the Gifted, 37*(1), 30–39. doi:10.1177/0162353214521492

Crothers, L., Field, J., & Kolbert, J. (2005). Navigating power, control, and being nice: Aggression in adolescent girls' friendships. *Journal of Counseling and Development, 83*(3), 349–420. doi:10.1002/j.1556-6678.2005.tb00354.x

Csikszentmihalyi, M. (1996). *Creativity: flow and the psychology of discovery and invention.* New York: Harper Perennial.

Csikszentmihalyi, M. (1998). Society, culture and person: a systems view of creativity. In R. J. Sternberg (Ed.), *The nature of creativity* (pp. 325–339). Cambridge, UK: Cambridge University Press.

Csíkszentmihályi, M. (2008). *Flow: The Psychology of Optimal Experience.* New York, NY: HarperCollins Publishers.

Cummings, L. (2013). How to challenge gifted students. *eHow* Retrieved from http://www.ehow.com/how_6569900_challenge-gifted-students.html

Cumming, T., Rodriguez, C., & Strnadova, I. (2013). Aligning iPad applications with evidence-based practices in inclusive and special education. In J. Keengwe (Ed.), *Pedagogical applications and social effects of mobile technology integration* (pp. 55–78). Hershey, PA: IGI Global. doi:10.4018/978-1-4666-2985-1.ch004

Dabrowski, K., & Piechowski, M. M. (1977). *Theory of levels of emotional development.* Oceanside, NY: Dabor Science.

Dacey, J., & Lennon, K. (2000). *Understanding creativity: the interplay of biological, psychological and social factors.* Buffalo, NY: Creative Education Foundation.

Dale, J. (2011, October 15). *Fairfax Education Summit.* Fairfax, VA: Fairfax Education Summit.

Dan Russell-Pinson. (2012). *Stack the States Lite (Version 2.3).* Retrieved from Apple App Store.

Compilation of References

Danahy, E. E., Goswamy, A., & Rogers, C. B. (2008). *Future of Robotics Education: The Design and Creation of Interactive Notebooks for Teaching Robotics Concepts.* Paper presented at the IEEE International Conference on Technologies for Practical Robot Applications. Woburn, MA. doi:10.1109/TEPRA.2008.4686687

Daniel, R. H., Matthew, T. M., & Thomas, P. H. (2007). Exploring the motivational trajectories of gifted university students. *Roeper Review, 29*(3), 197–205. doi:10.1080/02783190709554409

Darius, P. D. (2012). *Culturally relevant teaching: Hip-hop pedagogy in urban schools.* New York: Peter Lang.

Darling-Hammond, L., & Sykes, G. (2003). Wanted: A national teacher supply policy for education: The right way to meet the "Highly Qualified Teacher" challenge. *Education Policy Analysis Archives, 11*(33). Retrieved from http://epaa.asu.edu/epaa/v11n33/

Davidson, M., Evens, H., & McCormick, R. (1998). *Bridging the gap: the use of concepts from science and mathematics in design and technology at KS 3.* International Design and Technology Education Research and Curriculum Development (IDATER), Loughborough University of Technology. Retrieved January 1, 2013, from https://dspace.lboro.ac.uk/dspace-jspui/handle/2134/1419

Davis, G. (2003). Identifying creative students, teaching for creative growth. In N. Colangelo, & G. A. Davis (Eds.), *Handbook of Gifted Education* (3rd ed., pp. 309–324). New York: Pearson Education, Inc.

Davis, G. A., & Rimm, S. B. (2004). *Education of the gifted and talented* (5th ed.). Pearson Education.

Ddeubel. (2010, Nov 8). *VoiceThread in education – empowering students* [Blog post]. Retrieved from http://ddeubel.edublogs.org/2008/11/08/voicethread-in-education-empowering-students/

Deason, C., & Zhang, K. (2012) Technology-enhanced rap music pedagogy for history learning at an alternative school: impacts of a culturally-sensitive computer environment on at-risk teenagers. *Asian-Pacific Collaborative Education Journal, 8*(1), 39-58. Available at http://www.acecjournal.org/2009/Journal_Data/Vol8No1/201203.pdf

Dede, C., & Bjerede, M. (2011, February). *Mobile Learning for the 21st Century: Insights from the 2010 Wireless EdTech Conference.* San Diego, CA: Qualcomm. Retrieved from http://isites.harvard.edu/fs/docs/icb.topic1116077.files/!Wireless%20EdTech%20Research%20Paper%20Final%20March%202011.pdf

Dede, C. (2006, Spring). Virtual reality of learning. *Interactive Educator, 2*(1), 40–41.

Delisle, J. R. (1990). The gifted adolescent at risk: Strategies and resources for suicide prevention among gifted youth. *Journal for the Education of the Gifted, 13,* 212–228.

Demski, J. (2012, January). This time it's personal. *T.H.E. Journal.* Retrieved from http://thejournal.com/articles/2012/01/04/personalized-learning.aspx

Denzin, N. K. (1970). *The Research Act in Sociology.* Chicago: Aldine.

Department of Education. (2001). *No Child Left Behind (NCLB) Act.* Retrieved from www.ed.gov/nclb

Desbottes, A., & Nicholls, T. (2004). What is the impact of cross-phase, cross-curricular learning on gifted and talented pupils? *Educational Review, 18*(1), 79–84.

Diffily, D. (2002). Project-based learning: Meeting social studies standards and the needs of gifted learners. *Gifted Child Today, 25*(3), 40–43.

Dikkers, S., Martin, J., & Coulter, B. et al. (2012). *Mobile media learning: Amazing uses of mobile devices for learning.* Pittsburgh, PA: ETC Press.

Dimitriadis, G. (2001). *Performing identity/Performing culture: Hip-hop as text, pedagogy, and lived practice.* New York: Peter Lang.

Dissanayake, E. (1995). *Homo aestheticus: Where art comes from and why.* New York: Free Press.

Dixon, F., Cassady, J., Cross, T., & Williams, D. (2005). Effects of technology on critical thinking and essay writing among gifted adolescents. *Journal of Secondary Gifted Education, 16*(4), 180.

Dockstader, J. (1999). Teachers of the 21st century know the what, why, and how of technology integration. *T.H.E. Journal, 26*(6), 73–74.

Donnelly, L. (2007, January 1). Write away. *Teacher Magazine, 18*(04), 48.

Doppelt, Y. (2005). Assessment of project-based learning in a mechatronics context. *Journal of Technology Education, 16*(2), 7–24.

Doyle, A. E. (1999). Dishing the personal narrative: Its present classroom ignominy, its classroom potential. *Bridgewater Review, 18*(1), 20–23.

Drew, J., Esposito, M., & Perakslis, C. (2004). *Utilization of Robotics in Higher Education.* Paper presented at the 21st Annual Information Systems Education Conference (ISECON 2004). Newport, RI.

Drexler, W. (2010). The networked student model for construction of personal learning environments: Balancing teacher control and student autonomy. *Australasian Journal of Educational Technology, 26*(3), 369–385.

Ducamp, G. (2010). *Technology and gifted learners, presented to NCAGT conference.* Retrieved from http://www.slideshare.net/gjducamp/technology-and-gifted-learners

Duckworth, E. (2005). Critical Exploration in the Classroom. *New Educator, 1*(4), 257–272. doi:10.1080/15476880500276728

Duckworth, E. (2006). *The Having of Wonderful Ideas: and Other Essays on Teaching and Learning* (3rd ed.). New York, NY: Teachers College Press.

Dunleavy, M., & Dede, C. (in press). Augmented reality teaching and learning. In J. M. Spector, M. D. Merrill, J. Elen, & M. J. Bishop (Eds.), *The Handbook of Research for Educational Communications and Technology* (4th ed.). New York: Springer. doi:10.1007/978-1-4614-3185-5_59

Dunn, R., & Dunn, K. (1978). *Teaching students through their individual learning styles: A practical approach.* Reston, VA: Reston Publishing Company.

Dweck, C. (2006). *Mindset: The new psychology of success.* New York: Random House.

Dwyer, D. C., Ringstaff, C., & Sandholz, J. H. (1990). *Teacher beliefs and practices part II: Support for change. ACOT Report #9: Apple Classrooms of Tomorrow.* Advanced Technology Group, Apple Computer.

Compilation of References

Dykman, C. A., & Davis, C. K. (2008). Online education forum: Part two–Teaching online versus teaching conventionally. *Journal of Information Systems Education, 19*, 156–163.

Early Development Association (Ed.). (1998). *Collection of sayings on education by Masaru Ibuka*. Tokyo: Goma Shobo.

Eckstein, M. (2009). Enrichment 2.0 gifted and talented education for the 21st Century. *Gifted Child Today, 32*(1), 59–63.

Education of the Gifted and Talented-Volume1: Report to the Congress of the United States by the U.S. Commissioner of Education. (1971, Aug.). ERIC ED 056243.

EDUCAUSE Learning Initiative. (2009, May). *7 things you should know about... personal learning environments*. Retrieved from http://net.educause.edu/ir/library/pdf/ELI7049.pdf

eduPad Inc. (2013). *iTooch Elementary School (Version 4.6.1)*. Retrieved from Apple App Store.

Edwards, O. (2008). *Lego Mindstorms NXT Robots: Building Bonds with Bots - Learn science, technology, engineering, and math with robot-building projects*. Retrieved from http://www.edutopia.org/lego-mindstorms-robots-technology

Eguchi, A. (2007a). *Educational Robotics for Elementary School Classroom*. Paper presented at the Society for Information Technology and Education (SITE). San Antonio, TX.

Eguchi, A. (2007b). *Educational Robotics for Undergraduate Freshmen*. Paper presented at the Ed-Media Conference. Vancouver, Canada.

Eguchi, A. (2007c). *Educational Robotics for Undergraduate Freshmen*. Paper presented at the World Conference on Educational Multimedia, Hypermedia and Telecommunications. Vancouver, Canada.

Elkind, D. (2008). Forward. In M. U. Bers (Ed.), *Block to Robots* (pp. xi–xiv). New York, NY: Teachers College Press.

English, M., & Kitsantas, A. (2013). Supporting Student Self-Regulated Learning in Problem- and Project-Based Learning. *Interdisciplinary Journal Of Problem-Based Learning, 7*(2), 127–150. doi:10.7771/1541-5015.1339

EnsenaSoft. (2012). *US States (Match'Em Up History & Geography) (Version 1.0.12)*. Retrieved from Apple App Store.

Ertmer, P. A. (2005). Teacher pedagogical beliefs: The final frontier in our quest for technology integration? *Educational Technology Research and Development, 53*(4), 25–39. doi:10.1007/BF02504683

Ertmer, P. T., Newby, T. J., & MacDougall, M. (1996). Students' responses and approaches to case based instruction: The role of reflective self-regulation. *American Educational Research Journal, 33*(3), 719–752. doi:10.3102/00028312033003719

Evans, K. (2000). Multicultural counseling. In L. K. Silverman (Ed.), *Counseling the Gifted and Talented* (pp. 277–290). Denver, CO: Love Publishing Company.

Evelyn, J. (2008). The Miseducation of hip-hop discrimination in education. In *Pop Perspectives-Readings To Critique Contemporary Culture* (pp. 559–565). New York: McGraw-Hill.

Fan, S. (2010, April 8). *Why I'm falling in love with VoiceThread* [Blog post]. Retrieved from http://sinkorswim.posterous.com/why-im-falling-in-love-with-voicethread

Favre, L. R. (2009). Kinesthetic Instructional Strategies: Moving At-Risk Learners to Higher Levels. *Insights on Learning Disabilities*, *6*(1), 29–35.

Featonby, D. (2005). Toys and physics. *Physics Education*, *40*(6), 537–543. doi:10.1088/0031-9120/40/6/005

Feldman, D., Csikszentmihalyi, M., & Gardner, H. (1994). *Changing the World: A Framework for the Study of Creativity*. West Point, CT: Praeger.

Ferriter, B. (n.d.). *Using VoiceThread to communicate and collaborate.* Retrieved from http://www.learnnc.org/lp/pages/6538

Ferriter, W. M. (2011). Good teaching trumps good tools. *Educational Leadership*, *68*(5), 84.

Fleming, N. (2012). *Introduction to VARK*. Retrieved from http://legacy.hazard.kctcs.edu/VARK/introduction.htm

Florida Department of Education (FL DOE). (2013a). *Florida's frameworks for K-12 gifted learners.* Retrieved from http://www.fldoe.org/bii/Gifted_Ed/

Florida Department of Education (FL DOE). (2013b). *Florida's plan for K-12 gifted education.* Retrieved from http://www.fldoe.org/bii/Gifted_Ed/pdf/StateGiftedPlan.pdf

Fogarty, R. (1991). Ten ways to integrate curriculum. *Educational Leadership*, *49*(2), 61–65.

Ford, D. Y. (2003). Equity and excellence: culturally diverse students in gifted education. In N. Colangelo, & G. A. Davis (Eds.), *Handbook of Gifted Education* (3rd ed., pp. 493–505). New York: Pearson Education, Inc.

Fortus, D., Krajcikb, J., Dershimerb, R. C., Marxc, R. W., & Mamlok-Naamand, R. (2004). Design-based science and student learning. *Journal of Research in Science Teaching*, *41*(10), 1081–1110. doi:10.1002/tea.20040

Fortus, D., Krajcikb, J., Dershimerb, R. C., Marxc, R. W., & Mamlok-Naamand, R. (2005). Design-based science and real-world problem-solving. *International Journal of Science Education*, *27*(7), 855–879. doi:10.1080/09500690500038165

Fox, J. M. (2011). *Creativity 101: 4Ps of Creativity. Creativity Series 101*. International Center for Studies in Creativity, Buffalo State, University of New York. Retrieved January 1, 2013, from http://www.youtube.com/watch?v=UDy5eTqot1M

Frankel, R. (1998). *The adolescent psyche: Jungian and Winnicottian perspectives*. New York: Routledge.

Franklin Electronic Publishers, Inc. (2013). *AnyBook.* Retrieved from http://www.anybookreader.com

Freed, J. N. (1990). Tutoring techniques for the gifted. *Understanding our Gifted, 2*(6), 11-13.

Freeman, C. (2008). *Science stories: Using case studies in teaching critical thinking*. Washington, DC: National Science Teachers Association.

Frey, N., Fisher, D., & Gonzalez, A. (2013). *Teaching with tablets: How do I integrate tablets with effective instruction?* Alexandria, VA: ASCD.

Compilation of References

Fujinaga, T. (2006). Thoughts on early special education for gifted students. *Kyoiku to Igaku, 54*(10), 892–900.

Fuligni, A. J., Eccles, J. S., & Barber, B. L. (1995). The long-term effects of seventh-grade ability grouping in mathematics. *The Journal of Early Adolescence, 15*(1), 58–89. doi:10.1177/0272431695015001005

Gallagher, J. J. (1994). Current and historical thinking on education gifted and talented students. In P. O' Connell (Ed.), *National excellence: A case for developing America's talent. An anthology of readings* (pp. 303–213). Darby, PA: Diane Publishing Company.

Galton, F. (1989). *Hereditary genius: An inquiry into its laws and consequences.* New York, NY: McMillan and Co.

Gardner, D. P. (1983). *A nation at risk: The imperative for educational reform.* Washington, DC: National Commission for Excellence in Education.

Gardner, H. (1993). *Multiple intelligences.* New York: Basic Books.

Gardner, H. (1993). *Multiple intelligences: The theory in practice.* New York, NY: Basic Books.

Gardner, H. (1999a). *Intelligence reframed: Multiple intelligences for the 21st century.* New York: Basic Books.

Gardner, H., & Veenema, S. (1996). Multimedia and multiple intelligences. *The American Prospect, 7*(29), 75–84.

Gardner, P. L. (1997). The roots of technology and science: A philosophical and historical view. *International Journal of Technology and Design Education, 7*(1-2), 13–20. doi:10.1023/A:1008892400827

Garrett, R. M. (1987). Issues in science education: Problem-solving, creativity and originality. *International Journal of Science Education, 9*(2), 125–137. doi:10.1080/0950069870090201

Gay, G. (2002). Preparing for culturally responsive teaching. *Journal of Teacher Education, 53*(2), 106–116. doi:10.1177/0022487102053002003

Gee, J. P. (2004). *Situated language and learning: A critique of traditional schooling.* New York, NY: Routledge.

Gentry, J. (2008). E-publishing's impact on learning in an inclusive sixth grade social studies classroom. *Journal of Interactive Learning Research, 19*, 455–467.

Gentry, M. L. (1999). *Promoting student achievement and exemplary classroom practices through cluster grouping: A research-based alternative to heterogeneous elementary education. Research Monograph for Educational Research and Instruction.* Washington, DC: OERI.

Gentry, M., & Keilty, B. (2004). Rural and suburban cluster grouping: Reflections of staff development as a component of program success. *Roeper Review, 26*(3), 147–155. doi:10.1080/02783190409554260

Gentry, M., & Owen, S. V. (1999). An investigation of the effects of total school flexible cluster grouping on identification, achievement, and classroom practices. *Gifted Child Quarterly, 43*(4), 224–243. doi:10.1177/001698629904300402

George, J. C. (1972). *Julie of the Wolves.* New York: Harper-Collins.

Gilbert, J. K. (2005). *Constructing worlds through science education.* London: Routledge.

Gilbert, J. K., & Newberry, M. (2007). The characteristics of the gifted and exceptionally able in science. In K. S. Taber (Ed.), *Science education for gifted learners* (pp. 15–31). London: Routledge.

Gilbert, S. E., & Gay, G. (1985). Improving the success in school of poor black children. *Phi Delta Kappan, 67*(2), 133–137.

Giles, R. M., & Shaw, E. L. (2011). SMART Boards rock! Using technology to investigate geology with young children. *Science and Children, 49*(4), 36–37.

Gilman, L. (2013). *The Theory of Multiple Intelligence*. Indiana University. Retrieved from http://www.intelltheory.com/mitheory.shtml

Giroux, H. A. (1997). *Pedagogy and the politics of hope: Theory, culture, and schooling.* Boulder, CO: Westview.

Glesne, C. (2011). *Becoming qualitative researchers: An introduction.* Boston, MA: Pearson.

Goleman, D. (2006). *Emotional intelligence: Why it can matter more than IQ.* New York, NY: Bantam Press.

Goodhew, G. (2009). *Meeting the Needs of Gifted and Talented Students.* London, UK: Continuum International Publishing Group.

Green, A. (2011, February). Getting Started with LEGO Robotics. *D & T Practice,* 7-10.

Greene, M. (1995). *Releasing the imagination: Essays on education, the arts, and social change.* San Francisco: Jossey-Bass.

Gridmark Inc. (2009). *GridOnput.* Retrieved from http://www.gridmark.co.jp/english/gridonput.html

Güémez, J., Fiolhais, C., & Fiolhais, M. (2009). Toys in physics lectures and demonstrations - A brief review. *Physics Education, 44*(1), 53–64. doi:10.1088/0031-9120/44/1/008

Guildford, J. P. (1959). The three faces of intellect. *The American Psychologist, 14*(8), 469–479. doi:10.1037/h0046827

Guion, L. A., Diehl, D. C., & McDonald, D. (2011). *Triangulation: Establishing the Validity of Qualitative Studies.* Retrieved September 1, 2013, from http://edis.ifas.ufl.edu/pdffiles/FY/FY39400.pdf

Gura, M. (2013). *Student Robotics and the K-12 Curriculum.* Retrieved from http://www.edutopia.org/blog/student-robotics-k-12-curriculum-mark-gura

Gutiérrez, K., Baquedaño-López, P., & Tejeda, C. (1999). Rethinking diversity: Hybridity and hybrid language practices in the Third Space. *Mind, Culture, and Activity, 6*(4), 286–303. doi:10.1080/10749039909524733

Haberman, M. (2005). Raising teachers' salaries: The funds are there. *Education, 125*(3), 327–343.

Haigh, M. (2007). Can investigative practical work in high school biology foster creativity? *Research in Science Education, 37*(2), 123–140. doi:10.1007/s11165-006-9018-5

Hall, G. E., Loucks, S. F., Rutherford, W. L., & Newlove, B. W. (1975). Levels of use of the innovation: A framework for analyzing innovation adoption. *Journal of Teacher Education, 26*(1), 52–56. doi:10.1177/002248717502600114

Compilation of References

Hall, J., & Chamblee, G. (2013). Teaching algebra and geometry with GeoGebra: Preparing pre-service teachers for middle grades/secondary mathematics classrooms. *Computers in the Schools*, *30*(1-2), 12–29. doi:10.1080/07380569.2013.764276

Hammer, B. (1984). The artist as teacher: Problems and experiments. *Journal of Education*, *166*(2), 181–187.

Hansen, P. J. K. (2009). Analysing cases in technology and design education: How could designing and making technological products be a vehicle for enhancing understanding of natural science principles? *Design and Technology Education: An International Journal*, *14*(2), 45–52.

Harding-Smith, T. (1993). *Learning together: An introduction to collaborative learning*. New York, NY: HarperCollins College Publishers.

Hare D., Heap, J. L., & North Central Regional Educational Lab. (2001). *Effective teacher recruitment and retention strategies in the Midwest: Who is making use of them?* Naperville, IL: North Central Regional Educational Lab. (Eric Document Reproduction Service No. ED477648).

Hart, W. E. (2009). *The culture industry, hip-hop music and the white perspective: How one-dimensional representation of hip-hop music has influenced white racial attitudes*. (Unpublished Masters Thesis). The University of Texas in Arlington, Arlington, TX.

Hawk, T. F., & Shah, A. J. (2007). Using learning style instruments to enhance student learning. *Decision Sciences Journal of Innovative Education*, *5*(1), 1–19. doi:10.1111/j.1540-4609.2007.00125.x

Hebert, T. P., & McBee, M. T. (2007, Spring). The input of an undergraduate honors program on gifted university students. *Gifted Child Quarterly*, *51*(2), 136–151. doi:10.1177/0016986207299471

Hellweg, E. (2005). Hip-hop high the musical language of the street has new fans: Teachers, who are using it as a classroom tool. *Edutopia*, *1*(6), 4-7.

Hendler, J. (2000). Robots for the Rest of Us: Designing Systems "Out of the Box". In A. Druin, & J. Hendler (Eds.), *Robots for Kids: Exploring New Technologies for Learning* (pp. 2–7). San Diego, CA: Academic Press.

Higuchi, T., Hashimoto, N., & Okabe, S. (2013). *Attitude survey of parents and guardians on school education, 2012 Digest*. Tokyo: Benesse Educational Research & Development Institute.

Hisada, M. (1996). Special education for gifted students is practically child abuse. *Gendai*, *30*(7), 202–205.

Ho, Y. L. R., Lim, S. H., & Ho, B. T. (2005). *Differentiated Approach In Teaching Science To Normal (Technical) students*. Paper presented at CRPP International Conference on Education on 1stJune 2005 in The National Institute of Education. Singapore.

Hoang, T. (2007). Creativity: A motivational tool for interest and conceptual understanding in science education. *International Journal of Humanities and Social Science*, *2*, 477–483.

Hobgood, B., & Ormsby, L. (n.d.). *Inclusion in the 21st century classroom: Differentiating with technology*. Retrieved from http://www.learnnc.org/lp/editions/every-learner/6776

Hoffman, J. L., Wu, H.-K., Krajcik, J. S., & Soloway, E. (2003). The nature of middle school learners' science content understandings with the use of on-line resources. *Journal of Research in Science Teaching*, *40*(3), 323–346. doi:10.1002/tea.10079

Höhn, L., & Harsch, G. (2009). Indigo and creativity: A cross-curricular approach linking art and chemistry. *The School Science Review*, *90*(332), 73–81.

Hollingsworth, L. S. (1926). *Gifted children: Their nature and nurture*. New York, NY: MacMillan and Co.

Hong, W. (2010). *Puzzle Evolution HD (Version 2.0)*. Retrieved from Apple App Store.

Horne, J., & Shaughnessy, M. F. (2013). The response to intervention program and gifted students: How can it facilitate and expedite educational excellence for gifted students in the regular education setting? *International Journal of Academic Research*, *5*(3), 319–324. doi:10.7813/2075-4124.2013/5-3/B.48

Housand, B. C., & Housand, A. M. (2012). The Role of Technology in Gifted Students' Motivation. *Psychology in the Schools*, *49*(7), 706–715. doi:10.1002/pits.21629

House Energy and Commerce Committee. (2009). *H.R.2036-111ᵗʰ Congress: Jacob K. Javitz gifted and talented students education enhancement act*. Retrieved from http://www.govtrack.us/congress/bills/111/hr203

Howland, J., Jonassen, D., & Marra, R. (2012). *Meaningful learning with technology* (4th ed.). Boston, MA: Pearson.

Huber, S., & Ebner, M. (2013). iPad interface guidelines for m-learning. In Z. L. Berge & L. Y. Muilenberg (Eds.), Handbook of mobile learning (pp. 318-328). Florence, KY: Routledge.

Huffaker, D. (2005). The educated blogger: Using weblogs to promote literacy in the classroom. *AACE Journal*, *13*(2), 91–98.

Hung, D. (2003). Supporting current pedagogical approaches with neuroscience research. *Journal of Interactive Learning Research*, *14*(2), 129–155.

Hur, J. W., & Anderson, A. (2013). iPad integration in an elementary classroom: lesson ideas, successes, and challenges. In J. Keengwe (Ed.), Pedagogical applications and social effects of mobile technology integration (pp. 42-54). Hershey, PA: IGI Global.

Hutinger, P., & Johanson, J. (2001). *Learning modalities: Pathways to effective learning*. Retrieved May 10, 2013 http://www.pbs.org/teachers/earlychildhood/articles/learningmodalities.html

Hwang, S. J., Choi, J. W., Lee, E. K., & Lee, Y. J. (2013). Analyzing curriculums of university affiliated institutions for informatics gifted in Korea. In *Proceedings from IADIS International Conference ICT, Society, and Human Beings 2013*. Prague: IADIS.

Ikuta, S., Nemoto, F., Endo, E., Kaiami, S., & Ezoe, T. (2013). School activities using handmade teaching materials with dot codes. In D. G. Barres, Z. C. Carrion, & R. L.-C. Delgado (Eds.), *Technologies for inclusive education: Beyond traditional integration approaches* (pp. 220–243). Hershey, PA: IGI Global.

Ingersoll, R. M. (2007). Is there really a teacher shortage? In A. R. Sadovnik (Ed.), *Sociology of education: A critical reader* (pp. 159–176). New York: Routledge Taylor and Francis Group.

International Society for Technology Education's National Education Technology Standards. (2013). Retrieved from https://www.iste.org/docs/pdfs/nets-t-standards.pdf?sfvrsn=2

Ishitobi, R., Ezoe, T., & Ikuta, S. (2010). "Tracing" is "speaking": Communicating and learning using supportive sound books[in Japanese]. *Computers & Education, 29,* 64–67.

Ismail, M., & Tan, A. L. (2004). *Voices from the Normal Technical World – An ethnographic study of low-track students in Singapore.* Retrieved January 1, 2013, from http://conference.nie.edu.sg/paper/new%20converted/ab00565.pdf

Iwanaga, M., & Matsumura, N. (2010). *Talent and education: Toward a new horizon for individuality and talent.* Tokyo: NHK.

James, W., & Gardner, D. (1995). Learning styles: Implications for distance learning. *New Directions for Adult and Continuing Education, 1995*(67), 19–31. doi:10.1002/ace.36719956705

Jarvis, T. (2009). Promoting creative science cross-curricular work through an in-service programme. *The School Science Review, 90*(332), 39–46.

Jick, T. D. (1983). Mixing Qualitative and Quantitative Methods: Triangulation in Action. In J. Van Maanen (Ed.), *Qualitative Methodology* (pp. 135–148). Beverly Hills, CA: Sage Publications.

Johnsen, S. K. (2009). Best practices for identifying gifted students. *Principal, 88*(5), 8–14.

Johnsey, R. (1999). *An examination of a mode of curriculum delivery in which science is integrated with design and technology in the primary school.* International Design And Technology Education Research and Curriculum Development (IDATER), Loughborough University. Retrieved from https://dspace.lboro.ac.uk/dspace-jspui/handle/2134/1394

Johnson, H. R. (2001). Administrators and mentors: Keys in the success of beginning teachers. *Journal of Instructional Psychology, 28*(1), 44–49.

Johnson, L., Adams, S., & Cummins, M. (2012). *NMC Horizon Report: 2012 K-12 Edition.* Austin, TX: The New Media Consortium.

Johnson, L., Adams, S., & Haywood, K. (2011). *NMC Horizon Report: 2011 K-12 Edition.* Austin, TX: The New Media Consortium.

Johnson, S. K. (2011). *Identifying gifted students* (2nd ed.). Waco, TX: Prufrock Press, Inc.

Jonassen, D. H. (1991). Objectivism vs. constructivism: Do we need a new paradigm? *ETR&D, 39*(3), 5–14. doi:10.1007/BF02296434

Jonassen, D. H. (2003, August). The vain quest for a unified theory of learning. *Educational Technology, 43*(4), 5–8.

Jones, K. L. (2013). *Wonks, marathoners, and storytellers: Describing the participatory culture of NaNoWriMo.* (Order No. 3573433, Mercer University). ProQuest Dissertations and Theses, 262.

Kaneko, S., Ohshima, M., Takei, K., Yamamoto, L., Ezoe, T., Ueyama, S., & Ikuta, S. (2011). School activities with voices and sounds: Handmade teaching materials and sound pens[in Japanese]. *Computers & Education, 30,* 48–51.

Kanevsky, L., & Keighley, T. (2003). To produce or not to produce? Understanding boredom and the honor in under-achievement. *Roeper Review*, 26(1), 2–28. doi:10.1080/02783190309554235

Kang, S. H. (1997). Use of new media as constructivism-oriented learning environments. *Journal of Educational Technology*, 13(1), 117–131.

Kang, S. H., Cho, S. H., & Kum, M. R. (2000). The plausibility of cyber gifted education: A case study. *Korean Association for Educational Information and Broadcasting*, 6(1), 49–70.

Katei Kyoiku Shimbun. (2013). *Flipped classrooms as an escape from homogenous classes*. Retrieved from http://www.kknews. co.jp/maruti/news/2013/0204_4c.html

Kent, A. M., Feldman, P., & Hayes, R. L. (2009). Mentoring and inducting new teachers into the profession: An innovative approach. *International Journal of Applied Educational Studies*, 5(1), 73-95.

Kent, A. M., & Giles, R. M. (in press). The influential role of field experiences in a dual certification teacher preparation program. *The Field Experience Journal*.

Kershner, R., Mercer, N., Warwick, P., & Staarman, J. K. (2010). Can the interactive whiteboard support young children's collaborative communication and thinking in classroom science activities? *International Journal of Computer-Supported Collaborative Learning*, 5(4), 359–383. doi:10.1007/s11412-010-9096-2

Killion, J. (2002). *Assessing impact: Evaluating staff development*. Oxford, OH: National Staff Development Council.

Kim, J. (2011). Narrative inquiry into (re)imagining alternative schools: A case study of Kevin Gonzales. *International Journal of Qualitative Studies in Education*, 24(1), 77–96. doi:10.1080/09518390903468321

Klapp, J. (2000). Gifted grownups: The mixed blessings of extraordinary potential. *Roeper Review*, 23(1), 47. doi:10.1080/02783190009554062

Klein, N., & Shragai, Y. (2001). *Creativity and the design approach: a proposed module*. International Design and Technology Education Research and Curriculum Development (IDATER), Loughborough University of Technology. Retrieved from https://dspace.lboro.ac.uk/dspace-jspui/bitstream/2134/1337/1/klein01.pdf

Knafl, K., & Breitmayer, B. J. (1989). Triangulation in qualitative research: Issues of conceptual clarity and purpose. In J. Morse (Ed.), *Qualitative nursing research: A contemporary dialogue,* (pp. 193–203). Aspen.

Koch, J. (2005). Science stories: Science methods for elementary and middle school teachers (3rd ed.). New York, NY: Houghton Mifflin Company.

Kolberg, E., & Orlev, N. (2001). *Robotics Learning as a Tool for Integrating Science-Technology Curriculum in K-12 Schools*. Paper presented at the 31st ASEE/IEEE Frontiers in Education Conference. Reno, NV. doi:10.1109/FIE.2001.963888

Korea Education and Research Information Service (KERIS). (2003). *The plans for building cyber home learning system: The 6th educational research and development related systems*. KERIS.

Kozma, R. B. (2003). Technology and classroom practices: An international study. *Journal of Research on Technology in Education, 36*(1), 1–14. doi:10.1080/15391523.2003.10782399

Kramer-Dahl, A., & Kwek, D. (2011). 'Reading' the Home and Reading in School: Framing Deficit Constructions as Learning Difficulties in Singapore English Classrooms. In C. Watt-Smith, J. Elkins, & S. Gunn (Eds.), *Multiple Perspectives on Difficulties in Learning Literacy and Numeracy* (pp. 159–178). Australia: Springer. doi:10.1007/978-1-4020-8864-3_7

Krathwohl, D. R. (2002). A revision of Bloom's taxonomy: An overview. *Theory into Practice, 41*(4), 212–218. doi:10.1207/s15430421tip4104_2

Kristin, M. P., Stephen, L. W., Tracy, M. K., Amy, L. C., & Vannatter, A. (2010). Looking back on lessons learned: Gifted adults reflect on their experiences in advanced classes. *Roeper Review, 32*(2), 127–139. doi:10.1080/02783191003587918

Kristin, M. P., Tracy, M. K., Stephen, L. W., Vannatter, A., Claudine, C. H., Shepler, D., & Philip, A. P. (2011/2012). Major life decisions of gifted adults in relation to overall life satisfaction. *Journal for the Education of the Gifted, 34*(6), 817–838. doi:10.1177/0162353211425101

Kulik, J. A., & Kulik, C. C. (1984). Synthesis of research on effects of accelerated instruction. *Educational Leadership, 42*, 84–89.

Kulik, J. A., & Kulik, C. L. C. (1992). Meta-analytic findings on grouping programs. *Gifted Child Quarterly, 36*(2), 73–77. doi:10.1177/001698629203600204

Kumar, M., & Natarajan, U. (2007). A problem-based learning model: Showcasing an educational paradigm shift. *Curriculum Journal, 18*(1), 89–102. doi:10.1080/09585170701292216

Kumon Educational Japan Co. Ltd. (2010). *E-Pencil*. Retrieved from http://www.kumon.ne.jp/eigo/index.html?lid=eigo_002

Kuroishi, N., & Takahashi, M. (2009). A study on collaborations between the cram-school industry and public education: From present circumstances to future proposals. *Educational General Research. Bulletin of Japan Professional School of Education, 2*, 1–14.

Kuutti, K. (1996). Activity theory as a potential framework for human-computer interaction research. In B. Nardi (Ed.), *Context and consciousness: Activity theory and human- computer interaction* (pp. 17–44). Cambridge, MA: MIT Press.

Ladson-Billings, G. (1995). Toward a theory of culturally relevant pedagogy. *American Educational Research Journal, 32*(3), 465–491. doi:10.3102/00028312032003465

Laffey, J. M., Espinosa, L., Moore; J., & Lodree, A. (2003, Summer). Supporting learning and behavior of at-risk young children: Computers in urban education. *Journal of Research on Technology in Education, 35*(4), 441–458. doi:10.1080/15391523.2003.10782394

Lamb, A., & Johnson, L. (2009). The potential, the pitfalls, and the promise of multi-user virtual environments: Getting a second life. *Teacher Librarian, 36*(4), 68–72.

Last Day of Work. (2011). *Plant Tycoon (Verson 1.1.2)*. Retrieved from Apple App Store.

Latz, A. O., Speirs Neumeister, K. L., Adams, C. M., & Pierce, R. L. (2009). Peer coaching to improve classroom differentiation: Perspectives from Project CLUE. *Roeper Review*, *31*(1), 27–39. doi:10.1080/02783190802527356

Lave, J., & Wenger, E. (1991). *Situated learning: Legitimate peripheral participation.* Cambridge, UK: Cambridge University Press. doi:10.1017/CBO9780511815355

Lawless, K. A., & Pellegrino, J. W. (2007). Professional development in integrating technology into teaching and: Knowns, unknowns, and ways to pursue better questions and answers. *Review of Educational Research*, *77*(4), 575–614. doi:10.3102/0034654307309921

Lee, G. Y. (2003). *A study of community-centered cyber education for the gifted children of information science.* (Master's thesis). Gyeongin National University of Education.

Lee, J. H., & Hong, C. E. (2009). Development and validation of teaching-learning model for cyber education of giftedness. *Journal of Gifted/Talented Education*, *19*(1), 116-137.

Lee, J., & Lee, K. S. (2004). A study of e-Learning utilization to support elementary & secondary education. *The Journal of Korean Association of Computer Education*, *7*(5), 71-82.

Lee, K. W. L., Goh, N. K., Chia, L. S., & Wan, Y. K. (2006). Report on Creativity in Science Education. National Institute of Education, Nanyang Technological University.

Lee, Y. J., Kim, Y. S., Lee, E. K., & Kim, J. S. (2012). The evaluation research on gifted education continuity. *Korea Foundation for the Advancement of science & Creativity Report 2011-06.*

Lee, C. D. (2003). Toward a framework for culturally responsive design in multimedia computer environments: Cultural modeling as a case. *Mind, Culture, and Activity*, *10*(1), 42–61. doi:10.1207/S15327884MCA1001_05

Lee, K. W. L. (2001). Fostering Creativity in Science Education. *Review of Educational Research and Advances for Classroom Teachers*, *20*(2), 27–31.

Lee, M. (2007). Spark up the American revolution with math, science, and more: An example of an integrative curriculum unit. *Social Studies*, *98*(4), 159–164. doi:10.3200/TSSS.98.4.159-164

Lee, R. N. F., & Bathmaker, A. M. (2007). The use of English textbooks for teaching English to 'Vocational' students in Singapore secondary schools - a survey of teachers' beliefs. *RELC Journal*, *38*(3), 350–374. doi:10.1177/0033688207085852

Leh, A. S. C. (2000). Teachers' comfort level, confidence, and attitude toward technology at a technology course. In *Proceedings of Society for Information Technology & Teacher Education International Conference 2000.* AACE.

Lennex, L., & Nettleton, K. F. (2010). The Golden Apple: A Quest toward Achievement. In J. Yamamoto, J. Kush, R. Lombard, & C. Hertzog (Eds.), Technology Implementation and Teacher Education: Reflective Models (pp. 124-145). Academic Press. doi:10.4018/978-1-61520-897-5.ch008

LePage, P., Darling-Hammond, L., & Askar, H. (2005). Classroom management. In L. Darling-Hammond, & J. Bransford (Eds.), *Preparing teachers for a changing world: What teachers should learn and be able to do* (pp. 327–357). San Francisco: Jossey-Bass.

Lewis, T. (2006). Design and inquiry: Bases for an accommodation between science and teaching education in the curriculum? *Journal of Research in Science Teaching, 43*(3), 255–281. doi:10.1002/tea.20111

Lewis, T., Barlex, D., & Colin, C. (2007). Investigating interaction between science and design and technology (DandT) in the secondary school - a case study approach. *Research in Science & Technological Education, 25*(1), 37–58. doi:10.1080/02635140601053443

Lim, S. H. S., Lim, C., & Atencio, M. (2013). Understanding the processes behind student designing: Cases from Singapore. *Design and Technology Education: an International Journal, 18*(1), 20–29.

Little, C. A. (2012). Curriculum as motivation for gifted students. *Psychology in the Schools, 49*(7), 695–705. doi:10.1002/pits.21621

Lloyd, M. E. R., & Sullivan, A. (2012). Leaving the profession: The context behind one quality teacher's professional burn out. *Teacher Education Quarterly, 39*(4), 139–162.

Lock, J., & Lock, R. (1993). Revision raps: Elect this musical route to ease the pain in passin' GCSEs! *Journal of Biological Education, 27*(4), 2p. doi:10.1080/00219266.1993.9655342

Lofton, J. (2008). New ideas take flight. *CSLA Journal, 31*(2), 14–15.

Lopez, O. (2006). *Lighting the Flame of Learning for English Language Learners Through the Use of Interactive Whiteboard Technology* (White Paper, Su-2006-01). The Corporation for Public School Education K16. Retrieved from http://extranet.mypromethe−an.com/us/upload/pdf/ELL_WhitePaper.pdf

Lovecky, D. (1994). Exceptionally gifted children: Different minds. *Roeper Review, 17*(2), 116–120. doi:10.1080/02783199409553637

Lyall, M. (2010, July 28). *First ever virtual iPad app for dissecting of frog.* Retrieved from http://www.knowabouthealth.com/first-ever-virtual-ipad-app-for-dissection-of-frog/4557/

Mackin, J. (1996). A creative approach to physics teaching. *Physics Education, 31*(4), 199–202. doi:10.1088/0031-9120/31/4/014

Mahiri, J. (2000). Pop culture pedagogy and the end of school. *Journal of Adolescent & Adult Literacy, 44*(4), 382–394.

Manzo, K. K. (2010). Whiteboards' impact on teaching seen as uneven. *Education Week, 3*(2), 34.

Marland, S. P., Jr. (1972). Education of the gifted and talented: Report to the Congress of the United States by the U.S. Commissioner of Education and background papers submitted to the U.S. Office of Education (2 vols.). Washington, DC: U.S. Government Printing Office. (Government Documents Y4.L 11/2: G36)

Martin, F., Mikhak, B., Resnick, M., Silverman, B., & Berg, R. (2000). To Mindstorms and Beyong: Evolution of a Construction Kit for Magical Machines. In A. Druin, & J. Hendler (Eds.), *Robots for Kids: Exploring New Technologies for Learning* (pp. 9–33). San Diego, CA: Academic Press.

Marvel, J. (2007). Teacher attrition and mobility [electronic resource: results from the 2004-05 teacher follow-up survey / John Marvel ... [et al.]. Washington, DC: National Center for Education Statistics, Institute of Education Sciences, U.S. Department of Education.

Marzano, R. J. (2009). The art and science of teaching/teaching with interactive whiteboards. *Educational Leadership, 67*(3), 80–82.

Maslow, A. (1968). *Toward a psychology of being.* New York: Van Nostrand Reinhold.

Mataric, M. J. (2004). *Robotics Education for All Ages.* Paper presented at the American Association for Artificial Intelligence Spring Symposium on Accessible, Hands-on AI and Robotics Education. Retrieved from http://robotics.usc.edu/~maja/publications/aaaissymp04-edu.pdf

Matsumura, N. (2008). Education to discover true "talent": Special education for gifted students that has damaged children. Tokyo: Minerva Shobo.

Matthews, D. J., & Foster, J. F. (2005). A dynamic scaffolding model of teacher development: The gifted education consultant as catalyst for change. *Gifted Child Quarterly, 49*(3), 222–230. doi:10.1177/001698620504900304

Mayer, B. (2012). Get kids designing with student-created games. *School Library Journal.* Retrieved from http://www.slj.com/2012/08/opinion/the-gaming-life/get-kids-designing-with-student-created-games-the-gaming-life/

Mayer, R. E. (1999). Designing instruction for constructivist learning. In C. M. Reigeluth (Ed.), *Instructional-design theories and models: A new paradigm of instructional technology* (Vol. 2). Mahwah, NJ: Lawrence Erlbaum.

May, R. (1975). *The courage to create.* New York: Norton & Co., Inc.

McCombs, S., & Liu, Y. (2011). Channeling the channel: Can iPad meet the needs of today's m-learner. In M. Koehler & P. Mishra (Eds.), Proceedings of Society for Information Technology & Teacher Education International Conference 2011 (pp. 522–526). Chesapeake, VA: AACE. Retrieved from http://www.editlib.org/p/36322 on 10/28/11

McCormack, V. (2010). Increasing Teacher Candidate Responses through the Application of VoiceThread. *International Journal of Arts and Sciences, 3*(11), 160 – 165. Retrieved from http://openaccesslibrary.org/images/RLN147_Virginia_McCormack.pdf

McCormack, A. J. (1971). Effects of selected teaching methods on creative thinking, self- evaluation, and achievement of studies enrolled in an elementary science education methods course. *Science Education, 55*(3), 301–307. doi:10.1002/sce.3730550309

McCormick, R. (1997). Conceptual and procedural knowledge. *International Journal of Technology and Design Education, 7*(1-2), 141–159. doi:10.1023/A:1008819912213

McGonigal, J. (2011). *Reality is broken: Why games make us better and how they can change the world.* New York: Penguin Press.

Mchugh, R. (2005, October). Synching up with the iKid. *Edutopia, 1*(7), 33-35.

Meadows, M., & Murphy, F. (2004). Using technology in early childhood environments to strengthen cultural connections. *Information Technology in Childhood Education Annual,* 39–47.

Meckstroth, E. (1991, December). *Coping with the sensitivities of gifted children.* Paper presented at the Illinois Gifted Education Conference. Chicago, IL.

Compilation of References

Merchant, G. (2010). 3D virtual worlds as environments for literacy learning. *Educational Research*, *52*(2), 135–150. doi:10.1080/00131881.2010.482739

Mergendoller, J., Markham, T., Ravitz, J., & Larmer, J. (2006). Pervasive management of project based learning. In C. Evertson, & S. Weinstein (Eds.), *Handbook of classroom management: Research, practice, and contemporary issues* (pp. 583–615). Mahwah, NJ: Lawrence Erlbaum.

Metz, S. (2010). Create and Innovate! *Science Teacher (Normal, Ill.)*, *77*(6), 6.

Miller, D. P., Nourbakhsh, I. R., & Sigwart, R. (2008). Robots for Education. In B. Siciliano & O. Khatib (Eds.), Springer Handbook of Rootics (pp. 1283 - 1301). New York, NY: Springer-Verlag New York, LLC.

Milrad, M., & Spikol, D. (2007). Anytime, anywhere learning supported by smart phones: Experiences and results from the MUSIS project. *Journal of Educational Technology & Society*, *10*(4), 62–70.

Mimiduka, H. (2009). Report on additional analyses regarding Japanese students' academic achievement and learning conditions from the 2007 and 2008 surveys. *Ministry of Education, Culture, Sports, Science & Technology in Japan*. Retrieved from http://www.nier.go.jp/07_08tsuikabunsekihouko ku/07_08_tsuikabunseki_houkokusho_3_1. pdf

Ministry of Education (MOE). (2002). *The 1st comprehensive plan for gifted education promotion*. Seoul: Korea Government Printing Office.

Ministry of Education (MOE). (2004). *The master plan of education for excellence*. Author.

Ministry of Education (MOE). (2007). *The 2nd comprehensive plan for gifted education promotion*. Seoul: Korea Government Printing Office.

Ministry of Education and Science Technology (MEST), Korea Education and Research Information Service(KERIS). (2013). 2012 Adapting Education to the Information Age. Seoul, Korea: Author.

Ministry of Education Singapore. (2007). *Website, Science Lower Secondary NT syllabus*. Retrieved January 1, 2013, from http://www.moe.gov.sg/education/syllabuses/sciences/files/science-lower-secondary-nt-2008.pdf

Ministry of Education, Culture, Sports, Science, & Technology in Japan. (2008). *Report on a survey of the actual conditions regarding children's learning activities outside of schools*. Retrieved from http://www.mext.go.jp/b_menu/houdou/20/08/__icsFiles/afieldfile/2009/03/23/1196664.pdf

Ministry of Education, Culture, Sports, Science, and Technology. (2006). Main statement in the diet deliberation about the Fundamental Law of Education revision. Tokyo: MEXT.

Ministry of Education, Culture, Sports, Science, and Technology. (2007). Main report on Diet discussions on revisions to the Fundamental Law of Education. Tokyo: MEXT.

Ministry of Education, Culture, Sports, Science, and Technology. (2008). *Results of the additional analysis of the 2007 nationwide scholarship and learning conditions survey*. Retrieved from http://www.mext.go.jp/a_menu/shotou/gakuryoku-chousa/zenkoku/08020513/001/003.htm

Ministry of Education, Culture, Sports, Science, and Technology. (2012). *Super science high schools reference 1.* Retrieved from http://www.mext.go.jp/b_menu/houdou/24/08/__icsFiles/afieldfile/2012/08/09/1324481_1_1.pdf

Ministry of Education, Culture, Sports, Science, and Technology. (n.d.a). *Welcome to the Fundamental Law of Education data room!* Retrieved from http://www.mext.go.jp/b_menu/kihon/about/004/a004_03.htm

Ministry of Education, Culture, Sports, Science, and Technology. (n.d.b). *Universities implementing grade skipping for university entrance for the 2013 entrance exam.* Retrieved from http://www.mext.go.jp/a_menu/koutou/shikaku/07111318/001/002.htm

Ministry of Education. (2005). Culture, Sports, Science and Technology. In Guidebook for Starting School. Author.

Ministry of Internal Affairs and Communications Statistical Research and Training Institute. (2013). *Statistics of Japan.* Tokyo: Ministry of Internal Affairs and Communications Statistics Bureau.

Ministry of Trade, Industry, and Energy (MOTIE), National IT Industry Promotion Agency (NIPA), Korea Association of Consilience Education (KAOCE). (2013). *2011-2012 e-Learning White Paper.* Author.

Mishra, P., & Koehler, M. J. (2006). Technological pedagogical content knowledge: A framework for teacher knowledge. *Teachers College Record, 108*(6), 1017–1054. doi:10.1111/j.1467-9620.2006.00684.x

Misono, M. (2012). Enhancing the evaluations of science education programs. *Japan Society for Science Education, Annual Meeting Collection of Papers, 36,* 263-264.

Moo, S. N. (1997). Teachers' Perceptions of Normal (Technical) Students' Motivation and Classroom Behaviour. In A.S.C., Chang, S. C. Goh, S.N. Moo & A.Y. Chen (Eds.), Report on Motivation and Classroom Behaviour of Normal Technical Students. Singapore: National Institute of Education, Centre for Educational Research.

Moon, T. R., & Brighton, C. M. (2008). Primary teachers' conceptions of giftedness. *Journal for the Education of the Gifted, 31,* 447–480.

Moravcsik, M. (1981). Creativity in science education. *Science Education, 65*(2), 221–227. doi:10.1002/sce.3730650212

Morisano, D. M., & Shore, B. M. (2010). Can personal goal setting tap the potential of the gifted underachiever? *Roeper Review, 32*(4), 249–258. doi:10.1080/02783193.2010.508156

Morrisette, P. J. (2011). Exploring Student Experiences within the Alternative High School Context. *Canadian Journal of Education, 34*(2), 169–188.

Murata, H. (2013). Preparing for a harsh future – parents who value study: "School lives of junior high and high school students and the 2012 attitude survey. *Hosokenkyu to Chosa, 63*(2), 2–19.

Murcia, K., & Sheffield, R. (2010). Talking about science in interactive whiteboard classrooms. *Journal of Educational Technology, 26*(4), 417–431.

Mutou, T. (2006). Differences between early education and special education for gifted students. *Kyoiku to Igaku, 54*(10), 909–915.

Myers, I. B., & McCaulley, M. H. (1985). *Manual: A guide to the development and use of the Myers-Briggs Type Indicator.* Palo Alto, CA: Consulting Psychologists Press.

Naha, E., Schulman, T., Cox, P. F., Johnston, J., Moranis, R., Frewer, M., & Strassman, M. Buena Vista Home Entertainment (Firm). (2002). Honey, I shrunk the kids. Burbank, CA: Disney DVD.

Nakagawa, A. S. (2010, April 20). *Using Voicethread for professional development: Probeware training for science teachers.* Paper presented at the 15th Annual Technology, Colleges, and Community Worldwide Online Conference. New York, NY.

Nakashika, A. (2010). *Kyoto Scale of Psychological Development 2001.* Retrieved from http://www.prccs.otemon.ac.jp/item/clinic/clinic03_nakashika.pdf

Nakayama, N. (1997). *Intellect, scholastic attainments, and people skills that only parents can develop: Early special education for gifted students so as not to fail in elementary school.* Tokyo: Yosensha.

Nardi, B. A. (1996). Activity theory and human-computer interaction. In B. A. Nardi (Ed.), *Context and Consciousness* (pp. 7–16). Cambridge, MA: The MIT Press.

National Association for Gifted Children & Council of State Directors of Programs for the Gifted. (2011). *State of the states in gifted education 2010–2011.* Washington, DC: NAGC.

National Association for Gifted Children (NAGC). (2010). *Pre-K-Grade 12 gifted programming standards.* Retrieved from http://www.nagc.org/index.aspx?id=546

National Association for Gifted Children Standards in Gifted and Talented Education. (2013). Retrieved from http://www.nagc.org/index2.aspx?id=8188

National Association for Gifted Children. (2014). *Frequently asked questions: Question 2.* Retrieved from http//:www.nagc.org/index2.aspx?id=548

National Commission on Excellence in Education. (1982). *A Nation at Risk: The Imperative for Educational Reform.* Retrieved from http://www.ed.gov/pubs/NatAtRisk/risk.html

National Commission on Teaching and America's Future (NCTAF). (2003). *No dream denied: A pledge to America's children.* Washington, DC: Author.

National Governors Association Center for Best Practices & Council of Chief State School Officers. (2010). *Common Core State Standards for English language arts and literacy in history/social studies, science, and technical subjects.* Washington, DC: Authors.

National Institute of Mental Health. (March, 2014). *Attention deficit hyperactivity disorder.* Retrieved from http://www.nimh.nih.gov/health/publications/attention-deficit- hyperactivity-disorder-easy-to-read/index.shtml

National Mathematics Advisory Panel. (2008). *Chapter 6: Report of the task group on instructional practices.* Retrieved from http://www2.ed.gov/about/bdscomm/list/mathpanel/report/instructional-practices.pdf

National Novel Writing Month. (2012). *Year thirteen: A lucky number in our book.* Retrieved from http://nanowrimo.org/history#year-thirteen

National Research Council (U.S.). (2012). *A framework for K-12 science education: Practices, crosscutting concepts, and core ideas*. Washington, DC: The National Academies Press.

National Research Council. (2012). *A Framework For K-12 Science Education Practices, Crosscutting Concepts, and Core Ideas*. Washington, DC: National Research Council.

National Science Education Standards. (1996). Washington, DC: The National Academies Press.

National Society for the Gifted and Talented (NSGT). (2003). Retrieved from http://www.nsgt.org

Neihart, M., Reis, S. M., Robinson, N. M., & Moon, S. M. (2002). *The social and emotional development of gifted children: What do we know?* Waco, TX: L Prufrock Press.

Nemoto, F., & Ikuta, S. (2010). "Tracing" is "speaking": A student acquiring the happiness of communication using "Sound Pronunciation System"[in Japanese]. *Computers & Education, 28*, 57–60.

Nettleton, K. F., & Lennex, L. (2010). Technodiversity: Lessons learned from a diversity exchange. In N. A. Alias, & S. Hashim (Eds.), *Technology Leadership in Teacher Education: Integrated Solutions and Experiences* (pp. 69–84). Hershey, PA: IGI Publications.

Neumeister, K. S., Adams, C. M., Pierce, R. L., Cassady, J. C., & Dixon, F. A. (2007). Fourth- grade teachers' perceptions of giftedness: Implications for identifying and serving diverse gifted students. *Journal for the Education of the Gifted, 30*, 479–499.

Ng, I. S. P. (2004). Perspectives on streaming, EM3 pupils and literacy: views of participants. (Unpublished B.A. thesis). National Institute of Education, Nanyang Technological University, Singapore. Retrieved from http://hdl.handle.net/10497/2225

Ng, M. (1993). *The Normal (Technical) course. Videorecording. Singapore: Curriculum Development Institute of Singapore*. Singapore: Ministry of Education.

NGSS Lead States. (2013). *Next Generation Science Standards: For States, By States*. Washington, DC: The National Academies Press.

Nichols, A. (2010). VoiceThread and the World War II battle report. *School Library Monthly, 26*(6), 6.

Nickerson, L. (2009). Science Drama. *The School Science Review, 90*(332), 83–89.

Norman, E. (1993). Science for design. *Physics Education, 28*(5), 301–306. doi:10.1088/0031-9120/28/5/010

Nugent, S. A. (2001). Technology and the gifted: Focus, facets, and the future. *Gifted Child Today, 24*(4), 38–45.

O'Brien, E. R., & Curry, J. R. (2009). Systemic Interventions with Alternative School Students: Engaging the Omega Children. *Journal of School Counseling, 7*(24), 1–32.

O'Brien, T. (2011). *Even more brain-powered science; Teaching and learning with discrepant events*. Arlington, VA: National Science Teachers Association.

O'Connell-Ross, P. (1993). *National excellence: A case for developing America's talent*. Washington, DC: U.S. Department of Education, Government Printing Office.

Compilation of References

O'Dell, S. (1960). *Island of the Blue Dolphins*. New York: Houghton-Mifflin.

Oettingen, G., Honig, G., & Gollwitzer, P. M. (2000). Effective self-regulation of goal attainment. *International Journal of Educational Research*, *33*(7-8), 705–732. doi:10.1016/S0883-0355(00)00046-X

Office of Letters and Light Young Writers Program. (2010). *National novel writing month's young novelist workbook: Elementary school* (3rd ed.). Berkeley, CA: Office of Letters and Light.

Office of Letters and Light. (2012a). *For the press*. Retrieved from http://ywp.nanowrimo.org/press

Office of Letters and Light. (2012b). *Lesson plans*. Retrieved from http://ywp.nanowrimo.org/lesson-plans

Ogbu, J. U. (1992). Understanding cultural diversity and learning. *Educational Researcher*, *21*(8), 5–14. doi:10.3102/0013189X021008005

Oki Data Corporation. (2010). *Grid Layouter and Grid Contents Studio*. Retrieved from http://www.okidata.co.jp/solution/gridmark

Olthouse, J. M. (2012). Why I write: What talented creative writers need their teachers to know. *Gifted Child Today*, *35*(2), 116–121. doi:10.1177/1076217512437732

Olthouse, J. M. (2013). Multiliteracies theory and gifted education. *Gifted Child Today*, *36*(4), 246–253. doi:10.1177/1076217513497575

Olthouse, J., & Miller, M. T. (2012). Teaching talented writers with web 2.0 tools. *Teaching Exceptional Children*, *45*(2), 6–14.

Olympus Corporation. (1999). *Scan talk*. Retrieved from http://www.olympus.co.jp/jp/news/1999b/nr990823r300j.cfm

Oppliger, D. (2002). *Using FIRST LEGO League to Enhance Engineering Education and to Increase the Pool of Future Engineering Students (Work in Progress)*. Paper presented at the 32nd ASEE/IEEE Frontiers in Education Conference. Boston, MA. doi:10.1109/FIE.2002.1158731

Organization for Economic Cooperation and Development. (2011). *Education at a glance 2011: OECD indicators*. Retrieved from http://www.oecd.org/edu/eag2011

Ormrod, J. E. (1999). *Human Learning* (3rd ed.). Upper Saddle River, NJ: Prentice Hall.

Ostashewski, N., & Reid, D. (2013). The iPad in the classroom: three implementation cases highlighting pedagogical activities, integrating issues, and teacher professional development strategies. In J. Keengwe (Ed.), *Pedagogical applications and social effects of mobile technology integration* (pp. 25–41). Hershey, PA: IGI Global. doi:10.4018/978-1-4666-2985-1.ch002

Otta, M., & Tavella, M. (2010). Motivation and Engagement in Computer-Based Learning Tasks: Investigating key contributing factors. *World Journal on Educational Technology*, *2*(1), 1–15.

Ottenbreit-Leftwich, A., Glazewski, K., Newby, T., & Ertmer, P. (2010). Teacher value beliefs associated with using technology: Addressing professional and student needs. *Computers & Education*, *55*(3), 1321–1335. doi:10.1016/j.compedu.2010.06.002

Overberg, L. (2014). *Fan fiction reflection*. Course assignment. Used with permission.

Pajares, F. (1996, Winter). Self-efficacy beliefs in academic settings. *Review of Educational Research*, *66*(4), 543–578. doi:10.3102/00346543066004543

Palaniappan, A. K. (2007). Academic Achievement of Groups Formed Based on Creativity and Intelligence. In *Proceedings of the 13th International Conference on Thinking*. Retrieved January 1, 2013, from www.ep.liu.se/ecp/021/vol1/020/exp2107020.pdf

Papert, S. (1993). *Mindstorms - Children, Computers, and Powreful Ideas* (2nd ed.). New York, NY: Basic Books.

Papert, S., & Harel, I. (1991). *Constructionism*. New York, NY: Ablex Publishing Corporation.

Partnership for 21st Century Skills. (2008). *21st Cenutry Skills, Education & Competitiveness Guide – A Resource and Policy Guide*. Retrieved from http://www.p21.org/storage/documents/21st_century_skills_education_and_competitiveness_guide.pdf

Partners, W. (2011). *Sparklefish (Version 2.3)*. Retrieved from Apple App Store.

Pashler, H., McDaniel, M., Rohrer, D., & Bjork, R. (2008). Learning styles: Concepts and evidence. *Psychological Science in the Public Interest*, *9*(3), 105–119.

Patricia, A. H. (2001). Gifted teachers: Facilitators of becoming. *Roeper Review*, *23*(4), 189. doi:10.1080/02783190109554096

Patrick, H., Bangel, N. J., & Jeon, K. (2005). Reconsidering the issue of cooperative learning with gifted students. *Journal for the Education of the Gifted*, *29*(1), 90–108.

Paulson, G. (1987). *Hatchet*. New York: Simon & Shuster.

Pereira, L. Q. (1999). Divergent thinking and the design process. In P. H. Roberts & E. W. L. Norman (Eds.), Proceedings of the International Conference on Design and Technology Educational Research and Curriculum Development (pp. 224–229). Loughborough: Department of Design and Technology, Loughborough University. Retrieved from https://dspace.lboro.ac.uk/dspace-jspui/handle/2134/1403

Periathiruvadi, S., & Rinn, A. (2012). Technology in gifted education: A review of best practices and empirical research. *Journal of Research on Technology in Education*, *45*(2), 153–169. doi:10.1080/15391523.2012.10782601

Perkins, D. N. (1981). *The Mind's Best Work*. Cambridge, MA: Harvard University Press.

Perrone, K. M., Perrone, P. A., Ksiazak, T. M., Wright, S. L., & Jackson, Z. V. (2007). Self-perception of gifts and talents among adults in a longitudinal study of academically talented high-school graduates. *Roeper Review*, *29*(4), 259–264. doi:10.1080/02783190709554420

Petraglia, J. (1998). The real world on a short leash: The (mis)application of constructivism to the design of educational technology. *ETR&D*, *46*(3), 53–65. doi:10.1007/BF02299761

Pewewardy, C. (1993). Culturally responsible pedagogy in action: An American Indian magnet school. In E. Hollins, J. King, & W. Hayman (Eds.), *Teaching diverse populations: Formulating a knowledge base* (pp. 77–92). Albany, NY: State University of New York Press.

Phillips, G. (1984). *Growing hope*. Minneapolis, MN: National Youth Leadership Council.

Piaget, J. (1929). *The Child's Conception of the World*. New York: Harcourt, Brace and Company.

Piaget, J. (1954). *The Construction of Reality in the Child*. New York: Basic Books. doi:10.1037/11168-000

Piechoswki, M. M. (1991). Emotional development and emotional giftedness. In N. Colangelo, & G. Davis (Eds.), *Handbook for Gifted Education* (pp. 285–306). Needham Heights, MA: Allyn & Bacon.

Pinar, W. F. (1994). *Autobiography, politics and sexuality*. New York: Peter Lang Publishing, Inc.

Pinkard, N. (2001). *Lyric reader: Creating intrinsically motivating and culturally responsive reading environments*. Center from the Improvement of Early Reading Achievement (CIERA). Report #1- 013.

Pipho, C. (1998). A "real" teacher shortage. *Phi Delta Kappan*, *80*(3), 181–182.

Pizzini, E. L., Shepardson, D. P., & Abell, S. K. (1989). A rationale for and the development of a problem solving model of instruction in science education. *Science Education*, *73*(5), 523–534. doi:10.1002/sce.3730730502

Pleiss, M. K., & Feldhusen, J. F. (1995). Mentors, role models, and heroes in the lives of gifted children. *Educational Psychologist*, *30*(3), 159–169. doi:10.1207/s15326985ep3003_6

Plucker, J., & Runco, M. A. (1999). Deviance. In Encyclopedia of Creativity. San Diego, CA: Academic.

Polytechnic, N. (2012). *EducationZoo (Singapore Zoo) (Version 1.0.0)*. Retrieved from Apple App Store.

Pransky, K., & Bailey, F. (2003, January). To meet your students where they are, first you have to find them: Working with culturally and linguistically diverse at-risk students. *The Reading Teacher*, *56*(4), 370–383. doi:10.1598/RT.56.4.3

Prensky, M. (2002). The Motivation of Gameplay or, the REAL 21st century learning revolution. *On the Horizon*, *10*(1), 5–11. doi:10.1108/10748120210431349

Prensky, M. (2006). *Don't Bother Me Mom - I'm Learning!* St. Paul, MN: Paragon House.

Prensky, M. (2010). *Teaching digital natives: Partnering for real learning*. Thousand Oaks, CA: Corwin Press.

Preston, C., & Mowbray, L. (2008). Use of SMART boards for teaching, learning and assessment in kindergarten science. *Teaching Science*, *54*(2), 50–53.

Price, E. A. & Harkins, M. (2011). Scaffolding student writing. *Language & Literacy: A Canadian Educational E-Journal*, *13*(1), 14-38.

Project Bright Horizon. (February, 2014). *Gifted characteristics checklist for underrepresented populations*. Retrieved from http://www.cfsd16.org/public/_century/pdf/ProjectBrightHorizonGiftedCharacteristicsChecklist.pdf

Protheroe, N. (2003). Culturally sensitive instruction. Educational Research Service, 1-11.

Puccio, G. (2011). *What is Creativity? Creativity Series 101.* International Center for Studies in Creativity, Buffalo State, University of New York. Retrieved January 1, 2013, from http://www.youtube.com/watch?v=coJ2T0iI0tQ

Purcell, J. H. (1993). The effects of the elimination of gifted and talented programs on participating students and their parents. *Gifted Child Quarterly, 37*(4), 177–178. doi:10.1177/001698629303700407

Ramadas, J. (2009). Visual and spatial modes in science learning. *International Journal of Science Education, 31*(3), 301–318. doi:10.1080/09500690802595763

Ramos, E. (2010). Let us in: Latino under-represented in gifted and talented programs. *Journal of Cultural Diversity, 17*(4), 151–153. PMID:22303650

Ravitz, J. (2009). Summarizing the findings and looking ahead to a new generation of PBL research. *The Interdisciplinary Journal of Problem-Based Learning, 3*(1), 4–11. doi:10.7771/1541-5015.1088

Raviv, D. (2002). Do We Teach Them How to Think? In *Proceedings of the 2002 American Society for Engineering Education Annual Conference and Exposition.* American Society for Engineering Education Session 2630.

Reis, S. M., & McCoach, B. D. (2002). Underachievement in gifted students. In M. Neihart, S. M. Reis, N. M. Robinson, & S. M. Moon (Eds.), *The social and emotional development of gifted children: What do we know?* (pp. 81–91). Waco, TX: Prufrock Press.

Reis, S. M., & Renzulli, J. S. (2004). Current research on the social and emotional development of gifted and talented students: Good news and future possibilities. *Psychology in the Schools, 41*(1), 119–130. doi:10.1002/pits.10144

Reitz, S. (2011, Sept 3). *Many US schools adding iPads, trimming textbooks.* Retrieved from http://news.yahoo.com/many-us-schools-adding-ipads-trimming-text-books-160839908.html

Renzulli, J. S. (1998). *Three Ringed Concept of Giftedness.* Retrieved from http://www.gifted.uconn.edu/sem/semart13.html

Renzulli, J. S., & Reis, S. M. (2002). *The schoolwide enrichment model: Executive summary.* Retrieved from http://www.gifted.uconn.edu/sem/semexec.html

Renzulli, J. (1995). *Building a bridge between gifted education and total school improvement.* Storrs, CT: National Research Center on the Gifted and Talented.

Renzulli, J. S. (1978). What makes giftedness? Re-examining a definition. *Phi Delta Kappan, 60*(1), 180–184, 261.

Renzulli, J. S. (1982). Myth: The gifted constitute 3-5% of the population. *Gifted Child Quarterly, 26*(1), 11–14. doi:10.1177/001698628202600103

Renzulli, J. S. (1994). *Schools for talent development: A practical plan for total school improvement.* Mansfield Center, CT: Creative Learning Press.

Renzulli, J. S. (2012). Reexamining the role of gifted education and talent development for the 21st century: A four-part theoretical approach. *Gifted Child Quarterly*, *56*(3), 150–159. doi:10.1177/0016986212444901

Renzulli, J. S., & Park, S. (2000). Gifted dropouts: The who and the why. *Gifted Child Quarterly*, *44*(4), 261–271. doi:10.1177/001698620004400407

Renzulli, J. S., & Reis, S. M. (1985). *The school wide enrichment model: A comprehensive plan for educational excellence*. Mansfield Center, CT: Creative Learning Press.

Renzulli, J. S., & Reis, S. M. (1991). The reform movement and the quiet crisis in gifted education. *Gifted Child Quarterly*, *35*(1), 26–35. doi:10.1177/001698629103500104

Renzulli, J., & Reis, S. (2007). A technology based resource for challenging gifted and talented students. *Gifted Children*, *2*(1), 14.

Reyes, I. (2010). To Know beyond listening monitoring digital music. *Senses & Society*, *5*(3), 322–338. doi:10.2752/174589210X12753842356043

Rhodes, M. (1961). An analysis of creativity. *Phi Delta Kappan*, *42*(7), 305–310.

Rinn, A. N., & Plucker, J. A. (2004). We recruit them, but then what? The educational and psychological experience of academically talented undergraduates. *Gifted Child Quarterly*, *48*(1), 54–67. doi:10.1177/001698620404800106

Robinson, K. (2006). *Do schools kill creativity?* Paper presented at the Technology, Entertainment and Design (TED) Conference 2006. Retrieved January 1, 2013, from http://www.youtube.com/watch?v=iG9CE55wbtY

Robinson, K. (2006). Schools Kill Creativity. *TED Talk - Ideas worth spreading*. Retrieved from http://www.ted.com/speakers/sir_ken_robinson.html

Robinson, N. M. (2008). The social world of gifted children and youth. In S. Pfeiffer (Ed.), *Handbook of giftedness in children* (pp. 33–52). New York, NY: Springer. doi:10.1007/978-0-387-74401-8_3

Robinson, N. M., Lanzi, R. G., Weinberg, R. A., Ramey, S. L., & Ramey, C. T. (2002). Family factors associated with high academic competence in former Head Start children at third grade. *Gifted Child Quarterly*, *46*(4), 278–290. doi:10.1177/001698620204600404

Rock Liao, H. (2011). *Tiger Cam Lite (Version 1.3)*. Retrieved from Apple App Store.

Rodriguez, L. F. (2009). Dialoguing, cultural capital, and student engagement: Toward a hip-hop pedagogy in the high school and university classroom. *Equity & Excellence in Education*, *42*(1), 20–35. doi:10.1080/10665680802584023

Rogers, Y. (1997, August). *A brief introduction to distributed cognition*. Retrieved from http://mcs.open.ac.uk/yr258/papers/dcog/dcog-brief-intro.pdf

Rogers, C. (2008). A Well-Kept Secret - Classroom Management with Robotics. In M. U. Bers (Ed.), *Blocks to Robots: Learning with Technology in the Early Childhood Classroom* (pp. 48–52). New York, NY: Teachers College Press.

Rogers, C., & Portsmore, M. (2004). Bringing Engineering to Elementary School. *Journal of STEM Education*, *5*(3&4), 17–28.

Rogers, J. J., Lisowski, M., & Rogers, A. A. (2006). Girls, Robots, and Science Education. *Science Scope*, *29*(6), 62–63.

Rogers, K. B. (2002). Grouping the gifted and talented: Questions and answers. *Roeper Review*, *24*(3), 103–107. doi:10.1080/02783190209554140

Rogers, K. B. (2006). *A Menu of options for grouping gifted students*. Waco, TX: Prufrock Press.

Rogers, K. B. (2007). Lessons learned about educating the gifted and talented: A synthesis of the research on educational practice. *Gifted Child Quarterly*, *51*(4), 382–396. doi:10.1177/0016986207306324

Root-One, Inc. (2013). *StoryLines (Version 5.6)*. Retrieved from Apple App Store.

Ross, P. O. (1993, October). *National excellence: A case for developing America's talent*. Washington, DC: U.S. Government Printing Office.

Ryhammar, L., & Brolin, C. (1999). Creativity research: Historical considerations and main lines of development. *Scandinavian Journal of Educational Research*, *43*(3), 259–273. doi:10.1080/0031383990430303

Sage, J., & Steeg, T. (1993). Linking the learning of mathematics, science and technology within key stage 4 of the national curriculum, In *Proceedings of International Conference on Design and Technology Educational Research and Curriculum Development*. Loughborough University of Technology. Retrieved January 1, 2013, from https://dspace.lboro.ac.uk/dspace-jspui/bitstream/2134/1579/3/sage93.pdf

Saito, T. (2007). *"Grade skipping" not increasing for universities*. Retrieved from http://benesse.jp/blog/20071115/p3.html

Sak, U. (2004). Synthesis of research on psychological types of gifted adolescents. *Journal of Secondary Gifted Education*, *15*(2), 70–79.

Salman, K. (2013). *The one world schoolhouse: Innovation from "learning × technology"*. Tokyo: Diamond, Inc.

Sapon-Shevin, M. (2000/2001). Schools fit for all. *Educational Leadership*, *58*(4), 34–39.

Sarquis, J., Sarquis, M., & Williams, J. P. (1995). *Teaching chemistry with TOYS: activities for grades K-9. McGraw-Hill*. Learning Triangle Press.

Sato, Y. (1984). Special education for gifted students from zero years? Solitary child rearing and the baby classroom. *Sekai*, *466*, 225–235.

Saunders, R. (2005). *A comparison study of the academic effect of ability grouping versus heterogeneous grouping in mathematics instruction* (Doctoral dissertation). Arizona State University, Scottsdale, AZ.

Savery, J. R., & Duffy, T. M. (1995). Problem based learning: An instructional model and its constructivist framework. *Educational Technology*, *35*(5), 31–38.

Scarr, S. (1985). An author's frame of mind Review of *Frames of Mind: The Theory of Multiple Intelligences. New Ideas in Psychology*, *3*(1), 95–100. doi:10.1016/0732-118X(85)90056-X

Schillereff, M. (2001). Using inquiry-based science to help gifted students become more self-directed. *Primary Voices K-6*, *10*(1), 28-32.

Schultz, R. A., & Delisle, J. R. (2003). Gifted adolescents. In N. Colangelo, & G. A. Davis (Eds.), *Handbook of Gifted Education* (3rd ed., pp. 483–492). New York: Pearson Education, Inc.

Compilation of References

Schunk, D. H. (1991). Goal setting and self-evaluation: A social cognitive perspective on self-regulation. In M. L. Maehr & P. R. Pintrich (Eds.), Advances in motivation and achievement, (vol. 7, pp. 85-113). Greenwich, CT: JAI Press.

Schunk, D. H., & Swartz, C. W. (1993). Writing strategy instruction with gifted students: Effects of goals and feedback on self-efficacy and skills. *Roeper Review, 15*(4), 225–230. doi:10.1080/02783199309553512

Seigle, D. (2010). *Gifted students & technology: An interview with Del Siegle*. Center for Talented Development. Retrieved from: http://www.ctd.northwestern.edu/resources/displayArticle/?id=158

Seltzer, K., & Bentley, T. (1999). *The Creative Age: Knowledge and Skills for the New Ecomony*. London, UK: Demos.

Ser, D. (2004a). *I really not stupid (Part 1)*. NewsAsia, MediaCorp News. Retrieved January 1, 2013, from http://www.youtube.com/watch?v=HtfomNNKcmI

Ser, D. (2004b). *I really not stupid (Part 2)*. NewsAsia, MediaCorp News. Retrieved January 1, 2013, from: http://www.youtube.com/watch?v=GDx6WbOgKxM

Serpell, R., & Boykin, A. (1994). Cultural dimensions of cognition: A multiplex, dynamic system of constraints and possibilities. In R. J. Sternberg (Ed.), *Thinking and problem solving* (pp. 369–408). San Diego, CA: Academic Press. doi:10.1016/B978-0-08-057299-4.50018-9

Shank, R. C. (1999). Learning by doing. In C. M. Reigeluth (Ed.), *Instructional-design theories and models: A new paradigm of instructional theory* (Vol. 2, pp. 161–181). Malwah, NJ: Lawrence Erlbaum.

Sharkawy, A., Barlex, D., Welch, M., McDuff, J., & Craig, N. (2009). Adapting a Curriculum Unit to Facilitate Interaction Between Technology, Mathematics and Science in the Elementary Classroom: Identifying Relevant Criteria. *Design and Technology Education: An International Journal, 14*(1), 7–20.

Shaunessy, E., & Page, C. (2006). Promoting inquiry in the gifted classroom through GPS and GIS technologies. *Gifted Child Today*. doi:10.4219/gct-2006-11

Shetky, D. H. (1981). A psychiatrist looks at giftedness: The emotional and social development of the gifted child. *Gifted Child Today, 18*, 2–4.

Shneiderman, B. (2003). *Leonardo's laptop: Human needs and the new computing technologies*. Cambridge, MA: MIT Press.

Shukan, B. (2006). Difficulties of special education for gifted students: Survey of 1000 parents; the top three being swimming, English, and piano. *Shukan Bunshun, 48*(34), 146–148.

Shulman, L. S. (1986). Those who understand: Knowledge growth in teaching. *Educational Researcher, 15*(2), 4–14. doi:10.3102/0013189X015002004

Sidawi, M. (2009). Teaching science through designing technology. *International Journal of Technology and Design Education, 19*(3), 269–287. doi:10.1007/s10798-007-9045-1

Siegle, D. (2010). *Gifted Students & Technology: An Interview with Del Siegle*. Retrieved from http://www.ctd.northwestern.edu/resources/displayArticle/?id=158

Siegle, D. (2004). The merging of literacy and technology in the 21st century: A bonus for gifted education. *Gifted Child Today, 27*(2), 32–34.

Siegle, D. (2013). iPads: Intuitive technology for 21st century students. *Gifted Child Today*, *36*(2), 146–150. doi:10.1177/1076217512474983

Siegle, D., & McCoach, D. B. (2003). Factors that differentiate underachieving gifted students from high-achieving gifted students. *Gifted Child Quarterly*, *47*(2), 144–154. doi:10.1177/001698620304700205

Siegle, D., & Mitchell, M. S. (2011). Learning from and learning with technology. In J. VanTassel-Baska, & C. A. Little (Eds.), *Content-based curriculum for high-ability learners* (2nd ed., pp. 347–373). Waco, TX: Prufrock Press.

Silverman, L. K. (2000). The gifted individual. In L.K. Silverman (Ed.), Counseling the Gifted and Talented (pp. 3-28). Denver, CO: Love Publishing Company.

Silverman, L. K. (2014). Characteristics of Giftedness. *Gifted Development Center*. Retrieved from http://www.gifteddevelopment.com/What_is_Gifted/characgt.htm

Silverman, L. K. (1986). Parenting young gifted children. *Journal of Children in Contemporary Society*, *18*(3-4), 73–87. doi:10.1300/J274v18n03_08

Silverman, L. K. (1989). Invisible gifts, invisible handicaps. *Roeper Review*, *12*(1), 37–42. doi:10.1080/02783198909553228

Silverman, L. K. (1994). The moral sensitivity of gifted children and the evolution of society. *Roeper Review*, *17*(2), 110–116. doi:10.1080/02783199409553636

Silverman, L. K. (2000). The gifted individual. In L. K. Silverman (Ed.), *Counseling the Gifted and Talented* (pp. 3–28). Denver, CO: Love Publishing Company.

Singapore Department of Statistics. (2011). *Education*. Retrieved January 1, 2013, from http://www.singstat.gov.sg/pubn/reference/yos11/statsT-education.pdf

SingTeach. (2010). *Science Education for Gifted Learners*. Retrieved from http://singteach.nie.edu.sg/issue24-scienceed/

Sklar, E., & Eguchi, A. (2004). RoboCupJunior - Four Years Later. In *Proceedings of RoboCup-2004: Robot Soccer World Cup VIII*. Academic Press.

Sklar, E., Eguchi, A., & Johnson, J. (2002a). Children's learning from Team Robotics: RoboCupJunior 2001. In *Proceedings of RoboCup-2002: Robot Soccer World Cup VI*. Academic Press.

Sklar, E., Eguchi, A., & Johnson, J. (2002b). *Examining the Team Robotics through RoboCupJunior*. Paper presented at the the Annual Conference of Japan Society for Educational Technology. Nagaoka, Japan.

Sklar, E., Eguchi, A., & Johnson, J. (2003). Scientific Challenge Award: RoboCupJunior - Learning with Educational Robotics. *AI Magazine*, *24*(2), 43–46.

Slater, T. F. (1996). Portfolio assessment strategies for grading first-year university physics students in the USA. *Physics Education*, *31*(5), 329–333. doi:10.1088/0031-9120/31/5/024

Smith, J., & Dobson, E. (2009). Beyond the book: Using VoiceThread in language arts instruction. In T. Bastiaens et al. (Eds.), *Proceedings of World Conference on E-Learning in Corporate, Government, Healthcare, and Higher Education 2009* (pp. 712-715). Chesapeake, VA: AACE.

Smith, K. (2008). Teaching talented writers in the regular classroom. *Gifted Child Today*, *31*(2), 19–26.

Compilation of References

Smutny, J. F. (2001). Creative strategies for teaching language arts to gifted students (K-8) (ERIC Digest E612). Arlington, VA: ERIC Clearinghouse on Disabilities and Gifted Education. Retrieved from http://www.hoagiesgifted.org/eric/e612.html

Speece, S. (1993). National Science Education Standards: How You Can Make a Difference. *The American Biology Teacher*, *55*(5), 265–267. doi:10.2307/4449657

Spendlove, D. (2005). Creativity in education: A review. *Design and Technology Education: An International Journal*, *10*(2), 9–18.

Sprague, D. (2012). Use fan fiction with elementary students. *Learning and Leading with Technology*, *39*(7), 28–29.

Squire, K. (2010). From information to experience: Place-based augmented reality games as a model for learning in a globally networked society. *Teachers College Record*, *112*(10), 2565–2602.

Stahl, S. A. (1999, Fall). Different strokes for different folks? A critique of leanring styles. *American Educator*, *23*(3), 27–31.

Stainback, S., & Stainback, W. (1988). *Conducting a Qualitative Research Study. Understanding and conducting qualitative research*. Reston, VA: Council for Exceptional Children.

Stake, R. E. (1978). The case study method in Social Inquiry. *Educational Researcher*, *7*(2), 5–8. doi:10.3102/0013189X007002005

State of New Jersey Department of Education. (2005). *Curriculum and Instruction - Gifted and Talented Requirements*. Retrieved from http://www.state.nj.us/education/aps/cccs/g_and_t_req.htm

State of New York Department of Education. (2009). *Curriculum and Instruction - Gifted and Talented*. Retrieved from http://www.p12.nysed.gov/ciai/gt/

Steele, C. M. (1997). A threat in the air: How stereotypes shape intellectual identity and performance. *The American Psychologist*, *52*(6), 613–629. doi:10.1037/0003-066X.52.6.613 PMID:9174398

Steele, C. M. (2010). *Whistling Vivaldi and other clues to how stereotypes affect us*. New York, NY: Norton.

Stern, R. (2014, February 19). *Look who's talking now: VoiceThreads are a novel way to spark "classroom" dialogue*. Retrieved from http://www.chicagonow.com/gifted-matters/2014/02/look-whos-talking-now-voicethreads-are-a-novel-way-to-spark-classroom-dialogue/

Sternberg, R. J., Grigorenko, E. L., Ferrari, M., & Clinkenbeard, P. (1999). A triarchic analysis of an aptitude-treatment interaction. *European Journal of Psychological Assessment*, *15*(1), 3-13.

Sternberg, R. J. (1985). *Beyond IQ: A triarchic theory of intelligence*. Cambridge, UK: Cambridge University Press.

Sternberg, R. J. (1994). Comments on Multiple Intelligences. *Theory into Practice*, *95*(4), 561–569.

Sternberg, R. J. (1997). A triarchic view of giftedness: Theory and practice. In N. Coleangelo, & G. A. Davis (Eds.), *Handbook of gifted education* (pp. 43–53). Boston, MA: Allyn and Bacon.

Sternberg, R. J., Nokes, C., Geissler, W., Prince, P., Okatcha, F., Bundy, D. A., & Grigorenke, E. L. (2001). The relationship between academic and practical intelligence: A case study in Kenya. *Intelligence, 29*(5), 401–418. doi:10.1016/S0160-2896(01)00065-4

Stotsky, S. (2006). Who should be accountable for what beginning teachers need to know? *Journal of Teacher Education, 57*(3), 256–268. doi:10.1177/0022487105285561

Stouffer, W. B., Russell, J. S., & Oliva, M. G. (2004). Making the strange familiar: Creativity and the future of engineering education. In *Proceedings of the American Society for Engineering Education Annual Conference and Exposition, Engineering Education Researches New Heights* (pp. 9315-9327). Retrieved January 1, 2013, from: http://www.engr.wisc.edu/cee/faculty/russell_jeffrey/004.pdf

Super Duper Publications. (2013). *Using I and Me Fun Deck (Version 2.1)*. Retrieved from Apple App Store.

Tachibana, T. (1980). The joys of learning for the capable child: Memory that becomes stimulated from being provided with intellectual challenges. *Gekkan Kyoiku no Mori, 5*(4), 48-51.

TAKEN Publishing. (2003). *Tanaka-Binet Intelligence Scale V*. Retrieved from http://www.taken.co.jp/contents/vinet/vinet_top.htm

Teno, K. M. (2000). Cluster grouping elementary gifted students in the regular classroom: A teacher's perspective. *Gifted Child Today, 23*(1), 44–53.

Terasaki, M., Kaifu, T., Muchaku, S., Matsuzaki, Y., & Ishii, K. (1980). What is required now for "special education for gifted students": Conditions for schools to improve "individuality and ability". *Gekkan Kyoiku no Mori, 5*(4), 24-39.

Terman, L. M. (1959). *Genetic studies of genius* (Vol. 5). Stanford, CA: Stanford University Press.

Thompson, C. (2011). A dose of writing reality: Helping students become better writers. *Phi Delta Kappan, 92*(7), 57–61. doi:10.1177/003172171109200712

Thuraisingam, P. (2007). *Engaging the Normal Technical Stream Learner in the English language classroom*. Paper presented at the Redesigning Pedagogy Conference. Singapore.

Tomlinson, C. A. (1997). *The dos and don'ts of instruction: What it means to teach gifted learners well*. Retrieved from http://www.nagc.org/index.aspx?id=659

Tomlinson, C. A., Kaplan, S. N., Renzulli, J. S., Purcell, J. H., Leppien, J. H., Burns, D. E., et al. (2009). The parallel curriculum: A design to develop learner potential and challenge advanced learners (2nd ed.). Thousand Oaks, CA: Corwin Press.

Tomlinson, C. A. (1999). *The differentiated classroom: Responding to the needs of all learners*. Alexandria, VA: The Association for Supervision and Curriculum Development.

Tomlinson, C. A. (2001). *How to differentiate instruction in mixed-ability classrooms* (2nd ed.). Alexandria, VA: ASCD.

Compilation of References

Tomlinson, C. A. (2005). Quality curriculum and instruction for highly able students. *Theory into Practice*, *44*(2), 160–166. doi:10.1207/s15430421tip4402_10

Tomlinson, C. A., & Imbeau, M. B. (2010). *Leading and managing the differentiated classroom*. Alexandria, VA: ASCD.

Tomlinson, C. A., Kaplan, S. N., Renzulli, J. S., Purcell, J., Leppien, J., & Burns, D. (2002). *The parallel curriculum*. Thousand Oaks, CA: Corwin Press, Inc.

Tomlinson, C. A., & Moon, T. R. (2013). *Assessment and student success in a differentiated classroom*. Alexandria, VA: ASCD.

Tomlinson, C., Kaplan, S. N., Renzulli, J. S., Purcell, J., Leppien, J., & Burns, D. (2002). *The Parallel Curriculum*. Thousand Sands, CA: Corwin Press, Inc.

Torrance, E. P. (1966). *The Torrance Tests of Creative Thinking-Norms-Technical Manual Research Edition-Verbal Tests, Forms A and B-Figural Tests, Forms A and B*. Princeton, NJ: Personnel Press.

Torrance, E. P. (1974). *The Torrance Tests of Creative Thinking-Norms-Technical Manual Research Edition-Verbal Tests, Forms A and B- Figural Tests, Forms A and B*. Princeton, NJ: Personnel Press.

Torrance, E. P. (1987). Teaching for Creativity. In S. Isaksen (Ed.), *Frontiers of Creativity Research: Beyond the Basics* (pp. 189–215). Buffalo, NY: Bearly Limited.

Treffinger, D. J. (1978). Guidelines for encouraging independence and self-direction among gifted students. *The Journal of Creative Behavior*, *12*(1), 14–20. doi:10.1002/j.2162-6057.1978.tb00155.x

Trumbo, J. (2006). Making science visible: Visual literacy in science communication. In L. Pauwels (Ed.), *Visual culture of science: Re-thinking representational practices in knowledge building and science communication*. Dartmouth College Press, University Press of New England.

Truta, F. (2011). *3D iPad 'textbooks' now available from Kno*. Retrieved from http://news.softpedia.com/news/3D-iPad-Text-books-Now-Available-from-Kno-217950.shtml

Tucker, B. (2012). The flipped classroom. *Education Next*, *12*(1), 82–83.

Tugend, A. (2011). *The Role of Mistake in the Classroom*. Retrieved from http://www.edutopia.org/blog/benefits-mistakes-classroom-alina-tugend

U. S. Department of Education, National Center for Education Statistics. (2012). *The condition of education 2012 (NCES 2012-071)*. Washington, DC: U. S. Government Printing Office.

U. S. Department of Education. (2010). *Transforming American education: Learning powered by technology*. Retrieved from http://www.ed.gov/sites/default/files/netp2010.pdf

U.S. Department of Commerce Census Bureau. (2014). *(Lake) County, Kentucky State and County QuickFacts* [Data file]. Retrieved from http://quickfacts.census.gov/qfd/states/21/21205.html

U.S. Department of Education, Office of Planning, Evaluation, and Policy Development. (2010). *Evaluation of evidence-based practices in online learning: A meta-analysis and review of online learning studies (ED-04-0040)*. Washington, DC: U. S. Government Printing Office.

U.S. Department of Education. (1993). *National excellence: A case for developing America's talent.* Washington, DC: U.S. Government Printing Office.

University of Plymouth. (2006). *Distance education: Why distance learning?* Retrieved from http://www.plymouth.ac.uk/distance-learning

Vallis, K., & Williamson, P. (2009). Build your own board. *Learning and Leading with Technology, 36*(9), 18–20.

Van Tassel-Baska, J. L. (Ed.). (2008). *Alternative assessments with gifted and talented students.* Waco, TX: Prufrock Press.

VanTassel-Baska, J., & Stambaugh, T. (2007). *Overlooked gems: A national perspective on low- income promising learners.* Retrieved from http://www.nagc.org/index.aspx?id=17194

VanTassel-Baska, J. (2005). Gifted programs and services: What are the nonnegotiables? *Theory into Practice, 44*(2), 90–97. doi:10.1207/s15430421tip4402_3

VanTassel-Baska, J. (2010). *Patterns and profiles of low income gifted learners.* Waco, TX: Pufrock Press.

Vaughn, V. L., Feldhusen, J. F., & Asher, J. W. (1991). Meta-analysis and review of research on pull-out programs in gifted education. *Gifted Child Quarterly, 35*(2), 92–98. doi:10.1177/001698629103500208

Vernon, P. E. (1989). The nature-nurture problem in creativity. In J.A. Glover, R.R. Ronning, & C.R. Reynolds (Eds.), Handbook of creativity: Perspectives on individual differences. Plenum Press.

Viadero, D. (1995). Special Programs Found to Benefit Gifted Students. *Education Week.* Retrieved from http://www.edweek.org/ew/articles/1995/04/05/28gift.h14.html

Vialle, W., Ashton, T., Carlton, G., & Rankin, F. (2001). Acceleration: A coat of many colours. *Roeper Review, 24*(1), 14–19. doi:10.1080/02783190109554119

Vygotsky, L. S. (1978). *Mind in society: The development of higher psychological processes* (M. Cole, V. John-Steiner, S. Scribner, & E. Souberman, Eds.). Cambridge, MA: Harvard University Press.

Vygotsky, L. S. (1981). The genesis of higher mental functions. In J. V. Wertsch (Ed.), *The concept of activity in Soviet psychology.* White Plains, NY: M. Sharpe.

Wagner, T. (2012). *Creating Innovators – The Making of Young People Who Will Change the World.* New York, NY: Scribner.

Wallace, R. M. (2002, May). *Technology and science teaching: A new kind of knowledge.* Paper presented at the TIME conference. Battle Creek, MI. Retrieved from http://www.msu.edu/course/cep/953/readings/Wallace-TimeFinal.pdf

Wardle. (2009). Creativity in science. *School Science Review, 90,* 332.

Warne, W. T., Anderson, B., & Johnson, A. O. (2013, December01). The impact of race and ethnicity on the identification processes for giftedness in Utah. *Journal for the Education of the Gifted, 36*(4), 487–508. doi:10.1177/0162353213506065

Compilation of References

Warwick, P., Mercer, N., Kershner, R., & Staarman, J. K. (2010). In the mind and in the technology: The vicarious presence of the teacher in pupil's learning of science in collaborative group activity at the interactive whiteboard. *Computers & Education*, *55*(1), 350–362. doi:10.1016/j.compedu.2010.02.001

Washton, N. S. (1971). Creativity in science teaching. *Science Education*, *55*(2), 147–150. doi:10.1002/sce.3730550208

Waterhouse, L. (2006). Multiple Intelligences, the Mozart Effect, and Emotional Intelligence: A critical review. *Educational Psychologist*, *41*(4), 207–225. doi:10.1207/s15326985ep4104_1

Watson, A. (2012). NaNoWriMo in the AcadLib: A case study of national novel writing month activities in an academic library. *Public Services Quarterly*, *8*(2), 136–145. doi:10.1080/15228959.2012.675273

Weber, C. L., & Smith, D. (2010). Meeting the Needs of Gifted Students through Online Programs. *Distance Learning For Educators, Trainers, and Leaders*, *7*(2), 43–50.

Weir, L. (2008). VoiceThread extends the classroom with interactive multimedia albums. *Edutopia*. Retrieved from http://www.edutopia.org/voicethread-interactive-multimedia-albums

Welch, M., & Barlex, D. (2004). *Portfolios in design and technology education: investigating differing views*. Paper presented in DATA International Research Conference 2004. Retrieved from https://dspace.lboro.ac.uk/dspace-jspui/handle/2134/2864

West, R. W. (1981). A case against the core. *The School Science Review*, *63*(223), 226–236.

West, T. (1997). *In the Mind's Eye: Visual Thinkers, Gifted People with Dyslexia and Other Learning Difficulties, Computer Images and the Ironies of Creativity*. Amherst, NY: Prometheus Books.

Whale, S., Fisher, J., & Valenzuela, F. R. (2012). Promoting engagement and interaction through a technology supported learning activity. In *Proceedings of Ascilite Conference*. ASCILITE.

White, W. F. (1990). Divergent thinking vs. convergent thinking—a GT anomaly. *Education*, *111*, 208–213.

Wiebe, E. N., Clark, A. C., & Hasse, E. V. (2001). Scientific Visualization: Linking science and technology education through graphic communications. *The Journal of Design and Technology Education*, *6*(1), 40–47.

Williams, F. (1972). *Identifying and measuring creative potential* (Vol. 1). Educational Publications.

Winebrenner, S., & Devlin, B. (2001). *Cluster grouping of gifted students: How to provide full-time services on a part-time budget*. Eric Digest E538. www.ericec.org

Winebrenner, S. (2001). *Teaching Gifted Kids in the Regular Classroom*. Minneapolis, MN: Free Spirit Publishing.

Wood, P. F. (2008). Reading instruction with gifted and talented readers: A series of unfortunate events or a sequence of auspicious results? *Gifted Child Today*, *31*(3), 16–25.

World Book, Inc. (2012). *World Book's World of Animals (FREE Lite Edition) (Version 1.1.2)*. Retrieved from Apple App Store.

Wu, H., Lee, S., Chang, H., & Liang, J. (2013). Current status, opportunities and challenges of augmented reality in education. *Computers & Education*, *62*, 41–49. doi:10.1016/j.compedu.2012.10.024

Yamamoto, N. (1997). Grade skipping, skipping a grade for university entrance, and special education for gifted students: Current conditions in eight countries (or how an increasing number of young Japanese mothers are educating "geniuses"). *Sapio*, *9*(10), 116–117.

Yamasaki, H. (1980). "Special education for gifted students" beginning with Tanigaki's comments: Troubled feelings in the Ministry of Education with the Japanese teachers' union declaring its opposition. *Gekkan Kyoiku no Mori, 5*(4), 40-47.

Yin, R. K. (1989). *Case study research: Design and methods*. Beverly Hills, CA: Sage.

Ylvis. (2013). What Does the Fox Say?. *The Fox*. Parlophone Music.

York, S. (1991). *Roots and wings: Affirming culture in early childhood programs*. St. Paul, MN: Redleaf Press.

Zilmich, S. L., et al. (2012). *Using Technology in the Gifted and Talented Education Classrooms: The teacher's perspective*. (Doctoral dissertation). Retrieved from http://acumen.lib.ua.edu/content/u0015/0000001/0000903/u0015_0000001_0000903.pdf

Zorigian, K. A. (2009). *The effects of web-based publishing on students' reading motivation*. The University of North Carolina at Chapel Hill. ProQuest Dissertations and Theses. Retrieved from http://search.proquest.com/docview/304963123?accountid=12553

Zubrowski, B. (2002). Integrating science into Design Technology projects: Using a standard model in the design process. *Journal of Technology Education*, *13*(2), 48–67.

Zurita, G., & Nussbaum, M. (2007). A conceptual framework based on activity theory for mobile CSCL. *British Journal of Educational Technology*, *38*(2), 211–235. doi:10.1111/j.1467-8535.2006.00580.x

Zurmuehlen, M. (1990). *Studio art: Praxis, symbol, presence*. Reston, VA: National Art Education Association.

Zyngier, D. (2004, August). Putting young people at the center of the discussion: A review. *Primary and Middle Years Educator*, *2*(2), 3–11.

About the Contributors

Lesia Lennex received her EdD in Curriculum and Instruction from the University of Tennessee, Knoxville. She is a Professor of Education in the department of Middle Grades and Secondary Education at Morehead State University, Morehead, Kentucky. Dr. Lennex holds degrees in biology, anthropology, and curriculum and instruction. She researches, presents, and publishes in technology issues and integration for P-16 schools, NCATE online exhibit rooms, biology curriculum, and ethnobotany. Dr. Lennex was the Chair of Information Technology Education SIG for the Society for Information Technology and Teacher Education (SITE) 2008-2014 and an Adron Doran Fellow investigating 3D in P20 schools, 2009-2010. She was Distinguished Researcher 2012-2013 for Morehead State University. Dr. Lennex is a former high school teacher of biology, chemistry, physics, and ecology.

Kimberely Fletcher Nettleton has taught at both the middle and elementary school and served as a principal at a K-8 school before becoming an Assistant Professor in the Early Childhood, Elementary, and Special Education Department at Morehead State University. She is a firm believer in the healing power of chocolate. She is the Coordinator of the Professional Development School at Morehead. She received her BA from the University of Kentucky, an MA in elementary education from Georgetown College, an MA in School Administration from Morehead State University, and an EdD Curriculum and Instruction at the University of Kentucky.

* * *

Nazir Amir teaches in Greenview Secondary School in Singapore. He graduated with a Bachelor of Engineering (Hons) from the University of Surrey in the UK, and obtained his PhD from the National Institute of Education, Nanyang Technological University (NIE/NTU) in Singapore. Through action-research, Dr. Nazir has developed feasible classroom instructional approaches to present science content and foster creativity and inventiveness in ways that appeal to students in both science and Design & Technology (D&T) lessons. He has presented the instructional approaches and findings from his action-research work in peer-reviewed international journals, book chapters, conferences, and through conducting hands-on workshops for science teachers and university students at local and international platforms. Dr. Nazir was recently awarded the President's Award for Teachers in Singapore. Other teaching awards he has received include the 'Dean's Commendation for Research' by NTU, and the title 'Fellow of the Academy of Singapore Teachers' by the Singapore Ministry of Education for his contributions to the professional development of teachers.

Sangjin An, MEd, received his degree from the Korea National University of Education. Professional interests include programming education, computational thinking, learning science, and distance learning.

Judith Bazler is a Full Professor of Science Education at Monmouth University in West Long Branch, New Jersey, where she teaches both graduate and undergraduate students in elementary, middle level, and secondary science methods. Prior to Monmouth, she worked at Lehigh University as an Associate Professor and was the founder and CEO of the SMART Discovery Center, a hands-on science museum located in the former Bethlehem Steel Building. Her research interests range from a national study on NCATE accreditation in Science to her current research on App evaluation process for science and mathematics classes.

Jennifer Beasley is currently an Assistant Professor in Curriculum and Instruction at the University of Arkansas where she teaches courses in the Masters of Arts in Teaching program. Her professional contributions include serving as a regular columnist for the National Association for Gifted Children's publication Teaching for High Potential as well as Chair for the Curriculum Studies Network. Her research interests include: student engagement, teacher efficacy, curriculum design, and differentiated instruction.

Nancye Blair Black is an award-winning educator, speaker, author, and consultant who promotes dignity-driven educational practices that maximize each step of a child's developmental journey. Her accomplishments as an educational change agent have garnered her recognition as an International Society for Technology in Education (ISTE) Emerging Leader, PBS Teachers Innovation Award-winner, and featured educator in magazines, books, radio and television. Black currently serves as a school board member for the Lakeland Montessori Schools in Lakeland, FL; serves as President-elect for the Florida Society for Technology in Education (FSTE); chairs ISTE's Special Interest Group for 3D in Education (SIG3D); consults on several major education projects; and presents at conferences across the country. She is completing her graduate work in Computing in Education at Teachers College, Columbia University. Connect with Nancye Blair Black at www.nancyeblack.com.

Emily Bodenlos is a 2014 graduate in Elementary Education at Morehead State University. She is an Honors student and Undergraduate Research Fellow who has been researching 3D technologies in education for three years. She has presented research at the Mid-South Educational Research Association and International Society for Technology in Education conferences in 2012. Emily is passionate about the use of technology in education and looks forward to implementing technology in her own classroom.

Jeongwon Choi, MEd, has recently published (2013) The effects of gifted education on school achievements and academic skill in the *Journal of the Korea Society of Computer and Information,* and An analysis of the effectiveness of informatics gifted education in the *Korean Journal of Teacher Education.* Professional interests include computational thinking, learning science, distance learning, and puzzle-based learning.

Geri Collins has been an educator for the past 20 years. First in public education as a middle school teacher and currently as an Assistant Professor of Education in the graduate program of Tift College of Education, Mercer University. She received her doctorate in Social Studies Education at the University of Georgia with a focus on historical empathy as it relates to the learning process. Her research interests involve middle grades education, teaching with technology and social studies, which have all been topics of recent presentations locally and nationally.

Chris Deason is a Course Director (Associate Professor) at Full Sail University in Winter Park, Florida since 2008 where he teaches two courses in the Instructional Design and Technology Master of Science Program. These courses include *Instructional Design and Evaluation* and *Digital Media and Learning Applications.* Dr. Deason's research and writing interests include digital audio workstation-based hip-hop pedagogy, multimedia applications for teaching and learning, and uses of collaborative Web2.0 software for pedagogy. Prior to Full Sail Dr. Deason taught United States History and World History in Lubbock, Texas for eleven years as he worked on his Master's Degree and Doctorate Degree in the field of Educational Instructional Technology at Texas Tech University. He is happily married to his beautiful and supportive wife Kristi. They are raising their three girls Ariah, Tiva, and Julia in beautiful Orlando, Florida. Dr. Deason enjoys composing country songs, composing geo-political metal rap, skateboarding, and producing the Central Florida

Gardening Show with his family. The URL to his gardening show is http://www.youtube.com/user/CentralFlaGardening.

Amy Eguchi is an Associate Professor of Education at Bloomfield College in New Jersey, USA. She holds her MA in Child Development from Pacific Oaks College, EdM in Education from Harvard Graduate School of Education, and PhD in Education from the University of Cambridge and has an extensive teaching experience in educational robotics both with students and teachers in K-12 setting. She also teaches educational robotics to undergraduates. In addition, she runs a competitive robotics after school team at The School at Columbia University. She has been involved in RoboCupJunior, an educational robotics competition, since 2000, as the technical committee and organizing committee members, as well as the co-chair and general chair, in international, national, and local levels. In addition, she is a Vice President of RoboCup Federation representing RoboCupJunior and a member of the RoboCup Federation Board of Trustees. In addition, she has been involved in several international collaboration educational robotics projects including the CoSpace educational robotics projects with the Advanced Robotics and Intelligent Control Centre (ARICC) at Singapore Polytechnic, Singapore.

Rebecca M. Giles is a Professor of Education at the University of South Alabama in Mobile, AL where she serves as coordinator for the K-6 Teacher Education (BS), Early Childhood Studies (BS), Elementary (MEd and EdS), and Early Childhood Education (MEd and EdS) programs. Her teaching responsibilities include early childhood and language/literacy courses along with internship supervision. She has a Master's Degree from the University of Texas at Austin and a Doctorate of Philosophy in Curriculum and Instruction from the University of Southern Mississippi. Dr. Giles has spoken and published widely on a variety of topics related to teacher preparation and early childhood education and is co-author of *Write Now! Publishing with Young Authors, PreK- Grade 2* (Heinemann, 2007).

Letitia Graybill is Lecturer in education at Monmouth University where she instructs graduate as well a undergraduate students in methods of teaching science in the elementary and middle schools. Dr. Graybill had a long career in the New Jersey Public Schools prior to her work at Monmouth. In the public schools she supervised and taught science and mathematics. She retired from the New Jersey public school as Assistant Superintendent in charge of curriculum and personnel K-12.

Jeffrey Hall is an Assistant Professor in the Tift College of Education at Mercer University in Atlanta, Georgia. He is a former high school mathematics teacher, and currently teaches graduate courses in mathematics content, middle grades/secondary mathematics pedagogy, research methods, and assessment. His primary research interests include educational technology and mathematics education.

Mieko Horiguchi is an Associate Professor in the Department of Domestic Science at Otsuma Women's University, Japan. She studies and researches biochemicals on the promotion of health education focusing on anti-fatigue as well as practices development and its application of new tools for nurturing five senses related to nutrition. She took her bachelor's degree of dietitian at Otsuma Women's University and then took her doctor's degree of biological environment control at Tokyo University of Agriculture Graduate School. She has been in charge from 2000 of nutrition-related subjects and nurture of nutritionists. She organizes the volunteer circle to promote "Food and Nutrition Education" for the children and parents. Her fundamental principle is to nurture happiness through diet and to promote protection and inheritance of Japanese food culture, conducting various voluntary events relevant to food, nutrition, and health.

Shigeru Ikuta is a Professor at Otsuma Women's University, Japan, He is an education technologist, teacher educator in Science, and special educator with a focus on student learning and development on the basis of communication aids. He completed his graduate work and earned a doctorate in science at Tohoku University in Sendai, Japan. He had been working as a Professor of Computation Chemistry at Tokyo Metropolitan University for twenty-nine years and is honored to be an Emeritus Professor. He moved to University of Tsukuba and has started collaborative works with schoolteachers, affiliated with the University. He has been conducting many school activities in cooperation with the schoolteachers for more than nine years using original handmade teaching materials with dot codes and electronic books with Media Overlays in supporting the students both at the special needs and general schools.

Marcia B. Imbeau is currently a Professor in the department of curriculum and instruction where she teaches and directs the gifted and talented education program and teaches in the Master of Arts [MAT] program. She is actively involved with University/Public School Partnerships and teaches in a local school as a university liaison. Her professional experience includes serving as a field researcher for the National Research Center on the Gifted and Talented, teaching in the regular classroom, teaching in programs for the gifted, and coordinating university-based and Saturday programs for advanced learners. Imbeau has been a board member for the National Association for Gifted Children and has served as a Governor At-Large for the Council for Exceptional Children – The Association for the Gifted Division. Her research interests include differentiated instruction, curriculum development, gifted education, pre-service teacher education, student engagement, and action research.

Mikiko Kasai is a teacher at the School for Special Needs Education, Hirosaki University, Japan. She started as a schoolteacher at Aomori Prefecture School for the Blind. She moved to the present workplace via School for the Deaf, School for the Physically Handicapped, and School for the Children with Health Impairments. She is now the chief of junior elementary division, takes charge of the subjects of Japanese, Math, and the "Period of Group Movement," and studies how to promote the developments of recognition and techniques for the students with Mentally Challenged. She has been doing co-research works with Professor Shigeru Ikuta for more than four years, and has been creating the original handmade contents with new dot codes and electronic books with Media Overlays to promote the students' reading and joining abilities.

YoungJun Lee received his PhD in computer science from the University of Minnesota, Minneapolis, in 1994. He is currently a Professor in the Department of Computer Education and a director of Educational Information Institute, Korea National University of Education, Chungbuk, Korea. His research interests include intelligent systems, learning science, and technology education.

Noriyuki Matsunami completed his PhD at Tokyo Metropolitan University (TMU). He specializes in educational technology and is interested in methodologies of educational practice research development and the evaluation of information education at elementary schools. He is also well versed in school administration and elementary school education due to both his experiences as a supervisor of school education at the board of education in a ward in Tokyo and his experience as a teacher and curriculum coordinator at a public elementary school in Tokyo. He is a member of the Japan Society for Educational Technology, the Japanese Society for Science Education, and the Association for the Advancement of Computing in Education (AACE).

Diane Morton, MS Education, Director, The School for Young Children at the University of Saint Joseph, West Hartford, CT 06117 USA, is the former director at The School for Young Children at the University of Saint Joseph providing quality preschool services to over 100 families per year. She supervised 18 teachers and staff members. She has 13 years of experience in Administration of Early Care and Education programs. Ms. Morton was founder of Village Green Nursery School, a small community school located in Southington, CT. She has five years of experience at the higher education level developing courses, and teaching and advising students in her role as program coordinator for early childhood education at a local community college. Diane holds a master's degree in Mathematics Education and a bachelor's degree in Early Childhood Education both from Central Connecticut State University. She presented various workshops for early childhood education professionals throughout the State in the area of mathematics, early literacy, appropriate art experiences, and general program development.

Masahiro Nagai completed his PhD at the Tokyo Institute of Technology (TIT). He now serves as vice director at the Tokyo Metropolitan University (TMU) library and academic information center while also serving as a professor at the TMU's university education center. He specializes in educational technology and is interested in research methodologies on educational practice and development as well as methodologies on the evaluation of information education in Post-secondary institutions. He is also well versed in junior high school education because he was a mathematics teacher at schools in Chiba prefecture, Japan. He is a member of the Japan Society for Educational Technology, the Japanese Society for Science Education, and the Association for the Advancement of Computing in Education (AACE).

Fumio Nemoto is a teacher at the School for the Mentally Challenged at Otsuka, University of Tsukuba, Japan. He graduated in Department of Education, Faculty of Literature, Toyo University. He started as a part-time schoolteacher at Seibi Special Needs School, Suginami-ku, Tokyo, and moved to School for the Mentally Challenged at Otsuka, University of Tsukuba. He is the chief of senior high school division. He has developed many handmade teaching aids and tools to support individual needs and desires of each student. He has been conducting many school activities using communication aids and original handmade teaching materials with dot codes. He wants every student with disabilities to express his/her thoughts and feelings to others. He has been collaborating with Professor Shigeru Ikuta, Otsuma Women's University for more than eight years.

Masaki Ohtaka is a teacher at the Takashima Special Needs Education School, Japan. He graduated in Department of Special Needs Education, Faculty of Education, Tokyo Gakugei University. After working as one of the staffs of after school activities for special needs students for two years, he became a special needs schoolteacher at Shinjuku-ku, Tokyo. He is now working in a class for the students with autism. His major research field is "Teaching Method for the students with the perception ability of one-, two-, and three-year-old" in a cognitive assessment. He has been developing various varieties of handmade teaching aids for each student with an independent need and desire. He is an author of *Instruction and Handmade Teaching Aids for the Special Needs Students before Learning Characters and Numbers* (Meijitosho

Shuppan Co., 2010) and *Instruction and Handmade Teaching Aids for the Daily Life of the Special Needs Students* (Meijitosho Shuppan Co., 2014).

Jeanne Petsch has been working with pre-service art teachers in university settings for 20 years. This work includes extensive fieldwork in P-12 schools, alternative schools and community centers in the US and in Russia. Her research, involving the study of creativity and human development, has been published and presented in state, national and international publications and venues. She also continues to create and exhibit her artwork, understanding that to teach art meaningfully, she must experience art meaningfully. Her recent artistic explorations are in encaustic painting and collage. Petsch received a BA from Iowa State University in graphic design, an MA from the University of Northern Iowa in painting, an MAT from the University of South Carolina in Art Education, and a PhD from Florida State University in Art Education. She currently teaches Art Education at Morehead State University in Morehead, Kentucky.

Vanessa Dodo Seriki is an Assistant Professor of Teacher Education (Science Education). She teaches undergraduate and graduate courses in curriculum and instruction and teacher education, as well as a graduate course in studies in language and culture. Dr. Dodo Seriki's research interests include the use of culturally relevant pedagogy and cultural modeling in science education; the intersectionality of race and gender in education (including p-12, higher education, teacher education, and science education) as seen through the lens of critical race theory; effective teaching of science to students with exceptionalities; and accessibility of STEM education by all learners, particularly those underrepresented in the STEM pipeline.

Beverly Dixon Shaklee is a full-professor of Curriculum and Instruction as well as Director of the Division for Advanced Professional Teacher Development and International Education at George Mason University. She has taught in elementary and gifted child education, served on the board for the National Association for Gifted Children and conducted research on underserved populations of gifted children. She has numerous publications and presentations in gifted and international education.

Edward L. Shaw, Jr. is a Professor of Elementary Science Education at the University of South Alabama. His teaching responsibilities include elementary science education courses and curriculum development courses. He has a Master's Degree in Elementary Education from Columbus State University and a Doctorate in Science Education from The University of Georgia. Dr. Shaw has presented and published internationally and was selected as one of the Top 50 Professors in the first 50 years of the University of South Alabama.

Debra Sprague is an Associate Professor in the College of Education and Human Development at George Mason University. She is assigned to the Elementary Education Program and teaches courses that focus on technology integration and on differentiation. Her research interest focuses on the use of emerging technology to support teaching and learning. Dr. Sprague has experience teaching Special Education and English-As-a-Second Language on the Navajo Reservation in New Mexico. She served as the editor for the *Journal of Technology and Teacher Education* for ten years.

Douglas Steel is an Assistant Professor of Management Information Systems in the School of Business at the University of Houston-Clear Lake. He and his colleagues focus on the use of computer and information technology to solve business problems. Research interests include technology adoption, virtual teams, and computer self-efficacy.

Bridget Taylor has been an educator for 15 years, including 5 years as a gifted education teacher and 8 years as a teacher of middle level students. She currently teaches middle school language arts. She earned her master's degree in Educational Psychology with an emphasis on gifted and talented education at The University of Georgia. She is currently pursuing her doctorate in Curriculum and Instruction at Mercer University.

Cletus Turner is currently a sixth grade teacher at a rural middle school. He taught grades 6-8 at the same school for all of professional career as a teacher. He graduated with his BA from Berea College, an MA in Reading/Writing Endorsement from Morehead State University, and an EdS in Curriculum and Instruction from Morehead State University. He loves teaching students and cannot see doing anything else with his life.

Meta Van Sickle is a Full Professor at the College of Charleston. She earned her PhD is Science Education at the University of South Florida. She is the Department Chair for Teacher Education and teaches science methods. She is a past program director for the MEd in Science and Math for Teachers Program. Her major research interest is studying the ethics of care in science education and science for all. More broadly, she studies issues of race, class, and gender as it relates to policy and practice in schooling.

Kristen Waller is the Gifted and Talented teacher for Raceland-Worthington Independent Schools in Raceland, Kentucky. She has a Bachelor's Degree in Middle School Education from Ohio University Southern and a Master's Degree in School

Administration from the University of the Cumberlands. She is currently attending Morehead State University, because she loves everything about education and considers herself a professional student. She is married to her best friend and they have three children.

Jana Willis is an Associate Professor in the School of Education Instructional Technology and Curriculum and Instruction programs at University of Houston-Clear Lake. She designs, develops, and implements online and hybrid courses. She works with pre-service/in-service teachers on effective use of technology in the PK-12 curriculum. Dr. Willis works with a local school district's gifted and talented program, teaching 4th and 5th grade gifted students how to design and develop video games. Research interests include digital stories, technology integration, electronic portfolios, self-efficacy, and project/problem based learning. Scholarly works include international, national, and regional refereed/ non-refereed journal articles, edited book chapters, and professional conference presentations. She contributes to her field through editorial service on national and international journals, review of conference proposals, and member and committee involvement in state, regional, national, and international organizations.

Index

A

B

C

D

E

F